How Lives Change

How Lives Change

Palanpur, India, and Development Economics

Himanshu, Peter Lanjouw, and Nicholas Stern

OXFORD

UNIVERSITY PRESS

Great Clarendon Street, Oxford, OX2 6DP,
United Kingdom

Oxford University Press is a department of the University of Oxford.
It furthers the University's objective of excellence in research, scholarship,
and education by publishing worldwide. Oxford is a registered trade mark of
Oxford University Press in the UK and in certain other countries

© Oxford University Press 2018

The moral rights of the authors have been asserted

First Edition published in 2018
Impression: 1

Published in the United States of America by Oxford University Press
198 Madison Avenue, New York, NY 10016, United States of America

British Library Cataloguing in Publication Data
Data available

Library of Congress Control Number: 2018933898

ISBN 978–0–19–880650–9

Printed and bound in Great Britain by
Clays Ltd, Elcograf S.p.A.

To the people of Palanpur, past, present, and future

Table of Contents

Table of Contents

Part 4. Reflections

List of Figures

List of Tables

Introduction*

I.1 The Purpose of Research in Development

Development economics is, or should be, about the understanding of how and why lives and livelihoods change. The processes and pathways of development arise from the interactions of three elements—society, economy, and the behaviour of individuals—in relation to the opportunities they perceive and the environment in which they live. And the outcomes and forces at work concern the lives and activities of individuals, households, and communities. This understanding, together with the policies such an understanding can inform, is the purpose of our study and of the subject or discipline: the economics of development.

Decades of research into development, from the social sciences and humanities, have enriched our understanding of why some societies take longer to prosper than others or do so in different ways; or, indeed, why some decline, and similarly, why some individuals fare better than others. Our advance in understanding has usually been cumulative, with insights deriving from an array of focused investigations of specific questions in widely varying settings. Sometimes, although rarely, there are major changes in perspective; an example from economics more broadly would be Keynes' General Theory. One way or the other, our 'big picture' grows and changes. The advances of our understanding of the processes still at work in development may, and indeed often do, require us to look beyond the frontiers of mainstream economics and development studies. But, from whatever perspective, it is clear that some understanding of the forces at work is essential for the design and implementation of economic policy to overcome poverty and to promote sustainable and inclusive development.

This book is about understanding development, India, and policy. It aims to deepen our understanding in a very particular way: by close observation in

---

* This introduction was written by Himanshu, Peter Lanjouw, and Nicholas Stern.

great detail in one place, over a long period of time. It is about the key questions of development; it is precisely focused on how lives and livelihoods change. It brings ideas to experience and experience to ideas. It brings the big picture to the little picture and the little picture to the big picture. More specifically, it examines and integrates analytically the individual and the society, the village and the country, the micro and the macro, the intensely focused study and the subject of development economics. For all four, the interactions and insights go both ways.

Opportunities to ask the fundamental questions about economic development and change using long-term, detailed empirical studies of communities, households, and individuals, are rare. This book, and the work behind it, represents a sustained response to a special opportunity. We describe how we have been able to generate and analyse a unique data set, comprising detailed information on all households in the village of Palanpur (in Moradabad district of Uttar Pradesh, in north India). We use the results from one survey, covering all households, for each decade since India's Independence: seven in all, the first in 1957/8 and the most recent in 2015.

Around half the world's population of approximately 7.5 billion people live outside urban areas. Fifty years ago, it was around two-thirds and a half century from now, it will likely be around one third.[1] The determinants of livelihoods in villages, and how they respond to and drive change in the economy and society as a whole, are clearly of fundamental importance to an understanding of development and the making of policy.

This book is about the evolving nature of opportunities for the people of Palanpur as India changes and how markets and the behaviour of agents influence and are influenced by change. It examines the dynamics of interactions between markets and outcomes, with a strong focus on changing institutions.

The process of development in Palanpur is the story of the integration of a village economy with the outside world. Markets and institutions shape, interact with, and are influenced by social norms, economic structures, and geography. Some elements of conventional theory are helpful in understanding these changes; other theories and perceptions much less so. But the flow of learning is not just from theory to understanding of the evidence and phenomena we identify: the village's experience and development can help us understand how and in what direction some of the theories could and should develop.

Whilst this book, we trust, contributes to our understanding of the nature and processes of development in one village, it is not only about a village. It uses the village as a lens to understand and assess various theories of development in their social, political, and institutional contexts. And it goes further

---

[1] Fifty-four per cent of the world population was living in urban areas in 2014. This was only 30% in 1950 but is expected to increase to 66% by 2050 (UN, 2014).

and seeks to inform the role of, and scope for, public policy in shaping the lives of individuals and societies. It is intended to be useful to anyone interested in the nature and drivers of economic and social transformation and in how public policy might influence the processes at work, be they students, academics, practitioners, or just curious. Thus, we have tried to avoid the heavily technical and to keep the discussion accessible, whilst at the same time taking on some of the big conceptual and theoretical issues of our subject and times.

The long story of the work on Palanpur concerns the empirical foundations of developmental economics: it is built on individual data, carefully collected and analysed, spanning seven decades, household by household. Measurement requires theory; it also requires painstaking attention to detail and data quality. Some of our conclusions will be about lessons—learnt from the detailed, cross-checked, primary data in our surveys and research—for the reliability and design of the broad household surveys which loom so large in both national and academic data collection and in standard economic analyses.

The analysis presented here complements and takes forward the earlier work on Palanpur, including that reported in Christopher Bliss and Nicholas Stern's *Palanpur: The Economy of an Indian Village* (Bliss and Stern, 1982) and Peter Lanjouw and Nicholas Stern (eds), *Economic Development in Palanpur over Five Decades* (Lanjouw and Stern, 1998). These, in turn, build on the 1957/8 and 1962/3 studies by the Agricultural Economics Research Centre (AERC) of the University of Delhi, and reported in Nasim Ansari, 'Palanpur: A Study of its Economic Resources and Economic Activities' (Ansari, 1964). We hope that this book, as its predecessors, will contribute to wider discussions on development and growth.

The close study of, and residence in, a village is not simply a question of enhancing the accuracy and quality of data. This approach also means that we can get to know individuals and the society and its politics. At a number of points we will illustrate our ideas with stories of individuals; they are not merely data points with a particular number. And we shall set our arguments and inferences in the context of the ways in which the society and politics function. That local understanding of individuals and the community is a core feature of village studies, and it is all the richer in a longitudinal study where we can chart how fortunes develop over time.

I.2 Palanpur and India

The growth and changing structure of the Indian economy and the development of its institutions has had a profound effect on the development of Palanpur. *Zamindari* abolition came soon after Independence, with individual acts passed in each state and implementation differing across states. That, for Uttar Pradesh (UP), was in 1950. The intention was to transfer key ownership rights from the feudal landlord-cum-local ruler-cum-tax collector, the *zamindar*, to his tenants. These new ownership rights accrued to cultivators in a patchy way across Uttar Pradesh, but the process worked reasonably well in Palanpur. The greater confidence in ownership from this reform liberated investment by the landowners, particularly in irrigation in Palanpur, in the 1950s and 1960s. The technologies and methods of the 'green revolution', particularly the expansion of irrigation, fertilizers, and new seed varieties, fostered the advance and productivity of wheat in the later 1960s and the 1970s. And in the later part of the period under examination, from the mid-1980s onwards, the growth opportunities in nearby towns and outside agriculture have transformed economic opportunities. These opportunities have been largely related to the ability to commute to and from Palanpur, but non-farm activities within the village have advanced strongly, too.

Understanding change in Palanpur thus requires an understanding of change in India. At the same time, understanding change in Palanpur can help us understand drivers of change in India and how realities can differ from what they might seem to be in standard discussions, analyses, or data. The findings from Palanpur can also lead us to question directions of policy that are widely held or regarded as 'obvious', and to point to constructive ways forward which could open up new opportunities.

Thus, we shall devote part of our analysis early in the book to descriptions of change in India. Rather than provide a general commentary on India over the last seven decades, we orient that discussion of India around five core themes from Palanpur that emerged from our data and analysis. These core findings are set out briefly in Section I.4. They include: how off-farm opportunities, mainly in nearby towns and largely in the informal sector, have grown; how they have influenced mobility and inequality; how institutions at the local level are more dynamic than generally assumed; the weak progress of education and health and their relation to poor public services; and the importance of, and influences on, entrepreneurship and initiative in individual actions on investment in change.

Some of these observations of how India's overall development has influenced village life and livelihoods, and how the experience of a village helps us understand India, are reinforced from evidence elsewhere. But few other studies have the strength of the Palanpur detail or its length and, in some cases, the insights are fairly new. It is very rare for any longitudinal study to have detailed data of individuals and households for over two generations. We can, for example, examine intergenerational mobility for the quarter-century 1957/8 to 1983/4 and then again for the next quarter-century. Thus, Palanpur offers the unique opportunity to understand not only intra- and intergenerational mobility, but also changes in intergenerational mobility, and can combine quantitative data with knowledge of the individuals themselves, their choices, and the circumstances in which they live and work.

I.3 The Choice of Village and Earlier Work

The intensity of focus and the extended period of time require major resource inputs that would not be possible to replicate in a very large number of villages. Thus the choice of village is important. We do not want to argue that Palanpur is somehow 'representative' of India's approximately 600,000 villages, but it is important that it is not outstandingly unusual in any major way.

Notwithstanding the resource inputs necessary for such a study and that no single village could be fully representative, careful longitudinal study of the way in which lives and livelihoods of households and individuals change, taking careful account of the community in which they live, is surely of fundamental importance to understanding development itself, which is precisely concerned with this kind of change. There would be a certain hollowness to the study of development without some detailed longitudinal studies of the phenomena of change it is designed to illuminate.

The importance of 'institutional memory' amongst the community of researchers working over a long period requires someone to 'start young, live long, and seek younger partners'. Indeed, such research involves an 'overlapping generations' model for its researchers, where each new generation starts young and lives long.

We describe the earlier studies briefly in Chapter 1, to introduce the work and its foundations and to explain the choice of village and the 'overlapping generations' of the researchers. Greater detail on the earlier studies and the story they tell is contained in Chapter 2.

Christopher Bliss and Nicholas Stern led the 1974/5 study of Palanpur, collaborating with research investigators S.S. Tyagi Jr and V.K. Singh. The researchers lived in the village for most of the period September 1974 to June 1975. The study was described in the book *Palanpur: The Economy of an Indian Village* (Bliss and Stern, 1982).

Bliss and Stern chose to work on the topic of village India in 1974 for a number of reasons, not least that India was an important country in which close research was actually feasible. Bliss and Stern were enabled and encouraged by a number of good friends and fine academics (see acknowledgements in the Bliss and Stern book). The great majority of the Indian population lived, and still lives, outside towns and cities. Many theories and studies, prominent in academic discussions of development, concerned the functioning of rural economies (sharecropping, market linkages, efficiency wages, credit, class relations, and so on). And this was a time when the emphasis of development scholars was, understandably, moving away from large-scale and ambitious planning models towards trying to understand how economies worked, how markets and institutions functioned, and how people behaved within them. Further, it was a time when there was great interest in the 'green revolution', which was radically changing approaches to wheat production around the world, particularly in north India, from the late 1960s. It was also a time when there was intense discussion of how to model economic growth, including around theories in the tradition of the Lewis model of a dual economy,[2] which had been published 20 years previously. This was a story of development as a transformation from a primarily backward agrarian sector to a more advanced capitalist sector.

These broad motivations for focusing on village India and its development influenced the choice of village. The interest in tenancy and factor markets implied that we sought a village where tenancy was strongly present. The focus on the changes brought by the green revolution meant it was important to find a village with good-quality previous studies and where wheat was important.

In a sense, it should be obvious that those interested in development in the 1970s would go to Indian villages. As an academic, one seeks a place to work effectively and interact with others. And India was certainly very important among such countries; that is where the people were.[3] Debates were lively and polity was engaged, and the policy issues were of deep importance, including those around the movement away from planning and the green revolution.

For the good functioning of our relationships within the village, we wanted somewhere where we could live independently from a village household. We did not want to be associated with one particular group of villagers; we were fortunate to be able to live in a room above the seed store, originally desig-nated for a village-level worker who declined to live there. We also wanted to be far enough from Delhi for the village not to be strongly influenced by Delhi yet close enough to get there in a day's travel, because we were doing some teaching at the Indian Statistical Institute (the Delhi branch of which was located on the fifth floor of the Planning Commission).

With all of these criteria in mind, we searched specifically for earlier village studies amongst reputable Indian research institutions. This search generated a short list of villages which we personally visited, eventually choosing Palanpur as best fitting our list of criteria. High-quality studies for 1957/8 and 1962/3 had been carried out by the AERC of the University of Delhi. We were fortunate to be able to recruit from the AERC S.S. Tyagi Jr, the brother of S.S. Tyagi Sr,

---

[2] See Lewis (1954).
[3] Other examples prominent within applied research at that time included the countries of East Africa.

who had led the data collection for both the 1957/8 and 1962/3 studies. The AERC study was written up in a very thoughtful and careful way by Nasim Ansari of the AERC (see Ansari, 1964), and we have drawn heavily both on the original data and questionnaires and on that report.

The data collection for the 1983/4 study was led by Jean Drèze and Naresh Sharma, both of whom played a very prominent role in the analysis and writing. It was much more intensive and detailed than the 1974/5 study, with longer residence (15 months) and with especially close observation and knowledge of village life, institutions, and structures. Drèze and Sharma also led a smaller and shorter re-survey in 1993. The results were written up in Lanjouw and Stern (1998). Drèze and Sharma made major contributions to the chapters of that book and have maintained close interest in the work.

The data collection for the 2008/10 study was led by Himanshu, who also played a leading role in the analysis and writing. This was still more intensive than the 1983/4 study, with two years in the village and a bigger data collection team and ambitions. There were also more women researchers involved. The same team, based on the knowledge and structure developed for 2008/10, carried out a quick re-survey in 2015; given the foundation, it could nevertheless be quite detailed.

We should emphasize, as is clear from the history, that this was not originally planned as a structured longitudinal study. It developed that way over time. During this most recent period of work, we have invested much time and effort in getting the different studies across the years in a form which, for an extensive set of core variables, can be treated as a systematic, longitudinal panel data set, in the sense that families and individuals can be followed across the years and generations. This has great potential for further work. This book has a very strong emphasis on change over time, probably stronger than the earlier studies.

Further detail on the different surveys, including their different focus, and on Palanpur itself can be found in Chapters 1 and 2, respectively.

The book and the study have been conceived, designed, structured, coordinated, and written by the three of us (Himanshu, Peter Lanjouw, and Nicholas Stern) and we have played a central role in the analysis and writing of each chapter. Dipa Sinha has led the writing and associated research for Part 3, 'Society'. We have drawn on a number of papers and write-ups that have been contributed by various researchers associated with this round of the project, over its long journey of ten years. Some of the papers that we have used and referenced are available as working papers or as journal papers. We have collaborated closely, in some chapters, with other colleagues, and they, and their greatly valued contributions and authorship, are recognized at the beginning of the chapters. We acknowledge with gratitude the contribution of all researchers and participants in our work. More detailed acknowledgements can be found in Section I.7.

I.4 Some Key Findings on Change over Time

Five central themes or findings illustrate and organize what we have learned from the study and help understand the structure of our analysis, arguments, and the book itself. They are motivated, analysed, demonstrated, and discussed, and policy implications are drawn out, as we progress through the book. They are far from the only significant findings, but they are core. Their presentation in this Introduction will provide key guidance for the basic arguments and 'storyline' of what follows.

First, whilst the major driver of change in the first half of the period (1957/8 to 1983/4) was the intensification of agriculture, the major driver in the second half, increasingly so over time, has been the involvement in non-farm activities. These have been primarily in nearby towns, in informal activities such as unloading and loading in Moradabad railway yards, working in brick kilns, marble polishing, and the maintenance and repair of machinery. These jobs have largely been accessed by commuting from Palanpur rather than through migration. Sometimes they involve the household working together as a team (for example, in brick kilns), in which case they involve women. But generally, these have been male workers. So far, the majority of such jobs have not required any educational qualification of substance. Communication, via mobile or smartphone, has been important for learning about job opportunities and justifying the costs of travel. Some entrepreneurship and initiative in spotting and availing oneself of opportunities are also involved; some individuals react sooner, or are in a better position to react sooner, than others. Some are more successful than others. We raise the suggestion that policy should not inadvertently or otherwise curtail such informal opportunities without good cause. They matter greatly to the improvement of livelihoods and the growth of output. There are just a few regular, formal jobs performed by Palanpur villagers, and they require some education and, in a number of cases, special contacts, networks, or inducements. A further non-farm change of real importance is the rise of self-employment and small businesses, such as mentha oil pressing, a motorcycle repair shop, or some small retail outlets, many of which have been set up within the village itself.

Second, the drivers of growth as described are also drivers of mobility, as individuals and households create and respond to new opportunities. Thus, households of the Murao caste, traditional cultivating households, were on the whole amongst the most active in embracing new crop varieties and technologies and the green revolution. Eventually, however, most cultivating households adopted the improved seeds and other inputs. And prior to that, in the years after *zamindari* abolition, there had been active investment in irrigation by most households, allowing those not yet engaged in double-cropping (raising two crops a year on a piece of land) to do so. Thus, there was a process of catch-up as the village moved from around 50 per cent of land irrigated in the late 1950s to nearly 100 per cent by the 1970s. In the second half of the period, some households were quicker and more successful at getting involved in non-farming activities than others. The involvement in non-farm work has happened across castes, including amongst the major Dalit group, the Jatabs. But, as is often the case in this study, we find that there are even sharper differences within caste than across caste.

As a result of these effects, we see some rise in inequality in the second half of the study period arising from some moving faster and more successfully than others to avail themselves of non-farm opportunities. We pose the question of whether increases in inequality from such sources should be seen as counter to development. These increases in inequality appear in a Lewis or Kuznets model of growth, although they are very different here, since Lewis and Kuznets generally have in mind migration rather than commuting, focus on a transition to more formal sector jobs, and do not emphasize entre-preneurship and investment in the informal sector and in village agriculture.

Third, institutions and market structures influence outcomes. For example, as indicated, *zamindari* abolition, resulting in greater confidence in ownership rights and rewards to investments, led to strong investment in irrigation in the 1950s and 1960s. But we also see that institutions and structures themselves change as other opportunities, here non-farm, emerge. There is a two-way (endogenous) relationship between institutions and economic opportunities. In particular, tenancy arrangements in Palanpur have been changing as a result of off-farm activities, as we shall document in Chapter 6. This, for example, raises the policy question of whether further attempts at land redistribution or tenancy regulation (for instance, simplistic 'land to the tiller' policies) are advisable or necessary for change. The advance of non-farm activities may have significant effects on growth and poverty reduction and foster agricultural change, without such worrying side-effects as concealment and disruption of relations between owners and cultivators, or corruption in relation to land records which can arise from such policy initiatives. To raise a question is not to assume the answer, but it does require examination.

Fourth, human, political, and social development in Palanpur have moved at a markedly different pace and in different ways from economic develop-ment. Educational advances have been a very long time coming. Education has not been influential in the taking or creating of the great majority of new non-farm opportunities. On the other hand, in the last 15 years or so we are seeing the beginnings of progress, with many more children, including girls, now attending school. We suggest that whilst education has not yet become a driver of change, it may well become one soon, in particular if the quality of education can start to improve at a similar rate as school attendance. The process of education and better communication may improve the social and economic position of women, which remains very low, although there are some modest signs of change (see Part 3 of this book).

Fifth, the actions of entrepreneurship, initiative, and innovation at the individual level are key to understanding why some individuals or households perceive or react to opportunities before others. One of the great strengths of a village study is that individuals and households are more than a numbered data point or some random deviation from a regression line or fitted relationship. We know who they are and something about them. The ability to spot, invest in, and take advantage of opportunities really does vary across individuals, even though there will also be some systematic determining factors such as wealth, social position, health, caste, and so on. As Deng Xiao Ping is said to have put it, 'Some people get richer before others', and it is important to try to understand who they are and why.

These five broad findings do, we suggest, help us understand: (i) where India is going; (ii) models of and theories about development; and (iii) policy. And they will help structure the flow of our argument.

This book has the particular purpose of telling the story of lives and livelihoods of Palanpur over seven decades in a way that identifies drivers and outcomes of change, highlighting key forces, phenomena, and lessons. Whilst it tells our overall story in a way that we hope is persuasive and accessible, it is not a comprehensive account of all our work. There is an immense amount of underlying detail which is not presented in full here. We are providing working papers, mostly online, with some of this detail.[4]

We have also been producing more formal and technical research papers on particular issues and will continue to do so going forward. The data set we have put together is extraordinarily rich, both in terms of its longitudinal nature and also in terms of the great detail of quantitative and qualitative data produced in the 2008/10 study. And throughout the years we have paid great attention to data quality, including careful cross-checking and direct observation. We hope to do justice to the richness and quality of the data in forthcoming, more technical work. We shall also be publishing less formal work on aspects of policy and other ideas which we hope will bring the Palanpur conclusions and insights to a wider audience.

1.5 Reaction of Villagers

When we (Bliss and Stern) arrived in the village in 1974, there was some puzzlement as to why we would want to embark on such an exercise. The

---

[4] The working papers are available at http://sticerd.lse.ac.uk/india/research/palanpur/publications. asp.

question 'what is the purpose?' or in Hindi 'matlab kya hai' was frequently voiced. But soon there was some tolerance of, interest in, or even amusement generated from our activities. We were, we believe, moderately successful in following Clive Bell's advice, 'You must convince them that you are mad but harmless.'[5]

When we arrived in Palanpur for the sixth round of the survey in 2008, one of the first questions that we were asked was what the villagers would get by participating. This is an understandable question given that the village and villagers have been the subject of enquiry for over six decades by researchers, Indian as well as foreigners. The research teams over the years have tried to take great care not to influence the village life, economy, or society, even though most of the survey rounds have involved fairly long periods of stay.[6] While some villagers may have had expectations of material benefit directly or indirectly through government transfers, most of them were curious to know the outcome of the previous research and in what ways they have been part of the larger objective of informing and influencing understanding of development as well as policy.

It is difficult to say whether the previous two volumes, or the work involved, have had any measurable impact on policy of the Government of Uttar Pradesh or that of the government of India, but we are fairly confident they have not had a direct influence on policy or administration for Palanpur itself. Certainly it would be difficult to identify direct manifestations of this. Palanpur remains a relatively weak village in terms of infrastructure, schooling, and so on—in other words, those dimensions which could benefit from the preferences of local authorities—notwithstanding its economic progress, albeit modest, over the years.

Neither is there any reason to suppose that our presence changed the behaviour of those observed (the so-called Hawthorne effect[7]). We are not agricultural specialists, for example. And our interactions were slow and steady rather than founded on short-run performance measurement; furthermore, the publication of results occurred only with long lags.

On the whole, we think we have been successful in being observers of change rather than agents of change, and we trust that our research has not constituted a 'major shock' to the overall development of the village.

---

[5] Clive Bell, a friend and fine researcher, who had previously studied some villages in Bihar.

[6] One of the important issues, often discussed in anthropological and sociological surveys of this kind, is the impact of the continuous stay of research teams in villages. Other than the bias that it may introduce in the survey respondents, it is often argued that research teams cannot stay neutral and objective given the close association that they develop with the 'subject', particularly with long years of research.

[7] The Hawthorne effect refers to the change in behaviour of individuals/respondents as a result of being observed. The word was coined by Henry A. Landsberger (1958) based on his study of Hawthorne Works (a Western Electric factory outside Chicago).

1.6 Structure of the Book

There are four parts to this book, following the logic of the purpose of the study and the broad findings we have illustrated.

Part 1 (Chapters 1–4) lays out the foundations and establishes a point of departure for the subsequent analysis. We describe the importance of longitudinal village studies and our building of the evidence, the data, in Chapter 1. The broad features of the evolution of the village are set out in Chapter 2. In Chapter 3, we describe relevant aspects of the Indian economy, particularly as they relate to our five key themes as described. In Chapter 4, we point to theories of development, particularly in relation to India, that can help us understand our findings. We also indicate some implications of what we find for understanding and developing theory; we return to these implications in Chapter 13, the closing chapter of the book. With these four chapters in Part 1, we have the foundations of our investigations of the interplay among findings for Palanpur, India, and the subject of development economics, in other words, the issues highlighted in the subtitle of this book.

In Part 2, we set out detailed evidence from Palanpur to examine activities, markets, and outcomes, beginning, in Chapter 5, with change in agricultural activities. This includes the adoption of new crops and technologies, capital investment and increasing mechanization, the monetization of inputs, and the emergence of new markets. Inter alia, this tells a story of how increasing capital intensity in agriculture has enabled the release of labour. In Chapter 6, focused on tenancy, we analyse change in the markets for the services of land and labour. The market structures and institutions, often seen as rigid, have shown striking change as a result of the increase in non-farm activities. Institutions, including the functioning and form of markets, are endogenous. Then in Chapter 7, we analyse changes in non-farm activities, including the processes of commuting and migration. The consequences of all these changes for poverty, mobility, and inequality are presented in Chapter 8, which offers key aggregates or syntheses of the consequences of the various effects and drivers we have identified. We not only examine intragenerational mobility, but also exploit the longevity and detail of the data to look at intergenerational mobility and how it has changed.

In Part 3, we examine the village society beyond economics, narrowly defined. Health and education, or human development, constitute the subject matter of Chapter 9. Chapter 10 describes the lives, livelihood, and status of women in Palanpur, recognizing the changes but also that they appear more modest than might have been expected from or associated with the changes in incomes. In Chapter 11, we study developments in society and politics in Palanpur, exploring both inertia and change. Again, we see how institutions not only shape but also respond to changing economic circumstances.

The fourth and final section, on prospects and reflections, looks both forward and backwards. In Chapter 12, we speculate on future prospects based on the trends and structures we have identified. And we look back on the performance of the prognostications we made in the 1970s and 1990s, in our reports on our earlier studies. In Chapter 13, we offer, first, lessons for India, particularly concerning policy, and, second, lessons for theories of development.

I.7 Acknowledgements

A project such as Palanpur, with its ambition, detail, depth of engagement, and time span, can be carried out only with the involvement, assistance, and guidance of a large group of people. As with our previous studies of Palanpur, we have been extremely fortunate in the collaboration and support of both institutions and individuals. The acknowledgements for the earlier studies in Bliss and Stern (1982) and those of Lanjouw and Stern (1998) are of great and lasting relevance and should be read in conjunction with these.

The richness of data from the Palanpur study arises not just from the data collected in the recent rounds, but also from previous data carefully collected and assembled by various people who have been associated with this research since the first survey in 1957/8. The questionnaires from all the studies have been at the core of our work. The journal articles, working papers, reports, unprocessed monographs, and the two previous books have been a great source of ideas and motivation. They encouraged us to take the study to new areas and depths. We are fortunate to have maintained contact with almost all of those who have been associated with the study over its long time period and have benefited greatly from their guidance at different stages of the fieldwork. They have also been gracious and helpful whenever we needed advice, old materials kept by them, or simply wanted to discuss issues concerning data or the line of enquiry that we were pursuing. We are indebted to them for the valuable time and advice that they have offered throughout the course of the study.

Jean Drèze and Naresh Sharma spent time with us during the fieldwork for the 2008/10 round; they continued to guide and advise us at every step of the journey. Jean has also read drafts of several chapters and gave extensive and valuable comments. Jocelyn Kynch readily shared her notes and photographs from her earlier visits. Their roles in the earlier studies are described in Chapter 1. Christopher Bliss has provided helpful guidance at various points over the last decade.

We have been privileged to have the support of leading academic institutions while we worked on Palanpur, including, in the UK, the Universities of Oxford, Essex, Warwick from the mid-1970s to the mid-1980s. From then, its

UK home has been (with Nicholas Stern) at the London School of Economics (LSE) and, in particular, the Suntory and Toyota International Centres for Economics and Related Disciplines (STICERD). Its homes in India have been the Indian Statistical Institute from the mid-1970s to the mid-1980s, and in the last decade, the Centre de Sciences Humaines (CSH) in Delhi. We were very fortunate in the early days to have the guidance of the AERC of the University of Delhi. Peter Lanjouw's host institutions after STICERD have been the World Bank and the VU University Amsterdam; for Himanshu, Jawaharlal Nehru University (JNU) and CSH.

This round of work began at the LSE and CSH in 2007/8 and has continued (now in 2018) for ten years. We are enormously grateful to the India Observatory (IO) and STICERD at the LSE for their support throughout this period. Ruth Kattumuri, as Co-Director of the IO, has played a special role, and we owe her a great debt. CSH has been the main institutional home of the Palanpur researchers for the last ten years. The directors of CSH, Basudeb Chaudhuri and Leila Choukroune, went out of their way to accommodate our needs for space and infrastructure. The administrative team at CSH were very welcoming and helpful, both to researchers and to interns from various French academic institutions. We also owe a special debt to the research team at CSH, which patiently sat through numerous seminars and workshops and advised us on different aspects of the research.

We have been fortunate to have research associates from institutions across the world who have worked with us over the years and have enriched the research. Those in earlier studies were recognized in Bliss and Stern (1982) and Lanjouw and Stern (1998). Sue Stern, who drew the map and spent time in the village for the 1974/5 study, has continued to provide wise guidance and deep encouragement. The memory of the late Jenny Lanjouw, who was involved in the research of the 1980s and 1990s, has been a source of inspiration.

We have benefited enormously from collaborators in assembling the data, in the analytical work, and in the writing. Dipa Sinha has played a pivotal role and has led the analytical work and the writing in Part 3 of this book. All the work is built on the foundations of the data sets where collection, construction, and organization have involved tremendous effort over the whole period of study. A large number of students and research assistants have helped us on this vital data work during our stay at Palanpur and in the subsequent analysis at CSH, JNU, and LSE. Dinesh Tiwari, Neeraj Goswami, Gajanand Ahirwal, and Hemendra Ahirwar were the principal investigators in the village. Dinesh, with his years of experience and personal relationships, was helpful in setting up the base at Pipli village. Dinesh led the collection of data and also contributed to improvements in the design and structure of questionnaires. Neeraj left the research team halfway through for a permanent job with the Madhya Pradesh government, but Dinesh, Gajanand, and Hemendra shouldered the main responsibility of data collection. All four of them are anthropologists with years of experience of data collection in villages.

The other resident investigator was Ashish Tyagi, an economics student from JNU who also stayed in the village for the major part of the data collection exercise. Ashish, Florian Bersier, and Loïc Watine (interns from École Polytechnique) were also involved in cross-checking the data. While the primary resident investigators collected most of the data, we were joined by investigators who contributed in special surveys. Gautam Sinha helped us with the consumption schedules. We were fortunate to have a group of female colleagues who took on the responsibility of collecting data from female members of the household. Dipa Sinha led the data collection, along with M. Sangeeta, Archana Kesarwani, and Shilpi Rani, who collected the data on women, children, anthropometry, and adolescents. They also spent considerable time in the village conducting interviews. The 2015 survey was done on tablets, and the entire responsibility of designing and testing the software was on Gaurav Meena, alumnus of IIT Mumbai. He also stayed on and collected data for the 2015 survey along with Gajanand.

A number of researchers based at CSH Delhi were responsible for maintaining the data. They also worked on the analysis and writing. During the initial phase of data validation and preliminary analysis, Ashish Tyagi contributed in many ways. His detailed knowledge of the village and the surrounding area was helpful in maintaining the quality of the data collected. Ishan Bakshi, Aditi Banerjee, Tushar Bharti, Barkha Bhatnagar, Diya Bhatnagar, Ruchira Bhattacharya, Sidhharth Gupta, Bhavna Joshi, Japneet Kaur, Sidhharth Kaushal, Chaitanya Khandelwal, Manju Kumari, Gaurav Meena, Priyanka Pande, M. Sangeetha, Gautam Kumar Sinha, and Rishav Thakur have contributed to the analysis of data at various stages of the work during 2008–17. Vaishnavi Surendra helped us compile the data from different surveys into a format closer to panel formats, used for much of the analysis in the book. While some data from earlier surveys were available, there were some mistakes and missing entries. Fortunately, the availability of previous survey questionnaires allowed us to enter the data, correct where necessary, and organize using consistent definitions.

We were fortunate to have a regular flow of research students from some of the premier institutes of France who came to work on the Palanpur project. Some of them also did their Master's dissertations using Palanpur data, including Florian Bersier, Loic Watine, Rosalinda Copolleta, Camille Dufour, Aditya Kawatra, Soline Miniere, Floriane Bolazzi, and Violaine Pierre. Bertrand Lefebvre, doctoral student at CSH, was helpful in creating a geographic information system (GIS) map of the village. He also spent time in the village creating the village map and plots using modern cartographic techniques.

A number of research students at LSE have also worked on Palanpur, whether as part of their doctoral dissertation or as research assistants. Milad

Khatib-Shahidi and Tom O'Keeffe have used the Palanpur data as part of their doctoral research. The data from the 2008/10 survey and earlier surveys has also been used by researchers in India for their MPhil and PhD theses. Dipa Sinha and Ruchira Bhattacharya have used the Palanpur data in their PhD theses. Ishan Anand has used part of the data in his MPhil thesis. Pooja Sengupta, School of Planning and Architecture, and Vedanta Dhamija, TERI University, did their Master's dissertations based on Palanpur data.

Sarthak Gaurav has been associated with the Palanpur study as a post-doctoral fellow for three years, first at LSE and then at CSH, and has contributed to analysis, writing, and follow-up visits. Abhiroop Mukhopadhyay has been central to the analysis of migration data and has been an integral part of the team for the 2008/10 survey. The large volume of data collected has been managed and streamlined for analysis by Vaishnavi Surendra, Ashish Tyagi, Tushar Bharti, and Ruchira Bhattacharya.

For work on the creation of this manuscript, we are enormously grateful for the outstanding help and guidance of Shantanu Singh and Dipa Sinha. We have benefited greatly from the thoughtful and wise guidance of David Milner. Editors Katie Bishop and Adam Swallow and colleagues at Oxford University Press have provided very helpful advice. Thank you also to Elizabeth Stone, the copy editor, and S. Lakshmanan, Project Manager. Remarkably, Kerrie Quirk has been involved in preparing all three books. We are hugely grateful to her and to Lisa Duvar and Eva Lee at LSE.

We have discussed this work with many friends over the decade of this round of the Palanpur study and are grateful to them all. We should mention especially Isher Judge Ahluwalia, Montek Singh Ahluwalia, Yoginder Alagh, Sudhir Anand, the late Tony Atkinson, Oriana Bandiera, Abhijit Banerjee, Pranab Bardhan, Clive Bell, Sam Bowles, Terence Byres, Angus Deaton, Bruno Dorin, Chris Elbers, Maitreesh Ghatak, John Harriss, Barbara Harriss-White, Judith Heyer, Christopher Jalil-Nordman, Surinder Jodhka, Jens Lerche, Michael Lipton, Rinku Murgai, Jyoti Parikh, Kirit Parikh, Jean-Philippe Platteau, V.K. Ramachandran, Vijayendra Rao, Martin Ravallion, Gerry Rodgers, Abhijit Sen, Amartya Sen, Kunal Sen, Ravi Srivastava, Madhura Swaminathan, David Garces Urzainqui, and several other participants at different seminars and conferences where the Palanpur work has been presented.

A number of grants have made a sustained study of Palanpur possible over the years. The British Academy, the Nuffield Foundation, and the UK's Economic and Social Research Council (ESRC) played a crucial role in the early years. The Reserve Bank of India, the State Bank of India, and Yes Bank have contributed to the funding of the I.G. Patel chair at LSE held by Nicholas Stern. Since 1983 our principal funding source has been the UK's Department for International Development (DfID). We are deeply grateful to DfID, both for their support and for their patience. Studies such as ours take a long time.

Finally, as we said at the end of our preface to Lanjouw and Stern (1998), special thanks are due to the people of Palanpur for their patience, welcome, warmth, and good humour.

References

Ansari, N. 1964. 'Palanpur: A Study of its Economic Resources and Economic Activities (No. 41)', Continuous Village Surveys 1958–9. Agricultural Economics Research Centre, University of Delhi.

Bliss, C.J., and Stern, N.H. 1982. *Palanpur: The Economy of an Indian Village*, 1st edn. Oxford and New York: Oxford University Press.

Landsberger, H.A. 1958. *Hawthorne Revisited*. Ithaca, NY: New York State School of Industrial and Labor Relations.

Lanjouw, P., and Stern, N.H. 1998. *Economic Development in Palanpur over Five Decades*, 1st edn. New York and Oxford: Clarendon Press.

Lewis, A.W. 1954. 'Economic development with unlimited supplies of labour', *Manchester School of Economic and Social Studies* 22: 139–91.

UN (United Nations) (2014). 'World Urbanization Prospects: The 2014 Revision, Highlights (ST/ESA/SER.A/352)', Department of Economic and Social Affairs, Population Division.

Part 1
Foundations

1

The Study of Villages and the Understanding of Development

Building the Evidence*

1.1 Introduction: The Role and History of Village Studies

On the first page of his classic book, *Some South Indian Villages*, Gilbert Slater wrote, a century ago, in 1918,[1]

> Villages came before towns and even in the most industrialized countries, where all economic questions tend to be studied from an urban point of view, it is well to be reminded that the economic life of a town or city cannot be understood without reference to the lands which send it its foods and raw materials, and the villages from which it attracts young men and women. The importance of rural activities and of the village life in India, in view of the enormous preponderance of its agricultural population over that engaged in mining, manufacture, commerce and transport, is not likely to be overlooked.... (Slater (1918: 1))

Today, almost three-quarters of the world's population resides in developing countries, and a majority of them are in rural areas. It is surely clear that pathways of development cannot be understood without comprehending the functioning of villages or the process of integration of villages with urban areas.[2]

While the history of village surveys in India is over a century old, the Slater survey constituted the first systematic attempt at documenting the functioning

---

* This chapter has been written by Himanshu, Nicholas Stern, and Peter Lanjouw.
[1] Gilbert Slater was the first Professor of Economics at the newly created Department of Economics at Madras University. The first set of village surveys were conducted in 1916 in Tamil Nadu (then Madras). The year 2018 marks the centennial anniversary of the publication of *Some South Indian Villages*, perhaps the first book on Indian villages based on in-depth village study.

[2] This was also the primary concern for many development economists such as Lewis, Hirschman, and Kuznets. Insights from the functioning of village societies continues to enlighten many areas of contemporary development economics as well.

of a village economy through structured questionnaires.[3] This was also the beginning of a series of village surveys in different parts of the country by individuals as well as organizations.[4] These studies, which became numerous, were not only crucial in generating a picture of rural India and understanding the functioning of village economies and societies (a large number of them were undertaken by sociologists and anthropologists) but were also useful in laying the foundation for a robust statistical system later. Their contribution with regard to the design of appropriate questionnaires for large-scale surveys and the refinement of conceptual categories and sampling techniques were crucial in setting up the statistical system in India, particularly the National Sample Survey Office (NSSO), after Independence.[5]

Notable among these studies is the work of Bailey, who studied Bisipara village in Orissa (Bailey, 1957); Epstein, who studied Wangala and Dalena in Karnataka (Epstein, 1962); and Hopper, who studied Senapur in Uttar Pradesh (Hopper, 1965).[6] Findings from these were important in understanding the nature and functioning of rural economies, particularly the behaviour of individuals and households in the largely closed setting of a village.

They were also useful in providing insights for new theories. A large part of early Indian anthropology and sociology was built around evidence from village surveys, such as those by Dube (1955) and Srinivas (1955). While early village studies, except for the re-survey of Slater villages, were less focused on economic issues, systematic surveys of villages by the Agricultural Economics Research Centre (AERC) were useful in creating a pool of village surveys looking at agricultural production, credit, and tenancy relations (Dasgupta, 1975).[7] Later studies expanded the scope to the understanding

[3] There were studies commissioned by colonial governments to understand the society and economy of villages. For example, Dr Francis Buchanan was requested by the East India Company to report on the conditions in towns and villages in Madras, Mysore, Bihar, Bengal, etc., as early as 1800. See Mukherjee (1978) for details. The study by Harold Mann in 1915 of some households around Pune is perhaps the first recorded household survey in India.

[4] A comprehensive survey of village surveys in the early part of 20th century in India is available in Mukherjee (1978). Some of the notable village surveys conducted in the pre-Independence period are the surveys of the Punjab Board of Economic Enquiry (1920s), the Bengal Board of Economic Enquiry (1935), the Indian Statistical Institute (1937), Viswa Bharti (1946), the Congress Economic and Political Studies (1936), Gujarat Vidyapeeth (1931), the Gokhale Institute of Politics and Economics (1940), and so on.

[5] Both the Census of India and the NSSO undertook village surveys in the early 1950s and 1960s which were used to design large-scale surveys but also functioned as stand-alone surveys to analyse various features of rural economy. Particular mention must be made of the continuous village surveys of the AERC; this organization conducted surveys of villages in different parts of the country.

[6] The studies mentioned here are neither a comprehensive nor exhaustive list of village surveys, but are mentioned only to give an indication of the central role of village studies in understanding rural society and economy.

[7] It is important to note that the first two surveys of Palanpur were also part of the AERC village survey schemes. A large number of such villages were later re-surveyed by others, Palanpur experiencing the longest of these re-surveys.

of issues related to the workings of markets, individual behaviour towards shocks and risk, savings, investment decisions at the household level, informal credit arrangements, and interlinkages between various markets. Notable among these are the International Crops Research Institute for the Semi-Arid Tropics (ICRISAT) surveys,[8] which systematically studied a set of villages in southern India annually for almost a decade. Subsequent decades saw the areas of enquiry widen to include the choice of technology, adaptation of new technology (green revolution), non-farm diversification, poverty, and inequality.[9]

One of the reasons for the centrality of village surveys in understanding the functioning of economic, social, and political life in rural areas is that villages are the lowest administrative unit.[10] While village surveys have been used by many social scientists to understand various aspects of human behaviour as well as the social, economic, and political context, the approaches vary a great deal. A crucial distinction has usually been the object of research. In the case of sociologists and anthropologists this has been the village itself and its functioning as a social entity, whereas economists have tended to focus on the village as a site of research into specific questions about behaviour, markets, or outcomes.[11] While there have been differences in methodology and approach to the study of villages by anthropologists/sociologists and economists, topics of interest are common to these fields. In most cases, caste, social structure, institutional context, and economic conditions and outcomes appear as overarching themes. For the most part, the economics of rural tenancy, labour, and the credit market are best examined through the close economic study of particular markets, set in the context of a village.[12]

---

[8] The ICRISAT surveys covered eight villages primarily in Maharashtra and Andhra Pradesh, surveyed between 1975 and 1984, and then again in 1989, 1993, 2000, and 2001. For more details, see http://vdsa.icrisat.ac.in and Walker and Ryan (1990).

[9] For a collection of recent studies using village surveys, see Himanshu, Jha, and Rodgers (2016).

[10] There appears to be no standard definition of a village. Most researchers have used the notion of a village as understood by the resident of the village even though the exact boundary or the geographical limit of the village itself may vary depending on whether it is a *panchayat* village, census village, or revenue village (*panchayat* is the lowest level of administrative unit in rural India. It is governed by a village council elected by the residents). For a typology of villages as used in village surveys see Nagaraj (2008).

[11] While we should recognize that sociologists/anthropologists and economists have dwelt on interconnected issues without getting caught in specific disciplinary boundaries, such a generalization may not be off the mark for the majority of the village surveys in India. Bardhan (1989) is an important collection of work by various social scientists, who discuss the methodological differences and similarities of the approaches.

[12] Two of the important studies which have relied on village surveys to understand the function of rural markets are the Palanpur study (Bliss and Stern, 1982) and the ICRISAT surveys (Walker and Ryan, 1990) in India. Also see the Townsend village surveys in Thailand for analysis of rural markets through village surveys (Townsend, 2016).

Village surveys continue to thrive.[13] An important reason why the method of studying villages has continued to remain indispensable in many disciplines is the advantage it offers in analysing individual behaviour in relation to its institutional context. The fact that this has happened in an era where large-scale surveys (both private as well as government-sponsored) have grown in prominence, not only in terms of availability but also coverage, is testament to the usefulness of village studies.[14] The presence of large-scale surveys has not led to a diminishing role of village surveys but in fact has contributed to strengthening the field and the nature of enquiry used in such surveys. These large data sets have been a valuable source of information on general trends of levels of living as well as pointers to substantial changes in structures of income and assets in villages. All of this has led to both a sharpening of existing research questions and to the raising of new questions, which are then studied using village surveys. However, the complementarity in research questions has also been accompanied by some scepticism from practitioners of village surveys as to the quality of data collected by these large-scale surveys.[15] It is understandable that those who collect primary data for their own research with great care and effort over a long period of time and with much cross-checking are somewhat dubious about the data quality associated with a questionnaire that might be completed for a household in an afternoon or less, without much knowledge of the village and with only limited incentives for the collector of the data to focus on accuracy.

Corresponding scepticism by those using large survey data on the representativeness of findings from village surveys is not unheard of. Given that most village surveys are trying to understand and situate their observations within the social, political, and economic context of the villages they study, variances from some notional average are both natural and interesting. At the same time, there are enough village studies to observe patterns emerging across villages, each of which has its own history and social structure.

1.2 Longitudinal Surveys

A much smaller number of studies, mainly re-surveys of existing village surveys, have put the data to work to track the evolution over time of markets, poverty,

[13] An important testament to the recognition of the continued importance of village surveys is the emergence of a large number of village surveys in recent decades. See Himanshu, Jha, and Rodgers (2016) for details.
[14] The socioeconomic surveys of the National Sample Survey Office (NSSO), the National Family Health Surveys (NFHS), and the India Human Development Surveys (IHDS) are widely used sources of large-scale secondary data sets.
[15] See Harriss (1989) for a comparison of large-scale surveys and village survey and also on issues arising out of comparison between two data sources.

inequality, social relations, and institutional structures.[16] These longitudinal studies are few and have differences in terms of methods and findings, but they are vitally important sources for understanding the dynamics of change.[17]

Longitudinal village surveys rarely start as longitudinal surveys, and the nature of these village surveys does not remain constant. This is partly a reflection of the changing nature of the village society, but also of the emergence of new insights and data on the dynamics of change in rural societies. While rural areas and village societies in general have evolved as a result of the changing socioeconomic structure of the larger society in which they are located, they have also changed because of the evolving dynamics of production and distribution within the village itself. The external environment, be it government policy, political institutions, or markets, exercises a strong influence on village society. In that sense, villages have rarely been the closed society that some past studies might have sought or imagined, certainly much less so in recent decades. And each village responds to these external stimuli in its unique way. The changing nature of circumstances, issues, and objectives inevitably raise issues of comparability and methodology across survey years. Nevertheless, longitudinal studies remain an extremely valuable route to an understanding of the dynamics of change of institutions and associated individual and social outcomes. There are very few other ways of examining directly the central questions of development, namely how and why lives and livelihoods of individuals and households change over time.

Among the many revisit surveys, ICRISAT studies hold an important place for the frequency of data collected. The ICRISAT surveys examined eight villages in Gujarat, Maharashtra, and Andhra Pradesh, with the two villages in Andhra Pradesh covered intensively.[18] A similar study by Robert Townsend and others in some villages in Thailand has also followed villages for more than a decade.[19] Although these village surveys collected relatively high-frequency data (in the spectrum of village studies) for almost a decade, the relatively short time covered by these surveys is a major limitation to deriving conclusions on long-term changes in rural and village societies.

Among the set of longitudinal surveys in which villages have been studied intensively for a long duration, most have surveys separated by decades. The most notable among them are the Slater villages mentioned in Section 1.1.[20]

---

[16] For a useful survey on village studies on poverty and inequality, see Jayaraman and Lanjouw (1999).

[17] For detailed information on findings from some of the recent longitudinal village surveys, see Himanshu, Jha, and Rodgers (2016).

[18] See http://vdsa.icrisat.ac.in/ for details.

[19] For details, see http://townsend-thai.mit.edu/.

[20] Slater's villages were re-surveyed in 1936–7 under the supervision of P.J. Thomas and K.C. Ramakrishnan. The next re-survey of the villages was in 1961, led by Margaret Haswell. Some of these villages were also included in the AERC scheme of village surveys during the early

The Palanpur studies are, we believe, unique in their combination of longevity (now seven surveys covering seven decades), frequency (every decade since Independence), the detail of coverage of all households and many dimensions, and the quality of data (great efforts were spent on checking and cross-checking). The Palanpur surveys cover a larger number of dimensions and issues than other longitudinal surveys. And the long-term personal involvement of researchers constitutes the crucial ingredient of data quality in a village survey.

There are some other long-period studies: for example, the work on Karimpur dates back to 1925, and the village has been studied intensively by sociologists; but there are only a few survey years.[21] Another notable body of work is the study of Bihar villages by Gerry Rodgers and others (Sharma and Rodgers, 2015). Surinder Jodhka's study of villages in Haryana (Jodhka, 2016) and Ravi Srivastava's examination of a village in eastern Uttar Pradesh (Srivastava, 2016) highlight the changing agrarian structure and its linkages with the social structure in the changing agrarian economy. Jha and Thakur (2016) examine similar issues in north-east Bihar, playing close attention to the role of migration and external factors, such as macroeconomic policies. Turning to villages in south India, Harriss and Jeyaranjan (2016) have compiled results from long-term studies in Tamil Nadu and examine the changing economic and social relations in the village. Studies by Jan Breman (Breman, 2007) of south Gujarat villages and the study by Gilbert Etienne (Etienne, 2014) are also fine examples of long-term studies of the Indian village. We refer the reader to Himanshu, Jha and Rodgers (2016) for an examination of some of these studies and their insights into the transformations occurring in villages across India.

There are four issues we would emphasize in considering the advantages of village studies, particularly longitudinal village studies, over standard household surveys such as the Indian NSS. First, the village study can incorporate direct knowledge of external changes to the village which are relevant to understanding its development. For example, the abolition of the *zamindari* system and the associated increase in confidence in ownership rights fostered strong investment in irrigation in Palanpur. The story of how this reform played out in the village offers clear insight at the micro level into how successes and failures of reform arise. Second, the village study can involve direct observation of the workings and influence of relationships embodied in

1960s. Five of these villages were followed up by S. Guhan in the early 1980s. The most recent re-survey of the village Iruvelpattu was conducted by John Harriss, J. Jeyaranjan, and K. Nagaraj in 2008.

[21] Karimpur was first studied by William and Charlotte Wiser in 1925 and was followed by re-surveys by Bruce Derr and Susan Wedley in the 1970s and 1980s. See Wiser and Wiser (1971, 2001) and Wadley and Derr (1989) for details.

village society, politics, and institutions. These observations supplement our quantitative data to identify the drivers of change in Palanpur, understand their interlinkages and dependencies, and present a richer story of economic and social transformation. For example, the weaknesses of the formal credit system are clearly illustrated in Palanpur, where we see how brothers, who are active informal lenders, have colluded in the management and manipulation of formal credit institutions.

Third, the village study can allow detailed cross-checking of transactions from two sides, for example from the owner and tenant of land, from hirer and supplier of labour, or borrower and lender in the case of credit. This takes time, effort, and lengthy residence and has helped us ensure that our data is of high quality and accuracy. Fourth, we can come to know in a qualitative way the characteristics of a household and how its members behave. Thus, observations have personalities; they are people and not just a code number. We were able to track individuals as their fortunes changed, for better or worse, and recognize how these changes came about. Some were able to channel a spirit of entrepreneurship to move up the ladder, while others fell into poverty due to misfortune.

We will further illustrate these four advantages as we describe the data collection in the 2008/10 survey in Section 1.4 and in our discussion, in Section 1.5, of lessons for data assessment and design.

1.3 Palanpur Surveys

The choice of the village by Bliss and Stern in 1974, and its basis in the two preceding surveys of 1957/8 and 1962/3, was briefly described in the Introduction. The first two surveys were conducted by the AERC of Delhi University as part of the Continuous Village Surveys Programme. Their choice of Palanpur as part of this programme was due to the inclusion of the village in the Integrated Cooperative Marketing Scheme (ICMS) of the government of India.[22] Although the scheme was in its infancy, the follow-up survey in 1962 was expected to shed light on the functioning of the cooperative scheme in the village. The first survey, which served as the baseline, was a meticulous survey of all the households in the village, including the characteristics of the village and its surroundings. The second round in 1962/3 was a less extensive follow-up survey and again comprised a survey of all the households in

---

[22] Given that a large number of village surveys have been undertaken in recent years to evaluate public programmes, it is interesting to note that the first survey of Palanpur, sixty years ago, was part of the evaluation programme of government schemes. It is worth mentioning that Palanpur, during the first survey, was served by three cooperative societies: the Cooperative Credit Society, the Cooperative Seed Store, and the Cane Development Cooperative Credit Union.

the village. The findings of the first survey were set out in a report by Nasim Ansari, who was then affiliated with the AERC (Ansari, 1964). The fieldwork for both survey rounds was done by S. Tyagi Sr, the older brother of S.S. Tyagi Jr, the leading research investigator for 1974/5. S. Tyagi Sr advised on the 1974/5 survey and S.S. Tyagi Jr has stayed in touch with the surveys from 1974/5.

The first survey was essentially focused on agriculture-related issues, with details on landholdings, crop production, livestock, and labour utilization. It also had a small module on consumption expenditure which was repeated in the 1962 survey. Apart from the structured questionnaires and the detailed notes and comments in the questionnaires, descriptions in the Ansari report provide a valuable source of insights and information on the economy and society of the village. The second survey was a follow-up survey with the same investigator. Taken together, these surveys outline changes in the village economy immediately after the land reforms of early 1950s. These reforms were essentially *zamindari* abolition, transferring secure tenancy rights or ownership to those cultivating the land.[23]

The quality of data collected as part of the first two surveys (1957/8 and 1962/3) was one of the central reasons for Christopher Bliss and Nicholas Stern to select Palanpur village as a site for their re-survey.[24] The survey in 1974 was the beginning of the in-depth surveys of Palanpur. Unlike the first two surveys, which were one-shot surveys, the 1974 survey was spread over a period of nine months. The involvement of S. Tyagi Sr and S.S. Tyagi Jr, the former as advisor and the latter as leading research investigator for the 1974/5 survey, was instrumental in maintaining continuity in the survey process.

A particular feature of the 1974/5 survey round was the detailed accounting of agricultural income (including livestock) and input use in agricultural production. It also maintained details of the inputs used (fertilizer, irrigation, ploughing, etc.), along with labour utilization in the village. In some ways, the income estimates obtained through the detailed accounting in this round were more credible than those of the first two surveys. Where possible, data were validated on both sides of transactions.

Although this round did not collect data on non-farm activities in great detail, it did collect basic information on households not engaged in agriculture.

---

[23] The abolition of the traditional *zamindari* system of land ownership was one of the major reforms carried out in India in the first decade after Independence. It was aimed at taking surplus land from the erstwhile zamindars and redistributing it to landless farmers. It did have some impact—increasing investment in agricultural production in Palanpur. However, in many places, the social power exerted by the land-owning castes in the village constrained the effectiveness of the reform and, in Palanpur, the tenants who received the land were mostly from the upper castes in the village: the Thakurs and Muraos.

[24] Bliss and Stern were interested in studying the impact of the green revolution and therefore wanted to study a village with wheat as the predominant crop. An especially important criterion was the availability of good-quality data and past surveys for the village. See also the Introduction.

The 1974/5 survey was extensively analysed by Bliss and Stern, who used the data to test various theories related to the functioning of land, labour, and credit market. These theories included choices of how much land to rent in or out, attitudes to risk as reflected through choice of inputs, and the functioning of sharecropping (Bliss and Stern, 1982). One priority for the 1974/5 survey was to gauge the impact of the green revolution on the village economy; the data confirmed a sharp rise in agricultural productivity. The expansion of irrigation on village land, which went from 50 per cent irrigated in 1957/8 to almost all in 1974/5, represented the less productive and poorer households catching up to the more productive farmers. With the broad-based adoption of new seeds and technologies, the overall result was a lowering of the inequality of incomes across households.

The 1983/4 survey was even longer in duration, with Jean Drèze and Naresh Sharma staying in the village for almost 15 months. The quality of data collected was even more detailed and careful than earlier surveys, with valid-ation of data from both sides of a transaction which was even more extensive than 1974/5. Other than data on household characteristics and agricultural production, the survey also collected detailed data on labour use. This survey round also expanded its scope to include a small anthropometric study.[25]

A special strength of this survey was the wealth of qualitative data generated by the resident investigators. These not only included discussion question-naires and structured interviews but also one of the investigators, Jean Drèze, maintaining a daily diary of observations and events in the village. Other than data collected for all households, the survey also tracked a sample of house-holds for data related to labour use and agricultural production for almost a year. The data collected as part of this round were not only the best, up to then, in terms of quality, but also deepened the examination of other aspects of village society and economy, such as nutrition and non-farm activities.[26] Although 1983 was a bad agricultural year, with low rainfall compared to 1974, which was a good agricultural year, the incomes of the village continued to increase. This was partly a result of the expansion of non-farm employ-ment, with villagers joining the non-farm workforce in neighbouring factories and worksites. It was also a period which saw continued and rapid expansion in agricultural technologies. A clear indicator of this was the advent and expansion of new technologies for lifting water, such as bore wells and tube wells, as well as increased use of tractors. At the time of the 1983/4 survey, the expansion of non-farm employment was governed primarily by access to

---

[25] The 1983 survey also collected detailed data on credit, non-farm incomes, and anthropometric data to estimate indicators of health. These are discussed further in Parts 2 and 3.

[26] Earlier surveys also collected data on non-farm activities. However, since non-farm activities were not as dominant in village economy until 1983, the focus of earlier surveys was on agricultural activities.

networks and capital, such that better-off households were best placed to diversify in this way. Nonetheless, the increase in non-farm employment and income was an important point of departure in the Palanpur economy, which thus far had relied predominantly on agriculture.

The 1993 round was a small round, with data collection restricted to basic demographic data, employment data, land, and assets.[27] This round did not collect any information on incomes, but the data collected on other aspects of the village economy and society were useful in extending the analysis to 1993. The basic fieldwork was led by Jean Drèze and Naresh Sharma. Although this round was a small one, it did reveal the fragility of non-farm employment, documenting a sharp drop in regular non-farm employment compared to 1983.

The 2008/10 round, which collected data in great depth and breadth, was the longest in terms of residence in the village, in this case for about two years. The data collected were subjected to the same rigour as was seen in the case of 1983 data, with both sides of transactions recorded and validated after careful scrutiny. An important feature of data collection in this round was the expansion of the issues covered to include health, public services, education, gender, adolescent behaviour, children, and consumption expenditure. To maintain comparability, the schedules of enquiry were kept consistent with the 1983 and earlier rounds, except for the new survey issues where questionnaires were designed to provide comparability with other secondary data. The survey round collected a large amount of qualitative information through discussion questionnaires and through focus group discussions.[28] It also incorporated a measurement of well-being, through the Participatory Rural Appraisal (PRA),[29] for which the services of trained professionals were used.[30]

The most recent survey round was conducted in 2015 and is similar in scope to the 1993 round. For the first time, the surveys were conducted on hand-held devices for quick processing and verification of data. Basic household demographics and asset characteristics were preloaded in the software and the survey was canvassed with data transmitted online for checking and verification.

---

[27] These data were combined with data on ownership of consumer durables, collected by Peter Lanjouw in 1999.

[28] Although the resident investigators did not keep a daily diary, regular reports were prepared throughout the residency of the 2008/10 survey.

[29] PRA is a tool used by governments and civil society organizations for mapping and profiling a village society with active participation from the village residents. It has been used for village planning but has also evolved as a tool for understanding the evolution of poverty in village society. For details, see Mukherjee (1995).

[30] The PRA exercise was facilitated by volunteers from ActionAid India who had expertise in PRA.

1.4 2008/10 Survey

1.4.1 *The Start and the Investigators' Residence*

Previous surveys have been described in some details in the earlier books. The 2008/10 survey was the most extensive in scope and detail, lasting for two full years of residence and with a larger team. Data quality is of great importance, and we accordingly begin with a careful description of the data collection for this survey.

Although the actual fieldwork in the village started in May 2008, the preparatory work for the survey had begun in March 2008 at the Centre de Sciences Humaines (CSH).[31] This included assembling previous questionnaires and processed data, as well as arranging the logistics of the survey. We were fortunate to have all the previous survey questionnaires as well as material used in writing the previous books available at the London School of Economics (LSE). Fortunately, all the original questionnaires, as well as diaries and written notes, have been preserved for all the survey rounds of the Palanpur survey. Very few longitudinal surveys have the privilege of going back to old survey questionnaires. Although the research team had access to the old processed data and questionnaires, it required considerable effort to convert the old computer programmes and data formats into readable formats. The data collection was originally planned for one agricultural year. However, while the survey team was in the field, the meteorological department had predicted the possibility of a severe drought in 2009. We were tempted by the idea of extending the survey to study how villagers cope with adverse weather conditions. The extension also gave us the opportunity to collect more data, particularly qualitative data on various aspects of farming, credit behaviour, and engagement in non-farm activities.

The most immediate problem was to find a place for the survey team to stay in the village. While the earlier survey teams had used the seed store within the village as their base during the period of residency, by 2008 it had collapsed in many places and was no longer inhabitable. Although some of the village residents were generous enough to offer their houses, the research team made a conscious decision to avoid staying with any of the villagers.[32] Fortunately, we did manage to find an empty house available for rent in the neighbouring village of Pipli. This was around 500 metres or 10 minutes

---

[31] CSH is a research laboratory of the Centre National de la Recherche Scientifique (CNRS), located in New Delhi.

[32] This decision was in keeping with the practice in earlier surveys. The idea was not simply to avoid incurring obligation from village residents and thereby maintain independence. It was also a conscious decision to stay away from village-level local politics. Although issues of relationship between researchers and respondents in village surveys, particularly longitudinal ones, are commonly discussed in anthropological research, the objective was to maintain as much neutrality as possible. See Burawoy (2003) on observer and respondent relationship issues.

walk from Palanpur. This house continued to be our abode for the next two years and also for occasional visits to the village thereafter. The residence in Pipli was also used for a six-month stay in 2015 for the 'quick survey'.

With the availability of computers and printers and a basic internet facility, the research office at Pipli commenced work in May 2008. The first task was to identify the households as per the 1993 survey so as to maintain the longitudinal nature of the survey, but also to help in cross-checking and validating the data compared to the earlier rounds.[33]

1.4.2 *Investing in Quality: Collection and Checking of Basic Data*

The first round of data collection was the basic demographic module, which not only collected data on the demographic profile of household members, but also on ownership of land and assets, as well as a household history covering the intervening period, including significant events after 1993. Collection of data was easy thanks to the generous cooperation of residents. We wanted to be as careful and accurate as possible, so multiple checks were built into the survey process itself. While the survey questionnaire was canvassed by one of the resident investigators, it was cross-checked and verified using secondary data as well as random checking by another resident investigator. These were then cross-checked by two (French) research assistants, Loic Watine and Florian Bersier,[34] who cross-checked it with the data from the 1993 round.[35] It was finally checked by a research assistant in Delhi where the data entry was being undertaken. While this delayed the availability of data for analysis, the thorough checks at the time of data collection meant that there were fewer issues with regard to the comparability of data later on. The process of cross-checks continued throughout the survey process, although the quality of data from initial collection improved with time as familiarity with the subjects and techniques deepened.

1.4.3 *Instruments, Questionnaires, and Diaries: Examples of Income and Family Labour*

Among all the estimates that were collected as part of the survey, the most difficult was the collection of income data, because it covers so much of

---

[33] To ease matters, the survey team put household numbers on the main doors of the households based on the 1993 survey. We are grateful to the residents for allowing us to do so.

[34] Since the beginning of the data collection in 2008 until the writing of the book, we have been fortunate to have a regular stream of research students from some of the best institutions in France who visited CSH as interns or research assistants. Most of these had an economics background (from École Polytechnique) but also included sociologists, statisticians, and political scientists. Some of them also wrote their dissertations on Palanpur.

[35] Some of the obvious issues were missing household members, wrong entry of age data, and names not matching earlier rounds. They also flagged any unusual change in household characteristics, including land.

activity, is sensitive to definitions, and reflects flows over a period of time. While income estimates have been collected as part of village surveys for quite some time now, issues of comparability across surveys present particularly onerous challenges. Among various sources of income, income from cultivation has traditionally been collected using an accounting approach, with details of inputs and outputs collected. This was the practice in the earlier surveys of Palanpur. The 2008/10 survey was no different from earlier surveys in this regard, but special attention was paid to accounting for inputs for which no markets exist.[36] Of particular importance here was the use of household family labour. Although our survey instruments could not capture these details to our full satisfaction, we also employed a diary method to ultimately arrive at reasonably good estimates.[37] The use of diaries is also not new in the Palanpur context, with both the 1974 and 1983 surveys using diaries to collect information on input use in agriculture. We followed the same households that were used as sample households for diaries in the previous surveys, but also extended the coverage to include new households. This was particularly useful for estimating incomes of households where members were self-employed or which had multiple sources of income. The diary entries not only recorded the use of inputs, purchased or otherwise, but also labour use, consumption expenditure, and, in some cases, details on outside employment. The diaries were maintained in around 70 households for a period of 10 months covering both the agricultural seasons, *rabi* and *kharif*.[38] Of these, complete information was ultimately available for only 48 households, although we did make use of information on different aspects from all 70 household diaries.[39]

For most of the variables for which data were collected, the 2008/10 survey tried to maintain the conceptual framework as well as the methodology of data collection used in the previous surveys, particularly the intensive and

---

[36] Although most village surveys have some estimate of income from cultivation, there is no uniformity regarding the concepts used. This is particularly problematic for inputs for which imputation is needed. Generally, these are fixed capital, including land, where depreciation rates are difficult to define and compile, and even if they are available, lack of information on the date of purchase and asset quality is an issue. This is also an issue for seeds, water, and family labour. As much as possible, the cultivation income estimates in this book have tried to follow the standard methodology suggested by the Commission for Agricultural Costs and Prices (CACP) while maintaining comparability with earlier estimates of income.

[37] The diaries were kept with the households, with household members filling in specified information on a daily basis. The diaries were checked every week by the resident investigators. In those households where there were no adult literate members, the resident investigators would fill in the information by asking them about details of the previous week.

[38] The original list of sample households in 1983 included 36 households. These increased to around 50 because of the splitting of households. We added 20 more households to cover self-employed and wage labour households.

[39] In some cases, the diaries were incomplete because the household head left the village temporarily or gaps in data were not filled in. In some cases, we lost the diaries when they were torn up by monkeys in the village, and in two cases the diaries were eaten by buffaloes.

detailed 1983/4 survey. In some cases, changes in the nature of production necessitated changes of method, for example the greater monetization of inputs in agriculture, such as the development of a market for pumping water and the markets for various machines. A particular challenge was that definitions in earlier surveys were rather loose in the case of non-farm income. We used accounting methods for these incomes wherever possible. We also conducted special investigations of certain non-farm activities. The income estimates for those employed in marble polishing, brick kiln work, or repair shops were important examples. Particular attention was also paid to other sources of income such as informal moneylending, remittances, pensions, and other transfers. For most of these, we used different survey instruments where information was cross-checked from both sides of transactions. This was particularly the case for income from informal moneylending and remittances.

1.4.4 Coverage

The 2008/10 survey also made significant departures from earlier surveys in terms of coverage of issues. While some of these were necessary to improve the quality of analysis, some were entirely new. For example, consumption surveys were canvassed in the case of Palanpur after a gap of more than four decades. Information on consumption expenditure was collected as part of the first two surveys but not in the subsequent ones. In India, analyses of poverty and inequality have traditionally been based on consumption survey estimates.[40] The consumption survey in Palanpur was structured in a way which allowed us to have the broadest possible comparability with the National Sample Survey Office consumption expenditure survey estimates. We also followed a methodology of data collection spread throughout the year to cover flows as they occur and thus provide good estimates. Similarly, we also conducted a small survey based on the Socio-Economic and Caste Census (SECC) questionnaire.[41] These were also followed up with qualitative assessments of poverty in the village through the PRA technique. The PRA was administered by experts trained in the technique and the results were tabulated by the research team based in the village. Our indicators of nutrition and anthropometry this time included the entire village, unlike 1983, which involved only a sample.

---

[40] Official estimates of poverty and inequality in India are available only from consumption surveys. However, a few national surveys on income also exist. Notable among these are the income estimates from the IHDS of the National Council of Applied Economic Research (NCAER) and University of Maryland. The official poverty lines are based on consumption estimates.

[41] The SECC was a nationwide census carried out by the Government of India in 2011 to generate information for identification of beneficiaries of various government schemes. It included details on caste as well as other social indicators.

The second set of issues on which the 2008/10 survey has better and deeper coverage are issues related to human development. While some information on education and health was available in all the surveys, we have for the first time collected detailed information on education and health using separate survey instruments. On education, we collected information on the type of educational institutions and costs, including tuition fees and other related expenditures. On health, we collected information on expenditure, sources of expenditure, distribution, and access to facilities by the public and private sector. We were also fortunate to have a team of female researchers, which also allowed us to look at issues concerning women in greater detail. Information was collected not just on standard economic indicators, but also on mobility, decision-making, reproductive choices, intra-household behaviour, and domestic violence.[42] These were also followed up with detailed discussion questionnaires on adolescents, the elderly, and child labour.

Although the process of intensive data collection was limited to the 2008/10 period, several follow-up visits have been undertaken by the research team every year since.[43] These included not just visits to fill up gaps in the data from the 2008/10 survey but also to garner additional information on the changes in village in the intervening period. However, as considerable time had elapsed since the 2008/10 survey and because the period after 2008/10 showed significant changes in the behaviour of households, a small follow-up survey was conducted in 2015.

1.4.5 *The 2015 Survey*

This was similar in scope to the 1993 survey and was focused on collecting basic data on demography, employment, land, assets, education, and migration. However, as a considerable amount of work on cleaning data from the 2008/10 round had already been done, we could use the cleaned data for designing questionnaires as well as cross-checks built into the survey. These were, for the first time, conducted with hand-held devices. The availability of software-based data collection allowed us to cross-check the internal consistency of data quickly. We also included some open-ended questions which were based on the analysis that we had done so far. We have used the information from the 2015 survey in all the chapters that follow, wherever possible. However, for

---

[42] The task of collecting information from female members of households was led by Dipa Sinha along with a team of female researchers. The team was quickly able to gain trust of female household members and encourage them to cooperate with the survey process. Some of the questions, such as those concerning domestic violence and intra-household behaviour, were sensitive and so it was key there was a good level of trust between the respondent and research team.

[43] The follow-up surveys in some cases were intensive, with prolonged stays in the village for weeks and months. We have been visiting the village three to four times almost every year since 2010.

some of the variables, such as agricultural production, incomes, poverty, and inequality, the analysis is largely based on data up to the 2008/10 survey.

1.4.6 Institutions, Politics, and Society

The data collection on most of the variables used in the analysis was based on structured questionnaires. However, the data collection through these questionnaires was only a part of the overall evidence that we used in the analysis. A large volume of data and information was collected on aspects of society, politics, and institutions in the village, using different qualitative methods. The two-year period of residence and the subsequent follow-up visits allowed the team to engage with the villagers on a range of issues. Some of these were very personal and we have kept these confidential, but some of them were open discussions on the state of society and on politics at the state and national levels. We endeavoured to keep notes on most of these discussions. Researchers also made notes based on their own observations of events such as marriages, religious festivals, and markets in the village in which all of them participated. These accounts were not always in full agreement.

We also used structured discussion questionnaires which were focused on understanding the functioning of various economic, social, and political institutions. Notable among them were discussion questionnaires on tenancy, caste, village politics, credit, and gender issues. These were later coded and analysed. As part of our effort to understand institutional structures, we also conducted informal discussions in villages around Palanpur. Some of these discussions and structured questionnaires were also canvassed in urban areas where Palanpur residents would go to work. We paid special attention to the study of brick kilns, Moradabad railway yard, and marble polishers in Chandausi. We made repeated visits to these and several other sites to understand the nature of work and the functioning of the labour market. Wherever possible, we also conducted interviews with contractors, employers, and middlemen.

1.5 Quality Matters: Lessons for Data Assessment and Design

Sound information is a fundamental component of the analysis of any subject that seeks rigour, accuracy, and validity. This is even more so for the study of the processes of development, which are often situated in places witnessing rapid changes and with social and economic structures that can defy the simplicity that theory often seeks. Our journey through the years of data collection in a village setting helped us identify and understand the pitfalls of relying on secondary data or even one-time village surveys in testing theories of development. Some of these are important lessons for anybody interested in pursuing village surveys. But they are also of real importance for the design and implementation of large-scale surveys and for understanding national data.

We have learnt the value of accurate data from the experience of investigators of previous surveys who maintained meticulous diaries and records of the process of data collection. As there is considerable overlap between information collected through the structured questionnaires and qualitative surveys, the analytical strategy used in the book has been to employ a combination of data and qualitative information, along with the personal observations of investigators and researchers, to arrive at a better understanding of the village, its households, and its trends and patterns than would be available from standard quantitative questionnaires. In this section, we discuss some of the issues which are important for practitioners of village survey studies, but will also aid those who design, implement, and use large-scale surveys.

These lessons have become even more relevant as recent decades have seen a large expansion of primary surveys in development economics. Some of this is driven by the need to have controlled data on programme intervention,[44] which can be observed only through primary surveys. But the expansion has also arisen from those pursuing specific areas of enquiry which are not well informed by existing secondary data. This increase in primary data collection, however, has not been without its problems; due to the quality of data collected, conflicting results have often arisen. Differences may be due to the choice of survey instruments, methodology of data collected, purpose of investigation, and, lastly, the analytical strategy. Sampling errors can also be important, although for comprehensive village studies such as ours, sampling is not an issue. The absence of a generally accepted definition of variables used and the protocol for conducting these surveys has also contributed to each researcher using his/her own survey instruments and methodology.[45] The problem of faulty measurements affecting results is not limited to primary surveys but appears also in large-scale national surveys. A good example of this is the controversy that emerged around poverty estimates from the 55th round (1999/2000) of the NSSO.[46]

---

[44] For example, estimating the most effective price of mosquito nets in Africa for their maximum use via randomized control trials (RCTs) (Cohen and Dupas, 2010).

[45] Although there are exceptions such as Grosh and Glewwe (2000) on the Living Standards Measurement Study (LSMS) surveys. For a good survey on measurement problems, see *Journal of Development Economics*, 98, nos 1–2.

[46] The NSSO introduced two different recall periods for obtaining information on consumption expenditure for the 55th round, unlike the previous practice of collecting information on consumption expenditure based on a uniform reference period of 30 days. The problem was compounded by the design of questionnaire, where both these recall periods were used in the same block, thus contaminating the estimates of consumption expenditure. For details see Sen (2000) and Sen and Himanshu (2004a, 2004b). The issue of recall period is also flagged by Das et al.

1.5.1 *Credibility of Investigators*

All the researchers who have contributed to the analysis of Palanpur data have also been closely involved with collection of data. Some of them, including Nicholas Stern, Jean Drèze, Naresh Sharma, Himanshu, and Dipa Sinha, have lived in the village for extended periods of time.

One of the first lessons from our experience is that respondents' behaviour differs depending on the perceived credibility of the investigators, the purpose of the survey, and the methodology of data collection.[47] While we were fortunate that the previous team of researchers and investigators commanded great respect from the villagers,[48] this was not the case for all data collection efforts in the village.[49] The fact that the previous research team had maintained contact with the village over the years also helped us to start with some understanding and familiarity of the area.[50] The availability of previous data and questionnaires meant that we had a fairly good idea of the social composition of the village as well as the general background of agricultural production, the labour market, and so on.

1.5.2 *External Validation*

One of the big challenges in most village surveys (as for large-scale surveys) is the absence of a widely accepted statement of 'the true number' for the variable being collected. Each village is different and there is no way of using some external criterion for the validity of data collected, much less in

---

(2012) in their survey on doctor visits and income levels. They report differential recall effects across income groups with reverse sign of the gradient between doctor visits and per capita expenditures. They report greater use of health-care providers among the poor compared to the rich using weekly recall surveys in Delhi. However, the pattern is reversed when the surveys are done using monthly recall, with higher use of health-care providers among the rich compared to the poor.

[47] On being probed on differences in response to surveys, residents reported being cautious of random researchers if they felt the data could be used for targeting of benefits as part of government schemes. For example, identification of beneficiaries of housing benefit and social pensions depends on surveys by respective ministries. Villagers claimed that government surveys were often conducted by students, who are contracted to collect information on behalf of government agencies. They did, however, seem open to 'genuine' researchers.

[48] Our first visits were with Naresh Sharma, Jean Drèze, and Nicholas Stern, all of whom were held in high esteem for their integrity and commitment to the cause of research on Palanpur.

[49] The two previous books on Palanpur have prompted some other researchers to go to Palanpur for follow-up surveys. During our stay in 2008, a team of researchers from Lucknow University also came to the village with a view to undertaking a survey. The non-cooperation of the villagers forced them to abandon the survey within a week.

[50] Jean Drèze had been visiting the village almost on an annual basis. Nicholas Stern has also continued his association with the village and has been to the village many times between surveys as well, of course, as during surveys.

comparisons with secondary data.[51] While in some cases administrative or official data can be a useful benchmark, there is great degree of scepticism over official data, particularly that collected by government officials.[52] As a general exercise, we did compare most of our estimates with comparable estimates available from secondary data. This was done for population estimates with census estimates; agricultural cost estimates with CACP estimates; land data with revenue records; poverty, inequality, and consumption expenditure estimates with NSSO-based estimates; and anthropometry estimates with NFHS and Reproductive and Child Health (RCH) survey estimates.[53] We also compared the data collected with official and administrative records of the *anganwadi* centre,[54] school and Public Distribution System (PDS) records, Mahatma Gandhi National Rural Employment Guarantee Scheme (MGNREGS) records, and loan records from the cooperative bank. While our estimates matched broadly with independent survey-based estimates from NSSO and CACP, we did observe differences when compared to data reported as part of the Below Poverty Line (BPL) census.[55] We also observed differences in the data on school attendance reported by respondents compared to official school rosters.[56] The extent of variation in the data on school attendance was found to be higher for Muraos and other caste groups compared to Jatabs.

1.5.3 *Internal Consistency and Cross-Checking*

For Palanpur, or indeed any longitudinal village study, there are issues of internal consistency which can be divided into vertical and horizontal consistency. We define horizontal consistency as issues of consistency between the variable for which information was collected within the same round but as part of different schedules or at different points of time. On the other hand,

---

[51] While such comparisons are often resorted to, care must be taken to ensure comparability of definitions, concepts, and methodology between two surveys.

[52] Baird and Özler (2012) look at the differences in self-reporting by teacher and student compared to administrative data from schools. They find that self-reported data was much more accurate than those recorded by administrative officials.

[53] Wherever possible, our comparison was based on data from secondary sources at the lowest level of disaggregation. While we did have data below sub-district level from the CACP and census, other data sources were available only at district or state level.

[54] The *anganwadi* is a centre for rural mothers and children to provide health and nutrition services as a part of the Integrated Child Development Services (ICDS) programme. While providing various services to pregnant mothers and children, the officials also maintain data on various aspects of child nutrition and pregnancy.

[55] One of the exercises that we did was to validate the information collected as part of the government census for identification of programme beneficiaries. We did this using the BPL census in 2002 and the SECC 2011. While the data on BPL 2002 were found to be largely problematic except for the poorest households, we did find that the SECC 2011 data were not very different from the data collected by our 2008/10 survey.

[56] The village school attendance records showed a much larger attendance compared to our own random cross-verification.

vertical consistency meant consistency across survey rounds. Whilst consistency poses challenges, responding to those challenges strengthens data.[57] The criterion of ensuring horizontal and vertical consistency was applied for all the variables that were collected as part of the survey.

We paid special attention to some of the variables which were crucial to the analysis. These were generally information on land, tenancy, credit, income, consumption, employment, and anthropometry. For example, one of the first variables which required a considerable effort was information on landholdings. While this was collected as part of the demographic section of the survey, it was also collected in subsequent cultivation rounds. We did realize quite early that the data that were collected in the demographic module needed a cross-check. At the early part of the survey itself we managed to get the land records of the village from the block office. This was a voluminous 1500 pages of land records for each of the land parcels of the village. But it turned out that this information was of very little help.[58] We also used satellite imagery of the village land and started assigning parcels to households which claimed ownership. While this helped, we did have problems matching the satellite pictures to areas of land under ownership of each household. Finally, we used the old method of actually measuring each and every parcel of land. While this took some time, we did manage to establish ownership of land in the village together with accurate measures of land area. Thus we found that there was no substitute for direct observation in the village itself.

The actual measurement and mapping was done by Bertrand Lefebvre who was a geographer affiliated to CSH in 2008. When we were taking the measurements, some of the village residents accompanied us. We did report to them the discrepancy between information that they had reported to us and the actual land ownership. They said, 'If we knew that you are actually going to measure the land we would have informed you correctly, but we thought you were like usual researchers who come and collect data and disappear. There is no incentive for us to strain our minds and spend time and energy to give all the information accurately.' Not only did taking this action correct our land data, it also convinced the villagers of the sincerity of our intentions and greatly increased their cooperation in sharing details with us.

---

[57] A further effort was made to cross-check the data with available information from secondary sources but these differences were noted with no attempt to correct them. Throughout the book, we have made efforts to situate the Palanpur story in the broad context of developments in India, Uttar Pradesh, and Moradabad district. We have tried to use the available secondary data as much as possible in our analysis, attempting to maintain comparability with external data in terms of definitions, concepts, and units of measurement.

[58] The obvious issues were matching the names of land owners from the official records to those in our survey. The problem was partly that actual ownership of land was informally divided among split households but continued to show the father/mother as the owner even after the death of the parents, and also because land sales were not recorded or updated in the official records.

Table 1.1 provides data on land ownership obtained through the first schedule of demographic information, as well as information collected through subsequent cultivation schedules. The demographic schedule also has information on land ownership. The data on land ownership also happened to be the basic building block of our more detailed cultivation schedules over time. However, unlike the demographic schedule, the cultivation schedule used information at the plot level to gain detailed information on crops grown, inputs used, and output produced. The differences in information on land owned and cultivation suggest a pattern of higher differences in land cultivated than land owned. We also observe lower variation in the statistic among Muraos and Thakurs compared to Jatabs, where the extent of under-reporting is significant for all categories of land information except land leased-out.

Table 1.1 Land by caste from different schedules

Caste Group	Demographic Schedule (May–July 2008)				Cultivation Schedules (September–November 2008)			
	owned	leased-in	leased-out	cultivated	owned	leased-in	leased-out	cultivated
Thakur	577	89	122	544	595	174	230	539
Murao	763	108	124	747	775	210	138	847
Dhimar	41	21	2	60	55	25	0	80
Gadaria	150	13	23	140	173	53	50	176
Dhobi	27	38	0	65	38	48	5	81
Teli	97	62	10	149	94	106	26	174
Passi	44	0	32	12	45	0	35	10
Jatab	103	84	10	177	159	253	13	399
Other	4	3	1	6	34	0	0	34
All	1806	418	323	1901	1968	867	497	2338

These findings strike a cautionary note regarding the assumed quality of data from a standard large-scale household survey. Such surveys often collect information via an instrument similar to our first demographic schedule, and even then most likely involve less time and local knowledge than we had. Quick aggregate numbers can be unreliable with biases which are not uniform. Detailed and persistent investigation matters.

Similar inconsistencies were observed in the data on credit. The problem was a mismatch of information reported by borrowers and lenders. Among the borrowers, there was a general tendency to under-report loans taken from moneylenders for consumption purposes. For the moneylenders in the village, they were reluctant to share information on extent of loans or interest rates charged. We also observed discrepancies in the early phases of data collection on cultivation expenses and output in sharecropped plots. Some of these were later corrected, with detailed matching of information and persistent enquiry eliminating the discrepancies.

1.5.4 *Female Researchers and Investigators*

A significant omission in the research teams prior to 2008 was the near absence of female researchers and investigators.[59] While this did not exclude discussion of gender-related issues in previous surveys, it did constrain the survey team from collecting information on issues such as women's autonomy (see Chapter 10) and the perspectives of women in Palanpur more generally. The 2008 survey team was fortunate to comprise a large number of female researchers and investigators who collected and analysed data on various aspects of economic and human development in the village.[60] The presence of female researchers helped the survey team to establish contact with the women in the village. It was particularly helpful in collecting information on issues of women's participation in the labour market, their autonomy, reproductive behaviour, and marital relations. On issues of tenancy and the credit market, their perspective offered additional and valuable insight into the overall understanding of these markets. The process of data collection was not easy but we believe the presence of female researchers and the access to women respondents did add to our understanding of the various issues in the village.[61]

1.5.5 *Qualitative Data: Discussion and Diaries*

One of the unique features of the Palanpur surveys has been the extensive use of qualitative information collected by the researchers. Some has been collected through structured discussion questionnaires, but a large part has been made up of observations of researchers during the course of the stay in the village. A valuable source of information for the 1983 survey is the diary kept by Jean Drèze. While no such diaries were maintained during the 2008/10 surveys, the research team at the village managed to write weekly and fortnightly reports on several issues which were later used for analysis. So far, only a part of the qualitative information has been used in the 1983 as well as 2008/10 survey analyses, but such information remains useful for understanding the

---

[59] The 1983 survey included Jocelyn Kynch and Anindita Mukherjee, who analysed the data on nutrition and labour-market behaviour, respectively. The data on nutrition was collected by Jocelyn Kynch during a short visit to the village. Sue Stern visited during the 1974/5 study and carried out the mapping (as a former geography student). That allowed some informal interaction with women in Palanpur.

[60] During the majority of the 2008/10 survey period, there was a female researcher stationed in the village. Female researchers not only collected information on aspects of gender, but also on economic issues.

[61] It is generally not acceptable for male investigators and researchers to talk to female household members. While there is no social sanction to males talking to young girls and elderly women, married women largely stayed inside the home. Even for female investigators, the challenge was to ask questions without any interference from mothers-in-law or other senior female members of the household.

choices made by individuals and households with regard to tenancy, credit, and migration, as well as participation in the labour market. There are possibilities for further research here.

1.5.6 The 2015 Survey and More Modern Technology

While the 2008/10 survey involved a stay of two full years and data collection that was spread over various topics, the 2015 survey was much shorter, covering only six months. Furthermore, the 2015 survey was also different in nature from all the previous surveys since the entire survey was done on tablets and used pre-filled questionnaires. The use of pre-filled questionnaires on the tablet helped in faster processing of the data collected and also faster checking of inconsistencies. The 2015 survey was a limited survey, with the basic purpose of updating the basic information from the 2008/10 survey round. But the use of new technology allowed the research team to collect, validate, and analyse the data in a time-efficient way. In particular, the use of satellite data and cartography tools can be of help in future surveys, while tablets and software can help in weeding out inconsistencies.

1.5.7 Lessons

By describing the processes of checking and verification we used in Palanpur and the experiences from them, we have drawn out lessons which apply to village surveys, longitudinal village surveys, and large-scale survey data. Some lessons apply to all three and others to a subset of the three. We summarize them briefly:

(i) Pay attention to the perceived credibility and integrity of the investigators. Mutual respect matters greatly to the willingness of respondents to concentrate on the accuracy of responses.

(ii) Seek out external sources such as administrative data or other surveys. There will be differences which can be instructive.

(iii) Identify and exploit opportunities for checking for inconsistencies within the data. Where possible, check both sides of transactions, for example on credit. Mistrust the instant responses, such as for totals for land owned and cultivated, and where possible and necessary use direct measurement. Recognise that biases may not be uniform across groups and try to get some understanding of them.

(iv) Build a mixed group of investigators, male and female. This seems to matter not only for issues directly affecting women and their perceptions, but also for other data such as land and credit.

(v) Make use of qualitative data, discussion, and diaries. These are of great value not only in understanding perceptions and context but also in resolving discrepancies revealed from other cross-checks.

(vi) The use of modern technology allows not only immediate checking for some inconsistencies with data currently being collected, but also the reloading of existing information which allows for instant checks with past data.

From these six broad lessons and the examples that we have used to illustrate them, we must confess to considerable scepticism about those large-scale sample surveys that rely only on a few hours of interaction, where investigators have little knowledge of the context, little existing credibility, and only modest incentives to make the effort to record things accurately. This does not mean that we discard such surveys. We need them; but it does mean that we can and should make use of very intensive local studies to understand how biases can arise.

1.6 Capturing Change and Designing for Change

Finally, in this chapter we return to the issues raised at the beginning on the value of village studies and longitudinal village studies. We have explained our investments in trying to make data as reliable as possible and the issues of vertical consistency (across survey years) and horizontal consistency (within survey years). Data quality matters and much can be done in village studies to ensure that they provide a useful, interesting, and reliable check on evidence from large-scale surveys.

Longitudinal village studies have the key advantage of tracking change over time, a detail that permits the examination of the forces of change and the institutional context within which change takes place. Longitudinal studies speak to the central issue in economic development: how and why the lives and livelihoods of people change, improve, or deteriorate.

In order to follow this agenda of understanding and investigation, we must have some core variables which are collected consistently over the years. Where the surveys were not originally designed, as is currently the case, as longitudinal, that can involve a great deal of work. This was certainly true in the case of Palanpur and was a major call on our resources (e.g. in getting the earlier surveys into a comparable form). Access to the original questionnaires and to the earlier investigators and researchers has been a major advantage in this crucial task.

But the research is about change, and that means change has to be built into data collection. It would not make sense to insist only on common case variables. Technologies in agriculture change, external non-farm opportunities arise, new consumer durables, such as mobile phones, appear, new institutions arrive, new policy measures appear, and new political circumstances arise. That means the surveys themselves must change as the economy and society changes.

The argument that longitudinal village studies are of real, indeed indispensable, value in understanding development is, we think, overwhelming. We hope to add to the argument with the analyses, stories, and ideas offered in this book. Whether we have succeeded is for the reader to decide. For ourselves, we have learned an enormous amount and are already thinking about the next survey of Palanpur.

Acknowledgements

We have benefited enormously from the inputs provided by the research investigators Dinesh Tiwari, Gajanand Ahirwal, Hemendra Ahiwar, Ashish Tyagi, and Dipa Sinha. We have also benefited from the detailed records of data collection maintained by Jean Drèze and Naresh Sharma for the earlier surveys.

References

Ansari, N. 1964. 'Palanpur: A Study of its Economic Resources and Economic Activities', Continuous Village Survey 41. Agricultural Economics Research Centre, University of Delhi.

Bailey, F.G. 1957. *Caste and the Economic Frontier: A Village in Highland Orissa*. Manchester: Manchester University Press.

Baird, S., and Özler, B. 2012. 'Examining the reliability of self-reported data on school participation', *Journal of Development Economics* 98, no. 1: 89–93.

Bardhan, P. 1989. *'Conversations between economists and anthropologists: methodological issues in measuring economic change in rural India.'* Delhi and New York: Oxford University Press.

Bliss, C. J., and Stern, N. 1982. *Palanpur: The Economy of an Indian Village*. Oxford and New York: Oxford University Press.

Breman, J. 2007. *The Poverty Regime in Village India*. New Delhi: Oxford University Press.

Burawoy, M. 2003. 'Revisits: an outline of a theory of reflexive ethnography', *American Sociological Review* 68: 645–79.

Cohen, J., and Dupas, P. 2010. 'Free distribution or cost-sharing? Evidence from a randomized malaria prevention experiment', *Quarterly Journal of Economics* 125: 1–45.

Das, J., Hammer, J., and Sánchez-Paramo, C. 2012. 'The impact of recall periods on reported morbidity and health seeking behavior', *Journal of Development Economics* 98, no. 1: 76–88.

Dasgupta, B. 1975. 'A typology of village socio-economic systems: from Indian village studies', *Economic & Political Weekly* 10: 1395–414.

Dube, S.C. 1955. *Indian Village*. London: Routledge and Kegan Paul.

Epstein, T.S. 1962. *Economic Development and Social Change in South India*. Manchester: Manchester University Press.

Etienne, G. 2014. *Indian Villages: Achievements and Alarm Bells, 1952–2012*. Geneva: Graduate Institute Publications.

Grosh, M., and Glewwe, P. 2000. *Designing Household Survey Questionnaires for Developing Countries: Lessons from Ten Years of LSMS Experience*. Washington D.C. World Bank.

Harriss, J. 1989. 'Knowing about rural economic change: Problems arising from a comparison of the results of "macro" and "micro" research in Tamil Nadu', in P. Bardhan (ed.), *Conversations between Economists and Anthropologists: Methodological Issues in Measuring Economic Change in Rural India*. Delhi: Oxford University Press.

Harriss, J., and Jeyaranjan, J. 2016. 'Rural Tamil Nadu in the liberalization era: what do we learn from village studies?' in Himanshu, P. Jha, and G. Rodgers (eds), *The Changing Village in India: Insights from Longitudinal Research*. Delhi: Oxford University Press.

Himanshu, Jha, P., and Rodgers, G. (eds). 2016. *The Changing Village in India: Insights from Longitudinal Research*. Delhi: Oxford University Press.

Hopper, W.D. 1965. 'Allocation efficiency in a traditional Indian agriculture', *Journal of Farm Economics* 47, no. 3: 611–24.

Jayaraman, R., and Lanjouw, P. 1999. 'The evolution of poverty and inequality in Indian villages', *World Bank Research Observer* 14, no. 1: 1–30.

Jha, P., and Thakur, A. 2016. 'Thirty years on: work and well-being in rural Bihar', in Himanshu, P. Jha, and G. Rodgers (eds), *The Changing Village in India: Insights from Longitudinal Research*. Delhi: Oxford University Press.

Jodhka, S.S. 2016. 'A forgotten "revolution": revisiting rural life and agrarian change in Haryana', in Himanshu, P. Jha, and G. Rodgers (eds), *The Changing Village in India: Insights from Longitudinal Research*. Delhi: Oxford University Press.

Mukherjee, A. 1995. *Participatory Rural Appraisal: Methods and Applications in Rural Planning*. Delhi: Vikas Publishing House.

Mukherjee, R. 1978. 'On village studies in India', in A.R. Desai, *Rural Sociology in India*. Bombay: Popular Prakashan.

Nagaraj, K. 2008. 'A note on methods of village study', paper presented at Studying Village Economies in India: A Colloquium on Methodology, Madras Institute of Development Studies, 21 December.

Sen, A. 2000. 'Estimates of consumer expenditure and its distribution: statistical priorities after NSS 55th round', *Economic & Political Weekly* 35: 4499–518.

Sen, A., and Himanshu. 2004a. 'Poverty and inequality in India: I', *Economic & Political Weekly* 39: 4247–63.

Sen, A., and Himanshu. 2004b. 'Poverty and inequality in India: II: widening disparities during the 1990s', *Economic & Political Weekly* 39: 4361–75.

Sharma, A.N., and Rodgers, G. 2015. 'Structural change in Bihar's rural economy', *Economic & Political Weekly* 50, no. 52: 45.

Slater, G. 1918. *Some South Indian Villages*, vol. 1. New York and Oxford: H. Milford and Oxford University Press.

Srinivas, M.N. 1955. *India's Villages*. Bombay, Calcutta, New Delhi, Madras, Lucknow, London, and New York: Asia Publishing House.

Srivastava, R. 2016. 'Assessing change: land, labour, and employment in an eastern UP village, 1994–2012', in Himanshu, Praveen Jha, and Gerry Rodgers (eds), *The Changing Village in India: Insights from Longitudinal Research*. Delhi: Oxford University Press.

Townsend, R.M. 2016. 'Village and larger economies: the theory and measurement of the Townsend Thai project', *Journal of Economic Perspectives* 30, no. 4: 199–220.

Wadley, S.S., and Derr, B.W. 1989. 'Karimpur 1925–1984: understanding rural India through restudies', in P. Bardhan (ed.), *Conversations between Economists and Anthropologists: Methodological Issues in Measuring Economic Change in Rural India*. Delhi: Oxford University Press.

Walker, T.S., and Ryan, J.G. 1990. *Village and Household Economics in India's Semi-Arid Tropics*. Baltimore, MD: Johns Hopkins University Press.

Wiser, C.V., and Wiser, W.H. 1971. *Behind Mud Walls, 1930–1960*. Berkeley, CA: University of California Press.

Wiser, C.V., and Wiser, W.H. 2001. *Behind Mud Walls: Seventy-Five Years in a North Indian Village*. Berkeley, CA: University of California Press.

2

Palanpur

The Village through Seven Decades*

2.1 Introduction

The researchers working on the village of Palanpur and its development since the 1950s have attempted to tell its story through data and numbers. In this chapter we offer a broad, largely, but not exclusively, quantitative story of the village and how it has changed, to provide a feel for life and progress there and offer a context for the more detailed treatments that follow. We begin, however, with some brief, more personal, descriptions which span the years.

We start with an observation from the Ansari report (1964), which was the first report on the village. One of the reasons that Palanpur had been chosen as the site of research for the Bliss and Stern (1982) study was the quality of the initial data collection and scholarship, of which the Ansari report was an important part.

> The approach to the village gives quite a pleasant look because of the two gardens that the village has, which means a good number of trees around. The village habitat itself consists largely of mud houses and a few brick houses. On one side a big pucca building houses the seed store and the Integrated Cooperative Marketing Society.[1] A dharamshala (rest house), which is also a pucca building, stands just near the entry of the village and close to the railway station, presumably in order to be within the easy reach of the travellers . . . While from outside the village gives a pleasant look because of the gardens around it, from within it is quite shabby and dirty. Houses are mostly kuccha and have been built in a crowded manner. Lanes

---

* This chapter has been written by Himanshu, Peter Lanjouw, Nicholas Stern, and Dipa Sinha.
[1] A *pucca* (or *pukka*) house is generally brick, stone, or concrete. The word means solid, or permanent. A *kuccha* (or *kaccha*) house is generally mud.

are narrow and dirty with water often running through them because of lack of drainage facilities.

The fact that the village is well-linked with cities such as Moradabad and Chandausi does not seem to have been very significant from the point of view of the village economy. The nearness to the town of Bilari alone seems to have been important. This importance also has not arisen because of the fact that Bilari is a town but because of its having a sugar mill. (Ansari, 1964:3)

Ansari (1964) provides a view of Palanpur and the probable state of many other villages in post-Independence India. There were some signs of change and progress, in the seed store and the cooperative (which would play an important role in Palanpur in relation to the technical advances embodied in the green revolution). However, most other parts of the village were poor and dilapidated.

Sue Stern,[2] who visited Palanpur in 1974 and then again in 2002, presents her impression on the village and the changes that she saw in it in the following observation:

Our visit in 2002 was the first where we had been able to drive from Delhi to the village, although the last kilometres of the 'road' were rudimentary. The seed-store accommodation we had occupied in 1974/5 was now derelict. Sadly, the mango orchard, near the seed store, had been cut down, as had many other trees in and around the village. The presence of a few TV aerials was striking for a village that was without electricity in 1974.[3] Many more houses were pucca, where kaccha had predominated. The atmosphere in the village appeared somewhat more relaxed. More women were visible outside the home. The children looked better, physically, their clothes were less ragged and many more of them were wearing shoes or sandals. In agriculture where water had been mostly lifted by Persian wheels driven by buffalo, encouraged in their task by children, you now saw and heard diesel-engined pumping sets. The village did not feel as timeless as on my initial visit. (Sue Stern, July 2017)

During her first trip in 1974/5, Sue drew the map of the village lanes and houses/compounds using a protractor-compass and a pencil and pacing out the distances.[4] This involved spending time in each part of the village, always accompanied by a crowd of curious children. As a woman, she was welcomed more easily into the home by the women of the household (the other investigators in 1974/5 were all male). She returned briefly with her children, aged five, three, and one, in the spring of 1982, but then not again until 2002. Her comparison between 2002 and 1974/5 covers more than a quarter of a century.

---

[2] Sue (Susan) is the wife of Nicholas Stern.
[3] Electricity came to the village in the mid-1990s.
[4] See Bliss and Stern (1982).

This third snapshot of Palanpur by Jean Drèze,[5] on his visit to Palanpur in December 2014, also evokes change:

The village looks quite different now from what it looked like in 1983/4—almost like a tiny town, with brick houses, paved roads and drains almost everywhere (just a few mud houses are left). There are definitely more durables of all sorts—motorbikes, tractors, TVs, mobiles, some satellite dishes (and possibly laptops), even toilets (not sure how many—perhaps 15–20). Life looks less harsh—people have warm clothes, children look healthier, and there is also much greater connectedness to the outside world, especially for men, who come and go quite a lot (not just by train but also by road), and to some extent, even for women, if only through mobiles and television.[6]

The three descriptions cover more than half a century and capture important dimensions of change that will be subject to close attention in subsequent chapters. But the story is not one of unalloyed progress. In his account, Drèze moved on to bemoan the lack of social progress over the years, the closing of the village teashop—previously a popular gathering place for the villagers—and the general absence of public amenities and services that could contribute to a stronger sense of community in the village. These observations are also central to the story.

Palanpur is a small village in western Uttar Pradesh. It is not particularly unusual amongst India's half a million or so villages in its social and economic structure, but it cannot, of course, be seen as 'representative' in any formal sense. What makes Palanpur important for understanding the broad changes underway in rural India is that it is 'uniquely endowed' with data and studies. It is this uniqueness of longitudinal data over seven decades that has allowed a small village of a little over 1000 inhabitants in 2015 to become an observatory on the myriad ways in which the rural economy of India is affected by, and in turn affects, the broader economic policies and outcomes for the nation as a whole. And it can provide insights for the workings of and possibilities for public policy.

The original Palanpur study, and the choice of the village, was guided by the kinds of questions and objectives that have long engaged researchers and policy-makers concerned with understanding the possible paths of transition and growth of the rural economy. There has also, across the studies, been a concern to identify specific points in the history of Independent India which were of particular significance for the economic transformation of the village.

---

[5] Jean resided in the village for a duration of 15 months during the 1983/4 survey. He has maintained his contacts with the village and has been visiting Palanpur on a regular basis since the 1980s.

[6] Personal email to other members of research team following his visit on 14–15 December 2014.

Some of the changes in the structure of rural markets, and the evolution of the village economy in general, have led to shifts in emphasis across the years within the study itself. But, overall, the detail and nature of the data collected over the long survey period permit not only a reflection on the changes underway in village India, but also on underlying theoretical questions which have been crucial in explaining change in a primarily rural society and its linkages with the 'outside' world.

In this and Chapter 3, we use the data collected in a careful and structured way through extended stays to provide a description of the basic features of the village and its evolution in the last seven decades. The description, analysis, and inferences about change in the village are based not just on the analysis of quantitative data, but also on a wealth of information collected through informal discussions and diaries kept by the investigators. As described in Chapter 1, we are fortunate to be able to draw on the original questionnaires and on abundant original notes, diaries, and on annotations to the questionnaires, which are all in our possession. We also use previously published reports, working papers, published papers, and book chapters, as well as the two comprehensive books (Bliss and Stern, 1982; Lanjouw and Stern, 1998). We have also tried to incorporate data available from secondary sources wherever possible. These include not just data from the Population Census of India and the Socio-Economic Caste Census (SECC),[7] but also data from the revenue department, agriculture department, and the block office.[8] These sources have not only added a wealth of information on the village, but also have contributed, including via cross-checks, to improving the overall quality of the analysis.

The growing economic prosperity of the village in recent years is evident to anybody visiting it now. But there was little evidence of prosperity at the beginning of the survey.[9] Palanpur has travelled a long way from being a small village of some 500 residents with almost negligible connections with the outside world. The transition from only two *pucca* buildings, both public, in 1957/8 to having no *kaccha* houses in 2015 has been associated with a striking transformation of the economy of the village. The change has not only been visible in terms of houses and assets owned by villagers, but also in the changing nature of occupations, the population structure, the demographic profile, education, and social relations, some of which we describe in detail in subsequent chapters. Notwithstanding these changes, Palanpur remains a poor village in Uttar Pradesh, a poor state.

---

[7] These data are available at http://censusindia.gov.in/ and http://secc.gov.in/.

[8] A 'block' is one of the units of administration in most South Asian countries. As a subdivision of a district, it is usually composed of several villages.

[9] We have noted a very good description of the village as it existed in 1950s in Ansari (1964).

2.2 A Brief Description of the Village

Palanpur is a small village located in Bilari block of Moradabad district.[10] The location of this district was an important factor in deciding the initial choice of the village by the Agricultural Economics Research Centre (AERC) of the University of Delhi, for its Continuous Village Surveys Programme, but also underpinned the subsequent selection of the village by Christopher Bliss and Nicholas Stern for their re-survey of Palanpur in 1974. The village is located in the plains of the river Ganga and was one of the early bene-ficiaries of the 'green revolution' in the late 1960s.[11] But its physical location is also important with respect to more recent changes since the early 1990s. The village is near the town of Chandausi, which lies 13 kilometres to the south, and the city of Moradabad, which lies 31 kilometres to the north. A railway line connects the village to both of these urban centres, and villagers regularly make use of this connection. The railway line also connects the village to Delhi, some 220 kilometres away. Although there is a direct train connection, a trip to the capital is both costly and time-consuming. Even though the railway station lies alongside Palanpur village, it is named after a larger village, Jargaon, located four kilometres to the west.[12] The railway station also serves as the primary mode of transport for residents of neighbouring villages.

The railway line and the station have been present in the village since the first survey and have remained the primary means of access to the outside world for the villagers. In recent years, road access has also improved. Connectivity with the world outside the village has emerged as a major driver of change in the village in recent decades and has not only transformed occupational patterns, but also the operation of other village markets.[13] In the 1950s only two individuals were going out of the village to work; this has increased to over a hundred persons who now travel to surrounding areas for employment purposes. The radius of employment has also increased considerably, with workers now seeking jobs and working in distant centres like Agra (220 km) and Aligarh (120 km).

The population density, the associated proximity, and fairly straightforward connectivity to a variety of urban centres would apply to many or most

---

[10] More details on location and the surrounding villages is available in Bliss and Stern (1982) and Lanjouw and Stern (1998).

[11] The village was chosen in the first AERC survey for evaluating the impact of cooperatives on the village economy, as the village was serviced by four cooperative societies (Integrated Cooperative Marketing Scheme (ICMS), Cooperative Credit Society, Cooperative Seed Society, and Cane Development Cooperative Union).

[12] According to Census 2011, Jargaon has a population of 2680.

[13] We describe some examples of the integration of the agricultural market in Chapter 5.

villages in the region. Thus, access to outside jobs more often occurs through commuting than outright migration. Although migration rates from Palanpur have gone up in recent decades and are reflected in the slower growth rate of the village population, migration is still relatively uncommon in comparison to all-India or Uttar Pradesh averages.

According to official records in 2011, the village covers an area of 196 hectares, of which 161 hectares is available for cultivation. Ten hectares are non-cultivable waste land, and the remaining area is residential.[14] All of the cultivated area is irrigated, mostly through tube wells (diesel and electric). The small rivulet which used to encircle the village from two sides has now disappeared and the land has been brought under cultivation.

The railway station is the most visible landmark of the village. Other visible landmarks are the village primary school and the cooperative seed store. They are adjoining buildings. The seed store is now very run-down and has partially collapsed; it is in a dilapidated state and has mostly been closed. The village school has recently seen an expansion and now includes a middle school. It is a large complex and is the first building that one encounters when entering the village from the direction of Pipli village, around half a kilometre away on the main road into the village from Chandausi or Moradabad. The school also doubles up as the *anganwadi* centre.[15]

Most of the dwellings in the village are located on the eastern side of the railway track, while the station building and staff quarters for railway employees are primarily on the western side. In the last decade, a few private dwellings have come up on the western side beyond the railway quarters. The households on the eastern side are not strictly segregated by caste, but there is some clustering based on caste affiliation, with most houses built very close to each other. At the end of the residential area is the village pond. There are now some new constructions beyond the pond, most of which were built during the 2008/10 survey or later.

There is a communications tower at the south-east corner of the village, and the mobile phone connectivity is good. There is no medical facility, but the two medical stores are also used as private clinics by the two pharmacists. There are four temples, although there is not much religious activity around them except during festivals. There is, however, no mosque in the village, and the Muslim residents go to the mosque in the neighbouring

---

[14] Ansari (1964) records 200 hectares as village area, with 8.77 hectares as residential area, 8.55 as railways and roads, 4.49 hectares as forests, uncultivable waste, and permanent groves and orchards. The cultivated area of the village was 174.6 hectares.

[15] A rural mother and child care centre, initially part of the Integrated Child Development Services (ICDS) programme.

village of Pipli.[16] There are also three mentha extraction plants and an oil-pressing mill.[17]

Although the village became electrified in the 1990s, few households currently use electricity in their dwelling.[18] On the other hand, the village has 15 electric tube wells.[19] The supply of electricity has been erratic and is generally available for a six- to eight-hour duration, with changing shifts of day and night. A significant number of households now have televisions.[20] In 2015, there were over 50 dish antennas in the village.

2.3 Population, Caste, and Family Structure

2.3.1 Population and Caste

In the 2008 survey, Palanpur had a population of 1255 persons divided into 233 households. We define 'households' in relation to living arrangements, as a group of individuals living together, sharing a common hearth, and pooling their economic resources.[21] Population change for Palanpur is summarized in Table 2.1. Overall growth was slightly above that for India in the 1950s and 1960s, but substantially lower during the last 25 years. After adjustment for out-migration the population growth rate in Palanpur is very similar to India for the same 25-year period.

Compared to the beginning of the survey period in 1957, there is a clear trend of increasing concentration into the numerically populous groups. Smaller castes which comprised just over one-third of the total population in the first two decades have seen their share decline in the last three decades,

---

[16] The mosque in Pipli also has a *madrasa* (Muslim religious school) where some children from Palanpur study religious texts. The absence of a mosque in the village has been a long-standing issue for the Muslim residents.

[17] Mentha (*Mentha arvensis*) is a plant; mint oil is extracted from the leaves. Only one extraction plant was functioning by 2015. More information on mentha cultivation is presented in Chapter 5.

[18] Although electricity connection was available in the village, few households had metered connection in the village. Most households were using open hooks to draw electricity from electric lines.

[19] Electric tube wells are submersible pumps which run on electricity.

[20] Most of the time, the television sets were used for watching movies on rented CDs. The majority of TVs were run on batteries. Some households also used television sets for watching soap operas. Only two households reported watching news on the television during the 2008/10 survey.

[21] A possible ambiguity arising in this respect corresponds to a few cases of a joint family with several brothers who were living separately but cultivating jointly. Though such cases tend to be short-lived in the village, mostly occurring just after the partition of a joint household, we have treated such families as separate households. Our definition was applied in all survey years after 1983 and was also used for assigning numbers to every household in the village. Along with the information on continuing households, each survey year data set reports information regarding households that migrated into Palanpur from outside the village. These are considered as new households in the survey year following (or of) their migration. The households that migrated out of the village were excluded from our reference population in all the surveys conducted subsequently.

Table 2.1 Basic population indicators of Palanpur

	Year						
	1957/8	1962/3	1974/5	1983/4	1993	2008/10	2015
Population	528	585	790	960	1133	1255	1299
Number of households	100	106	117	143	193	233	224
Average household size	5.3	5.5	6.8	6.7	5.9	5.4	5.6
Female–male ratio	0.87	0.87	0.85	0.93	0.85	0.98	0.94
Annual growth rate of population	–	2.2	2.5	2.2	1.7	0.74	0.58
Migration-adjusted growth rate		2.3	2.7	1.9	2.2	1.9	1.8
Age distribution of the population (%)							
0–14	39	38	46	44	41	38	36
15–24	21	19	15	20	21	21	20
25–44	23	25	25	23	22	26	27
45–64	14	13	12	10	12	11	13
65 +	3	5	2	3	4	4	4

falling below one-fifth during the most recent survey round. The changing caste dynamics—influenced by the availability of caste and other support networks—both reflect and have influenced economic outcomes in the village. This changing diversity has been associated with changing caste relations, socially and politically as well as economically.[22] The caste composition by population is set out in Table 2.2.

Thakurs are the largest caste in the village numerically and they continue to be powerful economically.[23] They were the first ones to move into the non-farm sector in a major way, but have now been joined by other castes. Muraos, on the other hand, are seen as a cultivating caste and take pride in their agricultural skills. They were the largest caste group by 2015, with a population share of over a quarter. Jatabs,[24] at the bottom of the village hierarchy, remained economically and socially marginalized until around 2005, but are now seen as an increasingly important community within the village.[25] Their economic condition has also improved over the years, and no Jatab households now live in *kaccha* houses.[26] Some of them have even constructed two-storeyed houses, envied by some from other castes.

---

[22] Also see Chapter 11 for changing social and political relations in the village.

[23] Traditionally of the Kshatriya group, or warrior caste. Many of the local zamindars were Thakurs.

[24] A Dalit group. An earlier name for them in Palanpur was Chamars or leather workers. Jatabs are also the dominant caste group within the category of scheduled caste (SC) castes in Uttar Pradesh.

[25] During 2007–12, the Chief Minister of Uttar Pradesh was Ms Mayawati, a Jatab herself. She is the head of the Bahujan Samaj Party (BSP), working for the interests of SCs.

[26] Although poverty rates remain high, see Chapter 8.

Table 2.2 Distribution of households and population by caste

Caste Group	Year						
	1957/8	1962/3	1974/5	1983/4	1993	2008/9	2015
Households (N)							
Thakur	17	19	25	30	51	57	55
Murao	21	25	28	27	44	55	53
Dhimar	10	9	8	13	16	22	22
Gadaria	9	9	10	12	14	15	14
Dhobi	2	1	3	4	5	8	8
Teli	8	9	12	17	20	23	21
Passi	12	16	8	15	16	6	6
Jatab	16	13	14	19	25	39	37
Others	5	5	4	6	10	8	8
Total	100	106	112	143	201	233	224
Population (N)							
Thakur	104	125	174	217	283	287	302
Murao	117	133	178	217	294	304	345
Dhimar	56	53	59	74	82	113	106
Gadaria	42	45	68	83	89	91	89
Dhobi	6	2	22	27	31	46	59
Teli	47	57	71	92	109	143	148
Passi	56	70	63	79	62	20	27
Jatab	71	71	97	118	133	203	201
Others	29	29	58	53	50	48	22
Total	528	585	790	960	1133	1255	1299

The Muslim community is divided into two main castes of Teli and Dhobi.[27] Telis (oil pressers) have also seen a change in their economic fortune over time, with rising incomes. Much of this has been a consequence of various entrepreneurial activities (see Chapter 7). They are also among the most economically diversified caste group, with many of them engaged in non-farm occupations.

2.3.2 Family Structure

An interesting aspect of the demographic composition of Palanpur is that many or most households follow a cycle of formation, development, and partition. This cycle can be understood or categorized in terms of family structure. A key element in the structure is the 'patri-fraternal' joint family, where a male household head lives with his wife, son(s) and their nuclear families, and unmarried daughters, if any. Then there exist households known as 'split' households where the death of the male patriarch (household head) is followed by a partition of the joint family into separate households, typically consisting of

---

[27] The traditional occupation of Dhobis is washing clothes, whereas Telis are oil pressers.

nuclear families, with one of the brothers taking responsibility for the widow of the erstwhile patriarch. If the 'patri-fraternal' joint family survives the death of the head, it consists of a number of married brothers, their nuclear families, and their widowed mother. The eldest son typically becomes the head of the household. These cases of 'fraternal joint families' do not fall under the category of 'split' households. Palanpur conforms with the standard north Indian practice where, on marriage, a daughter goes to live in her husband's household.

Classifying by family structure only, households can be categorized into the following four categories: single-person, nuclear, stem, and joint households (for definitions, see notes to Table 2.3). The table provides the proportion of households of different types in the village. The increase in share of nuclear households (44 per cent in 1983/4, rising to 68 per cent in 2008/9) accompanied by a decline in the share of joint households (20 per cent in 1983/4, falling to 5 per cent in 2008/9) is mainly the result of the increasing number of partitions in households in Palanpur.

Analysis of the population data suggests that migration, while still limited, has been an increasing feature of development in Palanpur over the last two decades. Migration is an important theme in our study, and we have managed to collect some data concerning the identity and activity of outward migrants. We discuss migration to and from the village in Chapter 7. Our analysis points to an association with Palanpur residents' increasing access to outside opportunities. Although migration is becoming a significant feature of the village economy, we also emphasize the far more common and increasingly widespread practice of commuting to work in jobs outside the village. We anticipate that commuting will remain an important feature of the Palanpur economy in coming years.

Table 2.3 Proportion and number of households of different types, 1957/8 to 2008/9

Type of Households	Year					
	1957/8	1962/3	1974/5	1983/4	1993	2008/9
Single	6(6)	6(6)	3(4)	3(4)	3(6)	4(11)
Nuclear	45(45)	44(47)	41(48)	44(63)	54(104)	68(159)
Stem	28(28)	28(30)	29(35)	33(47)	31(60)	21(51)
Joint	21(21)	22(23)	28(33)	20(29)	12(23)	5(12)
Total	100(100)	100(106)	100(117)	100(143)	100(193)	100(233)

Note:
1. For any household, the 'basic couples' (see also note 2) consist of all ever-married members and their spouses (even if the latter are deceased or absent).
2. Single-person household is a household consisting of a single person. A nuclear household is a household with several members, but only one basic couple. A stem household has two basic couples, with one husband being the father of the other husband. A joint household is a household with two or more basic couples, where one husband is the father or brother of all the other husbands or all other households with several basic couples (Lanjouw and Stern, 1998: 18).
3. The figures for all years except 2008/9 are taken from Lanjouw and Stern (1998). We follow the same definitions as above for 2008/9. The 2015 survey was a shorter survey, and these data were not collected.
4. The figures in parentheses give the number of households.

Because of the increased outward mobility of Palanpur residents, the ways in which population acts as a driver of change have themselves seen gradual change. The growing importance of non-farm and outside opportunities has implied that the influence of population pressure on incomes of Palanpur residents has been fairly muted. This is not to dismiss the impact of population pressure via a decline in per capita land availability (also influenced by some land sales) as this is likely to have acted to catalyse the outward migration of some households. It has also been associated with the increasing importance of education as a means, we presume, at least in part, of accessing better livelihoods than the village can offer.

Some of the larger caste groups have taken advantage of their personal networks and caste affinity to expand into non-farm opportunities. We also note that caste affinities play a role with regard to tenancy and labour relations in agriculture, and the mechanization, and monetization of factor markets (see Chapter 6). While the trend towards non-farm diversification has led to a declining role of agriculture along with a weakening of traditional forms of caste hierarchy, caste has emerged as important proxy for trust in many of the transactions in the village. We do observe caste continuing to play an important role in the credit, tenancy, and non-farm labour market, but also in society, politics, and institutions in the village. We return to some of these issues in Section 2.6.[28]

2.4 Land, Assets, and Income

2.4.1 *Land*

Palanpur is basically a smallholder village in terms of land, with no single large landlord. Although there were a few households with landholdings above 100 *bighas* (around 15 acres or 6 hectares) during the first survey,[29] over the years the average landholding has gone down drastically in size. A major development over the last three decades has been the substantial decline in total land owned and operated by residents of Palanpur (see Table 2.4). Coupled with population growth, this has resulted in a marked increase in population pressure on land.[30] Over the entire survey period, per capita land availability, both owned and operated, has fallen by a factor of three.[31]

[28] We also discuss some of these issues in detail in Chapters 6, 7, 8, and 11.

[29] In Palanpur, 6.4 *bighas* make an acre or 4046.86 square metres. The term *bigha* is used to define different areas in different parts of India. 2.47 acres = 1 hectare.

[30] Throughout this chapter, land operated is the sum of land owned and land leased in, less land leased out, unless otherwise stated.

[31] In 1957/8 and 1962/3, following the implementation of the land reforms in the early 1950s, the category of 'land rented in from state' was considerable. However, this basically became land owned and this category has not been present in our data since the 1974/5 study. Ansari (1964) and

The story of the declining size of landholdings, which we discuss in detail later in this section, should be set in the context of the institutional changes that have taken place in the country. Legislation abolishing *zamindari* and other intermediary rights came in the 1950s. The effects in Uttar Pradesh were varied, with some *zamindars* managing to hold onto most of their land.[32] However, in Palanpur, most tenants did acquire their land. The zamindar was weak and ineffective.[33]

Various attempts at land redistribution after *zamindari* abolition in Uttar Pradesh have not performed well.[34] It is a similar story in Palanpur. There were two land consolidation operations in Palanpur; one completed a year before the first survey, and the second one a year after the 1983/4 survey. However, due to a lack of political commitment and bureaucratic incompetence (or possibly corruption) the outcomes were disappointing. For instance, in the first consolidation in 1956, six landless households received six *bighas* of poor-quality land each. In the second land consolidation operation in 1985, only about 20 *bighas* of land, less than 1 per cent of the total village land, was acquired by the government for redistribution to the landless and for village commons.[35] In 1993, a decade after 'completion' of land consolidation, the land distribution was actually far from complete as the land meant for the landless was being used for storage of cow dung and straw (Drèze et al., 1998: 192).

The decline in land owned (see Table 2.4) is largely explained by land transactions. We have assembled information on all land transactions in the village since 1993.[36] The analysis reveals that out of the 230 *bighas* of land sold between 1993 and 2008/9, the primary reasons for sales were debt repayment, paying for the marriage of a daughter, default on tractor loans, litigation, catastrophic health expenditure, and migration out of the village. Four households sold their land and left the village. There were four cases of default on tractor loans as the cause of land sales among Muraos. We have also

---

Bliss and Stern (1982) have descriptions of the process of land reforms in the village, which had been implemented before the first study commenced in 1957/8.

[32] The Uttar Pradesh *Zamindari* Abolition and Land Reforms Act was passed in 1951. The Act did not fix any limit on the area under personal cultivation of zamindars. However, land cultivated by an intermediary as his 'Sir (share-cropped)' or 'Khudkasht (self-cultivated)' was converted into 'Bhumidari (ownership)' land.

[33] He was, in some ways, a rather sad character, who in 1974 (some two decades after *zamindari* abolition) tried to borrow a small amount of money from Bliss and Stern.

[34] See Singh and Mishra (1964) and Shankar (2010).

[35] Drèze et al. (1998: 192) explore whether the sterilization of men (an unpopular population control policy emphasized at the time) was a precondition for eligible beneficiaries to receive their due land from redistribution. There is an anecdote of how, in December 1988, the *tehsildar* (local revenue officer) of Bilari informed the authors that redistribution would be possible if they brought a few 'cases' to the *tehsildar*, the term cases implying men to be sterilized.

[36] The land transactions in our list are not exhaustive, although we tried to track down each and every case of change in land ownership since 1993.

Table 2.4 Trends in land ownership, land operated, and demography, 1957/8 to 2008/9

	Year					
	1957/8	1962/3	1974/5	1983/4	1993	2008/9
Area owned (*bigha*)	2749	2715	2498	2612	2384	1968
Area operated (*bigha*)	2918	2789	2438	2705	2486	2326
Per capita land owned	5.2	4.6	3.3	2.6	2.1	1.6
Per capita land operated	5.5	4.8	3.3	2.8	2.2	1.9

Notes:
1. Area operated = area owned + area leased in − area leased out.
2. Ansari (1964) reports that 2618 *bighas* of land were operated inside the village in 1957/8.
3. 6.4 *bighas* = 1 acre; 16 *bighas* = 1 hectare.

documented instances of alcoholism and gambling contributing to distress sale of land. Between 2008/9 and 2014/15, there were a few further land transactions: four households reported selling about 17 *bighas* of land, while two households reported purchasing about 9 *bighas* of land. As seen in Table 2.4, there has been a relatively larger aggregate decline in land owned (27.5 per cent) compared to land operated (22.2 per cent) since 1957.

There has been a rise in the proportion of households that split in the village over the survey years, and this has exerted a strong influence on the distribution of the size of land owned by households. More than half of the households in 2008/9 derive from splitting of 1983/4 households. In addition, 27 households migrated out in the period between 1993 and 2009.[37] Most of those who migrated out sold their land to outsiders.

In Palanpur, the process of inheritance follows well-defined rules prevalent in most parts of India: when a male household head dies each of the sons is entitled to an equal share of his land (Drèze et al., 1998: 144).[38] In view of the living arrangements discussed in Section 2.3.2, there seems to be a continuity of land division traditions. As long as brothers reside together, actual division of the land usually does not occur following the father's death. However, the joint family usually breaks down after the father's death, and division takes the form of the division of each plot equally among all sons, as opposed to different sons getting different plots (Drèze et al., 1998: 144). In the special case where the son forms a separate household before the father's death,

[37] Chapter 7 examines in detail the role of non-farm activities in influencing out-migration from the village.
[38] The Hindu Succession Act of 1956 grants an equal share of inheritance to the deceased's wife and children, and his mother if she is alive and widowed. However, in practice the patrilineal system usually restricts daughters' access to inheritance. In a few cases where there are no sons and there is a married daughter staying outside Palanpur, the son-in-law migrated to the village along with the married daughter to cultivate the land to which his widowed mother-in-law and wife are entitled.

ownership rights remain with the father. However, in such cases, the father often concedes the use of a part of his land to his separated son (Drèze et al., 1998: 145),[39] although there are also a few cases of the father and the separated son entering into tenancy arrangements such as *batai* (sharecropping).

Figure 2.1 shows the changing percentage of each size/class of ownership holdings. There is a clear and strong trend towards marginalization in the distribution of ownership holdings in Palanpur, with a little over two-thirds of households being marginal in 2008/9. The trend and pattern of land ownership is also reflected in terms of asset ownership, particularly farm equipment. Thakurs and Muraos have substantially higher land and farm equipment ownership compared to Jatabs. However, concomitant with the general story of the increase in marginal landholdings, all the caste groups have witnessed a decline in the average land owned per household (see Figure 2.2). In 1974/5, at the peak of the technological transformation associated with the green revolution, Muraos surpassed the Thakurs in land-ownership status. They have maintained this position since. However, since 1983/4, there has been a tendency towards convergence in the average land owned by households of all castes, with a general decline in land per capita.

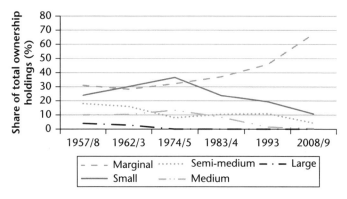

Figure 2.1 Share of land ownership in Palanpur by size/class, 1957/8 to 2008/10

Note: The land class intervals are defined in a way that makes them comparable with the classification followed in the National Sample Survey's (NSS) Situation Assessment Survey of Agricultural Households (SAS), as well as earlier rounds of survey in Palanpur. Marginal holdings are landholdings more than or equal to 0.1 *bighas*, but less than 15 *bighas*. Small holders have landholdings in-between 15–30 *bighas*. Semi-medium farmers have landholdings in the range of 30 to 50 *bighas*, while medium farmers have landholdings between 50 to 100 *bighas*, and larger farmers are those with holdings greater than or equal to 100 bighas.

[39] In the 1983/4 study, such inheritance was considered as *pre-mortem* inheritance, and the ownership was based on treating such transfers as 'virtual ownership' of the plots by the son. In the 1983/4 data, virtual ownership is considered as a form of ownership and in order to avoid double counting such land would not be included in the father's land-ownership calculation. This was not the case in the 2008/9 round. Virtual ownership as a separate ownership category was not used.

The changes in land-size distribution have implications for tenancy arrangements in the village as they have shaped the distribution of leased-in and leased-out land; an aspect which is central to the tenancy arrangements in Palanpur agriculture. These also have implications for cropping intensity and cropping patterns (see Chapter 5 for details). We discuss the changing nature of tenancy arrangements and agricultural production in Chapter 6. The role of tenancy can be seen by comparing Figures 2.1 and 2.3, where we see that small (as opposed to marginal) holdings are more prominent for cultivated than owned land.

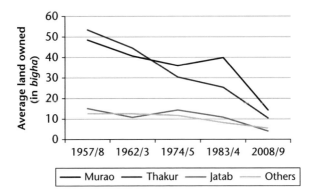

Figure 2.2 Average land ownership per household by caste in Palanpur

Note: The category 'Others' includes caste groups such as Dhimars, Gadariyas, Dhobis, Telis, Passis, and other caste groups who constitute 34% of the village population.

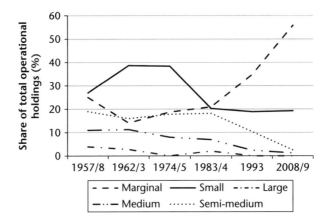

Figure 2.3 Size/class share of land operated in Palanpur, 1957/8 to 2008/10

Note: The land class intervals are defined in a way that makes them comparable with the classification followed in the NSS's SAS as well as earlier rounds of survey in Palanpur. Marginal holdings are landholdings more than or equal to 0.1 *bighas* but less than 15 *bighas*. Small holders have landholdings in the domain 15–30 *bighas*. Semi-medium farmers have landholdings in the domain 30–50 *bighas*, while medium farmers have landholdings between 50 to 100 *bighas*, and larger farmers are those with holdings greater than or equal to 100 *bighas*.

The irrigation before and during the green revolution led to double-cropping becoming the norm in the village by the mid-1970s. Since the end of the 1990s, the cropping intensity has increased further, with most households now using more water and growing two to three crops per year. The pressure on land has also led to changes in cropping patterns. While sugar cane and wheat dominated the cropping pattern in the first two decades, paddy emerged as a major crop after the spread, and improving quality, of irrigation. In the last two decades, villagers have increasingly adopted mentha as a cash crop.[40] The pressure on land has also led to further increases in irrigation intensity, and, with increasing availability of electricity, the number of tube wells has increased dramatically. This development, reflected over much of the Indo-Gangetic plain, has prompted a rapid decline in the water table as well as some land degradation (Kaur, Aggarwal, and Soni, 2011; Kaur and Vatta, 2015; Rodell, Velicogna, and Famiglietti, 2009). The pressures of population and size of holding have led to both increased intensity of cultivation and also the shift of labour out of agriculture towards the non-farm sector. The increase in machine intensity in agriculture, via water extraction and elsewhere, while allowing double-cropping, is also instrumental in a decline in labour requirement in agriculture. The release of labour from agriculture has allowed the villagers to take non-farm job opportunities both outside and inside the village.

2.4.2 Assets

An important visible indicator of the changing asset position of households is the quality of housing. As noted, the village now comprises only *pucca* houses, a significant change from a complete absence of private *pucca* houses in 1957. Much of the change in housing conditions has been relatively recent. Between 2008 and 2015, 39 households constructed new *pucca* houses, while 59 households upgraded and repaired their homes.

Most of the houses of better-off households have a courtyard surrounded by living rooms. The courtyard is also sometimes used as a storing space for agricultural output and fodder. Some better-off houses in the village are two storeyed, but the majority are single-storey structures. The richer households also have another house, a 'gher', exclusively for keeping the livestock. The majority of the households do not have a separate kitchen, with cooking generally undertaken in the courtyard using mud stoves powered by firewood or cow dung. Few households in the village have an LPG (liquefied petroleum

---

[40] Spearmint or garden mint, used largely for oil. For details, see Chapter 5.

gas) cooking stove.[41] Most of the superior houses have a handpump for domestic water use. The poorer households still depend on village handpumps for water.

Another notable feature of the housing situation in the village is the construction of toilets, with 57 households having constructed them after 2008. In 2008, there were only five households which had toilets. A majority of the toilets are located among the Thakur and Muraos households, with only a negligible percentage of households among Jatabs and Muslims possessing toilets. It should be noted, however, that there is a difference between having a toilet and using that toilet. As can be seen from Figure 2.4, one fourth of households which have a toilet are not using it. While 11 per cent of toilets are used exclusively by female members of the household, even in households where it is in regular use by all, the male members are less likely to use it.[42]

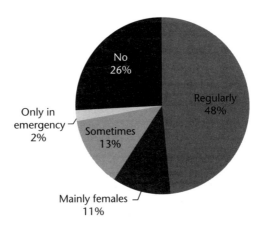

Figure 2.4 Per cent of households using toilets, 2015 (among those which own toilets)

When we began our fieldwork in 2008, the internal streets in the village were *kaccha* (mud with some bricks). There was only one main street in the village which was close to a *pucca* (brick and concrete) street. By 2015, most of the village streets were *pucca*. Most of these were created as part of the Mahatma Gandhi National Rural Employment Guarantee Act (MGNREGA)

---

[41] Some of those who do possess an LPG stove have not been using it due to the non-availability of cooking gas cylinders in the village.

[42] Our discussion with male members suggested various reasons for their reluctance to use the toilets. It varied from habit to feeling uncomfortable doing so. Some of them were also convinced that defecating in the field is good for their bowel movement.

Table 2.5 Possession of some durable assets in Palanpur (no. per 1000 persons)

Durable Asset	Year		
	1962/3	1993	2008/9
Bicycle	9	73	120
Motorcycle	0	2	15
Radio	2	45	65
Television	0	3	65
Sewing machine	3	22	51
Watch/clock	22	94	246

Note: Systematic and fairly comprehensive information on possession of household durables was collected only in the 1962/3, 1993, and 2008/10 surveys.

programme out of village development funds.[43] Very few streets were renovated using private contributions from residents. Drainage has also improved in the village, although most drains are open ones.

None of the households had a metered electricity connection in 2008/9, even though most houses have some access to electricity.[44] The electricity connection is through an open wire which latches on to the electricity supply lines of the village.[45] While the supply was irregular, it did lead to more households purchasing durable electronic goods. A more regular supply of electricity has increased the demand for durable assets such as televisions and computers. Most television sets in 2008 were used for watching films on rented DVD players. Only some households reported using the television sets for news or direct broadcasts. By 2015 the situation had changed. The village was dotted with satellite dish antennas, whereas there were none in 2008/9.[46]

Table 2.5 summarizes the possession of durable assets by the households in the village,[47] using data for 1962/3, 1993, and 2008/9. It shows very substantial increases in durables from almost negligible levels in 1962/3. And, as just noted, the growth continued strongly from 2008 to 2015. Whereas

---

[43] MGNREGA is a government scheme intended to guarantee a certain number of days of work at a given wage. It is often used for local infrastructure work such as building ditches or roads.

[44] However, those who were using electricity for tube wells had a sanctioned connection for which a flat fee was paid every month.

[45] During our stay, there were some cases of injuries due to electric shocks. The presence of monkeys, who would often hang on these wires, was a constant irritation for the villagers with regard to accessing electricity.

[46] Although direct-to-home broadcast started in 2003 in India, it acquired mass penetration only after 2008. Until then, households would use free-to-air broadcast channels through the individual antennas of cable operators. Only four households had the old-style antennas in the village and there was no cable service provider.

[47] Systematic and fairly comprehensive information on possession of household durables was collected only in the 1962/3, 1993, and 2008/10 surveys. Information on possession of selected durables was also collected in 2015, but was less comprehensive than the 2008/10 survey.

there were 15 motorcycles and 13 tractors in 2008, this increased to 65 motor-cycles and 26 tractors in the village in 2015. Tractors are primarily used in agricultural operations, but also for transportation. Just over 10 per cent of households owned tractors in 2015, a number that can be considered to be remarkably high for a total land area of around 400 acres or 160 hectares.[48]

These assets have been acquired either through purchase or through a gift, often as part of a dowry. Most motorcycles and television sets are gifts received as part of a dowry; ownership of these assets has continued to expand significantly.

There was a rise in other durable goods, too. There were a few refrigerators, and over 80 per cent of households had mobile phones in 2015. Growth in the use of mobile phones has been of great significance for all of India, and Palanpur is no exception. The improvement in telecommunications have helped integrate the village with the economy of the district. It has facilitated access to non-farm job opportunities outside Palanpur, which, as we discuss, has been crucial to the growth in household income (more in Chapter 7). Interestingly, the mobile phone has begun to replace other assets such as a watch or radio.

The increase in household assets is also reflected in the per capita possession of productive assets, including and beyond tractors. While the increase in productive assets and mechanization of farm produce was noted in the earlier surveys as well, it has gathered pace in recent years, including from 2008 to 2015, with increasing incomes and availability of credit from institutional sources (see Chapter 5 for details).

2.4.3 Income and Occupations

Total village income increased more than five times between 1957/8 and 2008/9 in real terms. The total village income in 2008/9 was Rs 17 million, up from Rs 3 million in 1957/8 in 2008/9 prices. Total village income, in 2008/9 prices, thus increased at an average of 3.44 per cent per year over the period between 1957/8 and 2008/9. During the first 25 years (1958–83), the rate of increase was 3.83 per cent per year, slowing down to 3 per cent per year over the next 25 years (1983–2008).[49]

Real per capita income increased more slowly, increasing by 2.4 times during the survey period. In terms of the growth rate of per capita income, there is an increase from 1.44 per cent per year during the first 25 years to

---

[48] See Table 5.4 in Chapter 5 for details on the possession of productive assets, including tractors.

[49] Growth rates are susceptible to the choice of initial and terminal years. Considering that 1983 was a bad agricultural year and 2008 was a normal year, the growth rates overestimate the increase in income growth in the latter half of the survey period compared to first half. Using 1974/5, which was a normal agricultural year, as the dividing year, the growth rate of per capita income has slowed from 2.6% per year between 1957/8 and 1974/5 to 1.2% between 1974/5 and 2008/9. The deceleration for total village income is 2.8% per year post-1974/5 period from 4.7% per year during the period before 1974/5.

2 per cent per year in the next 25 years. The fastest growth happened between 1962/3 and 1974/5, with total village income increasing at 6 per cent per year, and per capita income increasing at 3.7 per cent per year. This was also the period of intensification of the green revolution, and much of the growth in income was due to growth in agricultural earnings. Recall also that 1962/3 was a poor agricultural year, and 1974/5 a good one. The trend changed after 1983, with non-farm income contributing a larger share of the increase in total village income and per capita income growth. Table 2.6 gives the average per capita income by caste for all the survey years where income estimates are available.

Table 2.6 Real per capita income by caste (Rs, 2008/9 prices)

Caste Group	Year				
	1957/8	1962/3	1974/5	1983/4	2008/9
Thakur	6593	7419	10,879	9593	15,359
Murao	8014	7689	10,093	10,781	14,778
Dhimar	3461	3004	7667	7702	11,558
Gadaria	6047	7375	8257	8250	15,039
Dhobi	8031	26,575	5755	7861	7124
Teli	3679	3913	7704	7277	19,752
Passi	6407	5749	9417	7584	11,172
Jatab	4014	4015	6586	3962	8163
Others	3139	3832	6801	6524	7188
Total	5774	6010	8954	8309	13,628

Back-of-the-envelope calculations show that the average income in Palanpur in 2008/9 was just around the international poverty line (as defined by the World Bank International Poverty Line), one third of Indian average income and two thirds of average income in Uttar Pradesh. More precise calculations, using the Indian definitions of the poverty lines, are offered in Chapter 8.

Thakurs and Muraos have been among the caste groups with highest per capita income, while Jatabs have historically occupied the lowest income ranking in the village. However, by 2008/9 Telis emerged as the caste group with highest per capita income, thanks to their forays into non-farm activities. Muraos, the richest caste group in 1983, have moved to the third richest position after Telis and Thakurs, both of which have benefited from the non-farm expansion, the Telis more so than the Thakurs. In 1957/8, the Telis, along with Dhimar and Jatabs, had been one of the poorest caste groups; they have seen a steady increase in their income over the years, with a sharp acceleration over the last 25 years.

The other caste group which has seen a significant change in its fortunes are the Jatabs. They have seen their per capita income double in the last 25 years compared to almost stagnant per capita income in the first 25 years. Much of this growth in income is due to their greater involvement in non-farm employment, but they have also seen an increase in cultivation income due to their increasing participation in the tenancy market. We should also note that Jatabs fared particularly badly in the poor agricultural year 1983/4. They were involved in very few non-farm activities and were particularly dependent on agricultural labour. It is likely that a normal agricultural year then would have seen them with income per capita between Rs 5000 and 6000 (see Table 2.6).

The sharp increase in income of Telis and Jatabs in the period 1983/4 to 2008/9 has led to a significant rise in the income share of these two caste groups in this period (see Table 2.7).[50]

While Thakurs and Muraos continue to account for over 50 per cent of total income of the village, both their relative ranking and the contribution of other castes has changed over the years. The Passis, which accounted for around a tenth of income up until 1983/4, have moved out of the village. The decline in income share of Passis has been more than offset by the increase in share of Telis and Jatabs, particularly the Telis.

The changing composition of village income is a reflection of the rapid growth of non-farm income, which now accounts for around half of the total village income. With the growth of the economy in nearby towns and cities, opportunities outside the village have opened up, with commuting being the primary form of accessing these jobs. One significant recent

Table 2.7 Share (%) of total village income by caste group

Caste Group	Year				
	1957/8	1962/3	1974/5	1983/4	2008/9
Thakur	22.4	26.4	28.0	26.5	25.8
Murao	31.0	29.1	26.9	29.1	26.3
Dhimar	6.2	4.5	6.6	7.1	7.6
Gadaria	8.3	9.4	8.0	8.5	8.0
Dhobi	1.6	1.5	1.9	2.6	1.9
Teli	5.7	6.3	8.1	8.3	17.9
Passi	13.0	11.4	8.3	8.1	1.3
Jatab	9.3	8.1	9.4	5.9	9.7
Others	2.5	3.2	2.7	3.9	1.5
Total	100	100	100	100	100
Total village income (Rs 000) (2008/9) prices	3054	3516	6715	8118	17,100

[50] Although we should remember that this may be a little exaggerated by low agricultural incomes in the poor agricultural year 1983/4, which may have affected agricultural labour groups particularly strongly in that year.

development, in sharp contrast to the earlier phase of non-farm diversification, is the increase in non-farm activities amongst the Telis and the Jatabs.

Economic activity has seen extensive diversification towards non-farm enterprises and activities. The number of shops in the village has increased from 2 in the 1950s to over 15. Other than general *kirana* (grocery) shops, two medical stores, and a tailor, there is a small mechanic shop, providing repair services for tractors and motorcycles. The diversification away from cultivation has also been accompanied by increases in livestock and agro-processing. The village now has three oil-pressing machines. There was a poultry farm for some time between 2008 and 2015, although this has now closed. Indeed, not all innovations are successful. One of the Thakur households has been engaged in bee-keeping and manages a small plot of land for this purpose. There is now a dairy-processing machine in the village. Among those who are engaged in marble polishing, three households own the relevant machines.

The pattern of development of non-farm activities has also contributed to rising inequality in the village, because some get involved before others. The increase in income has contributed to a decline in poverty, with the poverty headcount ratio declining by more than half during the survey period. There has also been increasing mobility among the poorer households. We examine the details of inequality, poverty, and mobility in subsequent chapters, particularly Chapter 8.

2.5 Human Development and Public Services

Growth in incomes has not, however, been accompanied by increases in human development indicators in line with those associated with income change in other settings. In this sense, human development has performed less well than income. Although literacy has improved, the gender gap remains a critical issue, with far lower literacy levels for women than for men. Inequality in educational attainments is also reflected in lower literacy and school attendance among Jatabs relative to Thakurs. Nutritional status of men and women in the village has also not improved markedly; even in 2008 high levels of malnutrition were recorded in the village.[51] Immunization levels are also low, and institutional deliveries of babies were negligible even in 2008. Although we have noticed much more outward mobility in the village, this is not true for women.[52] One very rarely sees women working in fields or otherwise outside the house. Few girls have managed to gain access to higher education in colleges. Further observations on gender issues are offered in detail in Chapter 10.

[51] See Sinha (2011) for details.
[52] Apart from the standard movement of a bride to the husband's residence.

The relatively slow improvement in the circumstances of women, including in education and in health, are partly a consequence of the low importance they have in village society. The dominance of patriarchy and of the caste structure serves to preserve this low status. Health and education issues are not much discussed in the village, and there appears to be little local pressure for better public service delivery. The lack of public action has also contributed to low accountability of public institutions in the village.

The improvements in school infrastructure in the village and in the health infrastructure in the neighbouring villages indicate that there has been some increase in the local availability of public funds. Palanpur has been a beneficiary of increases in public spending over the years, including untied grants to the village *panchayat*,[53] and also as part of various central and state government schemes. But the performance of public services and institutions in the village is poor; in particular, the quality of education and health services remains disappointingly low. Human development, gender, and institutions are the subject matters of Part 3 of this book.

The primary reason the AERC chose Palanpur for the 1957/8 study was the presence of cooperatives in the village. Two such cooperatives existed in the village in 1958. By 2008, the seed store had almost closed down, with the building itself partially collapsed. Occasionally there has been some activity around distributing certified seeds, but even this service has come to a halt in the last few years. A similar situation prevails with the village cooperative society. The Cooperative Credit Society functions from one room and has not seen much activity in recent years.

The village in 1958 had no public institution other than the cooperatives. There was no school in the village, and the nearest one was located four kilometres away. By the 1970s, a primary school had been built, but enrolment was low. As of 2015, the village school offered facilities for students up to the eighth class. However, there has been a gradual decline in availability of teachers and other teaching materials. At the time of the 2015 survey, there were two permanent teachers and one contract teacher for the entire school, though their attendance was highly sporadic. Most of the classes are grouped together, and at any time only one or at most two classes are being held. The school also has a midday meal facility for primary students, but during our visits over several years the programme was non-operational for months at a time.

The village school is generally frequented by the poorer and Jatab households. Richer households prefer to send their children to a private school in Pipli. Palanpur used to have a private school before the 2008 survey, but that

---

[53] The village *panchayat* is the elected council. The elections are held every five years.

was closed down when the teacher was employed as a contract teacher in the village primary school. The weakness of the public schools has been associated with increasing demand for private schools; the most recent survey of 2015 shows almost two-thirds of Palanpur children who are enrolled at school go to private schools. The percentage is marginally higher for boys than for girls.

The school also acts as the ICDS centre, called the 'Anganwadi'. The *anganwadi* worker is a resident of the village, but the anganwadi barely functions, despite the village receiving food rations for distribution at the ICDS centre. The nearest health facility for the village is the Primary Health Centre (PHC) at Akhrauli (four kilometres away). This PHC was recently built but has only one Ayurvedic doctor and no allopathic doctor. The PHC barely functions, even though the building was renovated and other facilities were installed. Although Palanpur now has three pharmacists serving as 'doctors', the nearest public health facility for any emergency is Chandausi (15 kilometres away). Sometimes the villagers also go to Moradabad for emergency treatment, but they also turn to private health facilities in nearby towns. The village has an ASHA (Accredited Social Health Assistant) who is paid an honorarium for providing information on the government's various health programmes and facilities.

The situation of various government initiatives such as the MGNREGA and Public Distribution System (PDS) also remains variable. While MGNREGA has contributed to increasing access to non-farm opportunities in the village for many of the poorer households, it suffers from leakages, corruption, and exclusion of needy households. Notwithstanding its deficiencies, it has contributed to improvements in the village infrastructure through the renovation and upgrading of village streets and approach roads. The PDS also functions but was mired in controversy for major parts of our stay during 2008–15.[54] Only 20 households are eligible to draw subsidized rations from the PDS store but, in reality, just 8 households reported having received such subsidized rations.

2.6 Society, Politics, and Institutions

The social structure of the village is largely centred on caste. Even though caste-based rigidities have weakened over time, caste still remains important in understanding the economic and social evolution of the village. We

---

[54] During the 2008/10 survey, the villagers complained of leakages and corruption in the PDS to higher authorities. After some struggle, the corrupt dealer was removed, but it led to a situation of no PDS services for a large part of the survey duration because a replacement dealer was not appointed.

continue to use caste-based groups as the primary mode of understanding group behaviour, while using economic indicators for analysing activities, outcomes, and responses of different groups in the village.[55] The dominant castes among the village residents have been the Thakurs and Muraos. Thakurs who, as Kshatriyas,[56] have a higher social status than all other castes, are also the most affluent of the groups, with above average landholding and educational attainment. Over the years, the Muraos, who are traditionally the cultivator caste, have seen their economic status improve, even coming close to the Thakurs' and, in some respects, surpassing them occasionally during the green revolution years. However, they have fallen behind lately as non-farm activities have emerged more strongly as a major driver of change in the village.

Jatabs, sometimes previously described in Palanpur as Chamars or leather workers, are among the lowest of the caste groups by status. They are also the largest among the SC groups in the village.[57] Economically, they have been at the bottom of the village hierarchy, as largely manual workers. Their occupational profile continues to be predominantly manual casual work, but increasing involvement in non-farm work outside the village has seen their economic status improve over time. The emergence of the BSP in Uttar Pradesh politics also had its impact on the social status of the Jatabs. Between 2007 and 2012, Uttar Pradesh was ruled by Ms Mayawati, who belongs to the Jatab caste. During the same period the village was also declared an Ambedkar village,[58] with more funds being allotted to it for development work. The post of village Pradhan was reserved for an SC for the first time.[59] Access to the village council has clearly changed the behaviour of other castes towards them. During this period, the Jatabs not only saw their economic but also their social status improve. However, there still remains a considerable gap between the Jatabs and the rest of the village, even though our analysis (Chapter 8) shows that this gap may be narrowing. While this is clear in terms of economic outcomes, it is also clear through human development indicators such as education, immunization, nutrition, and access to public services.

---

[55] While visible forms of caste relations such as untouchability and caste-based occupational structures have broken down, caste relations continue to play dominant role in the day-to-day life of the village.

[56] Kshatriyas (or warriors) are one of the upper castes in the hierarchy of the caste system.

[57] Schedule Castes (SC), also known as 'Dalit', are the lowest, historically disadvantaged castes in the caste hierarchy. Recognized by the Indian Constitution as a separate group, they are protected against discrimination and are entitled for reservations in government jobs and in parliament. In Palanpur, the Jatabs constitute the major portion of the SCs. Dr Ambedkar was a prominent Dalit, a key figure in the Independence movement. A lawyer, he had a doctorate from the London School of Economics (LSE) and Columbia and is seen as the father of the Indian constitution.

[58] The Dr Ambedkar Gram Vikas Yojana (Dr Ambedkar Village Development Scheme) was initiated by the Mayawati government to prioritize development projects in villages that had a substantial SC population.

[59] *Pradhan* is the head of the elected village council. Most of the executive powers of the village council rest with the *pradhan*. He is also the executive authority for council finances.

Although the majority of the village residents are Hindus, there are two caste groups, the Telis and Dhobis, who are Muslims. The population of Muslims in the village has varied from 10 per cent in the first two decades to around 15 per cent as of 2015. With a similar population size as the Jatabs, Muslims have also been at the bottom of the village hierarchy economically as well as socially. However, they have also seen changing economic fortunes in recent years with increased involvement in non-farm jobs. The Telis have done particularly well. They are largely employed as manual labourers or in non-farm self-employment. There has not been any incident of communal violence in the village throughout the long survey period, although occasionally some tension has been reported by villagers along religious lines.

The existence of several caste groups has not resulted in the strict geographical segregation of households on the basis of caste or religion in the village, with households of all castes interspersed throughout the village.[60] While a majority of the poorer households (mostly Jatab and Muslim) have built their houses at the outer edges of the village, there is no clearly demarcated area for separate castes. In the common areas, such as the railway station and the village centre, one can see people of all castes gossiping and playing cards.

The only formal political or administrative institution in the village is the village *panchayat*. The nature and role of the village *panchayat* changed after the 73rd amendment, which gave it financial and administrative power. The village *panchayat* is now elected on a regular basis, with reservation for SCs and women by rotation.[61] Although caste-based solidarities are still dominant in village elections, the last two elections have also seen alliances between various caste groups. While there have not been many instances of the calling of a 'Gram Sabha',[62] there has been heated debate and discussion on the functioning of the *panchayat* among the residents. Informal institutions for collective functioning or action remain almost non-existent. Ansari (1964) as well as Lanjouw and Stern (1998) noted the role of caste *panchayats* in resolving local disputes in the 1980s. These are now almost non-existent although some Muraos and Muslims do claim that such groupings exist in other villages.

The absence of strong formal and informal institutions has been associated with very limited collective action by village residents on most of the issues

[60] While there was geographical segregation during earlier years, with Jatab houses at the outer side of the village, there are now some Thakur and Murao houses in those areas. Jatabs continue to remain mostly at the outer edge of the village.

[61] During our stay in 2008–10, the village headship was reserved for the SCs. It changed to women in 2010 when the next elections were held.

[62] Gram Sabha is the general assembly of village residents. Normally, the Pradhan and the village council are required to call a Gram Sabha every year to discuss the work of the *panchayat* and plan for future work.

concerning their village. Two examples of collective action during our stay were the impeachment of the Pradhan in 2008 and collective action by the villagers to get rid of monkeys in the village (see Chapter 11). Both these instances involved a general discussion and consensus among the villagers about the urgency of the situation, with some village elders taking responsibility for executing decisions. Other than these, there have been very few instances of the residents coming together for the common good of the village.

While there have been clear changes in caste relations,[63] there has not been much change in the status of women. Women are barely present in the social life of the village. Although there has been a significant recent advance in their literacy levels, they continue to remain largely absent from the labour market. Issues raised by women also remain largely absent from village discourse. The 2008/10 survey looked at the status of women in the village in some depth (see, in particular, Chapter 10).

Crime and violence are present in Palanpur, as they are in most communities. The only specific information in our surveys on violence concerns violence against women (see Chapter 10). We are also aware of a number of murders over the years. For example, during the 1974/5 survey, a man was shot to death at the railway station over a feud concerning sugar quotas. A frequent visitor to our residence in the seed store during that survey had been jailed over a murder arising from a land dispute. Sometime later, his sister-in-law was sent to jail for burning to death an infertile daughter-in-law. There were several other events over the years, but these illustrate both the types of quarrel that can arise and how they can turn to violence and death. Stories of thefts are quite common, and villagers take care to keep valuable assets, such as pumping sets and tractors, locked away.

2.7 Concluding Remarks

This brief description of the village and village life provides part of the context and background for the more detailed analyses of change since the 1950s that follow. It is important to remember that the changes in a village depend on its specific context and on its historical evolution of institutions as well as outside changes. Internal and external forces interact and combine to shape the development of the village and the change in fortunes of its members and households. In Chapter 3, we describe some of the external forces associated with the development of India since Independence and how, together with

---

[63] Open discrimination against lower castes seem to have reduced, and there is some evidence of Dalits moving up the economic ladder. See Chapters 7 and 11 for details.

the internal forces, they have shaped the economic development of Palanpur along some key dimensions.

We present, in Chapter 3, changes in Palanpur around the five key findings very briefly described in the Introduction. These concern: (i) the rise of non-farm activities; (ii) a recent rise in inequality associated with the mobility offered by these activities; (iii) the way in which institutions have both influenced economic outcomes and have been influenced by economic outcomes; (iv) the poor performance of human development; and (v) the role of entrepreneurship in determining change in lives and livelihoods and influences, together with constraints on it. Most have begun to emerge in our description of the village in this chapter. It is a story of dynamics and of change; but it is also a story of poverty, difficulties, and constraints. Nevertheless, it is growth of sorts.

We shall find that our key findings and central themes in the development of Palanpur are both influenced by change in India and reflect that change. Palanpur is not 'representative', but its development resonates with that of India as a whole.

Acknowledgements

Earlier versions of this chapter were presented at seminars at LSE, Jawaharlal Nehru University (JNU), and the Reserve Bank of India (RBI). This chapter also draws on the earlier publications of Himanshu and Stern (2011, 2016). We are grateful to Sue Stern and Jean Drèze for allowing us to use their personal reminiscences in this chapter.

References

Ansari, N. 1964. 'Palanpur: A Study of its Economic Resources and Economic Activities (No. 41)', Continuous Village Surveys 1958–9. Agricultural Economics Research Centre, University of Delhi.

Bliss, C.J., and Stern, N.H. 1982. *Palanpur: The Economy of an Indian Village*, 1st edn. Oxford and New York: Oxford University Press.

Drèze, J., Lanjouw, P., and Sharma, N. 1998. 'Economic development in Palanpur, 1957–93', in *Economic Development in Palanpur over Five Decades*. New York and Oxford: Clarendon Press.

Himanshu, and Stern, N. 2011. 'India and an Indian village: 50 years of economic development in Palanpur'. LSE ARC Working Paper 43, Asia Research Centre, London School of Economics and Political Science, London.

Himanshu, and Stern, N. 2016. 'How lives change: six decades in a north India village', in Himanshu, P. Jha, and G. Rodgers (eds), *The Changing Village in India: Insights from Longitudinal Research*. Oxford: Oxford University Press.

Kaur, S., and Vatta, K. 2015. 'Groundwater depletion in Central Punjab: pattern, access and adaptations', *Current Science* 108, no. 4: 485–90.

Kaur, S., Aggarwal, R., and Soni, A. 2011. 'Study of water-table behaviour for the Indian Punjab using GIS', *Water Science and Technology* 63, no. 8: 1574–81.

Lanjouw, P., and Stern, N.H. 1998. *Economic Development in Palanpur over Five Decades*. New York and Oxford: Clarendon Press.

Rodell, M., Velicogna, I., and Famiglietti, J.S. 2009. 'Satellite-based estimates of ground-water depletion in India', *Nature* 460, no. 7258: 999.

Shankar, K. 2010. 'Next step in land reforms in the context of UP', *Mainstream* 48, no. 9, https://www.mainstreamweekly.net/article1908.html (accessed 1 March 2018).

Singh, B., and Mishra, S. 1964. *A Study of Land Reforms in Uttar Pradesh*. Calcutta: Oxford Book Co.

Sinha, D. 2011. 'Nutrition status in Palanpur'. ARC Working Paper 51, Asia Research Centre, London School of Economics and Political Science, London.

3

India and Palanpur

A Story of Change*

3.1 Introduction

The seven decades over which we have examined development in Palanpur cover India's life as an independent nation. Its economy and society have been transformed, and India is a very different place today from what it was in 1957, when Palanpur was first surveyed. We cannot hope to document the economic history of this immense and varied country over the last seven decades in just a few pages. The purpose of this chapter is, therefore, not to try to present the contours of changes in the economy and economic policy of the country in any comprehensive way; it is a modest attempt at highlighting some of the changes in the country and in policy, particularly in relation to rural India, which have particular relevance for our understanding of the process of change in Palanpur.[1]

Economic and social policy and the structure of growth in India have significantly altered the shape of the village economy and society. Key events or changes in India's history include *zamindari* abolition, the green revolution, and an acceleration in economic growth, particularly since the 1980s, associated, at least in part, with the dismantling of some of the heavier aspects of planning and the 'licence raj'. Fundamental changes have been wrought by the combination of rapid population growth and slowly rising education levels, changing economic, social, and demographic structures, a transformation in

* This chapter has been written by Himanshu, Peter Lanjouw, Nicholas Stern, and Shantanu Singh.
[1] In this chapter, we build on the lessons and themes of the Palanpur story, outlined in previous chapters. Here we examine them in the context of the economic history of the country. We provide more detailed analyses of the themes and lessons in the individual chapters which follow. Each of the chapters in the book attempts to incorporate as much of the relevant changes in India, particularly rural India, as possible, using secondary data sources as well as other village surveys.

communications, and the liberalization and opening of the economy. More recently, a substantially altered governance landscape has taken root, in which improvements in access to information and to employment aim to strengthen civic participation and the accountability of public administrators and to empower weaker segments of society.

Across India there has been substantial growth in non-farm incomes in rural areas. Together with the non-farm sector growing much more strongly than agriculture, education levels are increasing and communications and mobility are being transformed. This movement to non-farm activities is a central feature of economic and social change in India as a whole. It is a process that is unfolding rapidly and is likely to continue over the next two or three decades. Agriculture's share, which was around 50 per cent of gross domestic product (GDP) in the years after Independence, is already less than 15 per cent and is likely to fall still further. The details of how these fundamental transformations take place and the consequences for the hundreds of millions of poor people in rural India are absolutely central to economic and social policy. Some of these concerns do find recognition in policy circles, and the emphasis on 'inclusive growth' in the last two administrations is an indicator of the seriousness with which public discourse in India is focusing on tackling these issues. Agricultural growth, with rural development and employment creation, are high on the economic and policy agendas.

Importantly, there has been broad political acceptance of the need to make growth broad-based and 'inclusive'. Some of the issues are seen not only in terms of potentially desirable benefits of growth, but as constitutional rights. Thus, along with increased expenditures on education, health, agricultural growth, and rural development, there has been some enactment of rights to the population. Some rights, such as the right to employment, enshrined in the National Rural Employment Guarantee Act (NREGA), right to food as part of the National Food Security Act (NFSA), and the right to education, have already been passed by parliament and are being implemented in some shape or form. There have been recent efforts to establish a right to health which would, if successful, constitute a significant landmark for a developing economy. These policy changes have been accompanied by decentralization of state power, with the 73rd amendment of the constitution, which gives a greater role to the village *panchayats* in the implementation of most of the programmes. This process has also meant that the village as a unit of administration continues to remain central, particularly for the challenge of inclusion.

These changes clearly cover a wide canvas, and we do not intend to analyse all of these in the limited scope of this chapter. We will rather seek to focus our discussion on the last three decades, since the 1990s, and on themes that find resonance in the Palanpur story. We will revisit earlier trends where necessary, but for the interested reader, an analysis of the prior changes in India's economy and their influences on the village economy is available in the two previous books on Palanpur.

As we proceed through this chapter, we will find that changes in the overall economic environment, in population, in health, and in education, together with those for agriculture, incomes, and wages, have also constituted crucial context for and forces behind change in Palanpur. Seven decades of data and close knowledge of Palanpur help to locate the macroeconomic growth story in a human context, providing a uniquely valuable opportunity to illuminate the story of India's growth.

In this chapter, we structure our analysis of change in India and in its villages in a way which links with our analysis of change in Palanpur. This chapter is thus organized around the five key themes on Palanpur which we described briefly in the Introduction to this book and in Section 2.7 of Chapter 2. Section 3.2 shows how the changing structure of the Indian and Uttar Pradesh economies, particularly with regard to income and occupational structure and the emergence of non-farm activities, has been an important driver of the village economy. This changing structure and new driver of growth is our first theme. These overall changes have contributed to both a new income structure and decline in poverty in the village, but have also been accompanied by rising inequality, which we examine in Section 3.3. Both the emergence of non-farm activities as a major driver of change and rising inequality are crucial to our understanding of the upward mobility of some households in disadvantaged communities, such as the Jatabs and Telis in Palanpur. These processes around mobility and inequality constitute our second theme. Section 3.4 focuses on the changing social and political structure, particularly the evolution of institutions. We examine the changes in institutional structures as they emerge not only from exogenous interventions from the state, but also from responses within the village society, economy, and polity to broader, aggregate changes in institutional structures. An important dimension of the institutional dynamism in the village revolves around the changing nature of caste relations. This institutional dynamics and endogeneity constitute our third theme. Section 3.5 looks, in the context of the changing economic structure, at human development outcomes, in particular, education, health, and gender relations. These weaknesses in human development, in relation to economic development, constitute our fourth theme. Section 3.6 examines the investment, entrepreneurship, and risk-taking involved in the decisions of households and individuals to alter core aspects of their lives and livelihoods. Because in India such entrepreneurship and initiative is a key aspect of change, we ask in this book why some households do better than others. Entrepreneurship is an important part of household and individual behaviour and change, even though the characteristics of the processes may look different from such manifestations in industry and firms. The role of entrepreneurship is our fifth theme. In Section 3.7 we set out the five themes, which are basic to understanding change in Palanpur, in a way that links them to the story of economic and social change in India.

3.2 Structural Transformation in India

India started its post-Independence economic history with an economic philosophy that took it on a route towards a mixed economy dominated by the public sector, although with recognition of an important role for markets and private capital. The argument was, in large measure, led by the ideas of Nehru and Mahalanobis.[2] The last three decades have seen a recasting of the structure and growth of the Indian economy, with a transition to a more open and globalized economic structure. Two features are of particular importance when discussing the Palanpur story. The first, at the macroeconomic level, is the overall increase in GDP and increased levels of per capita income. These increases have been, in large part, enabled by a shift away from agriculture to other sectors with higher productivity. Second, the shift in occupations has been accompanied by a trend towards greater urbanization, with the proportion of population residing in rural areas dropping from about 86 per cent in 1950 to less than 70 per cent in 2016.

The so-called 'Hindu' rate of growth of 3.5 per cent,[3] together with a population growth rate of over 2 per cent, over the period 1950–80, has long gone, with growth rates of the economy moving to 6 per cent per annum in the 1980s and the 1990s, and the annual population growth rate now down to 1.4 per cent and falling. The biggest acceleration in economic growth occurred in the post-2003/4 period, with growth rates averaging over 8 per cent. These have made India the second-fastest-growing (large) country after China during the first decade of the 2000s.[4] What is also remarkable is the recent resilience shown by the Indian economy in sustaining a strong rate of growth, despite the severe global slowdown after 2008. Although the growth rates have moderated in recent years, in India these continue to be higher than

---

[2] P.C. Mahalanobis, a statistician by training, was closely associated with the setting up of various institutions in India after Independence. But he is better known as the chief architect behind the second and third five-year plans, which led to the heavy-industry-led industrialization strategy being adopted by India.

[3] The term 'Hindu rate of growth' was coined by Raj Krishna to denote the low rate of growth of the economy in the first 30 years of planned economic development. The Hindu rate of growth referred to a low and stagnant growth rate of the economy in the first three decades of Independence compared to the high growth rate achieved by some of the Asian countries, notably the East Asian economies and South Korea. It has nothing to do with 'Hindu' religion.

[4] In recent years, India has emerged as the fastest-growing large country, overtaking China. However, the last five years have seen both countries decelerate in terms of growth rate.

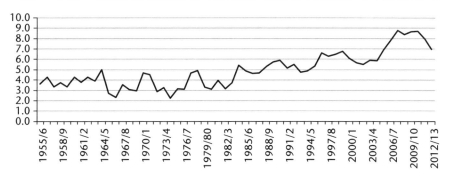

Figure 3.1 Annual growth rate of GDP at constant prices (2004/5 prices)

Note: Vertical axis is growth rate in % per annum.

Source: National Income Accounts, Central Statistical Organisation, Government of India.

other large countries, much higher than in the first decades since Independence, and much higher than developed countries. Figure 3.1 displays the growth rate of the Indian economy since Independence.[5]

While the movement of the economy to a higher growth trajectory since the 1980s marked a departure from the 'Hindu' rate of growth, the decline in population growth rates after 1980s meant that the increase in growth in per capita income was still more remarkable. Figure 3.2 shows the growth rate of per capita income. Over the last three decades it has risen from around 1 per cent per annum to 5 per cent or more: a powerful acceleration. It is striking that the division of the post-Independence period into two parts—1950s–1970s and 1980s onwards—at the top-down or macro level, in terms of growth, fits with the 'bottom-up' division in Palanpur into growth led by agricultural change in the 1950s–1970s, and growth led by non-farm activities thereafter.

The analysis of the reasons for the break in the trend of the aggregate growth rate, although useful and relevant, is not the main subject matter of this chapter. But what is relevant is how the growth was shared between rural and urban areas. On this count, the trend since the 1970s indicates a decline in the share of national GDP in rural areas.[6] Such a decline is not unexpected given that agriculture, which continues to remain important in the rural economy, has grown much more slowly than services and manufacturing.

---

[5] In 2014, the Central Statistical Office (CSO) changed the way GDP has been calculated in India. The new series is not comparable to the earlier series, and there has been no release of the back series. The GDP and associated data from the old series are available up to 2012–13. In most of the discussion in this chapter and elsewhere in the book, the data from the national accounts are based on the old series and are therefore restricted to the period up to 2012–13.

[6] The share of rural areas in total GDP of the country fell from 62% in 1970/1 to 47% in 2011/12. During the same period, the population share of rural areas fell from 80% in 1970/1 to 69% in 2011/12.

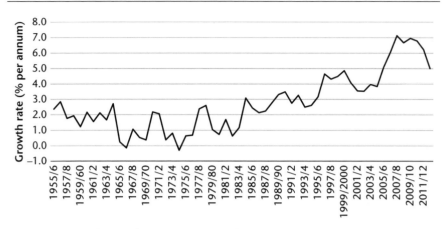

Figure 3.2 Growth rate of per capita income (constant 2004/5 prices) (5-year moving average)

Source: National Income Accounts, Central Statistical Organisation, Government of India.

Much of the acceleration in the growth rates since the 1980s has been on account of the higher growth of services and manufacturing; although the share of manufacturing in the national economy has not increased dramatically, services have grown more quickly. The growing importance of non-farm activities, including services, in rural areas is at the heart of the Palanpur story.

3.2.1 *Agriculture: Farm and Non-Farm*

Of particular interest is the performance of agriculture, which was central not just for the national economy in the early decades after Independence but also for Palanpur's economy. While agricultural growth rates mirrored the national income growth rates for most of the period after Independence, as seen in Figure 3.3, they do show considerable variation. Agriculture is vulnerable to weather. The opening up of the economy and its subsequent integration with the global economy has brought in new opportunities for growth in agriculture, but has also contributed to new forms of volatility, including via international markets.

Agriculture has grown at an average rate of 2.8 per cent per annum since 1950/1. The first decade saw agriculture grow at around 3 per cent, helped by land reforms and the expansion of irrigation. It fell to its lowest by the middle of the 1960s. A large amount of literature in the Indian context has analysed the reason for the deceleration of the agricultural growth rate and the crisis in agriculture in the mid-1960s. The explanations have varied from inadequate attention to agriculture in the first three five-year plans (due to a heavy focus on industry), to failures of land reforms, to dominance of non-market relations of production. Of course, agriculture is a risky business and very

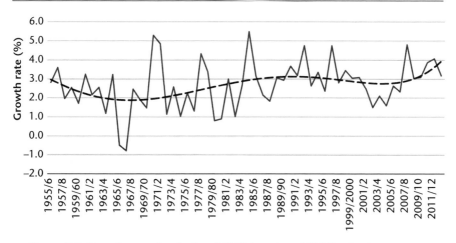

Figure 3.3 Growth rate of agricultural GDP (constant 2004/5 prices)

Note: Dotted line is polynomial trend line.

Source: National Income Accounts, Central Statistical Organisation, Government of India.

dependent on the weather; the mid-1960s saw bad monsoons and difficult weather conditions. With war and the collapse of five-year plans, this was a crisis period.

The crises in the mid-1960s led to some shift of focus back towards agriculture. The strategy of the so-called 'green revolution' in the mid-1960s led to a revival of agricultural growth which continued until the end of 1980s. Some have criticized the green revolution for its 'bias' towards wheat-producing regions and, it was argued, an inherent bias towards large and medium farms because of the necessary investment. Nevertheless, it did lead to India becoming self-sufficient in cereals by the end of the 1980s.[7] From a large importer of food grains in the 1960s, India turned into a net exporter of cereals by the middle of 1990s. And the so-called 'biases' were likely overdone. In Palanpur all farmers were involved, even though it was and is a backward village and some of them have very small holdings (see, for example, the discussion in Chapters 2 and 5, and also Bliss and Stern, 1982).

Although the green revolution was successful in raising the average rate of growth of agricultural output in India to over 3 per cent during the 1980s, such output remained lower than the growth rate of other sectors of the economy. This decline in output was not, however, accompanied by a similar decline in share of agriculture employment. This remained at over 50 per cent

---

[7] Food-grain production increased from 95 million tonnes in 1967/8 to 131 million tonnes in 1978/9 and increased further to 176 million tonnes by 1990/1. Per capita food grain availability increased from 409 grams per day in 1966 to 510 grams per day in 1991. Net food imports fell from 10.3 million tonnes in 1966 to 3.6 million in 1970.

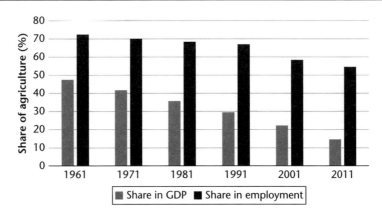

Figure 3.4 Share of agriculture in GDP and employment

Note: Vertical axis is share of agriculture in GDP in %, calculated for years with census data.

Source: National Income Accounts for share in national income; Registrar General of India for share in employment.

of total employment in 2011.[8] Figure 3.4 illustrates the evolving share of agriculture in national income and in employment over time.

That the agricultural share of employment has fallen so slowly is a phenomenon that has raised questions on the nature of structural transformation in India.[9] Agriculture is no longer the driving force of change in rural areas. The emergence and growth of the non-farm sector have not only changed the nature of the rural economy but have also altered the dynamics of rural labour markets. But there is considerable concern about the ability of the economy to generate adequate employment. Based on the usual status classification (principal and subsidiary status taken together), the total number of workers in the Indian economy as a whole increased from 398 million in 1999/2000 to 458 million in 2004/5, but then increased only marginally to 462 million in 2007/8, 463 million in 2009/10, and 473 million in 2011/12. Thus, additional employment generation between 2004/5 and 2011/12 was only 15 million as against 60 million jobs created between 1999/2000 and 2004/5.

The apparent slow pace of non-farm employment creation in the economy as a whole since 2004/5 has been a puzzling feature of India's growth. Even though non-farm employment did grow faster than agricultural employment in percentage terms, there was no significant decline in absolute numbers in the

[8] While census figures for 2011 show 54.6% of workers in the country were employed in agriculture (cultivators and agricultural labourers), the estimates of employment from the National Sample Survey (NSS) suggest that it had fallen below to 48% by 2011/12. Although the two data sources differ in terms of the share of workers in agriculture, the trends in employment and employment shared by both the sources are similar. The difference is mainly on account of the way a worker is defined in census and National Sample Survey Office (NSSO) employment–unemployment surveys.

[9] See Binswanger-Mkhize (2013) on the nature of the structural transformation of the Indian economy.

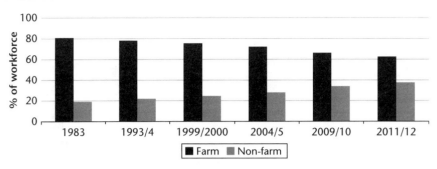

Figure 3.5 Percentage of workers in farm and non-farm sectors, 1983 to 2011/12
Source: Employment–unemployment surveys of NSS.

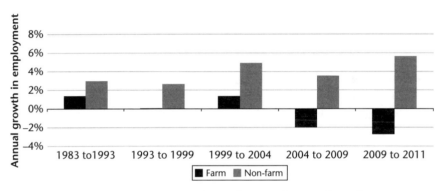

Figure 3.6 Percentage annual growth in employment by industry
Source: Employment–unemployment surveys of NSS.

agricultural workforce. Figures 3.5, 3.6, and 3.7 present some of the numbers underpinning this account, based on NSS quinquennial surveys. Figure 3.5 presents the percentage of workers in farm and non-farm sectors by usual status classifications. Figure 3.6 displays the growth rate of workers in farm and non-farm sectors, and Figure 3.7 gives the distribution of incremental jobs in farm and non-farm sectors.

Although the percentage of workers employed in the non-farm sector has increased at a faster rate this century than in the last (Figure 3.6), since 2004/5 it has also been accompanied by a decline in the absolute number of workers in agriculture for the first time in Independent India. But what is striking about this phase of non-farm diversification is the nature of jobs produced in the non-farm sector. The contribution of the manufacturing sector to rural non-farm employment has been very small. Preliminary evidence regarding the non-farm jobs created in the economy after 2004/5 reveals the uncertain nature of much of non-farm employment, most of which is casual

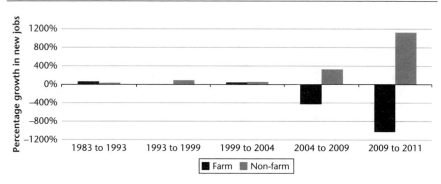

Figure 3.7 Percentage growth in new jobs in farm and non-farm sectors
Source: Employment–unemployment surveys of NSS.

employment, with construction accounting for the majority of new jobs.[10] While the period after 2004/5 was associated with rapidly declining rural poverty and appears to have been driven in large measure by non-farm employment expansion,[11] some have expressed concerns regarding the sustainability of this process. And the general perception is that that the scope for further growth in agricultural productivity may be limited, at least in some states. The rise in agricultural productivity appears to have been an important element in the release of labour to non-farm sectors, and this seems a likely force at work more broadly.

Diversification towards non-farm sources of employment is a familiar process in any country's economic development, but a puzzle in the Indian context has been that this process, particularly during periods of rapid economic growth, has been relatively slow.[12] It also remains unclear, at the all-India level, to what extent non-farm employment, across its various dimensions, is accessible to more vulnerable sections of society. Further research into some of the underlying mechanisms behind the observed changes in structural patterns of employment in rural areas is a priority.

Palanpur has seen similar changes to those at the all-India level in its own structure and can potentially provide some insights into the mechanisms at work. In our earlier work on Palanpur, we argued that the three main drivers of change in Palanpur have been population growth, development of agricultural technology, and expansion of non-farm employment opportunities outside the village. The green revolution in the late 1960s, and the consequent improvement in agricultural technology such as the use of high-yielding crop

---

[10] See Ghosh (2014), Thomas (2015), Mehrotra et al. (2014), and Himanshu (2015b).
[11] See Narayan and Murgai (2016), Datt, Ravallion, and Murgai (2016), Chatterjee et al. (2016), and Salazar et al. (2016).
[12] See Ghosh (2014), Binswanger-Mkhize (2013), Thomas (2015), and Himanshu (2015a).

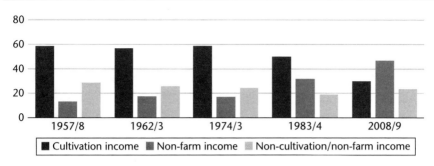

Figure 3.8 Share of farm and non-farm income in % total income in Palanpur
Note: Based on data from Palanpur surveys.

varieties, better irrigation facilities, and mechanization of agriculture, were originally associated with a reduction in income inequality in the village, particularly as irrigation increased from 50 per cent of the land in 1957/8 to close to 100 per cent in 1974/5.

As for Palanpur, notwithstanding the growth of non-farm activities in recent decades, agriculture remains of great importance to village livelihoods. Eighty-four per cent of Palanpur's households report income from agriculture. However, only 23 per cent of these households were dependent on agriculture alone. Figure 3.8 gives the share of farm and non-farm income in the village. Income from cultivation, which contributed to 60 per cent of total village income until the 1970s, started declining in the 1980s and now accounts for only one-third. Non-farm income now accounts for almost half of village income, and the balance comes from rent, remittances, pensions, transfers, and interest.[13] The decline in income from farming is similar to the trend seen in the data from the national accounts.

The decline in the share of agriculture in total income was a result of two factors in both Palanpur and at the national level. First, while agriculture investment and change in crops and techniques were successful in raising the average rate of growth of agricultural output to over 3 per cent in the 1980s, it remained lower than the growth rate of other sectors of the economy. Second, the non-farm sector saw higher productivity and earnings.

We look at the changing nature of agricultural production in Palanpur in Chapter 5. We identify the following key elements of the development process. First, while agriculture played a central role in income growth in earlier surveys, increasing non-farm and outside jobs have become more important to growth in recent periods. There have been important ramifications, as we shall see, for the agricultural development process. Second, there has been an intensification of farm capital in the form of farm mechanization that has

---

[13] For details, see Chapters 7 and 8.

been both land-augmenting and labour-saving. Whilst farm mechanization has raised agricultural productivity, it has also played a role in enabling the release of labour to non-farm activities. Third, there has been an increase in higher value crops, such as mentha, and improvements in farm practices. Notwithstanding that Palanpur is a backward village, villagers do show some dynamism and willingness to innovate and invest. The rise of non-farm income has played a crucial role in shaping the mobility of households.

The opportunities are different for different caste groups. History, culture, and tradition play a role. So, too, do forms of urbanization and government intervention. However, the rise of non-farm activities for Palanpur since the 1990s is also a story of different reactions from different people and of how entrepreneurship, innovation, and investment by village households through-out the long period of the study have shaped incomes. Agricultural invest-ment, particularly in irrigation, in the first part of the period, facilitated by greater confidence in land ownership following *zamindari* abolition, and in mechanization in recent decades, has been a strong feature throughout. The investments and involvement with change associated with new crops and new varieties, particularly of wheat, as part of the green revolution embodied major innovations for households. The spirit of entrepreneurship and innovation in new directions has continued in the last three decades. We have seen village residents move into poultry, bee-keeping, and dairy, making use of new tech-nology and investment, but also investing in non-farm activities, including marble polishing and repair services. Not all of these succeed, but the exposure to the outside world appears to have increased the appetite for risk-taking in the village. It has also shaped income distribution in the village, with many villagers willing to take risks in return for future rewards. All of these factors have altered the set of occupations for workers in Palanpur.[14]

3.2.2 Urbanization: Changing Economic Geography

The increase in outside jobs and opportunities being accessed by Palanpur residents has been accelerating since the 1983/4 survey. This trend has been noted across India and has been associated particularly with the emergence of small and medium towns as places of opportunity and drivers of rural non-farm diversification.[15] This is not just a feature of the area around Palanpur, but across the whole of India.

India has witnessed a strong increase in the rate of urbanization in the past few decades. Between 2001 and 2011, the urban population of the country grew by 32 per cent. As of 2015, India's cities are home to close to 420 million,

---

[14] We discuss the changing occupational composition of workers in Chapter 7.
[15] See Lanjouw and Murgai (2014), Gibson et al. (2017), Chatterjee, Murgai, and Rama (2015).

around one-third of the total population, with reports projecting this number to double to 800 million or more by 2050. This rate of growth, however, has been slower than that experienced by other countries, such as China (which went from 16 per cent in 1960 to 56 per cent in 2016). Binswanger-Mkhize (2013) attributes this slower rate of urbanization to the stagnant share of the manufacturing sector in the economy, which has, he suggests, played a role in fostering a period of 'jobless growth' in the urban economy and attenuated the pull-forces of migration.

This urban growth has occurred in spite of the failure of government, local and otherwise, to keep pace with urban investment, leading to inefficient, congested, polluted, and ill-planned cities and towns. Indeed, Indian cities and towns are now amongst the most polluted in the world, as World Health Organization (WHO) data make clear (WHO, 2014, 2016).

Datt and colleagues (2016) indicate that India's urbanization and structural change have been characterized by strong urban–rural and intersectoral linkages and argue that this feature of growth contributes to significant poverty reduction and an equalizing effect on distribution. This is a different story from Kuznets (see Chapter 4). This effect, they argue, is in addition to the role played by urban areas as absorbers of surplus agricultural labour.

It is very important to recognize that a major component of urban growth has been occurring in small towns and census towns, outside India's 'Tier 1' and 'Tier 2' cities. The number of census towns increased three times, with Census 2011 recording 3894 census towns as against 1362 in 2001.[16] The contribution of census towns to total urban population during this period increased from 7 per cent in 2001 to 14 per cent in 2011.

Recent literature has increasingly acknowledged the role of small towns and urban peripheries in creating jobs. Their growth has contributed to poverty reduction. Lanjouw and Murgai (2014) suggest that urban development contributes more to rural poverty reduction if urban economic growth arises from the small and medium towns than the big metropolitan areas.[17] Gibson and colleagues (2017) illustrate this using night-light data and conclude that it is urban growth on the extensive rather than the intensive margin that matters for rural poverty reduction. In effect, their analysis shows that it is the urban expansion which has been the key factor in rural poverty reduction after 2004–05. One of the ways that growth of secondary towns has helped in rural poverty reduction is through supporting employment diversification in

---

[16] Census towns are defined as towns based on the census definition of urban areas but are administratively treated as villages. A village is classified as census town if it has minimum population of 5000, a density of at least 400 per square kilometre, and at least 75% of their male workers are engaged in non-farm work.
[17] The argument flows from close connectivity between secondary towns and the rural hinterland, as such connectivity has a larger impact on rural poverty.

the rural areas. This has happened through using labour from the hinterland, but also by creating opportunities in the rural areas themselves.[18]

Much of the increasing integration of rural and urban in India, however, is associated with commuting rather than migration, somewhat in contrast to other developing countries. Data from the 2011 Census indicate that 48 per cent of all workers in India, working outside the agricultural sector, commute over a distance of at least 2 km for work. In the case of workers in rural areas, this metric increases to 5 km. Enabled by improved access to transportation and communication, these small towns and semi-urban areas have emerged as important intermediaries for the rural economy by providing connectivity to larger markets and spurring job creation in the non-farm sector. The high population density of much of India's rural areas, including the Indo-Gangetic plain where hundreds of millions of people live (and Palanpur is located), implies that local towns are also quite densely located across the region and can be readily accessed, within an hour or so, by a significant percentage of the rural population.

Palanpur's growth in the past seven decades broadly reflects these trends. The neighbouring towns have seen rapid growth in the last two decades, with their population growing at a rate of 3 per cent per annum or more. Growth in these areas has led to increased availability of jobs. These outside jobs and incomes have become ever-more important to Palanpur where, as we will see, most of the activity and income from outside jobs is associated with commuting. In Palanpur's case, Chandausi (roughly 13 kilometres distant) and the large town of Moradabad (about 31 kilometres) are particularly important as commuting destinations. The number of persons working outside Palanpur has increased from 8 in 1983 to 150 in 2015. The increasing importance of commuting has also altered the way various caste groups interact with the outside world. Migration over greater distances for longer periods has been increasing, but commuting is substantially more important. Most migrants belong to richer classes; there is very little migration amongst the Jatabs. Further, those households which were already in some regular job or in outside casual jobs seem to have a higher tendency to move away. The ease of transportation and access to communication services have helped the Jatabs and the poorer households come closer to the outside world and raise their incomes, but this has not been via migration.

It is interesting to compare this fundamental driver of change in Palanpur with Ansari's observation over sixty years previously, quoted at the beginning of Chapter 2: 'The fact that the village is well-linked with cities such as

---

[18] This is also clear from the analysis by Chatterjee, Murgai, and Rama (2015), which suggests that small towns have contributed significantly more in generating non-farm employment compared to large cities.

Moradabad and Chandausi does not seem to have been very significant from the point of view of the village economy.'

3.3 Mobility and Inequality

The growth impetus provided by the forces of globalization, liberalization, and technology provided a powerful stimulus to India's poverty reduction efforts. However, it is also important to note that such growth was accompanied by a deepening of economic inequality in India. Indeed, the nature of growth in the last two decades has seen a rise in income disparities in many or most countries. Public discussion, political debate, and policy-making is increasingly turning to issues around the distribution of income and wealth. Economists such as Tony Atkinson, Branko Milanović, and Thomas Piketty have used extensive data sets to try to understand the nature of this inequality and the channels through which it operates. For example, at a global level there has been much attention on results reported by Alvaredo and colleagues (2017) in the World Inequality Report, estimating that the top 1 per cent in Western Europe and the United States now account for 12 and 21 per cent of their national incomes, respectively.

Unfortunately, developing countries do not always offer the kind of detailed, quality data sets on incomes that are crucial to such studies of inequality. India is no exception, and this has hampered the development of literature devoted to understanding the nature of inequality in the country.[19] Even more scarce are data on intergenerational mobility, which might help gain insights into how fortunes move across generations. Such studies could, in principle, also inform how social factors impede income growth of individuals. The Palanpur surveys are a valuable source of data on such mobility, covering three generations of families and tracking their fortunes over decades. In other words, the data allow us not only to study intergenerational mobility but also the change in intergenerational mobility (see Chapter 8).

National-level studies such as the India Human Development Survey (IHDS) and the sample surveys conducted by the NSSO offer multiple perspectives on inequality in India. Data from the IHDS led to estimates of the Gini coefficient of income inequality in India in 2005/6 as 0.532, which marks it as a high inequality country (Lanjouw and Murgai, 2014). Jayadev and colleagues (2007) estimate that the Gini coefficient of inequality in per capital landholding in 2002 was 0.73, per capita asset holding was 0.65, while per capita holding of financial assets was 0.99, with large variations across regions, social

---

[19] In a recent study Chancel and Piketty estimate that the top 1% of Indians earn more than 20% of national income (Chancel and Piketty, 2017).

groups, and income categories. Across most dimensions they find a general upward trend in inequality. Inequality measures from a variety of sources looking at disparities in wealth, access to education, and nutritional outcomes all demonstrate similar tendencies.[20]

Economic disparities, some argue, through channels which include interaction with India's rigid social structure, can create severe impediments to the mobility of families across generations. Azam (2016) uses nationally representative IHDS data to find that households from the 'forward Hindu castes' experience the highest upward mobility and are significantly more mobile than those from disadvantaged backgrounds such as scheduled caste (SC)/ scheduled tribe (ST) or Muslim households. Moreover, he finds that urban households have better chances of improving their ranking in the national income distribution relative to rural households. Motiram and Singh (2012) also draw on IHDS data to report a high level of intergenerational persistence of occupation, indicating that families that are poor and unskilled are unable to push their children to higher-skilled or higher-paying jobs. They too find that upward mobility is easier in urban areas, as compared to villages. Asher and colleagues (2017) combine the Socio-Economic and Caste Census (SECC) data (2011) with the IHDS to report that despite advances in education across the board, intergenerational mobility has remained unchanged in the last 40 years in the country. They do, however, find a convergence in mobility outcomes between the general and historically disadvantaged (SC/ST) populations, indicating an improvement in mobility for the latter.

Palanpur's data broadly support these trends of rising inequality, which occur, in large measure, as a consequence of the rise in non-farm jobs along with an increase in wages. While income inequality declined between 1957/8 and 1974/5, it has been rising since then. This trend is not very different from that at the national level, with most indicators suggesting a decline in inequality until the 1980s, followed by a rise in inequality since the 1990s (Chancel and Piketty, 2017; Himanshu, 2015a). In Palanpur, the decline during the first two decades to 1974/5 was the consequence of two main factors. First, with the advent of green revolution technologies in the 1960s there was a significant expansion in the use and application of modern agricultural technologies, as well as the introduction of newer farming practices and better irrigation devices,[21] which applied across landholdings and embodied a

---

[20] See Himanshu (2007, 2013, 2015b) and Sen and Himanshu (2004).

[21] The distributional 'incidence' of the expansion of irrigation was particularly progressive in that, whereas previously only a few rich farmers were able to irrigate their land (using 'Persian wheel' lifting technologies which required complementary draft animal power), the green revolution saw an expansion of irrigation (through pumping sets) to all farmers, such that by 1974/5 all village land was irrigated. In terms of harvest quality in Palanpur 1974/5 was also a good agricultural year. As a result, 'errant' farming practices tended to be less severely penalized, leading to increased equality in the distribution of incomes.

Table 3.1 Estimates of inequality from NSSO consumption surveys

	Year				
	1983	1993/4	2004/5	2009/10	2011/12
Share (%) of various groups in total national consumption expenditure					
Bottom 20%	9.0	9.2	8.5	8.2	8.1
Bottom 40%	22.2	22.3	20.3	19.9	19.6
Top 20%	39.1	39.7	43.9	44.8	44.7
Top 10%	24.7	25.4	29.2	30.1	29.9
Ratio of average consumption of various groups					
Urban top 10%/rural bottom 10%	9.53	9.43	12.74	13.86	13.98
Urban top 10%/urban bottom 10%	6.96	7.14	9.14	10.11	10.06
Urban top 10%/rural bottom 40%	6.47	6.84	9.40	10.11	10.16
Gini of consumption expenditure (%)					
Rural Gini	27.1	25.8	28.1	28.4	28.7
Urban Gini	31.4	31.9	36.4	38.1	37.7
All-India Gini	29.8	30.0	34.7	35.8	35.9

Note: All estimates are based on Mixed Recall Period (MRP) estimates of consumption expenditure. Gini coefficients are expressed as percentages.
Source: NSS, Consumption Expenditure Surveys.

significant degree of catch-up, including from those who had little or no irrigation. Second, the distribution of land cultivated in Palanpur was more equal in 1974/5 than in other years. This was mainly a result of a fall in the proportion of land owned by Thakurs due to a few land sales.[22]

In the most recent Palanpur survey conducted in 2008/9 where income data is available, the Gini coefficient for income inequality had risen to 0.379—the highest level of income inequality observed over the entire study period. The trend for Palanpur of rising inequality during a period when access to non-farm jobs has increased, along with rising wages, is similar to trends for India as a whole. Table 3.1 provides broad estimates of some measures of inequality from the NSSO consumption surveys. These surveys suggest that while inequality in India looked fairly stable during the 1980s, it has risen since the early 1990s. Interestingly, since the mid-2000s inequality does not appear to have continued climbing as sharply, and indeed the last decade has seen particularly rapid poverty decline.[23]

As we mentioned in Section 3.2.1, and will examine further in Part 2 of this book, particularly Chapter 8, one of the drivers of the recent rise in inequality

---

[22] Moreover, during this year tenancy and sharecropping practices displayed a clear pattern of large landowners leasing out their land to those with smaller landholdings. In subsequent years that pattern tended to be more mixed, with the occasional observation of cases of 'reverse tenancy', where smaller landholders leased land to larger.

[23] Although Chancel and Piketty (2017) suggest that when non-coverage of the richest population segments in household survey data is corrected for, the trend of rising income inequality in India during the 2000s is maintained.

has been the differential success with which individuals and households have accessed non-farm jobs and activities. Whilst some caste groups have had better networks than others in finding these jobs, there has also been considerable within-caste variation. This growth of non-farm activity has represented new avenues for mobility and has brought about reduced poverty, rising incomes generally, and higher inequality.

On mobility, stories from Palanpur offer illuminating insights into the nature of the change that has allowed some social groups and households to move up the socioeconomic ladder, while others have seen a fall in their fortunes.

Although non-farm jobs were accessed by all Palanpur households, disadvantaged castes have benefited in particular after the 1990s compared to their ability to get involved in such activities in the past. The nature of non-farm diversification since the 1990s, essentially driven by casual jobs and particularly related to construction, has allowed lower castes to access non-farm jobs; outside activities had hitherto been seen as the preserve of educated and rich households. This is also true for self-employment. Some of the lower caste groups have had only a limited tradition as cultivators and own little land. But they have long experience of manual and demanding work. Many amongst them have responded to these new casual job opportunities. In addition to the Jatabs, other castes such as Telis and Gadariyas have moved into self-employed activities in a substantial way. Compared to the non-farm jobs in the years up to the 1980s, which were dominated by regular employment and therefore accessible to those with networks and skills, these casual jobs were accessible to the lower castes. The heavy physical requirement for some of them also discouraged some from higher groups, here the Thakurs and Muraos, from these activities.

We shall also examine, in Chapter 8, intergenerational mobility and will present some evidence that it has fallen. Recall that our Palanpur data, perhaps uniquely with their long time span, allow an examination of *changes* in intergenerational mobility. This declining intergenerational mobility of income alongside greater mobility among the disadvantaged may appear counterintuitive; however, this is not the case when one considers the nature of agricultural intensification in the first half of the survey period followed by non-farm diversification during the second. As noted, these non-farm activities have, on the one hand, become increasingly casual and informal and thereby more accessible to households at the bottom of the distribution, but on the other hand, access to opportunities is still significantly influenced by networks and family ties—particularly for the more remunerative and stable non-farm jobs. This whole process has become associated with rising within-caste inequality, as some people get involved in new opportunities before others. The probability of finding out about these new activities depends on a range of factors, including not only caste networks and wealth, but also social and economic preferences of different groups, abilities (physical and otherwise), and, importantly, differentials in initiative. One might expect a certain degree of persistence across generations in such assets and personal traits.

In contrast, recall that earlier change was driven in large measure by investment in land and agriculture, where there was a process of catch-up as all groups came to benefit from double-cropping brought about by investment in in irrigation and equipment. The particular nature of income growth during this episode was such that a household's economic position in the initial period was less likely to influence the next generation's outcome.

3.4 Informality, Formality, and Endogeneity of Institutions and Markets

India has gone through a series of changes in the structures that underlie its society and economy. Some of these changes have been gradual, such as the weakening of the hold of the caste system, while others have been abrupt, such as the abolition of the *zamindari* system designed to increase the ownership rights of tenants. Over the decades, Palanpur has shown remarkable adaptation to the changing economic environment, with village institutions reflecting the changes. The village has also been strongly influenced by large external stimuli, including the opening up of markets, access to outside jobs, and greater connectivity and communication. Before we examine and try to unravel the transformation that the village economy has experienced as a result of these changes, it is important first to understand the formal and informal structures of governance and institutions which shape its interactions and play a role in holding it together.

Institutions are defined broadly as the 'rules of the game in a society' (North, 1993: 2). They have been an increasingly favoured lens for economists since the mid-2000s to throw light on the dynamics behind the relationships between market participants. In the village economy, each economic and social interaction is influenced by a complex set of implicit and explicit rules, which can be seen as integral to the institutional structure. To facilitate our understanding of the changes we refer to here, we can group these institutions into three broad categories. The first category is the 'outside' institutions, including the machinery of government, politics, and external markets. The second is the set of economic institutions, particularly factor markets, within the village. The third is the social institutions within the village, including caste, gender, and social relationships.

As we go through the changes in these institutions, we recall and emphasize two major themes that emerge from Palanpur and run through our understanding. The first is an increase in informality in the non-farm economy. Contrary to predictions in our previous work on Palanpur, where we had imagined a more formally employed labour force in the future, the primary driver of economic growth has been the informal sector. The second major theme is the endogeneity of institutions, including in the social and governance domains, as well as in the economic, and particularly in the functioning of markets. Institutions not only shape economic and social outcomes, but are also shaped by the economic and social forces at work in the village. Together these factors intertwine in shaping the fortunes of the village. Institutions continuously interact with each other, influence one another, and generate forces that help us make sense of the seemingly haphazard processes of economic growth in Palanpur.

Institutions that we examine are divided into those that are outside or exogenous to the village and those within the village. The 'outside' institutions influence the village but are determined by factors which are uninfluenced by the village. These institutions include the machinery of the Indian government and its policies on the one hand, and market-based networks on the other. For the first 30 years of the Palanpur study, the government's policies on the green revolution and agricultural inputs and outputs, the set-up of cooperatives, and the abolition of *zamindari* together provided a positive impetus to growth in the village. Since the late 1980s, it is the opening up of the economy that has changed the way the village functions.

With an increase in urbanization in India, including smaller towns, villages now have greater access to the outside world. A significant rise in the connectivity and the availability of transport has no doubt also been an important driver of this change. Successive governments in India have invested major resources in the construction of road networks linking the big cities in the country. Projects such as the Golden Quadrilateral, linking the four big metro cities, and the construction of expressways within the state of Uttar Pradesh, linking Delhi to Lucknow, have allowed faster and cheaper access to domestic markets. At the same time, projects such as the Pradhan Mantri Gram Sadak Yojana, aiming to connect villages via all-weather roads, have helped create better infrastructure and connectivity for rural areas. This is significant, as research on the impact of road connectivity on employment and income growth has found that the construction of roads to previously unconnected villages can lead to substantial changes, with workers moving to new labour opportunities (Asher and Novosad, 2016) and a fall in the share of households working in agriculture.

The story behind the increase in connectivity would be incomplete without a discussion of the expansion of mobile telephony services in India. From none in 1995, to over 1.1 billion subscribers in 2017, the mobile revolution helped leapfrog generations of technology and enhance access to information and opportunity. While the penetration of telecom services in rural India lags behind that of urban areas, the changes brought about by the availability of fast and reliable telephony have been truly transformational for the rural economy and society. Jensen (2007) provides a powerful example from fisheries in north Kerala, where the introduction of the mobile phone helped eliminate gaps in information and create a more uniform market for fish. Fishermen were able to access a larger market for their catch and sell to the highest bidder. In Palanpur too, the mobile phone is a key element in providing the information that enables people to commute to work outside the village. A journey of 90 minutes or so each way may not be justified without some confidence there is work available that day, and a phone call can greatly increase that confidence.

The second and third categories of institutions we emphasize here are within the village. They are also endogenous in the sense that they influence outcomes, but they themselves change as they are influenced by outcomes. We look first at the *economic institutions*, which govern the markets for factor inputs. These include the norms and accepted practices around tenancy in agriculture, the labour market, providers of credit, and so on. Such institutions have changed dramatically, in large part in response to the exogenous changes coming to the village. We discuss these internal changes and the nature of their impact on the village economy in greater detail in subsequent chapters. We note here that some, but not all, of the adjustments can be seen as positive. The social and political institutions have also adapted and changed, and the interplay of power relations within the village has been complex.

Organizational structures for labour and land markets have been changing with the growth of off-farm activity. An increasing number of transactions are moving from traditional systems to a more marketed or cash-based structure. For ploughing, for example, tractors can now be rented. This is a major change from before, when it was not possible to rent draught animals. Those owning them would not allow others to use them, worrying about lack of due care, but were also not willing to take on a task which might appear as agricultural labour, deemed a low status activity, by ploughing other people's fields themselves. Sharecropping has declined and cash rents have risen as a fraction of land transactions. In part this is in response to outside activity reducing the ability to supervise farming, particularly important under sharecropping where incentive structures may be weaker than in other arrangements (see Chapters 4 and 6). But, also, those with outside jobs and a little land now have greater liquidity, and the marketization of inputs allows them to use that changed liquidity position to rent and cultivate land.

Changes in the nature and structure of the agricultural economy, together with rising non-farm activities, have reshaped the village labour markets. These changes have not been visible only in terms of occupational shifts,

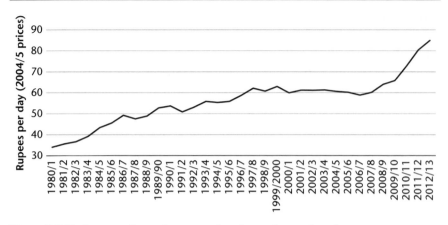

Figure 3.9 Real wages of casual wage workers in rural areas (men)
Source: 'Agricultural Wages in India' for data up to 1998 and Labour Bureau for data after 1998.

but have also contributed to changing modes of labour engagement with a rising share of piece-rate contracts and a growing preference towards cash contracts as compared to kind contracts. The second consequence of the changes in the labour market has been the impact it has had on wages. Figure 3.9 gives the rural casual wages rates for men in real terms at the all-India level from the Labour Bureau.

The trends appear to be common across India. There has been a sharp rise in casual wages across the country since the mid-2000s, although the exact determinants constitute a subject of intense debate. Much of the literature in the Indian context has pointed to increasing demand for labour in construction as the primary driver of wage increases, together with rising agricultural incomes, although this latter force appears to have been modest. The Mahatma Gandhi National Rural Employment Guarantee Act (MGNREGA) has also been highlighted as a factor contributing to wage increases, but the evidence is mixed, and the ways it may have contributed are still unclear.[24] Two other factors which have found support in the literature are the growing urbanization and integration of rural and urban labour markets and increasing education. While increasing integration with urban labour markets is a factor that contributed to wage increases in Palanpur, we have not found any support for education playing an important role so far in the village.

With the decline of the importance of the agricultural economy, as discussed, land and labour markets have undergone dramatic changes across India. As workers move into the non-farm sector and find opportunities in neighbouring areas, there has been a net movement to the informal non-agricultural economy.

---

[24] MGNREGA in principle gives workers the right to work for 100 days a year on public projects at specified minimum wage—in Palanpur in 2009 this was Rs 100/day.

Binswanger-Mkhize (2013) highlights that between 1999/2000 and 2004/5, the formal sector's share of employment declined from 8.8 per cent to 7.5 per cent. This has remained so until 2011/12. Even within the formal sector, there was a rise in the number of employees with casual contracts.[25] This movement was not along the lines expected by some. Many economists held the general expectation that as an economy develops, labour moves from the unorganized sector to the more advanced, organized sector. This was indeed the picture painted by Arthur Lewis in his seminal work on two-sector, or 'dual', developing economies, an idea developed by subsequent economists (see Chapter 4 for further discussion).

For the Indian economy, while it has seen an increase in the size in the formal sector, the growth in employment in the informal sector has been much more rapid and is still more pronounced in rural areas than in cities. India's National Accounts Statistics, in 2011/12, show 58.5 per cent of the total output of the country produced in the informal sector, with the share of sectors such as construction, mining, and quarrying increasing over the decades. The growth of labour productivity, too, was much higher in the informal sector in the past decade. Ghosh (2014) estimates that in the period between 1999/2000 and 2011/12, the annual growth rate of real output per employed person in the informal sector was 5.7 per cent, as opposed to 1.2 per cent in the formal sector.[26]

Examining this trend towards informalization more closely, data from the Labour Bureau show that almost half of Indians in all age groups are, by their definition, 'Self-Employed', with the rates of self-employment being higher in rural areas. While there might not be any change in the traditional preference for secure government jobs, there certainly are more workers who are investing their capital and establishing their own businesses. In part, this is indicative of an increasing role for entrepreneurship and innovation, although it may also reflect limited access to other opportunities.

Small and medium enterprises are encouraged by the government, through efforts aimed at easing access to credit and through business promotion schemes. Urban India has seen a spurt in 'start-up' businesses and capital-intensive enterprises that have brought disruptive innovation into the Indian markets. Indian companies like Flipkart, for example, compete with global behemoths like Amazon to connect the common trader and seller to larger markets. While rural Indian enterprises operate on a far smaller scale, there is a

---

[25] For example, in the manufacturing sector, the share of contract workers increased from 19% in 2000 to 32% in 2012.

[26] For an insightful essay on the informal economy in India, we refer the reader to Ajit Ghose's 2016 Presidential Address to the Indian Society of Labour Economics.

move towards greater entrepreneurship; people are branching out into new activities, taking decisions which are, for them, innovative and accepting risk. Palanpur has also seen residents taking risks and moving into new territories in search of better incomes. Non-farm self-employment now constitutes a significant employment category, unlike the past, where regular and casual employment were dominant forms of accessing non-farm jobs. Prior to the 2008/9 survey, such self-employment in the village was principally in the form of unskilled activities such as rope making, rickshaw pulling, or selling leaves. Outside these unskilled activities, self-employment consisted mainly of shopkeeping and tailoring. The 2008/9 survey round shows a substantial change in the nature of these self-employment activities. Self-employment accounted for about one-third of the total non-farm jobs in 2009; the activities included marble polishing, motorcycle and bicycle repair, flour mills, and tailoring. Some of these have gone well. A number of previous studies on India argue that the increase in self-employment has arisen as a result of distress-induced factors.[27] Whilst such stresses are present in Palanpur, including via population growth and reduced land per capita, the composition of self-employment activities in Palanpur clearly indicates a process of skill acquisition, initiative, and capital accumulation.

In subsequent chapters, we offer a discussion of how this story is unfolding in the context of Palanpur. We will see that the individual fortune and risk-taking capacity are important, but that village institutions such as caste and village identity continue to play important roles not just in land and labour markets in agriculture, but also in non-farm employment. Trust is stronger within family and caste. The emergence of caste-based networks, for messaging and inclusion in new non-farm opportunities, also suggests the importance of caste and other networks for villagers adapting themselves to situations of asymmetric information and market failure. These networks centred on caste and village affiliations are not just risk-sharing and information-sharing networks, but also can act as social safety nets in times of crisis.

Caste networks and trust are also important in relation to credit. Although the recent period has seen an increase in access to institutional credit in the form of the Kisan Credit Card scheme and access to commercial banks,[28] informal sources of credit continue to thrive. And relationships between the formal and informal can sometimes be troubling. For example, there is clearly collusion between formal and informal credit markets via the village credit

---

[27] For a discussion on the factors responsible for the growth of non-farm sector see Abraham (2009) and Himanshu (2011). Abraham (2009), using the 61st (2004/5) round of NSS, suggests that growth in non-farm employment in rural areas was probably a response to income crises in the farm sector.
[28] As the name suggests, the Kisan Credit Card scheme provides farmers with credit cards, to enable, in principle, quick, hassle-free access to small loans for agriculture and allied activities.

cooperative in Palanpur, which is run by the brother of the dominant money-lender in the village. New categories of informal moneylenders arise as activities change, including via employers in brick kilns and other non-farm enterprises. The provision of credit in these settings is as much to support families in distress as it is to foster a regular supply of labour, although the former could indeed help with the latter. While this form of labour tying (credit supplied by the employer) has not emerged as a major credit category, it can be a preferred option for some of the poorest households.

Integration with the broader economy, the influence of outside jobs, and changes in agricultural assets deployed has brought substantial change to land markets, too. While earlier land tenancy contracts were dominated by *batai*, or 50–50 sharecropping, *chauthai* (a quarter share of the harvest akin to wage labour, at least relative to the *batai* or 50–50 share) and *peshgi* (fixed cash rent) have grown in importance. There is some evidence that the bargaining power of tenants may have weakened as more potential tenants are available. Jatabs, for example, with their increased resources, are emerging as potential tenants where earlier they may have been seen as, and seen themselves as, only labourers. These observations indicate institutional and contractual arrangements which respond to a changing economy and society—in other words, they are not immutable traditional aspects of life. And they generate hypotheses about the changing features of an increasingly market-oriented economy which influence the varying contract forms.

The third and last category of institutions examined here encompass the *social structures of the village*, such as the family, caste, gender relations, the *panchayat*, and so on. These *social institutions* have undergone a great deal of change in the course of our studies, in part driven by economic growth. The exogenous changes influencing growth, employment, and economic outcomes filter down to adjustments in the institutions internal to the village, and these, in turn, have an impact on the economy. Power relations between caste groups, specific roles for women reserved in the *panchayat*, dispersion of employment, and migration through community networks all form the basis through which we seek to understand the changes in Palanpur. In contrast to its image of a slow, stagnant entity, we find that the village is dynamic and in a continual process of absorption of change. On the other hand, whilst understanding such change is critical to understanding Palanpur and India, we must emphasize again that we do not want to give the impression that Palanpur is some sort of rural powerhouse. It remains a backward village and, whilst incomes and living standards are rising, the pace of change is slower than in many other parts of India.

The economic changes brought about by the availability of non-farm employment has helped increase incomes, while the decline of the caste system has come with tensions that have allowed a resurgence of caste-based identities. Political parties have actively tried to capitalize on this change, leading to the emergence of caste-based political parties such as the Bahujan Samaj Party (BSP) and Samajwadi Party in Uttar Pradesh. The policy interventions that have allowed historically disadvantaged groups such as SC/STs to enter activities from which they were excluded, or for which they faced great barriers, are now allowing them to catch up with the general population in terms of education, occupation distribution, wages, and consumption levels. As found by Hnatkovska, Lahiri, and Paul (2012), these, together with the expansion of non-farm opportunities, have begun to bring some hope of rising living standards for these groups. But such change can bring stress in relation to others, who potentially feel resentment.

The gradual erosion in the social power of the upper castes has created discontent in various parts of India. Jats in Haryana, Patels in Gujarat, and the Marathas in Maharashtra have been recently involved in agitations for inclusion of their caste in the list of Other Backward Caste (OBC) for reservation in government jobs. In all three cases, these caste groups are not only numerically the largest population group but are also highly regarded for their cultivation skills. All three of them had seen their social and political status rise with the green revolution. All are now demanding reservation in government jobs and higher educational institutions for their communities.[29]

The relative failure of the dominant cultivating castes to access non-farm jobs, at least to the extent their social position might suggest, can be linked to two separate dimensions of the non-farm diversification seen in the country in recent years. First, most of the non-farm diversification has been in manual casual jobs which are less likely to be sought after or cornered by these castes given their status and aversion to working alongside lower caste groups. Second, even though these caste groups benefited from rising incomes in cultivation, this has not translated into improvements in educational outcomes. This slow progress in education has also made it difficult for them to find highly skilled regular jobs.[30] Deshpande and Ramachandran (2016) further suggest that the frustration within these communities is related to a perceived inability to compete with upper castes in urban areas.

While the social structures have changed in India, public institutions in Palanpur have fallen into an unfortunate state of disrepair. The seed store and the cooperative bank in the village were important village institutions and played a role in the advance of green revolution technologies and methods in the village up to the 1970s. The seed store building has now partially collapsed

---

[29] At least in the case of Marathas in Maharashtra, this has also taken the form of antagonism against the SCs, with demand for dilution of the existing legislation which provides protection of SCs from discrimination.

[30] See Himanshu (2015b), Jodhka (2016), and Deshpande and Ramachandran (2016).

and is virtually non-functional, and the cooperative bank was only marginally functional during our study period.

Across India, rising inequality has not only reinforced existing gaps between abilities to access public services, but has also been a result of the differential access to basic services. Sinha (2015) argues that the rise in inequality has been one of the factors contributing to lack of public action on essential services such as schools, the Public Distribution System (PDS), and health facilities. The weaknesses of public services in Palanpur are related to the failure or absence of collective efforts by the village community. In more cohesive villages or communities, collective action can be effective in improving standards of public provision.

An important aspect of the increasing democratization of the village council has been the increase in levels of awareness among the villagers. This was also partly helped by an increase in the quality of communication, particularly mobile phones and televisions. Interestingly, this increasing communication has also fostered group formation and caste alignments, with particular regard to the electoral prospects in the village council. While these have not led to the elimination of caste discrimination—far from it—village residents confirm that the level of discrimination is more muted. Policies such as reserved roles have also influenced the structures of power in the village; examples are the election of female or Dalit Pradhans.

3.5 Human Development: Education and Health

In India, the fact that rising incomes, both in the early decades of and after the green revolution years and since the 1990s, have not been associated with the transformations in human development outcomes seen in other countries has been seen by many as a problem for the country as a whole. On most indicators of nutrition, education, health, and gender, India's performance has been lagging behind not just countries of similar economic status, but also compared to its neighbours in South Asia.[31] Although on most of these dimensions there has been some acceleration in recent years, key indicators remain low by international standards. These have also varied regionally within India, with northern and eastern states further behind southern states such as Kerala and Tamil Nadu.[32] In public forums, there have been debates between economists on whether, in this context, the government should give particular

---

[31] A large literature exists which has analysed the weakness of improvements in human development outcomes in India. A good summary of this is available in Drèze and Sen (2013).
[32] For details on regional variation in human development indicators across states, see Sinha (2016).

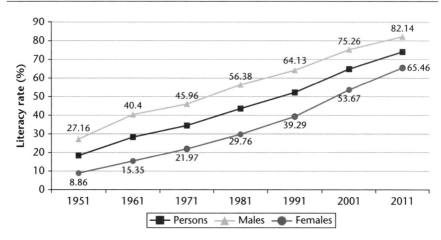

Figure 3.10 Literacy rates by sex
Source: Census of India.

priority to human development. Economists such as Jagdish Bhagwati and Arvind Panagariya (2013) have emphasized the argument that economic growth is necessary to generate the resources needed by a weak state to empower its citizens. Others, like Jean Drèze and Amartya Sen (2013), have stressed that human development is a necessary input for sustainable economic growth, as well as of great value in its own right.

Of course, the government continues to invest in both growth and human development simultaneously. At the country level, India is now seeing not only improvement in literacy rates but also in primary and secondary school enrolments. Figure 3.10 presents the trend in literacy rates for the population by gender. Figure 3.11 displays trends in enrolment rates for primary school by gender. Both these indicate significant progress, although female literacy rates continue to lag substantially behind male. However, the data on primary school enrolment does suggest that the trend is changing, with the enrolment rate of girls now at the same level as that of boys. The chart also suggests almost universal primary enrolment for both boys and girls. But these are far lower at higher levels of schooling, with the enrolment rate of boys at higher secondary level only 17 per cent and for girls, 12 per cent.[33] The education deficit at higher levels, as well as the gender gaps at higher levels, are likely to emerge as serious impediments for India's future.

The situation in Palanpur is no different in the sense that literacy rates have increased over the years. Literacy rates in Palanpur are lower than the national average, although they are comparable to rural Uttar Pradesh levels. In the case

---

[33] The higher secondary level of education in India refers to Class 11 and 12 (also known as intermediate education), or the two final years of school education.

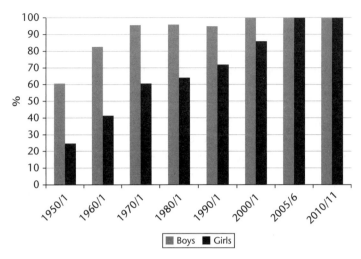

Figure 3.11 Enrolment rate in primary schools by sex
Source: Ministry of Human Development, Government of India.

of males as well as females, the growth in the literacy rate only picked up after 1993. Although the literacy rate of females has also picked up, it is still very low compared to rural India as a whole. What is also worth noting is that the Palanpur gender gap, which was increasing up to 2009, saw a reversal in the most recent survey round of 2015. While all the caste groups have seen an increase in educational attainment and literacy, there exists considerable variation across castes. Thakurs have always been the most literate of the major groups in the village, and they remain so. But other caste groups are now catching up with them. Telis now have almost comparable literacy levels as Muraos. However, it is the Jatabs who have shown the most remarkable improvement in literacy levels, starting from almost negligible literacy as recently as the 1980s, although female literacy rates continue to show only modest improvements. The education deficit and gender gaps for older age groups imply, however, that universal literacy is a long way off. Details are provided in Chapter 9.

On health, the story is quite similar to that for education. According to United Nations Children's Fund (UNICEF) data, as of 2012, India lags behind most other regions, including much of sub-Saharan Africa and other parts of South Asia, on child immunization rates. Its public health system remains weak. While the situation in Palanpur is similarly weak with regard to health status and access to health services, there is considerable variation across caste groups. The Jatabs continue to remain at the bottom as far as nutritional indicators are considered but also in immunization and institutional delivery of babies. Some of these issues are also ones on which there has been slow improvement nationally. We have detailed surveys on access to health and the health-seeking behaviour of the residents of Palanpur. Qualitative discussions have shown that forced reliance on private expenditure on health, as a result of weaknesses of the public system, continues to remain an important source of vulnerability for poorer households.

Our survey on credit also confirms the vulnerability of poorer households to such shocks, with many of them falling into debt traps after a major illness of a family member. The relatively slow improvement in supply of health services such as public health centres (until recently, the nearest health centre was 15 kilometres away) has also meant slow improvements in institutional deliveries (in the 2008/10 survey, only two institutional deliveries were reported in the entire sample of women who have delivered in the last five years). Overall, the slow pace of improvement in human development indicators remains a serious issue as far as improvements in the well-being of residents of the village are concerned. We provide a detailed discussion on these indicators and issues in Chapter 9.

Uttar Pradesh remains a laggard state in all aspects of human development, especially when compared to other states such as Tamil Nadu and Kerala. An aggregate metric for India can often be misleading in the face of these disparities. The close study of villages is important to building a deeper understanding of the state of human development in India.

The weakness of the social institutions is reflected in the poor indicators of health and education in Palanpur. Public institutions, such as schools, medical systems, village governance, food, and employment programmes, are weak and often troubled. Public services such as the school and the Primary Health Centre (PHC) are rarely operating as they should. While there has been a significant increase in central and state government spending on education and health, the increased spending has not yet translated into corresponding improvements in schools and public health facilities in Palanpur. The concentration of discretionary powers with the Pradhan and consequent rent-appropriating behaviour, including misappropriation of the funds meant for midday meals in schools, have weakened both health and schooling. Private alternatives are found in one way or another.

Women's voices remain largely excluded, although this is beginning to show some signs of change. Economic changes and political empowerment have been important in reducing caste-based oppression and have allowed lower-caste households to participate more freely in the village's economic and social life.

Women in general have been marginalized in the village economy and in the public sphere (see Chapter 10). And, in our own surveys, the general absence of a female investigator meant that until the 2008/10 survey, data on women were less complete than we would have wished. The 2008/10 survey not only included special surveys and questionnaires to measure and analyse women's participation in economic activity, but also enquired about several aspects of their autonomy and day-to-day life. Our analysis of the data suggests that there are improvements in the way women have been accessing public services, but women are still largely 'invisible' in the village economic sphere. Most of the economic engagement has been either as self-employed workers or as part of the family engagement in non-farm activities, such as work in brick kilns. While more girls are being put through formal education than in the past, their numbers lag strongly behind boys.

On the whole, while there certainly have been improvements over the past seven decades, the current position of women remains weak and vulnerable. We examine these indicators in greater detail and offer ideas for their improvement in later chapters in the book, particularly Part 3.

3.6 Entrepreneurship, Innovation, and Investment

Starting with a model of state-led development of heavy industry, the policies laid down by Nehru and Mahalanobis, particularly in the second five-year plan (1956–61), did not put entrepreneurial capitalism centre stage. In pre-Independence India, a few major private sector conglomerates, such as the Tatas and Birlas, had already established their presence and capacity across the country. Now, however, growth in industry was to be steered by the state in large measure, directed by the Planning Commission. And private investment opportunities that did arise were, in the main at least, for large investments—offered to family-run business houses by a bureaucracy that favoured experience over innovation. Nilekani (2010) provides a colourful history of India's affair with entrepreneurs. Reforms of India's agricultural sector, however, did offer new openings and opportunities that were not regulated by the state, and Indian farmers did embrace the change they enabled.

The policy environment started changing in the 1980s, with piecemeal reforms at first, eventually leading up to the landmark 1991 budget, where India finally shed its coyness towards wealth-making enterprises and embraced the possibilities offered by its young, dynamic business community. The approach continues to this day. Through efforts aimed at enhancing the ease of obtaining credit and promoting schemes for small and medium enterprises, the central and state governments actively promote entrepreneurship and woo business investors who can bring capital and expertise to India. Urban India has seen a spurt in 'start-up' businesses and enterprises that have brought disruptive innovation into the Indian markets.

We find that in Palanpur, and indeed we would suggest for much of India, the story of entrepreneurship provides a sound and helpful language for understanding key aspects of change, be this in non-farm diversification, agricultural investment, inter-household inequality, or intragenerational mobility. It is important to emphasize, however, that this language is different from much of the literature on entrepreneurship and innovation, which tends to dwell on firms and formal enterprises. Nevertheless, it provides a very useful lens for our study of the village economy and its alteration over the last seven decades. And the changes we examine do involve decisions, newness, innovation, and risk, the key elements of entrepreneurship, as individuals and households embark on activities which are, for the most part, very different from what they have practised before.

Contrary to the picture of a stagnant, unchanging rural backwater, the people of Palanpur have been constantly changing, adapting, and absorbing new ideas and technologies to create better lives for themselves and their families. And the way in which this change has occurred is through the routes of investment and innovation. We think of innovation here, for the household, as radical change in the methods and organization of production. A change in circumstances unleashes new opportunities, to which people respond. Individuals with initiative and an appetite for risk lead the way. Some will have advantages such as caste networks or greater income or wealth. In a few cases, education has made a difference. Others will have disadvantages such as poor health. Within all groups there are variations in initiative and entrepreneurship.

Investment has been crucial here, as households make decisions on how they might use capital, or their own time and effort, to achieve better livelihoods in the future. Agricultural investment, particularly in irrigation and facilitated by greater confidence in land ownership following *zamindari* abolition, has been a strong feature throughout. In the earlier decades, investment in much of north India (after the abolition of the *zamindari* system) was directed towards agriculture, with 'green revolution' technologies and methods bringing higher yields to farmers and with efforts and resources being directed towards obtaining the appropriate set of agricultural inputs such as fertilizers and seeds, as well as irrigation. In Palanpur, as we have seen, the expansion of irrigation during the early survey rounds facilitated double-cropping and higher productivity. Those who had previously 'lagged behind' in agriculture were able to 'catch up' to some degree. These investments and changes, with new crops and new varieties, particularly of wheat, embodied major innovations for households.

Notably, the investments were not necessarily enabled by the educational system in Palanpur (which remains in a dismal state even today), but through a process of learning-by-doing and learning-by-seeing (from others). The story, and the mechanics of this process, were in key respects as described in Griliches' (1957) path-breaking study of the diffusion of ideas and technologies in the context of rural USA.

In later decades, investments were directed towards further enhancing the use of capital in farming. Farmers invested in mechanization and purchased tractors, water-pumping sets, and threshing equipment. This fostered an auxiliary set of investments, with a deepening of the markets for renting out and maintaining these capital goods. In the past few decades, with growth in agriculture slowing, innovation in the non-farm sector has emerged as the primary engine of growth and, indeed, the avenue for entrepreneurship in the villages.

Some people take more initiative and risk than others. And as is the nature of risk, the entrepreneur is sometimes, but not always, rewarded. Perhaps, in the context of the fast-changing Indian economy and with the inherent vulnerabilities of agriculture, decisions to continue with traditional methods and occupations are also risky; but that is to incur risk by taking a more passive form, in contrast to actively trying to do things differently. As we have discussed in Section 3.2.3, the stories on mobility and inequality have been in large measure about individual households moving up or down the economic ladder, based on the decisions they took and the pay-offs they could get. Nanhe, whose story we share in subsequent chapters, is a good example of how individuals can move up the ladder, riding on their initiative and entrepreneurial instincts. Whilst some of this is symptomatic of fewer opportunities in agriculture and weakly growing formal employment, we have seen that the types of self-employment also suggest a major element of initiative and entrepreneurship.

In order to avoid being misunderstood, we should emphasize again, clearly and strongly, that we are not portraying Palanpur as a vibrant and dynamic example of Schumpeterian capitalism and growth, expanding at full throttle with extraordinary levels of innovation. It remains a backward village showing much slower growth than India as a whole. But its people do innovate, invest, and take risks to change their lives. And their powers of initiative vary. Understanding this is essential to understanding both change and inequality in Palanpur and India, as well as economic development more generally.

3.7 Concluding Comments: India, Palanpur, and the Five Basic Themes

India's transformation over the last seven decades has had a profound effect on Palanpur. The changes that we see in the data at the macroeconomic level find a reflection in the village economy. Just like India, Palanpur, too, is a society in flux, undergoing major changes in its society, economy, and culture. Examining these changes provides crucial understanding of the aggregate, its foundations, and the key elements driving change at the level of the nation.

While Palanpur is not, and could not be, a 'representative microcosm' of a large country such as India, it does provide a unique testing ground, showing how the events and policies of seven decades since Independence have influenced lives and livelihoods of individuals and households in a village—the basic element of much of Indian society. Palanpur surveys and the analyses of them have always been situated in the context of changing economic structures and policies. It is this interconnectedness of the lives of individuals in the village and the changing nature of economy and society outside which, in our view, makes this study fascinating. This kind of analysis is crucial to the understanding of the multiple ways in which markets, social structures, and livelihoods are affected at the most micro level by economic growth and development in a large country.

We have looked at India, in Sections 3.2 to 3.6 of this chapter, from the perspective of the five broad themes that we find to be central to the last few decades of the Palanpur story and which were described briefly in Section 3.1. The core of our first theme, as described in Section 3.2, is that a structural transformation is changing India, and Palanpur, from an agriculture-based economy to one that is driven by informal, non-agriculture-based growth. Outside influences such as the abolition of the *zamindari* system and the use of green revolution technologies and methods were earlier drivers of productivity growth in Palanpur. Now, improvements in yields are driven by increasing capital investments and mechanization, with a growing marketization of agricultural transactions. This also has the effect of enabling the release of labour and allowing more time for households to diversify their set of occupations. We have seen that this 'release of labour' has been in the directions offered by changes in the Indian economy and the opportunities created by urbanization, the deepening of an integrated market economy, and, in particular, informal non-farm activities, many of which are associated with construction. And those opportunities have, in large measure, been driven by local towns. This is a story of a new driver of growth—non-farm activities—associated with an integration and coming together of labour markets.

In Section 3.3, as our second theme, we examined mobility and inequality. Incomes have risen with these structural changes, as has inequality between households. Income from opportunities outside the village has been a key factor in the increasing inequality. Those households who were able to tap into opportunities outside the village but also into opportunities outside agriculture—the traditional mainstay of the village—have seen their incomes rise. Such households exist in all caste groups: there has been a strong increase in within-group inequality. On the other hand, many of those in the traditional cultivator caste of Muraos, gainers during the 'green revolution' years, have been more inward-looking than other groups and are no longer highly represented among the 'winners' in recent years, at least in terms of incomes or mobility. While the growth of external opportunities in this period has favoured, relatively speaking, those who were less dependent on agriculture, or who chose to be, the study does point to some success for those who were willing or able to take risks and embrace new opportunities compared to those who followed more conservative strategies. This is also one of the reasons behind some of the Jatabs, one of the historically most disadvantaged groups in the village, beginning to break out from poverty. Some of the Telis, a Muslim group who in the first two or three decades of the study were at the bottom of the distribution, alongside the Jatabs, have shown particularly strong entrepreneurship skills. The net result has been a significant decline in poverty and a rise in intragenerational mobility in Palanpur. This has been accompanied by rising income inequality, as some are quicker to seize opportunities than others.

Interestingly, the nature of the change described has led to some decrease in mobility across generations. The ability or willingness to participate in change was more widespread in the first period, as much of the new investment in irrigation (motivated in part by stronger land tenure after *zamindari* abolition) saw poorer households catching up, particularly via irrigation and double-cropping, with some of those who had invested previously. There was an equalizing factor at work in these dynamics. Those advantaged in the first period were not automatically those advantaged in the second. Advantages of networks and income in finding outside jobs and the lessening in importance of investment in irrigation, a mobility open to many in the earlier period, seems to have come with a decrease in intergenerational mobility. Some, such as the Thakurs, the highest group, seemed more able than others to operate these networks. Thus, finding and taking advantage of new opportunities has been influenced by both initiative or entrepreneurship, on the one hand, and privileged positions on the other, strands which are often interwoven.

Looking at the transformation in India and Palanpur through their social and economic institutions offers several valuable lessons in the importance of such institutions. That is our third theme, presented in Section 3.4. These institutions are very much endogenous to the system, as they shape economic and social outcomes and are, in turn, shaped by them.

Changes exogenous to the village, which we label as 'outside institutions', are interventions by, or due to, the actions of the Government of India or Uttar Pradesh that have a profound impact on the interactions between individuals. The abolition of the *zamindari* system, for example, generated greater land security, which encouraged more investment in agricultural inputs and fostered economic change.

The economic institutions of the village, those dealing in factor inputs, have had to adapt to the changing markets. Urbanization and an increase in connectivity, through investments in roads and mobile telephony services, have been crucial as facilitators of this change. The rural labour market in Palanpur is now much larger in scope, more cash-oriented, and also involves opportunities in the non-farm sector, leading to higher incentives and wages across all sectors. It is largely informal. Participation often involves a degree of entrepreneurship.

The land market, too, has undergone a significant change. The tenancy systems that had been in place until the 1980s are gradually giving way to a more cash-based structure. This is accompanied by the inclusion of social groups who were previously excluded from renting land, such as the Jatabs. The formal market for credit remains small, beholden to the influence of some upper-caste households, who also control the informal credit market.

Social institutions, including for governance and social action, remain weak in Palanpur as compared to other parts of India. While empowerment, defined as the ability to shape one's life, has increased, along with outside opportunities and human capital, it remains constrained by social and political arrangements, including gender and caste.

Empowerment and capability are also strongly constrained by weaknesses in education and health, arising in large measure from poor public systems. The slow changes in human development, relative to economic development, was the fourth theme, presented in Section 3.5.

Our fifth theme, in Section 3.6, concerned entrepreneurship and initiative. We argued that land pressures, via rising population, were making agriculture relatively less attractive as an occupation, and the growth of India, particularly in towns and cities near Palanpur, was creating new opportunities. More entrepreneurial households were seizing these opportunities before others. That was true in the village in earlier periods, too, with irrigation investment after *zamindari* abolition and involvement in the green revolution technologies and methods. Even in a backward village like Palanpur, and recognizing that some people have advantaged access to opportunities, entrepreneurship and initiative are important in understanding change.

Our analysis of this long and rich data set has enhanced our understanding of both the strengths and complexities of different theories of development. The village today is no longer a closed economy and is in one way or another influenced by global events such as the 2008 financial crisis and volatility in international commodity markets via their effects on India and on the markets which matter to the village. At the same time, the changing fortunes of villagers is as much a result of their own position in the village hierarchy, governed by caste and gender relations, as it is due to their ability to take advantage of the opportunities opened up by developments outside village. The period under study is one of fundamental change, from the *zamindari* abolition in the 1950s which brought land to farmers, to the green revolution of the 1960s and 1970s, to the increasing integration of village markets, notably labour markets, with a rapidly changing world outside the village, and the acceleration in growth of the Indian economy as a whole, since the 1980s. That same period has brought changes in economic policy, ranging from the reforms that moved away from the dominance of planning, starting in the 1970s and accelerating further during the 1990s, to institutional change which favoured certain groups in village governance.

Our task in this chapter has been to show how the main elements of change in Palanpur, summarized in part by the five themes set out in the chapter, have been influenced and shaped by change in India itself. And our understanding of change in Palanpur has, we trust, deepened our understanding of change in India. In Chapter 4 we relate Palanpur's experience to theories of development.

References

Abraham, V. 2009. 'Employment growth in rural India: distress-driven?', *Economic and Political Weekly* 44: 97–104.

Alvaredo, F., Chancel, L., Piketty, T., Saez, E., and Zucman, G. 2017. 'World Inequality Report, 2018', report presented at World Inequality Lab, 14 December.

Asher, S., and Novosad, P. 2016. 'Market access and structural transformation: evidence from rural roads in India', *Job Market Paper*, 11 January.

Asher, S., Novosad, P., and Rafkin, C. 2017. 'Estimating intergenerational mobility with coarse data: a nonparametric approach'. World Bank Working Paper.

Azam, M., 2016. 'Household income mobility in India: 1993–2011'. Economics Working Paper Series 1705, Oklahoma State University, Department of Economics and Legal Studies in Business.

Bhagwati, J., and Panagariya, A. 2013. *Why Growth Matters: How Economic Growth in India Reduced Poverty and the Lessons for other Developing Countries*. New York: PublicAffairs.

Binswanger-Mkhize, H.P. 2013. 'The stunted structural transformation of the Indian economy', *Economic and Political Weekly* 48: 5–13.

Chancel, L., and Piketty, T. 2017. 'Indian income inequality: 1922–2014: From British Raj to billionaire raj?' World Inequality Lab Working Paper Series No. 2017/11.

Chatterjee, U., Murgai, R. and Rama, M.G., 2015. Employment Outcomes along the Rural-Urban Gradation. *Economic and Political Weekly*, 50 (26), pp. 5–10.

Chatterjee, U., Murgai, R., Rama, M.G., and Narayan, A. 2016. 'Pathways to reducing poverty and sharing prosperity in India: lessons from the last two decades'. Working Paper 106902, World Bank Group, Washington, DC, http://documents.worldbank. org/curated/en/559851468910056173/Pathways-to-reducing-poverty-and-sharing-pros perity-in-India-lessons-from-the-last-two-decades

Datt, G., Ravallion, M., and Murgai, R. 2016. 'Growth, urbanization, and poverty reduction in India'. Discussion Paper 09/16, Department of Economics, Monash Business School, Australia.

Deshpande, A., and Ramachandran, R. 2016. 'The changing contours of intergroup disparities and the role of preferential policies in a globalizing world- evidence from India'. Working Paper 267, Centre for Development Economics, Delhi School of Economics.

Drèze, J., and Sen, A. 2013. *An Uncertain Glory: India and its Contradictions*. Princeton, NJ: Princeton University Press.

Ghosh, J., 2014. The curious case of the jobs that did not appear: structural change, employment and social patterns in India. *Indian Journal of Labour Economics*, *57* (1). pp. 1–18

Gibson, J., Datt, G., Ravallion, M., and Murgai, R. 2017. 'For India's rural poor, growing towns matter more than growing cities'. Policy Research Working Paper 7994, World Bank Group, Washington, DC.

Griliches, Z. 1957. 'Hybrid corn: an exploration in the economics of technological change', *Econometrica* 25: 501–22. DOI:10.2307/1905380.

Himanshu. 2007. 'Recent trends in poverty and inequality: some preliminary results', *Economic and Political Weekly* 42: 497–508.

Himanshu. 2011. 'Employment trends in India: a re-examination', *Economic and Political Weekly* 46: 43–59.

Himanshu. 2013. 'Poverty and food security in India'. ADB Economics Working Paper 369, Asian Development Bank.

Himanshu. 2015a. 'Inequality in India', *SEMINAR* 672 (August). Available at: http://www.india-seminar.com/2015/672/672_himanshu.htm (accessed 10 April 2018).

Himanshu. 2015b. 'Rural non-farm employment in India: trends, patterns and regional dimensions', in *India Rural Development Report 2013–14*. IDFC Foundation, Mumbai.

Hnatkovska, V., Lahiri, A., and Paul, S. 2012. 'Castes and labor mobility', *American Economic Journal: Applied Economics* 4: 274–307.

Jayadev, A., Motiram, S., and Vakulabharanam, V. 2007. 'Patterns of wealth disparities in India during the liberalisation era', *Economic and Political Weekly* 39: 3853–63.

Jensen, R. 2007. 'The digital provide: information (technology), market performance, and welfare in the south Indian fisheries sector', *Quarterly Journal of Economics* 122: 879–924. DOI:10.1162/qjec.122.3.879.

Jodhka, S. S. 2016. 'A forgotten "revolution": revisiting rural life and agrarian change in Haryana', in Himanshu, P. Jha, and G. Rodgers (eds), *The Changing Village in India*. Delhi: Oxford University Press.

Lanjouw, P., and Murgai, R. 2014. 'Urban growth and rural poverty in India 1983–2005', in N. Hope, A. Kochar, R. Noll, and T.N. Srinivasin (eds), *Economic Reform in India: Challenges, Prospects, and Lessons*. New York, Cambridge University Press.

Mehrotra, S., Parida, J., Sinha, S. and Gandhi, A., 2014. 'Explaining employment trends in the Indian economy: 1993–94 to 2011–12'. *Economic and Political Weekly*, 49(32): 49–57.

Motiram, S., and Singh, A. 2012. 'How close does the apple fall to the tree? Some evidence on intergenerational occupational mobility from India'. WIDER Working Paper.

Narayan, A., and Murgai, R. 2016. 'Looking back on two decades of poverty and well-being in India'. Policy Research Working Paper WPS 7626, World Bank Group,

Washington, DC, http://documents.worldbank.org/curated/en/841931468196177423/
Looking-back-on-two-decades-of-poverty-and-well-being-in-India (accessed 2 March
2018).

Nilekani, N. 2010. *Imagining India: Ideas for the New Century*. London: Penguin.

North, D.C. 1993. 'Institutions, transaction costs and productivity in the long run'.
Economic History Working Paper No. 9309004, EconWPA.

Salazar, B., Felipe, C., Desai, S., Murgai, R., and Narayan, A. 2016. 'Why did poverty
decline in India? A nonparametric decomposition exercise'. Policy Research Working
Paper WPS 7602, World Bank Group, Washington, DC, http://documents.wor
ldbank.org/curated/en/432721468197079833/Why-did-poverty-decline-in-India-
a-nonparametric-decomposition-exercise

Sen, A., and Himanshu. 2004. 'Poverty and inequality in India: I', *Economic and Political
Weekly* 39: 4247–63.

Sinha, D. 2015. 'Cash for food: a misplaced idea', *Economic and Political Weekly* 50:
17–20.

Sinha, D. 2016. *Women, Health and Public Services in India: Why are States Different?*
Critical Political Economy of South Asia. London and New York: Routledge India.

Thomas, J.J., 2015. 'India's labour market during the 2000s', in V.K. Ramaswami (ed.),
Labour, Employment and Economic Growth in India. Cambridge: Cambridge University
Press, pp. 21–56.

4

Theory and India*

4.1 Introduction

How do the livelihoods of individuals and communities change in the process of economic development? What drives those changes? What happens to distribution? Why is it that some people do better or worse than others? Those questions are, or should be, at the heart of economic enquiry. They are indeed at the heart of our research on Palanpur, where the nature of our data provides a unique opportunity to examine these issues in detail over the seven decades since the Independence of India. They were basic, too, to the classical economists Smith, Ricardo, and Marx, although their focus was for the most part on distribution between factors of production. Whilst growth and poverty reduction have remained centre stage for our subject, these questions on the dynamics of changing individual circumstances have not always been at the forefront of academic economics over the last two or three decades.

To understand change we require both evidence and data, on the one hand, and concepts and theories, on the other. It is the interweaving of, and inter-action between, the two that will provide our insights into the causes and consequences of change in Palanpur. What combination of theories and ideas provides the strongest insights into change in Palanpur? Can we see one set of ideas as predominant, or must we look to several sets in concert? Taken together, are the ideas sufficient for a strong and deep understanding of what we find? As we pursue these questions we shall learn not only about Palanpur, but also about economic theories of development, and that, too, is an important objective of this book.

Palanpur's context in terms of the economic changes in India as a whole will be a critical part of the enquiry and of any 'interchange' between theory and

* This chapter has been written by Himanshu, Peter Lanjouw, Nicholas Stern, and Shantanu Singh.

Palanpur's experience. And at the same time, the experience of Palanpur will help us understand that of India, given that around two-thirds of India's population is still rural based.

Some of the central strands of change in Palanpur—the key elements of which we wish to understand using economic theories of development—were introduced in the Introduction and were set out in more detail in Chapters 2 and 3. The core ideas of non-farm diversification, changes in inequality and mobility, the salience of endogenous institutions, and the stuttering progress of human development, as well as the spirit of individual initiative and entrepreneurship, together help us understand the changes sweeping across India in the past three decades. We now investigate how the same themes can inform theories of economic growth and development. Economic theories should help us understand the broad elements or key phenomena of change in Palanpur. And this context, of a not-atypical village in one of the most populous countries of the world, where the big majority of the population is rural, is surely a vital test of the usefulness of our theories. If not here, then where?

In this chapter we set out key elements of theory that correspond to and interact with these themes. The interaction is both ways. We have theories of change in mind, and we examine evidence relevant to these theories. And we identify key features of change in Palanpur and ask about relevant theories of change.

Our focus on the dynamics takes us to theories beyond those examined in the first Palanpur book by Bliss and Stern. For example, Chapter 2 on 'Theory and India' in the Bliss and Stern book (1982), reporting on the 1974/5 study, was primarily focused on the allocation of land, labour, and capital in agriculture. Rural factor markets were of strong interest to theorists at that time, for good reason. That interest remains in the present study, but we now have the much broader canvas of how lives and livelihoods change over time, including, particularly, growth and distribution, given the longer period and richer data. The theories we shall set out here are influenced both by the prominence of certain theories in shaping ideas in the profession and by the key findings we have identified.

Interestingly, in the last two decades of research in economics, and particularly development economics, we have seen a strong emphasis on institutional and behavioural economics. Indeed, as argued by the British Academy (see Besley, Stern, and O'Donnell, 2015), these two areas have been amongst the strongest new contributions to economics over the last two or three decades.[1] They are relevant here. Also, our discipline has seen much policy

---

[1] The award of the 2017 Nobel Prize to Richard Thaler for his contribution to behavioural economics is a testimony of the emergence of behavioural economics as an important area of research in economics.

literature on identifying the 'impact' of policies through carefully structured empirical investigation. Whilst this research has not been 'anti-theory', it has not always placed theory centre stage. And, given this literature's dependence on randomized control trials and the like, it is most unlikely to be applicable to studies which investigate detailed microeconomic change over seven decades. That would require a group of villages subject to a policy change, another group as 'controls', and all with data for seven decades. Given the research resources and the time horizons that would be required, it is improbable that will be achieved any time soon.

4.1.1 Plan of Chapter

In Section 4.2 we begin our assembly and review of relevant theory with models of growth and distribution, starting from and building on the classical economists Adam Smith, David Ricardo, and Karl Marx. The reason for beginning here is that they were concerned with the processes of transformation and investment of an economy with a growing industrial sector drawing on labour from an agricultural or backward sector. We also examine authors such as Arthur Lewis and Simon Kuznets, who, in part, followed in that tradition and examined questions of changing income distribution as part of the process of transformation. They shared a focus on the distribution of factor incomes. More recently, Thomas Piketty has discussed growth and distribution, drawing, in large measure, on this tradition. So, too, Branko Milanović. Given the centrality of agriculture and its change, we also discuss ideas and theories around the role of agriculture in economic growth and development.

Mobility, and theories thereof, are the subject of Section 4.3. Interestingly, the study of mobility seems to be deeper on concept and measurement than it is on economic theories of how mobility occurs.[2] Uncertainty in economic life concerning, for example, harvests or health, can play a strong role. Some behaviours, such as drinking and gambling, can derail and lead to downward mobility. The notion of a poverty trap, prominent in discussions of the 1950s (e.g. Ragnar Nurkse) and also in later literature (Banerjee and Mullainathan, 2010; Barrett and Carter, 2013; Dasgupta and Ray, 1986; Galor and Zeira, 1993; Ravallion, 2016), is an example of a theory of immobility. Social behaviour, including social constraints on empowerment, can prevent mobility. So can entrenched and vested interests.

---

[2] The review by Jäntti and Jenkins (2015) in the *Handbook of Income Distribution*, vol. 2A (edited by Atkinson and Bourguignon) provides a valuable conceptual overview as well as a review of empirical research on income mobility. Much of the evidence derives from developed countries. The contribution by Thomas Piketty (2000) in the *Handbook of Income Distribution*, vol. 1 (2000) provides a useful overview of theories of persistent inequality and mobility.

Institutions and society constitute the subject matter of Section 4.4. There is a long tradition amongst economic historians, including Joseph Schumpeter, Robert Putnam, Douglas North, Elinor Ostrom, and others, of putting institutions centre stage. They are in general concerned not only with the raison d'être and influence of institutions, but also with how they are built and change. Daron Acemoglu, Tim Besley, Simon Johnson, Torsten Persson, James Robinson, Dani Rodrik, and others have contributed to a more modern literature on institutions and economic development, with a strong emphasis on links between the nature of institutions and economic growth.

Institutions have a profound effect on what people recognize as possible, indeed what is possible, and thus on entrepreneurship and behaviour. There is therefore an intimate and interwoven relationship between entrepreneurship, behaviour, and institutions, which runs through our discussion.

At the same time, we must recognize that institutions are not a narrowly defined economic phenomenon, neither in the way they arise and change, nor in the outcomes they help generate. They are very much social and political, and we have to embrace political science, anthropology, sociology, and other social sciences if we are to understand economic and social change. Indeed, right through this book the economic perspective is entwined with the political and the social. We examine, in Section 4.4, some of the theories, of potential relevance for Palanpur, which bridge the social sciences. We include some aspects of behavioural economics in the discussion. The perceiving and taking of opportunities is shaped by how people behave, what they recognize, and what they feel able to do, all powerfully influenced by institutions. Behavioural economics has been a growing and fruitful area of economics in the last two or three decades.

Human development, capabilities, and empowerment are the subject of Section 4.5. The discussion embraces both the ideas of capabilities and 'development as freedom' (in the tradition of Amartya Sen) and ideas of empowerment (as in Stern et al., 2005).

In Section 4.6 of this chapter we examine theoretical and empirical work on entrepreneurship, innovation, and investment, again concentrating on authors concerned with longer-run processes of growth and change, including Joseph Schumpeter, Friedrich Hayek, Albert Hirschman, and Chris Freeman, and some of the 'Austrian School'. And in the India context, writers such as Scarlett Epstein and F.G. Bailey.

We comment in each section on relations with the broad strands of change in Palanpur as described. And in the concluding section we draw the discussion together, arguing that a satisfactory explanation of such changes would require all these theories to be collated and integrated. We argue further that, even together, they are inadequate in important respects and, in Part 4 of this book, point to possible directions for new ideas.

119

4.2 Growth and Distribution

The determinants of, and relationships between, growth and distribution in the process of economic development have long been at the heart of economic enquiry. Two hundred years ago, in a remarkable passage in the preface to his *Principles of Political Economy and Taxation* (1821: 3), Ricardo set out the 'principal problem in Political Economy' as follows:

> The produce of the earth—all that is derived from its surface by the united application of labour, machinery, and capital, is divided among three classes of the community; namely, the proprietor of the land, the owner of the stock or capital necessary for its cultivation, and the labourers by whose industry it is cultivated.
>
> But in different stages of society, the proportions of the whole produce of the earth which will be allotted to each of these classes, under the names of rent, profit, and wages, will be essentially different; depending mainly on the actual fertility of the soil, on the accumulation of capital and population, and on the skill, ingenuity, and instruments employed in agriculture.
>
> To determine the laws which regulate this distribution, is the principal problem in Political Economy: much as the science has been improved by the writings of Turgot, Stuart, Smith, Say, Sismondi, and others, they afford very little satisfactory information respecting the natural course of rent, profit, and wages.

The immediate and central focus of Ricardo's enquiry is the allocation of land, capital, and labour in agriculture, the rewards to these factors in terms of rent, profit, and wages, and how they move ('the natural course') over time. These allocations were indeed at the centre of the focus of the Palanpur study of 1974/5, as described in Bliss and Stern (1982), but we focused there less on the dynamics of distributional change than we do here. Ricardo, too, emphasizes 'the skill, ingenuity and instruments employed in agriculture', which would, of course, be concerned, in large measure, with technology and agricultural methods. Thus Ricardo goes straight into the driving forces around economic change emphasized in our work on Palanpur around the 1983/4 study: population, technology, and outside jobs (see Lanjouw and Stern, 1998). We have argued that all three have been fundamental in driving change in Palanpur, with the role of outside jobs becoming ever stronger as the Indian economy has grown and as communications have improved.

Ricardo's contemporary, Thomas Malthus, suggested that if per capita income were to rise above some 'subsistence level', the population would rise to negate any per capita income gain. It is possible that there may have been some kind of relationship between income per capita and population growth in the pre-Independence era in Palanpur; we have no evidence one way or the other. However, through our study period for the village, this somewhat pessimistic proposition does not hold. While population increased, from 528 in 1957 to 1255 in 2008/09, per capita income increased 2.4 times during the same period. Agricultural investment and technical progress, especially during the green revolution period, and individual effort in pursuing off-farm income have been the key determinants of increasing per capita income in Palanpur. On the other hand, Ricardo's language of skill and ingenuity, which gives space for entrepreneurship, initiative, and innovation, does find some resonance in Palanpur.

Ricardo, as with other classical economists including Marx, saw wages set at a subsistence level, at least in earlier stages of development, a level which allows for the reproduction of labour. He focused his attention on rent, which would be shaped by the fertility of the soil and the extensive margin of cultivation. Famously, he argued that the rent on the marginal land cultivated would be zero, because if it were above zero, it would pay to cultivate more land. The rent on any piece of land is then determined by how far its fertility is above the marginal piece of land cultivated. This was the 'Ricardian theory of rent' which has been extended in economics to other factors which vary in quality, from tennis players to brands.

In Ricardo's story, as population grew and more and more land was cultivated, the returns or rent for those owning land would rise. Ricardo was somewhat gloomy about growth prospects for precisely these reasons because he saw landlords, whom he regarded as having spendthrift or indolent tendencies and predilections, getting a rising share of income.

Here is a towering figure in our subject placing growth, distribution, and economic change at the centre of the agenda. However, later growth theory, after the pioneering work of Robert Solow (1956), moved away from the structure of the economy and the rewards flowing to participants, towards more aggregate and longer-run stories. It was seen primarily, in the first instance, as a story about advanced countries and, as a theory of aggregate growth, it said little about distribution. However, Arthur Lewis' seminal work on 'economic development with unlimited supplies of labour' (his famous article of 1954 and his splendid book, *The Theory of Economic Growth*, 1955), more or less contemporary with Solow's original growth paper, launched a period when dual economy models were prominent in discussions of developing countries (see, for example, Dixit and Stern, 1974; Stern, 1972). And subsequently, with the arrival of extensive aggregate data for a large number of countries in the 1980s and onwards, economics saw aggregate growth theory applied to a broad range of countries, including via innumerable cross-country regressions, not all of which were well structured or productive, or offering useful insights.

We shall examine dual economy models shortly, but we should first emphasize that, both in Ricardo (notwithstanding his introduction of skill and ingenuity in his argument) and in the dual economy models, there was very little focus on differences between people, in their choices, in their skills, in their entrepreneurship, and in their acquisition and ownership of capital. This is in sharp contrast to Ricardo's emphasis on differences in land. We shall see that both class and caste background *and* differences between people along various dimensions (including health and education) and entrepreneurship will together play a role in shaping the income, wealth, and well-being of households and how these change over time in Palanpur.

Lewis quite explicitly followed the classical tradition of unlimited supplies of labour at a fixed wage. In his case, however, he saw the subsistence wage not so much as the 'reproduction cost' of labour, but as the income available to a worker in a backward sector (or a modest mark-up thereon). Workers could 'fall back' on that sector and receive whatever average income was available there. He saw the backward sector as open to entry, using no capital, and being very large relative to a growing dynamic, capital-using, and profit-maximizing advanced sector. For this advanced sector, land did not play a role. Firms or enterprises in this sector faced a fixed wage and, in pursuit of profit maximization, employed people up to the point where the marginal productivity of labour was equal to that wage. The profit, or returns to the capitalists, was equal to the production less the wage bill (wage times employment). Much of that profit was invested, raising the marginal product of labour for given employment above the given wage and, thus, under profit maximization, expanding employment. He saw the advanced sector not necessarily confined to manufacturing, narrowly understood: the key features were the use of capital and profit maximization.[3]

This is a direct and appealing story of how a developing country can grow, which includes a very simple story of distribution. As the advanced sector expanded, profits grew both absolutely and as a share of the overall economy. Thus Lewis answered, in his terms, what was seen as one of the key questions in economic development at that time, of how savings rates in a developing country could be high enough to drive strong growth. Other economists, too, wrote on the importance of savings and industrialization (Nurkse, 1953; Rosenstein-Rodan, 1943; Sen 1983; Singer, 1952).[4] Savings out of profits have been fundamental to China's remarkable growth since the 1980s and have played a key role in the acceleration of India's growth (see also Chapter 3).

Some later models elaborated on Lewis' ideas by using two sectors, thought of as manufacturing and agriculture (including a relative price), with equilibrium

---

[3] See Gollin (2014) for a recent assessment of the Lewis model.

[4] The first three plans of Indian economy also had an explicit focus on savings and industrialization as the strategy of economic growth. The savings rate in the Indian economy doubled from less than 10% in the early 1950s to 20% by the early 1980s.

in product and labour markets and with markets for land used in agriculture. There were extensions to an open economy model, too, with key relative prices 'exogenously' determined on world markets (Dixit and Stern, 1974). Notwithstanding these extensions, the overall insights of the original Lewis story with development driven by the advanced sector have been the lasting contribution of the Lewis model and have played a powerful role in thinking about economic development and the mechanisms by which incomes grow. For example, recent discussion of future developments of the Chinese economy by a number of Chinese economists (Yiping and Tingsong, 2010; Zhang, Yang, and Wang 2011) have spoken of a 'Lewis turning point', referring to the exhaustion of the 'unlimited supplies' and a rising wage faced by the advanced sector. Again, as with Ricardo and Marx, the tradition upon which Lewis was drawing, that is, the examination of the distribution of the income between people as shaped, in large measure, by their differences, plays only a modest role, and it is class distributions that dominate the discussion.[5]

Kuznets built a largely empirical story, but his conceptual framework was based on a Lewis-like perspective on mechanisms of growth. He gives a clear and important summary of the structures and forces he has in mind in his story of industrialization and urbanization:

> The second source of the puzzle lies in the industrial structure of the income distribution. An invariable accompaniment of growth in developed countries is the shift away from agriculture, a process usually referred to as industrialisation and urbanisation. The income distribution of the total population, in the simplest model, may therefore be viewed as a combination of the income distributions of the rural and of the urban populations. What little we know of the structures of these two component income distributions reveals that: (a) the average per capita income of the rural population is usually lower than that of the urban; (b) inequality in the percentage shares within the distribution for the rural population is somewhat narrower than in that for the urban population—even when based on annual income; and this difference would probably be wider for distributions by secular income levels.

> Operating with this simple model, what conclusions do we reach? First, all other conditions being equal, the increasing weight of urban population means an increasing share for the more unequal of the two component distributions. Second, the relative difference in per capita income between the rural and urban populations does not necessarily drift downward in the process of economic growth: indeed, there is some evidence to suggest that it is stable at best, and tends to widen because per capita productivity in urban pursuits increases more rapidly than in agriculture. If this is so, inequality in the total income distribution should increase. (Kuznets, 1955: 7)

---

[5] Fields (1987) explores the impact on income inequality of economic development along a path traced out by the Lewis model. See also Elbers and Lanjouw (2001).

In Kuznets' story, in the early stages the vast bulk of the population is in the backward sector. They share a low standard of living and inequality is low. People start to move to a more advanced sector, here (a little differently from Lewis) with substantially higher wages. Average income rises. Inequality starts to rise as those who move to the more advanced sector gain higher incomes than those in the backward sector. They are few at first, but their numbers grow, and eventually, as they become numerically predominant amongst the labour force, inequality starts to fall. This is the Kuznets inverted U-curve of inequality plotted against time, as the numbers in the advanced sector rise.

But as we can see from the quote, his story of the inverted U-curve was richer than a simple combination of workers in one sector and workers in another. He was interested, too, in the combination of two income distributions, urban and rural. As we shall see in more detail and have already remarked, the Palanpur story is more complex and in key respects richer and more interesting. The villagers of Palanpur are involved in both urban and rural incomes simultaneously, and that involvement changes in nature and scale over time.

The inverted U-curve hypothesis prompted an entire literature of its own, with economists evaluating the existence of such a curve as more data became available for the global economy. While Kuznets was limited to the use of data from the UK, USA, India, Puerto Rico, and Sri Lanka, later empirical enquiries expanded the scope of examination as data from other countries became available. While some analyses seemed to support the hypothesis (Ahluwalia 1976; Ahluwalia, Carter, and Chenery 1979; Barro 2000; Bourguignon and Morrisson, 2002; Forbes 2000), other studies have been more ambiguous (Anand and Kanbur, 1993; Deininger and Squire, 1998). Some have voiced concern around the use of broad, cross- country empirical investigations on different sources of micro data. Working with such data requires large, sweeping assumptions which may not always be well founded (Anand and Segal, 2008; Banerjee and Duflo 2003). Interestingly, Kuznets himself was concerned with the fragility and the limited scope of the data he had used and advised caution in using the idea of the inverted U directly. He was, in fact, interested in using the limited data available to devise a theory that would provide a link between growth and income inequality for nations undergoing economic change (Fogel, 1987).

When we turn to Kuznets' more subtle story (beyond the simple inverted U) of combining two income distributions, we begin to get a little closer to the experience of Palanpur: the inequality within the labour force is central and comes about because some people get better employment before others, both within urban and rural sectors and across them. There are crucial differences and questions, however, which are illuminated, as we shall see, by the study of Palanpur's experiences. The involvement of Palanpur's villagers in the more advanced sector, at least that outside agriculture, advanced or otherwise, does not require a zero–one choice. Households and individuals mix their activities between sectors. And we can ask and, to some extent, answer how some get to participate in activities off-farm before others do. How those opportunities arise and are perceived, understood, and taken will be an important part of our story. So, too, will be consequences for relationships, markets, and opportunities inside Palanpur. Further, those opportunities are themselves varied and come with different requirements and risks.

Questions concerning how lives and livelihoods change and how distribution changes in the process should constitute a fundamental line of enquiry in the study of economic development. In pursuing these questions we should recognize that important insights come from the Kuznets tradition. It is a tradition that also has links to Deng Xiaoping, leader of China and its Communist Party from 1978/9, and the political driving force behind China's market-oriented reforms. In commenting on changing inequality in China, during a process of growth, transformation, and changing activities and institutional structures, he remarked 'we permit some people and some regions to become prosperous first, for the purpose of achieving common prosperity faster'.[6] This is sometimes paraphrased as 'some get richer before others'.

The classical tradition has recently been revisited by Thomas Piketty (2014) who has emphasized again, as in Ricardo and Marx, the factor distribution of income, although focusing more, as with Marx, on ownership of capital and returns to capital. He puts the focus on an increasing share of capital arising from, in his argument, a rate of profit greater than the rate of growth. If incomes for the population advance at the rate of growth and capitalists' incomes rise at the rate of profit (that would follow from high saving and investment rates out of profits) then the share of capital must rise.

There is much to be questioned in Piketty's argument or model, including patterns of ownership of capital. He has, in his argument, the ownership of capital very highly concentrated in a dominant, and indeed increasingly dominant, capitalist or ultra-rich class, whereas we know in many modern economies capital ownership, through property and pension funds for example, is fairly widespread. But problems with Piketty's argument are not our main concern here. Rather, we underline the fact that one of the most prominent recent works on growth and distribution retains the classical focus on the factor and class distribution of wealth and income.

Milanović (2016), too, has built on the idea that the paths of inequality and growth are related. Studying within and between country inequality, he suggests that there indeed is a strong relation between the two. And he

---

[6] Deng Xiaoping offered these insights into his vision for China in an interview with American TV correspondent Mike Wallace in 1986. Transcript available at http://www.chinadaily.com.cn/china/19thcpcnationalcongress/2010-10/25/content_29714454.htm.

suggests further that the curve that Kuznets described is actually a small part of larger, cyclical waves, which Milanović refers to as 'Kuznets waves'. By probing issues around inequality in the context of globalization, he also finds that enhanced mobility of capital has meant that unskilled labour in developed countries now finds itself competing with cheaper labour from developing nations. Indeed, questions of equity, alienation, and resentment around the changes brought by the processes of globalization are requiring us to re-examine our understanding of the processes of growth and distribution.

At the same time, we must recognize that the forces associated with changing technology are powerful, too. Often, the evidence suggests, they are still greater than those of globalization: for example, dramatic falls in retail sector employment in the USA this century are not the result of globalization. The interwoven forces of technology and market integration are powerful in Palanpur, as we shall see.

In other recent literature, too, there have been numerous attempts to create theoretical frameworks that can shed light on the relationship between growth and inequality. One strand of literature seeks to build on possible non-convexities in underlying economic functions or variables,[7] such as those associated with production, behaviour, or market structures (Aghion and Bolton, 1992, 1997; Banerjee and Newman, 1991, 1993; Bourguignon, 1981; Galor and Zeira, 1993). Galor (2011) has advocated a 'unified theory of growth', building on the idea that the primary driver of growth, in the course of the 20th century, has changed from physical to human capital. In the world of human capital, ensuring low levels of inequality becomes crucial to avoiding low-level equilibria in the macro economy. Another strand of theory has built on ideas of political economy to explain how inequality in democracies can lead to distortionary taxation, potential social conflict, and political instability (Alesina and Perotti, 1998; Alesina and Rodrik, 1994; Persson and Tabellini, 1994).

Some of the empirical literature on development in the last few years has dwelt on the processes of urbanization in developing countries and how these help with the reduction of poverty. Datt and colleagues (2016), Gibson and colleagues (2017), and Lanjouw and Murgai (2014) have studied India's urbanization and put forward compelling evidence on how small towns are an important catalyst in the country's growth story. They help reduce rural poverty through two channels—absorption of surplus rural labour and a more

---

[7] Convexity in production functions, for example, is essentially diminishing returns to scale. Increasing returns bring non-convexity. Functions can be locally convex in some regions and non-convex in others. Such a feature can bring multiple equilibria, low-level traps, instability, and various extremes, including very unequal distributions.

even spread of structural change and intersectoral linkages. Interestingly, the labour market changes associated with both of these channels have indicated a strong trend towards informalization. Regular and permanent jobs are being replaced by contractual work and self-employment, with the latter type of work often being more productive (Ghose, 2016). In Palanpur, too, we see individuals taking up informal opportunities off the farm to support their incomes, for example, in small shops and temporary jobs in neighbouring towns.

While it is tempting to see this empirical evidence as support for a simple interpretation of the two-sector model of structural change and development presented by Lewis and Kuznets, we find that the central story is not that of a wholesale shift from the backward to the advanced sector. Instead, the evidence points overwhelmingly to a story of gradual diversification. Ghose (2016) has, in fact, suggested that the whole notion of 'duality' in the economy might be a remnant of the way colonial rulers viewed and classified native economies. When seen without this potentially distortionary lens, it might be appropriate to point out that *informal is normal*.

In Palanpur, we find that households continue to be engaged in agriculture, but also use their labour to invest time and capital in off-farm opportunities. While jobs in neighbouring towns are now important for the rural economy, we do not find a large-scale migration of the population. Instead, we find that villagers—now enabled by advances in communications and infrastructure—commute for work from the village, for jobs that are neither formal nor in an advanced manufacturing sector. In fact, Gibson and colleagues (2017) find that the growth of small towns is a more powerful force in overcoming rural poverty than intensification of growth in metropolitan areas.

These distinctions are important. A simple-minded adherence to a two-sector story has led to a misunderstanding of the nature of growth, with a policy skew towards the organized manufacturing sector and large metropolitan areas. This has driven the focus of economics away from investments in the informal sector or in agricultural productivity. Such biases in the subject hold the power to distort the narratives that underlie the formulation of policies for a country's development.

4.2.1 Agriculture and the Story of Growth

The Bliss and Stern study of the village in 1974/5 was focused on the determinants and consequences of the allocation of resources in agriculture (Bliss and Stern, 1982). At the time that study was launched, there was strong interest in theories around the workings of agricultural markets. These included theories of sharecropping in relation to incentives and uncertainty, the linking of markets, class relations, and so on. It should be remembered that, at that time, agriculture would have been around 40 per cent of the Indian economy, employing perhaps 70 per cent of the working population.[8] There has been a long history of interest in the role of agriculture in economic development. As we have noted, for David Ricardo, writing two centuries ago in rural Gloucestershire in the UK, the role of the rent from land, both in the distribution of income and as a source of saving, was of central importance. For Marx, and later Lewis, as part of what they saw as the traditional or backward sector, agriculture was largely a source of labour for the more modern, capitalist sector which was the driver of both savings and investment. A number of writers have also stressed the role of agriculture in providing food for those outside agriculture, often thinking of a fairly closed economy (Dixit, 1973; Sah and Stiglitz, 1984).

In the 1940s Alan Fisher and Colin Clark developed fairly descriptive stories of 'stages of growth', as did Walt Rostow (Clark, 1940; Fisher, 1939; Rostow, 1960). For Fisher and Clark, the roles of 'the three sectors' (primary, secondary, tertiary, or agriculture, manufacturing, services), changed over time with first a movement out of agriculture into the other two and, then, progressively, a movement into the third. Both supply side (technological change) and demand side (via income elasticities) played a role.

Agriculture has thus had three critical roles in these stories: as a source of savings, of labour, and of food. All of these affect dynamics. Savings can, in principle, fund investment outside agriculture; the large labour supply in agriculture provides a pool of labour which can be drawn into more advanced sectors; and the availability of food allows that expansion to occur, although that will require increasing productivity per worker if food prices are not to rise too strongly and force up the real price of labour.

Some of these issues also arose in the famous debate on 'the Agrarian question' between Kautsky and Lenin on the role of agriculture in transforming a primarily agrarian economy into a modern industrialized country. The basic concern revolved around agriculture's ability to generate a surplus which could be used to finance investment in the modern sector. But it was also about changing the class character of the peasantry and creating a domestic market for industrial goods. The debate has long since died down in its classical form, but newer formulations arguing for changing the nature of production in agriculture have some relevance for developing countries.[9]

---

[8] Agriculture accounted for 39.5% of the national output in 1973/4 whereas the share of workers engaged in agriculture was 70.1% in 1971. The share of agriculture in national output in 2011/12 was 14.4% with the employment share at 54.6%. Output shares are based on national accounts and employment shares are based on Census of India data. However, based on National Sample Survey Organisation (NSSO) surveys of employment for 2011/12, the share of workers engaged in agriculture was 48%.

[9] See Byres (1986), Bernstein (2004), and Lerche (2013).

Debates on the nature of capitalistic production in agriculture have also been of long standing in India. Discussions on the 'mode of production' were prominent in the discourse on changes brought in by the green revolution.[10] However, given the complexity of the agrarian production system, linkages in the factor markets, many of which remain imperfect,[11] and the broader context of a rapidly changing non-farm economy, any attempt to study the role of agriculture in isolation is futile.

Debates on the relationship between farm size and productivity and on productivity issues and on share tenancy were central to the arguments for land reforms, which were seen by some as crucial to any successful transition of the agrarian economy to a capitalistic system. Bliss and Stern (1982) examined some of these issues in the Palanpur context.

Those writing in the early and mid-1950s on growth processes in economic development saw agriculture dominating the then current economic activity and saw deep and difficult obstacles to the emergence of an advanced economy. There was much talk of a poverty trap (e.g. Nurkse, 1953). Many, such as Rosenstein-Rodan and Nurkse, argued for a 'big push' and 'balanced growth' to generate demand; by this they meant major investments across the board. Some of the arguments had a strong Keynesian bent, and raising savings and investment rates were at the core of the discussion. For the most part, agriculture was not seen as a priority for such investment.

Soon after, in the 1960s and 1970s, a literature on agriculture in economic development emerged which took a somewhat different view, much of it arguing that investment and growth in agriculture was a necessary precursor to advance outside agriculture (by, for example, John Mellor and Michael Lipton). Part of the argument was that, in this way, labour could be released whilst maintaining food supplies; in addition, that extra productivity could help generate a source of savings. Further, the argument went, economic history showed that this was the sequence that has, in large measure, been followed both in the early stages of the development of the more advanced countries and more recently in developing countries. We shall see in Palanpur that investment to increase productivity in agriculture has indeed been associated with the release of labour.

The biggest of all examples are, of course, China and India. In China, the household responsibility system in agriculture was brought in fairly rapidly in the five or ten years from 1978/9, replacing the collective farming which had been imposed two decades or so previously. Agricultural productivity went up quickly, releasing labour and providing some contribution to initial savings for the township and village enterprises which quickly followed and which

---

[10] For an overview of the mode of production debate, see Patnaik (1990).
[11] See Bhaduri (1973).

were key drivers of the remarkable Chinese growth of the 1980s and 1990s (Lardy, 1978, 1983; Rosen et al., 2004; Saith, 2016).

In India, the green revolution period, covering the 15 years or so from the mid-1960s, showed strong investment in agriculture, and indeed we saw that investment in irrigation and double-cropping preceded that. India's economic growth can be broadly divided into two major periods—1950–80, when the prevailing philosophy of economic development had a directive state and strong public ownership at its core, with heavy restrictions on private enterprise, and 1980–2017, during which the country had attempted a series of partial reforms intended to promote faster economic growth.[12] The former period saw an unimpressive growth of around 3.5 per cent per annum, which was sometimes referred to as the 'Hindu rate of growth' (see Chapter 3). Growth started to pick up in the 1980s, to 5 per cent and more, with the country witnessing rapid growth after the 1991 reforms which began the liberalization of the economy (see Bliss and Stern, 1982; Joshi, 2017; Lal, 1988; Lipton and Longhurst, 1989; Ruttan,1977).

Thus the two biggest examples of economic development, India and China, do show agricultural advance preceding industrial advance and rising savings, investment, and growth rates, although the mechanisms at work are very different. And, as we have noted, Lipton, Mellor, and others emphasized that the story of agricultural advance before industrial advance applied to the advanced countries at earlier stages of their economic history.

These observations are largely at the macro level, and it is very interesting to compare them with the more micro experience in Palanpur. It is certainly true that agricultural advance in Palanpur preceded the involvement of the village outside agriculture. On the other hand, those groups which led the agricultural advance, for example the Murao group, were not those that led the advance into jobs outside agriculture. For the village as a whole, however, increasing labour productivity in agriculture since the late 1990s (after the green revolution period) appears to have played an important role in releasing labour. These are issues which will be further investigated in the chapters that follow.

The functioning of the individual markets relevant to agriculture has changed in Palanpur in fascinating ways. There has been less theorizing in the literature about how agricultural markets change over time than how they function at a given moment in time but, nevertheless, the changes can be understood in terms of the factors shaping these markets. Thus, for example, the supervision involved in letting out land under a sharecropping contract (because of its weaker incentives than some other contracts) becomes more

---

[12] Vijay Joshi offers an excellent *tour d'horizon* of the economic history of India from 1947 to 2016 in his book *India's Long Road* (2017).

costly if landowners have outside activities and a switch to a cash contract makes sense in terms of economizing on the work involved in that task of supervision. We shall see also (Chapter 6) that caste can be seen as a proxy for trust in the case of a sharecropping contract as supervision of tenant's labour becomes costly or difficult—someone in your own social group may be seen as less likely to shirk on agricultural responsibilities than someone who is socially more distant.

Labour and land markets have been transformed by changes in technology. An old literature saw 'tractorization' as making poor people still poorer, reducing demand for labour (Little et al., 1970; Turnham, 1971). But in Palanpur the availability of tractor services for hire has, together with the liquidity that comes from outside activity, enabled some of the Jatab group to hire land since they can rent-in tractor services, where previously they could not rent-in the services of draught animals. These ideas about the dynamics of growth, the role of agriculture, and the functioning and endogeneity of institutions in the growth process run through the book.

4.3 Mobility and Inequality

The study of development is about how lives and livelihoods change. Mobility is of the essence. The study of mobility in economics has been, in large measure, empirically based; the emphasis has not been strongly on theory, although we note some interesting ideas in this section. It has focused on mobility in dimensions such as income, wealth, education, and so on. Thus we ask how the income, wealth, or education of an individual are influenced by those in a preceding period or generation.[13] Mobility, once identified, can be compared across people, including, for example, across different socio-demographic groups. And we can examine how it might rise or fall over time. We can ask also how the nature of the mobility influences inequality or poverty. Such analyses are clearly data-dependent. Data on people's circumstances over extended periods are difficult or costly to assemble. Palanpur is a particularly good 'observatory' for studying mobility as it includes, very unusually, an ability to examine mobility across two generations and thus change in intergenerational mobility.

---

[13] Mobility can be considered from a variety of conceptual viewpoints (see Fields and Ok, 1999; Jäntti and Jenkins, 2015). The present discussion refers to mobility simply as changing incomes at the household or individual level. This is distinct from a perspective where mobility occurs only if there are positional changes: re-rankings of households or individuals. The former perspective can allow for upward mobility amongst the entire population, while the latter would require upward mobility to be matched by downward mobility.

Explanations of the causes of, or limits to, mobility have often been related to social and economic institutions and power relationships. Some studies in political economy or social theory point to methods by which social groups, for example caste groups or landowners in India, manage local or national power structures in their interests. Karl Marx (in his book *Capital*; see Marx (1951)) described how political and social superstructures would be erected to protect the interests of the capitalist class. Adam Smith, in *Wealth of Nations*, pointed to business groups or guilds in the 18th century in England who sought to control the entry to and the rewards for their professions (see quotes from Smith (1776) in Section 4.4 of this chapter). In his *Essay on the Influence of a Low Price of Corn on the Profits of Stock*, Ricardo showed how landowners would act to protect their interests, by inflating the price of food to benefit themselves, at the expense of the working class, and thus was in strong opposition to the Corn Laws (Ricardo, 1815).

In economics, theoretical frameworks on the cause and determinants of mobility have been offered, for example, by Atkinson, Gary Becker and colleagues, and Piketty (e.g. Atkinson, 1980; Becker and Mulligan, 1997; Becker and Tomes, 1979; Piketty, 1995). Becker and colleagues offered a simple, although uncomfortably narrow, approach; parents would invest in their children according to some family/dynasty objective function. The shape of the parental preferences would determine their investments in the assets and human capital of their children. Assumptions on mating patterns would also be relevant.[14]

Another influential framework in studying mobility has been the 'Great Gatsby Curve'—a negative relationship between inequality and intergenerational income mobility (Corak, 2013). It is suggested that societies with higher inequality are less likely to see economic mobility; one interpretation is that the better-off sections of society curtail the availability of economic progress for the poorer. The idea will be examined for Palanpur in Chapter 8.

A theory of immobility covering certain sections of the population lies in the idea of the 'poverty trap'. One possible explanation of such traps could be the presence of multiple equilibria, caused by the 'non-convex' shape of key functional relationships.[15] Early work on such traps focused on the importance of large-scale interventions by the state in the presence of traps arising

---

[14] See also Meade (1973). A survey of theoretical approaches to mobility is offered in Piketty (2000).

[15] This is an important but rather technical point. The existence of multiple points of stable equilibrium, deriving from non-convex functional relationships, or relationships which are convex over some parts of a domain but not over other parts, is explored in several branches of economics. For example, Kaldor (1940) uses them in his modelling of business cycles in 'growth and distribution'. Stiglitz (1986), too, has used them to illustrate the possibilities of multiple equilibria, some of which are 'bad' where there are failures of coordination in imperfect markets with informational problems.

from macro problems around savings and investment, which could get 'stuck' at low levels. This could be Keynesian in relation to investment demand, together with a lack of willingness or an inability to save. The aggregate trap theories have minor relevance to Palanpur (Nurkse, 1953; Rosenstein-Rodan, 1943).

More recent work has been focused on examining policy in relation to more micro understandings of 'vicious circles' or traps and implications for limits to mobility. One example of such vicious circles could be damaging behaviours, such as those associated with gambling or addiction to intoxicants. Expenditure on such items, rather than consumption or investment in human capital, can prevent an individual from escaping poverty (Banerjee and Mullainathan 2010; Bernheim, Ray, and Yeltekin, 2015). There are indeed examples in Palanpur.

Or the trap could be due to 'external frictions' or imperfections in the market such as gaps in the credit market (Banerjee and Newman, 1993; Galor and Zeira, 1993; Ghatak and Jiang, 2002). Another source of traps could be nutritional constraints on productivity where the lack of food imposes limits on the ability or effectiveness of work (Bliss and Stern, 1978a, 1978b; Dasgupta and Ray, 1986; Mirrlees, 1976; Stiglitz, 1976). Bliss and Stern (1982) examined both the theory and various sources of data, including those from the three Palanpur surveys then available. Hoff and Stiglitz (2016) also contribute here, coming from the perspective of behavioural economics. They highlight cases where social and psychological determinants trap individuals, and indeed societies, into cycles of inefficient behaviour, and they discuss how these can be broken.

There is a range of empirical examples of people or groups breaking out of poverty traps. Village studies such as those conducted by Bailey in Orissa, India, have provided cases of administrative and government jobs allowing individuals from lower castes to escape from poverty and from the oppression of the traditional social hierarchies (Bailey, 1957). Other examples include strong reaction when some constraint is relaxed (e.g. abolition of collectives and introduction of the household responsibility system in China, which resulted in a powerful response to incentives and increased agricultural prod-uctivity in the 1980s), or the market-oriented reforms in India in the early 1990s (much less dramatic than China). Such examples illustrate theory not simply by examining the consequences of alternative parameters within a given model, but by pointing to how things change when assumptions change and we move to very different models. There will be important examples from Palanpur. All too rarely in these models or approaches, how-ever, do we model the pace and process of movement from one new equilib-rium or growth path to another. Most economists would have argued that the introduction of the household responsibility system in China would increase output. But few could have provided a theory of how fast that change would be, or how associated stresses might play through.

Mobility can arise also from uncertainty and its influence on outcomes.[16] This can interact with behaviours and local institutions, particularly in relation to downward mobility. For example, a combination of sickness and difficulty in borrowing without collateral can lead not only to loss of income, but also to loss of land if a loan is secured against the land. Downward spirals can be noted, in all societies including Palanpur, associated with 'dissolute' behaviours such as drinking and gambling. The social custom of spending heavily on weddings and dowries for daughters can lead not only to a running down of capital and/or increased debt, but also thereafter to greater vulnerability to bad luck.

There are various possible relationships between mobility and inequality and these will play a strong role in understanding change in Palanpur. A few very simple theoretical observations linked to the measurement of mobility illustrate the possibilities.

An economy in which there is no income mobility at all, in the sense that the absolute income (or rank, if it is relative position at issue) is unchanged between two periods, will obviously have constant inequality.[17] On the other hand, a two-person economy with levels of income 0 and 1, and with one person at 0 and one at 1, could be called 'fully mobile' if between the two periods, the person at 0 went to 1 and the person at 1 went to 0; but inequality would be unchanged. It is clear that it is not simply mobility versus immobility, or greater mobility and less mobility, which shapes the course of inequality over time. It is the nature of the mobility. This will be a very important conceptual observation when it comes to understanding change in Palanpur.

Overall, taking these ideas to the Palanpur story, we can see the probability of being able to change income as routed through a number of factors, including: (i) circumstances and the nature of opportunities; (ii) communications and networks; (iii) special family or social positions; and (iv) entrepreneurship and initiative. For example, on (i), *zamindari* abolition together with ownership of land offered real opportunities for many to 'catch-up' in farming by investing in irrigation and double-cropping. On (ii), mobile phones made a difference to knowledge about work opportunities in the second half of the survey period. On (iii), wealth conveys advantages if bribes are necessary, and it enables acquisition of relevant capital, for phones or marble-polishing equipment, for example; both of these were relevant for some of these

---

[16] See Jäntti and Jenkins (2015) for further discussion.
[17] The relevant transition matrix has all zeroes off the diagonal. A transition matrix has an entry at row *i* and column j, which is the probability of moving from state *i* to state *j* in the period under consideration.

advantages accruing to Thakurs in Palanpur. On (iv), the Muraos were more entrepreneurial in agriculture early on, but did not seem to be well positioned in the second half of the period for the new opportunities; entrepreneurship can be specific both for groups and opportunities. These ideas will be investigated in Chapter 8 on mobility in Part 2 of this book.

4.4 Institutions, Society, and Behaviour

We understand or define institutions in terms of organizations and rules. Our focus is particularly on those strongly influencing economic and social behaviour and rewards. This should be taken to include what kinds of economic or social behaviour and interactions are seen as acceptable or problematic in relation to the society in which people find themselves, particularly in relation to the new opportunities they might contemplate or in the constraints they might perceive. Organizations and rules can be formal or informal and explicit or implicit.

4.4.1 Economics and Institutions

One clear example in this context is the arrangements for land ownership. *Zamindari* abolition in the 1950s gave greater security to farmers in their land ownership and rewards to investment. Hence, they increased their investment in their land, particularly via wells and irrigation.

A second example is in the ploughing of land. When this was done by he-buffalos or oxen, it was not possible to rent-in ploughing services. The owner of the animals would be reluctant to rent them out, unless managed by himself, for fear of misuse. But to do, or to manage, the ploughing himself could be seen as agricultural labour, which would be demeaning, especially if it were for someone regarded as lower in the social ranking. Sharecropping can be seen as a set of organizational rules to manage risk, in the absence of other options such as insurance, and in the face of problems in supervising and incentivizing labour. Thus, institutions both shape behaviour and initiative and are created in response to real issues, for example, by uncertainties and difficulties associated with incentive structures.

It seems that in the 1950s and 1960s some governmental interventions and institutional investment did have a positive influence. Further examples, beyond *zamindari* abolition, include the credit union and the sugar cooperative, which served to provide credit to the village and help protect the sugar industry. However, sugar mills are known to lobby the government to keep the prices of their input, sugar cane, low, while the credit unions can be strong-armed by small groups, locking the poorest out of the financial system.

Institutions can indeed be formal and informal and used and twisted beyond original intentions or anticipations. Whilst agricultural extension was weak by the time Bliss and Stern arrived in the 1970s, it had played a role in earlier years, and by 1974/5 new high-yielding varieties (HYV) of wheat were prevalent. And further land reform beyond *zamindari* abolition has taken place in the form of consolidation of fragmented plots into more viable holdings, although this has been fairly weak and ineffective. In the second half of the survey period, the performance of public interventions has been, at best, of varying success.

On the social front, domination of village politics by the two upper castes (Thakur and Murao) is no longer overwhelming, and employment guarantee schemes (Mahatma Gandhi National Rural Employment Guarantee Act, MGNREGA) have improved local village roads and drainage ditches. Village politics and society, and how they develop and change, are examined in Part 3 of this book.

Discussions of institutions are long-standing in economics. Adam Smith certainly did not see the 'invisible hand' working in a vacuum:

> People of the same trade seldom meet together, even for merriment and diversion, but the conversation ends in a conspiracy against the public, or in some contrivance to raise prices. It is impossible indeed to prevent such meetings, by any law which either could be executed, or would be consistent with liberty and justice. But though the law cannot hinder people of the same trade from sometimes assembling together, it ought to do nothing to facilitate such assemblies; much less to render them necessary. (Smith, 1776, Book I: 105)

Smith is believed to have been referring to the practices of trade guilds which were prevalent at the time. These guilds were the predominant institutional set-up around markets and were involved in a range of activities, from apprenticeship to control over entry into the markets. Smith's concerns around the dangers of potentially unscrupulous activities in these guilds can be seen, from today's perspective, as a concern about the functioning of institutions governing and sharing the markets.

A focus on institutions has appeared in relation to the working of cities where Robert Putnam, in his study of Italian cities and their economic and social functioning, showed how institutional and governance arrangements played a powerful role in understanding their economic histories (Putnam et al., 1983). And he showed that the influences could persist over very long periods. Elinor Ostrom demonstrated how institutional arrangements could be, and have been, created to handle problems of the commons or public goods (Ostrom, 2015). Douglas North, too (1971, 1991), contributed to the formalization of the ideas and language around institutions in economics.

Herbert Simon's work on firms (1984) also drew strongly on institutional relationships between ownership and control and was later developed into the behavioural theory of the firm. He questioned the helpfulness of modelling in terms of rational actors (at least as in the narrowly defined, fully informed, standard optimizing model in much of economics) and put forward ideas on 'bounded rationality' (see also Cyert and March, 1963).

More recently, economists such as Acemoglu, Besley, and Persson have made strong links between institutions and long-term economic growth (Acemoglu, Johnson, and Robinson, 2001, 2002; Banerjee and Iyer, 2005; Besley and Persson, 2011; Djankov et al., 2002; La Porta et al., 2008). These have often been in terms of legal and political structures. In this context, there has been particular emphasis on governance, or the manner of governing. Problematic or weak governance can reduce confidence in reaping returns from initiatives and thus reduce innovation, creativity, and investment.

Stern and others have argued (see, e.g., Stern, 2015; Stern, Dethier, and Rogers, 2005) that government-induced policy risk can be a very powerful barrier to investment and innovation. Studies of 'the investment climate' (see e.g. Stern, Dethier, and Rogers, 2005; World Bank, 2005) have demonstrated the central importance of these effects in shaping economic performance.

We should emphasize again the very close relationship between entrepreneurship, behaviour, and institutions. They shape, and are shaped, by each other. Their mutual relationships and endogeneities are a central feature of our work on Palanpur. And they are fundamental to understanding economic development.

The caste system, in villages across India, including Palanpur, and in urban areas, too, has remained one of the most important and enduring social institutions. The *jajmani* system of tightly defined occupations, duties to provide some services, and structured exchange relationships has historically moulded the economic and social interactions between individuals. Some economists have tried to explain the persistence of the institution of castes, others how relationships could change. In his survey of Bisipara in Orissa, Bailey examined the nature of interaction between caste and economic growth in the village, showing how the greater readiness of some castes to react to new opportunities (one example was brewing of alcoholic beverages) led to an improvement in their economic and social status (Bailey, 1957). George Akerlof (1976) drew on his experience of India to explain the persistence of caste in terms of the threat of severe punishment for violations of norms. More recent explorations of the nature of the caste system have focused on its behavioural underpinnings (Hoff, 2016). In a striking experiment in a village in Uttar Pradesh, Hoff and Pandey (2006) found that the awareness or salience of caste identities in children can have a significantly negative impact on their performance. This implies that the hierarchical identities such as caste may have an enduring effect on the formation of human capital.

Others have noted the importance of the caste system as a social network, as an enabler of access to economic opportunities and social insurance; it is clearly of great importance in relation to partners for marriage (Banerjee et al., 2013; Munshi and Rosenzweig, 2015).[18]

Interestingly, as more men take up jobs outside the village, women's working patterns have changed based on their caste affiliations. While Murao women are now more actively involved in agriculture, Thakur women, with that caste's acute awareness of status, still stay away from such work and, with the emphasis of that caste on agriculture, would rather lease land to other cultivators (see Chapter 10). Caste-specific norms hence create a variation in the village's response to new opportunities.

While the caste system has endured (albeit with some adaptation) in the village, other institutions, norms, and structures, both formal and informal, have changed substantially in response to a changing economic, social, and political environment. These are examined in relation to market structures in Part 2 of the book and to political and social institutions in Part 3.

However, some important institutional structures remain weak or absent. This is particularly true of common property resources such as the common pastures or village pond. Formal institutional mechanisms such as the *panchayat* and the *gram sabha* have been weak, and there has been no effort to create rules or mechanisms for private management of the common property resources.[19] We do not see any of Ostrom's eight principles of private management of the commons in the village.[20] An interesting example is the decline of the common land in the village which was used by the lower castes for raising pigs, hens, and goats. The absence of institutional mechanisms (formal or informal) to govern the use of common land has led to the disappearance of the common grazing land, forcing the lower castes to abandon rearing these animals. Lower castes were dependent on these animals for much of their protein intake, and this forced vegetarianism has led to changing dietary habits, with a sharp decline in protein intake among the poorer

---

[18] See Munshi (2016) and Hoff (2016) for more on the caste system and its economic underpinnings.

[19] *Panchayat* is a village council, the governing body at the lowest level. *Gram Sabha* (literal translation of village council) is the assembly of all adult members of the village.

[20] Ostrom (2015) laid down eight rules or principles, which are: define clear group boundaries; match rules governing use to local needs; ensure those affected by the rules can participate in modifying the rules; ensure the rule-making rights of the community are respected by external authorities; develop systems for monitoring members' behaviour; use graduated sanctions for rule violators; provide accessible, low-cost means for dispute resolution; and build responsibility for governing the common resource in nested tiers, from the lowest level up to the entire interconnected system.

households. There are no rules to manage the commons in Palanpur, and the lack of an institutional mechanism to deal with these continues to this day.[21] The absence of institutional structures where common interests could be debated and acted upon has also led to forms of economic individualism which are often damaging. A clear example relates to the case of the discharge of pollutants from the mentha factories which have been a health hazard but never an issue for collective action. The effluent discharge from the neighbouring paper mill has also been responsible for many eye infections in the village. The absence of collective action is evident in failures to raise demands for better functioning of schools, health services, and MGNREGA. Those who can afford find it easier to shift their children to private schools rather than to build coalitions for collective action.[22] This is not to say that villagers never respond to such calls for collective action. In Chapter 11, we shall elaborate on some instances of community-wide action for the public good.

4.4.2 Institutions: Beyond Economics

In the discussions of institutions in Section 4.4.1 we have, for the most part, although not entirely, focused strongly on economic ideas. Nevertheless, we have already emphasized the role of ideas outside economics in our discussion of the renting-in of draught animals, and also, to some extent, in some of the ideas around empowerment and behavioural economics. We must recognize that the social and political perspectives have to be interwoven with the economic if we are to understand change in Palanpur.

Thus, the study of change in an Indian village (and not just an Indian one) inevitably takes us beyond economics into politics and political economy, anthropology, sociology, psychology, and further. Gender issues, caste relations, and 'power plays' within the villages are all important examples, and they all have profound impacts for development and change. We cannot go into great theoretical detail. We offer just a few examples from disciplines outside economics. They are enough to show both that economics alone is insufficient to understand the processes of change in Palanpur and that other disciplines have to play a powerful role in understanding these changes. The examples are chosen to illustrate this point rather than offering more general observations on the insights that the other disciplines can bring.

---

[21] Drèze and Sharma (1998) also noted the absence of any institutional mechanism to regulate and preserve common resources during the 1983 survey. They discuss three examples: the village drainage system, delayed sowing as a response to bird and animal feeding, and the village school. For discussion on collective action in the village during the 2008/10 survey, see Sinha et al. (2016). Also see Chapter 11.

[22] On the role of inequality and collective public action, see Sinha et al. (2016).

The application of these ideas pervades this book, from tenancy to credit, to health, to schools, to the functioning of the *panchayat*.

One area where anthropologists, sociologists, and economists have much in common is the study of villages. Anthropologists have been involved in village studies for much longer than economists, although there are many overlaps of interest with regard to the issues of research.[23] Anthropological and sociological studies of villages and village institutions have contributed greatly to the understanding of social structures such as caste, kinship, and social and political institutions, which have a bearing on the functioning of markets and economic institutions. We have noted the anthropological origins of the inability to hire the services of draught animals.

The Wisers (Wiser and Wiser, 1971, 2001) showed some of the detailed effects of the restriction of possible activities for women, thereby severely inhibiting their potential economic contributions and life chances. Many of their observations apply strongly to Palanpur, although the passage of time has weakened their severity a little. Bailey showed how the absence of caste limitations enabled some groups to prosper via the production and sale of alcohol when that was permitted. The Muraos/Sudras, a cultivating caste, responded more quickly than others to the opportunities from *zamindari* abolition and the green revolution technologies and methods. Although caste hierarchies seem to have weakened over the years, the emergence of caste as an important proxy of trust has also strengthened caste bonding in many of the non-farm occupations. We also find caste and kinship play an important role in mitigating some of the supervision problems in Palanpur.[24] Bliss and Stern took care to consult with anthropologists and sociologists at the University of Delhi as they did their work on the 1974/5 study and with Scarlett Epstein and others in the UK before they began fieldwork.

4.4.3 *Political Economy*

We have already noted the interplay of institutions and individual behaviour in the management of common property resources. The institutional framework is not an exogenous construct, but a product of the social and political relations among households and groups in the village. Formal institutions such as the village council and the caste *panchayats* can, in principle, be effective institutions for resolving conflict as well as for designing and implementing rules for governance of social, political, and economic relations in

---

[23] Bardhan (1989) is an excellent collection of dialogues between anthropologists and economists on understanding and measuring change through village studies. Also see Bardhan and Ray (2008).

[24] See Chapter 6 for details.

the village. The implementation of the 73rd amendment in India created formal structures and rules of governance at the village level. These were subsequently strengthened by the state government by introducing provision of reservation for disadvantaged groups, such as the Dalits and women. While these have worked well in strengthening the democratic process and participation of disadvantaged groups in village affairs, they are open to elite capture. During our recent stay in Palanpur, the village has seen a Dalit and a woman as the head of the village council. In both cases, however, the old caste and male elite managed to maintain much of its dominance. Nevertheless, the politics are changing, and involvement has increased with the extra resources flowing through the *panchayat*.

Many of these problems of governance can be seen in terms of 'rent-seeking' behaviour, which has received much attention. We can see the issues as part of 'political economy', a branch of the subject which includes the examination of how interest groups can share the 'rules of the game' and outcomes. Anne Krueger (1974) studied the impact of rent seeking in societies and highlighted the extent of losses due to 'excessive regulations'. In India, for example, she estimated this rent to amount to 7.3 per cent of the country's national income.[25] Brennan and Buchanan (1985) also examined corruption and rent seeking as a product of the dominant rules and incentive structures in a society. For them, it was important to focus on the source of the problem and rewrite or eliminate these rules.

Mancur Olson greatly enriched this approach, both theoretically and through examples. He used the now famous metaphors of 'roving' and 'stationary' bandits to explain how rent-seeking behaviour, incentives, and the establishment of institutions for long-term economic prosperity are linked. The 'roving' bandit was a mercenary, interested in taking everything for himself from the land he targets, leaving nothing behind for the local population. A 'stationary' bandit, however, thinks over a longer term and has an incentive to leave enough in place to allow regeneration of resources. This encourages the bandit to set up institutions that encourage economic prosperity and also guard his territory against other bandits (Olson, 1993).

Baumol (1990) sees rent-seeking behaviour as a kind of unproductive entrepreneurial activity where the individual resorts to profit making through manipulation of the system of rules, rather than production or innovation. It hampers or shackles development because it misdirects a scarce resource, entrepreneurship.

Commenting on the extent of corruption within the systems of decentralized governance, a recent report by the Indian government (Ministry of

---

[25] Precision here is difficult and often implausible, but the argument that this is a major problem is convincing.

Panchayati Raj, 2013) did indeed highlight such rent-seeking behaviour in the systems of local rural governance, commenting on the distortion of the vision of Panchayat Raj into 'Sarpanch Raj'.[26]

4.4.4 Behaviour

For economics as a whole, whether examining issues in developing or developed countries, behavioural and institutional economics have arguably been the most fruitful developments since the late 1980s (see Besley, Stern, and O'Donnell, 2015). Interestingly, in the heyday of the market fundamentalism of the 1980s and 1990s, with its assertion that the perfectly competitive model had an overriding call on our attention, these key subjects were developing. We have discussed institutional economics in Sections 4.4.1–4.4.3 and we now turn briefly to behaviour. We cannot do full justice to such a big subject here and will only briefly highlight some special features relevant to development economics and particularly to our study of Palanpur. As we have emphasized, there is a strong overlap between institutional and behavioural analyses, and there has been a strong behavioural element in our discussion of institutions, for example in relation to caste.

Behavioural economics has drawn heavily on insights from psychology. It has largely been micro in its orientation, unsurprisingly given its focus on the behaviour of individuals, whereas the study of institutions has had a large element of macro, in the sense that some recent studies of overall differences in growth and performance, across country, cities, and regions, lean strongly in their analyses on differences in institutions, including legal and administrative. And many of the arguments in both behavioural and institutional economics focus on implications for entrepreneurship and initiative. Much of our understanding of change in Palanpur will be concerned with how these key elements interact, change, and shape outcomes, and their role in changing lives and livelihoods in the village.

A prominent figure in the rise of behavioural economics has been Danny Kahneman, a psychologist and economist who won the Nobel Prize in 2002, in large measure for his work with the late Amos Tversky. He has emphasized both the way in which people recognize and perceive opportunities and risks and how they respond. On the former, there has been great emphasis on cognition in terms of the matching of patterns and this, in turn, depends on what patterns one is used to or expects. This will, in large measure, be determined by experience and culture. As the reality changes, particularly

---

[26] *Panchayats* are comprised of a few members and a head, called the *sarpanch*. The *panchayats* in India, though ignored through the early decades, were empowered in 1992 to encourage a decentralized form of governance.

concerning opportunities, some people's cognition will change more quickly than others. There is, for some, a sort of inertia.

On the latter, 'loss aversion' has been a central idea. In other words, people, in their behaviour, show great reluctance to lose something they have. They appear to give that potential loss much greater weight in their decision-making than some apparently equivalent potential gain that they do not yet have. This can generate inertia, stronger for some than others, when new opportunities appear.

It should be clear, and has been demonstrated by experiments and in other ways, that these ideas have strong potential in helping understand behaviour in many circumstances. Examples in Palanpur would be the importance of learning-by-watching in the adoption of new varieties of wheat in the 1970s or 1980s, or the adoption of a new crop such as mentha since around the early 2000s. Some villagers, who sought out information and looked for experience beyond Palanpur, were early adopters. They can be seen as the entrepreneurs and innovators in the village context. Others, more conservative, 'familiarized' themselves by watching neighbours.

Karla Hoff has set out a number of examples relevant to or from developing countries in her work (see, for example, Hoff and Stiglitz (2016), and the references in Section 4.4.1). These include ways in which opportunities for women to work in call centres are gradually being better understood through the sharing of information and experience in different ways. Some of these result in the overcoming of individual or family reluctance to go forward to such jobs. Hoff offers other examples in terms of TV soap operas and the influence of the behaviour of leading characters. For example, if these characters made choices to lower fertility, then the receptivity of viewers to reproductive health services could change.

4.5 Human Development, Capability, and Empowerment

Some of the ideas around institutions, society, and behaviour in Section 4.4 have close links to ideas of capability (as in Agarwal et al., 2007; Nussbaum, 2000; Sen, 1999) and empowerment (see, e.g., Stern, Dethier, and Rogers, 2005). For Amartya Sen, capability refers to the ability to 'lead lives they have reason to value'. On empowerment, Stern has offered the definition of 'having the ability to shape one's life'. They are clearly close in logic and spirit. The second, in its concept and language, perhaps has a stronger focus on constraints, whether they be individual or social/cultural, with a policy perspective oriented, in part, to the overcoming of those constraints. The former has perhaps a stronger emphasis on human capital, in the sense that investments therein increase capabilities and widen the choices that an individual can make (Sen, 1999). But for both ideas, human capital and constraints are centre stage. To understand how societies and individual circumstances and well-being change, we must understand the determinants of human capital, capabilities, and empowerment and how those things change or might be influenced.

It is clear from these definitions that behavioural economics and the idea of capability or of empowerment have much to offer each other. Individuals can be strongly constrained by their perceptions of what is possible: these would depend on their education, health, and societal and family position. And their likely evaluation of and attitude to potential outcomes could be strongly influenced by the same factors.

A diagrammatic illustration of these ideas, in relation to empowerment, is presented here, taken from Stern, Dethier, and Rogers (2005: 102). The empowerment of an individual is determined by an interaction between her or his endowment, constraints imposed by socioeconomic surroundings, and their 'internal constraints', related to her or his preferences and perceptions of their role.

The ideas of capability and empowerment are important in understanding not only how development occurs, but also how we should measure development progress and structure policy. These ideas embody both means to development and ends or objectives of development. Thus an individual's capability or empowerment shapes how she or he acts and responds to circumstances and change. But enhancing capability/empowerment is itself an objective, irrespective of how the individual might use the enhanced ability to

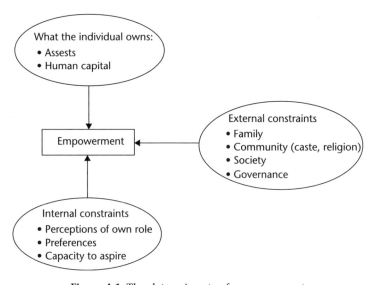

Figure 4.1 The determinants of empowerment

shape her or his life. The influence of such ideas on measurement has been direct. For example, the Human Development Index, introduced by Mahbub ul-Haq when at the United Nations (UN), was strongly influenced by Sen's ideas and advice. And these concepts subsequently influenced the specification of the Millennium Development Goals, which set objectives at the millennium for change measured over the period 1990–2015.

It is clear from this brief description of behavioural economics and capability/empowerment that the institutional environment, in terms for example of social or economic actions or rules and administrative and political arrangements, would be expected to play a strong role in behaviour.

The behaviour of agents within institutions and the institutional environment are especially important when considering the provision of public services of health and education. These two services are fundamental in the building of human capital for a country's development and in empowering its population. They have always been under scrutiny by development researchers and practitioners. We have learned that we must look beyond the provision of schooling and health care, narrowly measured in terms of facilities and staff. Based on a growing body of empirical and experimental evidence from research across countries, the current focus is presence, quality, and behaviour of teachers, medics, and staff more generally. Governance and social and cultural interaction with centrally provided services play a powerful role in shaping behaviour and delivery; see, for example, Rogers and others (Chaudhury et al., 2006; Suryadarma et al., 2006, Rogers and Vegas, 2009; Ree et al., 2015) on teacher performance and absence. The 2004 edition of the 'World Development Report' carried a detailed discussion on making public services work for poor people, with extensive evidence from the developing world.

4.6 Entrepreneurship, Innovation, and Investment

Economists thinking about entrepreneurship are likely to turn to Schumpeter (1954), although the idea has a long-lasting place in the history of economic thought. For example, Minniti and Levesque (2008) trace the concept back at least to Richard Cantillon, the Irish economist who in 1732 'identified entrepreneurship as the willingness of individuals to carry out forms of arbitrage involving the financial risk of a new venture' (Minniti and Leveqsue, 2008: 1).

In Cantillon's definition, he captures four elements which together constitute entrepreneurship: decision, change, risk, and originality. For Palanpur, we take those same four elements as constituting entrepreneurship, although the interpretation of 'originality' or 'new' in Cantillon's definition may be less strong than in some common uses of the term entrepreneurship today. For our study, the important thing is that the change is 'new' or 'original' for the individual, even though it may not be new for the village. We should be clear that we are not talking about originality or newness in the sense of some pioneering innovation in Silicon Valley. For Schumpeter, the possession of a strong or monopolistic position in an industry by a firm, and the associated rents, essentially invited innovative competition for those rents. The special position of the incumbent usually required the new competitor to come up with something which was different, something that could replace the old monopolistic position with a new or improved product or service. This was Schumpeter's story of creative destruction; he saw capitalist economics as dynamic, creative, and innovative. In his view, these economies would experience a sequence of disruptions and would not always, or perhaps rarely, be in static equilibrium. Existing monopolists would do what they could, using existing institutions and political influence to defend their position. Entrepreneurs, perceiving opportunities and acting on them, were the disruptors.

This process of creative destruction was, for Schumpeter, central to the initiation and advance of waves of technological change. He was directly concerned with how capitalism actually worked, with the role of large firms, and with the major strands and forces in economic history. Our enquiry in Palanpur is also concerned with the major strands and forces in economic development. But this is not a story of innovation in large firms, but of individuals acting to change their lives. And it is a story of whether and how the opportunities to do so can arise, together with how individuals perceive both those opportunities and their ability to respond.

Chris Freeman, a formidable economic historian of technological change, who has focused closely on processes of innovation, notes how Schumpeter, too, stressed the importance of the individual entrepreneur in his theories, dwelling on the centrality of the famed entrepreneurial spirit and individual action and how they linked up to the macroeconomic growth process (Freeman, 1994). Such emphasis allowed researchers in the Schumpeterian tradition to approach the fundamental questions around growth from a perspective of research and development and individual innovation.

Entrepreneurship, initiative, innovation, and investment loom large in a number of major stories or narratives of economic development, although in very different ways. Gunnar Myrdal shared the Nobel Prize in 1974 with Friedrich Hayek; famously, they had diametrically opposed views on many issues. Myrdal's view of Asia, published in the three-volume *Asian Drama* in 1968, was primarily based on ten years of working on India and was deeply pessimistic. It embodied a largely patronizing view of India as hopelessly fatalistic, and he saw Indians as lacking in the initiative and entrepreneurship necessary to change their lives. They were, in Myrdal's story, shackled by culture, attitudes, and institutions which maintained and reinforced inaction.

In our view, he was deeply mistaken. His work was also grossly mistimed. India was about to experience the green revolution, which did indeed involve much entrepreneurship and innovation, in the late 1960s and the 1970s, and its overall growth rate began to pick up in the 1980s. China's extraordinary growth started in the late 1970s, just a decade after *Asian Drama* was published.

For Palanpur, major changes of activity, entrepreneurship, and advances by villagers in terms of innovation and investment, in the first two or three rounds of our study, took place mostly around agriculture, irrigation, and new crops. Here, the ideas of Griliches (1957) and the diffusion of ideas and learning-by-watching are important. Griliches' early work in this regard was on agriculture. But the learning-by-watching in Palanpur featured strongly, too, in the recognition and seeking of activities outside agriculture, since the 1983 round.

Griliches' (1957) work provided a theoretical and empirical model to study the process and networks through which knowledge spread. Several modern studies have examined this further in the Indian context. Besley and Case (1993) and Foster and Rosenzweig (1995) carried out empirical studies on the ideas of learning-by-doing and learning from others, specifically looking at the spread of HYV seeds used during the green revolution period in India.

Economists such as Boserup (1965) and Hayami and Ruttan (1970, 1971) suggested that innovation in agriculture was, in large measure, driven by pressures exerted by an increasing population or scarcity of specific factor inputs.

Hayek (1945) placed entrepreneurship and the search for profit in an inherently uncertain world centre stage. For Hayek, with his teacher Ludwig von Mises, the doyen of the Austrian School, markets were processes of discovery and generators of new opportunities. Their ideas were subsequently taken forward by Kirzner (1973). To abandon markets in favour of planning was to suppress both freedom and growth: to stultify both political and economic life. The focus of Hayek and the Austrian School, however, was more on advanced than developing countries. For Myrdal, Hayek was dangerous in apparently justifying, perhaps celebrating, the inequalities of the capitalist system as natural, possibly virtuous, and the unavoidable outcome of the necessity of rewards for creativity and initiative.

On development, a contrast to Myrdal was embodied in the work of T.W. Schultz, Nobel Prize winner in 1979. For Schultz, and others of the Chicago School, all economic structures and transactions in place were efficient. As Robert Solow once put it in cartooning that approach, 'All that exists is efficient, because were it not efficient it would not exist.'[27] For Schultz, Hopper, Cheung, and colleagues, the Asian village, and the efficiencies which

---

[27] Verbal communication.

they believed it embodied, were just another example of this 'Chicago theorem'. It seemed that they were essentially asserting that full-blown neoclassical economic modelling was alive and well and residing in the villages of India.

Interestingly, in this simplistic vision there is little scope for entrepreneurship because all opportunities are instantly recognized and taken, because the alertness and speed of reaction of individuals are so strong and the system of economic competition so effective and vibrant. If everyone has entrepreneurship and initiative in full measure, then such concepts do not provide an analytic distinction between individuals.

For others, such as Hirschman (1977), entrepreneurship was neither absent (as in Myrdal), nor so universal that it was almost redundant in distinguishing one agent from another (as in Schutz et al.), but it was in short supply in developing countries. Hence his recommendation of policies to create 'backward and forward linkages' and his theory of 'unbalanced growth'. The limitations on entrepreneurship which he postulated required in his argument very strong signals of potential markets and profits to bring forth a response in terms of initiative and supply. Thus he stressed backward linkages. He defined these broadly as follows: the government would promote an activity which required inputs, perhaps imported initially, but local entrepreneurs, seeing a good market for their potential product, might then come forward with supply. In this sense it was a deliberate attempt to create strong market pressure, or disequilibrium, to bring forth an entrepreneurial response. With forward linkages, which he thought would be weaker, an easily available supply of an input at an attractive price might encourage activities which made use of that input. Interestingly, others saw 'linkages' through the spectrum of sectors (e.g. Mellor (1966) on agriculture) rather than from, more generally, in the Hirschman sense, via markets.

Palanpur has seen both forward and backward linkages, in the sense of Hirschman contributing to expansion of non-farm employment in the village. A good example is the installation of mentha extraction units in the village. The rise in mentha cultivation created a demand for these units, with three of them in operation in the village by time of the 2008/10 survey. The availability of tractors, initially bought for agricultural purposes, has also seen an expansion in transport services. There is now a well-developed market for transportation of freight as well as passengers in the tractors. Mechanization created a demand for repair services, with two repair shops in the village by 2015. Nanhe, whose story we shall discuss in detail in Chapter 7, lives in one of the best-off households in the village, having installed a mentha plant. He has also diversified into repair services and now runs a repair workshop in Chandausi.

It should be emphasized, however, that most of the above theory focuses on the entrepreneurship involved in entrepreneurs starting enterprises or firms to capture new opportunities which they had identified. In Palanpur the story is much more about individuals recognizing and pursuing opportunities, such as a new crop or a new variety in agriculture, or a job opportunity, however menial, outside agriculture. This difference between individuals and firms is important because firms compete and failed firms go out of business. These evolutionary forces are a big part of the story of how equilibria emerge, evolve, or are disrupted. The evolutionary forces do not work the same way with individuals. They can be more or less successful in endeavours, give up, or retreat. They are not usually eliminated, although some do end up richer or poorer than others. In some cases, however, the failure of individuals in their economic ventures can hasten or lead to their demise.

Entrepreneurship, the perceiving and taking of opportunities by individuals, turns on what individuals observe, how they interpret their observations, how they behave, and what they see as possible or appropriate for them. That clearly links strongly with behavioural economics and the ideas of empowerment, capability, participation, and inclusion.

4.7 Concluding Comments

This is not the place to anticipate all the conclusions in this book relating to theory and India. We have tried here to set out the theories that might be expected to bring some insights into the broad strands of change we identified in Section 4.1. The theories at issue are particularly those concerning change over time and dynamic processes, since that is the main theme of the study, corresponding to its very rich data set over seven decades. This contrasts with the corresponding chapter 'Theory and India' in Bliss and Stern (1981/2), which was focused on agricultural markets and resource allocation.

We have seen that many of the theories do offer real insight into processes of change, for example that of Kuznets, which links the temporal change of occupation and economic activity not only to the process of growth, but also to how inequality moves over time. On the other hand, we have seen that a weakness of the more aggregate theories is that they concentrate, in their aggregation, on class distribution of income rather than personal or household distribution of income. And some versions of them concentrate excessively on migration to formal sector manufacturing jobs, when so many of the activities that matter to individuals and households are informal, and in construction and services in nearby towns reached by commuting, not migration.

Further, many of the growth theories are deficient in that they fail to give a central place to investment and innovation by poor people. And many, but not all, are thin on institutions, political economy, and political and social structures, which will all be crucial to understanding change in Palanpur (see also Chapter 11).

To understand how personal and household income distributions change over time, we have to look more closely at analyses of initiative and entrepreneurship, together with their interaction with social structures. These ideas and studies do indeed provide insight into change in Palanpur, including in mobility and inequality. Variations in the ability or willingness to perceive and act on opportunities do seem central to the Palanpur story. At the same time, downward mobility can arise from ill-health, death, bad luck more generally, and also 'dissipation', such as drinking and gambling. We noted that theories of entrepreneurial activity tend, as in Schumpeter, to concentrate on firms rather than individuals, whereas in Palanpur, the individual and family in their local context are the key elements for study in relation to outcomes and actions.

In looking at the behaviours of individuals and understanding how they vary in relation to economic change, it is helpful to turn to theories of microeconomics, particularly behavioural economics, and to theories of institutions. These are two areas of economics that have progressed particularly strongly in the last two or three decades, and they do have much to offer to understanding change in Palanpur.

However, in order to put theories of market behaviour and institutions to work, we have to understand, and interweave our analysis with, the social and political systems in which people live and how these institutions and systems themselves develop. This interweaving is fundamental to understanding both processes and outcomes. We shall see that anthropology and sociology, political science and theories of governance and social institutions, and psychology all have much to offer in understanding economic behaviours, outcomes, and the process of economic development. And, as we bring to centre stage the role of institutions in influencing economic outcomes, we must recognize that the institutions themselves are strongly influenced by economic outcomes, whether they be in tenancy contracts or inter-caste relationships.

We shall argue that economic change in this village cannot be understood through one single story from economics, or indeed from outside economics. A single perspective such as, for example, that of Schultz, of Myrdal, or of Marx, will be thoroughly inadequate in explaining what we have found and in anticipating what might happen next. We have to equip ourselves with a broad knowledge of ideas and theories and a willingness to embrace many of them and discard others when they seem to offer little in the way of insights.

Palanpur's experience tells us much on how to theorize about development. As Frank Hahn put it, 'a theory is just a sentence in an argument'. We need many sentences and theories. And we also need to pay very careful attention to the context of the society and the broader features and drivers of change in

India as a whole. Too much of economic analysis is consumed by one idea or the theoretical or empirical enthusiasms of the moment. A view across the intellectual waterfront brings both extra breadth and extra depth. Palanpur has rich lessons for the study of economic development and for understanding the past, present, and future of India. We illustrate them throughout Parts 2 and 3, which follow. We draw them together in the final chapter of this book, Chapter 13, where, in particular, we revisit the theories set out in this chapter and ask where, in the context of analysis of Palanpur's experience, further research might be focused.

Acknowledgements

Some of the ideas in this chapter have been presented in earlier seminars and conferences at the London School of Economics (LSE) (Eva Colorni Lecture) and Reserve Bank of India (RBI) (I.G. Patel Lecture). We are grateful for comments and suggestions from the participants.

References

Acemoglu, D., Johnson, S., and Robinson, J.A. 2001. 'The colonial origins of comparative development: an empirical investigation', *American Economic Review* 91: 1369–401. DOI:10.1257/aer.91.5.1369.

Acemoglu, D., Johnson, S., and Robinson, J.A. 2002. 'Reversal of fortune: geography and institutions in the making of the modern world income distribution', *Quarterly Journal of Economics* 117: 1231–94.

Agarwal, B., Humphries, J., and Robeyns, I. 2007. *Capabilities, Freedom, and Equality: Amartya Sen's Work from a Gender Perspective*. Oxford: Oxford University Press.

Aghion, P., and Bolton, P. 1992. 'Distribution and growth in models of imperfect capital markets', *European Economic Review* 36: 603–11.

Aghion, P., and Bolton, P. 1997. 'A theory of trickle-down growth and development', *Review of Economic Studies* 64: 151–72.

Ahluwalia, M.S. 1976. 'Income distribution and development: some stylized facts', *American Economic Review* 66: 128–35.

Ahluwalia, M.S., Carter, N.G., and Chenery, H.B. 1979. 'Growth and poverty in developing countries', *Journal of Development Economics* 6: 299–341.

Akerlof, G. 1976. 'The economics of caste and of the rat race and other woeful tales', *Quarterly Journal of Economics* 90: 599–617.

Alesina, A., and Perotti, R. 1998. 'Economic risk and political risk in fiscal unions', *Economic Journal* 108: 989–1008.

Alesina, A., and Rodrik, D. 1994. 'Distributive politics and economic growth', *Quarterly Journal of Economics* 109: 465–90.

Anand, S., and Kanbur, S.R. 1993. 'The Kuznets process and the inequality: development relationship', *Journal of Development Economics* 40: 25–52.

Anand, S., and Segal, P. 2008. 'What do we know about global income inequality?' *Journal of Economic Literature* 46: 57–94.

Atkinson, A.B. 1980. 'On intergenerational income mobility in Britain', *Journal of Post Keynesian Economics* 3: 194–218.

Bailey, F.G. 1957. *Caste and the Economic Frontier: A Village in Highland Orissa*. Manchester: Manchester University Press.

Banerjee, A.V., and Duflo, E. 2003. 'Inequality and growth: What can the data say?', *Journal of Economic Growth* 8: 267–99.

Banerjee, A.V., Duflo, E., Ghatak, M., and Lafortune, J. 2013. 'Marry for what? Caste and mate selection in modern India', *American Economic Journal: Microeconomics* 5, no. 2: 33–72.

Banerjee, A.V., and Iyer, L. 2005. 'History, institutions, and economic performance: the legacy of colonial land tenure systems in India', *American Economic Review* 95: 1190–213.

Banerjee, A.V., and Mullainathan, S. 2010. 'The shape of temptation: Implications for the economic lives of the poor'. NBER Working Paper No. 15973.

Banerjee, A.V., and Newman, A.F. 1991. 'Risk-bearing and the theory of income distribution', *Review of Economic Studies* 58: 211–35.

Banerjee, A.V., and Newman, A.F. 1993. 'Occupational choice and the process of development', *Journal of Political Economy* 101: 274–98.

Bardhan, P.K. 1989. *Conversations between Economists and Anthropologists*. New Delhi: Oxford University Press.

Bardhan, P.K., and Ray, I. 2008. *The Contested Commons: Conversations between Economists and Anthropologists*. Oxford: Blackwell.

Barrett, C.B., and Carter, M.R. 2013. 'The economics of poverty traps and persistent poverty: empirical and policy implications', *Journal of Development Studies* 49: 976–90.

Barro, R.J. 2000. 'Inequality and growth in a panel of countries', *Journal of Economic Growth* 5: 5–32.

Baumol, W.J. 1990. 'Entrepreneurship: productive, unproductive, and destructive', *Journal of Political Economy* 98: 893–921.

Becker, G.S., and Mulligan, C.B. 1997. 'The endogenous determination of time preference', *Quarterly Journal of Economics* 112: 729–58.

Becker, G.S., and Tomes, N. 1979. 'An equilibrium theory of the distribution of income and intergenerational mobility', *Journal of Political Economy* 87: 1153–189. DOI:10.1086/260831.

Bernheim, B.D., Ray, D., and Yeltekin, Ş. 2015. 'Poverty and self-control', *Econometrica* 83: 1877–911.

Bernstein, H. 2004. '"Changing before our very eyes": agrarian questions and the politics of land in capitalism today', *Journal of Agrarian Change* 4, nos 1 and 2 (January and April): 190–225.

Besley, T., and Case, A. 1993. 'Modeling technology adoption in developing countries', *American Economic Review* 83: 396.

Besley, T., and Persson, T. 2011. *Pillars of Prosperity: The Political Economics of Development Clusters*. Princeton, NJ: Princeton University Press.

Besley, T., Stern, N., and O'Donnell, G. 2015. *Reflections on Economics*. London: British Academy.

Bhaduri, A. 1973. 'A study in agricultural backwardness under semi-feudalism', *Economic Journal* 83, no. 329: 120–37.

Bliss, C., and Stern, N. 1978a. 'Productivity, wages and nutrition: Part I: theory', *Journal of Development Economics* 5: 331–62.

Bliss, C., and Stern, N. 1978b. 'Productivity, wages and nutrition: Part II: some observations', *Journal of Development Economics* 5: 363–98.

Bliss, C.J., and Stern, N.H. 1982. *Palanpur: The Economy of an Indian Village*, 1st edn. Oxford and New York: Oxford University Press.

Boserup, E. 1965. *The Conditions of Agricultural Growth: The Economics of Agrarian Change under Population Pressure*. London: Allen & Unwin.

Bourguignon, F. 1981. 'Pareto superiority of unegalitarian equilibria in Stiglitz's model of wealth distribution with convex saving function', *Econometrica* 49: 1469–75.

Bourguignon, F., and Morrisson, C. 2002. 'Inequality among world citizens: 1820–1992', *American Economic Review* 92: 727–44. DOI:10.1257/00028280260344443.

Brennan, G., and Buchanan, J.M. 1985. *The Reason of Rules: Constitutional Political Economy*. Cambridge: Cambridge University Press.

Byres, T.J. 1986. 'The agrarian question, forms of capitalist agrarian transition and the state: an essay with reference to Asia', *Social Scientist* 14, nos 11/12: 3–67.

Chaudhury, N., Hammer, J., Kremer, M., Muralidharan, K., and Rogers, F.H. 2006. 'Missing in action: teacher and health worker absence in developing countries', *Journal of Economic Perspectives* 20: 91–116. DOI:10.1257/089533006776526058.

Clark, C. 1940. *The Conditions of Economic Progress*. London: Macmillan & Co. Ltd.

Corak, M. 2013. 'Income inequality, equality of opportunity, and intergenerational mobility', *Journal of Economic Perspectives* 27, no. 3: 79–102.

Cyert, R.M., and March, J.G. 1963. *A Behavioral Theory of the Firm*. Englewood Cliffs, NJ: Wiley-Blackwell.

Dasgupta, P., and Ray, D. 1986. 'Inequality as a determinant of malnutrition and unemployment: theory', *Economic Journal* 96: 1011–34.

Datt, G., Ravallion, M., and Murgai, R. 2016. *Growth, Urbanization, and Poverty Reduction in India*. Policy Research working paper no. WPS 7568. Washington, D.C.: World Bank Group. http://documents.worldbank.org/curated/en/571221468197063793/Growth-urbanization-and-poverty-reduction-in-India (accessed 10 April 2018).

Deininger, K., and Squire, L. 1998. 'New ways of looking at old issues: inequality and growth', *Journal of Development Economics* 57: 259–87.

Dixit, A. 1973. 'Models of dual economies', in J.A. Mirrlees and N.H. Stern (eds), *Models of Economic Growth*. London: Macmillan, pp. 325–52.

Dixit, A., and Stern, N. 1974. 'Determinants of shadow prices in open dual economies', *Oxford Economic Papers* 26: 42–53.

Djankov, S., La Porta, R., and Shleifer, A. 2002. 'The regulation of entry', *Quarterly Journal of Economics* 117: 1–37.

Drèze, J., and Sharma, N. 1998. 'Palanpur: population, economy, society', in P. Lanjouw and N.H. Stern (eds), *Economic Development in Palanpur over Five Decades*. New York and Oxford: Clarendon Press.

Elbers, C., and Lanjouw, P. 2001. 'Intersectoral transfer, growth, and inequality in rural Ecuador', *World Development* 29: 481–96.

Fields, G.S. 1987. 'Measuring inequality change in an economy with income growth', *Journal of Development Economics* 26: 357–74.

Fields, G.S., and Ok, E.A. 1999. 'The measurement of income mobility: an introduction to the literature', in J. Silber (ed.), *Handbook of Income Inequality Measurement*. Dordrecht: Springer.

Fisher, A.G. 1939. 'Production, primary, secondary and tertiary', *Economic Record* 15: 24–38.

Fogel, R.W. 1987. *Some Notes on the Scientific Methods of Simon Kuznets*. Cambridge, MA: National Bureau of Economic Research.

Forbes, K.J. 2000. 'A reassessment of the relationship between inequality and growth', *American Economic Review* 90: 869–87. DOI:10.1257/aer.90.4.869.

Foster, A.D., and Rosenzweig, M.R. 1995. 'Learning by doing and learning from others: human capital and technical change in agriculture', *Journal of Political Economy* 103: 1176–209. DOI:10.1086/601447.

Freeman, C. 1994. 'The economics of technical change', *Cambridge Journal of Economics* 18: 463–514.

Galor, O. 2011. *Unified Growth Theory*. Princeton, NJ: Princeton University Press.

Galor, O., and Zeira, J. 1993. 'Income distribution and macroeconomics', *Review of Economic Studies* 60: 35–52.

Ghatak, M., and Jiang, N.N.-H. 2002. 'A simple model of inequality, occupational choice, and development', *Journal of Development Economics* 69: 205–26.

Ghose, A. 2016. 'Presidential address', presented at the 58th annual conference of the Indian Society of Labour Economics, Guwahati, India.

Gibson, J., Datt, G., Ravallion, M., and Murgai, R. 2017. 'For India's rural poor, growing towns matter more than growing cities'. World Bank Group Policy Research Working Paper No. 7994.

Gollin, D. 2014. 'The Lewis model: a 60-year retrospective', *Journal of Economic Perspectives* 28: 71–88.

Griliches, Z. 1957. 'Hybrid corn: an exploration in the economics of technological change', *Econometrica* 25: 501–22. DOI:10.2307/1905380.

Hayami, Y., and Ruttan, V.W. 1970. 'Agricultural productivity differences among countries', *American Economic Review* 60: 895–911.

Hayami, Y., and Ruttan, V.W. 1971. *Agricultural Development: An International Perspective*. Baltimore, MD, and London: Johns Hopkins University Press.

Hayek, F.A. 1945. 'The use of knowledge in society', *American Economic Review* 35: 519–30.

Herbert, A.S. 1984. *Models of Bounded Rationality*, vol. 1: *Economic Analysis and Public Policy*, 1st edn. Cambridge, MA: MIT Press.

Hirschman, A.O. 1977. 'A generalized linkage approach to development, with special reference to staples', *Economic Development and Cultural Change* 25: 67.

Hoff, K. 2016. 'Caste system'. World Bank Policy Research Working Paper No. 7929, https://openknowledge.worldbank.org/handle/10986/25832 (accessed 12 March 2018).

Hoff, K., and Pandey, P. 2006. 'Discrimination, social identify, and durable inequalities', *American Economic Review* 96, no. 2: 206–11.

Hoff, K., and Stiglitz, J.E. 2016. 'Striving for balance in economics: towards a theory of the social determination of behavior', *Journal of Economic Behavior & Organization* 126: 25–57.

Jäntti, M., and Jenkins, S.P. 2015. 'Income mobility', in A.B. Atkinson and F. Bourguignon (eds), *Handbook of Income Distribution*, vol. 2. Amsterdam: Elsevier. DOI:10.1016/B978-0-444-59428-0.00011-4.

Joshi, V. 2017. *India's Long Road: The Search for Prosperity*. New York: Oxford University Press.

Kaldor, N. 1940. 'A model of the trade cycle', *Economic Journal* 50: 78–92.

Karl, M. 1951. *Capital*. London: Dent.

Kirzner, I.M. 1973. *Competition and Entrepreneurship*. Chicago and London: University of Chicago Press.

Krueger, A.O. 1974. 'The political economy of the rent-seeking society', *American Economic Review* 64: 291–303.

Kuznets, S. 1955. 'Economic growth and income inequality', *American Economic Review* 45: 1–28.

La Porta, R., Lopez-de-Silanes, F., and Shleifer, A. 2008. 'The economic consequences of legal origins', *Journal of Economic Literature* 46: 285–332.

Lal, D. 1988. *Cultural Stability and Economic Stagnation: India c.1500 BC–AD 1980*. New York: Oxford University Press.

Lanjouw, P., and Murgai, R. 2014. 'Urban growth and rural poverty in India 1983–2005', in N. Hope, A. Kochar, R. Noll, and T.N. Srinivasin (eds), *Economic Reform in India: Challenges, Prospects, and Lessons*. New York: Cambridge University Press.

Lanjouw, P., and Stern, N.H. (eds) 1998. *Economic Development in Palanpur over Five Decades*. New York and Oxford: Clarendon Press.

Lardy, N.R. 1978. *Economic Growth and Distribution in China*. Cambridge: Cambridge University Press.

Lardy, N.R. 1983. *Agricultural Prices in China*. Washington, DC: World Bank.

Lerche, J. 2013. 'The agrarian question in neoliberal India: agrarian transition bypassed?', *Journal of Agrarian Change* 13, no. 3: 382–404.

Lewis, W.A. 1955 [2013]. *Theory of Economic Growth*. London: Routledge.

Lipton, M., and Longhurst, R. 1989. *New Seeds and Poor People*, Johns Hopkins Studies in Development. Baltimore, MD: Johns Hopkins University Press.

Little, I., Tibor, S., and Maurice, S. 1970. *Industry and Trade in some Developing Countries: A Comparative Study*. London and New York: Oxford University Press.

Meade, J.E. 1973. 'The inheritance of inequalities: some biological, demographic, social and economic factors', in S. Howson, (1998) *The Collected Papers of James Meade Vol. II*. London: Unwin.

Mellor, J. 1966. *The Economics of Agricultural Development*. Ithaca, NY: Cornell University Press.

Milanović, B. 2016. *Global Inequality*. Cambridge, MA: Harvard University Press.

Ministry of Panchayati Raj. 2013. 'Towards holistic panchayat raj: twentieth anniversary report of the expert committee on leveraging panchayats for efficient delivery of public goods and services, volume 1: policy issues', Government of India.

Minniti, M., and Lévesque, M. 2008. 'Recent developments in the economics of entrepreneurship', *Journal of Business Venturing* 23: 603–12. DOI:10.1016/j.jbusvent.2008.01.001.

Mirrlees, J. 1976. 'A pure theory of under-developed economies', in L. Reynolds (ed.), *Agriculture in Development Theory*. New Haven, CT: Yale University Press.

Munshi, K. 2016. 'Caste networks in the modern Indian economy', in S. Dev and P. Babu (eds), *Development in India: India Studies in Business and Economics*. New Delhi: Springer.

Munshi, K., and Rosenzweig, M. 2015. 'Networks and misallocation: insurance, migration, and the rural–urban wage gap'. CReAM Discussion Paper Series 1516.

Myrdal, G. 1968. *Asian Drama*, 3 vols. New York: Pantheon.

North, D.C. 1971. 'Institutional change and economic growth', *Journal of Economic History* 31: 118–25.

North, D.C. 1991. 'Institutions', *Journal of Economic Perspectives* 5: 97–112. DOI:10.2307/1942704.

Nurkse, R. 1953. *Problems of Capital Formation in Underdeveloped Countries*. Oxford: Blackwell.

Nussbaum, M. 2000. 'Women's capabilities and social justice', *Journal of Human Development* 1: 219–47.

Olson, M. 1993. 'Dictatorship, democracy, and development', *American Political Science Review* 87: 567–76.

Ostrom, E. 2015. *Governing the Commons*. Cambridge: Cambridge University Press.

Patnaik, U. (ed.) 1990. *Agrarian Relations and Accumulation: The 'Mode of Production' Debate in India*. Bombay: Oxford University Press.

Persson, T., and Tabellini, G. 1994. 'Is inequality harmful for growth?', *American Economic Review* 84: 600–21.

Piketty, T. 1995. 'Social mobility and redistributive politics', *Quarterly Journal of Economics* 110: 551–84.

Piketty, T. 2000. 'Theories of persistent inequality and intergenerational mobility', *Handbook of Income Distribution* 1: 429–76.

Piketty, T. 2014. *Capital in the Twenty-First Century*. Cambridge, MA: Belknap Press of Harvard University Press.

Putnam, R.D., Leonardi, R., Nanetti, R.Y., and Pavoncello, F. 1983. 'Explaining institutional success: the case of Italian regional government', *American Political Science Review* 77, no. 1: 55–74.

Ravallion, M. 2016. 'Are the world's poorest being left behind?', *Journal of Economic Growth* 21: 139–64.

Ree, J. de, Muralidharan, K., Pradhan, M., and Rogers, H. 2015. 'Double for nothing? Experimental evidence on the impact of an unconditional teacher salary increase on student performance in Indonesia'. NBER Working Paper No. 21806

Ricardo, D. 1815. *An Essay on the Influence of a Low Price of Corn on the Profits of Stock, with Remarks on Mr. Malthus' Two Last Publications*. London: John Murray.

Ricardo, D. 1821. *On the Principles of Political Economy and Taxation*. London: John Murray.

Rogers, F.H., and Vegas, E. 2009. 'No more cutting class? Reducing teacher absence and providing incentives for performance'. World Bank Policy Research Working Paper No. 4847.

Rosen, D.H., Rozelle, S., and Huang, J. 2004. *Roots of Competitiveness: China's Evolving Agriculture Interests*. New York: Columbia University Press.

Rosenstein-Rodan, P.N. 1943. 'Problems of industrialisation of eastern and south-eastern Europe', *Economic Journal* 53: 202–11.

Rostow, W.W. 1960. *The Stages of Economic Growth: A Non-Communist Manifesto*. Cambridge: Cambridge University Press.

Ruttan, V.W. 1977. 'Green revolution: seven generalizations', *International Development Review* 19: 16–23.

Sah, R.K., and Stiglitz, J.E. 1984. 'The economics of price scissors', *American Economic Review* 74: 125–38.

Saith, A. 2016. 'Transforming peasantries in India and China: comparative investigations of institutional dimensions', *Indian Journal of Labour Economics* 59: 85–124.

Schumpeter, J. 1954. *History of Economic Analysis*. London: Routledge.

Sen, A. 1983. 'Development: Which way now?', *The Economic Journal* 93: 745–62.

Sen, A. 1999. *Development as Freedom*. Oxford: Oxford University Press.

Singer, H.W. 1952. 'India's five-year plan: a modest proposal', *Far Eastern Survey* 21: 97–101.

Sinha, D., Tiwari, D.K., Bhattacharyya, R., and Kattumuri, R. 2016. 'Public services, social relations, politics, and gender: tales from a north Indian village', in Himanshu, P. Jha, and G. Rodgers (eds), *The Changing Village in India: Insights from Longitudinal Research*. New Delhi: Oxford University Press.

Smith, A. 1776. *An Inquiry into the Nature and Causes of Wealth of Nations*. London: W. Strahan & T. Cadell.

Solow, R.M. 1956. 'A contribution to the theory of economic growth', *Quarterly Journal of Economics* 70: 65–94. DOI:10.2307/1884513.

Stern, N. 1972. 'Optimum development in a dual economy', *Review of Economic Studies* 39: 171–84.

Stern, N. 2015. *Why are We Waiting? The Logic, Urgency, and Promise of Tackling Climate Change*. Cambridge, MA: MIT Press.

Stern, N., Dethier, J., and Rogers, F. 2005. *Growth and Empowerment: Making Development Happen*. Cambridge, MA: MIT Press.

Stiglitz, J.E. 1976. 'The efficiency wage hypothesis, surplus labour, and the distribution of income in L.D.C.s', *Oxford Economic Papers* 28: 185–207.

Stiglitz, J.E. 1986. 'The new development economics', *World Development* 14: 257–65.

Suryadarma, D., Suryahadi, A., Sumarto, S., and Rogers, F.H. 2006. 'Improving student performance in public primary schools in developing countries: evidence from Indonesia', *Education Economics* 14: 401–29.

Turnham, D. 1971. *The Employment Problem in Developing Countries: A Review of Evidence*. Paris: OECD.

Wiser, C.V., and Wiser, W.H. 1971. *Behind Mud Walls, 1930–1960*. Berkeley, CA: University of California Press.

Wiser, W., and Wiser, C.V. 2001. *Behind Mud Walls: Seventy-Five Years in a North Indian Village*, updated and expanded edn. Berkeley, CA: University of California Press.

World Bank. 2003. 'World Development Report 2004: Making Services Work for Poor People. © World Bank. Available at: https://openknowledge.worldbank.org/handle/10986/5986. License: CC BY 3.0 IGO.

Xiaoping, D. 1994. *Selected Works of Deng Xiaoping*, vol. 3. Beijing: Foreign Languages Press.

Yiping, H., and Tingsong, J. 2010. 'What does the Lewis turning point mean for China? A computable general equilibrium analysis'. East Asian Bureau of Economic Research Macroeconomics Working Paper No. 22718.

Zhang, X., Yang, J., and Wang, S. 2011. 'China has reached the Lewis turning point', *China Economic Review* 22: 542–54. DOI:10.1016/j.chieco.2011.07.002.

Part 2
Economy

5

Changing Activities, Changing Markets: Agriculture*

5.1 Introduction

Agriculture has been central to the story of economic development in Palanpur. Agriculture is at the core of the Ansari report (1964) and of the first book on Palanpur by Bliss and Stern (1982), which documented the structure of agricultural production in detail. The green revolution was important in changing both the structure of economic growth and of production in Indian agriculture. The analysis of agricultural change in India, and its drivers and consequences, received much attention from a wide audience, ranging from those interested in understanding the Indian economy and its growth and structural changes, to those examining the structure of agrarian markets.[1]

Agriculture remains a key force for change and a source of dynamism in the village even today despite the declining importance of agriculture in village income. It was clear from the surveys up to 1983/4 that technological change in agriculture, demographic changes, and outside jobs were the 'primary' drivers of change in the village (Lanjouw and Stern, 1998). The decades since 1983 have seen the Indian economy undergo a structural transformation (see, for example, Binswanger-Mkhize and D'Souza, 2012).[2] While there has been a considerable decline in the share of agriculture in gross domestic product (GDP), the dependence on agriculture for employment has not fallen proportionately. At present, the share of agriculture in national GDP is less than

---

* This chapter has been written by Himanshu and Sarthak Gaurav.
[1] Considerable literature exists on the changing nature of agrarian production, much debated and discussed in the 1970s and 1980s. While a large amount of literature dealt with issues of changing modes of production in Indian agriculture, there was also a vibrant discussion on various theoretical issues such as tenancy, labour and credit market imperfections, and interlinkages between various markets. On debates on the mode of production, see Patnaik (1990). On production conditions in Indian agriculture see, for example, Bharadwaj (1974).
[2] See Chapter 3 for details.

15 per cent. However, even though agriculture is less relevant for growth, it still employs around half of the national workforce.

This period has also witnessed widespread economic reforms and liberalization of the Indian economy, beginning in the 1980s and accelerating strongly in the early 1990s, as a result of which there has been strong growth outside agriculture and greater integration of Indian agriculture with international markets. Some of these changes are also reflected in Palanpur, with non-farm employment and income now accounting for a significantly larger share of the total workforce and income of the village. We examine in this chapter the way agriculture has changed as a result of the process of transformation of the village economy and in response to opportunities in the 'outside world'. For Palanpur, the 'outside world' is primarily, but not exclusively, nearby towns in Uttar Pradesh. But, as we shall note, the Indian economy and the global economy are also of real importance to Palanpur and its agriculture.

In this chapter, we examine the process of agricultural development in detail and identify the factors that have played a significant role in shaping this process. In doing so, we present an account of the dynamics of agricultural development in Palanpur over seven decades. The evolution of agriculture in Palanpur involved and was shaped by the interactions amongst several factors, including demographic change, expansion of irrigation, intensification of cultivation, changing cropping patterns, farm mechanization, growing non-farm employment, 'marketization' of factors of production, and improvements in formal credit supply.

We identify five fundamental elements of the change in agriculture in Palanpur. First, *growing population pressure* and sale of land have meant that per capita land owned and land operated have declined significantly between 1983 and 2008–10. While the decline in land availability per capita has influenced changing patterns of tenancy, it has also affected choice of crops and cropping intensity. Second, while agricultural output, and to some extent outside jobs, played a central role in income growth in earlier surveys, *growing non-farm and outside jobs* have become more important in recent periods. The decline in the role of agriculture has implications not just for income distribution and inequality in the village but also for the labour and land markets. Third, we look at the role of agriculture in relation to social and cultural aspects of the village, particularly the *affinity of some of the caste groups in relation to agriculture*.

Fourth, the growth of non-farm activities has occurred in a period of *increasing capital intensity* in agriculture in the form of farm mechanization and intensification of inputs. The increased investment in labour-saving technology has both released labour for non-farm employment and contributed to increasing agricultural productivity. This release of labour from agriculture has been associated with both a growth of entrepreneurship and changes in the labour market. Fifth, along with the non-farm sector, agriculture has also seen *greater integration with the outside world*. This is true not only for sources of information on agricultural practices and access to markets outside the village, but also with regard to a changing labour market structure. For example, the increasing role of mentha cultivation in the village has been a result of this process of integration of the village agrarian economy with the outside world.

As with earlier analytical work on Palanpur, our purpose here is not restricted to documenting the changes in agricultural production in the village. It also explores the various dimensions of interaction between agriculture and non-agriculture as well as within agriculture, including across the various factors of production, land, capital, and labour. This is evident not only in the changing cropping patterns and intensification of mechanization and irrigation, but also in the evolution of factor markets. For example, the introduction of new forms of tenancy alongside the continuation of old forms, albeit on a smaller scale, also points to a degree of institutional dynamism. Palanpur's agricultural economy is responding to the globalization and liberalization of the Indian economy through the introduction of new crops such as mentha; its ability to transform itself, including the way its markets work, in response to new challenges of migration and outside employment are yet further signals of dynamism in a rural economy which in many other respects changes only slowly. At the same time, the developments in agriculture have also continued to influence the choice of livelihood and options for diversification of income and employment opportunities both as potential recipients of investment and sources of income.

While noting important elements of dynamism, the decline in the village's operated land and the deceleration in yield growth have been of real significance. It is important to situate agrarian change within larger changes, including the reforms and stresses experienced in the Indian economy since the 1990s. Some of the difficulties are also evident in the evolution of credit market and in the distress sales of land by the villagers.

While the percentage of total leased area has increased marginally, counter to the widespread prediction of those who expected a decline in tenancy, the changing nature of tenancy contracts, with specialized contracts such as fixed rent and labour contracts, have gained prominence, and this points to the importance of interaction among land and other markets. These changes confirm the inadequacy of attempting to characterize the nature of agricultural production in India in simplistic categories of 'semi-feudal' or 'capitalistic' modes of production.[3]

---

[3] See Rodgers and Rodgers (2001) and Sen (1981).

The complexity of the production system, the linkages in the factor markets, which remain imperfect, and the broader context of a rapidly changing non-farm economy also suggest that any attempt to study tenancy or farm-size productivity relationship in isolation would suffer serious limitations. We look at some possible explanations of the changing nature of tenancy in the village, highlighting the importance of the context and linkages, and thus the shortcomings of such stand-alone exercises, in Chapter 6.

Institutions matter but they are not static, and analysis of Palanpur agriculture offers an opportunity to look at changing institutional structures. These are reflected not just in labour markets, where labour contracts have changed markedly, with a shift towards piece-rate contracts and monetization of labour transactions, but also in markets for inputs and outputs. With increasing diversification towards non-farm activities, land owners have been faced with less time for supervising sharecropping contracts. On the other hand, outside activities have increased the income of Jatab households who are now more likely to lease land for sharecropping than before. The tenancy market has itself adapted, with the emergence of new forms of tenancy such as the *chauthai*,[4] but also an increasing share of cash contracts, or *peshgi*. Caste structure and kinship remain important in economic and social life but are changing their role in land contracts, both for sharecropping and tenancy. The dynamism in the land and labour market are examples of an institutional structure capable of adapting itself to a changing context. Whilst we have emphasized dynamism and change, we do not want to suggest that Palanpur is an extraordinary hotbed of ideas and innovation. It is changing, and individuals and households do show initiative. But it remains a backward village. There are other places in India that are changing a good deal faster.

This chapter is organized into four further sections. Section 5.2 describes some aspects of data collection and methodological issues. Section 5.3 sets out some of the basic characteristics of agricultural production in Palanpur as it has evolved through the seven decades. We analyse the changing structure of land, capital intensity, and the cropping pattern in the village. We also look at the evolution of yields and prices and the overall organization of production in the agricultural economy of Palanpur. We examine the changing nature of production in agriculture with respect to technology and the evolution of input markets. Section 5.4 describes the structure of cost of cultivation, incomes, and productivity. The final section discusses the changing nature of agriculture in the wider context of the changing village economy and some implications for income distribution.

---

[4] *Chauthai* has emerged as a new form of sharecropping, with the tenant getting one fourth of the output by supplying only labour. It is similar to a labour contract. For details, see Chapter 6.

The main objective of this chapter is to provide a structured description of the changing contours of agricultural production in the village economy, particularly in relation to the changing nature of land and the labour market and the accompanying evolution of incomes in the village. The purpose is to help understand the principal questions for this book, namely how lives and livelihoods have changed and the forces driving such change. The chapter does not present results of various technical details, nor formal tests for existing theories; these are available as separate working papers.[5]

5.2 Data and Methodology

The previous two books on Palanpur (Bliss and Stern, 1982; Lanjouw and Stern, 1998), along with the Ansari report (1964), provide a detailed account of the changes in Palanpur agriculture from 1957 to 1983.[6] Thus the main focus of this chapter is on changes in agriculture since 1983. However, we do refer to the previous data and analyses in our discussion, and return to some of the themes and ideas of the earlier studies. The new primary data used for analysis in this chapter are based on those collected during 2008–10.[7] The 2008/10 round of data collection was the longest running of all the survey rounds undertaken so far. It was spread over two agricultural years, 2008/9 and 2009/10.[8] Data for two *rabi* seasons (2008 and 2009) and two *kharif* seasons (2009 and 2010) were collected as part of the survey.[9] *Rabi* and *kharif* are the two major agricultural seasons in Palanpur.[10] The cropping pattern has largely been dominated by wheat in the *rabi* season and paddy in the *kharif* season, whose share has increased over time. The other major crop in recent years, which has accounted for one-quarter to one-third of the *kharif* area, is sugar cane.

Alongside maintaining continuity over the subjects of data collection, the fieldwork methodology was also similar to that applied in previous surveys of

---

[5] These papers are available at http://sticerd.lse.ac.uk/india/research/palanpur/publications.asp.

[6] Data on agriculture from the 1993 summary round are limited.

[7] While some data on landholding, tenancy, and cropping patterns were collected in the 2015 round, no data on costs, incomes, and input markets were collected in detail in 2015.

[8] The agricultural year refers to July–June, covering the *kharif* and *rabi* seasons as well as the crop cycle between *rabi* and *kharif*.

[9] The year 2008/9 was a normal agricultural one while 2009/10 was a drought year.

[10] *Rabi* crops are sown in November–December and harvested in March–April. The *kharif* season coincides with the south-west monsoon, and crops are sown in late June or early July and harvested in October–November. Sugar cane, which is an annual commercial crop, is usually harvested in February. In our discourse, we focus on major or principal crops and refer to changes in minor crops wherever necessary. There used to be a third season of short duration, between *rabi* harvest and *kharif* sowing, called *zaid*, where crops such as potatoes and pumpkins were planted. However, it has largely disappeared with the growing intensity of cropping, as the longer seasons usually overlap with each other.

1974/5 and 1983/4. However, in addition to the usual focus on agricultural practices, this round also collected extensive data on interlinkages across factor markets, in particular credit and tenancy. The methodology was largely questionnaire-based but was supplemented with a discussion questionnaire aimed at collecting qualitative information, including perceptions and motivations, on various aspects of agricultural production and tenancy. This was further supplemented by the information collected through daily diaries, which were distributed to a selected sample of households.[11] These were completed meticulously, and one of the uses of data from the diaries was to validate some of the information on expenditures and outputs in agriculture.

As with the previous surveys, a great deal of effort was spent on ensuring internal consistency across various rounds of questionnaires and also, for this round, validating the information collected through the questionnaires through secondary sources such as land records and through internal consistency checks. In particular, our data on the *rabi* crop of 2008, which was the first season we surveyed, is not as good as the subsequent rounds because of under-reporting of tenancy arrangements and land data. These were later made consistent with secondary data as well as through a physical verification of each plot. For the purpose of this chapter, we draw only on data for *kharif* 2008 and *rabi* 2009, which have been cleaned and validated and are free from abnormal weather fluctuations.[12] In subsequent analysis we have used only *rabi* and *kharif* as relevant seasons, although some plots of the village were also cultivated during the intervening period between these two seasons.[13]

One of the problems encountered during our survey was the differences in estimates of input use and outputs as reported by tenant and landlord. In the case of a conflict between the two estimates, the data were cross-checked again and, in most cases, these were resolved at the field level. However, in some cases, discrepancies did remain, and in those cases we have used the estimates provided by the actual cultivator. The exercises underline the great importance of data quality for us and how much time, care, and attention are necessary to produce accurate information.

While the land data were scrutinized in great detail using secondary data sources as well as physical verification, data on inputs used and outputs from

---

[11] The diaries were distributed to all the households which had been part of sample of households for which diary data was collected during the 1983 survey. In addition, diaries were also given to some agricultural labour households and non-farm households. The diaries were written by the respondents but were regularly checked by the resident investigators. The respondents were asked to report daily on labour used, inputs used, as well as output harvested and disposed.

[12] Although we collected data for *kharif* 2009, we have excluded it from the analysis given that 2009 *kharif* was one of the worst droughts of the decade.

[13] These crops were merged with *kharif* if they were sown before the *kharif* harvest, otherwise with the *rabi* season. Data for annual crops such as sugar cane were also collected and merged with agricultural year data.

cultivation were collected from questionnaires. Data on both inputs and outputs were collected in both quantity and value terms. In cases where output was self-consumed or home-produced quantities were used, values were imputed using locally prevalent prices in the village at the time of survey. No depreciation was ascribed at any stage. Information on labour use, both hired as well as family labour and exchange labour, was recorded in the questionnaire but are subject to recall problems in some cases. 'Days of labour use' has largely been taken as the actual number of days reported by the respondents. However, in some cases, information on labour use was also verified using diaries and cross-verification with tenants/landlords. The valuation of family labour, where needed, was at the locally prevalent wages which were taken to be the wages reported by the hired labourers. Since there is quite a bit of mixed cropping in Palanpur, the inputs were apportioned correspondingly across the two crops grown jointly. Unlike previous survey years, this time we also used secondary data sources such as the cost-of-cultivation surveys to validate and cross-check our data. As we show in Section 5.4, the data collected during our survey is very close to the aggregate and micro data reported by the cost-of-cultivation surveys.

5.3 Basic Features of Agriculture in Palanpur

Over the past seven decades, there have been many changes in Palanpur agriculture. Technological change has been pervasive. Persian wheels, as described in Ansari (1964), and still present in 1974/5, gave way to diesel-based pumping sets and, later, more powerful electric tube wells. Expansion of irrigation has enabled intensification of double-cropping and investment in new crops, such as mentha. Use of high-yielding varieties (HYV) and fertilizers has intensified, and the process of farm mechanization that was at an incipient stage in the 1970s has matured considerably. There have been conspicuous changes in tenancy arrangements, while labour and credit markets have undergone changes. This section describes the basic features of the agrarian economy of Palanpur as it has evolved over the years. Our discussion in this section is organized around the basic factors of production, land (Section 5.3.1), capital (Section 5.3.2), and labour (Section 5.3.3).

5.3.1 *Land and Cropping Patterns*

As described in Chapter 2, Palanpur is a smallholder economy with average landholding of less than 2 *bighas* per capita in 2009. Both land owned per capita and land cultivated per capita have declined to one-third of their levels in 1957/8. However, tenancy continues to remain important in the village.

Unlike previous years, when population growth was seen as the major factor behind the decline in landholdings, this no longer appears to be the only important explanation. A large part of the decline between 1983 and 2008/9 was driven by the decline in aggregate land owned by the villagers: a reduction of over 500 *bigha* between 1983 and 2008, from a total of around 2600 in 1983.[14] This is in contrast to the trend seen between 1962/3 and 1983/4 when land ownership by the villagers was rising. The decline in operational land-holding for the village as a whole is smaller because some of the land which is now owned by the outsiders is still cultivated by the residents of Palanpur. We have already described the basic features of landholding in Palanpur in Chapter 2. Institutional factors such as *zamindari* abolition have been important in shaping the evolution of landholding structure in the village; so, too, the functioning of and changes in institutions of tenancy.

Tables 5.1 and 5.2 give the land owned and land cultivated per capita by caste. Among the major caste groups, the largest decline in land owned per capita is seen in the case of Thakurs. Muraos had similar land ownership per capita as Thakurs in the beginning, but the decline for them is less rapid. The trend in land cultivated appears to be similar, but a noticeable change is the almost stable land cultivated per capita for Jatabs. An important attribute of the economic development in Palanpur has been the upward mobility of

Table 5.1 Land owned per capita by caste (*bighas*)

Caste Group	Year					
	1957/88	1962/3	1974/5	1983/4	1993	2008/9
Thakur	8.73	6.80	4.37	3.51	2.44	2.07
Murao	8.72	7.67	5.50	4.98	3.50	2.55
Dhimar	1.84	1.83	1.43	0.88	0.57	0.48
Gadaria	4.43	4.40	2.61	2.35	1.85	1.90
Dhobi	10	20	2.61	0.77	1.62	0.83
Teli	1.85	1.63	1.25	1.06	1.12	0.65
Passi	2.05	1.86	1.45	1.61	1.40	2.26
Jatab	3.38	3.44	2.08	1.84	1.29	0.78
Others	0.97	1.76	1.25	0.58	0.48	0.71
All Castes	5.20	4.65	3.27	2.70	2.10	1.57

[14] Analysis of land transactions suggests that most transactions have been a result of distress sales. These were primarily to repay loans outstanding to institutional sources such as banks and moneylenders in the village. The reason for taking out loans in many cases was marriage, court cases, and consumption loans. A significant fraction of the total amount of land sold went to one particular moneylender in a neighbouring village. The land had been mortgaged to the moneylender. Approximately 100 *bighas* of land, out of net sale figure of 500 *bighas* between 1983/4 and 2008/9, were acquired by this moneylender via this method. Another category of land sales occurred as a result of households completely migrating out of the village during this period. In only a handful of cases, were land sales made in order to acquire productive assets. .

Table 5.2 Land cultivated per capita by caste (*bighas*)

Caste Group	Year					
	1957/8	1962/3	1974/5	1983	1993	2008/9
Thakur	6.17	7.34	3.75	2.69	1.92	1.87
Murao	6.88	7.24	4.22	5.11	3.52	2.79
Dhimar	1.61	1.57	2.56	2.05	1.39	0.70
Gadaria	4.95	4.47	2.67	2.31	2.23	1.94
Dhobi	11.67	20	2.43	2.23	1.97	1.75
Teli	2.49	2.70	3.12	2.24	1.88	1.21
Passi	2.05	1.39	1.65	1.27	0.65	0.51
Jatab	3.44	3.96	3.08	1.90	1.38	1.97
Others	1.38	1.59	0.08	0.45	0.76	0.71
All Castes	4.41	4.76	3.20	2.76	2.13	1.86

Jatabs, a historically disadvantaged community with low land ownership on average. In the past, Jatabs were predominantly agricultural labourers on the farms of Thakurs and Muraos. However, since 1983/4, owing to increasing outside jobs and non-farm employment opportunities, Jatabs have experienced a general increase in their economic status. The increased income and liquidity from the non-farm work enables them to contribute to the cost of cash inputs, necessary under *batai*. It also enables them to hire in tractor services (ploughing is the obligation of the tenant), services which are now monetized and marketed. Thus they have been able to increasingly lease-in land for cultivation, particularly under *batai* (50–50 sharecropping) where previously they were excluded by lack of cash resources and ownership of the draught animals then necessary for ploughing.

In 2008/9, about half of the leased-in area of Jatabs was under *batai*. About a third of the land leased-in by Jatabs was under *chauthai* (the tenant-labourer receives one-quarter of the output).[15] In 2008/9, the leased-in area under *batai* contracts for Jatabs was almost comparable to that of the Muraos. Note that Jatabs are the only caste group with a considerable increase in the total cultivated area: from 254 *bighas* in 1983/4 to 399 *bighas* in 2008/9. As our analysis of economic mobility elaborated in Chapter 8 suggests, it is plausible that the increase of land leased-in for cultivation by the Jatabs is a consequence of their 'upward mobility' over the years. With increasing participation in non-farm jobs, they have been moving away from wage labour in agriculture, which has enabled them to reinvest a part of their increased earnings in agriculture. Therefore, at a time when most Thakurs have been moving away from cultivation as their outside jobs have increased, the active participation of Jatabs in cultivation through tenancy arrangements has

---

[15] We discuss *chauthai* and other tenancy contracts in Chapter 6.

resulted in them overtaking the Thakurs in terms of per capita land cultivated. We should remind ourselves that land owned and cultivated per capita, on average, is very small: two *bighas* is less than one-third of an acre and just 0.12 of a hectare.

The dual impact of decline in land ownership and increasing population pressure has led to reductions in the size of individual landholdings. On the other hand, the number of landless households shows a marginal decline compared to 1993—although there are now many more landless households than in 1984. The number of landless households is 14, 12, 17, 27, 44, and 42 in 1958, 1963, 1975, 1984, 1993, and 2009, respectively. The importance of *zamindari* abolition in the 1950s did play a role in making land available to a large section of the village. But the subsequent increase in gross cropped area and cropping intensity is a result of the large amount of private investment in irrigation and mechanization, both of which have contributed to muting the impact of population growth. Irrigation allows double- or triple-cropping and mechanization, while reducing overall labour needs speeds up the work between seasons so that sowing can be timely.

The opening of the village economy to outside opportunities has played a role in taking some pressure off agriculture with regard to sustaining the increasing population in Palanpur. Tenancy appears to work towards reducing inequalities in cultivated holdings arising out of unequal per capita land ownership. The percentage of leased-in land has increased to over one-third of total cultivated land compared to just over one-quarter in 1983/4.[16] The pressure on land has also led to more intensive cultivation of crops along with a shift towards high-value crops.

The village has seen a strong increase in cropping intensity, defined as the number of crops on a piece of land per year in the village. The first wave of increase in cropping intensity followed the rise in irrigation intensity, beginning in the 1950s, and the introduction of HYV wheat seeds from the late 1960s, which had a shorter growing season. The percentage of land irrigated was around 50 per cent during the first two survey years, but had increased to 96 per cent by the 1974/5 survey year. However, the last two decades have also seen a substantial increase in cropping intensity in the village. Increases in mechanization, as well as the introduction of new crops such as mentha, have allowed the villagers to cultivate their land more intensively than before.[17]

---

[16] While inequality in land ownership as measured by the Gini coefficient does not show any worsening over the years, there is a significant decline in the Gini coefficient for land cultivated. The difference between the Gini coefficient in 2008/10 for per capita land ownership and that for per capita operational holding is higher than any other survey year. However, despite the 'equalizing' effect of tenancy, per capita operational holdings are still marked by high inequality.

[17] Many farmers are now growing three crops a year in Palanpur. A few of them manage to grow four crops in a year, which includes short-duration mustard and lentils.

Table 5.3 presents the cropping intensity in the village. Increasing use of tractors for ploughing and levelling has reduced the time of many agricultural operations, while the increase in irrigation intensity has helped in cultivating mentha, which grows during the summer months of May and June.[18] The marginal decline in cropping intensity in 1962/3 and 1983/4 is due to the fact that these were rain-deficient years compared to other years, which saw normal or good rainfall.

Table 5.3 Cropping intensity in Palanpur

Year	Gross Cropped Area (*bigha*)	Net Sown Area (*bigha*)	Cropping Intensity
1957/8	2547	2331	1.09
1962/3	2807	2789	1.01
1974/5	3725	2438	1.53
1983/4	3881	2705	1.43
2008/10	4583	2338	1.96

Note: Cropping intensity is the number of crops on a piece of land per year.

The widespread changes in cropping practices, catalysed by increased irrigation, the green revolution in the late 1960s and early 1970s, as well as demographic change, have been described in detail in earlier studies (Bliss and Stern, 1982; Lanjouw and Stern, 1998). While the mid-1960s and early 1970s saw wheat as the central element in the agricultural transformation in the village, subsequent decades have seen paddy emerge as a major crop, along with sugar cane (continuing) and mentha. The trend towards cash crops and the finer cereals at the cost of coarser cereals is similar to the trend observed for the country as a whole. While tastes and preferences have contributed to the changing cropping pattern, this has also been in response to various factors such as the availability of irrigation, mechanization, labour market dynamics, and price responses. Table 5.4 summarizes the changes in cropping patterns in Palanpur in terms of area cultivated and share of total area cultivated for major or principal crops.

Wheat (*gehun*) has been central to the agricultural development of Palanpur, particularly following improvements in irrigation from the 1950s and 1960s, unleashed, in large part, by the strengthened ownership rights following *zamindari* abolition and the technological transformation ushered in by the green revolution in late 1960s and early 1970s. This is also evident from the

---

[18] One of the negative consequences of the increase in cropping intensity in the village and the region as a whole has been the impact on soil fertility and the water table. Although we do not have carefully collected data on water tables and soil quality, discussion with villagers confirms that the water table has gone down substantially in the last three decades. Barely any land in the village is left fallow and the land quality has deteriorated. Overuse of fertilizer has also contributed to increased salinity in the soil.

Table 5.4 Cultivation area for selected major crops in Palanpur

Crop	Year					
	1957/8	1962/3	1974/5	1983/4	2008/9	2015
1. Wheat						
Area cultivated (*bighas*)	879	767	1030	1573	1409	1324
% of total cultivated area	52	48	46	57	68	72
2. Mentha						
Area cultivated (*bighas*)	0	0	0	0	611	155
% of total cultivated area	0	0	0	0	29	8
3. Paddy						
Area cultivated (*bighas*)	70	274	125	266	651	658
% of total cultivated area	5	17	6	12	26	35
4. Bajra						
Area cultivated (*bighas*)	644	638	610 (730)	137 (363)	371	353
% of total cultivated area	46	40	29	6	15	19
5. Sugar cane						
Area cultivated (*bighas*)	391	430	463	886	673	627
% of total cultivated area	28	27	22	39	27	33

Note: (1) The figures in brackets include plots sown with mixed crops. In these cases the area figures are upper bounds on the effective areas.
(2) Proportion of area cultivated refers to percentage of area under the specified crop for the relevant season (*rabi* for wheat, *kharif* for paddy and *bajra*; *kharif* has also been taken as the reference area for sugar cane).

emphasis that Bliss and Stern (1982) gave to Palanpur's wheat economy in their study in 1974/5. The green revolution involved the greater use of HYV wheat seeds, together with increased irrigation and fertilizer use. Timely availability of HYV seeds from the seed store in the early years played an important role in the early 1970s.

However, there has been a decline in the acreage under wheat since 1983. A part of this decline in area can be attributed to the emergence of a high-value cash crop, mentha.[19] In the latest round, wheat and mentha intercrops were popular combinations in the cropping portfolio of Palanpur farmers.[20]

Among *kharif* crops, the growth of paddy (*dhan*) has been remarkable. This was anticipated after the 1974/5 survey (see Bliss and Stern (1982)). The area under paddy has increased around tenfold from its 1957/8 level. This has been mainly due to improvements in irrigation. The accumulation of pumping sets, along with the emergence of tube wells, aided the expansion of the area under paddy, notwithstanding that the soil in Palanpur was not particularly

[19] While discussing the reasons behind the expansion of mentha in Palanpur, we show that, if properly managed, it does not necessarily compete for acreage with either wheat or sugar cane. However, when mono-cropped and at times when price expectations are high, mentha does compete with wheat for acreage. Subsequently, we examine the role of changes in output prices, input costs, and profitability in the observed crop choices by farmers.

[20] In earlier rounds, mono-cropped wheat accounted for 70% of *rabi* acreage, whereas intercrops such as wheat-gram (*gochani*) and wheat-barley (*gehun-jou*) accounted for about 12% of the area.

conducive to high productivity from paddy.[21] Paddy benefits from the government's price support.[22] Paddy is not only water-intensive but also labour-intensive, largely because of transplanting.

The third important crop in Palanpur is sugar cane. Sugar cane is a high-value annual crop. It is labour-intensive, has high water requirements, is responsive to fertilizers, and is not particularly suited to the mostly sandy soil in Palanpur. Bliss and Stern (1982: 115) conjectured that the most obvious explanation for sugar cane acreage not increasing further was that many farmers did not command the resources in terms of capital and labour to make a success of this crop. However, there was an expansion of the area under sugar cane since 1974/5 because of improvements in the availability of formal credit and the increasing prosperity of Muraos in the subsequent decade, in particular because of their greater private investment in farming. The Muraos and Thakurs continue to be the dominant sugar cane growers, given their larger plot sizes and greater accumulated capital among the cultivating groups in Palanpur. The presence of two sugar mills in the vicinity (Bilari and Akrauli), along with the emergence of procurement of the produce directly from the fields by traders, further helped the growth of sugar cane. Relationships with traders and the mill are important in selling cane, and established contacts are an advantage.

Between the 1993 and 2008/10 surveys, the only new crop introduced in Palanpur was mentha, or peppermint/mint (*Mentha arvensis*).[23] It is usually sown in February and harvested from mid-May onwards. It is a water-intensive crop and requires about 10–15 irrigations during the crop cycle.[24] Mentha was

---

[21] Loamy soil is good for paddy as well as wheat. It is rare in Palanpur. Locals call it 'domat mitti'. Among non-price factors, improvements in irrigation and availability of hybrid seed varieties such as CR Dhan-701 and Arize 6444, along with *desi* or indigenous Basmati varieties such as Basmati Sugandha, Sharbati, and Mota Rani Kajal, have played an important role in the propagation of paddy in Palanpur.

[22] Rice and wheat are the two food grains which are included in the Public Distribution System (PDS). These are also supported by procurement operations of the government. Around 2008/9, almost 30% of rice and wheat produced was procured for PDS distribution.

[23] Mentha oil, obtained by steam distillation of mentha leaves, is used as an industrial input in toothpastes, mouth fresheners, medicines, drinks, mouthwash, chewing gum, and confectionery products. Mint leaves are used in beverages, jellies, and syrups. Mentha oil is also a natural source of menthol, which is one of the most actively traded commodities in the chemical markets in India—India is the largest producer and exporter of processed mentha products in the world. Mentha is primarily exported in powder, liquid, or crystal forms to China, Latin America, and Europe. Mentha oil futures are also actively traded in derivatives exchanges such as MCX (Multi Commodity Exchange) and NCDEX (National Commodity and Derivatives Exchange). Uttar Pradesh is the leading producer of mentha in India, with about 80% of the total production (as per MCX data in 2009). Mentha is cultivated extensively in the Indo-Gangetic plains in Uttar Pradesh, Uttarakhand, Haryana, Punjab, and Bihar (Kumar et al., 2011). The town of Chandausi in Sambhal district, which is an important urban centre for Palanpur residents, is one of the most important markets for mentha oil globally.

[24] Mentha requires considerable moisture, well distributed throughout the growing season. As it is rhizomatous (roots spread in the soil and new plants can grow from parts of the roots), roots do not penetrate deep in the soil, so light and frequent irrigations are useful. The sowing of the mentha crop begins with the intermittent rainfall during the *rabi* (winter) season.

introduced in Palanpur in the mid-1990s. The popularity of mentha in Palanpur is no accident. There are several factors that have played a role in the
diffusion of this cash crop in the village: first, Palanpur's proximity to the
town of Chandausi—one of the most important markets for mentha oil
globally. Second, greater access to groundwater through private investment
in irrigation in the form of pumping sets and tube wells/bore wells made the
planting of crops with high water requirements, such as mentha, more attractive. Third, mentha oil extraction in the village required no or minimal transportation cost; the extraction plant, which is now available in the village itself,
is in the vicinity of the farms. Fourth, storage is not a problem: the final
marketable product, that is, the oil, can be stored in large cans and kept in
the house. Fifth, mentha is sown in late winter, usually around February, and
grows until summer. Though mentha is generally considered a summer crop,
the practice in Palanpur is to only cultivate it for about 4 months (until early
summer) rather than the whole cycle of 8–12 months; this practice is enabled
by good irrigation and more intensive techniques. Better management of
other crops also allowed the cultivators to accommodate mentha. Mentha is
seen as attractive as a joint crop (intercrop) along with wheat and sugar cane.
The flexibility of the sowing season of mentha and it being a summer crop
allows time for wheat and sugar cane to grow first and take root. Mentha root
is then planted by hand (as in paddy transplantation) following a normal crop
spacing. This practice has allowed farmers to cultivate the land more intensively. Lastly, monkeys were a big menace in 2008/9, and their presence
affected farmers' crop choices at times. However, monkeys as well as other
pests stay away from mentha plants as the strong smell is a deterrent of sorts.

In spite of its growing popularity and profitability, mentha carries substantial
risks. It is susceptible to changes in weather. High temperatures or excess rain can
lead to substantial crop damages. Its high water requirements also necessitate
timely and adequate irrigation. Apart from being water-intensive, mentha is also
a labour-intensive crop. Furthermore, there are post-harvest risks, such as high
moisture content before oil extraction and risk of theft and fire of the stored oil.

A further critical post-harvest risk in growing mentha is the price uncertainty
farmers have to deal with every season. Mentha has contributed to the further
integration of Palanpur with the outside world, and that has come with the
exposure of farmers to the vagaries of international prices. There is considerable
international fluctuation in demand and supply, and speculative trading is rife.
This causes marked fluctuation in the prices received by Palanpur farmers.[25]

---

[25] As a case in point, in the winter of 2015 the price of mentha oil dropped to Rs 700 per litre,
from Rs 1200 the year before. Even in 2014 and the two previous years there was high price
variability. For instance, mentha oil prices reached an average of Rs 2570 per litre in March 2012
following a supply crunch despite high global demand, but prices crashed to Rs 716.50 per litre in

In the course of the diffusion of mentha in Palanpur, there seemed to be a general pessimism in 2015, which is in stark contrast to the conditions prevailing in 2008–10. The low 2015 prices made mentha unprofitable. Sugar cane has proven, for Palanpur farmers, to be a better crop in this respect, with more reliable prices, in due part to state-administered pricing.

We have details of all the crops grown in each study year, but we confine our discussion to major crops for brevity. Nevertheless, it is worth mentioning some aspects of two crops in particular—potato (*aloo*) and fodder crops—as their acreage has been shaped by non-economic forces. Potato has experienced wide fluctuation in its acreage over the years. In the 2008/9 survey, we found that there were only two *bighas* of potato cultivation (by Hazarilal, a Passi cultivator). The minuscule acreage was largely because of the activities of monkeys. During subsequent fieldwork, we gathered that potato acreage increased in 2014/15 following the eviction of monkeys from the village.[26] Another factor that has resulted in the increase in potato cultivation in 2014/15 is the introduction of 'potato diggers' that have mechanized harvesting.

Amidst the ongoing changes in land-use patterns in Palanpur, there has been a considerable reduction in the area under fodder crops, such as *jowar* (sorghum hay used as dry fodder), *berseem* (gives both green and dry fodder), *agola* (from sugar cane harvest), and other harvested grasses. Two factors can explain this phenomenon. First, there has been an unprecedented decline in the importance of bullocks and male buffaloes in Palanpur; an aspect we will return to while discussing tractorization in Palanpur. However, there has been a marked increase in the number of female buffaloes and cows, associated with the growth of dairy activity in Palanpur.

Dairy income is an important component of household income. About half of the households in the village have some dairy income from selling milk and milk products. A large part of this income is from selling to two milkmen in the village who act as aggregators of the dairy produce of Palanpur. On average, a household in 2008/9 sold milk and dairy products worth Rs 100 per day. Second, there has been a conspicuous decline in the village commons, which used to serve as grazing land for the livestock, and in arable land available for fodder production. With geographical limits to the expansion of arable land and growing population pressure on land, farmers have

July 2014 (D'Souza, 2014). There was also significant intra-annual variability and uncertainty in prices, making mentha cultivation much less economically viable.

[26] The monkeys particularly affected sugar cane and potato cultivation. Although monkeys were mentioned in the earlier rounds, they were never as serious a problem as witnessed during the 2008/9 round. *Nilgai*, or blue bucks, were observed destroying crops such as *arhar* (a ten-month crop) and maize in earlier rounds, and farmers devoted a substantial amount of time to 'watching' their fields. Farmers also resorted to late sowing, knowing well that it had disadvantages. However, there were difficulties in sowing together as people did not want to be the first to sow and see their seeds destroyed by *nilgai* and birds.

increasingly used the available landholdings (which get subdivided over time) for more intensive crop cultivation. Historically, Palanpur has experienced episodes of falling fodder supply whenever paddy acreage increased. The current demand for fodder in the village is mostly met from the crop residues and top feeding of livestock from shrubs and plants.

5.3.2 Capital, Technological Intensification, and Input Markets

Changes in cropping pattern are the result of various factors. Notable among them is the availability of new technology in the form of HYV seeds. Increases in irrigation and mechanization have also played a key role in the increase in cropping intensity and adoption of new crops. Bliss and Stern (1982) documented the changes in the early rounds, such as increasing use of Persian wheels for irrigation and the emergence of diesel-powered pumping sets.[27] The role of technology was highlighted as a major driver of change in Lanjouw and Stern (1998). This trend has accelerated on some dimensions in recent years, particularly in irrigation and traction (tilling and ploughing) technology. The increasing use of tractors has displaced animal power. While the number of bullocks and male buffaloes has fallen sharply, there is a marked rise in the number of cows and female buffaloes. Threshing has also become mechanized. In 1983/4, there were three threshers in the village, which increased to five in 2008–10. Table 5.5 reports the ownership of important agricultural assets in Palanpur between 1957/8 and 2008/9.

The increase in the number of tractors in Palanpur since 1983/4 is remarkable: from just 1 in 1983/4 (owned by a Murao farmer) to 13 in 2008/9. While

Table 5.5 Ownership of productive assets in Palanpur, 1957/8 to 2008/9

Year	Bullock + Male Buffalo	Cow + Female Buffalo	Persian Wheel	Pumping Set	Tube Well	Bore Well	Plough	Tractor
1957/8	124	74	10	0	0	0	78	0
1962/3	140	83	20	0	0	0	78	0
1974/5	164	109	24	10	2	14	61	0
1983/4	141	119	28	27	3	45	74	1
2008/9	51	242	0	86	13	17	34	13

Note: A diesel pumping set would fit on top of a bore well, which usually had a 10 cm diameter vertical pipe. Tube wells would be electric, with a larger diameter.

[27] The role of land reforms in incentivizing private investment in irrigation in Palanpur has been documented in detail in Ansari (1964) and Bliss and Stern (1982). The technology of Persian wheels in particular saw greater diffusion following the land reforms that occurred in the 1950s as the incentive problems associated with tenants digging wells for irrigation purposes under the zamindari system were overcome (see Lanjouw and Stern, 1998: 135).

such increases indicate increasing capitalization and farm investment (by Muraos and Thakurs especially), a demand for tractors as a prestige good appears also to be present. It has been observed that farmers take pride in the make and power of their tractors, a trait that appears to be present in some farmers and car owners around the world. Another factor is the improvement in availability of formal credit for tractor purchases.[28] Access to repair services/ spare parts in the nearby towns of Chandausi and Bilari is now straightforward. And there has been an increase in demand for tractors for passenger and freight services in the village. By 2015, there were 26 tractors in the village. For a land area of around 400 acres, this number is remarkably high and suggests underutilization and inefficiency. It will be interesting to see how the situation develops. Tractors are not particularly suited for passenger services; as of 2017, auto-rickshaws now come to the village and, as we saw in Chapter 2, there has been a large increase in cycles and motorcycles.

As in the process of tractorization, the mechanization of irrigation has been driven by private investment. Diesel pumping set purchases have mostly been financed through formal credit institutions since 1983/4. In 2008/9, the dependence on credit for acquisition of tube wells and diesel engines or pumping sets was high. About 14 per cent and 13 per cent of non-food credit was reportedly taken for tube well and pumping set purchases, respectively.[29] The development of a rental market for water-lifting services has contributed to the demand for pumping sets.[30] A consequence of the intensification of pumping sets in Palanpur and nearby villages has been a fall in the groundwater table. Anecdotal evidence by the researchers suggests that in 1974/5, one could reach water by digging to a depth of 10 to 20 feet. In 2014/15, the water table has declined to 45–50 feet. The elders in the village also confirm this trend. This problem of groundwater depletion is further worsened by the presence of factories in the vicinity,[31] such as the sugar mill in Bilari and the paper mill (now defunct), which extracted groundwater in large volumes.[32]

---

[28] For instance, Ram Avtar, a Murao farmer, borrowed Rs 400,000 for tractor purchase from Punjab National Bank (PNB) in Chandausi, initially borrowing Rs 100,000 in 2008 and the remaining in 2009 by mortgaging a total of 35 *bighas* of land. There are other examples, such as another farmer, Ganga Sahai, who borrowed Rs 23,500 from PNB. However, not all loans are from formal institutions—a Murao farmer borrowed Rs 85,000 from a relative for tractor purchase. However, many instances of default on tractor loans have occurred.
[29] We discuss some aspects of the credit market and its impact on investment in agriculture in Chapter 6.
[30] Such was the demand for diesel pumping sets in the village that the pumping set of a Dhobi cultivator, Idey, was hired out for over two hundred hours by several farmers in a cropping season.
[31] And their effluent has polluted water courses.
[32] There has also been an increase in the planting of eucalyptus and poplar in the village and in the region, both water-intensive trees, given the growing demand for wood to be used in household construction and furniture.

Table 5.6 Labour-saving technology in ploughing: tractors vs bullocks (2008/9 prices)

	Labourers	Man Hours	Bullocks	Bullock Hours	Rental Cost per *Bigha* (Rs) without Labour	Rental Cost per *Bigha* with Labour
Tractor ploughing	1	1	0	0	70	83
Bullock ploughing	1	8	2	8	20	120

Table 5.7 Labour-saving technology in irrigation: pumping sets vs Persian wheels (2008/9 prices)

	Labourers	Man Hours	Bullocks	Bullock Hours	Rental Cost per Acre without Labour	Rental Cost per Acre with Labour
Pumping set	2	5	0	0	240	305
Persian wheel	2	30	2	30	110	460

Note: 1 man day = 8 hours; 1 bullock day = 8 hours. Family usually provides labour for irrigation: frequently the cultivator and a child. The rental cost for a pumping set includes supervision by pumping set owner and fuel costs. Calculations are for irrigation of one acre of land, which takes around one hour with a pumping set. Labour is priced at Rs 100 per day using 2008/9 rates or Rs 13 per hour. Occasionally in 1983/4 a child would drive the bullocks working a Persian wheel.

Mechanization of farm operations is not only labour-saving, but also has important general equilibrium effects in terms of other markets and activities. For instance, while tractors enabled faster completion of land preparation activities, thereby being labour displacing, they could also enable a reduction in fallow periods—potentially leading to an increase in overall labour usage. Reduced fallow periods and the discontinuation of the practice of leaving land fallow, as seen in Palanpur in recent years, are in conformity with the findings of Bhalla (2001), who makes similar observations while discussing the patterns of land-augmenting mechanization in western Uttar Pradesh.

The trend of farm mechanization in Palanpur has not only enabled more intensive double-cropping, but has also freed up labour for other purposes.[33] Tables 5.6 and 5.7 provide a comparison of labour requirements and the costs of tractors versus bullocks and pumping sets versus Persian wheels. We compare costs using 2008/9 prices and wages. For the tractor market rates for ploughing, we base the calculations on 2008/9 data, because in 1983/4 the market for tractor services was not well developed. For the Persian wheel and pumping set comparison, we base the calculations on Bliss and Stern (1982), because Persian wheels went out of use in the decade or so following the

---

[33] See Hanumantha Rao (1972) and Binswanger (1986) for the logic of farm mechanization and its consequence on labour allocation in developing economy agriculture.

1974/5 study. All prices are adjusted to 2008/9 prices. The purpose of these labour and cost calculations is to characterize the nature of technical progress in broad terms, rather than to offer precise cost accounting.

In 1983/4, in order to plough a *bigha* of land with a pair of bullocks and a harrow/till, a farmer would toil for eight hours. By using a tractor the farmer could accomplish the same task (double-way harrowing/tilling) in about an hour. The rental price for a pair of bullocks for ploughing and levelling was about Rs 6 per *bigha* in 1983/4 (Rs 20 at 2008/9 prices). In 2008/9, a tractor could harrow/till a *bigha* of land in an hour, costing Rs 70.[34] If we add labour costs at the prevailing 2008/9 price, for both tractor and bullock ploughing we find that the cost per acre of using a tractor is much less than for bullocks: Rs 83 versus Rs 120 (see Table 5.6). Further, tractor-based ploughing has the substantial advantage of speed in task completion, which allows much greater flexibility in double- and triple-cropping, for example for timely sowing.

Back in 1974/5, most of the land was irrigated; diesel-powered pumping sets were being used along with Persian wheels to lift the groundwater for irrigation. The rental cost for a Persian wheel was around Rs 2 per *bigha* in 1974/5 (Rs 13 per acre) equivalent per acre to around Rs 110 at 2008/9 prices. Pumping sets were used where a bore well was available near the field. It took approximately thirty hours to irrigate an acre (6.4 *bighas*) by Persian wheel drawn around by bullocks (Bliss and Stern, 1982: 112). The rental rate for pumping sets in 1974/5 was Rs 5.5 per hour, equivalent to Rs 48 in 2008/9 prices, including the fuel and supervision by the pumping set owner. An acre took about five hours to irrigate by pumping sets, thus this cost was around Rs 24 per acre. We see, in Table 5.7, that counting labour at Rs 100 per day at 2008/9 rates, the cost of irrigation by pumping set is, at Rs 305 per acre, much lower than it would be if a Persian wheel was used at Rs 460 per acre. And note that this comparison excludes any cost of the bullocks. It is clear why pumping sets quickly replaced Persian wheels, which largely went out of use in the 1980s. The pumping set saved large amounts of labour time.

In Palanpur, the labour-saving technological change associated with machinery was accompanied by land-augmenting technological change in the form of HYV seeds and chemical fertilizers. There has also been concomitant improvement in irrigation, which is also land-augmenting. It should be borne in mind that while tractors can be labour-saving in a specific agricultural operation, as demonstrated, they are also land-augmenting as they enable shorter periods between harvesting and sowing. However, their net effect on labour demand would depend on associated practices such as intercropping and the intensity of irrigation. If tractorization increases cropping

---

[34] This includes the cost of renting a tractor per *bigha* for a single two-way harrowing/tilling operation and the cost of fuel.

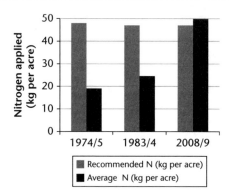

Figure 5.1 Recommended and actual nitrogen usage for wheat in Palanpur, 1974/5–2008/9

Source: The recommended level for 1974/5 is from Bliss and Stern (1982: 242). The source for other years is Government of India (2009).

intensity and crop productivity, the scaling-up of operations can be associated with greater labour utilization in agriculture at an aggregate level (Maggu 1982; Rao, 1972).[35]

As discussed at length in Bliss and Stern (1982), land-augmenting technologies such as HYV seeds and chemical fertilizers introduced during the green revolution period of the late 1960s and early 1970s were important elements of technical change in the village. In the first two surveys, fertilizer usage had not picked up in Palanpur, but it had increased by 1974/5, particularly for cultivation of HYV wheat varieties. Now fertilizer application is not only common practice, it has also intensified considerably.[36,37]

Figure 5.1 presents the change in the nitrogen application (kg per acre) in wheat production in Palanpur between 1974/5 and 2008/9 in comparison with the recommended levels. It is evident that there has been an increase in

[35] Agarwal (1984) separates farms by those which are tractor-hiring farms or bullock-hiring farms, as well as by ownership status, and shows that in Punjab agriculture, tractors have increased cropping intensity.

[36] Compared to the earlier rounds, there is more widespread use of synthetic fertilizers. For instance, in *rabi* 2008/9 season, the urea applied per *bigha* for mentha and sugar cane was 20.3 kg and 20.5 kg, respectively. Some fodder crops also had about 14 kg of urea followed by mustard and mentha, which had 8 kg and 9 kg per *bigha*, respectively. In terms of phosphatic fertilizers (DAP), wheat has the most intensive applications of about 7 kg per *bigha*, followed by mentha (5 kg per *bigha*), sugar cane (4.2 kg per *bigha*), and *masoor* (red lentils) (4 kg per *bigha*). Fodder and mustard have about 2.5 kg and 2.2 kg per *bigha*, respectively.

[37] Although the production and application of farmyard manure (FYM) has declined considerably, some farmers apply FYM to their sugar cane plots in particular. In earlier surveys, a thriving bullock economy contributed to the production of organic manure in the field. FYM was also considered as one of the most important factors in shaping tenancy arrangements in the village. For instance, if the landlord were dependent on the tenant for FYM, he would not be inclined to evict the tenant from a sharecropping arrangement. The duration of tenancy was also influenced by whether FYM was a part of the cost-sharing arrangement or not.

the intensity of nitrogen application, but only in the most recent round do we see the use of nitrogenous fertilizer for wheat approaching the recommended levels.[38] Nitrogen application is facilitated by the easy availability of subsidized urea through the Farmers' Service Society (FSS) in the village.[39] Ignorance about the appropriate NPK balance and how to match the soil quality with synthetic fertilizers is widespread.[40] In contrast to fertilizer usage, the application of pesticides, herbicides, and fungicides continues to be low, relative to recommended doses.[41] Pesticides are usually applied to paddy and sugar cane, if at all.

The average frequency of irrigation has gone up considerably. In *rabi* 2008/9, mentha averaged about ten irrigations,[42] and sugar cane five, wheat five, and potato six. Twelve irrigations in mentha cultivation were also common. Note that when mentha is jointly cropped with wheat, there are five irrigations along with wheat and seven after the harvesting of the latter. Fodder also involved high irrigation: about eight times on an average, while potato involved six. Analysis of the diary data of 58 households over the four seasons of 2008/10 supports the general observation of frequent and more intensive irrigation compared to 1983/4. Analysis of the cost of cultivation, presented in Section 5.4, also confirms the growing share of irrigation expenses in total cost of cultivation between 1983/4 and 2008/9. This is a picture of agriculture growing in intensity via cropping frequency, crop variety, mechanization and use of water, and so on.

The absence of functioning extension services in the village implies that most farmers learn about improved agricultural practices and modern agricultural technologies from other local farmers. In the 2008/9 survey, based on observed farm practices and a perception of villagers whose farming practices can be considered 'good', we identified 28 farmers who could be considered 'progressive' in the sense that they carry out 'good' farm practices.[43] Sixteen of the 28 progressive farmers are Muraos, 6 are Thakurs, 5 are Jatabs, 2 are

---

[38] Given the recommended levels of about 15 kg of urea per *bigha*, analysis of the wheat plots in 1983/4 *rabi* season reveals that the average dosage was approximately 8 kg, a little more than half of the recommended dosage. Three decades back, reliance on phosphatic and potassic fertilizers was also low. For instance, in the *rabi* of 1983/4, only one Murao farmer (Amar Singh) reported applying nitrogen, phosphorus, and potassium (NPK) fertilizers as basal fertilizer while sowing wheat in three *bighas* of land.

[39] The FSS is the local credit cooperative with an office in Palanpur. The FSS disburses fertilizers on credit, as well as cash credit, to members.

[40] Nitrogen (N), phosphorus (P), and potassium (K).

[41] Pest attacks continue to be low so crops are generally treated only when there is an attack.

[42] Ten to 15 irrigations in mentha were also not uncommon.

[43] There are no standard practices which qualify as 'good' farm practices. The information is based on a qualitative survey conducted among all farmers where they were asked to identify farmers with 'good' farm practices and also what may constitute 'good' farming practices. These included appropriate use of irrigation, good-quality seeds, fertilizer use based on soil quality and crops, and cropping pattern.

Gadariyas, 1 is Dhobi, and 1 is Teli. Notwithstanding the growing intensity and greater crop varieties, knowledge, skills, and talents in farming remain very varied.

5.3.3 Labour

One of the consequences of increasing mechanization has been the release of labour, in the sense of a reduction of labour per *bigha*. Table 5.8 presents a comparison of labour days per *bigha* in 1983/4 and 2008/9, confining our discussion to the *rabi* season. There has been a decrease in family labour days as well as hired labour days per *bigha*, the decline being higher for the former.

Changes in cropping patterns, farm mechanization, and agricultural wages jointly determine the labour utilization changes in Palanpur. For example, between 1983/4 and 2008/9, acreage under paddy, a labour-intensive crop, has more than doubled. Table 5.8 clearly shows a substantial reduction in labour per *bigha*.

Alongside changes in land ownership, tenancy, and mechanization, changes in labour market behaviour have also shaped the decisions of households regarding their involvement in agriculture. Prominent among the changes in the labour market has been a consolidation of the trend towards non-farm employment opportunities inside, as well as outside, the village. We discuss some of these changes further in Chapter 7. But from the perspective of the agricultural labour market, two things stand out. First, the category of agricultural labourer as a primary occupation has more or less disappeared from the village. While there were 17 households with primary involvement in agricultural labour in 1983/4, there are only 2 households that could be treated as agricultural labour households in 2008/9. Second, the availability of employment opportunities outside Palanpur, as self-employment and casual work, has reduced the dependence of casual labour households on agricultural work and has thereby contributed to a tightening of the labour market in agriculture. This second factor has been influenced not only by the increase in the number of landless casual labour households who have moved away from agriculture, but also by those who have regular employment and for whom dependence on agriculture is now a secondary choice.

Table 5.8 Average labour person days, per *bigha* in Palanpur, 1983/4 and 2008/9 (*rabi* only)

Year	Gross Cropped Area (in *Bigha*)	Family Labour Days (per *Bigha*)	Hired Labour Days (per *Bigha*)	Total Labour Days (per *Bigha*)
1983/4	3881.04	1.19	0.41	1.60
2008/9	4679.70	0.74	0.19	0.94

Along with the availability of public employment opportunities such as Mahatma Gandhi National Rural Employment Guarantee Act (MGNREGA), all this has meant that finding hired labour in agriculture is not as easy as it used to be. A related consequence of this has been a strengthening of the tendency towards exchange labour and tenancy to circumvent labour shortages. The increase in share of *chauthai* contracts (where a worker gets a quarter-share in the harvest) has partly been a response to labour shortages and rising wages in agriculture.

Overall, the tightening of the labour market has been striking over a period of substantial population growth. It is illustrated by labour days per acre in Table 5.8 and is further illustrated in Figure 5.2, which shows the land/worker ratio rising from 1993 (where 'worker' refers to a person engaged in agriculture, aged above fifteen).

As we shall see in Chapter 7 on non-farm diversification, between 1974/5 and 1983/4 the number of cultivators (primary occupation) increased from 144 to 152, with the number of agricultural labourers increasing from 7 to 11. This further increased considerably to 188 cultivators and 17 agricultural labourers, totalling 205 agricultural workers in 1993. Between 1992/3 and 2008/9, there was an absolute fall in the number of agricultural workers, with the number of cultivators falling to 134 and agricultural labourers falling to 6.[44] Thus the falling trend in land per worker associated with population growth continued for three and a half decades from 1957, but reversed in the early 1990s. The demand for non-farm work rose and was accommodated by the mechanization which released labour from cultivation. We speculate that this upward trend in the land–labour ratio will now continue, as has been the case in the period 2009–2015.

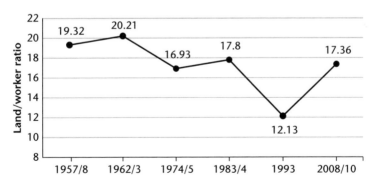

Figure 5.2 Land worker ratio (per *bigha*) in Palanpur

---

[44] In 2014/15, the number of agricultural workers fell further to 117: 113 cultivators and 4 agricultural labourers.

5.3.4 Productivity, Outputs, and Prices

In the preceding sections we described the changing nature of agricultural production. Increasing mechanization, the use of HYV seeds, and the spread of irrigation have not only contributed to the increase in cropping intensity, but also to improvements in yields for individual crops. Table 5.9 gives the change in yield (quintals of output per *bigha*[45]) of major crops over the survey years.[46]

Table 5.9 Yields (quintals per *bigha*) of major crops in Palanpur, 1957/8 to 2008/9

Year	Major Crop			
	Wheat	Paddy	*Bajra*	Sugar Cane
1957/8	0.37	0.14	0.38	11.46
1962/3	0.39	0.31	0.33	13.86
1974/5	1.40	0.93	0.50	15.33
1983/4	1.01	1.30	0.48	12.30
2008/9	2.90	1.90	0.95	24.70

There has been a general rise in productivity measured in terms of crop yields per *bigha*. Between 1957/8 and 2008/9, wheat yields have grown by about five times, while those for paddy have grown by nine times.[47] These increases, though striking, are not surprising given the introduction of HYV seeds and improved varieties following the green revolution, together with greater amounts of water and fertilizer. Moreover, 1983 was a particularly bad year and the outputs of most farmers were much lower than normal, making the rise between 1983/4 and 2008/9 more pronounced. In 1983/4, although the average wheat yield was depressed due to poor rainfall, the total wheat output was higher than in 1974/5 because of a significant expansion in the area under wheat.[48]

At the all-India level, there has been a spectacular growth in the yield of wheat during the same period. However, the relatively lower yield of wheat in Uttar Pradesh is a national concern. This becomes even more pertinent,

---

[45] A quintal is equal to 100 metric kilograms.

[46] We calculate yield by dividing physical quantity of output produced measured in quintals by the area of the crop cultivated. Throughout this chapter, yield implies quantity of output per *bigha* of land, expressed in quintals per *bigha* unless otherwise stated.

[47] See Lanjouw and Stern (1998: 285) for the performance of wheat in Palanpur in the early part of the study period.

[48] The central government announced the minimum support prices (MSP) for wheat in 1966/7. It is the price at which the government procures the produce and sets the floor for crop prices. Twenty-five crops are covered under the scheme. Since 1997/8, after the introduction of the Targeted Public Distribution System (TPDS), procurement based on MSP has only been provided for Common and Grade A paddy and wheat.

indeed of international concern, given the fact that India is second only to China in wheat production (FAOSTAT, 2013), and Uttar Pradesh has the highest area under wheat amongst India's states as well as the highest production. Productivity in Uttar Pradesh is much lower than Punjab and Haryana (Government of India, 2013).[49] The productivity growth in paddy has also been marked. In 2008/9, the state average was 21.71 quintal per hectare or 1.37 quintal per *bigha*. The corresponding figure for Moradabad division was 22.18 quintal per hectare, that is, roughly 1.39 quintals per *bigha*. Therefore, Palanpur has performed better than average for the district as well as the state in paddy productivity.[50]

Interestingly, *bajra* (pearl millet) yield has grown, notwithstanding a decline in its share, albeit slower than paddy and wheat. The increase in sugar cane yields is approximately two and half times over the whole period. As mentioned, the *kharif* of 1983 and *rabi* of 1983/4 had poor output due to average rainfall being much below normal, which explains the dip in the series for the year as well as making the subsequent rise more prominent.

The impressive rise in productivity of rice and wheat across the country has also led to a decline in prices in real terms for both these crops. Table 5.10 provides the prices of major crops grown in Palanpur over survey years. The decline started immediately after the green revolution and continued until the 1980s. While it has increased marginally in the case of rice and wheat, real prices are lower than corresponding prices in the 1970s. The increase in output following the green revolution was spectacular, changing India's food economy, from the country being a food importer to enjoying a situation

Table 5.10 Prices (in Rs per quintal) of major crops in Palanpur, 1957/8 to 2008/10

Year	Nominal				Real			
	Wheat	Paddy	*Bajra*	Sugar Cane	Wheat	Paddy	*Bajra*	Sugar Cane
1957/8	46.7	55.6	28.6	3.6	1444.7	1719.7	884.7	112.7
1962/3	53.5	42.5	37.8	3.9	1809.1	1438	1279	129.2
1974/5	130	120	130	8.5	1139.8	1050.4	1139.8	72.9
1983/4	135	137	125	14.5	848.2	858.2	785.3	89.5
2008/9	987.5	1092.9	540.1	124.1	987.5	1092.9	540.1	124.1

Note: (1) 1974 prices are based on prevailing market price and not the average price in the Palanpur data, as there are considerable missing data.
(2) Real prices are in 2008/9 rupees deflated by the Consumer Price Index for Agricultural Labourers (CPIAL).

[49] The yield of wheat in 2008/9 was 3.002 tonnes per hectare compared to Punjab (4.462), Haryana (4.390), India as a whole (2.907), China (4.762), and the world (3.086).
[50] In recent years, the average paddy yields for Uttar Pradesh in 2007, 2008, and 2009 were 1.30 quintal per *bigha*, 1.4 quintal per *bigha*, and 1.3 quintal per *bigha*, respectively. The lower yield in 2009 was due to severe drought.

of self-sufficiency by the early 1970s.[51] While the increase in production of rice and wheat certainly contributed to the decline in prices of these staple cereals, it was also helped by the expansion of the PDS, which included rice and wheat as its only cereals. However, the demand for rice and wheat for public procurement for the expanded PDS also led to generous increases in the MSP, which protected the real income of farmers.[52] To a certain extent, the focus of the MSP and PDS on rice and wheat has also contributed to an increase in area cultivated for these crops. Unlike rice and wheat, *bajra* has seen a relative decline in prices. Like most of India, *bajra* prices have suffered due to changing tastes and preferences, away from coarse grains towards finer grains.

The only crop which has not seen a decline in real prices is sugar cane. While there have been annual fluctuations, the trend has been one of stable real prices. It has seen a secular rise in recent years, partly because of the demand from the PDS, where sugar continues to be one of the commodities, but also because of organized action by farmers, who have agitated to get higher prices from the government.

5.4 Costs, Income, and Profits

5.4.1 *Output and Income*

Increases in productivity have not led to a corresponding increase in cultivation incomes. Cultivation incomes have grown more slowly in real terms than the growth of the real value of output (see the first two rows of Table 5.11). While price factors (see Table 5.12 on real price falls) explain a large part of the changing structure of costs and profits in cultivation, an important contributor has been the increase in farm costs. As the economy has become more monetized, the intensity of purchased inputs and cash-based transactions in agricultural inputs has gone up. The 2008/10 survey collected detailed information on cultivation practices along with details on inputs and outputs.

Our multivariate regression analysis across households suggests positive and significant returns to land owned, number of adult members in the household, and farm capital in the form of pumping sets for irrigation.[53]

---

[51] Food-grain production increased from 95 million tonnes in 1967/8 to 131 million tonnes in 1978/9, and increased further to 176 million tonnes by 1990/1. Per capita food grain availability increased from 409 grams per day in 1966 to 510 grams per day in 1991. Net food imports fell from 10.3 million tonnes in 1966 to 3.6 million in 1970.

[52] The MSP for wheat increased from 700 per quintal in 2006/7 to 1170 per quintal in 2011/12. Paddy MSP increased during the same period from 650 per quintal to 1110 per quintal. MSP of wheat at Rs 1000 per quintal in 2008/9 was higher than prevailing prices in Palanpur, whereas paddy MSP for 2008/9, at 930, was lower than prevailing market prices.

[53] Regression results are not reported in this chapter but are available in the Palanpur working papers. See http://sticerd.lse.ac.uk/india/research/palanpur/publications.asp.

In addition, our analysis of the determinants of cultivation income reveals that returns to land have increased remarkably during the study period. Pumping sets play a significant role in enhancing cultivation incomes. In terms of the role of caste affiliation, we find that in spite of a marked reduction in the share of agricultural income in total income for Muraos, they have significantly higher average real gross value of output per *bigha* as well as cultivation incomes compared to other groups in Palanpur. For the analysis of cost of cultivation as well as cultivation incomes, we confine our analysis to cultivating households. By cultivating households, we mean households that cultivated positive amounts of land in the reference survey years. Table 5.11 reports the summary statistics of some key variables used in our analysis.

Table 5.11 Summary statistics: households with cultivation incomes, 1957/8 to 2008/9

Mean per household	1957/8	1962/3	1974/5	1983/4	2008/9
Gross value of output (at 2008/9 prices)	21,628	23,475	49,529	46,400	40,873
Cultivation income (at 2008/9 prices)	21,009	20,756	42,174	39,659	28,040
Land cultivated (*bighas*)	34.26	29.02	26.08	26.20	12.09
Gross value of output per *bigha* (at 2008/9 prices)	631	809	1899	1771	3381
Cultivation income per *bigha* (at 2008/9 prices)	613	715	1617	1514	2319
Paid-out cost/value of output (per *bigha*) (%)	2.83	11.59	14.85	14.53	31.39
Number of adults in household	3.05	3.16	3.51	3.60	2.93
Value of livestock (at 2008/9 prices)	10,229	12,218	15,218	6350	13,158
No. of observations (households with cultivation information)	85	96	93	102	183

Note: The figures are averages for cultivation households and not the full population. CPIAL for Uttar Pradesh, with 2008/9 as the base year, is used for the calculation of real values.

Interestingly, while the average (per household) real value of output at 2008/9 prices has increased considerably over the full period, we find a decline in both the average real value of output and the average real cultivation income (the difference between real gross value of output and real paid-out costs) after 1983/4 (which, if we adjusted for the poor harvest that year, would likely have been higher than 1974/5). In both cases this is associated with a sharp decline in *bighas* per household as a result of household splitting (see Chapter 2), population increase between 1983/4 and 2008/9, and some land sales. The sharper drop in the latter suggests that real costs of cultivation have outstripped the growth of value of agricultural output between 1983/4 and 2008/9. This is largely because of the increasing cost of cultivation associated with greater farm mechanization, intensive irrigation, rising labour costs, and costlier purchased inputs, such as fertilizers.

There has been a marked growth in the real value of output per *bigha* of land, although real cultivation income per *bigha* has grown less quickly. Figure 5.3 shows the trend in real value of output per *bigha* and real cultivation

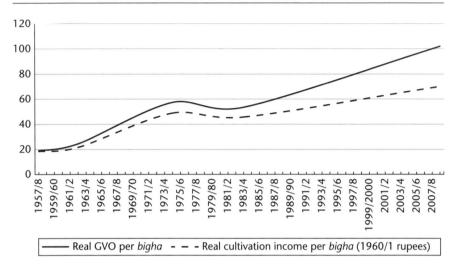

Real GVO per *bigha* - - - Real cultivation income per *bigha* (1960/1 rupees)

Figure 5.3 Real gross value of output and real cultivation income per *bigha* (at 1960/1 prices) in Palanpur, 1957/8–2008/9

Note: Cultivation income is the value of output less the purchased inputs, not including imputed values of machinery and family labour. This is comparable to cultivation cost A1 as per Commission for Agricultural Costs and Prices (CACP) classification, that is, all actual expenses in cash and kind incurred in production by the owner operator.

income per *bigha*. The two are close in 1957/8 and 1962/3, but subsequently diverge.[54] The share of paid-out cost was negligible in the early decades, but grew to reach 15 per cent by 1974 and 1983. Between 1983 and 2008/9 it almost doubled to 31.4 per cent.

However, with land cultivated per cultivating household declining during the survey period, real income per household from cultivation has increased only modestly between 1957/8 and 2008/9. While real income per *bigha* from cultivation increased by a factor of almost four, real income from cultivation per cultivating household increased by around one third. The most recent period, between 1983 and 2008/9, has seen real cultivation income per household decline by one third even though cultivation income increased by over 50 per cent. Slow growth of cultivation income since 1983 was associated with a decline in the share of agricultural income in household income.

The shift to non-farm employment and income sources has been associated with a search for new sources of income to supplement falling per capita or per household cultivation incomes. By 2008/9, most cultivating households,

---

[54] In earlier work (Lanjouw and Stern, 1998), there have been comparisons by taking averages from pairing the first two rounds and the next two rounds, as fluctuations in harvest quality were alternating. The 1957/8 period was a good one, but 1962/3 was below normal. While 1974/5 was good, 1983/4 was a drought year. The year 2008/9 was a normal year.

including the Muraos, undertake some non-farm activities along with agricultural activities.[55]

5.4.2 Cost of Cultivation over Survey Years

Table 5.12 gives a breakdown of various inputs and the real cost per *bigha* for the survey rounds. While there has been a rise in all cost components, particularly significant are the increases in real per *bigha* costs of irrigation, fertilizer, and hired labour; the increases in seed costs per *bigha* have been modest in comparison. The increase in the cost of inputs has been driven by both the rise in their prices as well as an increase in the intensity of their application. This is particularly true for increases in fertilizer application, as noted in Section 5.3.2. The increase in the cost of fertilizer has largely been a result of greater intensity of application rather than rise in per unit prices in real terms. Since fertilizer prices are administered and have been subsidized, any nominal price increases since 1983 have been modest. Indeed, this period has seen considerable reduction in real average fertilizer prices, particularly of nitrogenous fertilizers such as urea because of growing fertilizer subsidies (Gulati and Narayanan, 2003). While there have been attempts at rationalizing the fertilizer subsidy since the late 1990s, urea has largely remained unaffected, with its price continuing to be controlled.[56,57] The fertilizer subsidy had been introduced in the 1960s to introduce farmers to more 'modern' agricultural

Table 5.12 Real per *bigha* costs (per year, 2008/9 prices)

Year	Seed	Hired Labour	Irrigation	Fertilizer
1957/8	3.31	23.19	3.31	0.00
1962/3	86.14	33.13	16.57	9.94
1974/5	115.96	46.38	72.89	46.38
1983/4	235.24	96.08	212.04	271.68
2008/9	185.54	198.79	410.84	294.87

[55] The share of non-farm incomes in total income for Muraos, the traditional cultivating caste, is much lower than that of other caste groups.

[56] A nutrient-based subsidy regime was started in 2010. However, this affected only the complex fertilizers. Currently, the fertilizer subsidy is the second-largest component of government subsidy after food subsidy.

[57] Urea is sold at a statutory notified uniform sale price, while decontrolled fertilizers are sold at indicative maximum retail prices (MRPs). The New Pricing Scheme for urea units and the concession scheme for decontrolled phosphatic and potassic fertilizers since 2003 aims at incentivizing the fertilizer industry. The subsidies for institutionally determined prices are usually lower than the cost of production of a manufacturing unit. The subsidy to manufacturers is the difference between the cost of production and the selling price/MRP.

techniques. But the politics of phasing it out remains intense, and successive governments have failed to do so over the ensuing half-century.

The largest component of cost has been for irrigation, and this has also seen the highest increase. The growing costs are largely due to the increasing use of pumping sets, on the one hand, and more frequent irrigation, on the other.[58] Changes in cropping pattern have also played a role in raising irrigation costs per *bigha* of land. For example, the cultivation of mentha and paddy require particularly high irrigation, as noted. The substantial increase in hired labour costs per *bigha* can be attributed to growing real agricultural wages. Notwithstanding greater farm mechanization, such as increasing use of tractors for harrowing and tilling, hired labour is in high demand for transplanting paddy, fertilizer application, and harvesting operations. Harvesting in Palanpur continues to be manual, while all threshing is now fully mechanized.

Table 5.13 gives the share of paid inputs in the paid-out cost for each year. The general increase in the share of irrigation and fertilizer is evident. Hired labour has registered over a fourfold decline in its share. Recall that during this period there was a steep increase in agricultural wages and that average per *bigha* labour costs have risen sharply.[59] This reflects the impact of farm mechanization: more intensive irrigation using pumping sets, on the one hand, and reliance on tractors for ploughing, on the other.

Table 5.13 Share of inputs in cost of cultivation (%)

Year	Seed	Hired Labour	Irrigation	Fertilizer
1957/8	11.1	77.8	11.1	0.0
1962/3	59.1	22.7	11.4	6.8
1974/5	41.2	16.5	25.9	16.5
1983/4	28.9	11.8	26.0	33.3
2008/9	17.0	18.2	37.7	27.1

Note: Shares are percentage share of total cost comprising seed, hired labour, irrigation, and fertilizer. They add up to 100%.

5.4.3 Cost of Cultivation per Bigha for Major Crops

In the 2008/9 survey, we have rich data on quantity used and costs incurred on different agricultural inputs in the *kharif* and *rabi* seasons, which enable us to examine the agricultural production process in detail. Table 5.14 presents

---

[58] Electricity for agricultural operations is also heavily subsidized, apart from the diesel subsidies and cheap private irrigation equipment such as pumping sets and piping systems.
[59] On rising real wages, see Chapter 3.

Table 5.14 Input cost (Rs per *bigha*) for major crops, 2008/9

Crop	Paddy	Wheat	Mentha	Bajra	Sugar Cane
Seed	52.7	141.82	145.98	27.03	393.62
Fertilizer	192.3	217.23	242.02	21.82	148.46
Pesticide	15.86	7.6	0.66	0	2.38
Hired labour	267.47	56.1	174.33	49.36	105.91
Family labour	400	725	207.09	268.55	475
Hired tractor (harrowing)	32.42	29.33	26.41	35.64	14.21
Hired tractor (tilling)	19.07	22.12	19.79	25.21	9.41
Own tractor (harrowing)	2.19	3.48	2.81	1.43	67.86
Own tractor (tilling)	1.9	2.88	1.98	0.55	51.03
Diesel (harrowing)	31.18	27.65	24.64	33.15	17.1
Diesel (tilling)	24.21	26.81	23.68	29.89	15.28
Irrigation	341.59	234.27	546.82	9.25	627.67

Note: Costs reported adjusted for joint cropping and joint cultivation.

the per *bigha* costs (in rupees) of major crops in the *kharif* 2008 and *rabi* 2008/9 agricultural seasons. The high irrigation intensity of sugar cane, mentha, and paddy, along with that of wheat, is evident. Hired labour is most intensively used in paddy, which is particularly associated with the high labour requirements in transplanting activity. This is followed by mentha, which is also labour-intensive, particularly because of the high frequency of irrigation, as discussed earlier in this chapter. In contrast, there is high family labour utilization in the production of wheat. Family labour utilization in paddy and sugar cane are similar. While wheat and mentha have high fertilizer consumption, paddy has the highest pesticides/insecticides expenses in an environment where the overall use of pesticides/insecticides continues to be low. Insecticides are also applied to sugar cane when the pest pressure is high and farmers anticipate losses due to insect pests in a season.

In Palanpur, reliance on the outside market for sugar cane seeds is high. This reflects the high seed costs per *bigha* for sugar cane. Moreover, the sugar cane costs in our analysis include costs spread over different generations of sugar cane, as it is an annual commercial crop.[60] This distinguishes its seed costs from that of other crops; farmers often use home-grown seeds or roots (for mentha). As mentioned, dependence on the seed store for seeds has fallen strongly. With the failure of the seed store and greater integration of the village with outside markets, farmers are exposed to new and costlier seed varieties sold by merchants in nearby towns.

---

[60] Sugar cane is an annual crop. The crop, once harvested, regenerates and can be used for two to three harvests, with one harvest every year. The ratoon, or second-/third-generation sugar cane, is also called *pedi/tipedi* colloquially.

5.5 Conclusions: Agriculture in the Changing Palanpur Economy

Agriculture is the starting point of our analysis of changes in the economy of Palanpur. While agriculture now contributes much less as a proportion of the village economy than in the previous decades, it still plays a role in defining economic outcomes, such as growth and income distribution. Like most of the villages in India and in developing countries, Palanpur is going through a process of structural transformation. Such a process, accompanied by productivity increase in agriculture, is a natural change for poor societies whose economic activity was dominated by agriculture.[61] While agriculture has continued to show dynamism in the last two decades, the process of structural change in the village has also been driven by factors outside the village. In particular, the growth of non-farm activities in the village and outside has transformed the village labour and land markets and profoundly influenced the way agriculture is organized.

While agriculture in Palanpur continues to see further intensification of earlier trends of mechanization, greater input use, increasing cropping intensity, a move towards cash crops, and a decline in sharecropping, these have not been enough to counter the trend of declining per household income from cultivation in recent decades as the population has grown and households have divided. This has happened despite productivity per unit of land increasing for all crops. In terms of per capita income and per worker income, agriculture does not provide the same kind of income security or opportunities for growth that existed earlier. The demand for non-farm employment and income is a natural consequence in such a situation.

Alongside developments in the land and labour markets, there have also been new developments in other agricultural markets, notably the monetization of a significant portion of input costs, such as irrigation, harvesting, and threshing. There is now a growing market for the services of tractors and bore wells. Although there is no evidence of these markets exhibiting formal interlinkages, the increased monetization of input costs has meant that availability of cash is an increasingly important determinant of a household's ability to undertake cultivation.

The changes in agriculture have been driven not only by technological changes, but also by social and cultural factors. The impact of these changes

---

[61] Agricultural productivity growth through technical progress is central to the structural transformation process for two fundamental reasons. First, as household incomes grow, the share of food in the budget declines and that of non-food items (industrial goods and services) increases. This is a well-known empirical finding (Engel's law); the income elasticity of demand for food being less than unity. Analysis of consumption data in Palanpur available for first two rounds and the 2008/9 round confirms this. Second, when agricultural productivity reaches a high enough level, it releases labour and other resources for non-farm pursuits—activities that enable households to earn additional income.

has not been felt in the same way for all classes and caste groups in the village. While Thakurs have always enjoyed a higher status in the village, thanks to their larger landholdings, the Muraos, as the traditional cultivating group, committed earlier to the green revolution technologies and methods and were the biggest beneficiary of the growth of agricultural productivity. The attitude of Muraos is in contrast to the Thakurs. Aversion to manual labour has also meant that the Thakurs were the first major group to move out of agriculture, a trend that was already noticeable in the 1980s. On the other hand, in more recent decades, Muraos have (relatively) stayed put in agriculture and have been slow to recognize the opportunities that the non-farm sector offers. This has less to do with their aversion to manual labour or lack of capital and more to do with their cultural affinity to agriculture. While this trend has been changing gradually, they are still the caste group with the highest share of income from agriculture.

Some amongst the Jatabs and the Muslim groups have found the new form of agriculture difficult to manage. Increasing costs of cultivation due to monetization of input costs have put some of them at a disadvantage in the tenancy market. Others, however, are enabled by new income sources to participate in tenancy where they could not before.

Non-farm manual employment, which is often heavy and difficult, does have the attraction of greater freedom to choose one's employer and the nature of work, unlike agriculture within the village. It certainly has helped socially lower-ranked groups increase their incomes through a higher number of days of employment available outside of agriculture. And it has also helped push wages in the village higher and closer to the urban areas. For further discussion see Chapters 7 and 11.

The move of labour away from agriculture has also seen greater participation of women in agricultural occupations within the household boundary, but also occasionally outside. It is too early to argue that this process has led or will lead to fundamental change in the way the female labour market, which barely exists, works or will work in the village, but the trend is similar to the trend of feminization of agriculture seen elsewhere in the country. This appears to be emerging first amongst the Muraos.

We have described the evolution of markets for various inputs, including for water and traction. The availability of large numbers of pumping sets and tractors has created a market for water which was not there in earlier years. But it is the tractors particularly which are now contributing to non-farm employment as demand for freight increases in and around the village. It has also created a small market for repair services in Palanpur.

The emergence of the non-farm sector as the primary engine of growth does raise questions around the role of agriculture in future changes in the village economy. Capital investment will likely play an important and continuing role in increasing labour productivity and in releasing labour to non-farm activities. However, the current number of machines, together with the cropping intensity, may leave only limited opportunities for further growth in agriculture based simply on input intensity and increase in gross cropped area. Further growth in productivity may now depend on the availability of new seeds and new techniques of production. As always, in any activity or profession, the skills, talents, and commitment of cultivators show great variation, and there is real scope for productivity increase through catch-up of worse towards better. At the same time, we should note that these smallholdings likely preclude the kind of very small labour–land ratios we see in the very highly mechanized agriculture of many countries.

What is not in doubt is that agriculture will continue to play a strong role in the lives and livelihoods of the people of Palanpur.

Acknowledgements

This chapter has been written by Himanshu and Sarthak Gaurav and draws on earlier work: Tyagi and Himanshu (2011) and Himanshu and Stern (2016). We acknowledge the contribution of Ashish Tyagi, Vaishnavi Surendra, Tushar Bharti, and Japneet Kaur in the analysis and writing of the chapter.

References

Agarwal, B. 1984. 'Tractors, tube wells and cropping intensity in the Indian Punjab', *Journal of Development Studies* 20: 290–302.

Ansari, N. 1964. 'Palanpur: A Study of its Economic Resources and Economic Activities', Continuous Village Survey 41. Agricultural Economics Research Centre, University of Delhi.

Bhalla, S. 2001. 'Trends in employment in Indian agriculture, land and asset distribution', in K.S. Dhindsa and Anju Sharma (eds), *Dynamics of Agricultural Development*, vol. 1: *Land Reforms, Growth and Equity*. New Delhi: Concept.

Bharadwaj, K. 1974. 'Notes on farm size and productivity', *Economic & Political Weekly* 9: A11–A24.

Binswanger, H. 1986. 'Agricultural mechanization: a comparative historical perspective', *World Bank Research Observer* 1: 27–56.

Binswanger-Mkhize, H.P., and d'Souza, A. 2012. 'Structural transformation of the Indian economy and of its agriculture', in K.O. Fuglie, S.L. Wang, and E. Ball (eds), *Productivity Growth in Agriculture: An International Perspective*. Oxford: CABI Publishing.

Bliss, C.J., and Stern, N.H. 1982. *Palanpur: The Economy of an Indian Village*, 1 edn. Oxford and New York: Oxford University Press.

D'Souza, S. 2014. 'Mentha oil production to decline 20% on lower acreage', *Business Standard*, 4 September.

FAOSTAT. 2013. Food and Agriculture Organization of the United Nations Database, http://www.fao.org/faostat/en/#data (accessed 13 March 2018).

Government of India. 2009. 'Agricultural statistics at a glance', Ministry of Agriculture, New Delhi.

Government of India. 2013. 'Agricultural statistics at a glance', Ministry of Agriculture, New Delhi.

Gulati, A., and Narayanan, S. 2003. *The Subsidy Syndrome in Indian Agriculture*. New Delhi: Oxford University Press.

Himanshu, and Stern, N.H. 2016. 2. 'How Lives Change: Six Decades in a North Indian Village', in Himanshu, P. Jha, and G. Rodgers (eds), *The Changing Village in India: Insights from Longitudinal Research*. Delhi: Oxford University Press.

Kumar, S., Suresh, R., Singh, V., and Singh, A.K. 2011. 'Economic analysis of menthol mint cultivation in Uttar Pradesh: a case study of Barabanki district', *Agricultural Economics Research Review* 24: 345–50.

Lanjouw, P., and Stern, N.H. 1998. *Economic Development in Palanpur over Five Decades*. New York and Oxford: Clarendon Press.

Maggu, A. 1982. 'Tractorization in India: dispelling some myths', *Vikalpa* 7: 45–52.

Patnaik, U. 1990. *Agrarian Relations and Accumulation: The 'Mode of Production' Debate in India*. Bombay: Published for Sameeksha Trust by Oxford University Press.

Rao, C.H. 1972. 'Farm mechanisation in a labour-abundant economy', *Economic & Political Weekly* 7: 393–400.

Rodgers, G., and Rodgers, J. 2001. 'A leap across time: when semi-feudalism met the market in rural Purnia', *Economic & Political Weekly* 36: 1976–83.

Sen, A. 1981. 'Market failure and control of labour power: towards an explanation of "structure" and change in Indian agriculture. Part 1', *Cambridge Journal of Economics* 5, no. 3: 201–28.

Tyagi, A., and Himanshu. 2011. 'Change and continuity: agriculture in Palanpur', ARC Working paper number 48, London School of Economics and Political Science.

6

Tenancy in Palanpur*

6.1 Introduction

Land sales in agricultural communities are usually rare. They generally involve loss of social position, of security, and of collateral for credit. Transaction costs can be high. Sales are avoided if at all possible. On the other hand, there are often very active markets for the services of land, in other words, tenancy. Farmers in many parts of the world have historically depended on some form of tenancy arrangement to adjust the amount of land they cultivate to the family labour available and the inputs at their disposal, their commitments elsewhere, and their enthusiasm and skills. The village of Palanpur is no different.

Over the past seven decades, the village has changed immensely. The introduction of land reforms in the 1950s, technological progress and the green revolution technologies and methods of the late 1960s and the 1970s, the replacement of bullocks by tractors in the early 1980s, the growth of non-farm opportunities, and the mechanization of agriculture have all had a bearing on functioning tenancy arrangements and associated institutional structures. This chapter examines, in detail, the nature of and trends in tenancy in Palanpur. We explore how the evolution of tenancy in the village is associated with land ownership, landlord–tenant relations, castes, absent or missing markets, and employment in non-farm activities.

In comparison to the findings of Lanjouw and Stern (1998), many aspects of tenancy remain unchanged by the time of 2008–10 survey. The type of tenancy contract chosen continues to be affected by caste, the amount of land owned, and other inputs available to the landlords and tenants involved. There still seems to be no evidence, in sharecropping in Palanpur, of the tenant putting in less effort than he might have done on own-cultivated land because he receives only a half-share of output. Where this does occur,

* This chapter has been written by Himanshu, Tushar Bharti, and Japneet Kaur.

however, it is a problem sometimes known as 'shirking', a term we will some-times use here. Most of the sharecropping contracts continue to be between relatives, friends, or members of the same caste.

However, much has changed. The increase in non-farm opportunities in recent years has provided an additional source of income, encouraging some households to lease-out land and specialize in non-farm jobs. It has enabled others to lease-in more land via an increase in their capacity to invest in agriculture associated with their outside incomes. Increased mechanization has led to the introduction of labour-saving techniques. As a result, some households now find it easier to cultivate land on their own instead of leasing-out to others. Others, however, due to the higher costs of these inputs, find it difficult to manage land on their own and enter tenancy contracts to lease-out.

Our analysis highlights the importance of local institutional structures, particularly around land and labour markets, which continue to adapt to changing circumstances. The changing nature of tenancy and the emergence of new forms of land contracts are evidence of the dynamism of the rural society and its economic relationships. The emerging role of caste and com-munity networks as proxies for trust, together with the flexibility of land and labour markets, are important indicators of both the role of institutions in economic growth and development and how institutions are changed by economic growth and development.

The chapter is organized as follows. We begin by examining the trends in tenancy and different types of contracts in Palanpur. While we present data for all the rounds wherever possible, we focus on the last two major rounds of 1983/4 and 2008/10, where the data were most detailed. We attempt to explain these trends by describing how broader developments within and around the village over the survey rounds have affected the institution of tenancy. Section 6.3 then examines in more detail the patterns of tenancy and tenancy contract in rela-tion to caste and to the land ownership of the landlord and the tenant. Section 6.4 takes advantage of the discussion questionnaires, involving a sample of landlords and tenants, to present the various characteristics and traits of landlords and tenants and their perceptions and judgements surrounding their land and tenancy decisions. Section 6.5 presents and examines more closely some possible explanations of the emerging trends in tenancy in the village. We find that caste and communities play a prominent role in explaining patterns of tenancy contracts; this resonates with our findings in the labour market. We look at the idea of 'communities of trust'; landlords have a strong preference for making sharecropping contracts with tenants they trust, tenants who are their relatives, friends, from the same caste, or are in a patron–client relationship with them. Since these partners depend on each other outside the market of tenancy, shirking or other failures to fulfil commitments could have far-reaching consequences. As a result, social mechanisms reduce the need for constant and direct monitoring of the tenant's effort by the landlord. Section 6.6 concludes with some cautious predictions about how tenancy might evolve as an institution, within Palanpur and outside.

6.2 Tenancy in Palanpur over the Years

In Palanpur, as in the rest of the country, increases in non-farm opportunities have led to a decline in dependence on agriculture. However, in contrast to some other parts of India, the importance of tenancy as an institution has grown in the village.[1] In Palanpur, the area under tenancy as a percentage of the total cultivated area rose strongly from 10 per cent in 1957/8 to 34 per cent in 1983/4 (see Table 6.1). It has been fairly flat over the last 30 years to 2015. The percentage of total households engaged in some form of tenancy showed a rising trend from 1957/8 to 1983/4 and then declined from 77 per cent in 1983/4 to 48 per cent in 2015. While there has been a decline in this later period for both households leasing-out and those leasing-in as a percentage of households involved in tenancy, the decrease is considerably higher for the landlords. These changes reflect deep, underlying developments in the village's social and economic structure.

There are a number of reasons or factors behind these trends. First, since 1983/4, more and more land within the village is owned by outsiders.[2]

Table 6.1 Tenancy in Palanpur

Year	% Area under Tenancy	% Household in Tenancy	% Tenants	% Landlords
1957/8	10%	32%	25%	7%
1962/3	12%	45%	28%	17%
1974/5	23%	69%	39%	37%
1983/4	34%	77%	41%	52%
2008/9	37%	55%	36%	25%
2015	35%	48%	32%	18%

Note: % area under tenancy = area leased-in/cultivated area. The second column provides a proportion of total households in the village leasing-in or/and leasing-out land. The third and fourth columns represent the proportion of households leasing-in and leasing-out, respectively. If a household both leases in and leases out, we categorize the household both as a tenant and as a landlord. '% Landlords' excludes landlords from outside Palanpur.

[1] Walker and Ryan (1990) observed a decline in tenancy in the Indian International Crops Research Institute for the Semi-Arid Tropics (ICRISAT) villages during the 1980s in comparison to the 1950s. Rao and Charyulu (2007) found a further decline in tenancy in these villages in 2001–4, with an average of 14% of the area under tenancy in the six villages. As per the 59th National Sample Survey (NSS) round, the area under tenancy for the state of Uttar Pradesh is even lower, at around 10%.
[2] An increase in migration could be one possible reason for increased land sales. For example, Bidey's son (relative of Nasir) sold his 7.5 bigha of land to Dorilal Morya for Rs 10,000 per bigha and migrated to his ancestral village in Jargaon. Misfortune or excess are other reasons. Also see Chapters 2 and 5 for details on changing land ownership and land sales.

Table 6.2 Average landholdings per cultivator (in *bighas*)

	1983/4	N	2008/9	N
Land owned	16.18	137	11.90	122
Land cultivated	20.65	135	13.48	122
Land leased-in	10.77	94	9.85	58

Note: Cultivators are adult male individuals with their primary occupation as cultivation. The values are reported in *bighas*. N is the number of primary cultivators with non-zero land owned, cultivated, or leased.

This has led to an increase in the number of outsider landlords and a reduction in the landlords inside the village.[3] Second, the fragmentation of the land-holdings due to increased splitting of the households has sharply reduced the average land owned per household (Table 6.2), thereby, for most, reducing the incentive to lease-out. Third, the construction of new, bigger houses on the margin of the village might also have reduced the land available for cultivation. Fourth, mechanization of agriculture has enabled some households, who earlier used to lease-out land due to lack of labour, to cultivate their land themselves.

For the tenants, while land sales and mechanization could have led to an increase in the land leased-in, the increasing non-farm opportunities seem to have reduced the amount of labour they devote to cultivation, tilting towards a decrease in land leased-in. While earlier members of a household with a low land-to-labour ratio could have done little apart from leasing-in or working as agricultural labourers, non-farm opportunities now present attractive alternatives. Some of these non-farm jobs have led to the out-migration of a few households, thereby increasing the number of outsider landlords and decreasing the number of landlords and tenants inside the village.

For those who still wish to cultivate the land, non-farm income occurring outside peak periods for agricultural activity allows them to invest more in cultivation and ensure a contractual arrangement better suited to their needs. In Section 6.2.1, we look at how the changing economic landscape of the village has affected different forms of tenancy contracts; in Section 6.2.2, the role of size of holding and caste in relation to tenancy; and in Section 6.2.3, income and credit.

6.2.1 Types of Tenancy in Palanpur

There are three main types of tenurial arrangements in Palanpur: *batai*, *chauthai*, and *peshgi*. In *batai* (sharecropping) contracts, which remain the most

---

[3] Land leased-in from outsiders as a percentage of the total land leased-in increased from 22% in 1983 to 36% in 2008/9.

important, a tenant pays half the produce from the land to his landlord at the time of harvest. The landlord has to pay half of the cash inputs while the tenant, in addition to their share of cash inputs, is also responsible for all the labour inputs. Over the years, with increased use of cash inputs, like fertilizers and pesticides, and rental inputs, such as the cost of hiring pumping sets, tube wells, and tractors, the share of monetized inputs in cultivation has increased.[4] Also, seed cost for a few cash crops, like sugar cane, mentha, and potatoes, is now shared between landlords and tenants, where previously seed had been the responsibility of the tenant. This is an important way in which the sharecropping contract has changed over the years.

The second most important contract is *peshgi* (fixed-rent tenancy). In *peshgi*, a fixed amount of rent is paid by a tenant to his landlord either at the beginning of the season (cash-fixed-rent contract) or at the time of harvest (in-kind, fixed-rent contract). Third, there are *chauthai* contracts, which were first recorded during the 1974 survey.[5] Such contracts were also observed in 1983/4, accounting for 8 per cent of leased-in land. By the 2008/9 survey, *chauthai* contracts accounted for 15 per cent of all leased-in land. However, the terms of this contract have changed considerably over the years. In 1983/4, a *chauthai* tenant paid a quarter of the cost of all inputs, except labour and seeds, where he contributed half. The tenant received a 25 per cent share of the output in return. The *chauthai* contract in 1983/4 was almost like a special sharecropping contract with two tenants (one can think of the landlord as co-tenant as well as a landlord), rather than one individual contracted to do all the work.[6] As of 2008/9, a *chauthai* tenant fulfils all the labour requirements on the farm, incurs no other costs, and receives a one-quarter share of output. The *chauthai* contract in 2008/9 is almost like a piece-rated labour contract where the payment of wages is at the end of the cropping season with wages as share of output. However, we continue to treat *chauthai* here as a tenancy contract.[7] All the contracts in the village are oral contracts and are typically valid for one or two years. At the end of the term, contracts between long-standing partners are often renewed. Instances of contracts for one season, though noted, are rare and often temporary arrangements when owners are faced with temporary constraints in cultivating the plot themselves.

---

[4] See Chapter 5 for details.

[5] There is mention of only one *chauthai* contract in 1974.

[6] As Sharma and Drèze (1998: 467) note, 'chauthai: There are two partners (landlord and tenant). The tenant receives one-fourth of the produce ("chauthai" means "one fourth") and supplies one-fourth of the inputs (one half in the case of labour and seeds). One way of understanding this pattern of shares is to think of the chauthai contract as a sajha batai contract where the landlord is also one of the two co-tenants.' Unlike the 1983 *chauthai* contracts, which were a variant of *batai* contracts, by 2008/9, *chauthai* contracts had changed to a special type of contract.

[7] Similar tenancy contracts, which are like labour contracts, are seen in other parts of western Uttar Pradesh and Haryana. See Rawal (2006) for a description of *Siri* contracts in Haryana.

During the first two survey years, almost all the land under tenancy was under sharecropping—98 per cent in 1957/8 and 93 per cent in 1962/3. We focus on the next three 'thick' rounds of 1974/5, 1983/4, and 2008/9,[8] where the trends are clearly marked (see Table 6.3). In 1974/5, sharecropping was the main form of tenancy for all major castes. The area under tenancy and under all types of contracts increased from 1974/5 to 1983/4. Since then, the area under sharecropping has continued to decline, with a corresponding increase in the area under fixed-rent contracts. *Chauthai* contracts, too, have increased in number over this period. In *rabi* 1983/4, 78 per cent of the area under tenancy was under sharecropping contracts, 8 per cent was under *chauthai*, and 14 per cent under fixed-rent contracts. The corresponding figures in *rabi* 2009 were 56 per cent, 15 per cent, and 29 per cent, respectively. Although the fraction of sharecropping contracts in total has been declining over time, it is still the dominant form of land contract in the village and the participation remains quite evenly distributed across castes.[9] However, *peshgi* contracts are generally preferred by the wealthier castes of Thakurs and Muraos, with Telis also showing a preference for *peshgi* contracts by 2009. *Chauthai* contracts are generally used by the poorer tenant households, with Jatabs accounting for three-fourths of all *chauthai* contracts in 2009, unlike the *batai* variant of it in 1983, which was used by Thakurs and Muraos.

6.2.2 Tenancy, Size of Holding, and Caste

We analyse the trends in terms of size of holding and caste. Participation in tenancy remains fairly evenly distributed across caste (see Table 6.4).

Of the 53 households leasing-in under sharecropping in 2008/9, 30 of them had leased-in under sharecropping in 1983/4 as well.[10] For these 30 households, the area leased-in under sharecropping has also shown an increase from 218.2 *bighas* in 1983/4 to 239.5 *bighas* in 2008/9. For the remaining 23 households, 4 households were not in the village in 1983/4 and another 4 did not cultivate in the *rabi* season in 1983/4, 4 households did not participate in tenancy in 1983/4, 1 was involved in leasing-in but the information on the type of contract is not known, and the remaining 10 households leased-out. Amongst these, six of them leased-out under sharecropping.

For the 14 households who leased-in under sharecropping in 2008/9 but either leased-out or cultivated their own land in 1983/4, the reason for this

---

[8] The years 1993 and 2015 saw 'thin' rounds, in the sense that many fewer dimensions were covered—see Chapter 1.
[9] As per the 59th NSS round (for 2003), sharecropping remained the most prevalent form of tenancy in the country, covering 41% of the tenanted land. In the state of Uttar Pradesh, this number was still higher at 53%.
[10] These 30 households of 2008/9 had originally been 16 households in 1983/4 before splitting.

Table 6.3 Caste-wise distribution of area under tenancy contracts

Caste Group	Leased-in Land by Tenurial Contract (area in *bigha*)								
	1974/5			1983/4			2008/9		
	Batai	*Chauthai*	*Peshgi*	*Batai*	*Chauthai*	*Peshgi*	*Batai*	*Chauthai*	*Peshgi*
Thakur	74.5(95)	0(0)	4(5)	84.6(81)	5(5)	15.4(15)	108.5(62)	0(0)	65.24(38)
Murao	26(90)	0(0)	3(10)	103.8(63)	42(25)	19.5(12)	112.5(54)	14(7)	83.5(40)
Dhimar	44(97)	0(0)	1.5(3)	124.6(88)	16.5(12)	0(0)	7(29)	0(0)	17.5(71)
Gadaria	41(80)	0(0)	10(20)	81.4(93)	0(0)	6.4(7)	41(77)	0(0)	12(23)
Dhobi	18.1(58)	0(0)	13(42)	16.2(45)	0(0)	20(55)	37.5(79)	10(21)	0(0)
Teli	111.6(100)	0(0)	0(0)	100.6(78)	0(0)	27.75(22)	58(55)	7(7)	40.5(38)
Passi	17.5(71)	0(0)	7(29)	4(40)	0(0)	6(60)	0(0)	0(0)	0(0)
Jatab	104(93)	5(4)	3(3)	79.1(89)	0(0)	9.5(11)	119.5(48)	97(39)	32(13)
Others	3(100)	0(0)	0(0)	0(0)	0(0)	0(0)	0(0)	0(0)	0(0)
Total	439.7(90)	5(1)	41.5(9)	594.(78)	63.5(8)	104.6(14)	484(56)	128(15)	250.7(29)

Note: These figures are as per *rabi* season of each round, including sugar cane. Figures in parentheses present the percentage of their leased-in area under the particular contract for each caste.

Table 6.4 Household participation in tenancy

Caste Group	Year	
	1983/4	2008/9
Thakur	87%	63%
Murao	81%	64%
Dhimar	69%	14%
Gadaria	92%	47%
Dhobi	50%	63%
Teli	65%	48%
Passi	60%	67%
Jatab	89%	69%
Others	50%	0%
Overall	77%	55%

Note: Figures for *rabi* 2009.

Table 6.5 Land owned per cultivator (in *bighas*), 1983/4 and 2008/9

	Overall Village	Sharecropping Tenants
2008/9	11.9	9.6
1983/4	16.2	18.1

change seems to be the *land owned* by these households per cultivating member. As is clear from Table 6.5, these households had much more land per cultivating member in 1983/4 as compared to 2008/9. While there has been a decline in the land owned per cultivating member in these 25 years, the decline for the households who are leasing-in on sharecropping in 2008/9 is higher than the overall decline.

While sharecropping continues to be the most important type of tenancy contract, there has been a considerable increase in the percentage of tenanted area under the other two forms of contracts. In 1983, *chauthai* was a contract associated with the higher *castes*.[11] But this reversed in 2008/9; Jatabs and Dhobis, the two poorest caste groups in the village, accounted for 89 per cent of all leased-in land under *chauthai*. When we track the Jatab households cultivating leased-in land under *chauthai* in 2008/9 back to 1983/4, we find that all of these households were leasing-in under sharecropping in the earlier period.

One important reason behind this shift is the change in the terms of *chauthai* contract over the years. The cash costs of cultivating as a sharecropping tenant have increased, in part due to mechanization but also due to the monetization of various inputs (see Chapter 5). Some Jatabs and Dhobis, who are low on cash

---

[11] Only Thakur, Murao, and Dhimar leased-in under *chauthai* in 1983/4, with Muraos accounting for two-thirds of all *chauthai* land leased-in. And as we see in Section 6.3, much leasing is within caste.

resources, therefore prefer to cultivate under *chauthai*. This is not to say that the condition of Jatabs has deteriorated over the years. If anything, the increased participation of Jatabs, many of whom were agricultural labourers in 1983/4, both in non-farm activities and in the tenancy market suggests otherwise.

While non-farm opportunities have allowed poorer, low-caste households to earn additional income and lease-in land on sharecropping contracts, the richer, higher castes have increasingly shifted away from sharecropping to fixed-rent contracts. Fixed-rent contracts were almost non-existent in the first two rounds. They appeared in 1974/5 and had increased by 1983/4. Landlords in the village, who typically have more say in determining the form of tenancy contract,[12] report fixed rent to be the least profitable kind of contract. The small number of fixed-rent contracts, in 1974/5 and 1983/4, was therefore not a surprise. However, there was a significant increase in the percentage of land leased under this contract between 1983/4 and 2008/9. While landlords inside the village still primarily choose sharecropping contracts, *peshgi* is the contract of choice for absentee and outsider landlords and households with almost no labour for cultivation. Of the 67 contracts on fixed-rent terms, 46 have been leased-in by the villagers from outsiders.[13] The remaining 21 contracts are from 16 landlords inside the village. Amongst these contracts, 14 landlords have either one or no adult household member and 7 households specialize in non-farm occupations. This is consistent with the findings from discussions with the villagers that we examine in detail in Section 6.4. Among other reasons, poorer households inside the village also lease-out under *peshgi* when they face urgent cash requirements or lack able-bodied members to participate in cultivation.

Tenants, on the other hand, if they can manage the liquidity and risk, prefer fixed-rent contracts over other contracts due to higher profits and less interference from the landlords. However, leasing-in on a fixed-rent contract does require the tenants to be able to manage all the costs and risk of cultivation, thus only the socially and economically better-off tenants in the village have been able to move to fixed-rent contracts. Table 6.6 presents the distribution of the number of fixed-rent contracts between the landlords and the tenants in the two survey rounds of 1983/4 and 2008/9.[14]

The percentage of the contracts leased-in under fixed-rent contracts by the higher castes (Thakurs and Muraos) almost doubled between the two survey rounds (30 per cent to 59 per cent). The landlords leasing-out to these groups are mostly outside the village. Of the 12 contracts extended by the Thakur

---

[12] See Section 6.4.
[13] These figures are for *rabi* season of 2008/9.
[14] The number of contracts are crop- and plot-specific. For instance, if a landlord leases out ten *bighas* to a tenant who then cultivates wheat on five *bighas* and mentha on five *bighas*, we count it as two contracts.

Table 6.6 Fixed-rent contracts

		1983						
		Tenant Caste						
		Thakur	Murao	Gadariya	Muslim	Passi	Jatab	Total
Landlord Caste	Thakur		1					1
	Murao				1			1
	Gadariya		2		1			3
	Jatab	3			10		1	14
	Others	1	1	1	3	1	1	8
	Total	4	4	1	15	1	2	27

		2009						
		Tenant Caste						
		Thakur	Murao	Dhimar	Gadariya	Muslim	Jatab	Total
Landlord Caste	Thakur	13				1		14
	Murao		12	2		1		15
	Gadariya		2		4			6
	Muslim		2			3		5
	Passi		3	1	2	2		8
	Jatab	1				2	3	6
	Others	5	2	1	1		4	13
	Total	19	21	4	7	9	7	67

Note: Others includes 'other' castes inside the village as well as outsiders of unknown caste. Table entry shows number of contracts between landlords of caste shown in rows and tenants of caste shown in columns.

landlords, 6 of them are outsiders, and for Muraos, 12 of the 14 contracts are by outsider landlords. The share of Jatabs in the number of contracts shows a small increase from 7 to 10 per cent.

The number of plots leased-out by the Jatabs seems to have decreased substantially. In the past, households were constrained by lack of non-farm opportunities and limited access to credit. A household faced with cash constraints or lack of able-bodied male members could not do much more than leasing-out the land on fixed rent. We find that 8 of these 14 contracts by Jatabs in 1983/4 were offered by a single household, suggesting that lack of family labour or a cash requirement could have been the reason.

6.2.3 Tenancy, Income, and Credit

In addition to more outsider landlords leasing-out land on fixed-rent contracts, diversification of *income* due to a growth in non-farm opportunities has also played a role. It has increased the risk-taking ability of the tenants and provided a source of cash income to pay for costs of cultivation.[15] This has enabled the tenants to choose fixed-rent contracts more often. In fact, we find a high positive correlation between the percentage change in the area under fixed-rent contracts and the percentage change in the real non-farm income of the castes.

The detailed information collected about each of the households enabled us to track, across the survey years, the households who leased-in on fixed-rent contracts in 2008/9. The average real non-farm income per capita of these households has more than doubled between the two rounds, 1983/4 to 2008/9. In 2009, 35 households leasing-in under fixed rent contracts had an average non-farm income of Rs 6428 in current prices. These households can be tracked back to 22 households in 1983/4 with an average income of Rs 2428 in 2008/9 prices. These findings suggest that households might be using cash income from non-farm activities to pay the rents and cultivation costs associated with profitable fixed-rent contracts.

Tenants can also use *credit* as an alternative to non-farm income to pay the upfront rent and cost of inputs associated with fixed-rent contracts. The very high rates of interest charged by the village and the urban moneylenders make formal credit markets the only viable source of credit for investment in agriculture. However, accessing credit from formal sources requires some degree of literacy. Availability of land for collateral is also an advantage. Thakurs and Muraos, the two highest castes, are the most educated and own the highest amounts of land per capita. Consistent with this, as is clear from Table 6.7 for 2008/9, Thakurs and Muraos have benefited most from formal credit sources. A local Thakur family also controls some formal sector credit.[16] Superior access to formal credit is a key reason why these two caste groups have been able to secure a high number of fixed-rent contracts.

Table 6.7 Caste-wise distribution of credit sources, 2008/9

Caste Group	Total Hhds with Borrowings	Borrowing from Formal Means	Borrowing from Informal Means	Borrowing from Relatives	Borrowing from Landlords
Thakur	54%	32%	24%	19%	0%
Murao	75%	42%	49%	25%	2%
Jatab	69%	10%	51%	26%	3%
Others	45%	13%	30%	16%	1%

Note: Households as a % of total households in a caste. Multiple sources of borrowing for households occur.

[15] See Chapter 5.
[16] The dominant moneylender in the village is the brother of the manager of the local credit cooperative.

Table 6.8 Ratio of real per capita institutional credit to total credit, 1983/4 to 2008/9

Caste Group	Year			
	1983/4		2008/9	
	All Households	Pure *Peshgi* Tenants	All Households	Pure *Peshgi* Tenants
Thakurs	0.86	0	0.48	1
Muraos	0.53	0	0.74	0.68
Jatab	0.42	0.4	0.11	0
Others	0.62	0.17	0.18	0.14
Total	0.66	0.18	0.49	0.48

This becomes clear when we look at the caste-wise break-up of the ratio of per capita credit from formal sources to per capita credit from all sources in 1983/4 and 2008/9 for the households involved in pure *peshgi* contracts in Table 6.8.[17] Credit from formal sources as a percentage of total credit has declined from 1983/4 to 2008/9 for all households taken together and for all caste groups, apart from Muraos. Around 1983/4, corrupt Farmers' Service Society (FSS) officials provided easy loans to villagers in order to collect illicit administrative charges.[18] As of 2008/9, with the near dissolution of the FSS, the main source of formal credit in 1983/4, the share of formal credit in total credit has declined considerably. Additionally, 1983/4 was a drought year. The amount of in-kind loans taken from the FSS for consumption purposes, especially by the socially disadvantaged groups, could have been higher. This seems to be the case for Jatabs and others for whom the dependence on formal credit has decreased drastically. However, when we compare only pure *peshgi* tenant households across the two rounds, their dependence on formal credit has, in contrast, increased. This increase is greatest for Thakurs and Muraos, the two castes with the highest involvement in fixed-rent tenancy contracts.

Overall, it seems that improving non-farm opportunities, access to formal credit (particularly by Thakurs and Muraos), and the increase in the number of outsider landlords are the major forces behind the increase in share of fixed-rent contracts over time.

Apart from the three main contracts, there were a few special contractual arrangements evident. Two examples illustrate the flexibility in contracting arrangements depending on circumstances. Neighbours Divyanshu and Uday-bhan are on good terms with each other. Udaybhan had an urgent cash

---

[17] Pure *peshgi* households are those who, while they might have their own land, lease-in on *peshgi* contracts only.

[18] Lanjouw and Stern (1998) provide a detailed account of the prevalence of corrupt practices in the FSS.

requirement and approached Divyanshu, offering to lease-out land on a fixed-rent contract. Divyanshu accepted the offer. Divyanshu is new in the village and runs a medical shop; he has no experience of cultivation. He later leased-out the same land to Udaybhan on a sharecropping contract since he wanted a share in the produce. The second case is that of Udayveer and Asrat, who work together as casual workers in Moradabad. Udayveer had land but was short on labour due to his engagement in Moradabad. Asrat needed some land to cultivate. So Udayveer leased-out land under sharecropping to Asrat as a landlord and then became his partner in cultivation. It was as if two households leased-in from Udayveer.[19] As a result, Udayveer got 75 per cent share of the produce. These special contracts are also suggestive of the fact that non-farm growth has not only had an impact on the share of cultivation and tenancy in the village, but also on the contractual arrangements and terms of the contracts. In both these examples, it is the participation in non-farm activities by Divyanshu, Udayveer, and Asrat that led to these special arrangements, which were of a kind rarely encountered in the village before. Both these examples also suggest tenancy as an evolving institutional arrangement with changing social and economic structures, unlike its rigid portrayal in textbook examples.

6.3 Land Ownership, Caste, and Choice of Contract

We saw in Section 6.2 that the amounts of land and labour a household owns play a very important role, not only in the area of land sought for cultivation, but also in the choice of tenancy contract. We have seen that the presence of multiple contracts and the changing nature of contracts in tenancy suggest that there can be changes in institutional structures in response to changing economic pressures, opportunities, and needs. We have also noted that access to capital, credit, and labour is linked to choices in the tenancy market. And we have introduced the argument that caste plays a role in mediating the supervision problem associated with share tenancy by acting as a 'proxy for trust'. This section looks more closely at the choice of tenancy contract by land ownership and caste.

6.3.1 *Land Ownership and Tenancy Type*

In the presence of high transaction costs associated with land sales, households use tenancy contracts to adjust the area of land they cultivate to suit the amount of agricultural labour and other agricultural inputs the household

---

[19] This contract is similar to the *chauthai* contract in 1983.

owns. For a given amount of labour and other inputs, this would imply an inverse relationship between land owned and land leased-in. In practice, the situation is somewhat more complicated. Landless households find it difficult to lease-in land, especially on sharecropping contracts. In Palanpur, landless households have historically been particularly deprived.[20] Landlessness is, often, an indicator of a lack of the agricultural assets and cash necessary for timely payments for inputs and rents.[21]

Landless households' access to formal credit is also limited. Moneylenders consider landless households riskier and lend to them only at very high rates, if at all.[22] Lastly, their managerial ability and cultivation know-how is also often in question since many of them have historically been poor and have little experience at managing their own land. This makes it difficult for them to lease-in under *chauthai* as well. Landlords who agree to lease to these households often demand fixed-rent contracts since it guarantees them a fixed payment. In the past, not many of them were able to pay upfront. As a result, this section of the population was trapped in a vicious circle of poverty and inability to rent-in land.[23]

The extent of landlessness has reduced somewhat in recent years. In 2008/9, 18 per cent of households in the village were landless, in 1983/4, 20 per cent, and in 1993, 23 per cent. With the increase in non-farm opportunities, alternative occupations and sources of income have now become available to these households.[24] The average per capita income for this group in 2008/9, Rs 12,757, was not significantly different from Rs 13,775, the average per capita income of the landowning households. The corresponding figures in 1983/4 were Rs 5965 and Rs 8674. It seems that the increase in non-farm activities has resulted in a strong improvement in the relative position of landless households.

In Table 6.9, we categorize households in land-ownership quintiles and summarize the involvement of each land quintile in the tenancy market.

---

[20] This is true for landless farmers in other parts of Uttar Pradesh (Srivastava, 2008).

[21] Jograj, a landless Dhimar, acknowledges that he finds it difficult to lease-in land. Even though he has the capacity to manage land up to five *bighas*, he could rent only two *bighas*. Gangaram, another landless Jatab, has no resources and reports that he finds it difficult to lease-in. Mahipal, a landless Murao, admits that he finds it difficult to lease-in land. He asked for some land from Kishori but Kishori refused, saying that he would prefer to lease-out to a tenant with irrigation facilities.

[22] Jagat Pal, a landless Thakur, told us that if there is a need to borrow money, he prefers to go to his brother. He admitted that he could not get a loan from a moneylender since he does not have enough sources of income to pay back the loan. Parvati, a Murao widow, also preferred to borrow from relatives since they do not charge any interest, and she did not have the resources necessary to borrow from moneylenders in the village.

[23] Some of these households might have been in patron–client relationships with richer households in the past. While the force of such relationships has weakened, the reputation earned in the past sometimes is still instrumental in helping these households get some land on sharecropping contracts.

[24] Chapter 7 provides details of the non-farm opportunities available to them.

The majority of households (55 per cent) are involved in tenancy. In general, households with relatively lower ownership of land per capita lease-in land, and those with high land ownership per capita lease-out land, except for the lowest quintile, which has a large majority of landless households. The two relevant columns of Table 6.9 are columns 3 and 5, respectively, monotonically decreasing and increasing across quintiles excluding lowest quintile.[25]

The amount of land leased-in does not, however, decrease monotonically across the quintiles. It peaks at the fourth quintile. Lower down the order, in terms of rank by holding per capita, the desire to lease-in might be higher, but for some the qualifications as a tenant, in terms of liquidity and skill, may be weak. Others may also now be becoming more focused on non-farm activity. For households leasing-out, as expected, average land leased-out increases with land ownership per capita. It is easier to execute a desire to lease-out than a desire to lease-in.

A clearer picture emerges when we look at the distribution of leased-in area under different types of tenancy by land size class (Table 6.10). Consistent with Table 6.9 and the explanation just given, households in the first land quintile, even though low on land-to-labour ratio, are not able to lease-in much land. In contrast to households in other land quintiles, sharecropping is not the most important form of contract for this category. While some do lease-in under *chauthai*, the share of area under fixed-rent contracts of the total area leased-in is the highest for households in this land quintile.

Those in the second land quintile are not landless but own small amounts of land. While potential landlords might not be as sceptical of their managerial ability and cultivation compared to the landless, their ability to pay the fixed

Table 6.9 Participation in tenancy by land quintiles, 2008/9

Land per Capita Quintile	% Households in Tenancy Market	% Households Leasing-in	Average Land Leased-in (*bighas*)	% Households Leasing-out	Average Land Leased out (*bighas*)
1	26%	26%	6.88	2%	4.00
2	73%	60%	10.72	19%	2.86
3	53%	42%	9.68	22%	4.15
4	62%	28%	13.51	38%	4.8
5	61%	22%	11.35	46%	16.14
All	55%	36%	10.44	25%	8.41

Note: These are land owned per capita quintiles. A total of 43 of the 47 households in the first quintile are landless. Definitions here are same as Table 6.2.

[25] There is a peculiarity for the lowest quintile: the large majority of this quintile had zero land, and only one household in the first quintile leased-out (four *bighas* of land).

Table 6.10 Area (*bighas*) under tenancy contracts by land-ownership quintile

Land per Capita Quintile	*Rabi* 2008/9		
	Batai	*Chauthai*	*Peshgi*
1	36 (45.9%)	14 (17.8%)	28.5 (36.3%)
2	169.49 (54.5%)	80 (25.7%)	61.49 (19.8%)
3	134.5 (73.1%)	24 (13.0%)	25.5 (13.9%)
4	91.5 (52.1%)	10 (5.7%)	74.25 (42.2%)
5	52.5 (46.3%)	0 (0%)	61 (53.7%)
Total	483.99 (56.1%)	128 (14.8%)	250.74 (29.1%)

Note: Areas in *bighas*. Figures in parentheses are percentage shares across quintile groups. These figures are the leased-in areas under the particular contract for *rabi* season, including sugar cane.

rents and all input costs in time by themselves might still be limited. The poorer ones amongst them, and those who might be seen as having relatively better agricultural skill or acumen, therefore might enter *chauthai* contracts.[26] The less cash-constrained households from this quintile may not only find it easier to lease-in land under sharecropping, but also might prefer it to fixed-rent contracts where they have to pay an upfront fixed rent. Moreover, risk sharing might be a more important motive for households in this land quintile than those in higher quintiles. The choice of the contract is, to a great extent, a landlord's decision, unless the tenant is, for some reason, in a strong position to bargain. Landlords tend to prefer sharecropping to fixed-rent contracts due to the higher profits.[27] Potential landlords are not as doubtful of the ability of the households in the second quintile since they have managed cultivation on their own plots before. As a result, they find it profitable to lease to these tenants under sharecropping.

Many of those in higher quintiles will have all the necessary assets and acumen to be able to lease-in land under sharecropping. However, as we discuss in Section 6.4, fixed-rent contracts are the most profitable from the point of view of the tenants. Households in the top two quintiles are wealthier and more powerful. They are not only able to pay the rents and invest in inputs on time, but also enjoy a better bargaining position by virtue of their social and economic status. Fixed-rent tenants, in general, are wealthier. For example, in 2008/9, the average per capita income of all tenants was Rs 14,550, while those leasing-in on fixed-rent contracts had an income of Rs 17,220. Also, while fixed-rent contract tenants form 35 per cent of the total tenants, they own 50 per cent of the total assets owned by all tenants. For households for which the land may be seen as roughly in proportion to household labour, leasing-in

[26] A *chauthai* tenant with some land of his own might have a better idea of how to till, sow, irrigate, or weed as compared to a *chauthai* tenant with no land of his own.
[27] More on profitability of contracts in Section 6.4.

and out is mainly done in order to establish larger contiguous holdings and to obtain economies of scale with regard to the plot size.[28]

6.3.2 Caste and Tenancy Type

Caste has been an important element of almost every economic aspect in the village. Tenancy is no exception. As is clear from Table 6.11, all castes have continued to be actively involved in tenancy.[29] Most of the landlords continue to be from the two highest caste groups, Thakurs and Muraos. Their higher social and economic position often gives them a stronger say in the choice and terms of the contract. These positions count because interactions between individuals and castes occur all the time across many dimensions and are not confined to one particular contract. Thakurs continue to have a high participation in the leasing-out market, second only to the Passis (who have had extensive non-farm involvements for many years). Thakurs, with the highest amounts of land, have traditionally been at the top of the socioeconomic hierarchy and, it is argued, some of them may have an aversion to hard manual labour (Bliss and Stern, 1982). Leasing-out, then, may be a natural choice for them.

Table 6.11 Participation in tenancy by caste

Caste Group	Year					
	1983/4			2008/9		
	% Hhds in Tenancy	% Tenants	% Landlords	% Hhds in Tenancy	% Tenants	% Landlords
Thakur	87 (26)	30 (9)	70 (21)	63 (36)	28 (16)	46 (26)
Murao	81 (22)	56 (15)	41 (11)	64 (35)	42 (23)	25 (14)
Dhimar	69 (9)	31 (4)	46 (6)	14 (3)	14 (3)	0 (0)
Gadaria	92 (11)	42 (5)	67 (8)	47 (7)	27 (4)	20 (3)
Dhobi	50 (2)	50 (2)	25 (1)	63 (5)	63 (5)	25 (2)
Teli	65 (11)	59 (10)	29 (5)	48 (11)	35 (8)	22 (5)
Passi	60 (9)	20 (3)	53 (8)	67 (4)	0 (0)	67 (4)
Jatab	89 (17)	53 (10)	68 (13)	69 (27)	62 (24)	13 (5)
Others	50 (3)	17 (1)	33 (2)	0 (0)	0 (0)	0 (0)
Overall	77 (110)	41 (59)	52 (75)	55 (128)	36 (83)	25 (59)

Note: The definitions used here are the same as in Table 6.1. Figures in parentheses give, respectively across the columns, the number of households in tenancy and number of tenant and landlord households belonging to each caste.

---

[28] A Teli household leases in 13 *bighas* on *batai* and leases out 12 *bighas* of land on *batai*. On both the areas, wheat was sown in *rabi* 2008/9. The only difference in the two plots is the location. The land they lease-in is located near the station, near their own cultivated land, whereas the one they lease-out is more distant, located at Bhoodi.
[29] We focus on the last two detailed survey rounds here. See Lanjouw and Stern (1998) for this distribution during the survey rounds before 1983.

However, of late, both their dominance and their aversion to strong manual labour have weakened, contributing to a decline in the percentage of Thakur households leasing-out. The percentage of Thakur households that do not cultivate any land on their own but lease everything out has decreased from 20 per cent to 14 per cent, between 1983/4 and 2008/9. While this might look like a modest change, the numbers have to be interpreted while keeping in mind that increasing non-farm opportunities, from which Thakurs benefited considerably, could have otherwise led to an increase in the possibility of leasing-out land. This outcome, therefore, is the net of the two forces of outside opportunities, on the one hand, and caste/social attitudes and position, on the other.

Muraos, who have traditionally been a cultivating caste with a strong work ethic, continue to actively participate in cultivation and leasing-in. Increasing outside opportunities have led to the migration of Passi households in the village, with the number of Passi households declining from 15 in 1983/4 to 6 in 2008/9. Those who remain are mostly involved in non-farm jobs and prefer to lease-out land.

Jatab households, historically, have been the poorest in the village. In earlier rounds, many of them were observed to be working as agricultural labourers. Few had the agricultural resources and cash under sharecropping to lease-in land. Those with some land did not always own enough resources to cultivate it and, as a result, chose to lease it out. As of 2008/9, Jatabs were leasing-out less and leasing-in much more. Some Jatab households who have sold off a part or all of their land, perhaps under urgent cash requirement situations, now need to lease-in land. However, what really drives the trends for this caste group are improved markets, increased mechanization of agriculture, and access to alternative sources of income. Together these have allowed the Jatabs to have access to inputs and the cash to pay for them and thus to lease-in more land. While the land cultivated by the villagers went down from 2705 *bighas* in 1983/4 to 2326 in 2008/9, Jatabs were the only caste cultivating more land in 2008/9 (399 *bighas*) than in 1983/4 (254 *bighas*). Some of them reported that leasing-in land has become easier. Income earned from working in brick kilns during the off season provides members of this household with the means to pay for the costs of cultivation. Landlords may also sometimes offer non-farm jobs, like work in mentha extraction plants or as a construction worker, to tenants.

Consistent with the discussion in Section 6.2, Thakurs, Muraos, and Telis,[30] the wealthiest caste groups in the village, with resources to pay the upfront rent and the cost of all the inputs, lease-in under fixed-rent contracts more often. On the other hand, Jatab and Dhobi households, the poorest and most

---

[30] In the earlier survey years Telis were, with the Jatabs and the Dhobis, amongst the poorest groups.

resource-constrained caste groups in the village, are the only groups where the share of land leased-in under *chauthai* is more than that leased-in under fixed-rent contracts. Many of these households, especially Jatabs, have made a transition from being agricultural labourers, with uncertain and seasonal incomes, to being tenancy partners.

6.3.3 Choice of Tenancy Contract

Bliss and Stern (1982) find that the amounts of land leased-in or out in Palanpur were, in part, a result of incomplete markets for the services of draught animals.[31] Tractors had completely replaced the use of draught animals for land preparation by 2008/9, and a full-fledged rental market for tractor services existed in the village.[32] However, the land sales market and the agricultural labour market in the village continue to be far from perfect. Villagers, especially Thakurs, dislike working for others as agricultural labourers to this day. Women never work as agricultural labourers for others even though they might work on the land their household leases-in. There are no cases of agricultural workers from outside the village being hired to work inside the village. Similarly, no one from the village works on farms outside the village. As in many other parts of the developing world, there are no markets for agricultural managerial ability and cultivation skills or know-how. One cannot, therefore, easily adjust the amount of these inputs available to the land owned. Instead, individuals find it easier to adjust the size of land cultivated to these inputs through tenancy contracts.

The model presented in Bliss and Stern (1982), with some adjustments, is still useful in understanding the decisions regarding leasing and the choice of contract in Palanpur. Households now use tenancy to adjust the land area cultivated to the amount of family labour available for cultivation.[33]

Households with a higher number of adult males engaged in cultivation will want to cultivate more land to make good use of the labour available. If a household has adequate labour to cultivate the land it owns, it will neither lease-in nor lease-out. If the household labour falls slightly short of the adequate amount of labour required to farm the land owned, the household

---

[31] At that time, without owning draught animals, a household could not lease-in. If a household owned draught animals it would try to put them to good use, and since rental markets for them were very weak, leasing-in land was a partial response. Tenancy as a solution to missing or incomplete markets is also discussed in Bell and Zusman (1976), Braverman and Stiglitz (1982), Eswaran and Kotwal (1985), and Skoufias (1995).

[32] There have been some cases of workers going to work as farm labourers in other districts and states, but no one reported working as a farm labourer in neighbouring villages.

[33] See the Palanpur working papers for details of the econometric specifications. We do not include managerial inputs directly into our model due to the lack of good measures for these variables. See http://sticerd.lse.ac.uk/india/research/palanpur/publications.asp.

might lease-out land under *chauthai*. Since a tenant only gets a small share of the produce in *chauthai* contracts, his incentive to 'shirk' (apply less labour than he would working on his own land) might be higher than under *batai* or *peshgi*. Therefore, the household might require family labour to monitor the *chauthai* tenant. All decisions regarding the cultivation—the crop, the quantity or the timing of different inputs, including the tenant's labour input—are taken by the landlord. Leasing-out under *chauthai*, therefore, requires a significant amount of family labour.

If the household has some family labour but is short of the amount necessary to cultivate their land by a significant margin, it can opt to lease land out under a sharecropping contract. Given the higher share of output for the tenant, the tenant's incentive to shirk is smaller than that in *chauthai*. Hence, a lower level of monitoring is required. Even though the tenant does most of the work on the field, the landlord does need to be present occasionally when important decisions regarding the nature, quality, and quantity of inputs are being taken. While the requirement for family labour is not as high as in the case of own cultivation or *chauthai* leased-out contracts, it still is not zero. If the household is a long way short of the adequate amount of family labour, it might prefer to lease-out land on a fixed-rent contract. Also, tenants leasing-in from households with no adult male family member available for agriculture, either because there are no adult male members in the household or they are employed elsewhere, are in a stronger position to bargain for a fixed-rent contract.

Similarly, if a household has a small amount of excess labour, it would choose to lease-in land on a *chauthai* contract, as sharecropping and fixed-rent contracts require higher amounts of labour from the tenant. If the household has a significant amount of extra labour, it might choose to lease-in land on sharecropping contracts, where even though the landlord is involved in the cultivation process, the tenant is in charge of most of the work on the plot. For households with a substantial amount of excess labour, fixed-rent contracts seem more attractive as they require the largest amount of labour from the tenant of the three available types of contracts. Also, a good number of adult males in a tenant household may improve the bargaining position of the tenant household.

Holding constant the amount of land owned by a household, if the number of adult members available for cultivation in a household increases, the household is more likely to lease-in land. Depending on the magnitude of the increase, it might choose a *chauthai*, sharecropping, or fixed-rent contract. If there is a decrease in the number of adult members, the household is more likely to lease-out land, and again, depending on the magnitude, it might choose a *chauthai*, sharecropping, or fixed-rent contract. An increase in land owned by the household has the opposite effect as it decreases the labour-to-land ratio.

Even though the number of family members engaged in agriculture can be adjusted through variation in the number of members employed outside agriculture, recalling a member from a regular job may have large adjustment costs. Similarly, if there is extra labour in the short run, it is not easy to get a regular job immediately. Therefore, the number of individuals employed in the regular non-farm sector is, to a great extent, exogenous to the tenancy decision at the start of a given period.[34]

In our econometric analysis on the leasing decision,[35] we find that, controlling for the total number of adult males in the household, the higher the number of regular jobholders in the household, the more likely the household is a landlord. Since regular jobs subtract strongly from the time for cultivation, and given that households are very disinclined to sell their land, this result is in line with the prediction of the extended Bliss and Stern (1982) framework. Controlling for the number of regular jobholders, those households with a higher number of adult members are more likely to lease-in more land. Not all of the adult members are likely to find regular jobs. Some diversification might also be preferred. This, consistent with the model, should lead to an increased probability of leasing-in. As expected, the higher the amount of land owned, the lower the probability to lease-in. Availability of agricultural assets, like tube wells, ploughs, pump engines, or tractors, leads to an increase in the potential productivity of labour and expands the size of the desired cultivated area (again, whilst there are markets for both services and sales, they have some associated costs, particularly if one tries to act quickly).

Over the years, this association between tenancy choice and the labour and land variables have evolved to reflect the broad economic changes in and around the village. In 1983/4, only the richest households in the village owned tractors. Mechanization of land preparation gave them an edge. As a result, they were able to cultivate more land. By 2008/9, there were households in the village specializing in rental tractor services. Tillers and harrowers can be rented with the tractor at little extra cost. More recently, increased cash flow from diversification into non-farm activities has allowed the Jatabs to take in more land on lease on sharecropping contracts.

To understand better how the association of caste with contract choice has evolved over the years, we consider tenants and landlords separately. The higher-caste landlords were much more likely to lease-out on fixed-rent contracts in 1983/4. However, they were more likely to go for more profitable sharecropping contracts in 2008/9. With their increased involvement in

---

[34] Our definition of regular non-farm jobs in this case includes those who are self-employed in the non-farm sector and engaged full-time with little or no time to work in the fields.

[35] Details on the econometric results are available in the Palanpur working paper series, http://sticerd.lse.ac.uk/india/research/palanpur/publications.asp.

non-farm activities, they can now contribute their input shares relatively easily. Moreover, the aversion that Thakurs had towards agricultural labour has also, it seems, weakened. As tenants, they were more likely to lease-in land on sharecropping or *chauthai* contracts. Higher non-farm incomes have, again, enabled them to lease-in land on the more profitable fixed-rent contracts. Lower castes such as Jatabs and Muslims are now more likely to lease-in land compared to being agricultural labourers. As noted, in Palanpur fixed-rent contracts are more profitable from the point of view of a tenant, while sharecropping is more profitable for a landlord. In Section 6.5, we discuss further the profitability and risk associated with different contracts.

6.4 Perceptions of Landlords and Tenants: Discussion Questionnaires

To capture the perception of the villagers about a range of issues, such as the reasons for the choice of tenancy contract, a great deal of qualitative data was collected via a module of open-ended questions through 'the discussion questionnaire'. This kind of qualitative data constitutes a valuable source of insights into economic behaviour and is relatively rarely available. The discussion questionnaire was administered to a sample of 83 households representative of the village at the caste level.[36] Amongst these, 22 households were pure landlords and 49 were pure tenants. Another ten households reported being both landlord and tenant.[37] We excluded two households from our analysis as they did not fit any of these three categories.[38] Of the ten households who reported contracts as both landlord and tenant, we categorized them as a landlord or a tenant based on their answers to the discussion questionnaire.[39] After this reclassification, we had a sample of 81 households for our analysis, with 25 landlords and 56 tenants. Table 6.12 provides the distribution of different types of contracts for this sample.

The discussion questionnaire provides a rich source of information that contains the perspective of both landlords and tenants. We begin by presenting the responses of the landlord and tenants on the reasons for engagement in sharecropping. Figures 6.1a and 6.1b present the reason for leasing-in and leasing-out for tenants and landlords. Figure 6.2a and 6.2b give the reasons for

---

[36] The questions were asked to the main cultivating member of the household.

[37] A pure landlord is a farmer that does not lease-in any land for cultivation. Similarly, a pure tenant is one that does not lease-out any land.

[38] One household leased-in and leased-out the same land. Another leased-in from his brother and was free to decide the amount of crop he wanted to give his brother as rent.

[39] For example, if a household leased-in land on a fixed-rent contract and leased-out land on a sharecropping contract and answered questions meant for tenants, we categorized him a tenant.

Table 6.12 Distribution of discussion-questionnaire respondents

Contract Type	Landlords	Tenants	Landlords with Single Contract	Tenants with Single Contract
Batai	21	35	16	26
Peshgi	6	21	1	14
Chauthai	3	10	3	6

Figure 6.1a Major reasons for leasing-in land (for tenants)

Note: The figures are a percentage of the total number of tenants interviewed. Multiple options were allowed.

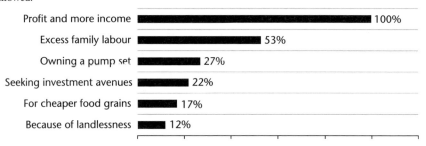

Profit and more income — 100%
Excess family labour — 53%
Owning a pump set — 27%
Seeking investment avenues — 22%
For cheaper food grains — 17%
Because of landlessness — 12%

Figure 6.1b Major reasons for leasing-out land (for landlords)

Note: The figures are a percentage of the total number of landlords interviewed. Multiple options were allowed.

Low family labour — 60%
Working capital shortage — 37%
Job, business, or outside work — 26%
Cash required — 17%
Unable to manage cultivation — 17%
Far-away land — 14%
Old age or sickness — 10%
Monkey menace on plot — 9%

Figure 6.2a Major reasons for preferring sharecropping (for landlords)

Note: The figures are a percentage of the total number of pure landlords who prefer sharecropping to fixed-rent lease in the sample. A total of 87% of the pure landlords prefer sharecropping to fixed-rent leases. Multiple options were allowed.

Higher profit than fixed-rent lease — 70%
Cost-sharing — 35%
Own family's labour low — 30%
Absence of immediate cash requirement — 20%
Cash rent not desired — 20%

Figure 6.2b Major reasons for preferring sharecropping (for tenants)

Note: The figures are a percentage of the total number of pure tenants who prefer sharecropping to fixed-rent lease in the sample. A total of 65% of the pure tenants prefer this. Multiple options were allowed.

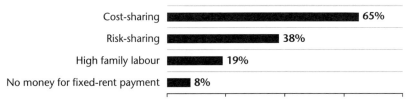

Table 6.13 Preference scores for different contracts

	No. of households (N)	Contract Type			Significance of Difference Results (t-value)		
		Batai	Chauthai	Peshgi	tvalue_bp (*Batai-Peshgi*)	tvalue_bc (*Batai-Chauthai*)	tvalue_cp (*Chauthai-Peshgi*)
Landlords							
All	23	2.43	2.04	1.21	5.43***	1.58	2.96***
Thakurs	9	2.78	1.83	1.28	9***	2.2**	1.25
Muraos	10	2.2	2	1.2	2.02**	0.69	1.71
Tenants							
All	49	2.21	1.25	2.38	−0.92	6.90***	−6.08***
Thakurs/Muraos	19	2.05	1.23	2.65	−2.16**	4.86***	−6.34***
Jatabs	15	2.6	1.73	1.66	3.69***	2.82**	0.21

Notes: tvalue_bp reports the t-stat for H_o: mean(*Batai*) - mean(*Peshgi*) = 0. tvalue_bc reports the t-stat for H_o: mean(*Batai*) - mean(*Chauthai*) = 0; tvalue_cp reports the t-stat for H_o: mean(*Chauthai*) - mean(*Peshgi*) = 0. (*$p < 0.1$; **$p < 0.05$; ***$p < 0.01$).

preferring sharecropping over other contracts by landlords and by tenants. For tenants, the incentive to earn more income is the predominant associated reason for engagement in tenancy. Those who have excess labour or agricultural equipment prefer to use tenancy to make good use of their available inputs, including labour. For landlords, tenancy provides the opportunity to circumvent the shortage of working capital or labour for cultivation.

For landlords, the preference for sharecropping is based first on the incentive of earning a greater profit and, second, on the ability to share costs. Cost sharing appears to be the major factor for tenants, while the second factor is risk sharing.[40]

---

[40] It is not uncommon for farmers to find themselves unable to provide timely inputs such as fertilizer or irrigation because they are running low on working capital. In *batai*, it is very common for one partner (be it landlord or tenant) to incur a cost in full, so that the cultivation operation can be completed on time, and to then be repaid by his partner later. This is normally an interest-free loan from one party to the other. For a self-cultivating farmer, working capital shortages imply that he would have to take a small loan from the village

One way to understand the choice of different contracts is by assigning ordinal ranking to different contracts. In Table 6.13, we assign a score of '3' to the most preferred choice and '1' to the least preferred choice of each respondent and then take an average for the scores of each contract choice over all respondents. If they were indifferent between two contracts, then both the contracts were assigned a score of '1.5' and if they did not mention a particular contract in their rankings, it was given a score of '0'.[41]

From Table 6.13 we can see that the landlords, on average, have a preference for sharecropping contracts. The predominant articulated reason in Figure 6.2a was profit, and we find that the higher profit for the landlord from sharecropping is verified in Figure 6.3, where we compare the profit of the landlords from sharecropping plots and fixed-rent plots, under three different profit definitions, for *rabi* 2008/9. Profit definition A is the difference between total product value and total paid-out cost.[42] Under definition B, profit is the difference between total product value and total cost of all inputs used, except family labour. This second definition includes an imputed cost for the inputs a farmer

Figure 6.3 Landlord profit from *batai* and *peshgi* plots, 2008/9

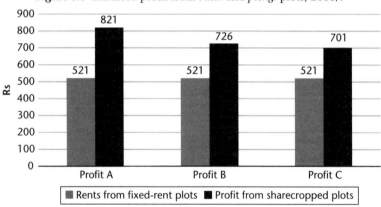

moneylender (with interest between 3 to 5% per month). In addition to the advantage of timeliness, where more than one input source or its finance might be available, there is the general argument that discussion may produce better decisions—'two heads may be better than one'.

[41] Every household was asked to express his/her preference for the contract. The maximum score that a household can get is 3. If the household expressed a clear preference, the preferred contract was given a score of 3. The remaining two contracts would get 0. In cases where the household expressed the same level of preference towards two contracts, the score was assigned as 1.5 for the two preferred ones and 0 for the contract not preferred. If no contract was preferred, all contracts were assigned 0.

[42] This refers to the cost of inputs for which a monetary amount was paid. It excludes the rental for own assets and wage payments for own family labour.

owns. Definition C includes an imputation for family labour hours in the cost definition.[43] The landlord's profit from sharecropping is higher under all three definitions of profit.

Even though some landlords do end up choosing fixed-rent contracts, they report having done so only when in urgent need of cash and having leased-out under sharecropping regularly before. One important characteristic of the fixed-rent contracts is that many of them were extended to the people in Palanpur by those who did not reside in Palanpur at the time of the survey.[44]

Between sharecropping and *chauthai*, landlords tend to prefer sharecropping. *Chauthai*, where the tenants have a lower share in the output and, therefore, greater incentive to shirk (as explained), requires more supervision. Of the 13 landlords who prefer sharecropping over *chauthai*, 10 (77 per cent) of them mention cost sharing and 3 (38 per cent) provide lower supervision costs as their reasons for this preference. The choice between sharecropping and *chauthai* also seems to depend on the capital inputs that the tenant owns and his experience with the management of these inputs. If the tenant owns capital inputs and, therefore, has experience in using these inputs, it seems reasonable to let him have a greater say in the cultivation decisions and lease land out under sharecropping.[45] Fixed-rent contracts seem to be the choice in cases where the landlord either is struggling for cash or is too low on labour to play the role of a sharecropping partner.[46]

The landlord's choice of contract seems relatively straightforward from the responses in the discussion questionnaire. Overall, landlords prefer sharecropping contracts to others. In cases where they believe that they have most of the necessary inputs, including the skill and family labour for supervision, but are a little short on labour for cultivation, *chauthai* seems to be the contract of choice. In some cases, where the landlord has very little skill or labour for supervision or is an outsider, fixed rent is the preferred form of contract.

Overall amongst the tenants, fixed-rent contracts seem to be the most preferred type, even though, from the indicator in Table 6.13, the difference

---

[43] Sharecropping is different from fixed rent in that there is an implicit loan from the landlord to the tenant in the form of postponed rents (sharing of the crop occurs at harvest time). The difference in profits for landlord from sharecropped and fixed-rent plots could be the interest charged on this implicit loan.

[44] Of the 67 contracts leased-in on fixed rents in *rabi* 2008/9, 66% of them were offered by outsider landlords.

[45] For instance, Neeraj Thakur prefers to lease-out on *chauthai* as he can provide his share of inputs and gets a higher share by using this contract. However, when the tenant, Hargyan, asked for land for sharecropping, Neeraj accepted as he was on good terms with Hargyan and Hargyan also had resources, such as an engine.

[46] Note that urgent cash requirements arise mostly in cases where there is a medical emergency, something that reduces family labour availability, or where there are no adult members in the family. Therefore, in essence, urgent cash requirements, most often, are closely related to labour shortage.

between fixed-rent and sharecropping contracts is insignificant. The tenants from different castes, however, seem to differ significantly in their preference. The higher castes, the Thakurs and the Muraos, seem to prefer fixed-rent contracts over sharecropping while the lower caste, the Jatabs, seems to have a clear preference for sharecropping.

This preference ordering is consistent with the economic and social structure of the village. Fixed-rent contracts are a preferred form of contract for tenants who possess the liquidity to pay the rent and input costs. In addition, such tenants believe they have the necessary skills but lack land in proportion to resources owned. The higher-caste tenants are more likely to own these resources. This is consistent with the findings in Section 6.3, where we observed a higher proportion of fixed-rent contracts being leased-out to higher castes.

The lower-caste tenants, often low on resources, prefer sharecropping as it gives them the opportunity to use the landlord's resources and skills and generate a higher profit than they would have otherwise managed. In addition, sharecropping in Palanpur works on the basis of the principle of reciprocity. A landlord and a tenant involved in a sharecropping contract are expected to help each other in times of trouble. Sadoulet, de Janvry, and Fukui (1997) find evidence of a similar arrangement between landlords and tenants in the Philippines. Jatabs occupy the lowest position in the social hierarchy and have the highest degree of poverty, illiteracy, and political isolation. Jatabs also have the lowest access to formal markets for inputs and credit (see Table 6.7 in Section 6.2 of this chapter). Sharecropping provides them with the opportunity to access these markets through their landlords.

In the past, there have been instances where agricultural inputs like fertilizers were obtained by Jatab tenants from the FSS on their landlords' account, and later, the costs and interest were divided between landlord and tenant.[47] For other inputs, such as diesel for irrigation and fertilizers, if a sharecropping tenant is unable to pay his share, the landlord pays for it at the time of the activity, then receives more than the originally agreed half-share of output after harvest. Jatabs are one of the poorest caste groups in the village and cannot always depend on members of their own caste to help them in times of need. Although the increase in non-farm opportunities has led to an improvement in the economic position of Jatabs, they still depend a lot on their landlords to help them. Thakurs and Muraos have traditionally been the richest and the highest in the social hierarchy. Therefore, a sharecropping partnership with them, from the point of view of the Jatabs, is not only one with familiar partners, but also the most secure that might be available to them.[48]

---

[47] See Lanjouw and Stern (1998) for details on the FSS.
[48] Similar arrangements to smooth consumption are observed by Rosenzweig and Stark (1989) and Mazzocco and Saini (2012) in other parts of India, albeit in different contexts.

The discussion questionnaire highlights that the choice of tenancy contract is largely the landlord's decision. Out of 13 landlords who preferred sharecropping contracts to others, all of them were able to lease-out under sharecropping. In comparison, out of the 24 tenants who preferred fixed-rent contracts, only 14 managed to lease-in land on fixed-rent contracts, and almost all of these leased-in from an outsider household or a household with no able adult male member. It would seem, therefore, that the contract choice for the tenants follows the following process. If a prospective tenant has most or all available resources, including money for rent and agricultural skills, but has a reasonable amount of extra labour in the household, he prefers a fixed-rent contract. Given this, if the landlord, depending on his own labour-to-land ratio, wants a fixed-rent contract, then fixed rent is the contract of choice. If the landlord does not agree to a fixed-rent contract, sharecropping is the contract of choice. If the tenant owns an adequate amount of labour for cultivation and some, but not all, of the other required resources, or if the tenant depends less on formal markets and more on the community for consumption smoothing and managing in times of emergency, sharecropping seems to be the most preferred form of contract. If the tenant has nothing except labour to offer and depends on the community in times of emergency, *chauthai* is the contract of choice. The fact that fixed rents are less profitable to the landlord and more profitable to the tenant is essentially saying that the landlord gets less for not taking a risk. And the tenant gets more for taking the risk. This is on top of and combined with the other argument about availability of inputs, cash, and so on.

In addition, the decision regarding the choice of crop on a sharecropped plot is also, most often, taken by the landlords. Of the 36 plots leased-out on sharecropping, the landlord decided the crop for 23 (64 per cent) of them. For six of them, it was decided upon mutually by both parties.

When we look at the characteristics that landlords seek in a sharecropping tenant, we find further insights into the forces at work.

Of the 16 pure landlords involved in sharecropping contracts, 13 mention a good relationship with and/or trustworthiness of the tenant as one of the most important traits that they look for (this is the 81 per cent in the first vertical bar of Figure 6.4). This is consistent with the findings of Drèze and Sharma (1998) for the 1983/4 round. For a sample of 11 landlords and 23 tenants, they found that 'Honesty' was the most important quality sought in their partners by both the landlord and the tenant. Landlords also preferred tenants who were hard-working and resourceful. Nearly all respondent households in 1983/4 who were involved in tenancy were engaged in sharecropping contracts (and 77 per cent of households were involved in tenancy, see Table 6.1).

In *chauthai* contracts, landlords look for hard-working tenants (see the third vertical bar in Figure 6.4), which is understandable given that *chauthai* is close to a pure labour contract and supervision cost is lower for tenants who are

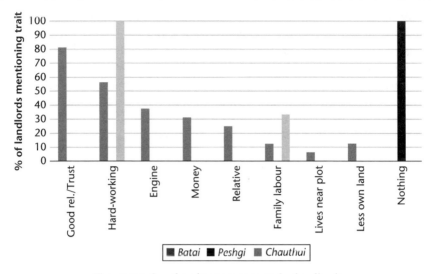

Figure 6.4 Sought-after tenant traits by landlords
Note: Multiple options were allowed.

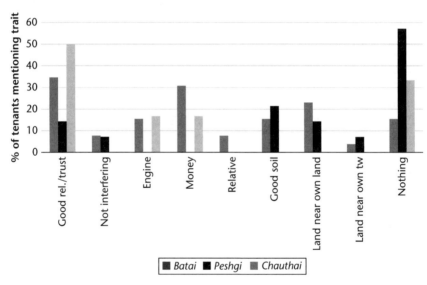

Figure 6.5 Sought-after landlord traits by tenants
Note: Multiple options were allowed; tw = tubewell.

likely to shirk less. For fixed-rent contracts, as might be expected, landlords do not seem to have a strong preference with regard to the traits of their tenants. The landlords get a fixed rent regardless of the effort or yield of the tenants.

Trustworthiness also appears as a strong characteristic sought after by the tenants in the choice of landlords for sharecropping contracts (see Figure 6.5).

Since contracts do not have a lot of scope for opportunistic behaviour by landlords, the trustworthiness of the landlord might arise from how likely he is to help the tenant during hard times. Access to money and to agricultural equipment such as pumping sets or tractors is also helpful in choosing a landlord, so that the commitment to cost-share is fulfilled reliably and with little fuss. However, for *peshgi* contracts, tenants look for good quality land or land near their tube well or their own plot.

These discussions not only help us understand the reason for the co-existence of different contracts at one point in time, but also explain the reason why one household might go for multiple contracts. The responses in the discussion questionnaire also qualify the leasing model from Section 6.3. Leasing behaviour, in terms of desired cultivated area (by a household) and in addition to its labour-to-land ratio, may also depend on preference for different types of contracts, ability to bargain, the availability of other assets, and the presence of trustworthy partners. For example, all else being equal, some households might choose to lease-out on sharecropping even though the labour-to-land excess might be best suited for fixed-rent contracts, as this could influence the availability of tenants. This also explains why households might prefer one portfolio of contracts to others which provide the same degree of labour-to-land adjustment.

We have seen that the preferences and reasons expressed in the 'discussion questionnaire' provide useful insights into the choice of tenancy contracts and the decisions of the households for the 2008/9 survey. The forces at work also help us to understand changes over time in the institutional structures of markets and how they function.

6.5 Sharecropping, Efficiency, and Institutional Dynamism

Many debates on tenancy have started with the 'Marshallian theory' of share-cropping: in the absence of contractible or enforceable effort, the disincentive created by the division of the marginal benefit of a tenant's effort renders the contract inefficient. Marshall recognized this issue (see, e.g., Bliss and Stern (1982) for a discussion) and thus further pointed to the necessity of the active involvement of the landlord. Cheung (1969) argues that this inefficiency can be eliminated if labour input can be specified and enforced through monitoring. The argument, however, in simple form, assumes costless supervision. Empirical studies, however, find evidence of both costly supervision (Jacoby and Mansuri, 2008) and no supervision (Shaban, 1987). Other arguments put forward and issues raised fall into three broad categories: (i) risk sharing; (ii) screening of workers with different abilities; and (iii) missing or incomplete markets for inputs besides land.

Cheung (1969) and, later, Stiglitz (1974) and Newbery (1975), argue that sharecropping contracts facilitate risk sharing between landlords and tenants. However, they do acknowledge that if a landlord was able to 'mix' contracts, that is, could divide his land between fixed-rent farming and his own cultivation, he would be able to achieve a similar level of risk sharing as in sharecropping.[49] Risk will always be important in agriculture, but there appears to be a lack of empirical evidence supporting the idea that risk sharing is the only motive behind sharecropping (Chao, 1983; Pant, 1981; Rao, 1971); although it would, in any case, seem odd to insist that risk was the only motive. Hallagan (1978) suggests that there may be information asymmetry about the entrepreneurial ability and quality of the prospective tenants, and contracts can act as screening devices where the tenants with the best ability get fixed-rent tenancy and those with worst work as agricultural labourers. Those in-between engage in share tenancy. However, this assumption of asymmetric information is unlikely to hold in a small village like Palanpur where people know each other fairly well, especially their tenants, and have a good idea of their abilities and traits. Screening models also fail to explain why the dominant contract would vary across regions governed by the same kind of institutions and why a tenant might lease-in some land on sharecropping contracts and some on fixed-rent contracts.

More recent studies have stressed imperfections beyond the land markets. Bliss and Stern (1982), Braverman and Stiglitz (1982), and Skoufias (1995) point out that imperfect markets for draught animal services, casual labour, or credit, and indeed the presence of all three imperfections, constitute reasons for households entering sharecropping contracts. Eswaran and Kotwal (1985) see such contracts as a response to the incomplete markets for management and supervision ability. However, the imperfect market argument fails to explain why the same tenant (landlord) leases-in (out) land on more than one kind of contract in a particular season (see Bliss and Stern, 1982; Shaban, 1987). Second, while these reasons might explain the existence of sharecropping, they do not explain why sharecropping tenants choose not to shirk, something observed in many parts of the world.[50]

Consistent with the findings of Bliss and Stern (1982) and Drèze and Sharma (1998) for previous rounds of the Palanpur survey, there seems to be little evidence of shirking by tenants in sharecropping contracts, in the sense of

---

[49] This equivalence requires a constant returns-to-scale assumption. However, the evidence on returns to scale is mixed. See Rudra (1968), Bardhan (1973), Cornia (1985), Townsend, Kirsten, and Vink (1998), and Wan and Cheng (2001).

[50] Tyagi and Himanshu (2011), Sharma and Drèze (1996), Sadoulet et al. (1994), Nabi (1986), Cohen (1983), Bliss and Stern (1982), Bardhan and Rudra (1980), Hossain (1977), Mangahas (1976), Huang (1975), Dwivedi and Rudra (1973), Chakravarty and Rudra (1973), and Rao (1971) all report evidence against the inefficiency of sharecropping. The evidence supporting the inefficiency of sharecropping is scarce in comparison to the amount of evidence against it.

lower output per *bigha* on sharecropped land as compared with own-cultivated land. In econometric analysis with the 2008/9 data, we again do not find any significant difference in the outputs between the sharecropped and fixed-rent plots. We also find no significant difference in the amount of input used or effort exerted by the tenants of sharecropped and fixed-rent plots.

Productivity per *bigha* does not directly measure the efficiency with which a set of inputs has been used. To examine that question, we compare the productivity or efficiency of sharecropped plots with that of fixed-rents plots using stochastic frontier analysis (SFA).[51] The technical efficiency parameter reported is the contribution of family labour to output.[52] It incorporates both the quantity and quality of this input. We use yield of a plot as the output and include irrigation, seed, fertilizers, and hired labour costs, expressed in per *bigha* terms, as inputs. Table 6.14 presents the findings from the SFA approach. The results are consistent with the hypothesis that sharecropping is not inefficient in comparison to fixed-rent plots. An examination of potential efficiency differences using non-parametric methods came to a similar conclusion.[53]

In Palanpur, the 'moral hazard' shirking or efficiency issue either does not arise or there are institutional structures in the village which help to take care of the problem. We suggest the latter.

An interesting story emerges when we look at the caste-wise distribution of sharecropping contracts between the landlord and the tenant. There seems to

Table 6.14 Technical efficiency using SFA for *rabi*, 2009

	Sharecropped Plots	Fixed-Rent Plots	Overall	t-value
Technical efficiency	0.626	0.643	0.633	−0.57
Number of plots	85	60	145	

[51] We use a parametric method, the SFA, to make the comparison. The SFA production function is a combination of ordinary least squares (OLS) production functions method and deterministic production functions used in data envelopment analysis (DEA). The DEA approach is a non-parametric approach to measuring technical efficiency by taking into account a given set of possible inputs and outputs. Assuming a particular combination of inputs used to produce a level of output as the most efficient combination, the method assigns a relative efficiency value to the other production units. For our purpose, we assume an output-oriented approach and variable returns-to-scale technology. While the OLS method assumes that all the deviations from the estimated function are due to measurement errors, the DEA method assumes all deviations are due to inefficiency. SFA reports two components, one for noise and the other for inefficiency, and, therefore, it is the most appropriate method for efficiency analysis here. Details of the estimation are available in the Palanpur working paper series.

[52] We use the yield of a plot as the output and include irrigation, seed, fertilizers, and hired labour costs, expressed in per *bigha* terms, as inputs. The part of input difference not explained by these inputs, therefore, is due to differences in family labour inputs (and, a random shock, in SFA).

[53] See the Palanpur working paper series, http://sticerd.lse.ac.uk/india/research/palanpur/publications.asp.

be a strong preference for a partner from the same caste, if someone is leasing-out on sharecropping. Table 6.15 presents what the distribution of area under sharecropping contracts in the two seasons in 2008/9 would have looked like if the matches had been made randomly, after controlling for land leased-in and leased-out by each caste. Table 6.16 presents the actual distribution. The area under within-caste contracts was 38.8 per cent of the total area leased-in under sharecropping in *rabi* 2009. However, under random matches controlled for area leased-in and leased-out by each caste, the percentage would have been 18.4. These are the sum of the diagonals in Tables 6.15 and 6.16, respectively.

This pattern of within-caste leasing has been observed in earlier rounds. In *rabi* 1983/4, the actual area under sharecropping within the same caste was 27.5 as against 11.4 expected under random matches. In *rabi* 1974, the figure was 28.1 instead of 8.3. Sharma and Drèze (1998) note the prevalence of

Table 6.15 Expected distribution (%) of sharecropped area, *rabi* 2009, under random matching

		Tenant						
		Thakur	Murao	Dhimar	Gadariya	Muslims	Jatabs	Total
Landlord	Thakur	10.8	11.2	0.7	4.1	9.5	11.9	48.1
	Murao	5.3	5.5	0.3	2	4.7	5.8	23.7
	Gadariya	1.8	1.8	0.1	0.7	1.6	2	8
	Muslims	1.4	1.4	0.1	0.5	1.2	1.5	6.2
	Passi	0.2	0.2	0	0.1	0.2	0.3	1
	Jatab	0.2	0.2	0	0.1	0.2	0.2	0.8
	Others	2.7	2.8	0.2	1	2.4	3	12.2
	Total	22.4	23.2	1.4	8.5	19.7	24.7	100

Note: The individual cell entries are obtained by taking as given the total amount of land leased-out (within the village) by each caste and assuming that this land is leased to different castes pro rata based on their share in the total number of households in the village. There were no tenants from 'other castes' or Passi and no Dhimar landlords in the village in 2009.

Table 6.16 Actual distribution (%) of sharecropped area, *rabi* 2008/9

		Tenant						
		Thakur	Murao	Dhimar	Gadariya	Muslims	Jatabs	Total
Landlord	Thakur	18.5	2.7	0	5	6.6	15.4	48.1
	Murao	1.2	11.9	0	0	4.6	5.9	23.7
	Gadariya	0	0	0	3.5	2.7	1.8	8
	Muslims	0	1.2	0	0	4.1	0.8	6.2
	Passi	0	0.8	0.2	0	0	0	1
	Jatab	0	0	0	0	0	0.8	0.8
	Others	2.7	6.6	1.2	0	1.7	0	12.2
	Total	22.4	23.2	1.4	8.5	19.7	24.7	100

same-caste tenancy, particularly among Thakurs and Muraos.[54] While the preference for same-caste members might be declining over time, it was still of importance in 2008/9.

Given the social structure of villages in India and the preference for trust-worthy tenancy partners observed in Palanpur, the choice of co-caste members and kin as partners is hardly surprising. In the discussion-questionnaire responses to questions on traits they look for in a partner (see Section 6.4), many report they prefer leasing to a friend or a relative. Such observations have been made in other parts of the world. According to Pollak (1985: 593): 'One would expect family governance to predominate in low-trust environments and in sectors utilizing relatively simple technologies.' De Janvry, Fukui, and Sadoulet (1997) studied the differences in sharecropping contracts between kin and non-kin in the Philippines. They reported direct monetary and in-kind transfers from the landlords to the tenants as the reason behind mitigation of the 'moral hazard' problem in case of kin. Kassie and Holden (2007) found that kin tenants in Ethiopia are less likely to cheat as they feel a stronger moral obligation to the landlord. Since relatives and same-caste members in Palanpur are dependent on each other in other walks of life and are called upon to help each other in times of need, there is an incentive to be constructive, collaborative, and deliver well in the contracts. That does not, of course, mean that all inter-actions within a caste or between landlord and tenant always work harmo-niously and well.[55]

Trust is central in explaining another relationship we find in Palanpur between a group of tenants and landlords. In Palanpur, as has been observed in many parts of the world, the poorest often enter into sharecropping contracts with the richer. As is clear from Tables 6.15 and 6.16, the percentage of the total sharecropped area leased-in by Jatabs from the Thakurs is significantly higher than that pre-dicted under ownership-adjusted random matching. These relationships have often been seen as a patron–client relationship, where the client gives priority to work at a patron's enterprise and, in return, the patron provides the tenant and his family members with security or other help over and above levels that might

---

[54] "The tendency to seek partners within one's own caste can also be seen to vary between different castes. For instance, Thakurs hardly lease-in land from non-Thakurs, the main exceptions being a few fixed-rent leases from Jatab households. This is consistent with the fact that Thakurs prefer to avoid the loss of prestige involved in sharecropping the land of a person of a "lower" caste (fixed-rent leases are considered as less problematic, because they give the tenant complete independence from the landlord). The tendency to seek a tenant in one's own caste is strongest among Muraos, for whom more than half of leased-out land remains within the caste" Sharma and Drèze (1998: 489).

[55] Caste can be interpreted as an extended version of family. In fact, in Palanpur, if one was to trace back current households sufficiently far, one might find that seemingly unrelated households from the same caste have originated from the same parent household.

be expected from a 'usual' employer.[56] The benefits that the poorer households enjoy in such contracts could be construed as 'efficiency wages', embodying the idea that better 'employment benefits' elicit stronger efforts. While such strong patron–client relationships have long departed, they have some bearing on trust between Thakur landlords and Jatab tenants even today. Elsewhere, Sadoulet et al. (1994) study two categories of sharecroppers that are observed to be as efficient as the fixed-rent and owner cultivators in two villages of Thailand. They observe that those under great income risk and in poverty and those in a long-term relation of gift exchange with their landlord have an incentive 'not to shirk'. However, they do not consider the relationships and understandings outside these gift-exchange contracts separately.

Based on these observations, and building on authors such as Arrow (1968), Akerlof (1970), and Ben Porath (1980), we argue that in settings with moral hazard, trust between partners plays an important role. Landlords and tenants choose their partners carefully from within these 'communities of trust' and depend on each other outside the tenancy market, for example, for assistance in times of need, in ways which can be both monetary and non-monetary in nature. Being an unreliable partner, or cheating, within the community of trust can, therefore, have far-reaching consequences. As a result, within these 'communities of trust' costly private monitoring is replaced by less costly social mechanisms.[57] The organization of such 'communities of trust' to overcome market limitations have been observed elsewhere in India (Foster and Rosenzweig, 2001; Mazzocco, 2012; Rosenzweig and Stark, 1989; Townsend et al., 1998).[58]

Observations consistent with this type of theorizing have also been made by Bliss and Stern (1982) and Lanjouw and Stern (1998). Here are two excerpts from the interviews with the farmers at the seed store that Drèze noted during his stay at Palanpur in 1983 as an investigator:

> [One of the farmers] said that most landlords would only lease to people from other castes if they cannot find someone within their own caste; but he seemed to attribute this behaviour to smoother 'contacts' and smoother flow of information within caste, rather than simply to a compulsory 'caste loyalty'. (13 October 1983)
>
> Roshan is . . . sick with fever for about a month . . . has two hungry kids and cannot work and has no assets . . . he could well die of exhaustion . . . His near relatives (also

---

[56] Kessinger (1974) observed a similar patron–client relationship in his study of a village of Vilayatpur, Punjab between 1948 and 1968. Gough (1952) found similar arrangements between Brahmas and Pallans in a village in Tanjore district of the erstwhile Madras state in the 1950s.

[57] Otsuka and Hayami (1988: 56) point out that: 'The fact that share[cropping] contracts are common in small agrarian communities that are characterised by intensive social interactions seem to reflect the existence of a relatively efficient enforcement mechanism in such communities.'

[58] Munshi and Rosenzweig (2003), Luke and Munshi (2006), and Munshi and Rosenzweig (2009) make a similar argument in their works on caste-based networks.

neighbours) seem more sympathetic and the women particularly might go as far as giving them some food (I guess his brothers are ready to lend him a limited amount of money, too). (14 October 1983)

Such observations are neither new nor unheard of from other parts of India. According to Lewis (1955: 169): 'A typology of peasant societies must include as a variable the role of kinship, that is, the extent to which the society is organised on a kinship basis.'

In his study of Ranikhera, a north Indian village, Lewis (1955) finds that there was great readiness to engage in cooperative activities within kinship and caste, similar to what we find in Palanpur. The villagers from Ranikhera, according to him, spent a great proportion of their time in some group activity, in smoking groups, in the extended family, in cooperative economic undertakings, and in caste councils. Caste members in Ranikhera were found to be bound by kinship, by common traditions, interests, and social inter-actions. Also, no faction rented out land to members of a different faction if there was someone from the same faction in need of land to till. However, as in Palanpur, the caste system was observed to be losing its force, with increasing off-farm employment opportunities in and around Ranikhera.

In his description of 'the Social System of a Mysore Village' in 1950, Srinivas (1951: 29–30) writes:

[S]ecuring labour on the basis of reciprocity depends on the ties of kinship, caste, neighbourliness, and friendship. A man must be friendly and ready to help another with his labour, time, resources and money, if he wants others to help him.

A word that is constantly heard in the village is daksinya, which be translated as 'obligation'. Every relationship between two human beings or groups is productive of 'obligation', and gives each of them a claim, however vague, on the other . . . A poor man can put others under his obligation by giving his personal labour and skills . . . Every rich man tries to 'invest in people', so that he can on occasion turn his following to political or economic advantage.

Discussing the changing structure of a depressed caste in Madhopur, a village in the state of Uttar Pradesh, Cohn (1955: 55) writes:

The relationships which were traditional between landlord and tenant tend still survive in Madhopur. These relationships involve much more than strictly economic considerations. The lessee of a Thakur is called a 'praja', literally a 'subject', 'dependent' or 'child' . . . The Thakur is considered to be responsible for the wealth of his tenants, and responsible for their care in need and ill health. A tenant in turn owes allegiance and support to his Thakur.

Cohn goes on to describe how this tie is dramatized at life-cycle ceremonies and how the tenant supports his landlord to the extent of doing violence to his adversary. The description of changes in Madhopur during the 1950s is strikingly similar to developments in Palanpur. Cohn writes how the construction of a railway line had led to better mobility and how residents from all castes were seeking work in cities. Elections brought political competition on a wider scale. All these developments led to a notable change in family structure, political behaviour, and attitudes towards caste status. These can all be observed in Palanpur, as well. Family ties grew looser and the importance of clan and village declined, much as is happening in Palanpur. But they have far from disappeared.

Steed (1955:121), studying Kasanda, a Hindu village in Gujarat, writes:

> One effect of strong local networks of relationships among the sub-castes was to insulate from the outside the social structure of the village as a whole... But in 1950, as the freer economic classes of peasant proprietors and hired labour grew in number, some of the old insularity of the sub-caste groups showed signs of giving away.

But does this mechanism of trust and obligation still ensure no shirking in the sense we have described? One could argue that communities of trust are nothing but networks, all the people that a farmer knows. If it is so, sharecropping tenants outside these communities of trust should be doing as well as those within a landlord's community of trust. Our comparison of input costs per *bigha* applied within these groups with those applied by sharecropping tenants outside a landlord's community of trust suggests communities of trust do as well, sometimes better, than non-related tenants in terms of value of inputs used. Similar analysis using SFA suggests that faith in these communities of trust is not misplaced and that they are more than mere acquaintance networks. Tenants within the communities of trust have higher technical efficiency, an indicator of a larger contribution of labour quantity and quality towards output, than those outside these communities.[59]

6.6 Conclusion

Tenancy continues, and is expected to continue, to be an important aspect of agriculture in Palanpur. There has been some decline in the percentage of households in the village involved in tenancy, but it is still a majority, and the overall percentage of village area under tenancy has been going up consistently. This change is associated with greater availability of jobs in the non-farm sector, with mechanization, and with the rising productivity of agriculture. Improvements in access to markets during 2008–15 and

---

[59] See the Palanpur working paper series, http://sticerd.lse.ac.uk/india/research/palanpur/publications.asp.

opportunities outside and inside the village have contributed to greater flexibility and ability to choose the preferred type of contract. Markets also seem to have played a significant role in allowing some, such as Jatabs and Telis, to loosen some of the constraints of the caste hierarchy in the village and have had an indirect impact on contract choice.

The changing nature of jobs, monetization of input markets, and mechanization have impacted the labour market and cropping patterns, and also changed the nature of tenancy contracts. The emergence of *chauthai* is a good example of the flexibility of labour–land contracts to changing requirements and abilities to undertake labour supervision, and to changes in labour availability within the household. The structure of contracts has evolved with the changing economy. But beyond the question of the type of contacts, there is also a question of with whom the contract is made. The institutions in land–labour markets bring features of the caste system to help handle issues of trust and supervision. At a time when caste-based traditional occupational structures seemed to be weakening, caste still appears to be an important element of the social and economic relations between landlords and tenants.

Sharecropping continues to exist and is the dominant form of tenancy contract because it carries benefits for both the landlord and the tenant.[60] Landlords try to keep unnecessary interference to the minimum and are willing to help the tenants if necessary. Tenants respond by cooperating in the cultivation process, by not shirking, and by using inputs in intensities similar to that on fixed-rent plots. There is no evidence of significant shirking by the tenants even though direct or intrusive monitoring by the landlord is rare. From our discussions with the villagers, both landlords and tenants, and the choice of partners across the years, we suggest that an apparently less costly social mechanism, in large part, replaces costly and constant private monitoring by the landlord. This mechanism operates via communities of trust for each partner, a group where the members depend on each other in other walks of life and when in need. However, the importance of such communities of trust has been reduced due to the greater penetration of formal markets, in particular for mechanized inputs, and greater liquidity from non-farm activities. With some availability of formal assistance from the state (such as the Mahatma Gandhi Rural Employment Guarantee Scheme (MNREGS) and the Public Distribution System (PDS)), individuals do not have to rely so much on informal linkages. However, life is uncertain and the state and markets do not always function well. The need for communities of trust and mutual support, and within them sharecropping, continues.

---

[60] As Higgs (1894: 8) says, 'It may be "the daughter of necessity", but is certainly not "the mother of misery".'

The markets of Palanpur are not ones where, as in standard neoclassical microeconomic theory, anonymous agents transact with each other's products, which are homogeneous and understood, at prices which are clear and well known. In Palanpur, as in many other regions around the world, the players in the tenancy markets are usually from the same village, share the same culture and customs, use the same common pool of resources, and depend highly on each other in ways which, often, bypass and even replace markets. And they live in a world where uncertainty and risk matter, and mechanisms to cope with them are limited. The sense of mutually supported reciprocity amongst villagers and fellow caste members also brings a fear of being ostracized if one cheats the village or the villagers. This creates a disciplining mechanism that limits shirking or using inefficient amounts of other inputs.

Mechanisms which enhance social discipline occur in other parts of the world (see, for example, Ostrom, 2015). Villages are small communities where members know each other well. Alignment and segregation along caste, ethnic, and religious lines are more intense than they are in urban areas. Within groups, households interact and depend on each other more than their urban counterparts. The existence of such 'disciplining mechanisms' within the community is facilitated by close interactions and high interdependence between the members of the village. Such systems of reciprocity can provide partial responses to absent or imperfect markets for credit, labour, draught animals, and so on. These systems continue in Palanpur and many other parts of the world. It is important that economists and social scientists try to understand them. That is possible only by close study within those communities.

Acknowledgements

This chapter has been written by Tushar Bharti, Himanshu, and Japneet Kaur, and draws on the earlier work by Tyagi and Himanshu (2011). The authors acknowledge the contribution of Vaishnavi Surendra, Ashish Tyagi, Gajanand Ahirwal, and Hemendra Ahriwar in data cleaning and analysis.

References

Akerlof, G. 1970. 'The market for lemons: qualitative uncertainty and the market mechanism', *Quarterly Journal of Economics*, 84, no. 3: 488–500.
Arrow, Kenneth J. 1968. 'The economics of moral hazard: further comment,' *The American Economic Review* 58, no. 3 (1968): 537–9.

Bardhan, P. 1973. 'Size, productivity, and returns to scale: an analysis of farm-level data in Indian agriculture', *Journal of Political Economy* 81: 1370–86.

Bardhan, P., and Rudra, A. 1980. 'Terms and conditions of sharecropping contracts: an analysis of village survey data in India', *Journal of Development Studies* 16, no. 3: 287–302.

Bell, C., and Zusman, P. 1976. 'A bargaining theoretic approach to crop sharing contracts', *American Economic Review* 66: 578–88.

Ben-Porath, Yoram. 1980. 'The F-connection: Families, friends, and firms and the organization of exchange,' *Population and Development Review*, 6, no. 1: 1–30.

Bliss, C.J., and Stern, N. 1982. *Palanpur: The Economy of an Indian Village*. Oxford and New York: Oxford University Press.

Braverman, A., and Stiglitz, J.E. 1982. 'Sharecropping and the interlinking of agrarian markets', *American Economic Review* 72: 695–715.

Chakravarty, A., and Rudra, A. 1973. 'Economic effects of tenancy: some negative results', *Economic & Political Weekly* 8: 1239–46.

Cheung, S.N.S. 1969. *The Theory of Share Tenancy*. Chicago: University of Chicago Press.

Cohen, P.T. 1983. 'Problems of tenancy and landlessness in northern Thailand', *The Developing Economies* 21, no. 3: 244–66.

Cohn, Bernard S. 1955. 'The changing status of a depressed caste', in M. Marriott (ed.), *Village India: Studies in the Little Community*. Chicago: University of Chicago Press, 53–77.

Cornia, G.A. 1985. 'Farm size, land yields and the agricultural production function: an analysis for fifteen developing countries', *World Development* 13, no. 4: 513–34.

Drèze, J., Lanjouw, P., and Sharma, N. 1998. 'Economic development 1957–93', in P. Lanjouw and N.H. Stern (eds), *Economic Development in Palanpur over Five Decades*. Oxford and New Delhi: Oxford University Press.

Dwivedi, H., and Rudra, A. 1973. 'Economic effects of tenancy: some further negative results', *Economic & Political Weekly* 8: 1291–4.

Eswaran, M., and Kotwal, A. 1985. 'A theory of contractual structure in agriculture', *American Economic Review* 75: 352–67.

Foster, A.D., and Rosenzweig, M.R. 2001. 'Imperfect commitment, altruism, and the family: evidence from transfer behaviour in low-income rural areas', *Review of Economics and Statistics* 83, no. 3: 389–407.

Gough, K. 1952. 'The social structure of a Tanjore village', *The Economic Weekly*, 4, no. 21: 531–6.

Hallagan, W. 1978. 'Self-selection by contractual choice and the theory of sharecropping', *Bell Journal of Economics* 9: 344–54.

Higgs, H. 1894. '"Metayage" in western France', *The Economic Journal* 4, no. 13: 1–13.

Hossain, M. 1977. 'Farm size, tenancy and land productivity: an analysis of farm level data in Bangladesh agriculture', *Bangladesh Development Studies* 5: 285–348.

Huang, Y. 1975. 'Tenancy patterns, productivity, and rentals in Malaysia,' *Economic Development and Cultural Change* 23: 703–18.

Jacoby, H.G., and Mansuri, G. 2008. 'Incentives, supervision, and sharecropper productivity', *Journal of Development Economics* 88: 232–41.

Kassie, M., and Holden, S. 2007. 'Sharecropping efficiency in Ethiopia: threats of eviction and kinship', *Agricultural Economics* 37: 179–88.

Kessinger, T.G. 1974. *Vilyatpur 1848–1968: Social and Economic Change in a North Indian Village*. Berkeley, CA: University of California Press.

Lanjouw, P., and Stern, N. 1998. *Economic Development in Palanpur Over Five Decades*. Oxford: Oxford University Press.

Lewis, O. 1955. 'Peasant culture in India and Mexico: a comparative analysis', in M. McKim (ed.), *Village India: Studies in the Little Community*. Chicago: University of Chicago Press.

Luke, N., and Munshi, K. 2006. 'New roles for marriage in urban Africa: kinship networks and the labour market in Kenya', *Review of Economics and Statistics* 88, no. 2: 264–82.

Mangahas, M. 1976. 'An economic theory of tenant and landlord based on a Philippine case', in L. Reynolds (ed.), *Agriculture and Development Theory*. New Haven, CT: Yale University Press.

Mazzocco, M. 2012. 'Testing efficient risk sharing with heterogeneous risk preferences', *American Economic Review* 102, no. 1: 428–68.

Mazzocco, M., and Saini, S. 2012. 'Testing efficient risk sharing with heterogeneous risk preferences', *American Economic Review* 102, no. 1: 428–68.

Munshi, K.D., and Rosenzweig, M.R. 2003. 'Traditional institutions meet the modern world: caste, gender and schooling choice in a globalising economy', *American Economic Review* 96, no. 4: 1225–52.

Munshi, K.D., and Rosenzweig, M. 2009. 'Why is mobility in India so low? Social insurance, inequality, and growth'. Technical Report, National Bureau of Economic Research.

Nabi, I. 1986. 'Contracts, resource use and productivity in sharecropping', *Journal of Development Studies* 22, no. 2: 429–42.

Newbery, D.M.G. 1975. 'The choice of rental contract in peasant agriculture', in L.G. Reynolds (ed.), *Agriculture in Development Theory*. New Haven, CT: Yale University Press.

Ostrom, E. 2015. *Governing the Commons*. Cambridge: Cambridge University Press.

Otsuka, K. and Hayami, Y., 1988. 'Theories of share tenancy: A critical survey,' *Economic Development and Cultural Change*, 37(1): 31–68.

Pant, Chandrashekar. 1981. 'Tenancy in semi-arid tropical villages of south India: Determinants and effects on cropping patterns and input use', ICRISAT Progress Report, No. 20, May 1981.

Pollak, R.A. 1985. 'A transaction cost approach to families and households', *Journal of Economic Literature* XX/II (June): 581–608.

Rao, C.H.H. 1971. 'Uncertainty, entrepreneurship and sharecropping in India', *Journal of Political Economy* 79: 578–95.

Rao, K.P.C., and Charyulu, D.K. 2007. 'Changes in agriculture and village economies'. Research Bulletin no. 21. International Crops Research Institute for the Semi-Arid Tropics.

Rawal, V. 2006. 'The labour process in rural Haryana (India): a field-report from two villages', *Journal of Agrarian Change* 6: 538–83. DOI:10.1111/j.1471–0366.2006.00134.x.

Rosenzweig, M.R., and Stark, O. 1989. 'Consumption smoothing, migration, and marriage: evidence from rural India', *Journal of Political Economy* 97: 905–26.

Rudra, A. 1968. 'More on returns to scale in Indian agriculture', *Economic & Political Weekly* 3: A33–A38.

Sadoulet, E., Janvry, A. de, and Fukui, S. 1994. 'Efficient share tenancy contracts under risk: the case of two rice growing villages in Thailand', *Journal of Development Economics* 45: 225–43.

Sadoulet, E., Janvry, A. de, and Fukui, S. 1997. 'The meaning of kinship in sharecropping contracts', *American Journal of Agricultural Economics* 79, no. 2: 394–406.

Shaban, R.A. 1987. 'Testing between competing models of sharecropping', *Journal of Political Economy* 95: 893–920.

Sharma, N., and Drèze, J. 1996. 'Sharecropping in a north Indian village', *Journal of Development Studies* 33, no. 1: 1–39.

Skoufias, E. 1995. 'Household resources, transaction costs, and adjustment through land tenancy', *Land Economics* 71: 42–56.

Srinivas, M.N. 1955. 'The social system of a Mysore village', in M. Marriott (ed.), *Village India: Studies in the Little Community*. Chicago: University of Chicago Press.

Srivastava, R.S. 2008. 'Rural labour in Uttar Pradesh: emerging features of subsistence, contradiction and resistance', *Journal of Peasant Studies* 26, nos 2–3: 263–315.

Steed, G. 1955. 'Notes on an approach to a study of personality formation in a Hindu village in Gujarat', in M. Marriott (ed.), *Village India: Studies in the Little Community*. Chicago: University of Chicago Press.

Stiglitz, J.E. 1974. 'Incentives and risk sharing in sharecropping', *Review of Economic Studies* 41: 219–55.

Townsend, R.F., Kirsten, J., and Vink, N. 1998. 'Farm size, productivity and returns to scale in agriculture revisited: a case study of wine producers in South Africa', *Agricultural Economics* 19, no. 1: 175–80.

Tyagi, A., and Himanshu. 2011. 'Tenancy in Palanpur'. LSE ARC Working Paper No. 47.

Walker, T.S., and Ryan, J.G. 1990. *Village and Household Economies in India's Semi-Arid Tropics*. Baltimore, MD: Johns Hopkins University Press.

Wan, G.H., and Cheng, E. 2001. 'Effects of land fragmentation and returns to scale in the Chinese farming sector', *Applied Economics* 33, no. 2: 183–94.

7

Changing Activities, Changing Markets: Beyond Agriculture*

7.1 Introduction

Economic development in a rural economy is generally associated with movement out of agriculture into non-farm activities and the growing importance of these activities in generating rural incomes. Productivity and wages in non-farm activities are often higher than in the farm sector, suggesting that increasing these activities could be a potent driver of growth and poverty reduction in rural areas (Fisher et al., 1997).

Rural India has seen significant growth of the non-farm sector during the past three decades. The share of the labour force in agriculture started declining in the mid-1970s, and by the mid-2000s the non-farm sector employed nearly 30 per cent of India's rural workforce. The average annual growth in non-farm employment was around 3 per cent during the 1980s and 1990s, and rose to over 4 per cent during the first decade of the 2000s. By 2011, employment in the non-farm sector had risen to nearly 40 per cent of the rural workforce (Himanshu et al., 2013).[1]

Given the size and the growth trajectory of non-farm activities, it is important to understand the nature of employment opportunities within this sector and the factors that govern access to and participation in such jobs. For example, while wages in non-farm activities are typically higher than in agriculture, it is generally observed that non-farm incomes are unequally distributed (Reardon et al., 2000). In this chapter we examine the dynamics of non-farm activities in Palanpur. We look at the factors that lie behind participation in the sector and that motivate workers to take on these jobs.

* This chapter has been written by Himanshu, Bhawna Joshi, and Peter Lanjouw.
[1] Based on National Sample Survey Organisation (NSSO) employment–unemployment surveys. Employment here refers to the usual status classification of NSSO. For details, see NSSO (2013).

The chapter also assesses the impact of non-farm activities on village income and its distribution. The span and the richness of our data allow us to track changes in the role of these activities over a long period of time, as well as in the evolving relationship between household or individual characteristics and involvement in non-farm activities.

We saw in Chapters 5 and 6 how investment in agriculture, particularly mechanization of irrigation, ploughing, and other activities, has enabled the release of labour to non-farm activities. We saw also how population growth had reduced the size of holdings and per capita opportunities within agriculture. That analysis will not be repeated here, but change in agriculture has been both an enabler and an incentive to non-farm activities.

We find that non-farm activities accounted for roughly two-thirds of total employment in Palanpur in 2015 (see also Figure 7.1 in Section 7.3.3).[2] Most non-farm employment growth can be attributed to an increase in casual employment opportunities, as opposed to regular, salaried jobs. This growth has been primarily driven, directly or indirectly, by the expansion of the construction sector. Self-employment growth has also been significant and accounted for nearly a third of non-farm employment by 2015.

Access to land is an important predictor of involvement in the non-farm sector. In the initial survey years, non-farm jobs were held largely by landless and near-landless households. Over time, as the village population has grown, the subdivision of landholdings has led to increased numbers of households with marginal landholdings and to a rise in the number diversifying out of agriculture. The process has been largely one of diversification rather than of complete withdrawal from agriculture, as many households combine various farm and non-farm activities. Growth of non-farm job opportunities has also led, as we saw in Chapter 6, to a change in tenancy patterns in the village: non-farm incomes have allowed some households who had been previously confined to agricultural wage employment due to a lack of cash for agricultural inputs, to now enter the tenancy market. Those households with substantial landholdings still participate less in the non-farm sector, but when they do they are best placed to access well-paid regular jobs, or they become involved in self-employment activities, which can require some capital investment.

At the household level, occupational diversification is associated with specific household- and individual-level characteristics. We find that, in Palanpur, the caste affiliation of a household has an important role in determining

---

[2] Employment here refers to the primary employment of an individual. Employment data for each individual was collected by months. Based on time criteria, primary employment was assigned to an individual based on the highest number of months spent in a particular employment. Most individuals engage in more than one activity. The activity on which the individual spent less time was considered a secondary activity. Those who spent most of the time not working were classified as non-workers or out of the labour force.

access to specific jobs, especially those in the regular non-farm sector. This appears to be largely due to the role of personal contacts and social networks in finding and availing oneself of opportunities. As a result, the highest-ranked castes in the village have acquired a disproportionate share of regular jobs, while the disadvantaged castes have minimal access. So far education does not appear to play a central role in determining access to the non-farm sector. This is likely due to the unskilled/semi-skilled nature of most non-farm jobs in Palanpur, which are regular and casual. Education may be necessary for some regular jobs, but such jobs make up a small part of the total.

There are two main components of the analysis presented in this chapter. The first component provides a sketch of the main sources of income in the village and shows how these have changed over the survey years. The subsequent part of the analysis attempts to identify some of the driving forces behind these long-run changes. The chapter is organized as follows. In Section 7.2, we describe some of the key features of the data supporting our analysis of involvement in non-farm activities. In Section 7.3, we document the growth of non-farm activities over the survey period. Section 7.4 relates the growth of agricultural wages in the village to growth of the non-farm sector. Section 7.5 gives a brief description of the major types of employment available to people in Palanpur. In Section 7.6, we examine the role of land endowment and caste affiliation of a household in determining access to and participation in non-farm activities. This section also deals with the role of education. Section 7.7 discusses the occupation structure of females in Palanpur. Section 7.8 examines migration and commuting patterns in the village over the survey period and documents the strong association of such flows with the process of rural non-farm diversification. In Section 7.9, we present a brief comparison of findings in Palanpur with those from other village studies. Section 7.10 offers a concluding discussion.

7.2 Data on Rural Non-Farm Activities

The Palanpur data allow us to track households and their activities over the entire survey period and to draw on the histories of all households in the village. In this chapter we focus primarily on data on occupation and income. For all survey rounds, the occupational classification is based on a time criterion, in the sense of a person's primary activity being determined on the basis of that activity to which he or she devotes the most time.

The data for 2008/9 deserve special mention as they are particularly rich. Information on employment and earnings, for this survey year, derives from three different sources. First, we have data from the household demographics survey module in which employment information for each individual in the household is reported based on the household head's perception of the occupation of the household members. In addition to this module, we have information on employment from a separate survey on employment that was conducted after the demographics survey. These employment data comprise the monthly activity of each individual in the household. Employment in any month is categorized as primary or secondary based on the time spent on each activity. Primary employment is defined as the activity where an individual spends most of his/her time in that particular month. Finally, for a sample of households we have detailed information on the daily activities of the members of the household entered in a diary format kept by a key informant in the household.

With the help of the first two sources and the diary data wherever available, we have been able to identify fairly clearly the primary and secondary employment of an individual for that year. In the end, the primary occupation of an individual in a year is defined as the activity which the individual pursues for the highest number of months during the year. The other activities that the individual is involved in are defined as secondary and tertiary activities accordingly.[3]

In all survey rounds that collected income data, income is calculated at the household level.[4] It includes (net) income from agriculture, various sources of non-farm employment (regular employment, non-agricultural labour income, self-employment, and other non-farm sources), agricultural labour income, rental income, remittances income, income from livestock, and *jajmani* income.[5] The data were collected with a reference period of one year and have been standardized across survey rounds. The data contain incomes from all the primary and secondary sources of employment for each of the households. All incomes are reported in real terms, deflated by the Consumer Price Index for Agricultural Labour (CPIAL) Uttar Pradesh at 2008/9 prices.

While the other rounds include information for all the households in the village, in the year 1974/5 the survey focused mainly on households that were involved in agriculture.[6] Based on this criterion, only 112 out of the 118 households present in the village were included in the survey. For the remaining six, we have data only on the number and characteristics of the family.

---

[3] In the case of outside jobs, we have information about the process of job search, how many days it took to find the job, and the number of days for which the job is obtained.

[4] The appendix to this chapter provides further details on income data.

[5] *Jajmani* refers to traditional caste-based occupations; that is, where certain castes take on specific jobs, such as Dhobi (washer-men), Gadaria (shepherds), Teli (oil pressers), Dhimar (water carriers), Passi (mat makers), and Jatabs (leather workers).

[6] These include households engaged in agriculture in any of the following senses: owning land, cultivating land, or providing agricultural labour.

Table 7.1 Broad classification of employment activities

Employment	Activities
Cultivation	Self-employment in cultivation
	Livestock production
Non-farm	Casual non-farm
	Self-employment (non-farm)
	Regular employment
	Jajmani
Non-cultivation	Non-farm
	Casual labour farm
	Mechanized farm activities
Not working	Student
	Domestic work
	Pension receivers
	Rent receivers
	Remittance receivers

Note: For details of incomes and classifications, see the appendix.

The head of these six households comprised two shopkeepers, a barber, a carpenter, a railway gang man, and a sweeper.[7] The surveys conducted in 1993 and 2015 were deliberately narrow/quick surveys and did not collect information on incomes. For these two rounds, occupational, but not income, data are available.

We follow standard definitions of cultivation, non-cultivation, and non-farm employment. Any work on one's own farm for the production of agricultural products, livestock production, or by leasing-in land is termed cultivation employment (see Table 7.1). The income derived from these activities is denoted cultivation income. Non-cultivation employment includes working on another's farm as an agricultural labourer, renting tractors or oxcarts used for cultivation, and employment in non-farm activities. Non-farm employment includes all economic activities other than those involved in the production of agricultural goods. It thus includes skilled or unskilled non-farm casual labour, work under the Mahatma Gandhi National Rural Employment Guarantee Scheme (MGNREGS), self-employment, jajmani (customary services), salaried employment, and employment in the mining, manufacturing, or government services sectors.[8] Any individual involved in non-market activities, such as

---

[7] See Bliss and Stern (1982: 5) for details on the data collection in 1974/5.
[8] These activities can be further classified depending on the terms of contract and the wage structure into the following categories. Casual labour non-farm includes unskilled activities on seasonal basis like Mahatma Gandhi National Rural Employment Guarantee Act (MGNREGA) workers, construction labourers, and casual workers in factories. The casual non-farm sector formed the major component of the rural non-farm economy in 2009. Regular jobs involve contract-based jobs either as temporary or as permanent employees on a salary basis in railways, government jobs, or as teachers, doctors, and so on. Self-employment off farm includes business units like marble polishing, repair or supply of machines, general stores, and other small enterprises.

domestic workers within the household, students, pension receivers, and rent or remittance receivers, is classified as not working.

7.3 Outside Jobs and Occupational Change in Palanpur

7.3.1 Non-Farm Activities Within and Outside the Village

Growing population, declining per capita land ownership, and reduced demand for labour due to farm mechanization have all been associated with efforts by residents of Palanpur to secure job opportunities outside agriculture. These include employment outside agriculture not only in Palanpur but also outside the village.[9] Within the village such activities include small 'petty' businesses, such as general shops, pharmacies, and tailoring. Many villagers have tried new forms of business and occupations over the survey period, such as beekeeping and mango cultivation.[10] Some, but not all, of these have been successful and have led to employment generation for others within the village.[11]

An interesting case is that of a Teli household headed by Nanhe, who owns 15 *bighas* of land. The household cultivated 46 *bighas* of land, including leasing-in 43 *bighas* and leasing-out another 12 *bighas* in 2008/9. Nanhe first found employment in a motorcycle repair shop in Chandausi. He worked there for a while and then returned to Palanpur where he opened his own repair shop. Over time, with the growth of his business, he was able to establish a flour mill and a mentha extraction plant. Assisted by these incomes from off-farm activities, the household has also been able to lease a substantial amount of land on *peshgi*. Higher incomes from non-farm sources are invested back in agriculture and generate higher farm income. By providing training to others, Nanhe has also helped other villagers establish their own repair shops.

Similar efforts have been made by other residents of Palanpur, and over time there has been an expansion of other business enterprises such as marble

---

[9] Examples of people who have moved out of Palanpur altogether for employment include a Dhimar, Siyaram, who works in a sugar factory in Jalandhar; and Mustaq, who first learnt the work of carpentry in Delhi and then imparted these skills to his sons who also now work as carpenters in New Delhi. The brother of Mustaq, Istiaq, had moved to Saudi Arabia for the same work and would often visit the village. A common perception amongst these villagers was that employment outside of Palanpur was definitely more remunerative than in Palanpur, as living standards of the family had improved. This also served as a source of inspiration for many others who wanted to search for employment outside the village. But migration is rare relative to commuting to non-farm activities.

[10] Currently three households from Palanpur are involved in the dairy business, purchasing milk from fellow villagers and selling it in nearby towns and villages.

[11] Another household in Palanpur tried pisciculture in the local pond. The business worked well in the beginning; however, over time, due to contamination of the water, the fish died. Residents from Palanpur try continuously to innovate and adopt new occupation strategies, as reflected in the growth of village business units.

polishing and motorcycle repair shops, generating higher incomes and non-farm employment expansion within the village.

7.3.2 Farm/Non-Farm Linkages

There exists a large body of literature emphasizing the linkages between agriculture and the non-farm sector. Some of this literature builds on Mellor's growth linkage technologies (Mellor, 1976). Mellor argued that increases in agricultural productivity and thus incomes of the farmers would be magnified by multiple linkages with the non-farm sector. These include production linkages both backward, via an increased demand for inputs such as ploughs, tractors, engines, and tools, and forward, via the need to process agricultural products. Mellor also pointed to the importance of consumption linkages via an increased demand for non-farm products.[12]

Linkages between agriculture and the non-farm sector certainly appear to be relevant for Palanpur. Increasing demand for technology which improves agricultural productivity can stimulate growth in the non-farm sector that can provide these inputs. We find, for example, that the increased use of mechanized agricultural technologies in Palanpur and the surrounding area, such as pumping sets and tractors, has led to an increase in the number of small businesses specializing in the repair and servicing of such machinery. Growth of household incomes driven by agricultural intensification has also led to changing consumption patterns, as households spend a smaller percentage of their income on food. In Palanpur we have found an increase in the number of general stores and motorcycle repair shops, related to the growing demand for non-food items. Conversion of household dwellings from *kaccha* (mud) houses to *pukka* (brick or cemented) households provides further and important evidence of changing consumption patterns. As has been noted, the expansion of such construction activities has resulted in the increase in brick kilns and marble polishing units in nearby towns and villages.

7.3.3 Occupational Trends in Palanpur

Until 1974/5 the economy in Palanpur was primarily agrarian, with over 70 per cent of employment in the farm sector. In recent decades, notwithstanding investment in agriculture and the growth in agricultural productivity and technology, the growth of the labour force in Palanpur has favoured the non-agricultural sector. By 2008/9 non-farm sector jobs accounted for

---

[12] For discussion on the linkages between agriculture and non-farm, also see Hazell, Haggblade, and Reardon (2010) and Chapter 4 of this book.

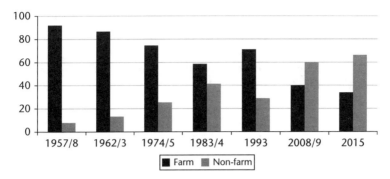

Figure 7.1 Composition of the farm and non-farm workforce

Note: The figure is based on the occupation composition of the adult male workforce in the village.

60 per cent of total jobs and rose further to 66 per cent in 2015, as shown in Figure 7.1.[13]

As noted, these findings for Palanpur resonate with national-level statistics.[14] Between 1993 and 2004 growth in non-farm sector employment outstripped that in agriculture at the all-India level.[15] Similarly, at the state level Ranjan (2008) draws on NSSO data and finds that the share of the non-farm sector employment in Uttar Pradesh rose from 17.8 per cent in 1987/8 to 20 per cent in 1993/4 and subsequently 30.1 per cent in 2004/5. It increased further to 40 per cent by 2011/12 (Himanshu, 2015). Himanshu and colleagues (2013) document that growth in non-farm sector employment in rural Uttar Pradesh accelerated even further during the second half of the 2000s.[16]

Prior to 1974/5, non-farm sector jobs in Palanpur largely comprised regular service on the railways. In addition, traditional caste-based *jajmani* services provided by, for example, washer men, oil men, blacksmiths, and barbers, also accounted for a significant share of non-farm activities. Such activities were undertaken by a few caste groups who were traditionally associated with these jobs, such as Dhobi (washer men), Teli (oil pressers), Dhimar (water carriers), and Gadaria (shepherds). Regular non-farm jobs in the first two survey years were mostly occupied by the Passis, who had migrated into Palanpur during

---

[13] An exception to the general trend of non-farm growth can be seen in the 1993 survey year. This is discussed further in this section and in footnote 22.

[14] Non-farm employment estimates provided here are for adult males (15+), unless otherwise stated. These are not strictly comparable to the non-farm employment estimates reported for India and UP which are for whole population. However, the trends are similar, that of accelerating non-farm employment.

[15] As compared to 64.4 million jobs created in the non-farm sector between 1993/4 and 2004/5, only 18.3 million jobs were created in agriculture. Also see Himanshu (2011), Dev and Evenson (2009), Jatav and Sen (2013).

[16] As against 5.85 million non-farms jobs created per year between 1993/4 and 2004/5, 7 million jobs were created per year between 2004/5 and 2011/12.

the 1940s and early 1950s, and who were already employed on the railways at that time. Given the paucity of non-farm job opportunities, agricultural labour represented the principal employment option for landless and near-landless households in the first two survey rounds. Those households with some land remained self-employed in cultivation either as cultivating land-lords or as cultivating tenants.

As Table 7.2 shows, there has been a gradual decline in the share of cultivation as a source of primary employment for households.[17] The other farm activity is casual agriculture labour, which had almost disappeared as a primary occupation by 2008/9. Together, these occupations account for just 26 per cent of all adult male occupations, or 34 per cent of the adult male workforce in 2008/9 (when the 'none' occupational category is removed from the calculation).[18] Expansion of non-farm jobs and growth of wages has resulted in a decline in hired wage labour in the village. The growth of agricultural wages and the decline in wage labour is discussed further in Section 7.3.4.

By 1974/5 a variety of manufacturing sector jobs were held by Palanpur villagers in nearby towns. These jobs included employment in a cloth mill in Moradabad, as well as oil and sugar mills in Bilari. The job opportunities had been eagerly seized upon by villagers, including some from caste groups that earlier had little or no role to play in the non-farm sector.[19] The cloth mill provided employment to 16 individuals in 1974/5.

While regular jobs were the most common non-farm sector jobs until 1983, these were overtaken by casual sector jobs in 2008/9.[20] Casual wage jobs accounted for almost 42 per cent of total non-farm sector jobs in 2008/9.

---

[17] The employment data is for male adults only and again has been carefully scrutinized and cross-checked to arrive at the final status of the individual. Other than an employment schedule, we also had supplementary schedules. Almost all the employment data are based on data for each of the months and activity patterns. A natural problem with this kind of classification is that the employment status is again a derived estimate and not a straight response from the respondent. We have followed the time-cum-priority criterion to assign the employment status. One consequence of this is that the individual identified as a casual labourer may not be engaged in casual wage work for 12 months; he may be involved in wage work for 6 months but working as self-employed for 5 months and unemployed or out of the labour force for 1 month. The status in our case will be casual labour. We do have information on child labour and female workers, but these are not included in this table. For female employment in Palanpur, see Chapter 10.

[18] If we look at the adult workforce, including males and females, in the village, cultivation accounts for 34.4%. The occupation composition for all adults in the village can be found in Table A.7.1.

[19] These primarily include those with some land in the previous years for whom cultivation was the only source of employment. Further details on the evolution of the employment structure based on caste are offered in Section 7.6.2.1.

[20] Himanshu and colleagues (2011), in their study of National Sample Survey (NSS) data, indicate that only 20% of the non-farm workforce held regular jobs in 2009/10. Nearly 40% of the rural workforce was employed as casual labourers. The declining share of regular jobs between 1983 and 2009/10 is striking: standard development models suggest a higher share of regular jobs. They attribute this decline to the absence of growth of social services employment where regular jobs would have been predominant.

Table 7.2 Occupation of adult males

Occupation	Year						
	1957/8	1962/3	1974/5	1983/4	1993	2008/9	2015
None	8 (4.65)	26 (14.05)	27 (12.27)	30 (10.38)	62 (17.71)	60 (15.19)	87 (20.23)
Cultivation & livestock	130 (75.58)	135 (72.97)	137 (62.27)	141 (48.79)	188 (53.71)	128 (32.41)	112 (26.05)
Casual labour (farm)	21 (12.21)	3 (1.62)	7 (3.18)	11 (3.81)	17 (4.86)	6 (1.52)	4 (0.93)
Casual labour (non-farm)	0 (0)	2 (1.08)	0 (0)	24 (8.30)	23 (6.57)	85 (21.52)	115 (26.74)
Regular employment	7 (4.07)	13 (7.03)	44 (20)	60 (20.76)	41 (11.71)	49 (12.41)	44 (10.23)
Self-employment (non-farm)	6 (3.49)	6 (3.24)	5 (2.27)	23 (7.96)	19 (5.43)	67 (16.96)	68 (15.81)
Total	172 (100)	185 (100)	220 (100)	289 (100)	350 (100)	395 (100)	430 (100)

Note: The table represents the number and proportion of adult males in each of the given occupations. The figures in parentheses represent the proportion of adult males in the given occupations.

The sharp decline in the number of regular jobs between 1983/4 and 1993 has been explained by Lanjouw and Stern (1998) as a consequence of the closure of the cloth mill in Moradabad, which accounted for more than a third of the regular jobs in 1974/5.[21] The rest can be explained by the out-migration of the Passi community from Palanpur after 1983/4. As noted, Passis held the majority of the regular jobs in the first two survey years (largely in the railways) and had subsequently expanded their regular non-farm employment beyond the railways to include manufacturing and steel polishing workshops. In 1974/5 and 1983/4 Passis accounted for 30 per cent and 25 per cent of the regular jobs, respectively.

The major decline in regular jobs between 1983/4 and 1993 led to an overall decline of non-farm employment, both in relative and absolute terms, in 1993. Between 1993 and 2008/9 there was some growth of regular employment, but not enough to overcome the fall in the regular jobs in the previous period. The share of non-farm jobs in the total workforce declined from 41 per cent to 29 per cent between 1983/4 and 1993, rising again to 60 per cent in 2008/9. The recovery in the relative share of the non-farm sector in 2009 in the total workforce was primarily a result of the strong growth of employment in the casual non-farm sector, which registered a compound annual growth of 9.1 per cent between the two survey rounds. An additional contribution to non-farm growth came from the expansion of self-employment, which saw a compound annual growth of 8 per cent between 1993 and 2008/9. Put together, self-employment and casual non-farm work accounted for 53 per cent of total employment by 2015.

The nature of regular jobs in 2008/9 remained more or less consistent with that of the previous rounds.[22] Common occupations across rounds included salaried jobs in the manufacturing sector, government, and the railways. Regular jobs remain highly sought after by villagers in Palanpur as these serve as a source of income stability and employment security.[23]

The casualization of the labour force in Palanpur, in the sense embodied in the figures mentioned, is closely linked to the expansion of construction activities. The construction sector employed as many as 42 per cent of total casual sector workers in 2008/9 in Palanpur. Its growth mirrors growth in the construction sector at the national level.

---

[21] Lanjouw and Stern (1998) mention that 17 cloth mill employees lost their jobs between 1983/4 and 1993. Had the cloth mills continued to employ 17 Palanpur villagers, the number of adult men with non-agricultural employment would have continued to rise in absolute terms between 1983/4 and 1993.

[22] The various regular jobs and the change in the type of regular jobs can be seen in detail in Table A.7.1.

[23] As explained by Himanshu et al. (2011), the regular sector jobs have a monthly or weekly payment basis as opposed to daily wage payments in casual activities and offer a modicum of employment security over the casual sector jobs.

The general trend in casualization has been confirmed by Himanshu and colleagues (2013) at the all-India level in their study of NSS data. They find that even though manufacturing and services are, for many people, the first that come to mind while considering the non-farm sector, by 2004/5 services provided employment for just over half of rural non-farm workers. Only one-third was in manufacturing; the remaining one-sixth was in construction. These shares have changed significantly over time. There has been a rapid rise of construction since the early 1990s: from 11 per cent of rural non-farm employment in 1993 to 18 per cent in 2004/5. The share of social services (public administration and community services, as well as health and education) shows a corresponding decline over the same period: from 26 to 18 per cent.

Another source of casual labour employment is MGNREGS, first introduced in 2005, that guarantees 100 days of employment to one adult male in rural households and a daily wage of Rs 100. The Act provides employment on public works projects such as road construction and other forms of infrastructure provision. The MGNREGS was introduced in Moradabad district and in Palanpur in 2007/8.[24] As many as 21 Palanpur villagers received a job card under MGNREGS. Between 2008 and 2009 some 18 to 20 villagers found some daily employment under the MGNREGS.

Also apparent from Table 7.2 is the recent growth in self-employment. The annual growth rate of self-employment was 4.4 per cent between 1983/4 and 2008/9. Prior to the 2008/9 survey, self-employment in the village was principally in the form of unskilled activities such as rope making, rickshaw pulling, or selling leaves. Outside these largely unskilled activities, self-employment consisted mainly of shopkeeping and tailoring in Palanpur. The 2008/9 survey round reveals a substantial expansion in the nature of these self-employment activities, including such activities as marble polishing, motorcycle and bicycle repair, and flour mills. A number of previous studies on India claim that the increase in self-employment has been largely due to 'distress-induced factors'.[25] However, the activities in Palanpur suggest a process of skill and capital accumulation by the residents that is more than simply a low-level, fall-back option as a result of distress.

Alongside the growth of these small businesses, Palanpur has seen a decline in the traditional caste-based *jajmani* services. By 2008/9 there was only one

---

[24] The work undertaken under MGNREGS can be significantly influenced by the village head. In Palanpur, the programme's operation suffered due to a lack of interest on the part of the *pradhan*. In 2008 the *pradhan* issued job cards only after receiving a bribe of Rs 50 from each applicant. Also, many of the upper-caste villagers refrained from taking part in the programme when the *pradhan* threatened to make people work on a sewage canal.

[25] For a discussion on the factors responsible for the growth of non-farm activities see Ranjan (2009) and Abraham (2009). Abraham (2009), using the 61st (2004/5) round of NSS, suggests that growth in non-farm employment in rural areas was probably a response to income crises in the farm sector.

surviving traditional worker in the village: Naresh, who belongs to the 'others' caste category. His household has no agricultural land, and Naresh is a barber (*nayi*) by tradition.

Our observations on the decline of *jajmani* occupations are in conformity with much of the literature on the process of rural transformation. For example, Ranis and Stewart (1993) argue that while new occupations emerge out of the process of rural transformation, traditional occupations such as those of village artisans may either disappear altogether or be transformed into a more modern form. In some cases, for example, that of rural black-smiths, the job has altered but still exists: previously primarily engaged in the production or servicing of hand tools, they now also produce or service animal-drawn equipment or farm machinery and irrigation equipment. In Palanpur too, the decline in *jajmani* occupations has been linked to changing technology, urbanization, and increased competition from more advanced self-employment units in urban areas, leading to declining prof-itability of traditional occupations (Drèze and Mukherjee, 1989; Lanjouw and Stern, 1998). Technological advancements, hand pumps for example, have also contributed to the disappearance of water carriers.

7.3.4 Non-Farm Income Trends in Palanpur

The growing importance of non-farm income in total village income is clearly evident from Table 7.3, which documents the decline in importance of culti-vation as a source of income in 2008/9 relative to earlier survey years.

The most powerful factor in the growth of non-farm income is self-employment. This grew at around 7.5 per cent per annum faster than village income as a whole between 1983/4 and 2008/9, or at around 12 per cent per annum overall since village income grew around 4–5 per cent.[26] It has been the strongest factor in income growth in Palanpur as a whole, registering a compound annual growth rate of 5.6 per cent in the share of income between 1957/8 and 2008/9. As mentioned, these activities consisted largely of *jajmani* services in the initial survey years. In the more recent rounds, self-employment refers to activities which may involve less traditional skills and some capital. Of particular importance have been entrepreneurial activities, including mentha pressing, repair facilities, and shops. Credit data revealed that six households in the village have obtained loans for non-farm business activities. These include loans of Rs 6000–10,000 for marble polishing machines and one loan of Rs 32,000 for the purchase of a flour mill. These

---

[26] Much of this was due to growth in profits from mentha pressing, from repair facilities and village shops, and so on. Business profits were not well measured in 1983/4, but these three activities were zero, or very small at that time.

Table 7.3 Income shares in Palanpur over time (%)

Income source		Year				
		1957/8	1962/3	1974/5	1983/4	2008/9
Household income	Cultivation	58.5	56.7	58.4	50.2	30
	Livestock income	19.8	21.5	22	13.7	10.4
	Non-cultivation (see breakdown)	21.7	21.8	19.6	35.4	59.6
	Total income share	100	100	100	100	100
Breakdown of non-cultivation income (% contribution to total income)						
Agricultural labour income	Casual labour—farm	7.3	3.5	1.8	1.5	0.9
Other non-cultivation income	Other farm income	1.2	0.6	0.1	2.7	10.7
	Rental	0	0.2	0.6	0	1.6
Non-farm income	Casual labour—non-farm	1.1	1	0	7	6.1
	Self-employment	1.3	3.5	1	3	19.8
	Regular employment	7.5	8.9	15.7	20	16.1
	Jajmani income	1.3	0.6	0.4	1	0.2
	Remittances	2	1.9	0	0.2	3.6
	Other non-farm	0	1.7	0	0.2	0.6

Note: For details on the income calculation, see Appendix at the end of this chapter. The figures represent the share of various sources of income in the total household income:
• Total non-cultivation income = agricultural labour income + other non-cultivation income (other farm income + rental income) + non-farm income.
• Total non-farm income = casual labour non-farm + regular income + self-employment income + *jajmani* income + other non-farm (remittances income + other non-farm income).
• Total household income = non-cultivation income + cultivation income + livestock income.
• The table does not include income details for 1993 as no data on income were collected.
• Livestock income = income from sale of milk.
• Other farm income = mechanized farm income + income from sale of livestock and livestock products, excluding milk.

units not only require initial capital investment, but can also lead to signifi-cant profits, as reflected in the share of income. Indeed, about two in five of the households in the richest income quintile are those with non-farm self-employment earnings.

Casual non-farm jobs accounted for 42 per cent of non-farm employment and 25 per cent of the total workforce in 2008/9. The percentage of income accounted for by these jobs has been between 6 and 7 per cent since 1983/4 but, of course, overall income has increased strongly (see Chapter 2), in large measure driven by non-farm, self-employment income.[27] Casual sector jobs

[27] Two caveats are in order as far as interpretation of income shares are concerned: (i) the low share of casual wage income in 2008/9 is likely due to better and robust estimates of self-employed and business income along with better estimates of remittances, rental income, and other income which drive down the share of income from casual wage labour. In absolute and real terms, average income from casual non-farm continues to show a large increase. As a share of total village income, it does get a lower share. (ii) The comparison with employment numbers is not strictly comparable because the income (particularly farm and non-farm business) is a household aggregate, whereas employment status is an individual attribute. In the case of farm and non-farm business, the gains/ profits from the enterprise is attributed to the member identified as the primary worker whereas in reality the enterprise may be run by contribution from most of the family members. This is similar

are typically daily wage contracts, often involving strenuous physical activity for fairly low pay. The growth of the casual non-farm sector is particularly important for the landless and disadvantaged sections of the village, for whom wage labour within the village is the only alternative choice of employment.

The share of Jatabs in such jobs has risen. Casual sector jobs, though not as well remunerated as regular jobs, are considered to be a better option than agricultural wage labour within the village. Casual jobs also generally allow for the household to have cultivation income (see Section 7.3.5). This preference is not only in terms of wages but also working conditions. Agricultural wage labour in the village is often considered to be a last resort option, particularly for higher-caste villagers who find such work demeaning. We should also note (see Section 7.3.5) that many of those taking advantage of new opportunities will still have farm incomes.

The income share from casual agricultural wage labour has declined from 7.3 per cent in 1957/8 to less than 1 per cent in 2008/9.[28]

7.3.5 Pluriactivity

Many studies show that involvement in the growing non-farm sector does not lead to a complete exit from agriculture. In some cases, it can lead to an increased participation in both farming and other activities, building on cash income from non-farm activities. Djurfeldt and colleagues (2008) argue that unlike in urban areas, where occupational transformation is generally associated with shifts between specific occupations by individuals, occupational change in rural areas usually takes the form of a shift to multiple occupations. This combination of activities within and beyond agriculture is sometimes termed 'pluriactivity'.[29] It is important to note that a majority of households in Palanpur belong to the small and marginal farm category;[30] with many households growing in size, working only on one's own land is unlikely to provide sufficient income to support a family. Rural households combine various farm and non-farm activities to both enhance their stream of incomes and to smooth total income in the face of the variability of agricultural income (see, for example, Reardon et al., 2006). Income diversification is likely to be particularly appealing to small and medium landowners.

to cultivation where it is difficult to assign the income to any particular individual or individuals. Most of the shops in the village are family enterprises but have not been captured adequately in our employment survey as far as their contribution to the running of business enterprises are concerned. There is some likelihood of underestimation of participation of family members in the running of non-farm enterprises, and this might show up as higher income per worker in the self-employed category.

[28] This fall in the share of farm labour income has come despite the rise in wages. See Section 7.4.
[29] Also see Unni (1998).
[30] This is defined by land ownership: those households with land between 0.1 and 30 *bigha* are categorized as small and marginal farm households.

We examine the number of income sources per household over the survey period in Table 7.4. Two-thirds of households had three or more sources of income in the year 2008/9 relative to just 20 per cent in 1957/8. The importance of pluriactivity can also be seen in Table 7.5. Only 4 per cent of households relied solely on cultivation for income in 2008/9 compared to 14 per cent in 1957/8. In 2008/9, 62 per cent of households generated income from farm and non-farm sources, up almost fourfold since 1957/8. Whilst cultivation may have declined as a primary source of income and employment, for a majority of non-farm workers it continues to serve as a secondary source.

The secondary occupation status of villagers, as shown in Table 7.6, provides further evidence that individuals often combine farm and non-farm activities to generate income. Participation in cultivation is highly seasonal.

Table 7.4 Number of sources of income per household

Year	Number of Sources of Income					
	0	1	2	3	4 and Above	Total
1957/8	0 (0)	21 (21)	59 (59)	19 (19)	1 (1)	100 (100)
1962/3	0 (0)	21 (19.81)	62 (58.49)	19 (17.92)	4 (3.77)	106 (100)
1974/5	1 (0.89)	13 (11.61)	38 (33.93)	46 (41.07)	14 (12.50)	112 (100)
1983/4	3 (2.10)	13 (9.09)	30 (20.98)	40 (27.97)	57 (39.86)	143 (100)
2008/9	2 (0.90)	26 (11.66)	47 (21.08)	86 (38.57)	62 (27.80)	223 (100)

Note: The figures represent the number of households with the given number of income sources. The figures in brackets represent the percentage of households with the number of income sources.

Table 7.5 Number of households depending on income source

Income Source	Year				
	1957/8	1962/3	1974/5	1983/4	2008/9
None	0 (0)	0 (0)	1 (0.9)	3 (2.1)	2 (0.9)
Pure cultivation	14 (14)	16 (15.1)	10 (8.9)	1 (0.7)	9 (4)
Pure non-farm	5 (5)	5 (4.7)	2 (1.8)	8 (5.6)	24 (10.8)
Others	10 (10)	6 (5.7)	16 (14.3)	32 (22.4)	14 (6.3)
Cultivation + non-cultivation	71 (71)	79 (74.5)	83 (74.3)	99 (69.2)	174 (78)
Total	100 (100)	106 (100)	112 (100)	143 (100)	223 (100)

Notes: The figures represent the number of households by source of income:
• The figures in the brackets represent the percentage of households.
• Others = non-cultivation – non-farm.
• Total = non-cultivation + cultivation + others + none + pure cultivation + pure non-farm.
• Pure cultivation households are those that derive income only from cultivation.
• Pure non-farm households include households deriving income only from non-farm sources.
• Non-cultivation households are those that derive income only from non-cultivation sources, which do not include non-farm.
• Cultivation + non-cultivation households earn income from cultivation and non-cultivation sources without earning any income from non-farm sources.
• The number of households in the year 2008/9 is 233; however, we lack complete information on income for 10 households. Therefore, we have included only 223 households in the above income analysis.

Table 7.6 Adult males' secondary occupation status

Occupation	Year						
	1957/8	1962/3	1974/5	1983/4	1993	2008/9	2015
None	127 (73.8)	147 (79.5)	187 (85)	209 (72.3)	288 (82.3)	177 (44.8)	195 (45.3)
Cultivation	12 (7)	6 (3.2)	3 (1.4)	32 (11.1)	12 (3.4)	163 (41.3)	172 (40)
Casual labour (farm)	18 (10.5)	15 (8.1)	21 (9.6)	21 (7.3)	18 (5.1)	16 (4.1)	7 (1.6)
Casual labour (non-farm)	7 (4.1)	1 (0.5)	2 (0.9)	17 (5.9)	19 (5.4)	21 (5.332)	30 (7)
Regular employment	7 (4.1)	10 (5.4)	4 (1.8)	2 (0.7)	1 (0.3)	2 (0.5)	2 (0.5)
Self-employment (non-farm)	1 (0.6)	6 (3.2)	3 (1.4)	8 (2.8)	12 (3.4)	16 (4.1)	24 (5.6)
Total	172 (100)	185 (100)	220 (100)	289 (100)	350 (100)	395 (100)	430 (100)

Note: Figures in brackets are percentages of households.

Growth of non-farm employment opportunities has allowed individuals to move away from specialization in a particular occupation and to adopt a more mixed profile. While in 1957/8 we observe that only 26 per cent of males were employed in some secondary occupation, this proportion increased to 57 per cent in 2008/9. Most such secondary jobs in 2008/9 involved cultivation. And in most of these cases, the respective primary occupation of the worker was non-farm employment. Easy access to different jobs is critical to such mixed occupations. In the Palanpur case, commuting to a nearby town or village makes it possible for villagers to combine non-farm work with care for their fields. Commuting is crucial for pluriactivity.

7.4 Farm and Non-Farm Wages in Palanpur

Wage rates in Palanpur vary across activities as well as the farm and non-farm sectors. As discussed, the major wage-remunerated activities in which residents from Palanpur take part include farm wage labour and casual non-farm daily wage activities including MGNREGS, construction, railway workers, and brick kiln labour. Many of these wages involve piece rates.

Agricultural wages have risen strongly since 1974/5. Over the entire survey period, agricultural wages grew at a rate of about 2.4 per cent per annum (Figure 7.2).[31]

The growth in farm wages in Palanpur appears to have been driven largely by the pull from the non-farm sector, especially the growth of casual non-farm

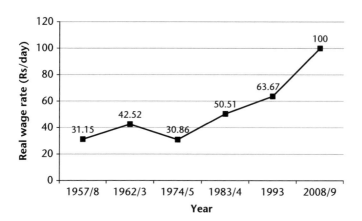

Figure 7.2 Real farm wages in Palanpur (2008/9 prices)

[31] The dip in real wages in 1974/5, despite the increase in land-augmenting technology such as the spread of irrigation, can be attributed to accelerating inflation in that year.

jobs post-1983/4 and the resultant tightening of the agricultural wage labour market. Strong growth in the construction sector led to multiple non-farm employment opportunities for villagers who would otherwise have worked mostly as farm labourers. The higher remuneration available in such casual non-farm jobs may have led to upward pressure on farm wages. Field discussions during the 2008/9 survey with a few Jatabs (the most important source of casual agricultural and non-agricultural labour in Palanpur) indicate that the availability of outside jobs made them more confident in bargaining for higher agricultural wages in the village.

Agricultural wage rates differ across different activities. Wages in weeding and sowing varied from Rs 80 to Rs 100 per day in 2008/9. For wheat harvesting, on the other hand, the wage rate was Rs 100 or, in the case of contractual labour, labourers were remunerated at the rate of 25 kg of wheat per *bigha* harvested. Women actively participate in wheat harvesting, usually as contractual workers. This wage structure in Palanpur is similar to that observed in neighbouring districts, such as Agra and Bareilly (Table 7.7). Wages are generally fairly uniform across workers within activities.

Wages in the casual non-farm sector vary depending on the type of job; there are piece rates as well as daily wage payments. Employment in the construction sector as casual construction workers, as part of the MGNREGS, and as a worker in manufacturing, typically involves daily wage payments. In construction, for example, the local wage rate in 2008/9 was Rs 120–150 per day plus one meal and a bundle of *bidi* with a matchbox.[32] On the other hand, work in the brick kilns and railway yards, and at marble polishing, is based on piece rates and can vary with the amount of work done by each individual. For example, in the railway yards the amount earned for one day depends on the amount of wagons unloaded. Labourers get 50 paise to 1 rupee per item, and workers can earn from 100 to 200 rupees a day.[33]

Results from other village studies also document the decline of agricultural wage labour employment and rising agricultural wages. Using data from three International Crops Research Institute for the Semi-Arid Tropics (ICRISAT)

Table 7.7 Farm wages in neighbouring districts of Moradabad (Rs/day)

District	2000/1	2001/2	2002/3	2003/4	2004/5	2005/6	2006/7	2007/8	2008/9	2009/10
Agra	62.67	64.44	60	60.72	61.15	64	80.50	82.50	98.74	100.71
Bareilly	55.36	57.07	61.01	62.67	67.88	–	60	95	99.69	100

Source: Agricultural wages in India, Ministry of Agriculture and Farmers Welfare, Government of India.

[32] A cheap cigarette made of unprocessed tobacco, wrapped in leaves.
[33] There are 100 paise in a rupee.

villages (Aurapelle, Shirapur, and Kanzara), Pal (1997) finds that in response to improved alternative employment options, there was a decline in the supply of farm labour. This led to an upward revision of farm wages in Shirapur and Kanzara so as to encourage participation in the farm labour market. The process was less marked in Aurapelle due to a lack of alternative employment or credit opportunities.

In all of the examples that follow, improved communication both by mobile telephone and via transport, have played a powerful role in facilitating participation in outside activities. With mobile phones, the probability of finding work can be assessed much more accurately, and lower transport costs reduce the necessary investment in search for and travel to work.

7.5 Some Examples of Casual Non-Farm Employment in Palanpur

7.5.1 Work in the Railway Yard (Malgodown)

One of the main sources of employment as casual labourers for those in Palanpur is work in the Moradabad railway yard. In 2008/9, about 10–15 males travelled from Palanpur to the railway yard on a daily basis. These workers usually work under a contractor who has contracts with several cement and fertilizer companies for unloading the wagons.[34] None of these contractors came from Palanpur, but the group of workers from Palanpur was led by Udayveer (a Thakur), who had contacts with the contractors and helped in getting Palanpur residents the work at the yard. Among the main contractors, there was one Muslim (Hamid) and one Sikh (Ram Swaroop Sardar) from Punjab. The contractors receive between 70 paise to Rs 1 per unloaded sack of 50 kg, and they pay the labourers 50 paise for each sack.

The labourers usually work in a group of ten, including a leader. As the wagons arrive, each group of labourers occupies or claims their wagon. Wagons near the *godown* (warehouse) are coveted because less effort is required in unloading these wagons and carrying the goods to the *godown*. Force and political power are important factors governing which rakes (i.e. wagon) a group can lay claim to. Group leaders who are better connected to the contractors are able to secure better claims than others. Palanpur villagers, under Udayveer, generally get rakes quite far from the *godown* since he is not very influential.

---

[34] ACC Cement, Ambuja Cement, Mehar Cement, J.P. Cement, TATA fertilizers, and IFCO are some of the companies with which the contractors at the railway yard usually set year-long contracts for the loading and unloading of goods.

After claiming the rakes, the group leader breaks the seal and receives a receipt after depositing it at the railway office. The leader receives the payment, Rs 0.5 per unloaded sack, and total earnings are equally distributed amongst group members. The most influential group leaders do not participate in the work, but do claim the earnings. On an average day the earnings per group member corresponded to around Rs 100 per day.

The work is heavy and tiring, and the earnings vary from day to day depending on the frequency of the trains and the number of groups. The work is highly competitive as there are several groups attempting to claim the rakes. Joining a group is also difficult and depends on contacts and influence. For Palanpur villagers, railway work is regarded as preferable to agricultural wage labour. It is seen as attractive for the poor amongst the Thakurs, as they would find working in the village as agricultural labourers highly demeaning. Workers from Palanpur involved in the railway yards at Moradabad are mainly Thakurs, Jatabs, and Muraos. Entry for other caste groups is difficult because Thakurs are generally reluctant to engage in manual labour alongside lower-caste villagers and currently have privileged positions as group leaders. However, Muraos tend to mix more easily with other caste groups.

7.5.2 Marble Polishing

Most of the marble polishing units exist in the nearby towns of Sambhal, Chandausi, and Moradabad. Work as marble polishers is usually obtained with the help of contractors living in these cities. The residents of Palanpur travel daily to the workplace and earn piece rates of Rs 7 for every foot of marble polished. Depending on their skill the workers can (in 2008/9) make Rs 300 to 500 per day. Work can generally be obtained for 15 to 20 days in a month, although in some seasons, such as festive seasons, work in marble polishing is less frequent. Workers involved in marble polishing generally have to invest in their own machinery. The required capital is roughly Rs 20,000. If workers lack the funds to purchase the polishing equipment, they are sometimes able to rent the machinery at a cost of Rs 1000 per month. About 20 households in Palanpur own marble polishing machines. Work in the marble polishing units gets affected by frequent power cuts. Sometimes workers have to pay high commission rates to the contractors in order to receive employment. No Jatabs work as marble polishers. This may be because they lack contacts with the contractors or because they are unable to fund the purchase or rental of marble polishing equipment. Employment in marble polishing is concentrated amongst Thakurs, Gadarias, and Dhimars. We generally classified it as self-employment, given that capital equipment is used and owned by the worker, together with the payment being in piece-rate form.

1. Bullock assisted ploughing during the 1974/5 survey Year

2. View of the village primary school in 1974

3. Thakur household compound and courtyard in 1974/5

4. View of crops damaged by caterpillars during 1983/4 survey year

5. Naresh Sharma in Sorghum field in 1983/4

6. Jean Drèze processing field notes during 1983 survey Year

7. The first copy of the first Palanpur book; SS Tyagi Jr and VK Singh, with Nicholas Stern, April 1982

8. Primary school lessons delivered outdoors in 1983/4

9. Village tailor at work in 1983/4

10. Naresh and Tyagi, Jr. conducting house visits in 1983/4

11. State of village lanes during brief visit in 1990

12. View of village and railway line during short visit in 1990

14. Village barber at work near railway line in 2009

13. Monkeys are frequent visitors to village. Here in 1990

15. Improved village lanes in 2009

16. Mobile phone network cellular tower in 2009

17. Delapidated state of village seed store during 2009 survey year

18. The data collection team in 2009, with guests

19. Mechanised irrigation during 2009 survey year

20. Jatab household compound and courtyard in 2009

21. A mentha oil-pressing mill in 2009

22. Murao household compound and courtyard in 2009

23. A NREGA road maintenance project in 2009

24. Upgraded school building facilities by 2009

25. Team of visitors during follow-up visit in 2012

26. Maintenance work on tractor in 2009

27. View of village pond and village buildings 2012

28. Teaching at village school during visit in 2012

29. Preparing fields for cultivation during visit in 2012

30. Poultry farming experiment at time of visit in 2012

31. View of fields during winter months in 2015

7.5.3 Brick Kilns

Brick kilns are located in several villages near Palanpur, notably Sirsi, which is 6 km from Palanpur, and Sambhal, some 20 kilometres away. The workers often travel on a daily basis to the kilns. Occasionally they seasonally migrate to the workplace, where they are provided with accommodation by the kiln owner. Workers in the kiln are often divided into different categories depending on the kind of work. The process of making bricks comprises the following steps:

1. Mixing of sand and water and shaping this into the form of bricks, which are then sundried.

2. The sundried bricks are then taken to the kiln for baking purposes. The bricks inside the kiln have to be arranged in a certain order for firing. The surface of the dry bricks has to be covered by sand before firing.

3. After the firing of bricks these are then unloaded from the kilns and the final bricks are then loaded onto trucks for outward carriage.

Workers usually work in teams with their families where the work is divided between the members. Children and women are often allotted the work of mixing the sand with water and shaping it into bricks. Work in the kiln is strenuous and hazardous and is usually carried out by the male members. The temperature inside the kiln where the bricks are placed is very high, as is the temperature on the surface, where the dry bricks are being covered with sand. The workers earn on a piece-rate basis and are paid Rs 170 per 1000 bricks produced. Usually several members from a single household will form a *toli* to undertake the work.[35] Generally one person can make 500 bricks during the span of a day, and a *toli* is able to produce 1500 to 2000 bricks per day. Workers can usually find work for around 25 days during a month and about 8 to 9 months throughout the year. The lean season coincides with the low sunshine period, during monsoons and winters. The brick kiln is closed down for weeks at a stretch during the foggy winter months or on cloudy days, when there is not enough sunshine to dry the bricks before firing them in kilns. Work in kilns is physically demanding, and few brick kilns comply with official health and safety regulations. Working for a prolonged period of time in these kilns can cause respiratory diseases and chronic fatigue. On the whole, brick kiln work is relatively unattractive and is carried out by the lowest and the most disadvantaged sections of the village. An attraction relative to agricultural labour is that work can be available for a high number of days per month and families can work together. In Palanpur all the brick kiln workers are Jatabs.

---

[35] A *toli* usually consists of a group of three or more members, where various activities involved in the process of brick making are distributed amongst the members.

7.6 Occupational Diversification, Entrepreneurship, and Household Characteristics

7.6.1 Land and Occupation

Non-farm employment is particularly important for households owning little or no land. Ranjan (2008), using data from two village studies in Muzaffarnagar district in Uttar Pradesh, Mubarakpur, and Kheritangan, notes an inverse relationship between land ownership and non-farm activities. With smaller landholdings, the pressure to seek non-farm work increases. Large landholdings may require greater management input, as well as agricultural labour, reducing the time available for other activities.

To explore occupation–land patterns in Palanpur, we divide households into five quintiles based on their per capita land ownership.[36] Considering first the 1957/8 survey year we can see clear evidence of an inverse gradient between landownership and non-farm employment (Table 7.8). In that year there were 13 adult males with either regular non-farm employment or engaged in non-farm self-employment. More than half (seven) of these were in the smallest per capita landownership quintile, and another two belonged to the second smallest landownership quintile. The few cases of non-farm employment in the third and fourth quintiles were primarily a result of non-farm activities linked to *jajmani* services.[37]

While, in 1957/8, 32 per cent of the households possessed landholdings larger than 30 *bighas*, with population growth this had declined to as low as 4.7 per cent in 2008/9. More than three-quarters of households were 'small and marginal' farmers with landholdings between 0.1 and 30 *bighas*

Table 7.8 Occupation composition of adult males in 1957/8 according to land quintiles

Occupation Class	Land Quintile					Total
	1	2	3	4	5	
None	2 (6.1)	0 (0)	1 (3)	3 (9.1)	2 (5)	8
Cultivation	8 (24.4)	26 (78.8)	30 (78.9)	28 (84.8)	38 (95)	130
Casual labour (farm)	16 (48.8)	5 (15.1)	0 (15.1)	0 (0)	0 (0)	21
Regular employment	4 (12.1)	2 (6.1)	1 (3)	0 (0)	0 (0)	7
Self-employment (non-farm)	3 (9.1)	0 (0)	1 (3)	2 (6.1)	0 (0)	6
Total	33	33	33	33	40	172

[36] Analysis of landholdings based on adult males per household yields qualitatively similar findings.

[37] As an illustration of this case, a Dhobi household with 20 *bighas* of land and a household size of three fell into the fourth quintile; it was involved in the traditional *jajmani* service of washer men along with cultivation. The household was the only one providing the customary washer-men service in the village.

in 2008/9. Indeed, there are no large landowners (with landholdings above 100 *bighas*) at all in the years 1983/4 and 2008/9. The decline in landholdings over the survey period has been associated with villagers across the per capita land distribution seeking alternative income earning opportunities (Tables 7.9 and 7.10).[38]

The case of the Murao household headed by Chachendra, in 2008/9, is instructive. In 2008/9 the household owned nine *bighas* of land and cultivated 4.5 *bighas* after leasing-out 4.5 *bighas*. In 1983/4 the household had owned about 100 *bighas*, falling to 30 *bighas* in 1993. The further division of landholdings between the three brothers after the death of Chachendra's father left him with less than 10 *bighas*, and as a result he turned to other income-earning options. His cultivation income is now much less than his earnings from work as a marble polisher.

Table 7.9 Occupation composition of adult males in 1983/4 according to land quintiles

Occupation Class	Land Quintile					Total
	1	2	3	4	5	
None	1 (2.6)	5 (7.6)	9 (12.7)	4 (6.4)	11 (21.1)	30
Cultivation	4 (10.5)	23 (34.8)	35 (49.3)	44 (70.8)	35 (67.3)	141
Casual labour (farm)	5 (13.2)	6 (9.1)	0 (0)	0 (0)	0 (0)	11
Casual labour (non-farm)	7 (18.4)	10 (15.1)	4 (5.6)	3 (4.8)	0 (0)	24
Regular employment	11 (28.9)	17 (25.8)	17 (23.9)	9 (14.5)	6 (11.5)	60
Self-employment (non-farm)	10 (26.3)	5 (7.6)	6 (8.4)	2 (3.2)	0 (0)	23
Total	38	66	71	62	52	289

Note: The entries in the table represent the number of individuals in each occupation and per capita land quintile in the years 1983/4. The total represents the number of individuals in each quintile.

Table 7.10 Occupation composition of adult males in 2008/9 according to land quintiles

Occupation	Land Quintile					Total
	1	2	3	4	5	
None	8 (14.3)	16 (17.2)	4 (4.8)	13 (15.7)	19 (24)	60
Cultivation	6 (10.7)	18 (19.3)	32 (38.1)	29 (34.9)	43 (54.4)	128
Casual labour (farm)	1 (1.8)	2 (2.1)	2 (2.4)	1 (1.2)	0 (0)	6
Casual labour (non-Farm)	19 (33.4)	27 (29)	16 (19)	16 (19.3)	7 (8.9)	85
Regular employment	8 (14.3)	13 (14)	12 (14.3)	9 (10.9)	7 (8.9)	49
Self-employment (non-farm)	14 (25)	17 (18.3)	18 (21.4)	15 (18.2)	3 (3.8)	67
Total	56	93	84	83	79	395

Note: The entries in the table represent the number of individuals in each occupation and per capita land quintile in the years 2008/9. The total represents the number of individuals in each quintile.

---

[38] For reference, Table 7.11 indicates the average and median *bighas* of land corresponding to the respective quintiles and years.

Table 7.11 Landholding size by land per capita quintiles

Land per Capita Quintile	1957/8		1962/3		1974/5		1983/4		2008/9	
	Mean	Median	Mean	Median	Mean	Median	Mean	Median	Mean	Median
1	0.3	0	0.3	0	0.2	0.1	0	0	0	0
2	2.2	2	2.1	2.1	1.6	1.7	0.7	0.7	0.6	0.6
3	4.4	4.3	3.9	3.9	2.9	2.9	1.7	1.7	1.2	1.2
4	6.6	6.6	6.2	6.1	4.5	4.3	3.5	3.7	2	2
5	14.3	12	13.3	11.8	9.5	7.7	8	6.4	4.7	4

Note: The figures represent the mean and median per capita landholdings in each of the quintiles.

Only in the very largest landholding quintile does it still appear that non-farm involvement is relatively unimportant: the number of adult males engaged in non-farm activities in the top quintile is lower than in the other respective quintiles (Tables 7.9 and 7.10). One important caveat to this observation, however, is that for the top quintile in both 1983/4 and 2008/9, there is regular non-farm employment. Such employment tends to be restricted to well-paid regular jobs, such as government jobs or skilled self-employment units involving significant capital equipment.

As is true for other parts of India, in Palanpur self-employment in cultivation by leasing-in land has not been a feasible option for the great majority of the landless.[39] In the absence of non-farm earning opportunities, agricultural wage labour is often the only option available. Indeed, in 1958, 48 per cent of adult males in the first quintile were employed as agricultural wage labourers. The demand for agricultural labour, however, varies across the year depending on the agricultural cycle and is often associated with lower wages as compared to other job options. Seasonality of demand for labour in agriculture often leads to involuntary unemployment during the slack periods. As an occupation, it is widely considered to be an activity of last resort.

The expansion of non-farm jobs has enabled, to some extent, the landless to overcome the low incomes and the instability associated with agricultural wage labour within the village. On the other hand, full withdrawal from the agricultural wage labour market is not necessarily common. Employment as casual wage labourers outside the village is generally based on daily contracts. These casual non-farm labourers often return to agriculture as wage labourers during the peak seasons and thereby derive income from agricultural labour as a secondary source of employment.

---

[39] The discussion in Chapter 6 on tenancy in Palanpur describes the obstacles to cultivation for landless households. It is difficult for the landless to bear the costs of cultivation given their lack of resources. At the same time, there is a lack of willingness on the part of landlords to lease-out land to the landless due to their lack of experience as cultivators as compared to those who own some land.

Tables 7.8–7.10 suggest that the increasing quality of activity available to self-employment business units in Palanpur has led to a penetration of self-employment amongst all the land quintile classes. As mentioned, self-employment in the years before 2008/9 largely took the form of petty business activities such as rope making, rickshaw pulling, or running one or two small shops within Palanpur. Generating meagre incomes, these were found to be concentrated amongst the lowest quintile. With the expansion of skill- and capital-intensive self-employment activities, these have now spread across all class quintiles including the upper quintiles. Examples include mentha pressing, machinery, repair shops (now much more numerous and with higher turnover), and marble polishing.

Households with higher land endowments may not need to diversify, although they may be in a better position to finance such diversification. Cultivation is the primary source of income for most of these households. Some of them, in part through contacts and networks, have found attractive regular non-farm jobs.

7.6.2 Social Networks and Occupation

The degree of occupational diversification depends on the opportunities available to households. The Palanpur data suggest that although caste-based traditional services have largely disappeared, caste continues to influence the occupational structure of the village. While the role of land ownership is important for the choice between farm and non-farm employment, access to specific jobs in the non-farm sector appears to be driven, to some extent, by caste affiliation. For example, Lanjouw and Stern (1998) indicate that the distribution of outside employment opportunities shows clear patterns of clustering around well-defined locations and socioeconomic groups.

We have seen that the village non-farm economy was traditionally based on *jajmani* services which were determined by the caste of an individual. However, with continuing economic development and growing urbanization in the region, traditional caste-based services have faded, and there are now new employment opportunities outside the village. Access to these outside jobs has been facilitated by networks, often based on caste and kinship. These networks act as a medium of mutual assistance in terms of information about job vacancies, or the transfer of skills and knowledge within the network, and monetary assistance during a job search or to cover for risk. Falco and Bulte (2013), in their study of social capital, claim that within kinship networks, moral obligations of reciprocity and sharing are supported by customs and norms and may allow individuals to claim and receive assistance in times of need. These expected behaviours and the social pressures for redistribution among kin provide a form of safety net as well as connections and opportunities for occupational diversification or advancement. Mutual trust and knowledge, clearly important in most activities where inputs are not directly observable and where teams and groups play an important role, may also be operating through caste and kinship groupings. We saw in Chapter 6 on tenancy that such 'communities of trust' played an important role in the matching of partners in land tenancy.

As most of the non-farm jobs are located outside the village, these networks are needed to find new job opportunities in those places. In some cases, unskilled workers receive a kind of training from family or friends already in the sector, or material help in the form of money or food. Initial entry by any individual into a job serves as a medium of contact for others belonging to the same network. The precise role of these networks varies depending on the type of employment. For example, self-employment units can be fostered by the accumulation and transfer of skills and capital within members of a particular network. This has happened in the case of Telis and repair shops. Regular jobs outside the village are made more accessible by a network of kinship or assistance in the form of accommodation. Those who have already secured a job outside the village are usually in a privileged position to help their friends, relatives, and fellow caste members by drawing on their knowledge of possible vacancies in their own place of employment. Employers may act similarly, using their existing employees as recruiting agents.

Suggestive of the importance of the kinship networks is that the pattern of expansion of regular jobs after 1974/5 was biased towards certain castes and occupations (see Table 7.12 for some examples).[40] Passis clustered in 1983/4 in steel polishing workshops, and Thakurs in 1983/4 in biscuit factories and as security guards in 2008/9.[41]

The search for jobs in the casual sector can be rather different, for example, where labourers sit in an *adda* (an informal gathering usually near the railway tracks in our case, where these job seekers come and wait to be selected by contractors and middlemen). The individuals who do get recruited are able to build relationships with the contractors and thereafter help members of the same group or family in obtaining these casual jobs. As explained, in the case of railway-yard work these networks play a very important role in the recruitment process. Moradabad has a labour *mandi*, a place where labourers gather together and are selected by contractors for particular jobs. The process seems to be competitive.

---

[40] Similar information of the caste concentrations in casual labour and several self-employment units can be seen in Tables A.7.2 and A.7.3.

[41] Thakurs were employed in bakeries, as this involved the processing of food. The lower-caste individuals could not be employed in this field due to social norms that exist in the village where people from higher castes do not sit, eat, or mix with people from lower castes, or accept food prepared by lower castes.

Table 7.12 Concentration of regular jobs

Regular Job Sector	Thakur	Murao	Jatab	Passi	Dhimar	Dhobi	Gadaria	Teli	Other	Total
1974/5										
Railways	0	1	0	1	1	0	2	3	1	9
Cloth mill	3	0	0	6	3	1	2	2	0	17
1983/4										
Cloth mill	3	3	1	7	1	0	3	1	0	19
Biscuit factory	6	1	0	0	0	0	0	0	0	7
Railways	0	0	0	2	2	0	2	2	2	10
Steel factory	0	0	0	6	0	0	1	1	1	9
2008/9										
Employee in a general shop	7	0	0	0	0	0	0	0	0	7
Private security guard	5	0	0	0	0	0	0	0	0	5
Railways	1	0	0	0	3	0	1	3	2	10

Note: The table represents the number of individuals in each occupation.

In the case of marble polishing, recruitment again takes place via contractors, and the workers often have to pay some commission to these contractors to get a job. Those in a weaker position may have to negotiate higher rates of commission to get employment. Since the piece rates for marble polishing are fixed, a higher commission can have an important bearing on final incomes earned.

An important aspect of the study of development concerns changes in the complex of social, political, and religious ties that characterize a village economy. With respect to the growth of the non-farm sector, we examine the evolution of *caste* ties in relation to the village occupational structure.

In Palanpur at the beginning of the survey period, land was predominantly held by Thakurs and Muraos who were primarily engaged in cultivation or as landlords leasing-out land.[42] Thakurs and Muraos were not active participants in non-farm activities. At the bottom end of the social hierarchy, the Jatabs had minimal access to land and also had little involvement in non-farm activities.[43] Wage labour in agriculture or employment as a cultivating tenant were the only sources of employment available for the Jatabs, and the latter was difficult without ownership of draught animals. The other caste groups

---

[42] The average landholdings have declined for all caste groups. Muraos now hold the highest average landholdings followed by Thakurs. Over time there has been a convergence of the landholdings between various caste groups.

[43] Non-farm jobs were mainly regular jobs, where the participation of Jatabs was negligible. They were also disadvantaged in terms of resources which might be necessary; for example, for bribes to acquire employment.

were employed as cultivating tenants or were involved in services often linked to traditional caste-based activities. Passis, who had migrated into the village prior to the survey period, had employment in the railways and other regular jobs around the village.

Over the years, the expansion of non-farm activities has created various employment opportunities for the villagers. Some caste groups have been able to embrace these more fully than others. Networks, often based on caste and kinship, have been important, with those for Thakurs being particularly strong.

Over the survey period, the Thakurs experienced a decline in landholdings as a result of population growth and a process of household splits and partitioning. However, the decline in landholdings and cultivation incomes was accompanied by a simultaneous increase in non-farm participation by Thakurs, as shown in Figure 7.3.

It seems that Thakurs were able to acquire some of the newly available regular jobs in 1974/5, including those in the cloth mill and the biscuit or bread factory in Chandausi, in part through better networks and influence than other caste groups. By 1983/4 Thakurs and Passis together held 50 per cent of the regular jobs, and by 1993 Thakurs accounted for 44 per cent of villagers' regular jobs. Although there had been a marked decline in the total number of regular jobs between 1983/4 and 1993 (following the closure of a cloth mill in Moradabad), the number of regular jobs held by Thakurs remained more or less the same between 1983/4 and 1993.[44] There was some recovery in the number of regular jobs between 1993 and 2008/9, and the Thakurs accounted for 45 per cent of these in 2008/9. Between 2008/9 and 2015 there

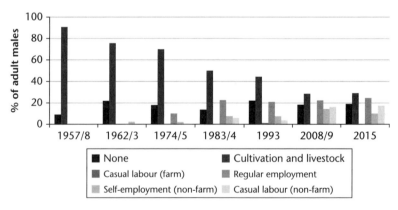

Figure 7.3 Occupation trends for Thakur adult males

---

[44] The closure of the cloth mill and decline in the availability of regular non-farm employment opportunities in 1993 led to significant out-migration by Passi families.

was an increase in the number of government jobs acquired by the Thakurs, such that by 2015 the Thakurs held 61 per cent of the total regular jobs in the village.

For a number of the Thakurs, it would appear that access to regular non-farm jobs has resulted from an ability to work the system. Bribes play a prominent role, and Thakurs are advantaged because they have greater resources. Presumably their networks are also of value in such processes. An example is that of Anil Singh who works as a security guard at a cell-phone tower. He paid a bribe of Rs 12,000 to get the job and now earns Rs 2,000 for work of 20 days per month. The job is available throughout the year and ensures a permanent income stream. Higher capital and better networks have also facilitated the growth of self-employment activities amongst Thakurs.

At the other end of the caste spectrum, Jatabs are under-represented in terms of regular non-farm employment. Lack of social acceptance, weakness of relevant networks, and monetary constraints in relation to bribes have been obstacles (Figure 7.4).

Even where Jatabs have occasionally gained access to regular non-farm employment, the nature of the work has been limited to such activities as working as a helper in a shop. Skilled and highly sought-after regular jobs such as government employment still remain inaccessible to the Jatabs. Similar considerations apply to any of the more attractive forms of self-employment, where opportunities for Jatabs are limited to largely unskilled and relatively unattractive occupations such as, for example, work as a rickshaw puller.

The picture is rather different in the casual non-farm job sector. This now forms the most important source of employment for the Jatabs. Casual jobs outside the village are quite unattractive to the more privileged and higher status villagers. They would not choose such work unless faced with severe

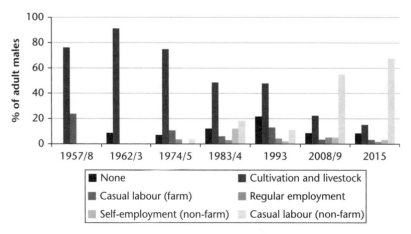

Figure 7.4 Occupation trends for Jatab adult males

constraints such as landlessness or having suffered some setback or hardship, such as the death of the household head or serious illness in the family.

Largely devoid of entry barriers, casual jobs provide an important source of employment for the Jatabs, who would otherwise be unemployed or employed as wage labourers within the village. Jatabs have been very eager to take advantage of new opportunities in the casual sector. A central example of this is work in brick kilns, as described in Section 7.5.3. Jatabs have made active use of this source of employment and have been able to establish a well-defined network with contractors from brick kilns in nearby towns. It is possible that over time this may result in strengthened networks and a wider range of contacts for Jatabs and eventually permit greater participation in other activities.

Declining land ownership and limited availability of regular job opportunities has also led other caste groups to seek employment in the casual non-farm sector. Thakurs appear to show some aversion to manual labour within the village for fear of damaging their social standing. One of the group leaders in the Moradabad railway yard (described in Section 7.5.1) is a Thakur from Palanpur, which shows that Thakurs have enjoyed easier access to such work; the group of casual workers employed in off-loading rakes in the railway yard is thus comprised mainly of Thakurs and a few Muraos. Another feasible source of casual labour employment for Thakurs is the marble polishing industry (described further in Section 7.5.2). Contacts with the contractors established by the initial entrants into this industry have allowed Thakurs to find employment either as casual labourers or self-employed workers (for those who have acquired their own marble polishing machines). Since work is undertaken outside the village for employers who do not belong to Palanpur, such employment does not compromise the social standing of Thakurs within the village. Employment as wage labourers within the village is still not considered an option for this caste, even if faced with acute landlessness and distress.[45]

The Muraos, the traditional cultivating caste, did relatively well in the early part of the survey period, with a strong commitment to investment in agriculture and the adoption of new techniques. However, the composition of their employment has changed with the declining size of holdings. By 2008/9, 61 per cent of Murao households were earning some non-farm income (Figure 7.5). Even so, few Muraos have exited from cultivation altogether; 40 per cent of the cultivators in the latest survey round belong to this caste. Because of their reluctance to engage in non-farm activities in the earlier part of the period, Muraos may have been handicapped in their ability to

---

[45] An interesting illustration of this case is that of Shri Pal Singh, a Thakur, who has two sons, both employed as casual wage labourers in the non-farm sector. The father of Shri Pal Singh owned 27 *bighas* of land, but 17 years ago one of his sons got asthma, and all of their land had to be sold for his treatment. There are five members in the household and no land to cultivate. The participation in casual jobs would appear to be an example of distress-induced employment.

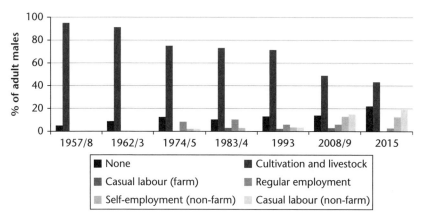

Figure 7.5 Occupation trends for Murao adult males

establish networks of contacts with the world outside the village, at least as compared to other caste groups. Muraos do not appear to exhibit aversion for specific jobs within or outside the village; their participation in non-farm work is fairly evenly distributed across all kinds. And, if circumstances are sufficiently difficult, they seem ready to work as wage labourers in the village.

Involvement in non-farm activities by the smaller caste groups varies and has followed differing trajectories. Gadarias (traditionally goat-herders), for example, are primarily involved in self-employment as represented by marble polishing and flour mills. In 2008/9, as a result of an earlier apprenticeship with the Thakur who introduced marble polishing to the village, the network of marble polishing also spread within the Gadarias, and four Gadaria household members now own marble polishing machines. Nearly 30 per cent of them remain involved in cultivating, and two of the biggest landowners belong to this caste group.[46]

A caste group that has emerged as particularly enterprising are the Telis. Traditionally oil pressers, the Palanpur Telis are Muslim. Telis own very little land and have actively sought involvement in the non-farm sector. In 2008/9 we saw a sudden increase in the number of business units amongst the Telis; these include flour mills, motorcycle repair shops, and a few marble polishing machines. This expansion of self-employment activities was kicked off by the Teli villager Nanhe (mentioned in Section 7.3.1), who received training as a motorcycle mechanic during a year-long sojourn in Delhi. When he returned to the village after a year, Nanhe started training other Palanpur Telis in this vocation. The result was the establishment of several motorcycle repair shops

---

[46] One of these households is headed by Triloki, who owns 34 *bighas* of land and cultivates 21.5 *bighas*. The household has also invested heavily in farm inputs. Another household, headed by Bhagpal, owns 40.5 *bighas* of land and is one of the biggest landowners.

in the village. Nanhe also branched out upon his return to Palanpur. The two Teli-owned flour mills in the village belong to him and his brother. In the Palanpur context, he is striking in his entrepreneurship.

The general perspective on the evolution and importance of rural non-farm employment in Palanpur has been examined, so far, on the basis of occupational trends. The broad conclusions hold also when we look instead at income shares. The evolution of income shares from overall non-farm sources across castes in Palanpur is displayed in Figure 7.6. For the three principal caste groups in the village (Thakurs, Muraos, and Jatabs), there is a strong upward trend for Thakurs and Jatabs, but less so for Muraos.

In 2008/9 Jatabs derived as much as 43 per cent of their income from non-farm work, of which 66 per cent was accounted for by casual sector jobs (Figure 7.7). Non-farm employment has led to an absolute increase in income

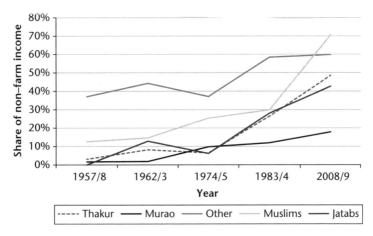

Figure 7.6 Share of non-farm income in total income over the survey period

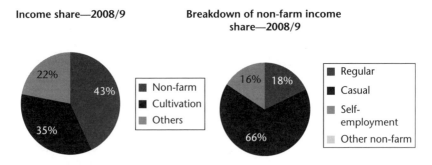

Figure 7.7 Income shares from various sources for Jatabs, 2008/9

Note: The figure represents proportions of income for Jatab households in 2008/9. Other sources of income include livestock income, rental income, and non-cultivation income, excluding non-farm income. Other non-farm includes remittances income plus other non-farm income.

levels and upward mobility of Jatab households. The impact of non-farm activities on poverty and mobility in Palanpur is explored in greater detail in Chapter 8.

7.6.3 Non-Farm Diversification and Education

The literature on rural non-farm employment in India has often emphasized the role of education in facilitating the growth of the sector.[47] It is argued that education plays a significant role not only in enhancing skills for specific jobs in the non-farm sector, but also in increasing awareness of employment opportunities, relevant business methods, where to seek information, modern agricultural practices, and government schemes and programmes. Overall, improved education can lead to a greater ability and a greater inclination towards movement out of agriculture.

Analysis of the Palanpur data points to a rather modest association between educational status and non-farm employment. Educational attainment in Palanpur has improved over the survey years. In 1957/8, literacy rates for adults were as low as 18 per cent for males and 0.05 per cent for females (Figure 7.8).[48] Over time, the level of male literacy has increased markedly; about 76 per cent of males were literate as of 2008/9. Female literacy has also increased, but at 33 per cent in 2008/9 is still lagging far behind the male

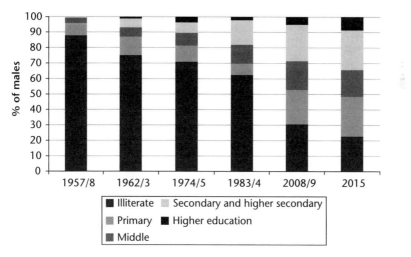

Figure 7.8 Education status of adult males in Palanpur

---

[47] For the importance of education see Basant and Visaria (1993), Eapen (1994), and Lanjouw and Shariff (2004).

[48] On literacy and education in the village, see Chapter 9.

levels. Although literacy rates have improved, overall education levels are still weak. Education above primary schooling is still low, at just 47 per cent of the males aged above fifteen in 2008/9.

Examination of the data from the first two survey years reveals that education did not play much of a role in governing access to non-farm jobs. As noted, many of these jobs, such as railway porters, domestic servants, and *jajmani* services, did not come with any educational prerequisites. There appears to be no difference in access to these jobs based on educational qualifications.

Given the growth of non-farm activities in the 1980s and the general increase in the educational attainment in the village, one might expect a change in the role of education in determining the occupation structure. However, in Palanpur we do not observe a stark change in this regard (Figure 7.9).

Figure 7.9 shows that the majority of non-farm workers in 1983/4 were illiterate. In 2008/9 it was a third, with a majority not educated beyond primary. These fractions are similar for adult males as a whole; see Figure 7.8. Although there has been significant growth of the non-farm sector this is largely made up of poor-quality jobs. Between 1983/4 and 2008/9 these have been casual sector jobs in construction and other manual labour activities where education does not seem to have played much of a role. Even the jobs in the regular sector are rather low in quality and sophistication. Accessing these seems to be largely determined by the household status and ability to pay bribes, rather than the education status of the applicant.[49]

Because most of the non-farm work available to Palanpur villagers requires few skills and little education, households often remark that they see little reason for providing their children with middle- and upper-level

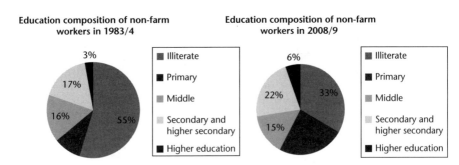

Figure 7.9 Education status of non-farm workers

---

[49] In their multivariate econometric analysis, Lanjouw and Stern (1998) observe a similarly weak correlation between non-farm employment and education.

schooling. Although even impoverished households recognize the desirability of college-level education as a means to securing a government job, they view this as insufficient to access such jobs and point to the burden of having to pay bribes in order to secure such employment. This is not to deny that a certain minimal level of education is essential for a few non-farm jobs in Palanpur (teacher or accountant in the seed store), but these positions remain rare.

7.6.4 Entrepreneurship

We have examined so far in this chapter the scale of expansion of non-farm activities, the nature of these activities, how the opportunities are identified and realized, and the rewards they offer. Those activities usually represent major change for the households. Those who want to engage in them have to seek them out. They have to invest their time in that search and they have to travel. They may incur opportunity costs in terms of foregone earning opportunities. They have to take risks. There are also, of course, 'push' factors in terms of declining opportunities in cultivation as a result of population pressure.

Not all members of the village, or members of a particular caste, have engaged in these activities. Some may feel less pressure to do so, but some may have more initiative and entrepreneurship in their commitment and ability to raise living standards for themselves and their family. The word entrepreneurship is often used in relation to firms and capital equipment. But it makes sense to use it here, too, in characterizing the initiative involved in seeking out new activities and ventures. It involves risk, searches, and investment of time and resources. Some are quicker to respond than others. We have seen very rapid growth in self-employment incomes between 1983/4 and 2008/9, associated particularly with initiatives such as mentha pressing, repair activities, shops, marble polishing, and so on. It has been, by far, the strongest form of income growth in the village. Even in casual non-farm jobs, many Jatabs have sought out jobs in brick kilns, a new and important source of income for them in addition to their income from agriculture. Entrepreneurship is surely an appropriate and useful description of what we have seen in Palanpur. And differences in entrepreneurship will help us understand the evolution of mobility and inequality in Palanpur, as we shall see in Chapter 8.

7.7 Women's Participation in the Non-Farm Sector

The labour force in Palanpur, in terms of remunerated or marketed work, is overwhelmingly male dominated. Figure 7.10 illustrates the very limited participation of women. Most of the women in Palanpur are engaged in

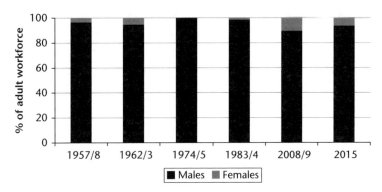

Figure 7.10 Gender composition of adult workforce

non-market activities and household-level domestic work; in work outside these activities, their participation rate, even in 2008/9, was only 11 per cent (see Chapter 10 for further discussion).

Some studies suggest that with the growth of the non-farm sector there has been a trend towards the feminization of cultivation.[50] In contrast, Ranjan (2008), using state-level data from NSSO, finds an increase in female participation in the rural non-farm sector. He finds that the proportion of female workers in the non-farm sector grew from 8.7 per cent in 1987/8 to 16.8 per cent by 2004/5. He suggests that reasons could include a decline in traditional prejudice against female labour and a fall in cultivation incomes, putting pressure on rural women to take up non-farm participation to sustain the family income. Neither of these trends appear to apply very strongly in Palanpur. Only 7 per cent of adult females were employed as cultivators in 2008/9 (Figure 7.11), although there is some evidence of rising participation amongst Murao women (see Chapter 10).[51]

Female remunerated employment has generally been seen as denigrating in the village, especially amongst the Thakurs. This observation has also been reported by Walker and Ryan (1990) in their study of ICRISAT villages. They report that within ICRISAT villages, a taboo prevents women from touching the plough, and men who do domestic chores are often ridiculed. Where women do work, their earnings are generally lower than for men. Low wages for women are often attributed to their lower physical strength.

But times are changing a little. Prior to 1993 there were no female workers amongst the Thakurs in Palanpur. By 2008/9, however, there were a few

---

[50] On the impact of non-farm growth on female occupation, see Binswanger-Mkhize (2012).

[51] Lanjouw and Stern (1998) note the possibility of under-reporting in the female occupational data. However, they find that even after allowing for some under-reporting, the picture of female labour force participation changes very little.

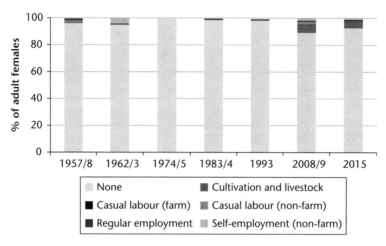

Figure 7.11 Occupation composition of females over the survey period

Thakur women working on family farms, self-employed as tailors, or with regular non-farm employment as *anganwadi* health workers. In case of the Muraos, female participation is restricted to cultivation; nearly 64 per cent of the women engaged in cultivation in the village belonged to the Murao caste in 2008/9. It is likely that the rapid rise in agricultural wages has led Muraos to increase the involvement of family labour, including women. Increasing male activity in non-farm jobs has been a factor too (see Chapter 10). Female participation in casual wage labour is largely confined to the lower-caste Jatab households. Occasionally, when a household is headed by a female due to the absence or death of male family members, women will also seek casual wage labour employment.

7.8 Migration, Commuting, and Links with the Outside World

A key feature of the expansion of rural non-farm activities in Palanpur has been the increasing connectivity of the village with the outside world. This expansion has been mainly via commuting by villagers to nearby towns and surrounding areas, but migration has also played a role. This interlinkage with the outside world has not only resulted in changing markets and institutions within the village, but has also changed the way the residents understand and deal with the world outside. While migration and commuting can be seen as a response by residents to pressure on land within the village, they can also be seen as a response to changes outside or exogenous to Palanpur. Urban areas around the village have expanded strongly in recent decades, drawing on rural areas for labour.

Improvements in transportation and communication infrastructure have allowed a growing pool of workers to access the outside labour market without moving permanently out of the village. In the past, the cost of travel or migration, the unfamiliarity of the urban milieu, and the uncertainty about opportunities served to deter poorer households from accessing the urban labour market. Over time, commuting has become less costly and complicated, allowing even the poorer segments of village society, notably Jatabs, to participate in outside labour markets. This has not only influenced the distribution of income (see Chapter 8), but has also shaped social networks based on caste, kinship, and neighbourhood, with castes beyond the Thakurs actively building up their own networks.

Migration involves substantial upfront expenditures on travel and the costs of a new place of residence. As a result, poorer households have traditionally been less able or inclined to migrate from Palanpur. With greater ease of commuting, some of the reasons to migrate are attenuated: outside jobs can be accessed while villagers continue to reside in the village. At the same time, with commuting comes a greater familiarization with the outside labour market and an ability to broaden one's circle of contacts. The costs of out-migration thus also decline. In Palanpur, we observe that during recent decades, households with some experience of regular or casual non-farm jobs have become more likely to migrate out of the village. Among the beneficiaries of improved access to outside jobs in the last two decades have been the Jatabs, and we do see an increasing number of Jatab individuals, and even entire households, deciding to migrate.

But it is not just economic factors that count. The nature of caste relations and cultural factors associated with caste identity also play a role in an individual or household's decision to migrate. This can be seen in the case of the Passi households in Palanpur. Passis were relatively recent arrivals in Palanpur, having migrated into the village from eastern Uttar Pradesh not long before the first Palanpur survey in 1957/8. At the time, most of these Passis were engaged as workers in the railways, and over time they had expanded their activities to other non-farm jobs. There have been several periods during which Passis left the village; their share of the village population has fallen from over 10 per cent in the 1950s and 1960s to only 2 per cent in the 2010s.

This caste has seen some decline in employment opportunities since the closure of a cloth mill in Moradabad after the 1993 survey, but that is not likely to be the only or even the main reason for leaving the village. Rather, the caste has never been fully part of village society and has generally been seen as more footloose than the other castes. It is likely that their connections to the outside world have always been greater than those of other Palanpur households, and that the costs of migration have thus been considerably lower for this group. The migration behaviour of this caste can be contrasted with that of the numerically dominant castes in Palanpur (Thakur, Murao, and Jatab), who have experienced far less out-migration. Indeed, Muraos are the caste group which has been the least mobile over the survey period. Their affinity to cultivation and land along with their relative hesitation in engaging in non-farm activities has meant that they have focused their activities on cultivation within the village rather than on the opportunities outside.

Migration and commuting decisions are also likely to be significantly influenced by the changing economic geography in and around Palanpur. Notably, there has been significant growth and expansion of nearby small towns. This resonates with what has been happening in the country as a whole (see Gibson et al., 2017). These small and medium towns are not just new centres of urban growth but have also emerged as new drivers of employment creation and poverty reduction in the rural economy (Gibson et al., 2017). Most of the new jobs continue to be dominated by informal employment and unorganized enterprises.

7.8.1 *Migration Out of Palanpur*

Information on migration has been collected in Palanpur throughout the survey period, with the exception of the 1974/5 survey year. The 1957/8 and 1962/3 surveys included a separate questionnaire on migration. These are also available in the 1983 and in 1993 surveys, albeit in a slightly different form. The data collection effort in 2008/9 was particularly comprehensive. It not only covered information on migrants from the village, but also attempted to contact out-migrants and collect information on them.

Migration by complete households was uncovered by tracking the original household in the earlier survey year and then matching it with households in the subsequent round. Households that were not observed in the subsequent survey are treated as migrants. A possible source of error associated with this method relates to those households that migrated after a particular survey but returned to the village before the subsequent survey. Such households would not be counted amongst migrating households.

Individuals that moved out of the village for study or employment are treated as migrants. Female members of households who move out because of marriage are not treated as migrants; it is the usual practice for a newly married wife to join her husband's family. To be counted as a migrant, an individual had to be out of the village for over six months. In the 2008/10 survey, a separate schedule was fielded to capture seasonal migrants who move out of the village individually or as complete household to work for some parts of the year. This is common in the case of households and individuals engaged in brick kiln work. Such households and individuals have been treated as normal residents for the purpose of the survey. As far as possible, similar information on employment and place of migration has also been collected for the 2015 round.

A caveat is in order at this stage regarding the interpretation of trends in migration. Since the data used in this book cover a long period of over 60 years, some systematic attrition bias in later years cannot be ruled out. Other things being equal, for this reason one might expect to observe a declining inclination to migrate: those who were so inclined will have done so already, and those who remain are likely to possess some latent disinclination to leave. Of course, other things are changing rapidly, including opportunities, understanding of the workings of the world outside the village, communication, travel costs, and so on.

Table 7.13 provides an overview of households that migrated during the survey period. Migration by entire households has been observed since the first survey period of 1958–64, when nine households migrated after the 1957/8 survey.[52] However, as a proportion of the population of households, the most intensive household-level migration occurred between 1964 and 1975. This was the period when the influence of the green revolution technology was at its peak and, for this reason, the migration of large number of households from the village is perhaps surprising. In that year, however, Passis accounted for two-fifths of the migrating households. As described, the

Table 7.13 Migration of entire households

Caste Group	Year					
	1957/8 to 1962/3	1962/3 to 1974/5	1974/5 to 1983/4	1983/4 to 1993	1993 to 2008/9	2008/9 to 2015
Thakur	0	1	2	4	6	0
Murao	0	3	2	0	6	0
Dhimar	2	1	0	4	1	3
Gadariya	0	1	1	0	1	0
Dhobi	1	1	0	1	0	0
Teli	0	0	0	1	1	3
Passi	0	6	1	2	7	1
Jatab	3	0	0	0	4	5
Others	3	2	1	0	1	3
Total	9	15	7	12	27	15
Total base year households	100	106	117	143	193	231
Migration Rate	1.50	1.29	0.66	0.84	0.93	0.93

Note: The migration rate is defined as the number of households, per hundred households in a base year, migrating out per year.

[52] The Ansari report (1964) mentions that four households were temporarily absent from the village in 1958.

position of the Passi caste within Palanpur society is somewhat unusual as they had moved to Palanpur only relatively recently and were clearly less vested in the village and its agriculture. Passis migrated again in large numbers after the 1993 survey.

Overall, Table 7.13 reveals a decline in the migration rate (per household) in the village since the first two decades. Although the absolute number of households migrating per year has risen (from around 1.2 per year 1958–1984 to 1.7 per year 1984–2015), this is slower than the increase in the number of households.[53] Over the entire survey period 85 households have moved out of the village. Passis represent the single largest group of migrants, with 17 households accounting for 20 per cent of all migrating households. Among other caste groups, Dhimars have also been significant migrants. This caste has also engaged significantly in non-farm activities. Because Thakurs, Muraos, and Jatabs have been less likely to migrate relative to other caste groups, there has been a rising concentration of the three largest caste groups in the village population. These caste groups accounted for 55 per cent of village population in 1958, but as much as 66 per cent by the 2015 survey round.

Table 7.14 reports the distribution of the primary occupation of migrating households in the base year and indicates that most of the migrating house-holds had some exposure to non-farm employment. In the first two decades, migrant households also included some that had depended on *jajmani* income. The decline of the *jajmani* system in the village put pressure on these households to seek employment elsewhere. None of the households in the first three decades who migrated out were engaged in casual employment. This is also reflected in zero migration of Jatab households after the 1964 survey. However, in the last three decades, casual labour households engaged

Table 7.14 Primary occupation of migrating households in base year

Occupation	Base Year					
	1957/8	1962/3	1974/5	1983/4	1993	2008/9
Cultivation	3	4	3	1	6	1
Casual labour	0	0	0	2	7	5
Regular work	1	2	2	5	4	2
Self-employed non-farm	0	4	1	3	7	3
Other	4	5	1	1	3	2

[53] We should note that the number of people per household has fallen. And the table refers to migration of whole households; individuals can migrate from within the household.

in non-farm employment have experienced migration and are among the most prominent occupation group in the last three decades.

Negligible migration of Jatab and casual labour households in the first three decades likely reflects the difficulty of settling into a new place of residence outside the close-knit village society. Migration to urban areas often requires substantial outlays for settling in. Casual labourers and poorer households are typically unable to afford such costs or to navigate the urban environment. Some idea of the functioning of the urban labour market is also needed. On the other hand, those with some exposure to the labour market beyond the village find it easier to move out. The process of migrating is not sudden and often involves one member of the household first moving and settling in before subsequently being joined by his family.

While migration of entire households has been low in the village and does not show any increase in the rate per household over time, individual migration has increased over the years. Table 7.15 presents the changes in population between survey years in relation to relevant reasons, excluding individuals migrating as part of the migration of their entire household. As is clear from the table, the annual migration rate per 1000 persons has increased from around four in the first two decades to six to seven in the next two decades, rising to ten in the last decade. The proportion of women migrating is much lower than for men. Closer scrutiny of the data also suggests that female migrants are mostly relatives of migrating adult members. There are no cases of woman migrating alone.

The caste pattern of individual migrants is similar to that observed for migrating households, with Passi, Dhimar, and other smaller castes more strongly represented than Thakurs, Muraos, and Jatabs. However, the last two decades, since the late 1990s, indicate a rising trend of Jatabs, and also Telis, migrating out of the village. The analysis of migrating individuals by their primary occupation in the previous round also suggests that most migrants had some exposure to non-farm employment outside the village.

7.8.2 Commuting

The growth of non-farm employment in Palanpur has been facilitated by its proximity to the large town of Chandausi and the city of Moradabad. In addition, there are smaller towns in the vicinity (e.g. Bilari) and workplaces like brick kilns and sugar factories located within the surrounding rural areas. Hazell and colleagues (2010) note that with the growth of towns, villagers from surrounding areas are increasingly able to find employment opportunities in such towns and either to commute to them for work on a daily basis, or for periods of short duration (less than six months). This process is clearly seen

Table 7.15 Population changes in the village over the survey rounds

Year

	1957/8 to 1962/3			1962/3 to 1974/5			1974/5 to 1983/4		
	Male	Female	Total Persons	Male	Female	Total Persons	Male	Female	Total Persons
Inside village	240	189	429	240	141	381	333	240	573
Married out	0	16	16	0	48	48	0	49	49
Migrated out	9	1	10	12	13	25	19	12	31
Dead	25	30	55	39	38	77	40	34	74
Total	274	236	510	291	240	531	392	335	727
Annual migration/1000 persons	5.5	0.7	3.3	3.7	4.9	4.3	5.4	4	4.7

	1984 to 1993			1993 to 2009			2009 to 2015		
	Male	Female	Total Persons	Male	Female	Total Persons	Male	Female	Total Persons
Inside village	383	293	676	362	240	602	553	494	1,047
Married out	0	98	98	0	132	132	0	63	63
Migrated out	43	19	62	74	20	94	72	17	89
Dead	48	39	87	79	47	126	24	20	44
Total	474	449	923	517	437	954	649	594	1243
Annual migration/1000 persons	9.1	4.2	6.7	8.9	2.9	6.2	15.8	4.1	10.2

Note: Every individual surveyed in a survey round is tracked in the subsequent survey and is assigned one of four statuses: (i) inside village, if the surveyed individual is surveyed again in the village in the next round; (ii) married out, primarily women who move out of the village after marriage; (iii) migrated, if the individual is alive but is living away from the village for a period longer than six months; and (iv) dead, if the individual has died between the two survey rounds. For example, there were 236 females in the village in 1958. Of these, 189 were found to be residing in the village in 1964, 16 had married out, 1 had migrated out, and 30 had died.

in Palanpur, where Table 7.16 documents the increasing number of outside non-farm jobs held by villagers.[54]

Over the years, not only did the number of residents accessing outside jobs increase, but the radius of locations to which they commuted also increased. While, in the first four decades, villagers would go to the nearby towns such as Chandausi, Bilari, and Moradabad, they are now going to Aligarh and Agra in search of jobs. Working in places as distant as Aligarh and Agra (which are 125 and 210 km away, respectively) would not be possible on a daily basis. Recall that we do not count being away for less than six months as being migration. Figure 7.12 illustrates the radius of destinations that Palanpur villagers

Table 7.16 Location of non-farm jobs

Location	Year					
	1957/8	1962/3	1974/5	1983/4	2008/9	2015
Outside	7 (38.9)	14 (50)	41 (83.7)	86 (76.8)	133 (59.9)	150 (62.8)
Inside	11 (61.1)	14 (50)	8 (16.3)	26 (23.2)	89 (40.1)	89 (37.2)
Total	18	28	49	112	222	239

Note: The table presents the number of non-farm jobs inside and outside the village. The figures in the parentheses present the percentage of non-farm jobs inside and outside the village.

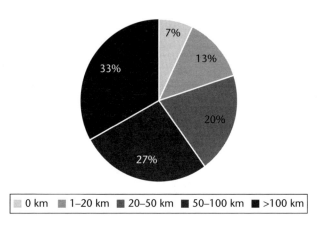

| ▨ 0 km | ▨ 1–20 km | ■ 20–50 km | ■ 50–100 km | ■ >100 km |

Figure 7.12 Distance to place of employment

Note: The figure represents the proportion of jobs within each of the peripheries in 2008/9: (i) in Palanpur, distance (0 km); (ii) Pipli, Bilari, Akrauli, Nagaliya, Sahaspur, Jargaon, Bhoori, and Chandausi (within 20 km); (iii) Moradabad, Kundarki, Sirsi, and Sambhal (20–50 km); (iv) outside but in Uttar Pradesh (50–100 km); (v) outside Uttar Pradesh or further than 100 km.

---

[54] Lanjouw and Stern (1998) state that in the period up to 1993, the expansion of non-farm activities mostly took the form of regular or semi-regular wage employment outside the village. Between 1957/8 and 1993 the number of these jobs grew from 11 to 49. Most of these jobs occurred outside the village, in areas within commuting distance from Palanpur.

commuted to in 2008/9. Movement to the more distant destinations is typically triggered by a search for higher-income earning opportunities. Such movement leads to increased knowledge about opportunities and can also serve as a source of information and motivation for others within the village to travel outside for work. In some cases, work as farm labourers outside the village in places such as Punjab is also seen as an attractive opportunity: agricultural wages are higher and demand is strong, while high-caste villagers can avoid the dishonour of working as farm labourers within the village.[55]

While commuting has helped Palanpur residents to find employment outside, it has also helped them acquire information and know-how which has been used to set up non-farm enterprises within the village and the immediate surroundings. Indeed, non-farm jobs within the village rose strongly between 1983/4 and 2008/9.

7.8.3 Determinants of Outside Employment and of Migration

Mukhopadhyay (2011) employs econometric methods to analyse the determinants of migration and commuting in Palanpur. Probit models are estimated to ascertain which household- and individual-level characteristics and circumstances are particularly strongly associated with the likelihood of seeking work outside the village.[56] The estimates from models which were focused on commuting indicate that a particularly robust correlate of outside job involvement is the amount of land owned. The more land owned by the individual's household (controlling for the total number of adult members in the households), the lower the probability that they will work outside the village. Lower land ownership, and household and per capita income, will push people to seek non-farm activities. The result is consistent with the discussion in Section 7.6.1 on non-farm involvement and landholding patterns. There is little evidence that the relationship between land owned and outside job involvement has weakened over time. This has an important implication for the Palanpur economy. It implies that the lower average landholdings in 2008 would make non-farm activities outside the village more likely. A further important finding is that the number of male adults is insignificant. This suggests that it is the size of landholding of the household that matters and not necessarily the land/labour ratio.

A further finding of interest is a changing association between education outcomes and non-farm involvement outside the village. In 1983/4 a positive

---

[55] An example is that of a Thakur household headed by Chandrapal, who migrated out with his wife Munnu Devi to Punjab, where they found employment as regular agricultural labourers. They moved out to achieve a higher income as well as to avoid the shame of working as casual labourers within the village.

[56] Detailed results and estimation strategy are discussed in Mukhopadhyay (2011).

correlation with education indicated that people with higher education were more likely to work outside Palanpur. This appeared largely due to the relatively abundant regular jobs held by villagers in that year: jobs that required some education. However, many regular jobs were lost after 1983 with, for example, the closure of a cloth mill and biscuit factory. In both 1993 and 2008, education had no significant marginal effect on the probability of working outside. The opportunities outside Palanpur were shifting away from regular jobs in the later survey rounds and towards more common casual wage jobs and self-employment that had few educational prerequisites.

Moving on from commuting, probit regressions were also estimated to examine the determinants of migration over the two periods 1983–1993 and 1993–2008 (Mukhopadhyay, 2011). There are contrasting results between the two periods. In the first period, those with more land were found to migrate out less. Those household members who did migrate were generally better educated. Larger households (in the base year) were less likely to migrate, suggesting that it was not only, in this period, pressure on land that made people migrate. People in regular/semi-regular jobs inside the village were less likely to migrate, while those who were involved in non-farm work outside the village in 1983 were more likely to migrate during the subsequent decade.

In 1993–2008, interestingly, some of the estimated effects changed. Most importantly, if an individual was working outside the village, he was now more likely to remain living in the village—a reflection, possibly, of the changing composition of outside jobs towards casual employment. Land ownership remained a significant variable post-1993, although the models now emphasized the higher propensity of migration amongst those with little land (rather than a higher propensity to remain in the village amongst those with more land). Education did not appear to play a role, indicating little difference between educated and uneducated people in their propensity to migrate—possibly also reflecting the lack of an education premium in outside employment options. The relative scarcity of regular non-farm employment opportunities outside the village, coupled with generally improving education outcomes, may have weakened the importance of education as a predictor of migration. In this period, pressure on land and low income seemed to be the most important factors pushing villagers to leave.

7.8.4 Migration, Commuting, and the Role of the Village

It is possible that the growing practice of commuting outside the village for work, together with continuing migration away from the village altogether, have led to changes in the way that Palanpur is perceived by its inhabitants. Whereas in earlier decades the village was naturally regarded as a relatively closed economy with tightly linked social, political, and economic ties, the village increasingly came to be seen more as a place of residence and a familiar community. Whether, and to what extent, perspectives are changing in this way is likely to vary with the degree to which households remain engaged in cultivation and other village-specific activities. It is also important to note that despite a growing propensity to move outside the village, it is also quite common for workers who have migrated to return at some point. It seems that it is regarded as important to maintain village ties while becoming increasingly connected economically with the outside world. Such perspectives might stem not only from the insecurities of the urban informal labour market, but also from the social and cultural ties of households.

The 2008/9 round of data collection in Palanpur included a survey of the 41 households who had migrated out earlier but had subsequently returned. This survey provides insights into the migration process from the perspective of the subjects themselves: a series of open questions was built into the questionnaire. The 'returners' are unlikely to be a random sample of original migrants out of the village, but their perceptions are interesting.

The main reasons for returning to Palanpur were reported to be employment related: inability to find a new job, the end of the contract, or the failure of the enterprise in which the worker was employed. However, reverse migration can also be a more personal choice prompted by social and familial reasons, health issues, and preferences related to the conditions of life and work in the village.[57] Reverse migration is sometimes also seen as part of a deliberate strategy to work hard while young and to create enough capital for survival in the village during one's later stages of life. Migration, according to the stories of the interviewees, often means hard working conditions and a lower quality of life in the place of employment.[58]

Occupational and spatial mobility do not necessarily imply social mobility (Lerche, Guérin, and Srivastava, 2012; Srivastava and Bhattacharya, 2003). Rural workers often feel compelled to accept non-farm employment that is precarious and irregular. Breman (2013) argues that rural non-farm

---

[57] Dorilal spent five years in Haryana with his wife, son, and daughter, but returned after it became difficult to continue working there. Lakhpat, fifty-five years old, referring to his life in Haryana where he worked for two years to pay back the debt for his daughter's marriage, complains, 'It was too much work, long working hours. Any cultural and religious activity could not be performed there because I was all the time busy in my work. No time for any social activities in that society.'

[58] Banney complained about the pollution in Lucknow, 'The air is very smoky in the street so I can't stay there.' Thirty-one-year-old Pramod, who spent six months in Moradabad with his family doing casual labour, also complained of hard work and the restrictions of urban society. Twenty-five-year-old Ramesh, a seasonal migrant in agricultural labour, like many other workers, complained about the very poor living conditions in the working camps, 'Living facility is not good. 8–9 persons live in a room like cattle.' Harichandra, forty-two years old, experimented as a seasonal worker in a construction site, but after one and half months decided to return to cultivation in Palanpur, 'I got tired of doing cooking, cleaning and all the housework after returning from work.'

workers can be seen as a mobile and flexible workforce characterized by great vulnerability. Partly, in his view, this is due to the skills mismatch in the labour market that he sees emerging as a result of the massive conversion of the rural labour force from farming to non-farm activities.

From this perspective, such vulnerability could be aggravated by exploitative practices in the complex chain of recruitment. Recruitment for much non-farm employment is through a middleman/contractor who is often known to the job seekers and may come from the same village. These contractors often act as moneylenders who will pay advances to workers in an effort to lock-in the workforce for the duration sought by the employer. In Palanpur, such practices are not uncommon in the case of brick kiln work and are also occasionally seen with casual wage labour employment in Moradabad. Contractors usually recruit from within their networks, where trust and reputation partially compensate for the absence of formal contracts. As a result, workers often share common characteristics, such as geographical origins, religious community, and caste, with the contractors. The emphasis Breman (2013) puts on non-farm workers as a vulnerable group may be somewhat misplaced in the context of commuting and diversification. The people in non-farm casual work and non-farm self-employment in Palanpur are not powerful. However, the diversification away from agriculture and the new opportunities are, for them, ways to manage overall risk and not only to increase incomes. They are not solely 'non-farm casual' workers in isolation: they have a base in the village and alternative activities in the village or in the vicinity.

Of all respondents from the migration survey in Palanpur, over half declared that they had received help during the migration process in acquiring a job or receiving accommodation, loan, or food. Most were helped by family and fellow caste members.

7.9 Comparison with Other Village Studies

Given our description of the income and employment dynamics in Palanpur, as well as the understandings of the main drivers of these changes we have proposed, we now consider some of the insights that come from other village studies of rural India.

An important longitudinal village survey in India has been conducted by ICRISAT since 1975. One study based on the ICRISAT data examines the villages of Aurepelle and Dokur in the Mahbubnagar district of Andhra Pradesh and points to a process of rural livelihood diversification (Deb et al., 2002). As is the case in Palanpur, these villages have seen a decline in the importance of cultivation as a source of employment. Agriculture has always been a risky activity, and households are increasingly participating in non-farm sources of income in order to diversify risk. Increasing population pressure on landholdings has also played a role. Deb and colleagues (2002) point to an increased tendency amongst households to engage in multiple activities. In both villages there has been an increase in the number of sources of income. In Aurepelle in 1975, households were recorded in the survey as drawing on at most three sources of income. By 2001 a majority of farmers (59 per cent) had between two and four sources of income, and 16 per cent of households had five or more sources of income. Similar trends were observed in Dokur.

Pressure on agricultural incomes with rising population has led to residents from both Aurepelle and Dokur looking beyond their village for employment opportunities. Migration has emerged as a common strategy. A lack of employment opportunities for better-educated villagers is cited as a reason to migrate. Unlike Palanpur, there appear to be relatively few opportunities for daily commuting. In this regard, Palanpur's close proximity to the cities of Moradabad and Chandausi has worked in its favour.

Such proximity is common, however, in the densely populated Indo-Gangetic plain and in many other parts of India. A dense rural population is a key foundation for local towns, while the growth of the latter—in terms of populations and incomes—means they provide jobs and markets that can be accessed by commuting.

Migrants in Aurepelle and Dokur have brought back information about migrant labour opportunities and have thereby encouraged other people to migrate. Migrants helped their neighbours to find work and passed on knowledge about conditions of work and pay.

A study on the diversification of rural incomes in three villages (Ananthavaram, Bukkacherla, and Kothapalle) in Andhra Pradesh has been carried out by Swaminathan and colleagues (2008). The authors note that the degree of income and occupational diversification is highest in the village located along a major highway north of the city of Telangana.

Kajisa and Palanichamy (2006), in their study of several villages in rural Tamil Nadu, document a significant rise in non-farm diversification since the mid-1990s. The expansion of non-farm employment has led to a rise in agricultural wages. The increase in the two sources of income has led to some decline in poverty. Unlike in Palanpur, the authors observe a role for education in determining access to non-farm jobs as well as in the greater farm management associated with increased mechanization.

In a study by Ranjan (2009) of two villages in Uttar Pradesh, Kheri Tangan and Mubarakpur, it was found that many middle and higher caste villagers are, by and large, regularly employed. Of the total, 42.9 and 20.8 per cent of these villagers are in regular jobs in the two villages, respectively. On the other hand, villagers from the lower social strata (Muslims, scheduled caste, tribes, and other backward classes), are casually employed. Similar patterns are observed for self-employment, where the backward and socially lower-caste people pursue low-skill and low-investment occupations that are relatively less remunerative. Landlessness, lack of productive assets, and low education levels are amongst the factors resulting in distress-induced employment for these groups.

In a study of the Slater village Iruvelpattu in Tamil Nadu, Harriss and colleagues (2010) confirmed the decline of traditional caste-based *jajmani* services. While 28.5 per cent of households could be described as non-agricultural in 1981, this number had increased to 40 per cent by 2008. Harriss and colleagues (2010) found that middle- and upper-caste villagers are increasingly migrating out of the village altogether. There has also been some migration amongst the lower-caste Dalits, but not to the same degree. As a result the village economy and society both are becoming increasingly Dalit. While middle and upper castes have moved into salaried non-farm occupations, Dalits can be found more commonly employed in labouring occupations, such as construction, or employed in brick fields and brick kilns in places near the village. While agricultural labour was an important source of employment for the Dalits in the 1980s, this had lessened by 2008 due to the emergence of other non-farm occupations.

Overall, we find that non-farm activities have been playing a pivotal role in the transformation of the economies of a number of Indian villages other than Palanpur. The extent of diversification depends on multiple factors, but proximity to urban centres does seem to be important. At the micro level, the drivers of diversification vary across rural groups depending on the agrarian structure, education levels, and the kind of opportunities that are available in the non-farm sector. In the presence of pressures such as population growth, declining cultivation income, inequality in land ownership, discrimination based on caste, and lack of profitable income opportunities within the village, the non-farm sector becomes an important route to securing alternative sources of income.

7.10 Conclusion

Non-farm activities are now central to the Palanpur economy. While over 80 per cent of households still derive some income from cultivation, over time agriculture has come to generate a smaller fraction of village income and is now a less potent driver of economic growth. Recent decades have seen growing demand for labour in the non-farm economy in rural India as a whole. In Palanpur we see that there have been divergent rates of growth between farm and non-farm jobs, with the latter accounting for nearly 60 per cent of the total workforce. These activities also made up nearly 50 per cent of total village income in 2008/9, with agriculture around one-third (see Table 7.3). Many more households now have more than one type of job, and some have several.

Given the importance of the non-farm sector, the major aim of this chapter was to understand the growth of this sector and the various factors responsible for this. As we saw in Chapters 5 and 6, the increase in the population, the decline in per capita landholdings, and the releasing of agricultural labour through mechanization has facilitated, incentivized, and accompanied a process of strong intensification of non-farm activities by the labour force in Palanpur. Better access to towns and cities via improvements in railways and communications infrastructure, particularly mobile phones, has helped villagers find jobs and has led to a growing number travelling outside Palanpur for their employment.

We find that there has been substantial change in the range and nature of the non-farm jobs available. While these jobs were restricted mainly to traditional caste-based *jajmani* services and a few regular jobs in the railways during the first two survey years of the 1950s and 1960s, there has been a significant expansion over time beyond the network of traditional services. Non-farm employment is now found in a range of establishments such as the cotton factory, sugar mill in Bilari, paper factory in Nagalia, marble polishing units in Chandausi, casual labour in brick kilns, and so on.

The jobs in the non-farm sector can largely be categorized into two kinds: low-paying casual and menial activities and more attractive and higher-income opportunities. Casual wage non-farm jobs would fall under the first category while the latter includes well-paid regular jobs (often government provided) as well as some profitable self-employment units. But the lower-paying jobs are more remunerative than agricultural labour, and many allow for more frequency of employment whilst retaining the flexibility to work in agriculture. Some activities, like marble polishing, lie between the two ends of the spectrum.

The casual non-farm sector has registered the highest growth in employment in recent decades, notably in activities related to the construction sector. The rate of growth in casual employment has been followed in employment terms by self-employment. Self-employment has seen the fastest income growth in Palanpur by a substantial margin. The entrepreneurship has been striking. Contrary to what had been anticipated in Lanjouw and Stern (1998; reporting on the 1983/4 and 1993 studies), regular wage jobs have declined both relatively and absolutely, and there has been very little growth in the number of these jobs after the early 1990s. See Chapter 12 for some current speculations on the future.

In the face of declining per capita landholdings and lower cultivation incomes, households have pursued a broad spectrum of livelihood strategies. Our analysis indicates that participation in the non-farm sector varies across households depending on the size of their landholdings and caste affiliation. Casual non-farm employment is the primary source of employment for the landless and the near-landless, as the rewards from agricultural labour become less attractive relative to the opportunities outside. For households with landholdings above 30 *bighas*, non-farm participation is still less common, although there are a number engaged in relatively high-earning, regular employment or particularly remunerative self-employed enterprises.

A majority of households in Palanpur now belong to the small and marginal land farm category and, for these, non-farm activities are playing an important role both in increasing income and diversifying risk. Dependence on cultivation has fallen, and the constraints on income related to land have loosened. Although households rarely exit fully from cultivation, the extent of participation in it is determined by opportunities in the non-farm sector. Those with well-paid regular jobs reduce their involvement in cultivation significantly while those with casual sector jobs remain more dependent on cultivation in order to maintain levels of income and to manage variability.

While land endowment plays a role in the basic occupational decision concerning participation or not in non-farm activities, access to these jobs, especially regular jobs, is also influenced by the caste affiliation of an individual. Access to regular jobs is often determined by an ability to pay bribes, as well as influence, contacts, and networks based on caste and kinship. As a result, such jobs tend to be held by relatively advantaged caste groups such as the Thakurs. The historically disadvantaged Jatabs, on the other hand, are poorly placed to find regular non-farm employment. Caste networks also play a role in some casual non-farm jobs, as we saw in the example of work in the Moradabad railyards, where Thakurs were predominant.

Recent decades have seen a marked increase in participation by Jatabs in the casual wage non-farm labour force, where there are few barriers to entry. This process has led to improvements in their economic circumstances: almost all Jatabs owned *pukka* houses in 2008/9,[59] whereas almost all their houses were *kaccha* in the earlier decades of the surveys; many have moved out of poverty as conventionally measured (see Chapter 8).

The traditionally cultivating caste of Muraos originally displayed some resistance to non-farm participation—preferring to focus efforts and attention

---

[59] Income mobility is examined in greater detail in Chapter 8.

on cultivation. But declining agricultural incomes over time (due to declining per capita landholdings) has led some of them to belatedly pursue opportunities in the non-farm sector.

There is little evidence to show that education plays a key role in determining access to non-farm jobs. Most of the jobs available in the non-farm sector are unskilled in nature, and formal education does not appear to be essential. We speculate in Chapter 12 on how long this lack of importance of education for job acquisition may continue.

Women are greatly under-represented in the non-farm labour force of Palanpur, and indeed in the entire labour force of the village. There are examples where women work alongside their husbands in non-farm activities—for example, as part of a family group in the brick kilns—but it appears that social restrictions on women working for wages as non-farm labourers, salaried employees (except for some government jobs), or entrepreneurs, continue to hold. In the same way, economic activities in agriculture within the village are also circumscribed for women, although there is some indication of increasing cultivation activity for Murao women as participation in non-farm activities by Murao men starts to increase (see Chapter 10).

While full migration from Palanpur is not particularly common, and is not yet increasing as a proportion of households, the related practice of villagers commuting from Palanpur on a daily basis, or for periods of short duration, is both common and increasing over time. Commuting permits villagers to continue to reside in Palanpur and maintain some involvement in cultivation, while they access an ever wider range of non-farm job opportunities in the surrounding area and nearby towns and cities. Migration seems increasingly associated with declining land per household. It can be facilitated by caste and family networks.

Starting small service enterprises, such as oil pressing, motorcycle repair, shops, and so on, also involves initiative, risk, and investment of time and often a little capital. And so, too, do casual non-farm activities. Some pursue these new opportunities earlier and with more success than others, by showing greater commitment and initiative. Whilst luck, capital, and connections play a role, so does entrepreneurship. As we noted in Chapter 4, quoting Deng Xiaoping, 'some get richer before others'. We saw, for example, that whilst caste matters, there is great variation within caste. We have also seen that self-employment income has been by far the fastest growing in Palanpur. Some of the entrepreneurial activity has been impressively successful. To add to Deng Xiaoping's phrase, 'and some get more rich than others', we shall explore issues of mobility and inequality in Chapter 8.

The expansion of the non-farm sector in rural India is of great importance because of the potential role it can play in generating rural employment, reducing poverty, and diversifying risk. The features of the non-farm sector in relation

291

to Palanpur, and its evolution over time, resonate both with observations from other village studies and with all-India evidence from secondary data. It is very important not to underestimate the importance of rural non-farm activity in India and its association with the growth of smaller towns and cities.

And there are already signs that migration will accelerate as population pressures increase, the outside and local urban economies expand rapidly, and the villagers of Palanpur get to know more and more about opportunities. The role of education in the finding of these jobs, so far very limited, is likely to increase.

Chapter 8 examines the evolution of poverty, inequality, and mobility in the village during the seven decades covered by our study period in light of the forces identified in this chapter and in Chapters 5 and 6. Its argument and analysis depend strongly on the story that has unfolded in this chapter. Other questions and speculations concern what will happen next. We will suggest in the two concluding chapters of this book that the non-farm rural sector is crucial to India's growth in the coming decades and that the recognition of this critical driver of growth and poverty reduction should be reflected in policy.

Appendix
Note on Income Data in Palanpur

The income data for Palanpur presented in Chapters 2, 5, 7, and 8 begin with the construction of household income for the agricultural year July 2008–June 2009. There is no separate schedule on income in the Palanpur surveys. The data on income were put together using different schedules on cultivation, non-farm enterprises, employment, migration and credit, and so on. Details on income from cultivation have already been described in Chapter 5. The data on non-cultivation income have been compiled using the information provided in schedules along with that collected through diaries. There is some imputation involved in some of the income estimates; particularly for businesses and also for casual labour where the information on number of days worked has been used to scale up the estimate for the year. Thus, the income data have been carefully built up using several of these data sets to arrive at an annual income for a common reference period of one year. The same procedures have been applied to data for previous years to arrive at a comparable estimate of income across survey rounds. In a few exceptional cases it was not possible to construct a convincing measure of household income due to incomplete data. This applies in the case of 1 household in 1974/5, 3 households in 1983/4, and 12 households in 2008/9.

The imputation of casual wage income has been based on the number of days worked as a casual worker and the wage rate in the activity. Information on the number of days worked in a month was asked from every respondent who reported working as a casual wage worker. In cases where the respondent was unable to recall the exact number of days, we have used 25 days in a month. Workers mix various types of activities during a year, moving from casual wage work to self-employed, and also cultivation. Most of the casual non-farm labourers also reported themselves to be working as self-employed in some months; most of these are in agriculture during the peak agricultural season, but some also as non-farm self-employed. The total income of a worker is the sum total of all his income received from different activities.

While interpreting the income trends, the following needs to be kept in mind. Self-employment for income purposes includes marble polishers, drivers, shopkeepers, moneylenders, those who provide repair services, doctors, commission agents, mentha plant workers, tailors, contractors, tutors, oil mill workers, flour mill workers, paddy mill workers, those who collect and sell milk, those who provide hand-drawn/animal-drawn carts, rickshaw pullers, middlemen, metal polishers, brokers, vendors, and eatery owners. Marble polishing has been included in self-employed for the reason that it is an activity by an individual with an independent contract with a client, it involves some use of capital assets, payment is by piece rate, and costs fall on the individual doing the marble polishing. Only those individuals who are strictly working for an employer are treated as casual wage workers.

The total self-employed income consists of two parts. Income of self-employed individuals (professionals, etc.) and income from business. The income from self-employed activities is a small component of total self-employed income. It is even smaller than non-farm casual labour income. The main part of self-employed income is income from businesses, which comprises income from transportation (freight and passenger), moneylending, and all shops, including medical stores, tailors, carpenters, profits of mills (mentha, oil, paddy), repair shops, eateries, and so on. Income from businesses constitutes over 85 per cent of self-employed income.

Profits of business enterprises have been clubbed together with self-employed for comparability purposes as the former were not available in previous years. Our esti-mates of business enterprises is better than earlier years because extra effort was made to collect such data. We have data on profits of all shops, mills, repair shops, and other enterprises. This was achieved using both the diary method and an accounting approach wherever the respondent was cooperative. While it was not possible to use the latter to arrive at a firm estimate of income, care was taken to include all aspects of costs of the business to arrive at its net profits. As can be observed in Table 7.3, the share of self-employed income is very high compared to earlier years.

There was underestimation of business income in earlier years. Given the focus on agriculture in earlier surveys, no attempt was made to collect detailed information on the profits of non-farm enterprises; there is no category of business income in earlier years. However, there is no doubt that the growth of business income is genuinely very rapid and impressive. The business activities included for 2008/9 and mentioned were entirely absent or very small in 1983/4. Their expansion plays a very important role in Palanpur's development.

Table A.7.1 Regular wage employment outside agriculture, 1957–2009 (no. of persons with stated job)

Occupation	Year					
	1957/8	1962/3	1974/5	1983/4	1993	2008/9
Regular jobs involving skills						
Teacher	0	0	0	3	4	2
Medic	0	0	1	0	0	0
Mechanic	1	1	0	0	0	0
Electrician	0	0	0	0	0	0
Insurance salesman	0	0	0	0	0	0
Cook	0	0	0	0	0	0
Skilled work in bakery	0	0	0	0	0	0
Clerk in factory	0	0	1	0	0	0
Accountant	0	0	0	0	1	1
Compounder under doctor	0	0	0	0	0	1
Carpenter	0	0	0	0	0	1
Assistant in map making	0	0	0	0	0	1
Paid training/internship	0	0	0	0	0	1
Para-teacher	0	0	0	0	0	1
Asha (community health worker)	0	0	0	0	0	1
Regular jobs involving limited training or skills						
Anganwadi manager	0	0	0	0	2	1
Chowkidar (watchman)	1	2	1	3	2	0
Permanent railway employee	2	6	9	10	10	10
Non-permanent railway employee	1	0	0	0	0	0
Permanent servant	4	2	2	0	0	0
Cloth mill employee	0	1	16	19	0	0
Bakery employee	0	0	0	7	2	1
Security guard or policeman	0	0	0	2	2	11
Coal depot employee	0	0	0	1	0	0
Sugar mill employee	0	0	1	1	0	0
Bank employee	0	0	1	0	1	0
Permanent coolie	0	0	0	1	0	0
Steel plating and service in steel factory	0	0	0	9	4	3
Helper in general store/shops	0	0	0	0	0	9
Service in *tehsil* (administrative area of a district)	0	0	1	1	0	0
Unspecified regular job	0	1	12	2	1	1
Liquor factory employee	0	0	0	0	1	0
Silverware factory	0	0	0	0	1	0
Service in a sweet shop	0	0	0	0	1	0
Service in ice factory	0	0	0	0	2	0
Service in brass factory	0	0	0	0	1	1
Catering services	0	0	0	0	0	1
Worker in mentha factory	0	0	0	0	0	1
Service in paper mill	0	0	0	0	0	1
Service in tile factory	0	0	0	0	0	1
Employee petrol pump	0	0	0	0	0	1
Coolie	0	0	0	1	0	0
Hawker	0	0	0	0	0	1
Village head	0	0	0	0	0	1
Contractor electricity department	0	0	0	0	0	1
Tractor driver	0	0	0	0	0	1
Total	9	13	45	60	35	55

Note: In some years, these also included regular jobs within the village.

Table A.7.2 Caste-based concentration in casual labour, 2008/9

Occupation	Caste Group									Total
	Thakur	Murao	Jatab	Dhimar	Gadaria	Dhobi	Teli	Passi	Other	
Brick kiln	0	0	20	0	0	0	1	0	0	21
Marble polishing	4	2	0	0	1	0	1	0	0	8
Railway yard	4	4	0	0	1	0	2	0	0	11
Construction	1	2	4	1	0	0	2	0	0	10

Table A.7.3 Caste-based concentration in self-employment, 2008/9

Occupation	Caste Group									Total
	Thakur	Murao	Jatab	Dhimar	Gadaria	Dhobi	Teli	Passi	Other	
Marble polishing	6	2	0	4	6	0	2	0	0	20
Flour mill	0	0	0	2	0	0	5	0	0	7
Motorcycle repair shop	0	0	0	0	0	0	4	0	0	4

Acknowledgements

This chapter has been written by Himanshu, Bhawna Joshi, and Peter Lanjouw, and draws on earlier work on employment and migration by Mukhopadhyay (2011), Himanshu and colleagues (2011; 2013), and Himanshu, Joshi, and Lanjouw (2016). The analysis of migration trends depends on work done by Abhiroop Mukhopadhyay and Floriane Bolazzi. We also acknowledge the contribution by Priyanka Pande, in cleaning and analysing income and employment data.

References

Abraham, V. 2009. 'Employment growth in rural India: distress-driven', *Economic & Political Weekly* 14, no. 16: 97–104.

Ansari, N. 1964. 'Palanpur: A Study of its Economic Resources and Economic Activities', Continuous Village Survey 41. Agricultural Economics Research Centre, University of Delhi.

Binswanger-Mkhize, H.P. 2012. 'India 1960–2010: structural change, the rural nonfarm sector, and the prospects for agriculture'. Paper presented at the FSI Stanford Symposium (2012), USA. Available at: http://citeseerx.ist.psu.edu/viewdoc/download?doi=10.1.1.406.2420&rep=rep1&type=pdf (accessed 10 April 2018).

Bliss, C., and Stern, N. 1982. *Palanpur: The Economy of an Indian Village.* Oxford and New York: Oxford University Press.

Breman, J. 2013. *At Work in the Informal Economy of India: A Perspective from the Bottom Up.* Delhi: Oxford University Press. Deb, U.K., Nageswara Rao, G.D., Mohan Rao, Y., and Slater, R. 2002. 'Diversification and livelihood options: a study of two villages in Andhra Pradesh, India'. Department for International Development (DFID), UK.

Di Falco, S., and Bulte, E. 2013. 'The impact of kinship networks on the adoption of risk-mitigating strategies in Ethiopia', *World Development* 43: 100–10.

Djurfeldt, G., Athreya, V., Jayakumar, N., Lindberg, S., Rajagopal, A., and Vidyasagar, R. 2008. 'Agrarian change and social mobility in Tamil Nadu', *Economic & Political Weekly* 43, no. 45: 50–61.

Drèze, J., and Mukherjee, A. 1989. 'Labour contracts in rural India', in S. Chakravarty (ed.), *The Balance between Industry and Agriculture in Economic Development.* London: Macmillan.

Eapen, M. 1994. 'Rural non-agricultural employment in Kerala: some emerging tendencies', *Economic & Political Weekly* 29, no. 21: 1285–96.

Fisher, T., Mahajan, V., and Singha, A. 1997. *The Forgotten Sector.* London: Intermediate Technology Publications Ltd.

Gibson, J., Datt, G., Murgai, R., and Ravallion, M. 2017. 'For india's rural poor, growing towns matter more than growing cities', Policy Research Working Paper No. 7994, the World Bank.

Harriss, J., Jeyaranjan, J., and Nagaraj, K. 2010. 'Land, labour and caste politics in rural Tamil Nadu in the 20th century: Iruvelpattu (1916–2008)', *Economic & Political Weekly* 14, no. 31: 47–61.

Hazell, P.B.R., Haggblade, S., and Reardon, T. 2010. 'The rural nonfarm economy: prospects for growth and poverty reduction', *World Development* 38, no. 10: 1429–41.

Himanshu. 2011. 'Employment TRENDS in India: a re-examination', *Economic and Political Weekly* 46, no. 37: 43–59.

Himanshu, Lanjouw, P., Murgai, R., and Stern, N. 2013. 'Non-farm diversification, poverty, economic mobility and income inequality: a case study in village India', *Agricultural Economics* 44(4–5): 461–3.

Himanshu. 2015. 'Rural non-farm employment in India: trends, patterns and regional dimensions', India Rural Development Report 2013–14, IDFC Foundation.

Himanshu, Joshi, B., and Lanjouw, P. 2016. 'Non-farm diversification, inequality and mobility in Palanpur', *Economic and Political Weekly* LI, no. 26–7.

Himanshu, Lanjouw, P., Mukhopadhyay, A., and Murgai, R. 2011. 'Non-farm diversification and rural poverty decline: a perspective from Indian sample survey and village study data'. LSE Asia Research Centre Working Paper No. 44.

Jatav, M., and Sen, S. 2013. 'Drivers of non-farm employment in rural India: evidence from the 2009–10 NSSO round 10', *Economic & Political Weekly* 29: 14–21.

Kajisa, K., and Venkatesa Palanichamy, N. 2006. 'Income dynamics in Tamil Nadu, India from 1971 to 2003: changing roles of land and human capital', *Agricultural Economics* 35: 437–48.

Lanjouw, P. and Shariff, A. 2004. 'Rural non-farm employment in India: access, incomes and poverty impact', *Economic and Political Weekly* 39(40): 4429–46.

Lanjouw, P., and Stern, N. 1998. *Economic Development in Palanpur over Five Decades*. Oxford: Clarendon Press.

Mahendra Dev, S., and Evenson, R.E. 2009. 'Rural development in India: rural, non-farm, and migration'. Stanford Centre for International Development Working Paper No. 187.

Mellor, J. 1976. *The New Economics of Growth: A Strategy for India and the Developing World*. Ithaca, NY: Cornell University Press.

Mukhopadyay, A. 2011. 'Stepping out of Palanpur: employment outside Palanpur. From short visits to long-term migration and how they are linked'. Asia Research Centre Working Paper No. 46, London School of Economics, London.

Pal, S. 1997. 'An analysis of declining incidence of regular labour contracts in rural India', *Journal of Development Studies* 34(2): 133.

Ranis, G., and Stewart, F. 1993. Rural nonfarm activities in development: theory and application, *Journal of Development Economics* 40(1): 75.

Ranjan, S. 2008. 'Determinants of rural non-farm employment: microlevel evidence from Uttar Pradesh', *Social Scientist* 36, no. 5: 22–50.

Ranjan, S. 2009. 'Growth of non-farm employment in Uttar Pradesh: reflections from recent data', *Economic & Political Weekly* 44, no. 4: 63–70.

Reardon, T., Berdegué, T.J., Barrett, C.B., and Stamoulis, K. 2006. 'Household income diversification into rural nonfarm activities', in S. Haggblade, P. Hazell, and T. Reardon (eds), *Transforming the Rural Nonfarm Economy*. Baltimore, MD: Johns Hopkins University Press.

Reardon, T., Taylor, J.E., Stamoulis, K., Lanjouw, P., and Balisacan, A. 2000. 'Effects of non-farm employment on rural income inequality in developing countries: an investment perspective', *Journal of Agricultural Economics* 51, no. 2: 266–88.

Srivastava, R. and Bhattacharya, S. 2003. 'Globalisation, reforms and internal labour mobility: analysis of recent Indian trends', *Labour and Development* 9(2): 31–55.

Swaminathan, M., Rawal, V., and Sekhar Dhar, N. 2008. 'On diversification of rural incomes: a view from three villages of Andhra Pradesh', *Indian Journal of Labour Economics* 51, no. 2: 229–48.

Unni, J. 1998. 'Non-agricultural employment and poverty in rural India: a review of evidence', *Economic & Political Weekly* 33, no. 13: A36–A44.

Visaria, P., and Basant, R. 1993. *Non-Agricultural Employment in India: Trends and Prospects*. New Delhi: Sage.

Walker, T.S., and Ryan, J.G. 1990. *Village and Household Economics in India's Semi-Arid Tropics*. Baltimore, MD: Johns Hopkins University Press.

8

Poverty, Inequality, and Mobility in Palanpur*

8.1 Introduction

Poverty reduction has long been a priority for successive Indian governments and tops the list of global objectives enshrined in the Sustainable Development Goals set out by the United Nations (UN) in 2015. Inequality has also been of growing concern in societies around the world, including in India, in part because of its association with social tensions. Social and economic mobility are widely regarded as key characteristics or indicators in relation to equality of opportunity. It is rarely the case that one is able to examine these issues together, in detail, and over an extended period. Our study of Palanpur, with its detailed information on individuals and households stretching over seven decades, provides a possibly unique opportunity. We can go beyond a description of what has happened over the study period to households in the village. Armed with our close knowledge of the village economy and society, and setting change in the village in the context of a changing India, we can also offer explanations of possible drivers of the striking changes we find. And at the same time we are able to illustrate our findings with stories of individual experiences; people are not just data points, but individuals with their own experiences and problems.

Our focus on the experience of a small village offers rare and at times provocative insights into processes first described by classic development economists such as Arthur Lewis (1954) and Simon Kuznets (1955), as described in Chapter 4. We observed the detailed workings and consequences of agricultural intensification during the 1960s and 1970s, followed, thereafter, by accelerating involvement in the wider rural non-farm economy. These broad forces of change are not unique to Palanpur and have been observed at the level of rural India as a whole, as described in Chapter 3. In Palanpur, however,

* This chapter has been written by Himanshu, Peter Lanjouw, and Priyanka Pande.

we are able to enquire into the distributional consequence of these processes. We observe that, overall, they have been associated with growth in per capita incomes and with falling poverty amongst villagers. They also appear to underpin evidence of growing social mobility, where previously disadvantaged social groups that had seemed 'trapped' at the bottom of the income distribution are increasingly able to lift themselves out of poverty and also see their income status improve in relative terms. A number of villagers, drawn from different economic and social groups, have prospered via self-employment, often starting small enterprises and showing entrepreneurship. The process has brought rising income inequality in Palanpur. It is possible that this growth in income inequality, together with the changing of groups' relative status, could create stress in social cohesion in the village and could also point to new, emerging pressure points governing access to economic opportunities. It has been noted, for example, that high inequality countries tend to display relatively low intergencrational income mobility (Corak, 2013; Krueger, 2012). In Palanpur, tentative evidence consistent with this association can also be found. Despite rising incomes, falling poverty, and ongoing diversification of the Palanpur economy, incomes of the current generation of sons appear to be fairly closely associated with those of their fathers, even more so than for the previous generation.

In the face of falling poverty and rising inequality, the role of caste differences, including differences within a particular caste group, is particularly pertinent. We point to the rise in the relative position of the Jatab caste, historically ranked at the bottom of the village economic hierarchy, and illustrate how this movement has been, in part, matched by the relative decline of the Muraos, a historically cultivating caste. The expansion of non-farm employment opportunities, including self-employment and new enterprises, is found to have catalysed the rise in economic mobility, but has also contributed to growing dispersion in the distribution of income. At the same time, land fragmentation, population pressure, and sluggish growth of agricultural output has also meant that agriculture is playing less of a role in explaining inequality or upward mobility of households. We suggest that the Muraos' social and cultural affinity with cultivation has played a role in their hesitation around involvement in the non-farm sector, and hence their relative stagnation as the village economy has diversified. Although our results on declining intergenerational mobility of income alongside greater mobility among the disadvantaged might appear counter-intuitive, they can be understood through the nature of non-farm diversification, which, on the one hand, has become increasingly casual and informal and thereby more accessible to households at the bottom of the distribution, but, on the other hand, is still significantly influenced by access to networks and family ties—particularly for the more remunerative regular non-farm jobs. In the process of growth of non-farm activities, some have taken advantage of opportunities before others and some people and ventures have been more successful than others. Although our analysis covers the entire survey period between 1957/8 and 2008/9, we focus in our discussion of the village economy most closely on its features and dimensions at the time of the most recent detailed survey, conducted in 2008–10.[1]

The rest of the chapter is structured as follows. In Section 8.2, we document the extent, profile, and evolution of poverty over time and discuss the ranking methodology that permits us to broaden our focus on poverty beyond income and consumption poverty. Section 8.3 describes inequality trends observed over time. In Section 8.4, we look at income mobility, both intra- and intergenerational, in the context of experiences of non-farm employment. Section 8.5 considers some of the social factors and individual behaviours and circumstances that determine the vulnerability of households to economic shocks. Section 8.6 concludes.

8.2 Poverty Dimensions and Trends

8.2.1 *Measuring Standard of Living*

The affluence of households in a village can be understood in a number of ways and can be determined or shaped by a variety of factors. In broad terms, most of these factors would be common knowledge among the village population. A household's income, assets, expenditures, health and nutritional status, members' occupation, and other social indicators would all be seen, in some shape or form, as influencing its economic status. The interplay of these aspects is important in understanding, defining, and measuring the prosperity of different households.

In our study of changing social and economic conditions in the village, we generate rankings based on five different measures of well-being. These include quantitative measures such as income, consumption expenditure, and ownership of assets. We also used qualitative measures; one which takes into account the resident investigators' perspectives on living standards and a second that captures the relative socioeconomic status of households from the villagers' own standpoint. The differences in various ranking methodologies highlight the role and relative importance of different characteristics in defining and identifying poverty and provide a multidimensional view of poverty

---

[1] For additional detailed analyses see Bliss and Stern (1982), which focuses primarily on the 1974/5 survey year, and Lanjouw and Stern (1998), which incorporates data from both the 1983/4 and 1993 survey years, providing an in-depth examination of socioeconomic transformation and trends seen in Palanpur up to the early 1990s.

and the circumstances of poor people that is broader than that available from a single dimension. Though each of these measures gives us relevant and interesting insights into the standard of living of village households, there are merits and demerits to each of them. We begin our discussion with the use of current incomes as a measure of ranking the households. This methodology has a long history and has been a long-standing topic of debate.

The use and effectiveness of income as a basis for ranking households must take into account the following arguments.[2] First, the choice of unit of measurement—an individual, a family, or a household—will depend on the objective of the study and the availability of data. It is important to choose the appropriate unit with care, and each carries problems. For instance, in our study, a household defined as a group of individuals pooling their economic resources and sharing a common hearth, is used as the income earning unit. One possible problem with this definition could be if households considered as separate using the above definition are involved in the same occupation, for instance, joint cultivation. In such cases, we make use of the farm definition for income estimation and equally divide the income from cultivation.

Second, the data on income are subject to the time period being used and are sensitive to seasonal/annual variations. In particular, agricultural incomes are significantly influenced by factors such as input costs, weather conditions, and availability of irrigation facilities. The seasonal and annual vagaries associated with agricultural output might lead to highly variable incomes, and income in a particular year may therefore only imperfectly capture the longer-term economic well-being of households.

Third, what constitutes income can be difficult to establish. A household may be involved in production, consumption, and investment. It may also have sources of income other than cultivation. In such cases, the estimation of household income becomes an increasingly difficult exercise, particularly in relation to inputs or outputs which are not marketed and for which imputation is required. In our case, given our span of many decades, it is also imperative to maintain consistency in our income calculation across all survey rounds. This requires following a consistent definition of income and making certain approximations for missing or inaccurate information. And there are difficulties associated with the fact that the surveys were not originally conceived as a longitudinal study.

Fourth, there is no perfect reference period, especially in a rural village like Palanpur. While some earnings are for seasonal activities, others, such as regular employment in factories, might be based on an annual cycle. Problems

---

[2] See Bakshi (2008) and Rawal (2008) for issues in measurement of incomes during household surveys. Also see appendix 3 in Lanjouw and Stern (1998) and the appendix to Chapter 7.

also arise if the cultivation cycle extends to more than a year, as is the case, for instance, with sugar cane.

Finally, given that incomes are self-reported, there is a possibility that incomes may be misreported. For instance, sources of income such as interest earnings and earnings from illegal activities are likely to suffer from under-reporting and are difficult to cross-check. Despite these limitations, we think that our data on household earnings, and our ability to cross-check and validate information to a degree that is not generally available with large-scale studies, provide us with a fairly good idea of the economic well-being and the extent of income poverty among Palanpur households in a given year.

To summarize, the Palanpur surveys include information on income for all survey years except 1993 and 2015.[3] These two years are therefore largely omitted from the analysis of this chapter where it has a stronger focus on income; thus, we cover here five of the seven survey years. Chapter 7 describes the specific components of income captured in the surveys and the manner in which they are put together to yield a measure of household income, high-lighting in particular how this measure captures the growing importance of non-farm income sources.[4] In order to maintain consistency across rounds, the underlying definition of income that we employ remains largely constant across survey years, barring a few minor differences. In terms of data quality, the data for 2008/9 are the most extensive and reliable since they involved the most far-reaching and exhaustive exercise of data collection. The investigators, along with the researchers, were able to carry out multiple cross-checks and clean the data on income from various sources.[5] Next in terms of quality are the data for 1983/4, which, again, were comprehensive and subjected to extensive quality control during the fieldwork. These data are followed by the 1974/5 round in terms of reliability—this round expanded the scope of income to include non-cultivation income, but involved a certain amount of approximation for some income sources. Finally, the income estimates for 1957/8 and 1962/3 are based on single-round interviews conducted during the survey and also involve some approximations for certain income sources. Overall, the estimates of income are reasonably comparable across all survey rounds and follow the basic definition of income as net returns to all labour and household assets.[6] In our view, they are all of a good quality relative to

---

[3] The re-surveys of the village conducted in 1993 and 2015 were carried out for a short duration and were intentionally less ambitious in terms of information collected. We are unable to report any income-based welfare measures for these survey years.

[4] For further discussion, see chapter 6, Bliss and Stern (1982), and the appendix of chapter 3, Lanjouw and Stern (1998). See also the appendix in Chapter 7, this volume, for details of income data.

[5] For further details on the data sources and the cleaning process, refer to Chapter 1.

[6] Considerable effort has been made to organize the data of previous years in order to arrive at comparable and consistent estimates of incomes for all the survey rounds.

most surveys, with the data for 1983/4 and 2008/9 being very unusual in terms of the cross-checking and validation involved.

The data on income were calculated at the level of the household. Data were collected for each of the income-generating activities at the household level for a reference period of one year. The income definition includes incomes from agriculture, various sources of non-farm employment (regular employment, non-agricultural labour income, self-employment, and other non-farm sources), agricultural labour, rents, remittances, livestock, and *jajmani* (customary services). The data definitions and methods maintain consistency across rounds and include incomes from all the primary and secondary sources of employment for each household. All incomes were reported in real terms, deflated by the Consumer Price Index for Agricultural Labourers (CPIAL) for rural Uttar Pradesh at 2008/9 prices.

For the purpose of comparing income against other indicators of living standards, we focus on rankings. Using data available on per capita household income, we generate quintiles of such income (at 2008/9 prices) for each survey except 1993 and 2015. In this way we generate rankings based on income where every individual is ranked from 1 to 5; 1 being in the lowest quintile and 5 in the highest. Distributions, deciles, and quintiles are over individuals. A household with, say, five people, contributes five individuals for this distribution, each with the per capita income of the household.

It is often argued that welfare rankings based on a measure of household consumption are more informative or reliable than income-based rankings. It is sometimes suggested that accurate consumption data are easier to collect and that they are able to provide a longer-term perspective on living standards. Though our consumption expenditure data are less complete and comprehensive than our income data, we explore contrasts between income and consumption rankings later in this chapter.[7]

In a third approach to assessing economic well-being, we generate rankings of households based on asset ownership using information on productive assets, consumer durables, and land owned by the households. We apply principal component analysis (PCA) to create a 'wealth' index.[8] Every asset is assigned a weight depending on its variation in the village and an asset score is generated for every household. Using this method, we get a ranking based on ownership of assets that can also be expected to provide some representation of longer-term economic position.[9]

---

[7] The data on consumption expenditure are available only for three rounds of survey conducted in 1957/8, 1962/3, and 2008/9.

[8] For more details see Filmer and Pritchett (2001). They used the method of PCA to estimate wealth levels using asset indicators as dummy variables.

[9] There is no information on the value of assets, quality, and the rate of depreciation. Also, the data on consumer durables is available for the 1962/3, 1993, and 2008/9 rounds only. For this

The asset position and purchasing power of households is likely to be common knowledge, at least in broad terms, among the inhabitants of a small village like Palanpur. They are also subjects of keen interest amongst villagers. As Piketty (2014: 2) writes:

> Peasants and nobility, worker and factory owner, waiter and banker: each has his or her own unique vantage point and sees important aspects of how other people live and what relations of power and domination exist between social groups, and these observations shape each person's judgment of what is and what is not just. Hence there will always be a fundamentally subjective and psychological dimension to inequality.

Palanpur villagers live in a close-knit community where individuals know a great deal about others. With a long residence in the village by investigators, much of such local knowledge is absorbed and can be considered together with direct observation. We attempt to capture this local knowledge via yet another household classification exercise—one based on an 'observed means' classification carried out by the resident investigators. Clearly here, 'means' should be understood as having the ability to command resources. During the course of their long stay in the village in 1983/4 and 2008/9 for data collection, the field investigators were able to establish some rapport with the villagers; that is, to observe their lifestyles and to learn about relevant specific circumstances that may not be straightforwardly captured in formal survey instruments. Thus, they were in a position, based on these experiences and evidence, to construct a ranking of overall prosperity for every household. In the 1983/4 round of survey, the classification exercise was undertaken by Jean Drèze and Naresh Sharma. They first classified households into seven groups and categorized them as follows: 'Very Poor', 'Poor', 'Modest', 'Secure', 'Prosperous', 'Rich', and 'Very Rich' (see Drèze, Lanjouw, and Sharma, 1998; Lanjouw and Stern, 1991, 1998). Drèze and Sharma did this independently. They intended their categorization to be an attempt to capture the asset and wealth position of households as well as their access to various resources. With the exception of a few discrepancies, Drèze and Sharma's rankings were broadly consistent. In the final stage of classification, the rankings were combined into five quintiles of roughly equal sizes designated as follows: 'Very Poor', 'Poor', 'Secure', 'Prosperous', and 'Rich'.

This ranking procedure was repeated during the 2008/9 survey round. This time, four investigators independently categorized households into the same five groups, without insistence that the households be evenly distributed across groups. Again, the independent rankings of the investigators were remarkably

---

reason, we use dummy variables for asset ownership; for instance 1 if the household owns the asset and 0 otherwise. For land, we generate quintiles of land owned per capita in each survey year.

consistent. Nonetheless, there were a few instances where the investigators ranked the households differently. To take one example, Mohan Lal, son of Ram Avtar, was ranked as 'Rich' by two of the resident investigators in 2008/9 as he lived with his father, although with a separate kitchen and budgetary arrangements. The family cultivated the owned land jointly, had access to family labour, owned a tube well, and earned a decent living. On the other hand, Mohan Lal was the sole earning member of his nuclear family and mostly worked outside Palanpur. As a separate household, he did not have any assets of his own and the land was still in the name of his father. These latter considerations prompted the two other investigators to rank Mohan Lal as 'Poor'. While the first two investigators took into account Mohan Lal's full family circumstances and the future prospects of inheriting wealth from his father, the other two ranked him solely on the basis of his current economic status. Ambiguities such as these that emerged during the exercise of ranking observed means were resolved on a case-by-case basis, following close scrutiny of the specific circumstances of the respective households. Overall, the broad consistency observed in the independent rankings of the investigators confirms the view that the relative position of households in the scale of economic affluence is well understood in the village and became fairly clear to the investigators residing in the village over an extended period of time (Lanjouw and Stern, 1998).

A final classification approach builds on participatory rural appraisal (PRA) methods that were implemented by a group of trained professionals whose aim was to quantify villagers' perceptions of the overall well-being of households. The following characteristics were used as well-being criteria: land, quality of house, marital status, age, illness/disabilities, assets, livestock, occupation (labour/work/service), and so on. The villagers were asked to rank every household in the village under each category based on their personal knowledge and judgement. Since this ranking was based on villagers' perceptions and every individual has a subjective opinion about other households, imposing any strict group-size criteria violates the basic principles of the method. As a result, PRA rankings do not necessarily divide the population into equal groups. The exercise was undertaken as part of the India-wide Participatory Socio-Economic Survey 2010. A sample of participants was selected, comprising both men and women and belonging to all major caste groups. The sample was constructed to be representative of the village population. The participants classified the 234 village households in 2008/9 into five different categories—'Very poor' or 'khaane tak ko thikana nahi' (28 households); 'Poor' or 'roj kamaate roj khaate' (91 households); 'Medium' or 'khaate peete log' (59 households); 'Rich' or 'chain se jee rahe' (26 households); and 'Very rich' or 'mauj aa rahi hai' (30 households). The Hindi phrases capture the investigators' general observation/remarks.

We examine in Table 8.1 the correlation of rankings arising from the different classification approaches.

Table 8.1 Correlation matrix of various rankings, 2008/9

	Income	Consumption	Asset Scores	Observed Means	PRA
Income	1				
Consumption	0.364	1			
Asset scores	0.4066	0.2293	1		
Observed means	0.4644	0.1528	0.6945	1	
PRA	0.4086	0.1336	0.5821	0.7094	1

We can see that there exists a high degree of correlation between qualitative rankings of observed means, PRA, and rankings generated using asset scores. These rankings are all likely to reflect wealth and potential income sources. On the other hand, we find that there is less correlation between income (and particularly consumption) with the other indicators. This is probably due, in part, to the fact that current incomes are more prone to annual/seasonal variation. Consumption appears to be particularly poorly correlated with both income and the other ranking indicators. The definition of consumption employed here follows that applied in the National Sample Survey Organisation (NSSO) nationwide surveys. Treatment of housing and the use-value of owned consumer durables is fairly problematic in this definition, and it may be that at the village level these limitations significantly affect the ability of the consumption indicator to usefully rank households in terms of overall living standards.[10]

8.2.2 The Evolution of Poverty and its Profile

In this section, we take a closer look at the evolution of poverty in Palanpur and at changes in the profile of poor people over time. We focus on the correlates of poverty—including the economic and social characteristics of the households such as the demographic composition, caste position and relations, ownership of assets, and their participation in labour markets—and ask how the association between these correlates and poverty has evolved over time. We base our assessment on household income per capita and focus on the bottom two quintiles of the population in the village in each respective year. In addition we make reference to investigators' own assessments of the overall well-being of households in Palanpur, and we supplement our assessments with specificities from individual household histories.

In India, national-level poverty estimates are based on National Sample Survey (NSS) consumption expenditures. The only survey round in the

---

[10] The low correlation between income and consumption may partly be statistical given the limitations of capturing income data and underestimation in some income categories, such as illicit income or income from usury. Further, consumption is a smoothed measure, unlike income, with lower variation over time or relative to shocks than income.

Table 8.2 Estimates of poverty HCR in Palanpur

Year	Poverty HCR		Mean Income/Consumption (annual; per capita, in rupees)	
	Income	Consumption	Income	Consumption
1957/8	85.1	80.4	5774	7357
1962/3	83.6	74	6010	8079
1974/5	56.7		8954	
1983/4	58.3		8309	
2008/9	38.3	38.3	13,628	12,788

Note: Mean income/consumption are at 2008/9 prices deflated by CPIAL for respective years. HCR is the headcount ratio. The poverty line employed here is based on the official poverty line for rural Uttar Pradesh from the Planning Commission (Planning Commission, 2009). This line yields a consumption–poverty rate of 38.3% in Palanpur in 2008/9. To determine a comparable income-poverty line, the per capita income level associated with a poverty rate of 38.3% in 2008/9 was obtained and then deflated back using CPIAL price indices to obtain the income poverty rates for the earlier years.

Palanpur study for which a comparable consumption measure was collected is 2008/9. Applying a poverty line of Rs 700 per capita per month at nominal prices in 2008/9, we find that just over 38 per cent of the village population lay below the poverty line in 2008/9.[11] We do have consumption expenditure estimates, although not fully comparable, for 1958 and 1964 as well. However, given that we have income estimates on a comparable basis for most of the survey years (except 1993), we are also able to estimate poverty based on income.[12] Table 8.2 provides these estimates of poverty as well as estimates of mean income and consumption expenditure.

Poverty in Palanpur was very extensive in the early survey years—over 80 per cent of the population was classed as poor during the first two rounds. The growth in incomes associated with expanding irrigation in the late 1950s and the 1960s, as well as the green revolution technologies and methods in the late 1960s and early 1970s, led to a sharp decline in poverty, with the headcount ratio falling to less than 60 per cent by 1974/5 and remaining at roughly that level in 1983/4. Poverty then fell again sharply after 1983, with non-farm

[11] The poverty measures in Table 8.2 are derived from the nominal poverty line obtained by adjusting the official Planning Commission poverty line (Planning Commission, 2009) using the CPIAL for Uttar Pradesh. The poverty line for rural Uttar Pradesh according to the Tendulkar Committee is Rs 663.70 and the estimated headcount rate in 2009/10 is 39.36%. The poverty line applied in Palanpur is based on the Tendulkar poverty line and corresponds to the line estimated for western Uttar Pradesh.

[12] The latest poverty estimates are based on Tendulkar Committee report. However, these are not available for years before 1983. We estimate the poverty lines for previous years by deflating it using the CPIAL for the survey years. Also, the income poverty line has been generated for 2008/9 so as to arrive at an estimate of poverty using income distribution, which gives the same estimate of poverty headcount ratio as the consumption poverty estimate when applied to consumption expenditure distribution. The income poverty lines for previous years have been obtained by deflating the income poverty line of 2008/9 by the CPIAL.

employment playing an important role in improving the fortunes of many, including those at the bottom of the distribution. A similar picture emerges when we look at mean consumption/expenditure estimates which changed only moderately in the first two decades, but had increased strongly by 2008/9. We should bear in mind in looking at the course of poverty over that time that the quality of agricultural years varies (see Chapters 1 and 2). In particular, the harvests in 1957/8, 1974/5, and 2008/9 were reasonably good, but were bad in 1962/3 and 1983/4.

Table 8.3 documents the percentage of population in each caste group classified as poor in income terms in the respective survey years. Thakurs and Muraos have historically seen the lowest poverty rates. The relative prosperity of Thakurs and Muraos increased after the expansion of irrigation and the green revolution, with both caste groups showing a sharp decline in poverty between 1962/3 and 1974/5. By 1983/4, Muraos were the least poor caste group, less poor even than the Thakurs. At the other end of the distribution, the expansion of irrigation and the green revolution did little to lift the Jatabs out of poverty. The most recent interval—between 1983/4 and 2008/9—saw some decline in poverty amongst the Jatabs, although 70 per cent remain in poverty, considerably higher than any other group. On the other hand, with the declining rate of agricultural growth, Muraos have not seen any significant further decline in poverty since the late 1980s. Indeed, the Thakurs have regained their pole position in terms of lowest poverty and have been joined by the Telis and Gadarias, two groups that have also seen a particularly sharp reduction in poverty in the last three decades. These latter two caste groups were also amongst those with the highest involvement in non-farm employment in 2008/9, including in self-employment and starting small businesses.

Another way to look at the characteristics of the poor in Palanpur is to employ a relative poverty line. As poverty in Palanpur, by our definition, in

Table 8.3 Poverty by caste

Caste Group	Year				
	1957/8	1962/3	1974/5	1983/4	2008/9
Thakur	73.1	81.6	45.7	46.9	22
Murao	78	70.7	37.4	33.3	32.2
Dhimar	98.2	100	70.7	60	47.8
Gadaria	95.2	57.8	64.6	61.9	25.3
Teli	100	100	59.2	74.2	23.9
Passi	75.8	85.7	44.1	55.2	40
Jatab	94.4	95.8	82.3	100	72.4
Total	85.1	83.6	56.7	58.3	38.3

Note: For poverty lines used see footnotes 12 and 13.

2008/9 affects nearly 40 per cent of the population in the village, we take this as our threshold to identify the relatively poor in each respective survey year. In Table 8.4 we focus on those belonging to the bottom four deciles of the per capita income distribution in the various survey years. Households are categorized on the basis of their demographic composition, occupation, land ownership, and caste. For each year, the first column gives the number of households in the lowest four deciles with the particular characteristic. The second column indicates what percent of the population in the village with the respective characteristic are amongst the poor. In 2008/9, the likelihood of being poor (among the bottom 40 per cent of the population) is particularly high amongst households: without land; without land and without a regular job; with family members working as agricultural labourers; without an adult male in the household; or in a female-headed household. In that year, 64 per cent of the Jatab households belonged to the bottom four deciles of the income distribution, closely followed by Dhobis (63 per cent)

Table 8.4 Proportion of Palanpur households in the four lowest deciles of per capita income scale

Household Characteristics	Year									
	1957/8		1962/3		1974/5		1983/4		2008/9 (1) (2)	
	No.	%	No.	%	No.	%	No.	%	No.	%
With regular job	3	0.25	2	0.12	19	0.45	15	0.27	14	0.26
Landless	7	0.54	4	0.31	7	0.64	16	0.55	22	0.55
Landless without regular job	6	0.55	4	0.4	2	0.5	12	0.71	18	0.56
Agricultural labour	16	0.62	13	0.76	23	0.72	35	0.56	22	0.47
Landless agricultural labour	3	0.5	1	0.33	4	0.8	12	0.71	4	0.8
Without adult male	1	1	1	0.17	0	0	5	0.19	6	0.43
Landless without adult male	1	1	1	0.25	0	0	2	0.67	3	0.75
With widow	12	0.43	9	0.33	6	0.3	16	0.5	21	0.4
Widow without adult male	1	1	1	0.25	0	0	5	0.83	5	0.56
Thakur	4	0.24	3	0.16	7	0.28	8	0.27	12	0.21
Murao	3	0.14	6	0.24	7	0.25	6	0.22	22	0.4
Dhimar	7	0.7	8	0.89	4	0.5	7	0.54	11	0.5
Gadaria	2	0.22	3	0.33	4	0.4	4	0.33	4	0.27
Dhobi	0	0	0	0	2	0.67	2	0.5	5	0.63
Teli	6	0.75	6	0.67	7	0.58	6	0.38	7	0.30
Passi	5	0.42	6	0.38	1	0.13	7	0.47	2	0.33
Jatab	10	0.63	8	0.62	10	0.71	16	0.84	25	0.64
Other	3	0.6	3	0.6	3	0.75	2	0.29	6	0.75
All households	40	0.4	43	0.41	45	0.4	58	0.41	94	0.4

Note: Due to the fragmentation of households, the number of households in the bottom four deciles has increased from 58 in 1983/4 to 94 in 2008/9.

and Dhimars (50 per cent). Households with a regular job or belonging to the Thakur caste are visibly better off than the rest. An interesting observation is that between 1983/4 and 2008/9, among the Muraos the share of households in the bottom four deciles has gone up from 22 to 40 per cent, while among the Jatabs it has fallen from 84 to 64 per cent.

Though a number of characteristics are strongly and consistently associated with poverty in all survey years, it is noteworthy that the poor are far from a homogeneous group in the village. For instance, a landless household may find job opportunities outside agriculture and be able to attain a decent standard of living. Such an observation would apply, for example, to the case of Naubat Singh, who worked at a 'chakki' (or milling) service in Bilari in 1983, and at that time was ranked among the poorest households in Palanpur. He was the sole earning member of the family, having two sons and one daughter, and found himself compelled to sell his land in order to pay off debts acquired for his daughter's marriage. Later, he managed to get a marble polishing machine and by 2008/9 he hired labour and took up floor-finishing work in Chandausi and Moradabad. In that survey year he was ranked in the top quintile of the 2008/9 income-based household rankings. Naubat Singh's case illustrates well how a landless household was able to make use of the opportunities in the non-farm sector and achieve upward mobility.

Even in the case of households without an adult male and with a widow as the head, the circumstances in which the household is left after the death of the male earning member largely determines the condition of the household. Geeta, wife of the late Charan Singh, is one such example. Her husband was murdered in 2004 at the age of thirty-seven while he was sleeping on the rooftop with his entire family. After her husband's death, Geeta started cultivating, with the help of her two daughters, the household's land. She also owned a small 'kirana' (grocery) shop and sent her daughters to schools in Akrauli and Palanpur. Based on our income rankings and 'observed means' she was ranked as 'Rich' and 'Secure' respectively in 2008/9. In contrast, Naraini, widow of Om Prakash, had to face the harsh realities of life after her husband's death at the age of thirty-nine in 2002. His unknown illness had lasted for six years, during which they had to sell off their two *bighas* of land. After his death, Naraini worked as an agricultural labourer to support her family. A year or so later, her son Khem Karan, who worked as a marble polisher, died at the age of twenty-one as a result of an accident at work. Naraini was compelled to rely on her relatives for help when she could not find sufficient work in Palanpur. She would sometimes even visit her family home in Sarai Berni near Chandausi to work as an agricultural labour. Death of one's husband, in Naraini's case, translated into a downward spiral from which escape proved impossible, driving her ever deeper into poverty.

311

Table 8.5 Occupational structure by income deciles, 2008/9 (%)

	Agricultural Labour	Casual Labour	Cultivation	Not Working	Regular Employment	Self-Employment
Bottom four deciles	3.1	30.5	39.1	10.9	7	9.4
Top four deciles	0	12.7	28.9	14.5	17.9	26

Note: Income deciles are generated using household income per capita. The table includes only male adults of fifteen years and above.

As has been emphasized throughout this book, the change in village occupation structure has played an important role in changing the living standards of the people of Palanpur. In Table 8.5 we document that involvement in non-farm employment is strongly associated with higher incomes: amongst the non-farm activities for the bottom 40 per cent of households, only casual non-farm wage labour appears to occur with any frequency.

Individuals belonging to households in the bottom quintiles were mostly involved in cultivation or casual labour activities. In the face of declining per capita incomes from cultivation (see Chapter 5), households did try to diversify out of agriculture by taking up casual labour activities in and around the village. While the additional incomes no doubt helped to protect against further declines in living standards, the modest earnings from casual non-farm wage activities were unable to lift these households out of the lower income quintiles. On the other hand, the households in the higher income quintiles were able to sustain incomes from cultivation if their landholdings were sufficiently large. Further, with their higher status and better network connections, they were often able to gain access to higher-paying, regular non-farm jobs. Households in higher income quintiles also find it easier to move into non-farm self-employed activities (which require capital) due to their asset position; even so, for some, who were originally at the bottom end, particularly amongst the Telis, the more entrepreneurial have been successful in self-employment and small enterprises.

8.3 Income Inequality

While the early survey years did not reveal particularly rapid progress in terms of declining poverty and rising average incomes, the evidence points to important gains following the adoption of the green revolution technologies and methods in the 1960s, 1970s, and early 1980s. Overall, progress then continued via the accelerating process of rural non-farm diversification, although rates of growth of per capita incomes were lower than for India as a whole. Real per capita incomes in the late 2000s were markedly higher than in the beginning of the survey period, and poverty decline has been significant, notably between 1983/4 and 2008/9.

The Palanpur study is uniquely placed to shed light on another important dimension for understanding social and economic structures and the place of individuals within them, namely, overall income inequality. Unlike most empirical analyses of distributional change at the village level, the Palanpur study has taken as its reference domain not just a sample of households in a particular village or locality, but the entire population of the village. All households were surveyed and interviewed, and income data were collected for the entire population for five out of the seven survey years. The availability of income data for the complete population allows us to examine the distribution of income in five survey years and to analyse changes that have taken place. Such an assessment can shed important light on the functioning and evolution of village institutions (such as village governance) and can help identify and interpret possible pressure points in the social fabric of the village. As we will see in Section 8.4, an understanding of how both poverty and inequality have evolved over time is also of great value when we attempt to interpret and understand patterns of income mobility. Understanding the path of inequality, and the forces that drive it, can provide valuable insights into the workings of the processes of economic development.

8.3.1 *Inequality Levels and Trends*

For our inequality analysis, we treat the individual as the basic unit and make no adjustment for household demographic composition. This means that if the household size was 'h', we attributed household income divided by 'h' to each of the household members; calling it 'individual income'. Table 8.6 presents various measures of inequality calculated on the basis of this indicator, for

Table 8.6 Inequality of individual incomes

Measures of Inequality	Survey Years				
	1957/8	1962/3	1974/5	1983/4	2008/9
Gini coefficient	0.336	0.353	0.272	0.310	0.379
Coefficient of variation	0.650	0.755	0.530	0.578	0.769
Atkinson Index					
e = 1	0.173	0.191	0.137	0.170	0.229
e = 2	0.319	0.344	0.206	0.366	0.444
Theil L measure					
GE(0)	0.19	0.213	0.147	0.186	0.26
No. of observations	529	585	750	977	1255
No. of households	100	106	112	143	233
No. of individuals (households) with missing income	0	0	5(1)	8(3)	37(12)

Note: Households with missing incomes were dropped from our calculations (see appendix in Chapter 7). On definitions, see Cowell (2011).

each of the survey years.[13] We observe that in the period between 1957/8 and 1962/3, the Gini coefficient rose from 0.336 to 0.353. This trend saw a reversal in the subsequent round of survey conducted in 1974/5. The remarkable decline between 1962/3 and 1974/5 was the consequence of three principal factors. First, with the investment in irrigation in the 1960s and the advent of green revolution methods in the late 1960s and the 1970s, there was a significant expansion in the use and application of modern agricultural technologies and an introduction of newer farming practices and better irrigation devices. The distributional 'incidence' of the expansion of irrigation was particularly progressive in that whereas previously only a few, better-off farmers had been in a position to irrigate their land (using 'Persian wheel' lifting technologies which required digging and maintaining a large well and complementary draught animal power), this period saw the expansion of irrigation to all farmers. By 1974/5 all village land was irrigated. The arrival of diesel pumping sets to replace Persian wheels was part of this process as they were mobile, could be rented out easily, and used if a bore well (usually around 10 cm diameter and cheaply constructed) was close by. Second, that year was also a particularly good agricultural year in terms of harvest quality in Palanpur. As a result, those who had spent less on inputs were less at risk from lower or negative incomes in the face of a bad harvest. And 'errant' farming practices (late sowing, poor weeding, etc.) tended to be less severely penalized.

The third factor to contribute towards an equalization of income in 1974/5 was that the distribution of land cultivated in Palanpur was more equal in 1974/5 than in other years. This was mainly a result of a fall in the proportion of land owned by Thakurs due to a few land sales. Moreover, during this year tenancy and sharecropping practices displayed a clear pattern of large landowners leasing-out their land to those with smaller landholdings. In subsequent years that pattern tended to be more mixed, including an increasing number of cases of 'reverse tenancy', in the sense of households with smaller holdings leasing-out to those with larger. One reason for this could be greater involvement of those leasing-out in non-farm activities.

Between 1974/5 and 1983/4 inequality increased, but remained lower than its 1957/8 and 1962/3 levels. A combination of factors helps to explain the rise. With the ongoing intensification of agriculture, the Muraos as a group, already with the Thakurs amongst the more prosperous groups, experienced improved relative prosperity due to higher returns from cultivation.[14]

---

[13] The different measures reflect varying degrees of sensitivity to income changes along different parts of the income distribution (see Foster and Sen, 1997, for a useful review).

[14] Muraos, a traditional cultivator caste, were, on average, amongst the earlier to take advantage of the green revolution technologies and methods.

By 1983/4 the Muraos had even surpassed the Thakurs in terms of per capita income. In addition, in 1983/4, new non-farm employment opportunities were becoming increasingly available and were taken up mostly by villagers from economically better-off backgrounds. Due to a disappointing harvest in 1983/4, the income gaps were further widened between those who derived some earnings from outside and those who were entirely dependent on agriculture. And there was wider dispersion within cultivator incomes, influenced by spending on inputs and the relative impact of the poor harvest.

In the most recent survey conducted in 2008/9, the Gini Index, at 0.379, was at its highest level compared to all other survey years.[15] This is true also for alternative inequality indices, such as the Atkinson Index or the Theil L measure (see Table 8.6), which put more weight on the lower end of the income distribution. Lorenz curves for each respective year are displayed in Figure 8.1.[16] The Lorenz curve for per capita income in 2008/9 lies furthest from the line of equality (45 degree line) relative to other years.[17] At the other

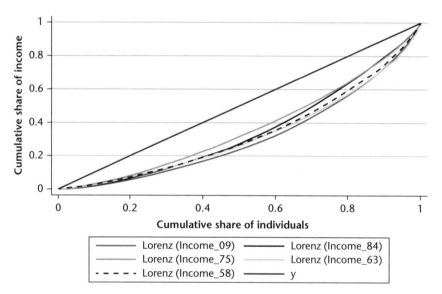

Figure 8.1 Lorenz curves, 1957–2008

Note: Income in all years refers to per capita incomes; y = x is the line of equality.

---

[15] Consumption Gini in Palanpur in 2008/9 was 0.274, which is also the highest. The Gini of consumption expenditure in 1958 was 0.213 and 0.263 in 1964.

[16] Lorenz curves plot the cumulative share of total income received by the bottom x% of the individuals ranked by income. The further a given Lorenz curve lies from the diagonal (line of equality) the greater the extent of inequality in the corresponding income distribution. If the Lorenz curve for distribution B lies fully outside and does not intersect with that for distribution A then inequality in distribution B is unambiguously higher than in distribution A (Atkinson, 1970).

[17] Although there is no Lorenz dominance, implying that at least some measures of inequality might rank 2008/9 differently relative to other survey years (Atkinson, 1970).

extreme, the Lorenz curve drawn for the income distribution in 1974/5 lies closest to the 45 degree line. These results are in line with our discussion of overall inequality trends, indicating that these have not followed a monotonic path over the whole study period.

The sharp increase in inequality between 1983/4 and 2008/9 merits further examination. While changes in inequality across the early survey rounds can be understood in terms of the impact of expanding irrigation and green revolution technologies and methods on agricultural incomes, as well as the varying efforts or abilities of Palanpur households to create improvements in agricultural productivity, the distribution of income in later survey rounds is more significantly influenced by the expanding non-farm sector. This can be readily ascertained on the basis of income decompositions that assess the contribution of different sources of income to overall income inequality. We turn to such a decomposition analysis in Section 8.3.2.

8.3.2 Inequality Decomposition by Income Sources

In order to investigate which factors are associated with the rise in inequality between the 1980s and late 2000s, we decompose the Gini Index of Inequality by income sources.[18] We follow a basic framework where the Gini coefficient for total income inequality G can be represented as:

$$G = \sum_{k=1}^{k} S_k.G_k.R_k$$

Where S_k represents the share of source k in total income, G_k is the Gini coefficient corresponding to the distribution of income from source k, and R_k is the Gini correlation of income from source k with the distribution of total income ($R_k = Cov\{y_k, F(y)\}/Cov\{y_k, F(y_k)\}$, where F(y) and F(k) are the cumulative distributions of total income and of income from source k).[19] Our basic welfare indicator for the individual is the per capita income of the household to which he or she belongs. The income components we examine are income from cultivation, non-farm sources, and other sources.[20]

Table 8.7 presents our findings. The share of income from non-farm sources in total income has increased over the survey period from 13 per cent in 1957/8, to 46 per cent in 2008/9. In contrast, the share of cultivation income has declined from almost 50 per cent in 1983/4 to 30 per cent in 2008/9. In addition, there has been increasing divergence in non-farm incomes which

[18] See Shorrocks (1982), Lerman and Yitzhaki (1985), Stark, Taylor, and Yitzhaki (1986).
[19] See Lopez-Feldman (2006).
[20] Total income = cultivation income + non-cultivation income; non-cultivation income = non-farm income + other sources. See Chapter 7.

Table 8.7 Inequality decomposition by income sources

Inequality in Source of Income k (Gini Coefficient (G_k))

Year	Cultivation Income	Non-Farm Income	Other Sources	Total
1957/8	0.468	0.825	0.539	0.336
1962/3	0.475	0.836	0.576	0.354
1974/5	0.434	0.685	0.450	0.272
1983/4	0.529	0.598	0.510	0.310
2008/9	0.499	0.645	0.598	0.379
Share of total income (S_k)				
1957/8	58.5%	13.3%	28.2%	1
1962/3	56.7%	17.5%	25.8%	1
1974/5	58.4%	17.0%	24.6%	1
1983/4	49.9%	31.7%	18.5%	1
2008/9	30.0%	46.4%	23.6%	1
Contribution to overall Gini coefficient				
1957/8	63.9%	8.7%	27.4%	1
1962/3	55.0%	19.2%	25.8%	1
1974/5	76.6%	3.7%	19.8%	1
1983/4	63.9%	22.9%	13.3%	1
2008/9	19.7%	58.4%	21.9%	1

Note: The table does not report the value of R_k, the Gini correlation of income from source k with the distribution of total income (for details, see Section 8.3.2).

Table 8.8 Inequality decomposition of non-farm income by kind of occupation, 2008/9

Non-Farm Income Source	Share of Total Non-Farm Income (%)	Source Gini	Share (%)
Non-agricultural labour	13.3	0.83	6.2
Regular employment	34.9	0.90	38.6
Self-employment	42.8	0.86	46.6
Remittances	7.8	0.95	7.1
Other non-farm income	1.2	0.99	1.4
	100	0.69	

Note: The last column gives the share of each income source in explaining inequality in non-farm incomes in 2008/9.

can be observed from the rise in the non-farm income source Gini (G_k). It increased from 0.60 in 1983/4 to 0.65 in 2008/9. These two factors, along with the Gini correlation coefficient, give the contribution of various income sources to overall inequality. In 2008/9, the contribution of cultivation income was 20 per cent, while that of non-farm income was 58 per cent. The corresponding figures in 1983/4 were 64 per cent and 23 per cent, respectively. The rise in the contribution of non-farm income to inequality is dramatic in those 25 years.

Further investigation into the contribution of various non-farm activities to non-farm income inequality is presented in Table 8.8. Inequality of each of the respective subcomponents of non-farm income is uniformly high—the

Gini exceeds 0.80 in all cases. Of the five possible non-farm income sources, the contribution to overall non-farm income inequality is greatest from regular employment and self-employment activities. These activities have become increasingly concentrated among certain groups of the village population. Overall, the expansion of the non-farm sector has been playing a significant role in explaining the rise in income inequality, and within the non-farm sector, the changing mix of income sources and employment activities has also been important. Further discussion of the impact of the process of rural non-farm diversification on economic well-being is offered in Section 8.4.3. One important entry point is the association of caste with this process, although entrepreneurship is not confined to just one or two castes. We turn to this question in Section 8.3.3.

8.3.3 Inequality Decomposition by Caste Groups

Given the salience of caste to an understanding of a variety of aspects of economic and social life and change in Palanpur, it is of interest to enquire to what extent caste might be seen as lying at the heart of income differences across the village and whether such an assessment has changed over time. We find that in Palanpur, income inequality appears to be largely a within-caste phenomenon, rather than being one driven primarily by differences in average incomes across castes.

In Table 8.9, we provide a decomposition of the Theil L measure of inequality by population subgroup for each of the survey years. The Theil L measure is an attractive measure for this purpose as it is neatly decomposable by population subgroup and is also sensitive to changes in income among the poorest.

We find that the contribution of within-caste differences has increased from 72 per cent in 1957/8 to 87 per cent in 2008/9. In other words, if we eliminated all income differences between individuals belonging to the same caste in 2008/9 (by allocating to them their respective caste-wise average per capita income) and we then recomputed inequality based on this new distribution of

Table 8.9 'Classic' inequality decomposition by caste

Year	Theil L Measure GE (0)	Within-Caste Component (%)	Between-Caste Component (%)
1957/8	0.1896	72	28
1962/3	0.2125	72	28
1974/5	0.1468	87	13
1983/4	0.1861	78	22
2008/9	0.2601	87	13

Note: The general entropy (GE) class of inequality measures with a parameter value of 0 yields a summary measure of inequality often referred to as the mean log deviation or Theil L measure (see Cowell, 2011).

income, our new estimate of income inequality would be only 13 per cent of the original value: 87 per cent of the inequality originally observed—attributable to differences across individuals within their respective caste—would be eliminated.

Thus, the evidence points to large and growing differences in incomes across households within the respective caste groups. Caste groups are far from homogeneous, and it is pertinent to ask what lies behind the growing income differences between households of the same caste. We probe this question by examining some of the specific factors at work in the more prominent castes of the village.

We look first at the Thakurs. Historically, the high-ranked Thakurs were the large landholders in the village. They tended to lease out their land, or cultivate it using hired labour, as they were generally reluctant to engage in manual labour within the village.[21] Over time, both their position of authority and their aversion to manual labour appear to have weakened. One possible explanation could be the rising cost of hired labour in cultivation. In addition, declining per capita landholdings in the village is likely to have nudged them towards cultivation of their own land.[22] Given these changes in the cultivation environment, one would expect a significant decline in leased-out land. While some decline has occurred, it has been rather modest to date.[23]

Part of the explanation could lie in the expansion of non-farm employment opportunities. In keeping with their perspective, connections, and status, the Thakurs have been quite alert to regular employment opportunities outside the village, in part, we suppose, due to the relatively attractive work conditions and better salaries that accompany such occupations. As a result of their comparatively high economic and social status, more extensive asset ownership, stronger social networks, and better educational qualifications, the Thakurs have been well placed to take up these opportunities. This is reflected in the declining importance over the past 25 years of cultivation income as a share of total income and the increase in the share of income from non-farm sources for Thakurs as a group.[24]

Involvement in non-farm activities is far from uniform amongst Thakurs, however. Access to, awareness of, and interest in non-farm opportunities varies markedly across households. Anecdotal evidence from individual households' experiences helps to illustrate the heterogeneity of opportunities and constraints faced by Thakur villagers. The example of Thakur Ram Pal Singh is interesting. He and his father were both murdered by *dacoits*

---

[21] Lanjouw and Stern (1998).

[22] Himanshu et al. (2013).

[23] See Chapter 6.

[24] The share of cultivation income in total household income of Thakur households was 55% in 1983/4. This came down to 30% in 2008/9. On the other hand, the share of income from non-farm sources has gone up from 26% in 1983/4 to 49% in 2008/9.

('outlaws') in December 1976. Naresh Pal Singh, the son of Ram Pal Singh, became the head of the household and resided in the village at the time of the 1983/4 survey with his family of nine, including his brothers and sisters. The household was ranked in the second-lowest income quintile at that time. Between 1993 and 2008, the household split into five separate households. Kushal Pal, one of Naresh Pal Singh's brothers, completed his education through correspondence. He started teaching in a private school and was subsequently appointed as a 'shiksha mitra', or contract teacher by the government. His income ranking went up from being designated as 'poor' in 1983/4 to 'prosperous' in 2008/9. Another brother, Mahesh Pal, completed his BA and found work as an accountant at the Farmers' Service Society (FSS) in Palanpur. Yet another brother, Kuldip, also completed his BA and started working as an assistant to a doctor in Chandausi in 2006. The latter two households were both classified as 'rich' based on their income rankings in 2008/9. In this particular case, a Thakur household experienced a massive shock in the form of sudden death of family members and the partitioning of the household. Yet, with the help of education and a network of connections, several family members were able to access well-paying, stable, non-farm jobs. It is important to point out that while, overall, education has not (yet) appeared to exercise a strong impact in Palanpur in shaping job opportunities, this particular Thakur household was clearly able to leverage its education credentials to gain access to regular employment outside the village. This type of example might become more common in the future.

Thakur Prithi Pal Singh was, in 1983, working in a bakery and lived together with his three brothers, Surendra Pal, Hari Om, Birendra Pal, and his mother. His father had died in 1979 from tuberculosis, and the household had had to sell most of its landholdings of 60 *bighas* to pay for his treatment in Moradabad, Sambal, and Agra, over a period of 12 years. As a result, the household was ranked very poor in 1983/4. In the early 1990s, Prithi Pal Singh left for Delhi with his family after finding work in a plastic factory. Later in 2009, the remaining household split into two separate households headed by Surendra Pal and Birendra Pal. Due to their small (remaining) landholding, the two brothers decided to alternate in cultivating their land each year and sought to supplement their income via employment outside Palanpur. Surendra Pal found work at a shoe shop in Chandausi and Birendra Pal obtained work in a bakery in the same town. The remaining brother, Hari Om, migrated out to Ambala with his family in 2001 and found work in a liquor factory there.

Not all accounts end on a similarly positive note. A Thakur household headed by Jagdish in 1983 showed extreme downward mobility in the subsequent decades. Jagdish was aged forty in 1983/4, worked as a security guard, and headed a family of seven members (comprising Jagdish and his wife, two sons, aged twelve and nine years, and three daughters). He inherited his father Gaidan Singh's land after the latter's death in 1981. With a land ownership of 27.7 *bighas* and based on a cumulative ranking of income, assets, and observed means, Jagdish's household was classified as 'rich' in 1983/4. In 1993, Jagdish was employed as a private security guard, while Makkhan Singh of the neighbouring village of Bhoori cultivated his land under a leasing arrangement. Jagdish's daughter Geeta had died during childbirth due to complications and his wife Kamla Devi had subsequently passed away from a heart attack in 1989, after reportedly suffering severe distress from her daughter's death. In 1993 Jagdish's son Jagat Pal was away from Palanpur, undergoing training to become a security guard. His second son, Raj Kumar, worked as a steel polish worker in Moradabad. By 2009, the household size had shrunk to two members: Jagat Pal and his sister, who later got married. A chain of events that took place after 1993 led to their economic downfall. After Jagdish's death in 1998, Jagat Pal and Raj Kumar decided to sell their house and land. In 1999 Jagat Pal discovered his wife was having an affair, leading to their separation. This was followed by more deaths in the family. Their sister Suneeta committed suicide due to problems with her family members in 2002. Raj Kumar also committed suicide in 2004 by taking poison. By 2009, Jagat Pal had given up on life and had opted to become a wandering hermit.

The second main caste in the village, ranked just below the Thakurs, are the Muraos. Muraos are generally considered to be hard-working and devoted to their traditional occupation—cultivation. Their growing prosperity up to the 1980s closely accompanied the intensification of agriculture in the village. In subsequent years, as a result of reluctance to move out of agriculture and to pursue non-farm employment, the Muraos have seen their fortunes stagnate alongside the slowing of growth in agricultural income. In per capita terms, land owned and cultivated have fallen drastically over the survey period (see Figure 8.2), leading to a fall in per capita cultivation income.[25] Though cultivation and livestock remain their primary source of income, some of the Muraos have recently started exploring opportunities outside agriculture. This is evident from the rising per capita share of non-farm income shown in the right panel of Figure 8.2 and to some extent explains the rising divergence in incomes amongst the Muraos.[26] Those who take up jobs outside agriculture are mostly involved in self-employment or casual labour activities. The remainder are still largely dependent on agriculture.

Even when a small caste group, such as the Telis, is considered, one is struck by the great heterogeneity in their income and employment trajectories. The

---

[25] For a detailed discussion, see Chapter 5.
[26] As drawn from the discussion in Section 8.3.2 on the higher contribution of income from non-farm sources to overall inequality.

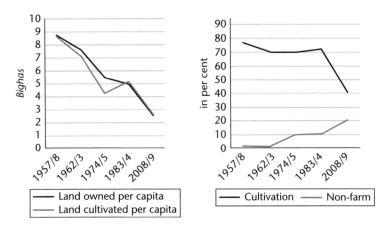

Figure 8.2 Trends in landholding size and per capita income shares from different sources for Muraos, 1957/8–2008/9

Note: We take the total land owned by Muraos in each of the survey years and divide it by the total number of individuals in the Murao caste that year. Land cultivated is land owned + land leased-in − land leased-out.

share of Telis in total village-wide non-farm income increased dramatically from 9.5 per cent in 1983/4 to 21.8 per cent in 2008/9.[27] This rise derives from a significant increase in self-employment activities amongst the Telis. This is evident from the fact that in 2008/9, among male adults above the age of fifteen, two-fifths were self-employed.[28] How this can translate into dramatic upward mobility is vividly captured by the example of Nanhe, described in Chapter 7. He is a striking example, but there are several more who have done well from self-employment amongst the Telis. But contrasting experiences of extreme destitution amongst the Telis can also be found. For example, a single-member Teli household headed by Banke Mir, aged sixty-one, is among the poorest households in Palanpur. He owns two *bighas* of land which he leases out to his grandson on a sharecropping basis. His wife died in 2005 due to old age and both his daughters have married. Due to poor health he finds it difficult to work as a labourer and knits rope cots ('charpoy') to meet his daily expenses.[29]

While within-group differences are large and have increased over time in Palanpur, there has been a decline in income differences between caste groups. This observation applies even when we subdivide the population into

[27] For shares in village non-farm income of various caste groups in 1983/4 and 2008/9, see Appendix Table A.8.1.

[28] In 2008/9, the employment structure of Teli adult males aged fifteen and above was as follows: 22% in cultivation, 15% in casual labour (non-farm), 41% in self-employment, 17% in regular jobs, and the remaining 5% not working.

[29] 'Charpoy' is a light bedstead used in India, which consists of a web of rope or tape netting.

just two groups: Jatabs and the rest of the village. Jatabs have historically been the most socially and economically disadvantaged group in the village. They generally own little land, live in shabby dwellings, and have historically earned most of their income from casual labour and subsistence farming. In earlier rounds, illiteracy was nearly universal, and only few Jatabs had managed to obtain regular jobs outside the village. Their condition saw very little advancement during the initial rounds of the survey period. Despite being involved in cultivation, the Jatabs were unable to increase their land endowments and continued to face many forms of discrimination.[30]

Lanjouw and Rao (2011) study caste-based dynamics using the Elbers, Lanjouw, Mistiaen, and Özler (ELMO) procedure for investigating group differences in inequality.[31] They point out that between-group inequality depends on three factors: number of subgroups, their relative sizes, and the difference in mean income across them. In conventional inequality decompositions the between-group share compares the observed between-group inequality with an extreme benchmark, namely, total inequality. This is an extreme benchmark because total inequality can be understood as the between-group inequality that would occur if every household in the population constituted a separate group. Elbers and colleagues (2008) propose replacing total inequality with the maximum between-group inequality that could occur given the number and size of the groups under consideration. In the case of the two-way Jatab versus 'others' subdivision of the population, this maximum between-group inequality would occur if these two groups were entirely non-overlapping in their incomes and fully partitioned the observed income distribution.[32] Between-group inequality in such a hypothetical partitioned income distribution can be readily calculated and can be taken as the benchmark against which actual between-group inequality can be compared. We implement this procedure and report findings in Table 8.10.

We find that in 1983/4 a comparison of the Jatabs versus the 'rest' of the village indicates that the Jatabs were 36 per cent of the way towards 'standing fully apart from the rest of the village', up from 11 per cent in the previous rounds. In the period leading up to 1983/4 the Jatabs as a group were clearly falling behind the rest of the village. This process saw a reversal in the period between 1983/4 and 2008/9. The Elbers and colleagues (2008) statistic declined from 36 per cent to 20 per cent in 2008/9, indicating a significant degree of 'catch-up'.

---

[30] Lanjouw and Rao (2011).
[31] Elbers et al. (2008).
[32] Elbers et al. (2008).

Table 8.10 Inequality decomposition (Jatabs versus rest of the village)

Year	Inequality Decomposition		
	Overall Inequality Theil L Measure	ELMO Partitioning Index (%)	Inequality Contribution from 'Classic' Decomposition (%)
1957/8	0.190	11	5
1962/3	0.213	10	5
1974/5	0.147	11	4
1983/4	0.186	36	16
2008/9	0.260	20	9

Note: The ELMO Index compares observed between-group inequality relative to the maximum possible between-group inequality given the actual group definition sizes under consideration (based on Elbers et al., 2008).

Similar, but less pronounced, results are observed when 'classic' decomposition methods are applied (see Table 8.10). Together, the results provide strong evidence of an improvement in the condition of Jatabs as a group, relative to the rest of the village population. The growth of the non-farm sector clearly lies behind this positive evolution. The expanding availability of non-farm jobs has provided opportunities to individuals belonging to various groups to look beyond their historical agricultural occupations and to explore new ventures. Within the Jatab caste, a growing dispersion in incomes is becoming increasingly evident and can likely be attributed to the acquisition by some Jatabs of non-farm jobs, although others have been unable to shift out of casual labour in the agricultural sector.

A Jatab household headed by Ganga Ram provides a useful example of how Palanpur villagers struggle to lift themselves out of poverty and secure a decent standard of living. In 2008 Ganga Ram spent most of his time outside Palanpur working as a casual labourer in Chandausi with his father and brother Som Pal, while the family stayed in Palanpur. By 2009, the entire family had followed Ganga Ram and had found work in nearby brick kilns or as agricultural labourers. The only exception was Charan Singh (Ganga Ram's eldest son). He, along with his wife and daughter, remained in the village and is cultivating the family's land. He is also supplementing his income by working as a construction labourer. Of all the Jatab households in the village, this is now the richest and also the most diversified out of agriculture.

A contrasting experience is that of Bhoori, wife of Dansar. Bhoori became a household head after her husband's death in 1998. She has three sons, all of whom separated from the family and formed new households in 1998. One son, Ramji Mal, stayed in Palanpur and remained largely committed to cultivation. His son Jeetpal, aged fifteen, worked for a while as a construction labourer. However, Jeetpal was murdered under mysterious circumstances and was found buried in a sandbank. Bhoori's second son, Ram Jasrath, became a social activist and migrated to Chandausi along with his wife. The third brother, Ram Niwas, initially worked in a motor repair shop in Bilari but then moved back to Palanpur and found work cultivating leased-in land and as an agricultural labourer. Bhoori was left alone to be taken care of by her daughter Gyanvati, a widow, who cultivated two *bighas* of owned land in Palanpur. In 2008/9 the household could barely manage to make ends meet and rarely received any help from the sons. Circumstances in the past have had a huge influence on present living conditions, and Bhoori's family now finds itself stuck in a downward spiral.

There are many more examples of household histories to help us understand the reasons for widening income gaps between households belonging to the same caste groups. Whilst there is no doubt that Jatabs as a group have well below average incomes and are more likely to be poor, caste is becoming a less important predictor of relative economic position in the village. Key to understanding the process has been non-farm diversification, which has allowed villagers to move out of their traditional occupations and to look for alternative livelihood sources. However, factors such as luck, health, and individual initiative, have clearly also played a role.

A caste that has moved up still more strongly than the Jatabs, as we have seen, is the Telis, a Muslim group (see Table 8.3). For them, a key driver has been self-employment and small businesses, rather than casual non-farm employment. Further exploration of these issues follows in Section 8.4.

8.4 Economic Mobility

The unique feature of the Palanpur data—in which we follow all households in the village over successive survey years—allows us to broach questions of economic mobility in addition to the analysis of inequality of Section 8.3. One entry point into such analysis is to compare the relative income position of the households in one period with their position in the second period. We take this to be an indicator of income mobility and use it to group households into three categories: upward mobility, downward mobility, and immobility (when households remain in the same ranking). Our focus is on rankings in terms of per capita income quintiles. In other words, a household with income Y and with N people is represented in the income distribution by N persons each with income Y/N. Thus it is a distribution of individuals (although derived from households as just described). In that context, we mention here an important caveat. As we generate income quintiles for every survey round based on the income distribution in that round, the change in rank may not necessarily indicate a change in real per capita income of the household. Mobility, as indicated using this method, refers explicitly to changes in relative position in the income distribution and does not look at absolute increases or declines in incomes.

8.4.1 *Intragenerational Mobility*

We examine intragenerational mobility by looking at changes in the individual rankings in the income distribution between adjacent surveys (for which we have income data). For rankings in the previous period we use the data for the households from which they come; we have to 'match' using family and household information. Often, the head of the household remains the same, but identification can be complicated by deaths and the splitting of households.

Panel D in Table 8.11, for example, shows the cross-tabulation of individual per capita income rankings between the two survey rounds of 1983/4 and 2008/9. The diagonal entries indicate the share of individuals who continued to be ranked in the same quintile in both rounds. For instance, 20 per cent of those who belonged to the highest income quintile in 1983/4 remained there in 2008/9. There was higher mobility among the bottom quintiles, with only 8 per cent of households in the lowest quintile for both 1983/4 and 2008/9. On comparing the share of households moving up or down between the two periods, we find that there is a higher incidence of downward mobility. One possible explanation for this could be the downward mobility of Muraos, who constitute a significant share (24 per cent) of the village population (see further in Section 8.4.2).

Over the entire survey period since the 1950s, there is some evidence of increasing mobility of households across income quintiles, with the share of households ranked in the same quintile between two rounds falling from 28 per cent in 1957–62 to 20 per cent in 1983–2008. This is also accompanied by decline in rigidity at the top, with the share of households in the top quintile who managed to maintain their relative ranking in the village declining from 56 per cent during 1957–62, to 40 per cent during 1962–74 and 20 per cent during 1983–2009 (Table 8.11). One of the factors that seemed to have contributed appears to be the decline in landholding and the relatively weak role played by agriculture compared to non-farm work, which has emerged as a new source of potential income increase. While access to non-farm jobs has been uneven, with the relatively affluent and socially networked being more successful in finding regular, high-paying jobs, the spread of non-farm activities to lower-ranked households in more

Table 8.11 Cross-tabulation by income quintiles

Panel A: 1957/8 and 1962/3

Quintiles of real per capita income in 1962/3

		1	2	3	4	5	Households in 1962/3	Households in 1957/8
Quintiles of real per capita	1	0.22	0.33	0.28	0.11	0.06	18	17
income in 1957/8	2	0.33	0.38	0.19	0	0.10	21	19
	3	0.25	0.20	0.15	0.35	0.05	20	19
	4	0.18	0.09	0.23	0.23	0.27	22	18
	5	0.06	0.06	0.11	0.22	0.56	18	18
Households in 1962/3		21	21	19	18	20	99	91

Panel B: 1962/3 and 1974/5

Quintiles of real per capita income in 1974/5

		1	2	3	4	5	Households in 1974/5	Households in 1962/3
Quintiles of real per capita	1	0.16	0.21	0.11	0.32	0.21	19	19
income in 1962/3	2	0.16	0.37	0.16	0.21	0.11	19	18
	3	0.19	0.19	0.23	0.19	0.19	26	21
	4	0.18	0.14	0.27	0.27	0.14	22	16
	5	0.25	0.05	0.25	0.05	0.40	20	15
Households in 1974/5		20	20	22	22	22	106	89

Panel C: 1974/5 and 1983/4

Quintiles of real per capita income in 1983/4

		1	2	3	4	5	Households in 1983/4	Households in 1974/5
Quintiles of real per capita	1	0.23	0.23	0.35	0.08	0.12	26	21
income in 1974/5	2	0.30	0.19	0.22	0.19	0.11	27	21
	3	0.15	0.12	0.19	0.27	0.27	26	23
	4	0.08	0.28	0.12	0.28	0.24	25	21
	5	0.10	0.14	0.19	0.14	0.43	21	20
Households in 1983/4		22	25	25	26	27	125	106

Panel D: 1983/4 and 2008/9

Quintiles of real per capita income in 2008/9

		1	2	3	4	5	Households in 2008/9	Households in 1983/4
Quintiles of real per capita	1	0.08	0.35	0.23	0.23	0.12	26	18
income in 1983/4	2	0.28	0.21	0.16	0.14	0.21	43	22
	3	0.20	0.12	0.27	0.17	0.24	41	22
	4	0.14	0.20	0.24	0.20	0.20	49	23
	5	0.08	0.18	0.20	0.34	0.20	50	22
Households in 2008/9		33	42	46	46	42	209	107

Note: Each cell gives the share of number of individuals belonging to the quintile of row year, and ranked according to the quintile of column year. Individuals are deemed to have the per capita income of their households. The total number of households matched between two rounds of survey is less than the actual number of households. For instance, the number of matched households in 1962/3, 1974/5, 1983/4, and 2008/9 are 99, 106, 125, and 209 respectively, as against 106, 112, 143, and 233—the actual number of households. This is because some households migrate out, some die out, and others go missing from subsequent rounds of survey. Households that are not present in the previous round of survey are not included in the subsequent round of survey. To take into account splitting of households, all the split households are matched with the ranking of their original non-split households in the previous round.

recent years has also allowed at least some of those at the bottom to improve their fortunes.

The mobility trends discussed can be further explored via the analysis of transitions across welfare quintiles based on the observed means classification for 1983 and 2008–10 as described in Section 8.2. The observed means classification is available only for the 1983 and 2008/10 survey years, so we are unable to say anything about the extent of upward and downward movement, based on this criterion, for earlier periods. On the other hand, the observed means classification is less susceptible to idiosyncratic fluctuations in incomes and therefore may be more robust for tracking the movements of individuals and their households across survey rounds. As with income, for the distribution of individuals by 'observed means', if we have a household ranked as 'poor' with five members, then the distribution contains five 'poor' people corresponding to that household. The observed means rankings confirm a larger percentage moving down in welfare ranking than moving upwards. Given that the period between 1983 and 2008–10 is lengthy, overall mobility is high: only 23 per cent maintain their respective ranking in the village, with 32 per cent moving upwards compared to their ranking in 1983 and 45 per cent moving downwards.[33]

Table 8.12 displays the movement of individuals and their households according to the observed means classification in 1983/4 and 2008/9. As with the income classification, the transition matrix by observed means also confirms a relatively high percentage maintaining their ranking among the better off in 1983 (28 per cent of the rich and 26 per cent of the prosperous

Table 8.12 Cross-tabulation of households by 'observed means' (investigator rankings) between 1983/4 and 2008/10

Observed Means Household Rankings in 2008–10

		Very poor	Poor	Secure	Prosperous	Rich	Matched households	Households in 1983/4
Observed	Very poor	0.13	0.42	0.39	0.06	0.00	31	20
means	Poor	0.17	0.13	0.57	0.03	0.10	30	19
household	Secure	0.10	0.31	0.27	0.19	0.13	52	24
ranking in	Prosperous	0.05	0.19	0.40	0.26	0.10	42	22
1983/4	Rich	0.02	0.11	0.34	0.25	0.28	61	22
Households in 2008–10		17	48	81	39	31	216	107

Note: The total number of households (216) matched between the two rounds of survey is less than the actual number of households (233) in 2008/9.

[33] It is important to mention here that unlike the 1983 classification of households in nearly equal-sized classes, the observed means classification in 2008–10 did not attempt to create equal-sized groups.

group, see cells on the diagonal of the transition matrix in Table 8.12). At the bottom, the percentage of very poor or poor in 1983 who continue to remain very poor and poor is only 13 per cent in both categories (see diagonal in Table 8.12). As with income quintiles, this suggests greater mobility by those at the bottom of the rankings than amongst the top two categories.

8.4.2 Caste and Intragenerational Mobility

One of the striking results of the inequality decomposition by caste has been the decline in between-caste inequality and increase in within-caste inequality. Further refinement using the ELMO decomposition with Jatabs versus the rest also confirms the decline in between-group inequality, with Jatabs managing to reduce the overall gap between them and the rest of the village. These findings are also confirmed by our analysis of mobility across rankings of households using income as well as observed means.

Thakurs and Muraos have traditionally dominated the group of richer households in the village, while the Jatabs have remained the prominent caste group among the poor. While the relative rankings of various caste group remained fairly stable until the 1980s, the more recent interval between 1983/4 and 2008/9 shows Jatabs moving up the economic ladder. Forty-four per cent of Jatab households moved up from their respective quintile based on income in 1983 (Table 8.13).The relative decline of Muraos as a group is also confirmed, with 61 per cent of Murao households experiencing downward mobility, while only a quarter have shown upward mobility. We also find almost half of the Teli and Passi households have moved up the economic ladder in the last 25 years.

Table 8.14 looks at mobility patterns between castes. Among those who have moved up from their respective ranking in 1983, Jatabs (21 per cent) are the second largest group after Thakurs (30 per cent). Similarly, among those experiencing downward mobility, the Muraos comprise the largest share at around 35 per cent. There has thus been a significant improvement in the relative position of Jatabs, matched by a relative decline in the position of Muraos in the last 25 years.

These trends find further confirmation from analysis of the movement across rankings based on observed means (see Table 8.15). The dominance of Thakur and Muraos among the relatively well-off is once again seen from the fact that no Thakur and Murao household was ranked as very poor in 1983/4. On the other hand, there was no Jatab household which was classified as prosperous or rich. The situation changed in 2008/9 with at least some Thakur and Murao households then appearing as very poor. While there were

Table 8.13 Within-caste group mobility based on real per capita income rankings, 1983/4 and 2008/9

Caste Groups	Number of Households	Upward (%)	Downward (%)	Same (%)
Thakurs	55	40	44	16
Muraos	54	26	61	13
Dhimars	17	18	47	35
Gadariyas	15	27	33	40
Dhobis	6	17	67	17
Telis	20	50	30	20
Passis	6	50	17	33
Jatabs	34	44	35	21
Others	2	50	50	0
Total	209			

Note: The number of households matched (208) is less than the actual number of households (233) in 2008/9. The mobility of households is relative to their respective economic position in the previous round of survey, i.e. 1983/4.

no poor households in 1983/4 among the Muraos, a little over one-fifth of Murao households were classified as poor in 2008/9. As against this, with no Jatab households classified as prosperous and rich in 1983, 8 per cent were classified as prosperous by 2008/9. But what is striking is that only 8 per cent of Jatab households were classified as very poor in 2008/9 as against three-quarters classified as very poor in 1983. The analysis of mobility of households by caste is further confirmation of our results, based on inequality decomposition, that Jatabs as a group seem to have made some progress in catching up with the rest of the village. The rise of Jatabs in the rankings is a reflection of fundamental changes in Palanpur's economic and social structures.

At the same time, we must note the remarkable rise of the Telis at the top end. In Table 8.15 we see that there were no Teli households in the rich group in 1983/4, but they made up 23 per cent of households in that group in 2008/9. That is, in large measure, a consequence of the entrepreneurship of some of the Telis.

8.4.3 *Intergenerational Income and Occupational Mobility*

Yet one more unique feature of the Palanpur study is its ability to offer a window into mobility patterns across generations. Given that we have data for all the individuals and households over seven decades, the Palanpur study allows us to look at the change in occupational patterns as well as ranking of households over generations. There are three main aspects that determine the economic outcomes achieved during an individual's lifetime. First, the 'circumstances' such as caste, gender, wealth of the family into which he or she is born. Second, people's 'efforts' or 'talents' in terms of the initiative

Table 8.14 Between-caste group mobility based on income rankings, 1983/4 and 2008/9

Caste Group	Share of Households in Village (%)	Upward mobility		Downward mobility		No change	
		Number of households	Households in caste group as a percentage of all households with upward mobility in the village (%)	Number of households	Households in caste group as a percentage of all households with downward mobility in the village (%)	Number of households	Households in caste group as a percentage of all households with same ranking in the village (%)
Thakurs	26	22	30	24	26	9	21
Muraos	25	14	19	33	35	7	17
Dhimars	8	3	4	8	9	6	14
Gadariyas	7	4	5	5	5	6	14
Dhobis	3	1	1	4	4	1	2
Telis	10	10	14	6	6	4	10
Passis	3	3	4	1	1	2	5
Jatabs	16	15	21	12	13	7	17
Others	1	1	1	1	1	0	0
Total	100	73	100	94	100	42	100

Note: This table compares the share (in %) of households of different castes in each income mobility group (upward/downward/same) with their share in total households in the village. For example, while 21% of the households that saw upward mobility were Jatab, Jatab households comprise 16% of all households. Similarly, 35% of households experiencing downward mobility are Murao households, while their share in total households is 25%.

Table 8.15 Distribution within caste groups by observed means, 1983/4–2008/9

Caste Group	2008/9 % of Households per Category					No. of Households	Caste Group	1983/4 % of Households per Category					No. of Households
	Very Poor	Poor	Secure	Prosperous	Rich			Very Poor	Poor	Secure	Prosperous	Rich	
Thakurs	5	11	35	25	25	57	Thakurs	0	27	23	27	23	30
Muraos	4	22	38	18	18	55	Muraos	0	0	22	37	41	27
Dhimars	14	36	27	9	14	22	Dhimars	15	46	31	8	0	13
Gadariyas	0	13	53	27	7	15	Gadariyas	0	25	25	17	33	12
Dhobis	25	25	25	25	0	8	Dhobis	25	25	25	0	25	4
Telis	22	17	26	13	22	23	Telis	38	31	19	13	0	16
Passis	0	33	50	0	17	6	Passis	40	7	13	20	0	15
Jatabs	8	41	44	8	0	39	Jatabs	74	16	11	0	0	19
Others	13	25	13	38	13	8	Others	33	17	0	33	17	6
No. of households	19	54	84	41	35	233	No. of households	31	28	28	28	27	142

Note: There are 233 households in 2008/9 and 142 households in 1983/4 included in the table. The columns are categories based on investigators' ranking very poor; poor; secure; prosperous; rich.

and work that they put into sustaining a livelihood. Third, good or bad fortune, including health and outcomes of risky activities in agriculture or elsewhere and the extent to which behaviour, such as gambling, involve exposure to risk. Inequality of outcomes attributed to 'efforts' or 'talents' are sometimes regarded differently from those associated with family background or ill-health.[34]

A large literature exists that looks at the extent to which family background plays a role in a child's future.[35] In some of these studies, the focus lies primarily on income and evaluates what is called 'the intergenerational elasticity in earnings', which captures the strength of the association of income earnings across generations.[36] For example, an intergenerational elasticity in earnings of 0.6 means that a 1 per cent increase in father's income is associated with a 0.6 per cent higher income for the son. In other words, a higher elasticity means a stronger correspondence between a father's income and that of his son, therefore implying, in this sense, less mobility. In cross-country comparisons, estimates of these elasticities sometimes attempt to control for other phenomena in a multivariable analysis. Such analyses commonly use father–son (rather than, say, mother–daughter) comparisons, as the data tend to reflect gender structures in the society.

Corak (2013) focuses on the father–son relationship and evaluates the elasticity of the son's lifetime earnings with respect to the father's lifetime earnings. He introduces the idea of 'the Great Gatsby curve', which plots the relationship between the intergenerational elasticity of income and a cross-sectional measure of income inequality, the Gini coefficient. The Gatsby curve shows a positive relationship across countries, where higher inequality in a given country at a given point in time is associated with lower intergenerational mobility (a higher intergenerational elasticity of earnings) in that country.

Using the very long time span of our data, we enquire into the mobility across generations in Palanpur. The long period of surveys covering income data for 1957/8 to 2008/9 allows us to not only look at father–son intergenerational income elasticity over one generation, but also to track, and assess *changes* in, this elasticity over two generations.

We calculate the intergenerational elasticity in income for two periods of at least 25 years: 1957/8–1983/4 and 1983/4–2008/9. For each period we identify father–son pairs, where sons in the latter period belong to the twenty-five to thirty age group. The per capita income of the household in the initial period

---

[34] See, for example, Motiram, Sripad, and Ashish Singh (2012).
[35] See, for example, Corak (2006), Solon (2008), Lefgren, Lindquist, and Sims (2012).
[36] Corak (2013).

Table 8.16 Intergenerational elasticity in earnings and inequality, 1958–2009

	1958–84 (1)	1984–2009 (2)	1958–74 (1984) (3)	1974(1983)–2009 (4)
Number of observations (in the age group 25–35 years)	58	100	58	100
Gini coefficient in terminal year	0.336	0.379	0.235	0.379
Intergenerational elasticity	0.328	0.396	0.294	0.441

Note: Columns 3 and 4 represent the elasticity replacing the income for 1983/4 by an average of 1974/5 and 1983/4, because 1974/5 was a good agricultural year and 1983/4 was a bad year.

is assumed to be the father's income. In other words, if the son lies in the age group mentioned and is part of the household in 2008/9, then the per capita income of the household in 1983/4 is considered to be his father's income. The following model is estimated:

$$\log(\text{income}_{son}) = \alpha + \beta\log(\text{income}_{father}) + \epsilon,$$

where income_{son} is the per capita household income in the latter period and income_{father} is the per capita household income in the former period. Table 8.16 reports the estimated elasticities.

Our findings are consistent with Corak's (2006) observation of higher income inequality being associated with a higher intergenerational income elasticity (and thus lower mobility). We observe an increase in the intergenerational elasticity over time, along with a rise in overall inequality as measured by the Gini coefficient. Because 1983/4 was a bad year in terms of agricultural production, we assess the robustness of this result by recalculating the elasticities by taking the average of incomes of 1974/5 and 1983/4. The increase in intergenerational elasticity is even more pronounced in this case. Figure A.8.1 in the appendix at the end of this chapter plots the Gini coefficients of the terminal year and the value of intergenerational elasticity—the figure known as the 'Gatsby curve'.

Interestingly, the estimates of intergenerational elasticity of 0.396 and 0.441 for the 1983/4–2008/9 period are broadly in line with the findings from Atkinson, Maynard, and Trinder (1983), who report an earnings elasticity of 0.436 between sons and fathers in the town of York over the period 1950 to 1975–8. As an indication that 0.4 can be seen as quite a high elasticity, representing a strong effect, Atkinson, Maynard, and Trinder (1983) note that it is similar to the result obtained from their data when income is replaced by height.

The persistence of positions by income is presumably influenced strongly by inheritance passed on to successive generations, notably land in the case of an agrarian economy like Palanpur. However, the emergence of non-farm as an alternative source of income has generated an opportunity for some households to break the rigidities in income and wealth transmission. As noted, the nature of non-farm diversification has not only varied across caste and income strata, but there has also been an evolution in the extent to which households from different groups have been able take advantage of non-farm occupations, as well in the nature of non-farm jobs that have become available. Jatabs and households at the lower end of the income strata have now gained access to some non-farm activities, but they are mostly of casual nature. It is important to recognize, however, that although non-farm employment has become accessible to a wider population, the importance of networks and assets has not disappeared and may well have increased. In particular, access to regular, well-paying, non-farm jobs remains concentrated amongst Thakur and other advantaged households who have better access to networks and can finance 'entrance fees' or bribes where these might be seen as necessary (furthermore, in a few cases, education is relevant). Even among the Jatab and other relatively backward castes, we do observe some reliance on networks and relatives in accessing non-farm jobs. The story emerging from our examination of intergenerational mobility, and finding evidence of some decline, is thus not inconsistent with increased intragenerational mobility of Jatab and other caste groups. Broadly speaking, the new non-farm opportunities do open up possibilities for upward mobility and within any group some move to take these opportunities more quickly than others. Nevertheless, income and social status increase the likelihood of obtaining these non-farm jobs, and this effect becomes more important in overall structures as the number of non-farm opportunities rises.

In this context, it is useful to briefly scrutinize the nature of non-farm diversification. We consider the occupation of children in relation to their parental occupations between 1983/4 and 2008/9.[37] The various occupations are classified into the following broad categories: not working, student, cultivation, agricultural labour, casual labour (non-farm), regular employment, and self-employment. Table 8.17 presents the current occupations of fathers and their sons for 1983/4 and 2008/9. One of the striking results from this analysis is the concentration of casual labour jobs in 2008/9 compared to 1983/4. Only 40 per cent of casual non-farm labourers in 1983/4 had a father also working as a casual non-farm labourer in 1957/8, but 54 per cent casual

---

[37] This analysis is only for those households where both parent and children are alive. In Appendix Table A.8.2, we take individuals who were the son of the household head 1983/4 and who themselves became a head of a household in 2008/9 and compare their occupation in 2008/9 with that of the head of their household (their father) in 1983/4. We also include sons in 1983/4 whose father remains the household head in 2008/9 and compare their occupation in 2008/9 with that of their father in 1983/4.

Table 8.17 Transition matrix of fathers' and sons' occupation categories, 1983/4 and 2008/9

	Occupation	Student	Cultivation	Agricultural labour	Casual labour	Regular employment	Self-employment
				Sons (2008/9)			
Fathers (1983/4)	Not Working	0.08	0.38	0	0.08	0.23	0.23
	Cultivation	0.21	0.40	0.05	0.16	0.10	0.10
	Agricultural Labour	0	0	0	0	0	0
	Casual labour	0.15	0.08	0.15	0.54	0.08	0
	Regular employment	0.39	0.19	0	0.17	0.17	0.08
	Self-employment	0.25	0.25	0	0.25	0.06	0.19
				Sons (1983/4)			
Fathers (1957/8)	Not working	0	0.33	0	0.17	0.17	0.33
	Cultivation	0.05	0.58	0	0.06	0.31	0
	Agricultural labour	0	0	0	C	1.00	0
	Casual labour	0.20	0	0	0.40	0.20	0.20
	Regular employment	0.18	0.09	0.18	0.18	0.36	0
	Self-employment	0	0	0.33	0	0.67	0

Note: Entries in the table are fractions moving from the status in the row to the status in the column. For the first block of the table, the sons' occupation class (present and surveyed in 2008/9) in the age group fifteen to fifty is matched with fathers' (head of household) occupation in 1983/4. For the second block of the table, the sons' occupation class (present and surveyed in 1983/4) in the age group fifteen to fifty is matched with fathers' (head of household) occupation in 1957/8. Total number of sons matched with their fathers in 2008/9: 141; total number of sons matched with their fathers in 1983/4: 104. Sons falling under the category of 'not working' were students.

non-farm labourers in 2008/9 are in households where the father was also a casual non-farm labourer in1983/4. On the other hand, if we compare the bottom and top panels in Table 8.17, we see that the transmission of parental occupation has been weaker in 2008/9 compared to 1983/4 for cultivators and regular non-farm workers.

8.5 Household and Social Structure in the Face of Change and Shocks

So far we have looked at the trend in inequality and mobility across households. Our analysis, based largely on income, has emphasized the role of both economic and social factors in explaining upward and downward mobility of households and the course of inequality in the village. While changes at the village level, in agriculture through land reforms and technological intensification, or via integration of the village with the larger economy, have played a pivotal role in the evolution of inequality and mobility in the village, we do find that individuals react and respond very differently to these changes. And they vary both to the extent that they experience adversity and shocks and how they react to such events. The movement of households in relative economic well-being or status depends also on personality and temperament of household members, on social networks, on bad luck such as ill-health or deaths, and, importantly, on the ability of the household to deal with such misfortune.

Various studies have looked at the kinds of factors that drive movement of households out of conditions of poverty in different social contexts.[38] Sen (2003), in his study of 379 rural households in Bangladesh surveyed in 1987/8 and 2000, contrasts the fortunes of ascending households (those who manage to escape poverty) and descending households (those who fall into poverty). He shows that escapees overcome structural obstacles by pursuing multiple strategies such as agricultural diversification, off-farm activity, migration, and so on. In contrast, the descents into poverty were largely associated with life-cycle changes and unforeseen crises such as flooding and ill-health. In terms of specific patterns of poverty persistence, Krishna (2011), in his study of 18 villages in Rajasthan, India, between 1977 and 2010, shows that a meagre inheritance, combined with a succession of adverse events, such as chronic and serious illnesses, deaths of major income earners, disability,

---

[38] For example, Fuwa (2007), Motiram and Singh (2012), Hnatkovska, Lahiri, and Paul (2012, 2013).

abandonment in old age, and indebtedness, often drive households into chronic poverty from which escape becomes particularly difficult.

Previous work on Palanpur has identified the role of 'dissipation' (e.g. drinking and gambling) and vulnerability to external shocks as important reasons for declining well-being. Detailed analysis of households which have seen downward mobility suggests that death of a male head, drinking and gambling, illness–both acute and chronic, criminality, and court cases, have all been important factors contributing to households moving down the village economic and social hierarchy. On the other hand, having the willingness and initiative to explore better opportunities and working hard towards the acquisition of technical skills, often combined with a bit of luck, can have a significant positive impact. In what follows we highlight some of the factors that have been particularly relevant in accounting for changing fortunes of households in Palanpur. It is important to note, however, that the accounts are illustrative rather than exhaustive.

As was seen in Section 8 of Chapter 2, one of the important changes in the village has been the change in structure of households. Partly driven by population pressure and fall in fertility rates, partly due to the changing nature of production and occupation structures, and partly from change in preference and convention, there has been a trend towards a nuclearization of households. Unlike agriculture, which was organized jointly, most non-farm activities do not require joint-family labour.[39] The joint-family system was helpful not only in organizing agricultural production, but also in dealing with economic shocks, for example, if one brother is ill, the other brother could carry on with the cultivation. A joint family may have an advantage over nuclear families in terms of greater access to family labour. It may provide greater social influence if it is more strongly bound into a larger network of kin and neighbours, thereby facilitating improved access to resources. The division of assets such as land, farm equipment, and residence, together with a lower family size, can imply that the members of the nuclear household seek to manage or reduce risk via other routes, including attempts to diversify their sources of income and occupation.

One consequence of the splitting of households has been the increase in vulnerability of elderly people. Most splits that happen after the death of the household head lead to surviving members, particularly widows, becoming more vulnerable to external shocks. Although in most cases, the widows continue to live with one of the nuclear families, there are instances of widows being separated as independent households.[40]

---

[39] Sometimes, for brick kilns for example, the nuclear family will work together, but there would be no special reason for a joint family to work in this way.

[40] See Drèze (1990) for further discussion.

Additional factors that appear to be important for the downward movement of households—drinking and gambling—continue to be significant. While there does not appear to be any clear association between drinking and economic status, there are instances where drinking addiction, particularly by the earning member, has led to debt and the subsequent sale of assets, including land. We further find evidence of major disruption or shocks, such as sudden death, court cases, chronic illness, and marriage/dowry expenses, leading to debt traps. Since most of these debts are financed by moneylenders at high rates of interest, households can find it difficult to escape from the trap.

Detailed analysis of individual household histories also throws up interesting cases of households that have managed to change their economic fortune. One of the findings has been that households that have greater exposure to the outside world respond more readily to non-farm opportunities. The outside exposure and the desire to broaden experience help households to diversify as well as to improve their economic status. Non-farm activities that have arisen since the 1983/4 survey round became central features of the Palanpur economy after villagers had acquired the necessary skills in different locations. Villagers have also tried many other things, such as beekeeping, fish farming, dairy businesses, and so on, although not always with equal success.

While new skills and an entrepreneurial drive have contributed to employment diversification and rising incomes, it is difficult to point to systematic evidence of education acting as an important driver of change so far. It has been relevant only in a very small number of regular jobs. Educational attainment in Palanpur has improved over the years, but from a very low base, and thus continues to remain weak. However, we do see education outcomes improving more rapidly in the 2015 survey and some evidence that it is becoming increasingly important in accessing non-farm regular jobs. While this evidence still remains fairly thin, there are straws in the wind, on which we speculate further in Chapter 12.

8.6 Conclusion

The richness of data covering all households in the village for a span of many decades allows us to track changes in poverty, inequality, and mobility at a level of detail not normally available from secondary data sources. We take advantage of the richness and quality of the data on income and economic status to analyse the trends in inequality and employ standard as well as modified decomposition techniques to separate the drivers of income inequality. The close attention to detail and the long time spent in the village also give us an opportunity to use individual examples and to set household change in social context. And it has allowed us to use 'observed means', economic status as assessed by research investigators resident in the village, to classify households and analyse household and individual mobility across groups over time.

The analysis clearly brings out the rise in per capita incomes and the consequent fall in poverty in recent years. Consistent with all-India trends, the rise in incomes has also been accompanied by increasing inequality in the later decades of the study period. Also consistent with all-India experience, we find acceleration in the trend towards non-farm employment diversification. This has been accompanied by a change in the composition of the non-farm sector since 1983/4, with a rise in the share of casual labour and self-employment activities and a fall in regular employment. Overall there has been, in the later decades of the survey period, a divergence in incomes and a rise in inequality. However, the expansion of non-farm activities has also led to some increase in participation of disadvantaged castes in these activities. This has not only increased overall incomes of the disadvantaged castes, notably the Jatabs, but has also contributed to narrowing of the gap between the Jatabs, as a group, and the rest of the village. The Telis have moved up markedly, in large measure through self-employment and entrepreneurship. The decline in contribution of between-group inequality, however, has been muted by increasing contribution of within-group inequality during the same period. Although greater dispersion of non-farm jobs across caste groups has been an important driver of mobility of households, particularly those at the bottom of economic ladder, these jobs are, to an important extent, still governed by access to networks, as well as the acquisition of assets for some self-employment activities. Initiative and entrepreneurship, which varies across households and individuals, has been associated with different speeds of reaction to the new opportunities; for some individuals, not just from the formerly rich groups, there has been considerable success.

The role of individual entrepreneurship has emerged as an important factor in upward movements. That this is true, and has been expanded, enabled, and reinforced by the growing non-farm activities, is a key conclusion from our work.

The emergence of non-farm activities as a key driver of economic inequality and mobility has also been at the relative expense of agriculture as a share of activity and income. While the growth in per capita incomes in the first three decades was driven by agricultural intensification, particularly via irrigation, following land reforms in the first decade and the advent of green revolution technologies and methods in subsequent decades, the role of agriculture in shaping individual/household trajectories has weakened over time. This has also meant that the early adopters of the technological innovations, such as the Muraos, have, in the later part of the survey period, fallen behind, in relative terms, with agriculture no longer driving the growth of incomes to the extent it did earlier. However, it is important to recognize the significant remaining role of agriculture, since it continues to engage a substantial section of village population, including amongst households that have diversified into the non-farm sector. Furthermore, some of the non-farm activities are associated with capital goods which have been acquired, including those used in agricultural production, and the liquidity to incur costs necessary in cultivation.

At first glance, our story of broad-based income and employment mobility and diversification might appear to be in tension with our analysis of inter-generational mobility. Consistent with cross-country patterns, where higher inequality is associated with lower intergenerational mobility, we find for Palanpur some evidence of declining mobility in the sense of a closer associ-ation between the incomes of fathers and sons for the later part of the survey period. We argue that an important part of the explanation for this result lies in the nature of non-farm expansion, which, even though accessible to a large and growing population, remains strongly influenced by access to caste-based and family networks. Involvement in the new forms of self-employed employment, such as marble polishing and repair activities, continue to be influenced by good networks of relatives and caste connections. The same is true for lower-end casual labour such as brick kiln work, which relies on caste affiliations. Whilst new opportunities open up and some entrepreneurial characters amongst poorer groups are responding, being from a more privil-eged group improves the chances of being able to take those new opportun-ities. We should note again, however, that notwithstanding these caste, family, and network effects, there are some individuals who have done well. Most strikingly, a number of Telis, a previously poor Muslim group, are now at the top end of the income distributions, in large measure through their entrepreneurship.

Finally, we should stress, and have stressed, the important sources of downward mobility. Instances of death of a household head, drinking and gambling, illness–both acute and chronic, criminality and court cases, and more, can wreak real damage and possibly generate a downward spiral from which escape becomes very difficult.

Appendix

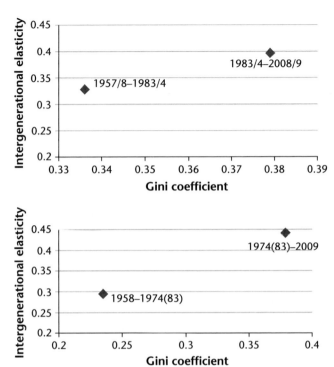

Figure A.8.1 Great Gatsby Curve for Palanpur

Note: Elasticities and Gini coefficients are discussed in Section 8.4. In the second diagram, incomes for 1974/5 and 1983/4 are averaged because 1974/5 was a good agricultural year and 1983/4 was bad.

Table A.8.1 Shares of village non-farm income of various caste groups, 1983–2009

	2008/9	1983/4
Thakurs	32.2	19.8
Muraos	10.9	8.1
Dhimars	13	12.4
Gadariyas	6.4	8.8
Dhobis	0	1.7
Telis	21.8	9.5
Passis	2.4	23.2
Jatabs	10.7	5.8
Others	2.5	10.8

Table A.8.2 Transition matrix for fathers' occupation 1983/4 and sons' occupation 2008/9

Occupation		Sons (2008/9)					Total
		Student	Cultivation	Agricultural labour	Casual labour	Regular employment	Self-employment	
Fathers (1983/4)	Not working	0.20(1)	0.40(2)	0	0	0	0.40(2)	5
	Cultivation	0.01(1)	0.42(33)	0	0.18(14)	0.14(11)	0.24(19)	78
	Agricultural labour	0	0	0	0.50(1)	0	0.50(1)	2
	Casual labour	0	0	0.13(1)	0.50(4)	0.25(2)	0.13(1)	8
	Regular employment	0.20(3)	0.20(3)	0	0.07(1)	0	0.53(8)	15
	Self-employment	0	0	0	0.67(4)	0.17(1)	0.17(1)	6
								114

Note: The figures in parentheses give the number of individuals.

Acknowledgements

This chapter has been written by Himanshu, Peter Lanjouw, and Priyanka Pande, and draws on earlier work in Himanshu and colleagues (2013) and Himanshu, Bakshi, and Dufour (2011). We acknowledge the contribution of Vaishnavi Surendra in the cleaning and analysis of income data.

References

Atkinson, A.B. 1970. 'On the measurement of inequality', *Journal of Economic Theory* 2, no. 3: 244–63.

Atkinson, A.B., Maynard, A.K., and Trinder, C.G. 1983. *Parents and Children: Incomes in Two Generations*. London: Heinemann.

Bakshi, A. 2008. 'A note on household income surveys in India', paper presented at Studying Village Economies in India: A Colloquium on Methodology, Chalsa, West Bengal, India, December.

Bliss, C., and Stern, N. 1982. *Palanpur: The Economy of an Indian Village*. Oxford and New Delhi: Oxford University Press.

Corak, M. 2006. 'Do poor children become poor adults? Lessons for public policy from a cross country comparison of generational earnings mobility', *Research on Economic Inequality* 13: 143–88.

Corak, M. 2013. 'Income inequality, equality of opportunity, and intergenerational mobility', *Journal of Economic Perspectives* 27, no. 3: 79–102.

Cowell, F. 2011. *Measuring Inequality*, 3rd edn. Oxford: Oxford University Press.

Drèze, J.P. 1990. 'Widows in rural India'. LSE STICERD Development Economics Research Program Discussion Paper No. 26.

Drèze, J.P., Lanjouw, P., and Sharma, N. 1998. 'Economic development 1957–93', in P. Lanjouw and N.H. Stern (eds), *Economic Development in Palanpur over Five Decades*. Oxford and New Delhi: Oxford University Press.

Elbers, C., Lanjouw, P., Mistiaen, J., and Özler, B. 2008. 'Reinterpreting between-group inequality', *Journal of Economic Inequality* 6, no. 3: 231–45.

Filmer, D., and Pritchett, L. 2001. 'Estimating wealth effects without expenditure data—or tears: an application to educational enrollments in states of India', *Demography* 38, no. 1: 115–32.

Foster, J., and Sen, A.K. 1997. *On Economic Inequality*. Oxford: Clarendon Press.

Fuwa, N. 2007. 'Pathways out of rural poverty: a case study in socio-economic mobility in the rural Philippines', *Cambridge Journal of Economics* 31, no. 1: 123–44.

Himanshu, Lanjouw, P., Murgai, R., and Stern, N. 2013. 'Non-farm diversification, poverty, economic mobility and income inequality: a case study in village India'. World Bank Policy Research Working Paper Series 6451.

Himanshu, Bakshi, I., and Dufour, C. 2011. 'Poverty, inequality and mobility in Palanpur: some preliminary results', Asia Research Center, Working Paper No. 45.

Hnatkovska, V., Lahiri, A., and Paul, S. 2012. 'Castes and labour mobility', *American Economic Journal* 4, no. 2: 274–307.

Hnatkovska, V., Lahiri, A., and Paul, S. 2013. 'Breaking the caste barrier: intergenerational mobility in India', *Journal of Human Resources* 48, no. 2: 435–73.

Krishna, A. 2011. 'Characteristics and patterns of intergenerational poverty traps and escapes in rural north India'. Chronic Poverty Research Centre Working Paper No. 189.

Krueger, A. 2012. 'The rise and consequences of inequality in the United States', speech at Center for American Progress, Washington, DC, 12 January.

Kuznets, S. 1955. 'Economic growth and income inequality', *American Economic Review* 45, no. 1: 1–28.

Lanjouw, P., and Rao, V. 2011. 'Revisiting between-group inequality measurement: an application to the dynamics of caste inequality in two Indian villages', *World Development* 39, no. 2: 174–87.

Lanjouw, P., and Stern, N. 1991. 'Poverty in Palanpur', *World Bank Economic Review* 5, no. 1: 23–55.

Lanjouw, P., and Stern, N. (eds). 1998. *Economic Development in Palanpur over Five Decades*. New Delhi and Oxford: Oxford University Press.

Lefgren, L., Lindquist, M., and Sims, D. 2012. 'Rich dad, smart dad: decomposing the intergenerational transmission of income', *Journal of Political Economy* 120, no. 2: 268–303.

Lerman, R., and Yitzhaki, S. 1985. 'Income inequality effects by income source: a new approach and applications to the United States', *Review of Economics and Statistics* 67, no. 1: 151–6.

Lewis, A.W. 1954. 'Economic development with unlimited supplies of labour', *Manchester School of Economic and Social Studies* 22: 139–91.

Lopez-Feldman, A. 2006. 'Decomposing inequality and obtaining marginal effects', *Stata Journal* 6(1): 106–11.

Motiram, S., and Singh, A. 2012. 'How close does the apple fall to the tree? Some evidence on inter-generational occupational mobility in India', *Economic & Political Weekly* 47, no. 40: 56–65.

Piketty, T. 2014. *Capital in the Twenty-First Century*, tr. A. Goldhammer. Cambridge, MA, and London: Belknap Press of Harvard University Press.

Planning Commission. 2009. 'Report of the Expert Group to Review the Methodology for Estimation of Poverty', Government of India, http://planningcommission.nic.in/reports/genrep/rep_pov.pdf (accessed 19 March 2018).

Rawal, V. 2008. 'Estimation of rural household incomes in India: selected methodological issues', paper presented at Studying Village Economies in India: A Colloquium on Methodology, Madras Institute of Development Studies, 21 December.

Sen, B. 2003. 'Drivers of escape and descent: changing household fortunes in rural Bangladesh', *World Development* 31, no. 3: 513–34.

Shorrocks, A. 1982. 'Inequality decomposition by factor components', *Econometrica* 50, no. 1: 193–211.

Solon, G. 2008. 'Intergenerational income mobility', in S. Durlauf and L. Blume (eds), *The New Palgrave Dictionary of Economics*, 2nd edn. London: Palgrave Macmillan.

Stark, O., Taylor, J., and Yitzhaki, S. 1986. 'Remittances and inequality', *The Economic Journal* 96, no. 383: 722–40.

Part 3
Society

9

Human Development

Education, Health, Public Services*

9.1 Introduction

The story of human development in Palanpur is similar to that of Uttar Pradesh and much of rural India: there has been economic growth, although slower than India as a whole, but advances in human development have been disappointing relative to what has been achieved elsewhere with corresponding growth (for example, see Drèze and Sen, 2013). Bangladesh, for example, is a much poorer country than India, but has managed to achieve a lower infant mortality rate (IMR) and higher life expectancy despite having worse human development indicators in the early 1990s. And Bangladesh has achieved this with slower economic growth than India.

Within India, Uttar Pradesh is a state which ranks amongst the lowest in terms of human development indicators, as well as per capita income. The increase in real per capita income between 1993 and 2008 is about 2.3 times for both Bangladesh and Uttar Pradesh. In contrast, while the IMR halved during this period in Bangladesh, it reduced by only about 30 per cent in Uttar Pradesh. The change in life expectancy is also slower (see Table 9.1).

The trends in Palanpur are similar to the rest of the state. While there has been substantial improvement in human development indicators in the village, particularly after the 1983/4 survey, Palanpur still lags behind the rest of the country and state. The literacy rate (of persons aged seven and above) in Palanpur increased from 26 per cent in 1984 to 63 per cent in 2015 (see Table 9.2).[1]

---

* This chapter has been written by Dipa Sinha and Ruchira Bhattacharya.
[1] Literate refers to all those who can 'read and write'.

Table 9.1 Selected economic and human development indicators

	India		Uttar Pradesh		Bangladesh	
	1993	2008	1993	2008	1993	2008
Per capita gross national income, PPP US$	1270	3620	929	2087	990	2330
IMR	82	50	94	67	88	44
Life expectancy	59	66	57	63	60	69

Source: World Bank database for India and Bangladesh. Sample Registration System and Central Statistical Organisation, Government of India for Uttar Pradesh.

Table 9.2 Literacy rates (%) across survey years in Palanpur (7+ years)

Year	Total	Male	Female	Gender Gap
1958	8.4	14.5	1	13.5
1964	20.4	34	3.5	30.5
1975	21	33.5	5.5	28.1
1984	25.6	39.9	9.2	30.6
1993	32.8	50.5	13.1	37.5
2009	53.8	73.6	33.1	40.6
2015	62.7	80.3	44.2	36.1

Note: Literacy being defined as being able to 'read and write'. The figures are based on self-reporting. This is also how the Census of India defines literacy.
Source: Computed by authors using village survey data. Gender Gap calculated as the difference between the male and female literacy rates for each year.

However this 2015 figure is lower than the corresponding figure for Uttar Pradesh (69.7 per cent according to Census 2011[2]).

It is more difficult to comment on changes in health outcomes in Palanpur. We do not have mortality indicators from the earlier rounds of the survey to make comparisons. And sample size and other data issues make it difficult to estimate these. However, using data on birth histories, some estimates have been made of the IMR in the village and this shows (see Section 9.3) that while the IMR has declined since 1993 (from 160 to 93), it is still higher than comparable figures for the rest of rural Uttar Pradesh. There is a reduction in fertility rates and increase in age at marriage. Health expenditures are high, with most people depending on the private sector for health care. On this aspect of human development, as with others, Palanpur is making significant progress, but is still far behind the rest of the state (see Section 9.3).

In this chapter, we discuss the trends in education (Section 9.2), health (Section 9.3), population, and nutrition (Section 9.4) in the village. There are no longitudinal data available for some aspects, and in other instances the population of the village is too small to be confident that we are picking up real

[2] http://censusindia.gov.in/.

population-level trends. Keeping these limitations in mind, we offer some analysis of the reasons why the changes in human development seem out of step compared with those from economic growth. The chapter also describes the state of basic public services in the village. In conclusion, we discuss how these are interconnected and what one can speculate about the future based on these trends.

9.2 Literacy and Education

The literacy rates in Palanpur have historically been low; similar to the rest of the state of Uttar Pradesh. However, there was a remarkable rise in the literacy levels in the village after 1993, and it continued to rise until 2015. While only one-third of the village population was literate in 1993, the literacy rate in 2015 was almost two-thirds (63 per cent). More remarkable is the rise in the literacy rate for males, with over 80 per cent of the male population in the village now being literate. On the other hand, even though the female literacy rate more than tripled between 1993 and 2015, it is still far behind, with only 44 per cent of females being literate in 2015.

The gender gap in literacy rate was rising until 2009, but shows a decline from 2009 to 2015. The increase in the male literacy rate was much faster than female literacy in the earlier periods. Even if the literacy rates continue to change at a similar pace for females, it will still take some time before they catch up.[3] On the other hand, it is important to note that although Palanpur is relatively behind the state and the country in terms of literacy, this increasing trend is likely to have significant effects on other aspects of village economy and society in the years to come.

The rise in literacy is very uneven, not only across gender but also caste. Almost 40 per cent of the village population remained illiterate in 2015; most of them belong to lower castes and are women.[4] Tables 9.3 and 9.4 present the data on literacy rates by caste and gender for the various survey rounds. Differences by caste in literacy rates have always existed, for both men and women. Although the differences across castes remain large, what is also striking is the huge increase in literacy rates for Jatabs between 1993 and 2009. The literacy rate for Jatab males increased from 24 per cent in 1993 to over 51 per cent in 2009 and 64 per cent in 2015. In the case of females, there was not one amongst the Jatabs who was literate until 1993, when the literacy rate increased to 22 per cent, and to 34 per cent in 2015. Amongst females,

---

[3] For a caste-wise breakdown of gender gaps, see Chapter 10.
[4] A total of 73% of the illiterate in the village are female. Over 20% of the illiterate persons in the village are Jatabs, while their share in the population is 14% (7+ years).

Table 9.3 Literacy rates (%) by caste (7+ years), male

Caste Group	Year						
	1958	1964	1974	1984	1993	2009	2015
Thakur	34.1	58.5	59.2	60	67.6	82.6	87.3
Murao	10.4	27.8	40	46.3	53.2	78.9	84.4
Muslims	4.2	20	7.9	26.8	36.1	73.7	83.8
Jatab	3	12.1	5.4	7.5	23.7	51.3	64.2
Others	14.1	35.4	28.9	40	53.7	74.1	76
Total	14.5	34	33.5	39.9	50.5	73.6	80.3

Source: Computed by authors using village survey data.

Table 9.4 Literacy rates (%) by caste (7+ years), female

Caste Group	Year						
	1958	1964	1974	1984	1993	2009	2015
Thakur	0	8.9	12.7	15.1	28	48.3	52.3
Murao	0	0	3.1	1.3	3.7	28.3	50
Muslims	0	0	0	2.1	0	26	32
Jatab	0	0	3.1	0	0	21.7	33.8
Others	3.2	4.8	5.8	16.5	19.3	33.9	43.9
Total	1	3.5	5.5	9.2	13.1	33.1	44.2

Source: Computed by authors using village survey data.

a large rise in literacy rates post-1993 can also be seen among Muraos and Muslims. While Murao females had almost caught up with Thakurs in 2015, Jatabs and Muslims, despite the improvements, remain far behind. Therefore, while there has been an increase in literacy rates amongst all castes, with a significant jump after 1993, the gaps between the Jatabs and the rest amongst males, and between Jatabs, Muslims, and the rest amongst females, remain very wide. The male literacy rate for Jatabs in 2015 (64 per cent) was lower than for Thakurs (68 per cent) in 1993. The female literacy for Jatabs in 2015 (34 per cent) was not much higher than that for Thakurs in 1993 (28 per cent). In this sense, there seems to be a 25-year lag period in literacy rates for the Jatabs.

These caste-wise differences are strong and at the current pace of change it will take a long time for the gaps to close. If we look at literacy in children aged between seven and eighteen, as seen in Table 9.5, we find that in 2009 less than 50 per cent of Jatab girls were literate; their literacy rate is roughly similar to the level achieved by Thakur girls in 1993. In 1993, no Jatab girls were literate, so there certainly has been an improvement. Compared to Thakurs, there seems to be a 15-year time lag for Jatabs in terms of girl's education. Considering the intergenerational effects that women's education can potentially have, such

Table 9.5 Caste group literacy rates (%) among 7–18 years

Caste Group	Year							
	1984		1993		2009		2015	
	Boys	Girls	Boys	Girls	Boys	Girls	Boys	Girls
Thakur	55.6	18.2	76.9	44.1	89.1	92.3	100	100
Murao	48.8	3	60	4.4	88.1	65.9	91.4	93.4
Teli	38.1	7.1	43.8	0	100	73.9	95.8	60
Jatab	15.4	0	38.1	0	81.5	46.7	83.3	55.3
Overall	43.4	13.7	60.1	18.2	89.4	65.8	90	77.8
Number of observations	182	153	168	154	180	161	194	207

inequality in literacy can have long-lasting impacts on the overall inequality of both incomes and human development.

The rise in literacy is not the same as a rise in education levels in the village. The level of education achieved has implications for skill levels and employment opportunities. In 2015, among those in the fifteen to twenty-four age group, only 43 per cent of males and 20 per cent of females had completed elementary school.[5] While some of them were still pursuing education, most are either illiterate or educated only up to the primary level. Looking at the twenty-five to thirty-four age group, only 2 per cent of females and 30 per cent of males have completed elementary education or beyond. The levels of educational attainment are probably still too low to show much impact on employment opportunities. However, with increasing participation in higher education amongst the younger generation, this can be expected to change in the future.

Reflecting the trend of increasing literacy rates over time, the literacy levels are higher amongst lower age groups; amongst those aged under twenty-five, they are much higher (see Table 9.6). Across India, one can expect the demand for education in relation to different kinds of jobs to rise as work profiles shift and as new groups entering the labour market become more literate. In the case of women, the literacy level is lower, with only 30 per cent of the women in the twenty to twenty-four age group being literate. However,

[5] By the age of fourteen, children are supposed to have completed 'Class 8'. Primary school consists of classes 1 to 5 (ages six to eleven); middle or elementary school is classes 6 to 8 (ages eleven to fourteen). The Right to Education Act in India guarantees free and compulsory education up to age fourteen/Class 8. Two years of pre-school (ages four to six) is provided by the ICDS (Integrated Child Development Services) scheme. Secondary school is Classes 9 and 10 (ages fifteen to sixteen). At the end of Class 10, students take a board examination and are given a certificate. Completing Class 10 is the basic minimum requirement for a number of jobs. All education beyond Class 10, is referred to as 'Higher Education'. This includes Classes 11 and 12 (also known as higher secondary or intermediate education) and college education towards undergraduate or graduate degrees and diplomas.

Table 9.6 Literacy rates by age, 2009

Age Groups	Men		Women	
	N	%	N	%
7 to 10	55	83.6	68	69.1
11 to 14	62	91.9	43	69.8
15 to 19	80	91.2	69	52.2
20 to 24	59	81.3	56	30.4
25 and above	249	51	254	10.6
Total	505	68.5	490	32

Note: N is the number of observations, 'Total' is the weighted average of all observations.

Table 9.7 Students in private schooling (%), 2009–15

Caste Group	2009		2015	
	Boys	Girls	Boys	Girls
Thakur	35	24	63	62
Murao	35	16	61	49
Others	31	10	59	40
Muslims	33	9	74	54
Jatab	27	0	35	9
Total	33	14	58	46

Note: Table only refers to those below 12th standard.

amongst younger females the literacy levels are above 65 per cent, and this can be expected to make a difference in the next few decades. Future mothers will be more literate, and this will likely have a ripple effect on the health and education of future generations. It also could result in a change in the work profile of women, with more women demanding jobs outside the home. Currently, very few women in Palanpur report being part of the workforce.

Along with caste and gender differences and low levels of educational attainment, another clear trend is of increasing privatization of education. This is more visible between 2009 and 2015. In 2009 only 33 per cent of boys and 14 per cent of girls were in private schools (see Table 9.7), while in 2015 the proportions rose to 58 per cent for boys and 46 per cent for girls. Further, the proportions of students in private schools in Palanpur also point to caste-wise differences and gender gaps. Although, on average, male children are more likely to be sent to private schools, in the upper castes the gender gap is smaller. In fact, within the Thakurs the percentage of girls in private institutions is almost equal to the percentage of boys.

The availability of a private school at close proximity could be a reason for this sharp increase for girls. Most of the girls in private schools are going to Pipli, a village adjacent to Palanpur, where a new school was recently opened. The rest of the children are at private schools in nearby villages, about three to four kilometres away. Until recently, most households were not very comfortable sending their daughters to schools that were not in the village, especially after they had reached puberty. Parents had safety concerns for girls having to walk through the fields or uninhabited areas between villages to reach school.[6] However, in recent times a number of girls have been going to schools outside the village, and arrangements have been made for them to walk/cycle in groups.

9.2.1 *Education Facilities in Palanpur*

One important reason for the shift to private schools is the poor quality of the government school in Palanpur. The problem in Palanpur is not so much the poor physical state of the school, but rather the absence or shortage of teachers. There has been a government primary school in the village since the 1970s. The school was later upgraded to span the full elementary level (up to Class 8) in 2012. The school is situated at the entrance to the village, across the road from the railway station. This allowed our survey teams to easily observe its functioning.

In 1974/5 Palanpur's government primary school had three teachers and one headmaster (see Bliss and Stern, 1982: 4). It also served the nearby villages of Bhoori and Pipli. Facilities were very poor, and most of the teaching took place outside in the open. After 1974/5 the number of teachers fell, apparently due to the adoption of a policy of spreading teaching posts more evenly between villages. By late 1992 the school had only one teacher. In 1993 a new directive from the UP government prevented teachers working in primary schools in their own villages, resulting in the transfer of the local teacher and recruitment of two teachers from outside the village. The survey team of 1993 found that this had led to an improvement in the attendance of students, though the performance of the school remained poor. The government school in Akrauli had better infrastructure and staff, and some parents sent their children there, mostly boys, as parents did not want to send their daughters such a distance (Drèze and Sharma, 1998: 73).

The expansion of basic education in Palanpur has been considerably slowed down by the poor functioning of the village school. In fact, around the end of the survey period the village school remained virtually non-functional for more than ten years, due to systematic absenteeism and shirking on the part of the local

---

[6] When we went back to the village in 2015, parents were concerned about sending their daughters to Akrauli (for high school) because there had been a recent incident of a girl from the neighbouring village Pipli being raped on her way back from school.

teacher. The most extraordinary aspect of this situation is that there has been no concerted effort to do anything about it. Admittedly, the scope for putting pressure on the village teacher has been somewhat reduced by the fact that, for much of the relevant period, he was the son of the village headman.

The situation was very similar when we began the survey in 2008. There were four teachers in the school, two of them were regular teachers from outside the village while the other two were Shiksha Mitras from the same village.[7] The two permanent teachers were very unreliable and rarely attended school. They later got transferred out. One of the Shiksha Mitras was reliable but she also left once she got married. The other local teacher was known as a miscreant in the village and was often seen near the school in a drunken state. By the end of the survey (2010) he was the only teacher left, even though five teacher posts had been sanctioned by the government for the school. When we went back in 2015, there was again a permanent teacher appointed in the school. He seemed to be reliable but was finding it difficult to manage so many classes alone. The *anganwadi* worker (the person appointed to work at the early childcare centre) often helped out by teaching the lower classes so that the schoolmaster could manage the higher ones.

In terms of infrastructure, the school building has seen major improvements since the previous survey in 1993. There are four classrooms, separate toilets for boys and girls (albeit often non-functional), and a kitchen for cooking the midday meal. Some of the rooms are kept locked, and different classes are merged together, with only two rooms being opened. The toilets are always locked. In 2008, the midday meal had not been served for many months even though grain and money for the meal were being supplied to the village for this purpose. It was alleged that the Pradhan,[8] who was also in charge of the grain and money that came for the midday meal, siphoned off the funds. It was only a year after we began this round of survey in the village that the midday meal in the school was restored. This was one of the changes brought in by the new *panchayat pradhan*.[9] Although the children started attending the school more regularly, they would often be found playing outside waiting for mealtimes.

For high school, the nearest government school is in Akrauli village, about three kilometres away. For university education, the nearest institutions are located in Chandausi (13 kilometres away, the nearest town and former block

---

[7] Shiksha Mitras are para teachers who are paid less and who have lower qualification requirements. They are appointed for a fixed period. The understanding was to employ such teachers in the short term to fill the gaps in teacher availability in primary schools. Data for 2009/10 show that 38.4% of all government teachers in UP are para teachers and, of them, only 33.4% have received professional training (DISE, 2011).

[8] This *pradhan* was later replaced. See Chapter 11 for details.

[9] The person elected after the previous *pradhan* was impeached. See Chapter 11 for details.

headquarters) and Moradabad (31 km away, the district headquarters). As mentioned, some children in Palanpur also attend private schools. These schools are in nearby villages such as Amarpur Kashi (4 km away). By 2015, a new school had been opened in Pipli (1 km away) where a number of children from Palanpur were now going. While education in the government schools is almost free, in private schools the average fee was Rs 650 per child per year, as per data collected in 2009. Up to 2005, there was a small private school running in Palanpur village itself, and this used to function fairly regularly. This school, however, closed down because the two teachers running it got jobs in government primary schools.

While there is an increase in literacy rates, as seen at the beginning of this section, there is still much to be desired as far as quality of schooling and equity in access is concerned. Those who can afford it are moving to private schools, and it is the poorer and lower social groups who remain in the government school. While it is difficult to ascertain the quality in the private schools, they offer regular teaching, and this is often argument enough for the parents.

9.3 Health and Population

We have less complete data on health outcomes in the village than for education. Education data are available from all rounds of survey, as the literacy and schooling details were collected as part of the basic demographic information for all members of the household. On the other hand, health indicators were not included in the earlier rounds. Moreover, it is difficult to estimate basic health indicators, such as child mortality rates or life expectancy, for a village with a small population such as Palanpur due to issues related to sample size. However, in this section the available data on health and population are presented. While these data and analysis are limited, what they indicate is that, as in the case of education, progress leaves much to be desired. Fertility rates have fallen, and there is some increase in the age at marriage. These developments will have contributed to a reduction in population growth as well as freeing up women's time for potential non-household activities. At the same time morbidity levels seem to be high, as are expenditures on catastrophic health events. As in the case of education, the situation in Palanpur is also slightly worse than the rest of the state of Uttar Pradesh.

As we have remarked, estimates of the IMR suggest that although there has been a decline, it is high compared to the rest of the country and even to the rest of rural Uttar Pradesh. The IMR is a widely used indicator of the general health of a population and health-care services available to it. The estimated IMR in 1993 was 160 deaths per 1000 live births (Drèze and Sharma, 1998) and for 2009 was 93 deaths per 1000 live births.[10] In both years this estimated IMR is considerably higher than the IMR for rural UP (139 in 1991 and 66 in 2009).[11] While the ratio of the IMR for Palanpur to that for UP was 1.15 in 1993, it increased to 1.4 in 2009.

9.3.1 Fertility and Age at Marriage

The fertility rate in the village is high, although falling. It is quite common for a woman to have four or more children. However, as we will see in Chapter 10, the ratio of children to adult women is declining, suggesting declining fertility rates. The age at marriage is seen to have an impact on fertility rates (by reducing the reproductive period) as well as IMRs (by increasing age at first pregnancy, as early pregnancy is riskier). The age at marriage for men and women in the village shows an increase.

The age at marriage was not directly asked in the 1993 survey, but the marital status of all village inhabitants was reported. Figures 9.1 and 9.2 indicate that there was a change in the average age at marriage between 1993 and 2008, for both men and women. In 1993, 18 per cent of Palanpur girls aged fifteen to seventeen were married (1 girl aged fifteen, 1 sixteen, and 5 aged seventeen among the 40 girls in this age group), whereas none of the girls in this age

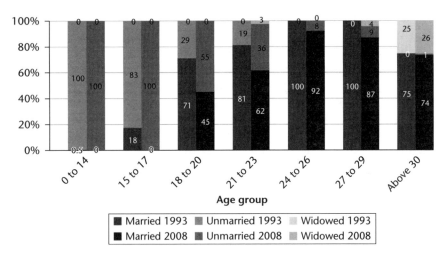

Figure 9.1 Marital status of women in Palanpur, 1993 and 2009

---

[10] The earlier IMR estimates were computed using the 'children ever born, children surviving' method (Drèze and Sharma, 1998). The latest estimates of IMR are calculated using formulae based on the World Bank's Child Survival Rate (see Pierre, 2011).

[11] The IMR of rural UP and Palanpur have been discussed in Lanjouw and Stern (1998). The IMR data for 2009 is from the Registrar General of India.

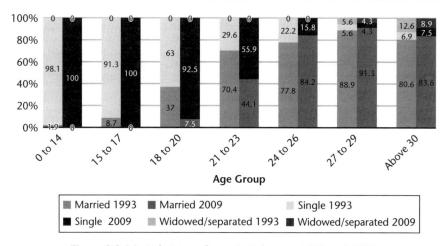

Figure 9.2 Marital status of men in Palanpur, 1993 and 2009

Table 9.8 Average age of women at marriage (based on response to 2008/9 survey)

Age Group	Mean	Std. Dev.	Freq.
17–24	17.9	1.87	54
25–31	17.5	1.88	58
32–8	16.4	2.16	56
39–50	16.1	1.88	56
Overall	17	2.08	224

group was married in 2009.[12] The corresponding figures for men in 1993 were lower than women, at 8.7 per cent married in the fifteen to seventeen age group, which fell to zero in 2009. Similar differences were also seen in the eighteen to twenty and twenty-one to twenty-three age groups. A total of 71 per cent of girls aged eighteen to twenty were married in 1993 compared to 45 per cent in 2009, and 81 per cent of girls aged twenty-one to twenty-three, compared to 62 per cent in 2009. For men, the figures were 37 per cent in the eighteen to twenty age group in 1993, which went down to 7.5 per cent in 2009.

In the 2009 survey, women were asked for their age at marriage. Based on these data, as reported by the women themselves, we can see that there has been an increase in the mean age at marriage. In Table 9.8, the mean age at marriage for

---

[12] This compares unmarried girls in Palanpur (as it would be difficult to know precisely at what age they were married and left the village) to newly married women who came to Palanpur. It could be the case that parents in Palanpur like their boys to marry young girls and send their own daughters after marriage when they are older, but qualitative data suggest there is little difference in age at marriage in Palanpur and in the surrounding villages.

Table 9.9 Sex ratios in Palanpur

	Year						
	1957/8	1962/3	1974/5	1983/4	1993	2008/10	2015
Population	528	585	790	960	1133	1255	1299
Female–male ratio	0.87	0.87	0.85	0.93	0.85	0.98	0.94
Child sex ratio	0.98	0.88	1.01	1.23	0.75	1.1	0.78

women who are currently in the thirty-nine to fifty age group was around 16.1, whereas the mean age at marriage for women in the seventeen to twenty-four age group was 17.9. Looking at a caste-wise break-up, it is seen that the mean age at marriage is highest among Thakur women, followed by the Muraos, with the lowest mean age at marriage being amongst the Jatabs. Interestingly, we see that while the mean age at marriage is 18.5 for literate women, it is 16.6 for illiterate women, indicating that schooling/education might be an important factor.

9.3.2 Sex Ratios

The ratio of females to males ('sex ratio') in any given population is a sensitive indicator of the status of women in that society. For most of the world, it is seen that the sex ratio usually favours women,[13] as the life expectancy for females is, in general, higher. However, India has had a history of low sex ratios, with fewer females compared to males. There has been a rising trend for India since 1991; the sex ratio in India was 927 females per 1000 males according to the 1991 Census and went up to 933 in 2001 and 940 in 2011. This is because of an increase in female life expectancy in the last few decades. However, what is worrying is that the child sex ratio (ratio of number of females per 1000 males among children under six years of age) has been decreasing (Census 2011). In Palanpur the sex ratio is also very low, with the female–male ratio being lower than the Indian average, another indicator of the poor status of women in the village.

During the different rounds of survey from 1957 to 1993, the female/male ratio was around 0.86 (i.e. 860 females per 1000 males), as seen in Table 9.9. In 1983/4, a much higher female/male ratio of 0.93 (930 females per 1000 males) was recorded. The 2008 survey also found a high female–male ratio of 0.98, which was closer to that of 1983/4 than any of the previous survey years. The figure for 2015 is close to that for 1984. Drèze and Sharma (1998) had drawn attention to this upward blip and suggested

---

[13] Except in some Asian countries. This phenomenon has been called one of 'missing women' (Sen, 1990), indicating deep gender inequalities in Asian societies.

that this could be due to sex-selective migration (males moving out); but this was not investigated further.[14]

Normally, child sex ratios globally are around 950.[15] While more boys than girls are born (because, it has been argued, females usually have a greater chance of survival) this ratio tends to improve in favour of girls (John et al., 2008). In Palanpur, the female–male ratio among children under six years of age shows a lot of fluctuation, and this might be because of the small size of the village.

Drèze and Sharma (1998: 51), based on earlier surveys in Palanpur, mention that 'age-specific female–male ratios strongly suggest that child mortality rates are much higher among girls than among boys, a common pattern for this region'. Watine's (2008) analysis for Palanpur shows that 220 out of 268 females born between 1993 and 2008 survived (i.e. 82.1 per cent), whereas in the case of males, 214 of 244 born survived (i.e. 87.7 per cent). Pierre (2011), based on her study of Palanpur data, finds that although the difference between male and female IMRs is not statistically significant, there are other indications of son preference and better medical treatment for boys. The gap between pregnancies is smaller if the older child is a girl, girls are less likely than boys to be taken to a private health centre in case of fever or animal bites, and girls are less likely to be taken to the *anganwadi* centre compared to boys.[16]

In some parts of India, there appears to be a declining female to male ratio at birth, associated it seems with the increasing practice of sex-selective abortions.[17] In Palanpur, we did not hear of the existence of such a practice or any case where this was done.[18]

---

[14] The decline in sex ratio in 1993 appears to be an outlier since the trend is towards an increasing female–male ratio over the survey years. This could probably be due to measurement error, since the 1993 data was collected using a short schedule for shorter duration. However, we do note, as seen from Table 7.15 in Chapter 7, that the rate of migration after 1983 has increased sharply, with migration rate of males being higher than females.

[15] The child sex ratio in India according to the 1991 census was 945, which fell to 927 in 2001 and a further low of 914 in 2011. According to Census 2011, the child sex ratio in Moradabad is 903, and overall sex ratio is 909.

[16] Most women, while discussing fertility preferences, said that they would like to have at least one boy. An extreme example is of Devki Nandan and Ombati, a Murao couple, who had six daughters when we conducted the survey in 2008. Ombati was then pregnant and she clearly stated that it was for a son that they were trying repeatedly. Their seventh child was also a girl.

[17] Census data has also shown that the areas where the child sex ratios have been worsening are in fact areas that are prosperous and also have shown improvements in female literacy. Another factor that is seen to be contributing to this phenomenon is the aggressive 'family planning' programme of the governments and the resultant two-child norm, leading to a situation where people do not want more than two children and at the same time want to make sure at least one of them is male (John et al., 2008). One does not yet witness the 'two-child norm' being so prevalent in Palanpur. Maybe this is also one of the reasons for the village not showing declining child sex ratios. At this stage, all of these are speculative explanations, and further analysis is required before a more definitive conclusion can be reached.

[18] Abortion is, of course, a highly sensitive issue and not something that we would expect to be easily told about. The survey did not include any direct questions on this. The female researchers also spent much less time in the village than the males, perhaps insufficient to develop the kind of

9.3.3 *Illness and Treatment*

In the 2008/10 survey, a special round was conducted on episodes of illness and health expenditure. There are no comparable data from the previous rounds, and with a small sample it is also difficult to make any generalizations. The percentage reporting ailments during the last 15 days (21 per cent) is much higher than the figures that are available for rural Uttar Pradesh (10 per cent) from the National Sample Survey (NSS). Although the questions asked were exactly the same as in the NSS, it is difficult to say whether this reflects truly higher morbidity in the village or whether it is a result of better reporting because of familiarity with the investigators.

Of the persons who reported any ailment in the last 15 days, 90 per cent sought treatment, and among those who sought treatment, 92 per cent went to a private source. In almost 60 per cent of these cases, the complaint was of fever. Other common issues were injuries, diarrhoea, and respiratory ailments. Five per cent of persons reported hospitalization in the last 365 days, of whom 86 per cent went to a private hospital. The median duration of stay was two days. Almost 10 per cent of the villagers had been bitten by an animal in one year preceding the survey. Most of these were monkey bites, followed by dog bites.[19] There were three persons suffering from tuberculosis during the survey (2008/10).

In 2008/10, 99 per cent of all children under six had received at least one dose of polio drops, but only 38 per cent had received at least one dose of DPT vaccine (they are supposed to get three).[20] Less than 40 per cent of the children had immunization cards. On childbirth, over 90 per cent of the women delivered at home in 2008/10. While we do not have exact data for the previous years, based on the survey in 1984, Drèze and Sharma (1998: 53–4) wrote, 'Family planning practices are quite limited in Palanpur leading to high fertility rates and short birth spacing...A delivery almost invariably takes place at home with the help of a local *dai* (midwife) with no formal training...No publicly-provided maternal health services are conveniently available.' The survey in 2015 collected data on the number of births since 2008 and the place of delivery. A total of 67 per cent of the births post-2008 took place at home, showing a shift towards medical institutions.

---

rapport for such sensitive information to be shared. However, even in the time spent in the village such a rapport was established with some of the women in the village. From conversations with these women, the impression was that access to ultrasound was still very low for women in the village compared to other areas. Access to any kind of antenatal care is also very low. So it is quite unlikely that sex-selective abortion is rampant. The only instance of abortion that was shared was the case of a woman who decided to abort her child as this was her sixth pregnancy and she felt that she and her husband were too poor to afford another child. She secretly had an abortion, not even informing her husband. In this case, the foetus was a male.

[19] In 2008/10 the village had a serious monkey problem which was later resolved by complaints to and action by the forest department.

[20] Diphtheria, pertussis (whooping cough), and tetanus.

With the appointment of an ASHA (Accredited Social Health Activist) in the village in 2009 and the introduction of a monetary incentive by the government for institutional deliveries (Janani Suraksha Yojana), there was an increase in people accessing institutions for delivery. A further reason could be the non- availability of midwifery services in the village. Midwifery as a skill is not being passed on to younger generations any more. During the 2008/10 survey there was only one midwife in the village. Her daughters-in-law had not learnt the skill from her and were not interested in taking on this role. This woman was also not being approached by all the households during the survey period, as there was a political mobilization in the village against her son, who was the Pradhan, the head of the village council,[21] and so people who were vocally against him did not trust her to provide proper care. Some women said that they would not have gone to an institution had there been another midwife in the village.

For primary health care, residents of Palanpur went mostly to (unqualified) medical practitioners in the village. There were two such practitioners (one lives in Palanpur and the other comes from the neighbouring village of Pipli); neither had received any formal training. They prescribed a range of medicines from painkillers to antibiotics, and in their 'clinics' they maintained a stock of most common medicines. There were also others offering services in the village who did not have 'clinics' but were called 'doctor'; they prescribed medicines for common illnesses. For further consultations, villagers went to the government hospital in Chandausi (13 km) or private clinics in Bilari (8 km). However, government hospitals are often considered as not accessible or not available (with absentee doctors and long waiting times). Most of the sick persons go to private hospitals, either in Chandausi or Moradabad. For certain illnesses people also approach traditional medicine (Ayurveda/Vaidya/Hakim) practitioners.

An auxiliary nurse midwife (ANM) is supposed to visit the village twice a month to provide maternal child health services and some primary health care. During 2008/10 she usually came only once a month as part of the Pulse Polio campaign. At other times, even if she came to the village, people complained that they were not informed of her visits.

There is an *anganwadi* centre in the village for meeting the health, nutrition, and education needs of children under six years of age (childcare centre of the government ICDS programme[22]). The *anganwadi* worker and helper were

---

[21] See Chapter 11 for details.

[22] The ICDS scheme has the following objectives: (i) to improve the nutritional and health status of children in the zero to six age group; (ii) to lay the foundation for proper psychological, physical, and social development of the child; (iii) to reduce the incidence of mortality, morbidity, malnutrition, and school dropout; (iv) to achieve effective coordination of policy and implementation amongst the various departments to promote child development; and (v) to enhance the capability of the mother to look after the normal health and nutritional needs of the child through proper nutrition and health education. These objectives are sought to be achieved through a package of services comprising:

sisters and had been working there for over twenty years. They may have been appointed because at that time they were the only ones in the village with a high school education. The *anganwadi* centre functioned even more poorly than the school. It did not have a building of its own and mainly operated out of the school. The *anganwadi* worker was sometimes seen taking classes for the older children enrolled in the school.

In 2009, only about 9 per cent of the eligible women said that their children had ever been given any supplementary nutrition from the *anganwadi* centre, and less than 5 per cent reported their children having ever been weighed. The situation earlier was similar: 'None of the six services (of ICDS) mentioned [in footnote 22]... are actually supplied at the anganwadi except sporadic doses of nutritional support. In 1993, many Palanpur residents were not even aware of the fact that an anganwadi has been set up in one of the Kayasth homes' (Drèze and Sharma, 1998: 189). The *anganwadi* worker also complained of irregular supply and poor quality of materials, as well as a lack of support from higher authorities.

A few months after the completion of the 2008/10 survey, a Primary Health Centre (PHC) was opened in a nearby village (Akrauli, 3 km away). While this PHC had excellent infrastructure in terms of the building and the space, later visits showed that it was understaffed (only one Ayurvedic doctor, one laboratory technician, and one pharmacist) and had limited supplies: the operation theatre and labour room had neither staff nor furniture. Overall, the health services available for people of Palanpur are very poor.

9.3.4 Health Expenditure

The quality of services is low and the burden of health expenditure on people in the village is high. The expenditure on treatment was much higher when people went to private facilities (which cost an average of Rs 6259 per hospitalization case, see Table 9.10) compared to public facilities (Rs 839). However, people preferred private care, with most saying that they did so because they were not satisfied with the quality of care in a government hospital (72 per cent). The other reasons given were that the health centre was too far away and that there was a long waiting period before getting any care (Pierre, 2011). The survey in 1983/4 also found that public facilities, however, are rarely used by Palanpur residents. The main reasons for this seem to be that they have little faith in the

(i) supplementary nutrition; (ii) immunization; (iii) health check-ups; (iv) referral services; (v) pre-school non-formal education; and (vi) nutrition and health education. These services are provided through an *anganwadi* centre (each centre has an *anganwadi* worker and helper). Based on Supreme Court orders, the ICDS is a universal scheme, with *anganwadi* centres in every village and open to all children under six. For further details on the ICDS scheme see http://wcd.nic.in http://www.righttofoodcampaign.in/

quality of the services provided. They resent the brusque behaviour of the health staff and expect to be asked to pay for services that are supposed to be free (Drèze and Sharma, 1998: 189–90).

The survey on health expenditures in 2009 showed that the share of out-of-pocket expenditure to total consumption expenditure in Palanpur is 5.9 per cent, which is slightly higher than the share for all India (5.1 per cent according to NSS 2004/5). Further analysis showed that while the rich spent, in absolute terms, a higher amount on health care, the burden was higher amongst the poor, as the rich spend a smaller share of their non-food expenditure on health than the poor.[23] It was also the case that, for similar kinds of illnesses, the better off were more likely to go outside the village for treatment than those who were poorer. The poorest households depended most on borrowings to finance health expenditure, while those who were richer were able to dig into their savings or use their current income to finance episodes of hospitalization (see Table 9.11).

Table 9.10 Illness and access to treatment in Palanpur, 2009

Outpatient Care		Inpatient Care	
% persons reporting any ailment during the last 15 days	21	% persons hospitalized during the last 365 days	5
% with ailment accessed some treatment	90	**Source of treatment**	
Source of treatment		Government	13.8%
Government	8%	Private	86.2%
Private	92%	Average expenditure (government)	Rs 835
Average expenditure per treatment	Rs 231	Average expenditure (private)	Rs 6295

Table 9.11 Source of finance for inpatient expenditures in the last 365 days

Quintiles (from consumption survey)	Primary Source of Financing Quintiles (%) of Households			
	savings/income	borrowings	from relatives	other
Poorest 20%	45	45	10	0
2nd poorest 20%	42	25	8	25
Middle	57	29	0	14
2nd richest 20%	75	25	0	0
Richest 20%	72	14	7	7

[23] For detailed data and analysis, see the internship report of Pierre (2011) based on Palanpur health expenditure data.

9.4 Nutrition

9.4.1 *Data*

The heights and weights of all the residents of Palanpur who were available and willing were taken during a period of one week in November 2009. While this is very valuable information, there are issues of sample size and quality of data that need to be mentioned. Heights and weights of 1127 persons (out of 1265 residents of Palanpur) were collected. In this chapter, we use the data related to children under five years of age and adults over twenty. The first group was chosen because that is the standard age group used to study child malnutrition, with anthropometric norms given by the World Health Organization (WHO). The second group was chosen as the analysis on adult nutrition status based on data from the 1983/4 survey included those above twenty (Kynch, 1998). In Palanpur in 2009, there were 170 children under five years of age and 645 adults above twenty. Among the 645 adults of the relevant age group, measurements for 562 persons were taken during the survey.[24] Among the 170 children under five, heights and weights were measured for 166 children. However, in this chapter we use only the data for 134 children for whom we had all other relevant information, including date of birth (at least month and year) and their mother's characteristics (i.e. those whose mothers were interviewed in the 'women's round').[25]

There were two other problems with using the child anthropometry data. First, it is important to know the exact date of birth for children to be able to estimate the standard anthropometric measures such as height-for-age and weight-for-age. As has been the experience with most studies involved in collecting the dates of birth in rural India, in Palanpur, too, it was only in very rare cases that parents could recall the exact date of birth of children. A lot of time was spent in trying to arrive at the precise month and year of birth using local events and festivals as reference points. The data were also then triangulated with the information that the *anganwadi* worker had. However, since the ICDS is almost non-functional in the village, she did not have records for many children.

---

[24] The remaining persons were not included as they were either not available or not willing to participate. They included 48 females and 35 males. Of the 562 whose measurements are available, the data for 4 persons has not been used in the analysis because of errors.

[25] Further, those whose anthropometric indicators were outliers were removed. According to the WHO norms (WHO, 2006), children having a weight/height for age z-score that is more than −2 standard deviations (SD) away from the mean of the international reference population are considered to be undernourished. Further, weight/height for age and weight-for-height/length z-scores that are less than -6SD or greater than 6SD compared to the reference population are usually not included on grounds of biological implausibility (as defined by the WHO norms). These could be because of measurement errors; therefore, they have been removed.

Second, the entire exercise of collecting heights and weights of young children was quite tedious and raised some doubts in our minds on how accurate our measurements were. Most children would cry and refuse to stand/sit still even for the few seconds required to get their weights and heights recorded. Some adults also did not see a point in this exercise and therefore were not very encouraging. Many adults were, however, more interested in having their own weights measured, and so were older children. While we were wary before starting the measurements because we were told by some that people in this area believed that weighing children would attract 'the evil eye', and that we should expect a lot of resistance from the parents and especially grandparents, this was not the case. The actual problem was that it was difficult to find flat surfaces on which to place the weighing machines and then to get the children to cooperate. So, while sitting in the little basket for weighing, children would constantly move, and while getting their heights measured, would not stand up straight. We did our best to get the most accurate measurements, given the obstacles, and have used only the data that we felt confident about. It is hard to judge whether our problems were worse or better than 'normal' for this kind of exercise.

While these limitations to the data must be kept in mind, it is also important to note that the results we get are not wildly dissimilar to the measures from secondary sources for the district and the state. And on the whole, we believe we may have applied tougher standards, closer checking, and more care in general for data collection across the board in Palanpur than for many other studies and surveys. Therefore, we suggest they can be used to derive at least some broad conclusions on the status of nutrition among children in Palanpur and the factors which might be affecting it.

The village survey in 1983/4 also measured heights and weights, providing some degree of comparison over time. However, the 1983/4 nutrition survey was restricted only to a sample of cultivator households and therefore is not strictly comparable to the present data. The nutrition survey in 1984 covered 239 persons in the 36 sample households. The Body Mass Index (BMI) was calculated for all adults,[26] and measures for stunting (height-for-age) and underweight (weight-for-age) for children. Whilst we will make the best use we can of earlier data on nutrition it is, nevertheless, very limited. In spite of the data gaps, what emerges from both rounds of survey is that the levels of malnutrition in Palanpur are high. While there might have been some improvement over the last 25 years, the 2008–10 data show that levels of

---

[26] BMI is a simple index of weight-for-height that is commonly used to classify adults as underweight, overweight, or obese. It is defined as the weight in one kilogram divided by the square of the height in metres (kg/m^2). BMI values are age independent and the same for both sexes.

malnutrition among children are still high. This is also true for rural Uttar Pradesh in general.

9.4.2 Malnutrition in 2009

The figures for malnutrition that we get for Palanpur from our survey in 2009 are presented in Table 9.12. According to this, 58.2 per cent of children under five years of age are underweight, and 68.6 per cent of them are stunted.[27] Further, about half the adults (51.5 per cent men and 48.7 per cent women) have a BMI less than 18.5, which is considered to be 'normal'. Based on these data, the situation in Palanpur is worse for both adults and children than the all-India (rural) and Uttar Pradesh (rural) averages; a higher percentage of children are stunted and underweight, and a higher percentage of adults have a low BMI. Further, the difference in stunting and underweight prevalence among girls and boys in Palanpur is striking and much larger than the gap between girls and boys seen in all India (rural) and Uttar Pradesh (rural). The malnutrition level for girls is much higher in Palanpur than in rural India or rural UP. Such a gap is not seen in the case of adult BMIs. However, as will be seen in Section 9.4.3, this probably has a lot to do with the small sample size for Palanpur and may be a reflection of other confounding factors, such as the socioeconomic status of the family.[28]

Table 9.12 Malnutrition in India, Uttar Pradesh, and Palanpur

	India*	Uttar Pradesh*	Moradabad**	Palanpur (2009)[#]
% children underweight	45.6	44.1	72.7	58.2
			(56)	
% girls underweight	41.9	43.7	(54.1)	63.4
% boys underweight	43.1	41.2	(56.4)	52.4
% rural children stunted	50.7	58.4	N/A	68.6
% girls stunted	48	57.5	N/A	71.8
% boys stunted	48.1	56.2	N/A	65.1
% rural men with BMI less than 18.5	38.4	41.5	N/A	51.6
% rural women with BMI less than 18.5	40.6	38.9	N/A	48.7

*Source: NFHS-3 (IIPS, 2007). (The data for all India are from the India report of NFHS-3 and the data for Uttar Pradesh are from the UP-state report of NFHS-3); the data related to children are for children under five years of age (0–59 months).
**Source: DLHS 2002–04 (IIPS, 2006; average for UP is 55.3). Figures in brackets in the column are the average figures for UP from the DLHS report.
Data from the Palanpur village survey. Data collected in November 2009. The data related to children are for children under five years. The data related to adults are for all adults above twenty.

[27] 'Underweight' is low weight-for-age, and 'stunted' is low height-for-age. Both are defined as those whose height/weight lie more than two z-scores away from the mean when compared with the WHO reference population. These are the standard definitions used by WHO as well as the Government of India.
[28] This is based on data related to 71 girls and 63 boys.

9.4.3 *Adult Malnutrition in 2009 Compared with 1984*

Based on 'the International Classification of adult underweight, overweight and obesity according to BMI' given by the WHO, those with a BMI of less than 18.5 are considered underweight. Among underweight populations, those with BMI less than 16 are classified as having severe thinness, BMI between 16 to 16.99 moderate thinness, and BMI between 17 and 18.49 as mild thinness (WHO, 2011). The 1984 data are for 101 adults above twenty from a few sample households, while the 2009 data are for 541 adults above twenty from all households. In Table 9.13 we see that the percentage of adults who have a BMI of less than the cut-off has fallen over the last 25 years. However, while there was an improvement among men, there has been a slight increase in below-normal BMI among women (47.2 per cent in 1984 and 48.7 per cent in 2009). Nevertheless, the earlier observation of more adult men having a below-normal BMI than adult women continues to hold with this round of survey as well. Using the current internationally accepted cut-off for underweight of 18.5, male undernutrition is higher than female undernutrition, with 51.6 per cent of men and 48.7 per cent of women having a BMI of less than 18.5. The figure for malnutrition for men in 1984 looks implausibly high and may be due to sampling or measurement problems.

As we do not have further information on diets, work patterns, and health status, it is difficult to draw conclusions on possible causes and implications. What can be said overall from these data on adult BMIs is that there seems to be an improvement in male nutritional status since 1984 (especially at lower cut-offs), while at the same time it needs to be said that the number of persons who have a below-normal BMI is still very high.

Table 9.13 BMI for adults*: comparison with data from previous survey in Palanpur

Cut-off[a]	Men		Women[^]		Total Adults	
	1984[#]	2009[**]	1984[#]	2009[**]	1984[#]	2009[**]
WHO current cut-off for underweight adults: 18.5	87.5	51.6	47.2	48.7	66.3	50.2
Total N	48	273	53	268	101	541

Note: *Adults defined as all those above twenty years of age; [#] based on data collected during the 1983/4 Palanpur village survey (Kynch, 1998). **Data from the Palanpur village survey. Data collected in November 2009. The data related to adults is for all adults above twenty in the sample households.[29] ^ 'Women' include pregnant and lactating women—the cut-off points may be too low for such women.

[29] Following FAO (2010)/WHO (2011), 'cut-off' refers to the lower limit of *normal* adult BMI.

369

9.4.4 Child Malnutrition in Palanpur: Caste and Education

As noted, for young children anthropometric indicators in relation to age are considered more reliable as reflections of nutrition status than for adults. As seen in Section 9.4.3, the child malnutrition levels (using reference height and weight as given in WHO (2006)) in Palanpur are higher than available data for Uttar Pradesh as a whole. This is not entirely surprising, as in many other social indicators as well, Palanpur seems to be worse off than the UP average. Furthermore, direct observation does suggest that many children in Palanpur appear to be less healthy than elsewhere in the district. General levels of hygiene are low. Although there are not many visibly severely malnourished children in the village, many children look undernourished and/or have skin infections, running noses, and so on.

Looking at the breakdown of child nutrition status by caste, we find that Thakurs (upper caste) and 'Others' in general have lower levels of underweight and stunting than the rest of the castes (see Table 9.14).[30] The highest number of malnourished children can be found among the Jatabs (who belong to the scheduled castes (SC)). What is surprising, however, is that the level of malnutrition among the Muraos (a land-owning agricultural caste) is also quite high, almost similar to that among the Jatabs, although economically they are probably closer to the Thakurs. However, the causes for malnutrition in Palanpur include not just economic status but also childcare practices, the mother's education, and so on. What needs to be examined is whether there is something specific among Muraos, in terms of their childcare practices and so on, that makes children in these households more malnourished. At the same time, with the small sample size and measurements at one point of time, there should be caution concerning the conclusions that can be drawn.

Table 9.14 Child malnutrition in Palanpur: by caste (2008/10)

Caste Group	Underweight		Stunted	
	N	%	N	%
Thakur	17	53.1	20	62.5
Murao	22	62.9	25	71.4
Jatab	20	69	21	72.4
Muslims	11	52.4	16	76.2
Others	8	47.1	10	58.8
Total	78	58.2	92	68.6

[30] For details on different caste groups in Palanpur see Lanjouw and Stern (1998).

Table 9.15 Child malnutrition in Palanpur: by sex and mother's literacy status

	Underweight		Stunted	
	N	%	N	%
Sex of the child				
Female	45	63.4	51	71.8
Male	33	52.4	41	65.1
Total	78	58.2	92	68.7
Mother's literacy status				
Illiterate	67	58.8	82	71.9
Can read/read & write	11	55	10	50
Total	78	58.2	92	68.7

There is a large difference in malnutrition levels between male and female children, with 63.4 per cent of female children being underweight compared to 52.4 per cent of male children (Table 9.15). Further, it should be noted that while National Family Health Survey (NFHS) data for the entire state of Uttar Pradesh also shows that female underweight children are more common than male underweight, the difference between the two is not very wide. Given that our sample is quite small and the measurement is at one point of time, we must be cautious about the extent of gender discrimination reflected in the gap. We note, however, that such a gap was also noticed in the survey conducted in 1984. The previous round of survey found that 'a significantly higher percentage of girls than boys were severely malnourished, by the weight-for-age criterion' (Kynch, 1998: 428).

Also, as seen in many other studies,[31] in Palanpur there are more malnourished children among those born to illiterate mothers than to those who can read or read and write. The difference is starker in the case of stunting (see Table 9.15), which is a stronger indicator of chronic undernutrition than being underweight. However, there are very few literate mothers in Palanpur, and caution is necessary in interpreting the results, as well.

9.4.5 Childcare Practices

An immediate factor that could be considered to be affecting child's nutrition status is whether appropriate childcare practices are being followed or not. Important among these are early and exclusive breastfeeding and timely introduction of complementary feeding. In these aspects it is also seen that

---

[31] For example see Mishra and Retherford (2000), Moestue and Hutley (2008), and Miller and Rodgers (2009). The author's own calculations using NFHS data for all Indian states and controlling for other socioeconomic factors of the family also confirms this positive relationship between a mother's education and child nutrition.

Table 9.16 Child malnutrition in Palanpur: childcare practices

Childcare and Feeding	%
% children given (human) colostrum	10
% start complementary feeding (solid/semi-solid) by 7th month	15
% children/women who got no benefit from ICDS	87

Note: The first breast milk (colostrum) is highly nutritious and has antibodies that protect the newborn from diseases. Late initiation of breastfeeding not only deprives the child of valuable colostrum, but becomes a reason for the introduction of pre-lacteal feeds (that is, something other than breast milk) like glucose water, honey, *ghutti*, animal milk, or powdered milk that are potentially harmful and contribute to diarrhoea in the newborn (IIPS, 2007). This also triggers a cycle of malnutrition and infection.

Palanpur performs poorly. Only 10 per cent of the women said that they gave their babies colostrum milk (Table 9.16), and only about 15 per cent reported timely introduction of complementary feeding. It is believed locally that colostrum feeding is harmful to the babies, and therefore it is squeezed out before feeding the baby. Further, it is also believed that the mother does not produce enough milk initially, and therefore most children who are breastfed are, for the first couple of days, given pre-lacteals such as sugar-water and *ghutti*.[32] Data from the NFHS shows that in Uttar Pradesh 96 per cent children are given pre-lacteals (IIPS, 2007).

Further, from observation in Palanpur, one saw that young children were rarely given appropriate food when solids were introduced. This was because of the lack of both resources and awareness. In general, diets in Palanpur are poor in variety, with most eating only 'roti' (a wheat flatbread) and 'vegetables' (in insufficient quantity). The ICDS scheme, which is supposed to provide supplementary nutrition for young children and counsel mothers on these issues, is non-functioning. Of all the women with young children, only about 13 per cent said that they ever received any service, including supplementary nutrition, from the ICDS. For Uttar Pradesh, as a whole, NFHS reports that only 22.3 per cent of all children under six receive any services from the ICDS (IIPS, 2007).

The two most significant immediate causes of malnutrition are inadequate dietary intake and illness, and these tend to create a vicious cycle a malnourished child, whose resistance to illness is compromised, falls ill, and malnourishment worsens. Children who enter this malnutrition–infection cycle can quickly fall into a potentially fatal spiral as one condition feeds off the other. Malnutrition lowers the body's ability to resist infection by undermining the functioning of the main immune-response mechanisms. This leads to longer, more severe, and more frequent episodes of illness. Infections cause loss of appetite,

---

[32] Something like gripe water, made using local herbs.

malabsorption, and metabolic and behavioural changes. These, in turn, increase the body's requirements for nutrients, which further affects young children's eating patterns and how they are cared for (UNICEF, 1998).

Lack of hygiene, sanitation, and clean drinking water leads to infections, which in turn contribute to malnutrition. Although not much systematic data are available, from observation it can be said that Palanpur performs poorly in these aspects. Of the 217 households in Palanpur in 2009, only 19 households had a toilet with a septic tank/flush system, 5 households used a covered drainage system,[33] and all the households use drinking water from handpumps. As seen in Chapter 2, after 2009, a number of toilets were constructed in the village, with 57 households having toilets according to the 2015 survey.[34]

9.4.6 Diets

A related issue which has an impact on health and nutrition is the diet of people in the village. Indian diets have generally been observed to be poor in protein and fat intake, with the diets being largely cereal-based.[35] Apart from low intake of protein, Indian households have been observed to consume lower than the required amount of lipids or fats (Dorin, 1999). The agricultural practices and incomes of the households also affect these diets. In Palanpur, we observe that consumption baskets are biased towards carbohydrates and are low in fat content—a feature similar to the rest of India. Most meals consist of either chapatis (made of wheat) or rice with some vegetables (usually potatoes). On some days, there would also be some dal (pulses). For a few months in a year, post-harvest, some households shifted to *bajra* as the main staple, if they cultivated it. The pulse consumption was also largely from own cultivation.[36] For the major land-owning castes, a larger proportion of nutrients come from own production. The landless or non-cultivator castes have very low proportion of nutrients from home-grown stock. The total fat, protein, and calorie consumption of these castes is also lower than other major castes. As seen in Table 9.17, carbohydrates make up over 70 per cent of the average diet in Palanpur.

---

[33] There is no underground drainage facility in the village.

[34] It should be noted, however, that there is a difference between having a toilet and using that toilet, see Figure 2.4, Chapter 2.

[35] The dietary guidelines for Indians of the National Institute of Nutrition (NIN, 2011) state that, 'A balanced diet should provide around 50–60% of total calories from carbohydrates, preferably from complex carbohydrates, about 10–15% from proteins and 20–30% from both visible and invisible fat.'

[36] Diets have clearly not changed very much since the mid-1980s. Commenting on their diets in 1984, Jean Drèze wrote, "No doubt hardship is on the increase in the village at this time. People manage to eat; but what they eat is another matter, and untreated sickness is another frequent drama.'—Jean Drèze, Diary, vol. 22, Palanpur, 2 September 1984, p. 70.

Table 9.17 Balance of nutrients in Palanpur diets, 2009

Caste Group	% of Average Total Calories from:		
	Carbohydrate	Protein	Fat
Thakur	70.1	11.2	18.7
Murao	72.8	11	16.2
Jatab	75	11.5	13.5
Muslim	73	11.7	15.3
Overall	72.3	11.2	16.5
Recommended	50–60	10–15	20–30

Note: Recommended levels as per WHO (2007).

Table 9.18 Contribution of own production to calories and protein intake, 1958 and 2009

	Calories (1958) (kcal per day)		Calories (2009) (kcal per day)		Protein (1958) (gms per day)		Protein (2009) (gms per day)	
	Total	% non-market	Total	% non-market	Total	% non-market	Total	% non-market
Thakur	2797	77.2	2633	59.6	84	94	74	68.9
Murao	2560	89.2	2588	72	79	96.2	72	80.6
Muslims	2123	81.5	2511	48.2	72	86.1	74	51.4
Jatab	2329	82.7	2393	47.3	78	88.5	68	55.9
Overall	2277	75.6	2478	56.7	73	83.6	70	64.3

Note: 'non-market' includes consumption from own production and PDS.

Calorie consumption data can be estimated from the consumption expenditure data that are available for 1958 and 2009. As seen in Table 9.18, per capita calorie consumption on average has increased in the village from 2277 kcal to 2478 kcal per day in the 50-year period from 1958. In both years, and for proteins as well as calories, Thakurs have had the highest consumption. Jatabs consumed the lowest calories in 2009, while the Muslims' calorie consumption was even lower than Jatabs in 1958. The only caste group which has seen a decline in calorie consumption is the Thakurs, which can be explained at least partially by declining need (as people move on to less strenuous jobs). On the other hand, in the case of protein consumption, all caste groups have seen a decline (except Muslims,[37] who also show a higher increase in calorie consumption).

Compared to 1958, the contribution of non-market sources to calorie and protein consumption has declined significantly for all caste groups. In terms

[37] As a group, Muslims in the village, as of 2009, have the highest average per capita income and they are also the group that has seen the greatest increase. Their self-employment income has risen strikingly through their entrepreneurial activities. See Chapter 2.

of ranking, Muraos had the highest proportion of their consumption coming from non-market sources in both the years, which is a reflection of their close involvement in agriculture. The increased dependence on markets for proteins is also an outcome of declining availability of common pastures and resultant reduction in livestock ownership.[38]

Over the decades, as occupation has diversified and the economy has monetized, the consumption basket has shifted towards more food purchased from shops, which is often less nutritionally rich than what was traditionally consumed. Nevertheless, consumption remains predominantly from non-market services. Thus, production matters. Earlier households used to produce coarse grains, pulses, and dairy products only for consumption. Over the past half-century, with input intensification—irrigation, fertilizer, tractor usage, and so on—the production system has shifted towards a culture of predominantly wheat in winter and rice in summer. Amongst crops purely for cash, earlier it was predominantly sugarcane and later mentha.[39] Livestock production has also been limited to dairy, with a decline in meat and fish production. The decline in consumption of livestock products may also be due to the increase in prices.

9.5 Conclusion

Much like the rest of Uttar Pradesh, Palanpur has experienced some improvements in human development outcomes during this period. There have been improvements in literacy rates since the late 1990s, although they remain much lower than in rest of the state and country. Health outcomes show slow progress. Malnutrition remains a concern, and diets are poor. Public services are inadequate and in some cases showing decline.[40]

While human development in Palanpur is showing some improvements, inequities on the basis of income, caste, and gender remain. Jatabs still lag far behind compared to Thakurs when it comes to education. Although gender gaps in literacy rates appear to be closing, they are still high. Health expenditures pose a higher burden on the poor. Food consumption is still better amongst Thakurs compared to the rest. Malnutrition is higher amongst girls. There is some evidence also of discrimination in accessing health facilities, with boys more likely to be taken to higher health facilities for the same kind of illness than girls. While better health and education could contribute

---

[38] The number of goats, pigs, and chickens in the village currently is very low. See Chapter 4.
[39] On the increasing share of cash crops at the cost of food production in Palanpur, see Chapter 5.
[40] See also Chapters 2 and 11 for a discussion of public services.

favourably to employment opportunities and overall living standards in the future, the role they could play in perpetuating inequalities remains an issue. There are also important inequalities in access to services. With public services generally failing, there is an increased dependence on the private sector, access to which depends on ability to pay. While there have been increases in investments in education and health by central and state governments through various programmes, they are mainly reflected in better buildings and infrastructure, but not quality of services. There are large gaps in the functioning of public services. Both schools and health centres are under-staffed, absenteeism of staff is a huge problem, and the quality of services is largely poor. In Palanpur, as in Uttar Pradesh, there has been barely any public protest against such poor services although people individually express dissatisfaction over the state of affairs.

Inadequate services for education and health in the village have until now failed to become important public concerns for Palanpur's residents. People who are able to afford them use private services to overcome the lack of public facilities. As a result, they appear to place lower value on the improvement of village public services. Those who depend on public services are poorer socio-economic groups and are unable to mobilize efforts to seek improvements. They also aspire to move to the private sector as soon as they are able to afford it. This observation on the poor state of public services and also the absence of collective action in the village has been discussed in previous work on Palanpur. It was argued that the limited reach of collective action in Palanpur is responsible for some of the failures of its development experience (Sinha et al., 2016). The highly fragmented nature of the village society offers few rallying points for collective action. We return to some of these arguments in Chapter 11, on society and politics.

Acknowledgements

This chapter has been written by Dipa Sinha and Ruchira Bhattacharya. It draws upon Sinha (2011) and Sinha and colleagues (2016), and has benefited from contributions by Ruth Kattumuri, Gajanand Ahirwal, and Dinesh Tiwari.

References

Bliss, C.J., and Stern, N. 1982. *Palanpur: The Economy of an Indian Village*. Oxford and New York: Oxford University Press.

DISE (District Information System for Education). 2011. 'U-DISE Unified District Information System for Education', http://udise.in/ (accessed 19 March 2018).

Dorin, B. 1999. 'Food policy and nutritional security: the unequal access to lipids in India', *Economic & Political Weekly* 34, no. 26: 1709–17.

Drèze, J., and Sen, A. 2013. *An Uncertain Glory: India and its Contradictions*. London: Penguin.

Drèze, J., Lanjouw, P., and Sharma, N. 1998. 'Economic Development in Palanpur, 1957–93', in P. Lanjouw and N. Stern (eds), *Economic Development in Palanpur over Five Decades*. New York and Oxford: Clarendon Press.

FAO (Food and Agriculture Organization). 2010. 'Fats and fatty acids in human nutrition: report of an expert consultation', FAO Food and Nutrition Paper No. 91, http://foris.fao.org/preview/25553-0ece4cb94ac52f9a25af77ca5cfba7a8c.pdf (accessed 19 March 2018).

Harriss, B., Gillespie, S., and Pryer, J. 1990. 'Poverty and malnutrition at extremes of south Asian food systems', *Economic & Political Weekly* 25, no. 51 (22 December): 2783–99.

IIPS (International Institute for Population Sciences). 2006. 'District Level Household Survey (DLHS-2), 2002–04', Mumbai, India.

IIPS (International Institute for Population Sciences). 2007. 'National Family Health Survey (NFHS-3), 2005–06', Mumbai, India.

John, M.E., Kaur, R., Palriwala, R., Raju, S., and Sagar, A. 2008. *Planning Families, Planning Gender: The Adverse Child Sex Ratio in Selected Districts of Madhya Pradesh, Rajasthan, Himachal Pradesh, Haryana, and Punjab*. New Delhi: ActionAid and Canada's International Development Research Centre (IDRC).

Kynch, J. 1998. 'Nutrition', in P. Lanjouw and N.H. Stern (eds), *Economic Development in Palanpur over Five Decades*. New Delhi and Oxford: Oxford University Press.

Lanjouw, P., and Stern, N.H. (eds). 1998. *Economic Development in Palanpur over Five Decades*. New Delhi and Oxford: Oxford University Press.

Miller, J.E., and Rodgers, Y.V. 2009. 'Mother's education and children's nutritional status: new evidence from Cambodia', *Asian Development Review* 26, no. 1: 131–65.

Mishra, V., and Retherford, R.D. 2000. 'Women's education can improve child nutrition in India'. NFHS Bulletin No. 15.

Moestue, H., and Hutley, S. 2008. 'Adult education and child nutrition: the role of family and community', *Journal of Epidemiology and Community Health* 62: 153–9.

NIN (National Institute of Nutrition). 2011 'Dietary guidelines for Indians: a manual'. National Institute of Nutrition, Indian Council for Medical Research, Hyderabad.

Pierre, V. 2011. 'Health inequalities in Palanpur'. Master's dissertation, Department of Quantitative Economics and Finance, École Polytechnique, France.

Sen, A.K. 1990. 'More than 100 million women are missing', *New York Review of Books*, 20 December, http://www.nybooks.com/articles/1990/12/20/more-than-100-million-women-are-missing/ (accessed 19 March 2018).

Shetty, P.S. 1984. 'Adaptive changes in basal metabolic rate and lean body mass in chronic undernutrition', *Human Nutrition: Clinical Nutrition* 38C: 443–51.

Sinha, D. 2011. 'Nutrition status in Palanpur', in 'India's economic "revolution": a perspective from six decades of economic development in Palanpur, a north Indian village'. Department for International Development Research Paper.

Sinha, D., Dinesh, T., Ruchira, B., and Ruth, K. 2016. 'Public services, social relations, politics and gender: tales from a north Indian village', in Himanshu, P. Jha, and

G. Rodgers (eds), *The Changing Village in India: Insights from Longitudinal Research*. New Delhi: Oxford University Press.

UNICEF (United Nations Children's Fund). 1998. *State of the World's Children*. New York: UNICEF.

Watine, L. 2008. 'Will we have another child?: Fertility behavior in rural areas of north India, an empirical study of the village of Palanpur'. Masters dissertation, Department of Quantitative Economics and Finance, École Polytechnique, France.

WHO (World Health Organization). 2006. 'WHO child growth standards: length/height-for-age, weight-for-age, weight-for-length, weight-for-height and body mass index-for-age: methods and development', Multicentre Growth Reference Study Group, Geneva, http://www.who.int/childgrowth/publications/en/ (accessed April 2011).

WHO (World Health Organization). 2007. 'Protein and amino acid requirements in human nutrition'. WHO Technical Report Series No. 935, http://apps.who.int/iris/bitstream/10665/43411/1/WHO_TRS_935_eng.pdf?ua=1 (accessed 20 March 2018).

WHO (World Health Organization). 2011. 'BMI classification', http://apps.who.int/bmi/index.jsp?introPage=intro_3.html (accessed April 2011).

10

Women

Possibilities and Constraints*

10.1 Women in a Changing Village

In the six decades since the first survey round in Palanpur (1957/8), the last decade or two have in many ways been the most significant in terms of changes in women's lives in the village. The burden of household work has fallen with the adoption of new technologies. For example, women who were involved in tasks involving hard, time-consuming physical labour, such as manual grinding of flour (*chakki*), now have some extra time after the introduction of flour mills. Most have a handpump within the household or nearby and no longer have to walk long distances to fetch water. Fertility rates have fallen, with women having fewer children and therefore spending less time pregnant or caring for children. With many households in possession of a television set and/or a mobile phone, there is greater access to information and to the 'outside world'. There is increasing participation of girls in education. The primary school in the village had a female teacher for some time, and most primary-school-aged girls are now in school. Many girls walk to nearby Akrauli to attend high school, and some of them even travel by train to attend college in Chandausi or Moradabad. School-going children, especially daughters, have new aspirations and expose their mothers to new ideas.[1]

Long-time visitors to the village have reported noticing more women outside their houses in Palanpur than earlier.[2] Many older women in the village talked about how they could not even sit down or speak if their fathers-in-law

---

* This chapter has been written by Dipa Sinha and Ruchira Bhattacharya.
[1] Where all married women used to wear a saree, now some of the younger daughters-in-law have moved on to a *salwar kameez*, while the younger unmarried girls can be seen in jeans.
[2] Observations by Sue Stern, who visited the village in the 1970s and 1980s and then again in 2002 and 2008. See Chapter 2.

were anywhere around. But now younger women, despite continuing to practise *purdah*, can sometimes give their opinion on household issues. The village in the last decade has for the first time also seen a couple, belonging to different castes, eloping. They got married and returned to the village. They were isolated for some time but have now been accepted by their families. There was another woman in Palanpur who had been widowed. She was living with her parents and fighting a legal battle with her husband's family for her share in his property.[3] She had the complete support of her parents. Thanks to reserved seats for women in *panchayat* elections, the village now has a female Pradhan. However, her position is largely nominal as she and her husband live outside the village, and a nephew in the village exercises authority.

These are all stories that demonstrate how much has changed in Palanpur. Much of this change was probably unthinkable, even in the early 1980s. Despite these changes, however, there remains much more that could be improved. Household and care work are still predominantly carried out by women. The drudgery of this work remains high. Women spend most of their time in domestic work—cooking, taking care of children, cleaning, and so on. Literacy is still at a low level, and barely any women work for pay. While there has been great change in other aspects of village life, including the economy (see earlier chapters) and politics (see Chapter 11), the pace of change in women's roles both in society and within the household is slow.

Initial visits to Palanpur by the new team of researchers in 2008 indicated that women's lives in the village had not changed much over the decades of the survey. There were still very few women seen out on the streets, *purdah* was still practised, very few worked outside the home for a wage, and so on. There is very little physical mobility, with most women confined to the boundaries of the household. Strict *purdah* is widely practised (especially amongst the upper castes), marriages are patrilocal and patrilineal, and dowry is the norm. Domestic violence is prevalent. Most families do not consider the village a safe place for young girls. Women are absent from decision-making roles in the village society; their issues rarely become public issues. Therefore, while there have been some significant changes in women's lives, it is also the case that, on most dimensions, women in Palanpur continue to be largely invisible in economic, social, and political life.

As seen in Chapter 9, in terms of education there has been an impressive change in the village since the late 1990s, for both men and women. The fertility rates are lower, and therefore women have more time to participate in economic activities. These changes might be expected to increase women's

---

[3] This woman's natal village is Palanpur, whereas her marital village is a slight distance away in the same district. While she went to live with her husband's family post-marriage, after his death she moved back to Palanpur.

participation in the workforce as well as their status both within the household and outside in the coming years. While movement on these fronts is still slow, we might see significant change in the role of women in the village in the next few decades. Women constitute almost half of Palanpur's population, and how the village grows and changes in the future is closely linked to the fate and role of women.

10.2 Data

Data on women's education and workforce participation are available for all the rounds, with differing levels of detail. Each survey round conducted a census of the village and collected some basic demographic data in relation to all members. While planning the latest survey (2008/10) in Palanpur, it was recognized from the beginning that a deeper understanding of the village required some more systematic data collection on women's lives.[4] Although fully comparable data were not collected in the earlier surveys, there is considerable qualitative information and anecdotal evidence related to women. Further, some information, such as on schooling/literacy, employment status,[5] marital status, and so on, is available from the household survey data. These data from earlier surveys are used to make some comparisons. Along with the general household information that was collected during the 2008/10 study period, this chapter uses data gathered from all ever-married women aged fifty or less based on a specific 'women' questionnaire. Information was collected on birth history, women's work outside home, autonomy, mobility, and domestic violence. Women with any children under six were also asked questions related to ante- and post-natal care, breastfeeding, child immunization, and participation in childcare services. Data on age, education, family structure, and so on were available from the household survey.

All the data related to the women questionnaire were collected by female researchers, and therefore there was a fair degree of comfort in sharing information. However, it must also be mentioned that it was difficult to talk to women alone as often other (female) family members would also be present. This was many times out of curiosity but also, in the case of younger and recently married women, there was almost always a 'chaperone' (usually the

---

[4] In earlier Palanpur studies, there were a few visits by women involved in the research programme to the village (including Sue Stern, Jenny Lanjouw, and Jocelyn Kynch) but no extended data collection by women. This placed limitations on the access of past researchers to hold discussions with women in the village.

[5] As mentioned in Drèze and Sharma (1998), there is a problem with employment data because this is mostly reported by men in the family who might undervalue a lot of the work done by women. This time around we also asked the women directly what work they did. Even this was not detailed enough to get a good estimate, but is definitely a step forward.

mother-in-law and sometimes a younger sister-in-law). This made it difficult to discuss 'sensitive' issues, especially those related to domestic violence, dowry, decision-making within the household, and so on. On the other hand, due to the extended time spent in the village, the researchers developed a good rapport with some women with whom more personal discussions took place. And even if there were other women present, older women (those with children) were quite open about discussing many issues. Small details about the social contexts in which the survey was administered make a large difference to the quality of data, as we have argued in Chapter 1. Time and rapport have been crucial in ensuring that the data we collect in Palanpur have been of the highest possible quality; this is of particular importance in relation to understanding the role of women in the village.

10.3 Fertility

Whilst we do not have the detailed birth data to estimate fertility rates, there is sufficient evidence to show that, on average, women are giving birth to fewer children over time. Two crude measures are presented here to help understand fertility trends in the village. First, the ratio of children under fifteen to adult women in the village shows a decline from 1.9 in 1975 and 1.7 in 1993 to 1.3 in 2015. The gross fertility rate (GFR) is another indicator used by demographers. GFR is the ratio of births in a year to the number of women of reproductive age. Since we do not have detailed data on births, in Table 10.1 we look at the ratio of children aged less than a year per 1000 women in the reproductive age group (fifteen to forty-nine years), which also shows a sharp decline after 1993 (see Table 10.1).

Therefore, on the whole there are indications of declining fertility levels in Palanpur. It should be noted that this fertility rate is still high; it is quite common for women to have four or more children. Not many women use contraception.[6]

Table 10.1 Indicators of fertility rates

	Year						
	1958	1964	1975	1983	1993	2009	2015
Ratio of children under 15 to adult women	1.50	1.42	1.94	1.94	1.68	1.39	1.27
GFR (modified)*	171.2	135.7	137.8	134.6	130.5	106	91.3

Note: * Ratio of children aged less than one year per 1000 women in the reproductive age group.

[6] We do not know much about condom usage among men. The local 'doctor' did inform us that he also sold condoms and that some men in the village bought them.

Some of them have undergone sterilization procedures,[7] some of them still wanted children and did not use contraception, and some of them used contraceptive pills or condoms. The mean age at first pregnancy (miscarriages included) is 19.5 years. This corresponds to the average for rural India (19.5) when comparing with National Family Health Survey (NFHS) data (IIPS, 2007). We see that although there is a rise in the age at marriage, the age at first pregnancy does not seem to have increased over time, as it is around nineteen years of age for all age groups of women.

10.4 Education: Literacy and Schooling

Among important factors that give women a voice and agency within the family and the community are education and workforce participation. While education has an intrinsic value, it is also well established that female education, even more than male education, has a positive effect on the well-being of the entire family, especially of children. This is because women are the primary caregivers in a family, and an educated woman can take informed decisions, has a greater role in the decisions of the household, and is able to access available public services better. In this and other ways, increased maternal education is seen to have a major influence on reduced child mortality. Further, education is seen to have an impact not only through the characteristics of the individual mother, but also through the educational level of society as a whole (for example, Caldwell, 1979; Kravdal, 2003; Sinha, 2016; Ware, 1984).

Palanpur has seen a tremendous increase in literacy rates since the 1957/8 survey. However, serious gender gaps remain. While the male literacy rate increased from 14 per cent in 1957/8 to 77 per cent in 2015, the female literacy rate increased from almost nil (1 per cent) to 43 per cent during the same period. Up to 1993, the level of female literacy in the village was negligible, with only 8.7 per cent of females literate.[8] It is only in the last two decades that

---

[7] Kanti, a young Thakur woman, discussed her sterilization with us. Before the pregnancies, she used contraceptive pills her husband gave her. After having two boys, she wanted a girl so they had a third child, who was also a boy. They then decided not to have any more children. She was informed of a government sterilization programme through the ANM (Auxiliary Nurse Midwife) who came to administer polio drops for her children. She is happy with her and her husband's decision.

[8] 'Literate' refers to all those who can 'read and write'. This status differs from education level, as persons without formal schooling are included as literate if they can 'read and write'. 'Read and write' is a category based on the respondent's reporting. As for education level, those reporting no school education or who cannot read and write are 'illiterate', those with education till 5th standard are clubbed as 'primary', between 6 to 8th standard are clubbed as 'middle', 9th to 12th standard are 'secondary and high school', and beyond 12th standard are clubbed as 'higher educated'. Those below primary education would come under illiterate in 'literacy status' if they could not 'read and write'. It is taken in relation to individuals aged over seven.

Table 10.2 Gender gap in literacy rates (%), by major caste groups

Caste Group	Year						
	1958	1964	1975	1984	1993	2009	2015
Thakur	34.1	49.6	46.5	44.9	39.6	34.4	35
Murao	10.4	27.8	36.9	45	49.5	50.5	34.4
Muslims	4.2	20	7.9	24.7	36.1	47.7	51.8
Jatab	3	12.1	2.3	7.5	23.7	29.5	30.4
Overall	13.5	30.5	28.1	30.6	37.5	40.6	36.1

Source: Primary survey data from Palanpur.

an expansion in female education can be seen. However, it is also the case that even as late as 2015, less than half the girls/women in the village were literate.

The change in the 'gender gap' in literacy rates can be seen as an indicator of how fast women are catching up with men. As seen in Table 10.2, the gap was increasing until 2009, with a faster increase in the male literacy rate than the female. Although there was some reduction in the gender gap in 2015 it was still high at 36 percentage points. There is continuing gender bias in access to education in Palanpur (for further information, see Section 9.2 of Chapter 9).[9]

Usually when literacy rates are low, the gender gap is also low. The gender gap increases as literacy rates rise initially, and then there is a reduction in the gender gap as women also catch up. Such a trend is also seen for Palanpur, as shown in the caste-wise breakdown of the data in Table 10.2 where the gender gap is the least amongst the Jatabs. The gender gap among Muraos reduced the most between 2009 and 2015, while it remained more or less the same for Thakurs and continued to increase for Jatabs and Muslims. In each of the communities, education has first come for the males and then for females. Jatab women therefore face the dual disadvantage of caste and gender, with only 34 per cent of Jatab females literate in 2015.

To get an indication of the level of education among women and how this has changed over time, in Figure 10.1 we look at the highest level of education completed among women above eighteen. As can be seen, most women who are literate are educated only up to the primary level. There are very few adult women in the village who have completed high school. When we segregate the trends in women's education by caste, it becomes clear that the women of upper-caste households such as Thakurs and Kayasths were the earliest to enter schooling. Although the numbers before 1993 were almost negligible, they were enough to observe a caste-based gap in education within the women of Palanpur. Even after 1993, when almost all the castes except Jatabs

---

[9] 'The gender gap' in literacy rates in Uttar Pradesh and Moradabad based on Census 2011 is around 20%.

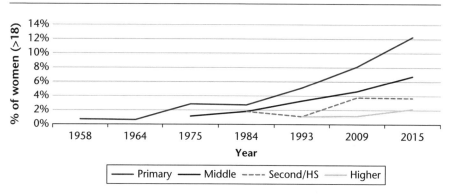

Figure 10.1 Level of education: women above 18 years
Source: Primary survey data from Palanpur.

showed some level of education among women, it was those of other upper castes and Thakurs who entered higher education, that is, beyond primary school level.

In 2009, there were four women who had completed class 12. Of these, one belonged to the Kayasth community and was working as the *anganwadi* worker at the local *anganwadi* centre.[10] Her sister also studied up to high school but did not pass her 12th standard examinations. The other two belonged to the same Thakur household, and one of them was unmarried, while the other was the daughter-in-law of the head of the household; neither was engaged in any employment. By 2015, beyond these four, seven more girls in the village had completed class 12. Three more belonged to a single Thakur family, that of Naresh and Mahesh (one of whom came in as a daughter-in-law). None of these girls were engaged in any employment. One of the daughters-in-law used to work as a school teacher before she got married and came to Palanpur. While there are now a few girls in the village who have completed schooling and some who have even been to college, there are no employment opportunities for them. There do seem to be some 'pioneer' families who encourage female education; in almost all these cases both parents have some education.

10.5 Women's Employment Participation in Palanpur

All seven of the surveys, from the initial round onwards, listed the primary and secondary occupations of all individuals in the village, including all members of the household. The respondent to this round of data collection

---

[10] The *anganwadi* (roughly translated as 'courtyard') is a part of the Integrated Child Development Services (ICDS) scheme by the central government. It acts as a hub for child welfare, nutrition, and health programmes within the village.

was usually the male 'head of the household'. As in other such survey data there is an underestimation of work done by women. However, these data seem reasonably reliable as long as mainstream definitions of employment participation are being used.[11]

Primary occupation is defined as one which the person has been doing for the major part of the year, and secondary is what is done for less time. The 'major time' criterion is similar to that used in official data sets such as the National Sample Survey (NSS). Activities in which the respondents were engaged for more than six months in a year were categorized as 'primary' activities. If the engagement was less than six months, it was classified as a secondary or subsidiary occupation.

For women, the secondary employment status was particularly important because of the fragmented nature of their work. Since most of the farming and livestock activities are seasonal and done for few hours early in the morning or late in the evening, women's activities under these official criteria almost never show up as 'primary activity'.

The overall participation of women in the workforce in this village has always been very low (which is also the case for the region of western Uttar Pradesh in general). Women in Palanpur are engaged in several different kinds of unpaid work, including care work, and spend a significant amount of time in household work. Other than the tasks of cooking, cleaning, taking care of children, and so on, much time is spent on the preparation of dung cakes, which is the primary source of fuel in the village. Except for young married women from the Thakur caste, the rest also spent time in cutting fodder for the cattle that they own and in general in looking after the animals. Occasionally, some women are seen in the fields doing agriculture work as well.[12] When the Mahatma Gandhi National Rural Employment Guarantee Act (MGNREGA) came into the village some women participated, but otherwise it is rare to find women in Palanpur engaged in paid work (except for those working in government schemes like the *anganwadi* workers,[13] ASHA,[14] or para-teachers).

---

[11] There are valid criticisms on the way women's work is estimated in mainstream surveys. It generally excludes work done within the home boundary and also excludes unremunerated work which may be productive but for home consumption. While obviously problematic, for comparability and consistency this definition has been adopted here. For details on the underestimation of women's work, see Sinha (2016).

[12] There are barely any instances of women working in the fields as wage labour. What is, however, seen is that during certain operations such as weeding and harvesting women work on family farms or leased-in land. This is observed mainly in the case of Muraos and Jatabs. Thakur women, other than in exceptional circumstances (such as in the case of widows), do not work in the fields.

[13] *Anganwadi* workers run the *anganwadi* centre. The job involves conducting pre-school education, nutrition and health counselling, growth monitoring, supplementary feeding, and making health referrals.

[14] 'ASHA', or Accredited Social Health Activist, is a health worker selected and trained from within the village under the central government's health programme. An ASHA is trained to be the interface between the rural community and the public health system.

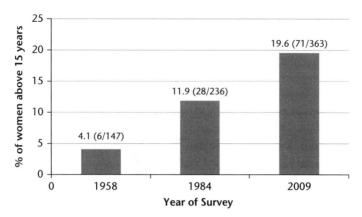

Figure 10.2 Number of women workers (primary and secondary) above 15

Note: Absolute numbers in brackets. WPR (P&S) is women's participation rate primary and secondary.

Source: Primary survey data from Palanpur.

In terms of the occupation data for the village, while a small proportion of women are classified as 'workers' on the basis of primary and secondary occupations, the long-term trend is one of increasing women's workforce participation: it has risen from 4 per cent in 1957/8 to 20 per cent in 2008/9 (see Figure 10.2). One of the reasons this has been recorded in Palanpur might be improved data collection. Although it is difficult to quantify this, we illustrate such data issues from some comparisons between the information from male heads of household and the smaller survey that was conducted in 2009 in the village with a sample of women in the reproductive age group. This survey asked women for information related to any work done by them in the seven days prior to the survey being conducted. Forty-two women who were shown as not being part of the workforce in the occupation data as reported by male heads of households were doing some work on the farms based on the data from this 'women's round'. Of these 42 women, 24 (belonging to Murao and Jatab castes) had done some paid work on others' land.

With the caveat that at least some of the apparent increase in women's workforce participation in Palanpur is a result of better definitions and data collection, in this section we examine the changing structure of economic activity in the village and how this is related to women's workforce participation. For instance, it is possibly the case that with a shift of male employment from farm to non-farm, more women are now increasingly engaged in cultivation. Further, the nature of the changes has been such that there are more opportunities for paid employment activities such as harvesting or weeding in agriculture, or in brick kilns outside that are taken up in groups, usually by the family or a couple as the payment is on a piece-rate basis. The other area where

Table 10.3 Number of women in primary/secondary occupation (above 15 years)

Caste	1958	1964	1984	1993	2009	2015
Thakur	0	1	0	1	5	5
Murao	0	0	7	3	24	13
Jatab	0	0	4	5	16	5
Muslim	2	2	4	1	8	4
Other	4	6	13	7	18	4
Total	6	9	28	17	71	31
Total population of women above 15	147	168	236	303	363	394

Source: Primary survey data from Palanpur.

Table 10.4 Number of women by type of primary occupation

Primary Occupation	Thakur		Murao		Jatab		Muslim		Total	
	2009	2015	2009	2015	2009	2015	2009	2015	2009	2015
Own cultivation	1	1	14	13	1	1	1	2	22	17
Casual labour					5	3	1		9	3
Self-employed	3	1					2	2	7	5
Regular	1	2							3	5
Total	5	4	14	13	6	4	4	4	41	30
Women above 15	96	97	87	109	45	79	52	60	363	394

Source: Primary survey data from Palanpur.

women are joining the workforce is in the government sector and home-based self-employment in the form of tailoring or running a shop at home—but these are few. The activities have a caste-wise pattern which influences the possible avenues for women's participation in the workforce.

As can be seen in Table 10.3, the highest number of women showing workforce participation (either primary or secondary) in recent years are Muraos, followed by those from other small caste groups and Jatabs.[15] There are a higher number of Thakur women reported as being workers compared to earlier, but this is still very low. From Table 10.4 (on primary occupations), we see that all women reporting any occupation other than domestic work among Muraos are in cultivation. Muraos are a caste strongly related to agriculture, and here it is acceptable for women to go to work in the fields, especially their own. We see that there was a major increase in women's participation for all castes (Table 10.3) between 1983/4 and 2008/9, but it is strongest for Muraos with cultivation as the only primary occupation (Table 10.4).

---

[15] As seen in previous sections, Murao women have also registered the greatest increase in educational outcomes.

Table 10.5 Per cent of adult men in cultivation

Caste	1984			2009		
	Total	Cultivation	% Cultivation	Total	Cultivation	% Cultivation
Thakur	61	31	50.8	93	27	29.0
Murao	63	47	74.6	92	47	51.1
Muslims	34	16	47.1	53	16	30.2
Jatab	29	13	44.8	53	13	24.5
Village Total	264	131	49.6	373	125	33.5

Note: Village Total also includes other castes not mentioned in the table.
Source: Primary survey data from Palanpur.

Between 2008/9 and 2015, there was a decline in female workforce partici-pation among all castes. This is in line with the trend observed nationally and partly could be attributed to more women in the working age group now attending educational institutions. The percentage of women above fifteen attending educational institutions increased from 4.1 per cent in 2009 to 6.3 per cent in 2015.

While Murao women always contributed to agriculture to some extent, it can be seen that with a shift in employment to non-farm jobs among Murao males (see Table 10.5), more women are participating in cultivation. While such a shift to non-farm activities is also observed for Thakur men, Muraos appear more committed to holding on to agriculture.[16] Thus, Thakurs with strong non-farm activities tend to have leased-out land (see Chapter 6), and Muraos have tended to increase women's participation in cultivation.

Therefore, in the case of Muraos, the 'feminization' of agriculture argument would seem relevant to explaining the rise in participation of women in culti-vation.[17] For instance, Sombati and Omvati, both belonging to Murao house-holds, were recorded as being engaged only in household work in the previous rounds, but in 2009 were shown as cultivators. During this period, the primary occupation of their husbands changed from cultivation to non-farm casual labour. Similarly, with Chanderkali (Passi), her husband's primary occupation was cultivation in the previous rounds but changed to working in and owning a cycle repair shop in 2009. Table 10.5 and Figure 10.3 further illustrate this point by showing that the increase in casual non-farm employment amongst Muraos, and corresponding decline in cultivators among Murao males, is sharp between 1984 and 2009, which is also the period that saw an increase in female participation in cultivation. The rise of the participation of Murao

---

[16] Thakurs had higher land ownership both in terms of land owned and operated per capita than the Muraos in the 1950s and 1960s; but since the 1970s this has reversed, with the gap increasing over time.

[17] On the trend of feminization of agriculture in India see, for example, Binswanger-Mkhize (2013).

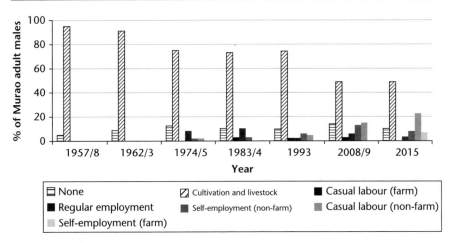

Figure 10.3 Employment diversification: Murao males (the cultivators)

Source: Primary survey data from Palanpur.

women in cultivation is simultaneous with the decline of Murao men in cultivation (from roughly 75 per cent in 1984 to 51 per cent in 2009, see Table 10.5). Between 2009 and 2015 there was stagnation in non-farm employment for Murao males as well as in cultivation for Murao females.[18]

It is in situations of acute necessity that a Thakur woman in Palanpur would decide to break the norm of not working outside the home. Thus, Thakur women in Palanpur who are in cultivation are widows who have no support from the extended family and do not have adult male children.[19] These women handle farming activities mainly to keep the land under their control till their children grow up. They are also treated with suspicion by the rest of the community. Although the level of education among girls and women is growing rapidly among the Thakurs, this has not translated into greater workforce participation.[20] This has as much to do with supply-side factors of women having low mobility as with demand-side factors in the sense that the kind of jobs that are seen as acceptable for these women are just not available in and around the village.

The other category where women are working is casual labour, although this just applies to Jatab women. Most Jatab men and women are engaged as casual labourers. The most common non-farm occupation for Jatab families is as labourers in brick kilns. This work is seasonal, where the entire family migrates

---

[18] For further details on employment patterns in Palanpur, see Chapter 5.

[19] Even the woman who was engaged as the cook for the midday meal scheme in the local school is a widow.

[20] The ASHA worker in the village is from a Thakur household. Her husband lost his job and their family had no other source of income when the Thakur 'elders' of the village decided to offer her the ASHA post. So in this instance there was a need and also an acceptable job available.

for three or four months a year, and everyone contributes to the work; they are paid by the number of bricks they make. It is possible that there is an under-estimation of women working in brick kilns, as formally it is the man who takes up the job, but most women also contribute. Many Jatabs who are in cultivation are tenant farmers in *chauthai* contracts, which are in large measure labour contracts (with one-quarter share), where once again it makes economic sense for the entire family to work. Within Jatabs there has been a strong increase in casual labour in non-farm activities. Jatab women, too, have entered the workforce as casual labour; often this has been distress related. The restrictions on women's mobility and employment are also the lowest among Jatabs. Further, the level of education among Jatabs is the lowest, with barely any adult literate women among Jatabs in the village.

Finally in 2009, amongst the five women workers from Thakur households, four are in the category of self-employed or regular jobs/working for government. These are basically women working as tailors or in small shops run from their own homes. Those in government employment were an ASHA worker in 2009 and the ASHA worker and a midday meal cook in 2015.[21] From conversations with various members in Thakur households, both men and women, it is clear that it is acceptable for women to work only if the jobs are 'respectable'; working for the government, preferably as a teacher or officer, is seen as something that women can do. Otherwise, there is a strong preference for women to remain and work within the household boundary.

Other than the causal factors of men moving out of agriculture and the availability of acceptable jobs, most women who enter the workforce can be seen as influenced by, or classified in, one of three categories on the basis of the change in status compared to the previous round of survey: (i) those who have been widowed; (ii) suitable opportunities being available for women with some education; and (iii) cases where the economic status of the household changed (with an improvement resulting in women withdrawing from the workforce, and a decline leading to women joining work). We examine these in turn.

10.5.1 *Widows*

A category of women where, irrespective of caste, there is a higher workforce participation is widows without adult children. Of all the women in employment in 2009, nine are widows. Of these women, six were in the village in

---

[21] Between 2009 and 2015, there was one girl from a Thakur household who briefly worked as a para-teacher in the village government school. She later moved to another village when she got married and worked as a teacher in a school near her marital village.

1984 and were married and not working. In 1993, out of the nine, seven were in the village, all of them were married and not working. It is only in the 2009 round that they show up as 'workers', and the change in their status from the previous rounds is that they are now widowed. Looking at the data for the village, it is seen that for all women who are in the age groups of fifteen to sixty, the workforce participation rate is 20 per cent. However, this rate for widows is 32 per cent (8 out of 25). The workforce participation rate for widows excluding Thakurs (where the restrictions are highest) is 40 per cent (7 out of 18).

In 1964 out of the 11 women with any reported source of income, 6 were widows. Surja Devi, a Passi woman from the village, started working after her husband's death in 1964. Hardai, a widow in 1958, was not reported as working, but in 1964 she was working as a coal trader.[22] Her son was an agricultural labourer in the village in 1958 but by 1964 he had migrated out of the village. Similarly, two Passi women, Champa and Ramkali, and Leelavati, the only Murao woman who was cultivating in 1984, started working after losing their husbands. Of the 32 women with a primary occupation (excluding 'new' residents) in 2009, 7 started working after their husbands died, and 4 started cultivating after male members of their family shifted to non-farm activities.

10.5.2 Availability of Opportunities for Educated Women

The level of education and literacy among women is low in the village. But, as seen in Chapter 9 (and Table 10.6), there has been an impressive increase in

Table 10.6 Per cent of literate women and level of education

Data for Women over 15 Years	Literacy Rate	Level of Education			
		Primary	Middle	Secondary	Higher
1958	1	0.7	0	0	0
1964	1	1.2	0	0	0
1975	6	4.4	1.3	0	0
1984	6	3.1	1.6	2.3	0
1993	11	5.8	3.5	1	1
2009	22	10.3	7.1	4	1.1
2015	37	13.6	6.9	4	1.7

Source: Primary survey data from Palanpur.

---

[22] The coal was sometimes obtained by illicit removal from steam trains stopped at Jargaon Station.

the literacy rate in the village between 1993 and 2009, which continued after 2009. Thirty-seven per cent of women above fifteen in the village were literate, and 6 per cent had completed secondary or higher levels in 2015. However, there are no job opportunities available for women who are educated, even though in discussions with them it emerged that they are willing to undertake some kinds of work.

Barring the para-teacher posts (which have now gone, as regular teachers have been appointed) and *anganwadi* workers, there are no jobs in the village that require education as a qualification for entry. In 1993 Shobha Devi and Lovely Devi (sisters, belonging to the only Kayasth family in the village) were the only two women with higher education. Both of them got jobs at the local *anganwadi* and continue to work there. In 2009, Suman, a Thakur woman with elementary education, started working as the ASHA under the National Rural Health Mission. Preeti, a Thakur woman who had completed her MA, worked in the local school as a para-teacher for some time. There have been no other such employment opportunities in the village.

10.5.3 *Change in Household Fortunes*

Decline in the households' fortunes over time has also been a reason for women entering the labour market, but women also seem to withdraw when their situations improve. Sometimes a husband's death and downward mobility may coincide, but in some households women started working even when the husband had sufficient work to earn enough for sustenance, but household income per capita had fallen. In 1964, out of the 11 working women, Bhagwati, a Dhimar woman, was observed to start working after her family's per capita income declined to Rs 74 (1960–1 prices) from Rs 100 in 1958. A similar case was observed for two Muslim women from the same family where the mother-in-law, Munno, worked as non-farm labourer in 1958, and in 1964 her daughter-in-law, Chhoti, joined her as their per capita income went down.

In 2009 at least eight households with working women showed decline in per capita income compared to earlier rounds. Suman, the only Thakur woman working in regular employment, was in one such household. Similarly, out of those women who had not endured any loss of working male members (due to either migration or death), three Murao women started working as their household's income declined. Asha and Sheela, who are from Jatab households, also saw a decline in real household income since 1983. In these two households, their total household income (including income from brick kilns) was less than Rs 2000 per month, about one-fourth the Palanpur average.

10.6 Autonomy, Decision-Making, Mobility, and Exposure to Media

With increasing education, there might be an expectation of enhanced autonomy for women within and outside the household. Since data on these aspects are not available from the previous rounds, we are somewhat limited as to what can be said in a quantitative manner on how these aspects have changed within the village over time. However, in the survey in 2009 the women's round collected some data on issues related to autonomy and decision-making, and it shows that like the rest of this region, such indicators point to a weak status of women in Palanpur.

In order to assess how household decisions are made and also to understand some direct indicators of 'autonomy', some questions were asked of women on decision-making within the household, physical mobility, domestic violence, exposure to media, and so on. Defining and measuring 'autonomy' or 'empowerment' is a complicated issue. For many feminists, the value of the concept lies precisely in its 'fuzziness' (Kabeer, 2000). The terms used in the literature are many and sometimes not well defined. The most frequently used term of 'status of women' is also defined differently depending on the authors (Mason, 1986). Some focus rather on the *prestige*, that is, the respect or esteem accorded to women because of their gender, whereas others concentrate on women's *power* or *empowerment* and *freedom*. We focus on the term women's *autonomy*, defined as 'the extent to which [women] have an equal voice in matters affecting themselves and their families, control over material and other resources, access to knowledge and information, the authority to make independent decisions, freedom from constraints on physical mobility, and the ability to forge equitable power relationships within families' (Jeejeebhoy and Sathar, 2001: 688).

In Palanpur, norms on mobility and work for women are intrinsically linked with the caste status of the household, as in much of India, particularly north India. Among Thakurs, norms of *ghunghat* (covering head and face, part or fully with cloth) and restricted mobility for women are the strongest. New brides are extremely limited in their ability to go out of their homes, and generally women do not go to work on their farms or collect firewood/fodder, and so on. These tasks are done by the men of the household. Thakur women do a lot of livestock-related work, but this is usually within the household boundaries.

Muraos, being a caste focused on cultivation, have an attachment to land and farming. Amongst Muraos, while there also is a tendency towards restricting women's mobility, women working on their own farms is considered acceptable. For example, in response to questions on mobility asked to married women, among Muraos 72 per cent said they can go to the fields alone while only 28 per cent of Thakurs said so.

Table 10.7 Indicators of autonomy among women in Palanpur, 2009

Indicator	% (N: 224)
Economic decision-making	
Have a say in spending	73
Have cash in hand for expenses	88
Have land in own name	8
Have a bank/post office account in own name	19
Mobility (can go the following places alone)	
Local market	31
Village doctor	62
Fields outside the village	54
Relative's house	63
Village temple	71
Nearby shrine	21
Parents' house	50
Health centre	35
Exposure to media (ever)	
Read newspapers	6
Listen to radio	26
Watch TV	33
Ever gone to cinema	12
Participation in civic life	
Visited government office (outside or in Palanpur)	14
Voted in last elections	79

Note: Number of observations N = 224.
Source: Primary survey data from Palanpur.

Jatabs have the least restrictions on mobility for women. They are also the poorest caste group in the village with most of them being landless and depending on wage labour for work. Even among Jatabs it is rare to see women working in paid jobs independently. Most of their work is on farms as agricultural labour and in brick kilns, as mentioned; in both cases, the labour contract is with the man, on a piece-rate basis, and the entire family works.

It is, however, important to keep in mind that talking about 'the' status of women as if along a simple scale may not be appropriate; it is in many ways a multidimensional concept (Mason, 1986, 2005), spanning social, economic, political, and psychological factors. Some women may have more power in the private sphere and less in the public one, whereas for others it would be the other way a round. We present some different indicators, using data from the women questionnaire, separately, without trying to construct one single indicator of women's autonomy. These are assembled in Table 10.7 and discussed in turn.

10.6.1 *Economic Decision-Making*

An important aspect of women's autonomy is whether they have some control over how the household resources are spent. As seen in Table 10.7, whereas three out of four women reported that they have a say in household expenditures, and 88 per cent do get cash in hand, only 8 per cent have any land in their name, and only 19 per cent have a bank account. In contrast, of all the households in the village, 53 per cent reported having at least one bank account, and 81 per cent owned some agricultural land.

10.6.2 Mobility

Traditionally, a woman is not allowed to go out alone and should be accompanied either by her husband or by someone else of her in-law family. We asked women whether they could go alone to a list of commonly visited places. The place where women can most often go alone is the village temple (70 per cent), followed by the village doctor (62 per cent), relatives or friends in the village (61 per cent), and fields outside the village (53 per cent).[23] One woman out of two can go alone to visit her parents (49 per cent), but this varies considerably across women in the village, and some parents may live quite far away. The places where fewest women can go alone are a health centre outside the village (33 per cent), the local market in the village (31 per cent), and a shrine or market outside the village (21 per cent).

While almost 70 per cent of the women said that they visited their parents once or twice a year, with the increasing availability of mobile phones women are now more in touch with their parents and other natal family. When asked how they would send a message to their parents in case of an emergency, 90 per cent of the women said that they would do so by phone. By 2015, the number of phones and mobile connectivity in the village had increased even more. Greater communication with the parents' family could improve women's fall-back position within the household.[24] In earlier times, women were not in touch with their parents for long periods, but now many spoke about how they would regularly call them.

The main determinant of mobility seems to be caste. As expected, Jatab women are the freest to go where they want to in almost every category. As also expected, Thakurs are at the bottom of the list in terms of mobility, except for the category temple in the village (where, obviously, Muslims rarely go),[25] or a health centre outside the village. One Thakur woman out of two can go to relatives or friends in the village, whereas almost all Jatab women can do so. Putting together the data on all the different places, for about 16 per cent of

---

[23] Women would go to fields outside the village to take meals to workers, to do farm work, to gather/cut grass for the cattle. Since there are very few households in Palanpur which have toilets, women also have to go to the fields to relieve themselves.

[24] On fall-back position see Agarwal (1997).

[25] The temple in the village is Hindu, and there is no mosque in the village. The nearest mosque is in the neighbouring village, Pipli (see also Chapter 11).

women there is no place where they can go to alone (mostly newly married women). But it also shows that every case is different, that the distribution within the village is not extreme—that is, women who can go everywhere versus women confined to their own house—and that a lot of intermediate cases do exist.

10.6.3 *Exposure to Media*

Women were asked whether they read newspapers or magazines, listen to the radio, or watch television, and, if they did, how frequently they did so. Fourteen women (6 per cent) said that they ever read the newspaper, of which 1 does it every day, and 3 at least once a week; 57 women (26 per cent) listen to the radio, most of them (40 women) almost every day; 74 women (33 per cent) watch television, half of them almost every day, 16 of them at least once a week, and 21 less than once a week. We also asked the women whether they had ever gone to a cinema hall or theatre to see a movie, and only 24 women (12 per cent) said they had.

Over half of Palanpur women are not exposed to media at all. One out of five has access to one type of media, one out of five to two types, and the remaining 5 per cent of the women to three or four. It has to be kept in mind that possession of a television or a radio is correlated with wealth and often with higher caste, as it can be expensive. Furthermore, a significant percentage of televisions and radios were acquired through dowries.[26]

By 2015, the village had a number of households with DishTV. Women mostly watched daily serials ('soaps') or Hindi films, and on the radio listened to songs from Hindi films. Although they did not watch 'news' or other informational programmes, watching TV gave them an exposure to the 'outside world'. Some women also told us that they got to know about immunization, childcare, and so on from radio advertisements. It is difficult to say how increasing exposure to media, mainly through television, could shape preferences of women.[27] While watching TV is indeed giving women exposure to information and different lifestyles, the popular Hindi daily soaps have also often been criticized for their regressive portrayal of women.[28] In most cases the films and TV shows are located in urban settings and might seem alien to the women in Palanpur. Since satellite television came in only after the 2009 survey, we do not comment on this in detail.

---

[26] Information on sources of acquisition of durables was collected in detail.
[27] On institutional and cultural factors shaping preferences, see Fehr and Hoff (2011).
[28] For example, see Stanley (2012), Malhotra and Rogers (2000), Bhandari (2017).

10.6.4 Civic Life

A total of 79 per cent of Palanpur women voted in the last elections (*panchayat* elections), which is an impressive participation rate by most international standards. In general, it is observed that in India the participation rates in elections, especially local elections, are high for both men and women. When asked if they had ever been to a government/*panchayat* office in their village, or in a government office outside the village, 86 per cent of women said no. Only 2 have ever been there in the village, and 29 outside the village. The women were also asked whether they had ever attended a Gram Sabha or any such meeting in the village or ever attended a public meeting/political meeting/rally outside the village, but there were no positive answers for the first question and only two for the second one. There was a whole section about women's participation in any kind of associational activities, including self-help groups, Mahila Mandals,[29] and so on. But none of the women reported being part of any association.

10.6.5 Domestic Violence

It is common knowledge in the village that domestic violence (in the form of physical violence where husband beats the wife) is prevalent in Palanpur. While we did not go into the factors affecting domestic violence, which many studies have done (for example, Eswaran and Malhotra, 2009; Jejeebhoy, 1998), in the survey with women we tried to get some basic information. Some of this is reported in Table 10.8.

Women were first asked about their opinion on domestic violence, and this was followed up with a question on whether they had ever experienced any

Table 10.8 Domestic violence

% of women who felt husband beating wife is justified if:

Reasons for domestic violence	%
Wife is disrespectful to in-laws	76.3
Wife neglects household chores	74.3
Wife is disobedient	76.7
Wife beats children	55.3
% of women reporting being:	
Never beaten	48.2
Beaten regularly	10.3
Beaten sometimes	33.5

[29] Mahila Mandals are women's associations in a village.

violence from their spouses. Sometimes women were forthcoming with further details, but we did not probe unless they volunteered. Further, there was no insistence if women did not feel comfortable responding. However, there were not too many such instances.

In the first set of questions the woman was given hypothetical situations where a husband beat his wife in response to wife's behaviour, and was asked whether he was justified in doing so. As seen in Table 10.8, 76 per cent of the women felt that such violence was justified if the woman was disrespectful towards her in-laws, and a similar proportion felt that there was justification if a woman neglected her household chores or was 'disobedient'. However, when asked if the husband could beat a wife for mistreating their children, fewer women (55 per cent) said that this would be acceptable.

In relation to their personal experience of violence, 52 per cent of women in Palanpur said that they have ever been beaten by their husbands, among whom 20 per cent said that this happened *regularly*, and 65 per cent said *sometimes*. It is hence far higher than that reported as the rural India average of 36.1 per cent and the Uttar Pradesh average of 42 per cent (NFHS-3, IIPS, 2007). This could well be because of better reporting in this study. About 12 women did not answer the question. However, given that it is such a sensitive topic, it is surprising that so many women talked openly about it. It is nevertheless plausible that among the 48 per cent who said they were never beaten, some of them actually were, but did not want to talk about it. While there are no previous data on this, conversations with older women suggest that there is a decline in domestic violence, and women used to be beaten more often.

10.7 Conclusion

Many studies that have looked at reasons for the wide interstate variations in human development within India have pointed to the low status of women in north India, compared to relatively more open societies in south India, as an important determining factor for north India's continuing backwardness, especially in comparison with the southern states (Drèze and Gazdar, 1997; Drèze and Sen, 2002; Malhotra et al., 1995; Ramachandran, 1997). Women's status has been seen as an explanatory factor for crucial demographic changes, especially in the context of differences in fertility levels in north and south India (Dyson and Moore, 1983; Jejeebhoy, 1991). Better women's status is also understood to be one of the driving factors of better human development outcomes as well as more effective social services in states such as Tamil Nadu and Kerala in comparison to Uttar Pradesh and Bihar (Drèze and Sen, 2013; Sinha, 2016). Uttar Pradesh continues to perform very poorly in comparison with the rest of the country, as far as basic indicators, including on education and workforce participation, are concerned. For instance, the female literacy rate in Uttar Pradesh, at 59.3 per cent, is significantly lower than the all-India average of 65.5 per cent (Census, 2011), and the state ranks 31 out of 35 states in India. The female literacy rate of Moradabad district is much lower at 47.9 per cent. Similarly the female work participation rate (rural) of Moradabad district is 9.9 per cent (10.8 per cent), whereas it is 16.7 per cent (18.3 per cent) for Uttar Pradesh as a whole, and the all-India average female work participation rate is 25.5 per cent (30 per cent).

Uttar Pradesh has one of the poorest human development outcomes in the country, and Moradabad is amongst the weakest districts in Uttar Pradesh in this respect. In terms of economic prosperity, however, Moradabad district is above average for the state. Palanpur, in Moradabad district, more or less reflects this situation at the village level. The gender norms of western Uttar Pradesh are largely common through the region, with some caste and class differences. As with most other aspects of village life, Palanpur is not particularly unusual in its treatment of women. Drèze and Sharma (1998), based on the previous surveys in Palanpur village, described briefly the lives of women in Palanpur and the differences observed across caste. Similar to other villages in that region, Palanpur was a deeply patriarchal society, very unequal, where women had very little role to play in public life, were rarely seen outside of their homes, practised *purdah*, and could make little contact with 'outside men' or those outside the family.[30] Literacy and workforce participation among women was also very low. Most women were married off at a young age, with repeated pregnancies and poor access to health care. Women usually did not get a share in property (either from parents or in-laws) and had few freedoms. While much of this remains relevant even now, there are also some changes.

As seen in this chapter, there is an increase in female education. Other positive changes are to do with an increase in age at marriage, decline in fertility, and improved access to information. However, there are still many ways in which women's status is very low in Palanpur. Within the household, the inequalities remain stark, the extreme manifestation being the extent of domestic violence. The household as well as the village is also a very unequal space for women, with change coming only slowly, especially when compared to the economic changes that the village has gone through. Bargaining within the household also depends on a woman's fall-back position and, as we have seen, this is weak. Women's employment opportunities in Palanpur remain extraordinarily limited, especially in terms of any sort of skilled or well-remunerated employment. Further, much of the ability

---

[30] On gender relations in north India also see the references listed in Drèze and Sharma (1998).

of women to develop their potential is still linked to their social position in terms of class and caste, as well as the gender norms related to mobility.

In terms of the future, however, there is much potential for change in this aspect of village life. With more girls being sent to school, one might expect some changes in the labour market, with more women being available for work, as well as changes in intra-household relationships, with women having a greater say. Exposure to mass media and the outside world can also contribute to the process of improving women's status in the village. Proliferation of mobile phones can further contribute to changing dynamics, as women can be in touch with their parental family with greater ease. It is support from the parental family that is, in large measure, the 'fall-back position'. With education and exposure, we may also see an increase in the age of marriage and maybe even terms of marriage. These forces may increase as mobile phones become smartphones.

If change continues as it has in recent years, the rising status of women may reinforce the caste-based inequalities that exist, since it is particularly higher-caste girls who are getting an education. It will be interesting to see how public institutions respond to a situation of changed gender relations, whether politics in the state will address women's issues, and whether newer services/institutions will be created for women. Some external changes, such as reservation of posts in the *panchayat* elections, have resulted in Palanpur getting its first woman Pradhan. While there are doubts about the power wielded by her, it certainly sets a welcome precedent, one that might encourage more women to take on political roles. Overall, one can speculate that the improvements in education and health amongst women would eventually result in long-lasting changes for both the economy and human development in the village.

Acknowledgements

This chapter has been written by Dipa Sinha and Ruchira Bhattacharya; it draws on earlier work on Palanpur (see Sinha and Coppoletta, 2011; Sinha et al., 2016).

References

Agarwal, B. 1997. ' "Bargaining" and gender relations: within and beyond the household', *Feminist Economics* 3, no. 1: 1–51.
Bhandari, P. 2017. 'Towards sociology of Indian elites: marriage alliances, vulnerabilities and resistance in Bollywood', *Society and Culture in South Asia* 3, no. 1: 108–16.

Binswanger-Mkhize, H.P. 2013. 'The stunted structural transformation of the Indian economy', *Economic & Political Weekly* 48, nos 26–7: 5–13.

Caldwell, J. 1979. 'Education as a factor in mortality decline', *Population Studies* 33, no. 3: 395–413.

Census. 2011. 'Provisional population totals', http://censusindia.gov.in/ (accessed 20 March 2018).

Drèze, J., and Gazdar, H. 1997. 'Uttar Pradesh: the burden of inertia', in J. Drèze and A. Sen (eds), *Indian Development: Selected Regional Perspectives*. New Delhi: Oxford University Press.

Drèze, J., and Sen, A.K. (eds). 2002. *India: Development and Participation*. New York: Oxford University Press.

Drèze, J., and Sen, A.K. 2013. *An Uncertain Glory: India and its Contradictions*. London: Penguin.

Drèze, J., and Sharma, N. 1998. 'Palanpur: population, society, economy', in P. Lanjouw and N. H. Stern (eds), *Economic Development in Palanpur over Five Decades*. New Delhi and Oxford: Oxford University Press.

Dyson, T., and Moore, M. 1983. 'On kinship structure, female autonomy and demographic behaviour', *Population and Development Review* 9, no. 1: 35–60.

Eswaran, M., and Malhotra, N. 2009. 'Domestic violence and women's autonomy: evidence from India'. University of British Columbia Working Paper.

Fehr, E., and Hoff, K. 2011. 'Introduction: tastes, castes and culture: the influence of society on preferences', *The Economic Journal* 121, no. 556: F396–412.

Jejeebhoy, S.J. 1991. 'Women's status and fertility: successive cross-sectional evidence from Tamil Nadu, India', *Studies in Family Planning* 22: 217–30.

Jejeebhoy, S.J. 1998. 'Wife-beating in rural India: a husband's right? Evidence from survey data', *Economic & Political Weekly* 33: 855–62.

Jejeebhoy, S.J., and Sathar, Z.A. 2001. 'Women's autonomy in India and Pakistan: the influence of religion and region'. *Population and development review* 27, no. 4: 687–712.

Kabeer, N. 2000. 'Resources, agency, achievements: reflections on the measurement of women's empowerment', in S. Razavi (ed.), *Gendered Poverty and Well-Being*. Oxford: Blackwell.

Kravdal, O. 2003. 'Child mortality in India: exploring the community-level effect of education'. Health Economics Research Programme, University of Oslo, Working Paper No. 4.

Malhotra, S., and Rogers, E.M. 2000. 'Satellite television and the new Indian woman', *Gazette* (Leiden, Netherlands) 62, no. 5: 407–29.

Malhotra, A., Vanneman, R., and Kishor, S. 1995. 'Fertility, dimensions of patriarchy, and development in India', *Population and Development Review* 21, no. 2: 281–305.

Mason, K.O. 1986. 'The status of women: conceptual and methodological issues in demographic studies', *Sociological Forum* 1, no. 2: 284–300.

Mason, K.O. 2005. 'Measuring women's empowerment: learning from cross-national research', in D. Narayan-Parker (ed.), *Measuring Empowerment: Cross-Disciplinary Perspectives*. Washington D.C.: World Bank Publications.

Ramachandran, V.K. 1997. 'On Kerala's development achievements', in J. Drèze and A. Sen (eds), *Indian Development: Selected Regional Perspectives*. London and New York: Oxford University Press.

Sinha, D., and Coppoletta, R., 2011. 'The invisible half-women's status in Palanpur'. ARC Working paper No. 50, Asia Research Centre, London School of Economics and Political Science.

Sinha, D. 2016. *Women, Health and Public Services in India: Why are States Different?*, Critical Political Economy of South Asia. New Delhi: Routledge India.

Stanley, A. 2012. 'On Indian TV, "I Do" means to honour and obey the mother-in-law', *New York Times*, 12 December, http://www.nytimes.com/2012/12/26/arts/television/indian-soap-operas-ruled-by-mothers-in-law.html?pagewanted=all (accessed 20 March 2018).

Ware, H. 1984. 'Effects of maternal education, women's roles, and child care on child mortality', *Population and Development Review* 10: 191–214.

11

Society and Politics

Inertia and Change*

11.1 Introduction

In this chapter, we examine the village as a society. We will look at structures and stories emerging from Palanpur that describe how quickly things are changing in some areas, and how they remain static in others, sometimes painfully so. Through the analysis, we seek to understand how the relations between different social groups have changed, recalling that gender has been discussed in Chapter 10. We examine how the interactions of institutions and politics with economic change can help explain the nature and evolution of village society and relationships.

As we have shown in Parts 1 and 2, the last seven decades have brought a transformation in the village from being a place that was largely based on agriculture to one that is increasingly diversifying into non-farm activities. Currently, a major part of the income in Palanpur comes from the non-farm sector, and much of this is from outside the village. Improved transportation and communications with the development of roads and rail, and increased ownership of motorcycles, television sets, and mobile phones, have opened up new dimensions of engagement with the outside world.[1] The flow of information has become easier and faster.[2]

---

* This chapter has been written by Himanshu and Dipa Sinha.
[1] On the role of the communications revolution and its impact on social life in a western Uttar Pradesh village, see Kumar (2016).
[2] We note several relevant changes in Palanpur even though the penetration of television and other social media is limited in the village. While it is difficult to attribute changes in village society to the influence of television, we did find in our discussion that women in Thakur and some Murao households were regular viewers of television serials. The younger generation used the television to watch films on rented DVD players. There was only limited use of television for gathering information or keeping track of news.

Commuting is now the primary mode of accessing outside jobs, and the radius of the catchment area for jobs has increased in recent decades. The relative decline of agriculture and the emergence of non-farm outside jobs have contributed to altering social relations which were earlier centred around the agrarian economy. The changing occupations have influenced the way various caste groups interact with each other. Recent literature on caste in rural India has highlighted how, on the one hand, traditional caste structures are changing radically in relation to occupational structures and economic activities, but, on the other hand, social hierarchies on the basis of caste remain strongly entrenched (Jodhka, 2016, 2017). Others have argued that what we see now is the beginning of the end of the village (Gupta, 2005; Jodhka, 2016). We explore the implications of these perspectives for Palanpur while also taking them a step further and interrogating how developments in institutions and politics in the village have affected changing caste relationships and economic structures, together with how a changing economy and caste relations have influenced politics and institutions.

Along with occupational diversification, we have also seen that there has been some decline in caste diversity in the village in the sense that smaller castes are slowly moving out of the village. The composition of the village is changing as the population share of the major castes is rising. Is it the case that the smaller castes have had problems integrating in the village, or is it that it is easier for them to leave because their ties to the village, both in terms of assets and relationships, are not as strong? Further, while the Thakurs and Muraos have mostly dominated political structures in the village, recently, scheduled caste (SC) groups such as Jatabs have been asserting their caste identity not only in the economic sphere by taking on new economic activities, but also politically. The emergence of caste-based political formations in the state, such as the Bahujan Samaj Party (BSP) and the Samajwadi Party (SP), has also led to strengthening of political alignments within caste groups in the village as well as in neighbouring villages.[3]

While analysing these changing social relations, this chapter also looks at the state of public institutions. We find a decay in the quality and provision of public services and the absence of any significant collective action to change this situation. There is an increasing demand for the 'public services' of education and health amongst all the castes in the village. This is being manifested particularly in a higher number of children being sent to school. As seen in Chapter 9, the weakness of public provision is reflected in rising

---

[3] The emergence of caste-based parties and political mobilization along caste lines since the early 1990s has remained an important feature of politics in Uttar Pradesh. The two major parties which have ruled the state for the majority of the last two and half decades are the SP, which derives its strength from the other backward castes (OBC), mainly Yadavs, and the BSP, representing the interests of Dalits, mainly Jatabs.

numbers going to fee-paid, private schools. More people are accessing health-care facilities, too, but through fee-paid, privately owned facilities. The seed store has now physically collapsed and is largely non-operational in terms of services; so too the cooperative function it housed.

This is not to say that the government has withdrawn completely from the village. In fact, the period after 1993 saw a major rise in the amount of funds being made available. The school, for example, has expanded up to the secondary level, and now has a number of classrooms, toilets, and a kitchen. Lakhs of rupees come to the *panchayat* every year under various government schemes including the Mahatma Gandhi National Rural Employment Guarantee Scheme (MGNREGS), social security pensions, school meals, and so on.[4] However, the funding does not always meet the articulated objectives, to put it mildly. Funds disappear, and the services remain of low quality and are hard to access. In Section 11.7, we analyse how the caste and gender relationships can explain, at least partly, the lack of accountability or demand for public services in the village.

11.2 Caste and Occupation

The changes in the occupational structure of Palanpur households are features of all castes. Traditional caste-based *jajmani* occupations are beginning to disappear, and newer kinds of jobs in the non-farm sector have emerged. These new jobs are both inside and outside the village. As a result, the relationship between caste and occupational structure is also changing with all castes being engaged in a wide range of occupations. While in the earlier rounds, one could identify a single major occupation as being of special importance for each caste, this is not the case anymore. From a situation where no Thakur or Murao was working as a casual labourer and very few Jatabs were anything but casual labourers, we now have a number of Thakurs also working as casual labourers, Jatabs leasing-in land for cultivation, and some Muraos moving out of agriculture. However, at the same time there is still some caste-based pattern in occupation, and therefore it is premature to argue that the relationship between caste and occupation structure has completely disappeared in Palanpur.[5] Further, now that the links with the outside are stronger than ever before, any analysis has to take into account processes

---

[4] Approximately 10–12 lakhs per annum is the figure we arrived at based on estimates of the amounts that came into the village for the major schemes such as MGNREGS, pensions, midday meals, and an untied grant of Rs 3 lakh.

[5] Jodhka (2017), based on his survey of villages in Bihar, argues that the new economy dominated by non-farm activities is also characterized by persistence of differential incomes and discriminatory practices based on caste.

outside the village and their relationship with village structures to explain what is going on inside.

Overall, the contribution of agriculture to the economy of Palanpur has reduced considerably. While the Muraos are still strongly committed to agriculture, Thakurs, who were the first to move into non-farm occupations, are increasingly moving away from cultivation. On the other hand, more Jatabs now own or lease-in land. There are some Murao households now which have moved away from cultivation as their main source of income, and for a few non-farm casual labour has even become their main source of income. The Ansari report based on the survey in 1957/8 stated that between them, Thakurs and Muraos owned all the land in the village, and Jatabs were found to be exclusively tenants (Ansari, 1964). Now, although there is still great inequality in land ownership, some Jatabs own the land they cultivate. Further, while Jatabs cultivated (own land or leased) about 9 per cent of all village land in 1983, this proportion almost doubled to 17 per cent in 2009. This was in large measure associated with a decline in the Murao share from 41 per cent to 36 per cent and with smaller caste groups such as Dhimars and Passis moving out of the village and thus relinquishing their land.

The relative decline in agriculture has not only been linked with occupational choices in the village, but also changes in social relationships. Most of the caste-based relationships had deep roots in the agrarian production system. The system of sharing of produce as part-payment for labour was an integral part of the village labour market. With the emergence of widespread non-farm employment, piece-rated contracts are becoming dominant, with most transactions taking place in cash. For example, in the head-loading work at Moradabad, a group of ten workers are assigned a railway truck for unloading and paid for completing the task. Further, agricultural operations are also becoming increasingly monetized. One of the implications of these changes in occupation and payment structures is the decline in patronage that the higher castes and land-owning families had on lower castes and landless labourers. Gupta (2005), based on his visits to western Uttar Pradesh, argues that the decline in agriculture has not only affected occupational choices, but has also contributed to changing the culture in villages, which had been largely based on agricultural transactions. Similar observations are made by Harriss and Jeyaranjan (2016) using their analysis of longitudinal data of several south Indian villages.[6] Jodhka (2016), based on his re-survey of Haryana villages, also highlights the decline of structures of village identity centred on economic relations rooted in agriculture.

---

[6] Harriss et al. (2016) use the term 'post-agrarian' to define the nature of villages in the last two decades.

In Palanpur, too, the move towards non-farm activities has had an impact beyond the observed changes in income and occupation. Along with the weakening of agriculture, there is also a change in the caste-based norms on division of labour. In agriculture there were set caste-based norms on the roles households could play; for example, it was almost impossible for Thakurs to work as agricultural labourers or for Jatabs to own land. For the new occupations there is some amount of caste neutrality in the task itself, which has allowed people to diversify. In jobs outside the village, people are now working with those from other castes more than they did before. Further, the fact that many of these jobs are located outside the village also makes it easier for people to shed their traditional roles and undertake something new or different without feeling the intensity of social pressure that can arise within the village.

Notwithstanding these changes, we still see broad occupational patterns by caste, as we described in Parts 1 and 2 of this book. Wage labour remains the highest among Jatabs and cultivation highest among Muraos. While earlier these were maintained by social norms as well as asset ownership, now there is a further avenue through the role that networks and connections play in getting outside jobs. Therefore, a Thakur group leader in the railway sheds in Moradabad prefers to have other Thakur or upper-caste members in his group. The group leader contacts those of this own caste when there is a work opportunity. Mutual trust and teamwork are a key ingredient of this work. Thakurs who are seeking work would perceive that this activity does not imply loss of social status, in contrast to working as labourers in the village, which they find unacceptable. Other factors such as better education and more resources have also advantaged Thakurs in acquiring whatever few regular jobs might arise.

Such networks are seen to play a role in other occupations as well where other castes are dominant—such as marble polishing, repair shops, security guards, and so on. The Jatabs still continue to be at the bottom of the ladder, with many of them working in brick kilns as their main source of non-farm diversification. Work in the brick kilns is of the most unpleasant and often exploitative kind. In many cases, they have to move away from the village for a few months each year and all the members of the household have to work to make the most of this opportunity as the payment is on a piece-rate basis. That enables women and children to contribute, something which is more difficult in the village context. This feature of work opportunities for the whole family, together with greater regularity than agricultural labour, makes such work attractive, notwithstanding its unpleasant nature. Other than brick kilns, the Jatabs are also engaged in some other non-farm occupations but mostly as wage labourers. However, on the positive side, such access to outside jobs and cash incomes have now made it possible for Jatabs to lease-in land for cultivation and pay cash for necessary inputs, such as ploughing by tractor.

Thus, the new occupational structures have to some extent depended on and reinforced caste networks. Caste networks have also emerged as an important factor affecting migration behaviour, with migrants from the same caste often acting as a source of information by helping with contacts for jobs, arranging for accommodation, and so on. In many aspects of the new economy, and in managing change, trust plays an important role and caste remains a determinant of how much one person trusts the other. The power of social sanction is also greater within castes. Such intra-caste economic dealings based on trust are evident in not just non-farm jobs, but also in tenancy choices.[7] Similar issues arise in lending and borrowing.

Therefore, while changes in the occupational structure are driving a transformation in the dynamics between the castes, it is still too early to claim that caste does not play a role in determining a household's economic opportunities or its social status. The phrase 'greater equality' amongst the castes can be overdone. If we look at the big sectors into which non-farm diversification is taking place—brick kiln (Jatabs), repair services (Muslims), working in railway yards or *mal godam* (Thakurs), and marble polishing (mixed, with Muslims playing a strong role), there is still some caste concentration, and caste networks are used to bring people into the net. In 1983 such networks were seen to be working for the Thakurs but not for others; they have now become of use for other castes as well.

11.3 The Village as a Residential Unit

The changing nature of the village economy, with its declining share of agriculture and the emergence of the non-farm sector, also has implications for the village as an economic and social unit. One of the reasons that anthropologists as well as economists were attracted to villages as the unit of observation was the nature of village society. The village was seen as an autonomous unit centred around its economy, which was primarily agrarian.[8] Mahatma Gandhi considered villages as the unit of economic planning and a strong society for his conception of economic growth and development.[9]

Many villagers now have jobs outside the village, and it is seen that commuting and not migrating is the most common form of accessing these jobs. The rise in commuting should be seen in the context of a population which is

---

[7] See Chapters 5 and 6 for details.

[8] Even in official statistics and administrative rules, villages continue to be seen as agriculture-dominated units. One of the important criteria of reclassifying a village into a census town is that more than three quarters of workers in the village should be engaged in non-farm occupations.

[9] The Gandhian model was based on self-reliant villages with most of the consumption and production happening within the village.

mobile but yet rooted to village life. With most non-farm outside jobs being informal in nature and wages higher than in agriculture but not greatly so, the cost of staying away from the village in the urban areas is certainly a reason why commuters prefer to stay in the village. However, the choice of village as a residential unit for those who prefer to work outside—with only a small share of their economic transactions in the village—is not just an economic one. It is also a reflection of the uncertainty of the informal job market outside the village. The village continues to provide social networks and some form of community security or insurance.

Our discussion with migrants outside the village suggests that most either continue to maintain strong links with the village or would like to re-establish links with it. It not only remains as their roots or identity in an anonymized urban world, but is also the fall-back option in case of economic difficulty or uncertainty. For most social engagements, be it marriage or religious and social events, the identity of the village is still important. For most migrants, marriages are still arranged by relatives in the village and, for some of them, they do hold the ceremony in the village. Overall, there has been a recasting of the role that village society used to play in an individual's life. While it is less important than earlier as far as economic relations are concerned, the social relations which define identity and the notions of home and belonging remain strong.

11.4 Changing Social Relations: Caste

Within the village, both the changing occupational structure and the development of institutions such as elected village *panchayats* are contributing to changing social relations between castes. The Ansari report on Palanpur observed that the 'inter-caste differences in the economic plane in the village are much less marked than in the social plane' (Ansari, 1964:30). This could be said to be more or less true in the village even today. However, in a comparative perspective, economic differences are much smaller than earlier, and social hierarchies are also undergoing change. From an outsider perspective, the village seems to be fairly calm, with no apparent inter-caste or inter-religious tensions. In terms of living arrangements, the households of major caste groups are not fully segregated. Further, Muslim households are scattered throughout the village. Although the majority of Jatab households are situated at the northern side of the village around the pond, some Thakurs and Muraos have also built houses there. The Thakur and Murao households otherwise mostly live near the railway station. There is also no apparent restriction on drinking water from public handpumps. Different (male) caste members can be seen chatting and gossiping with each other. There are no visible signs of the kind of untouchability which was practised earlier in the village.

Nevertheless, amongst the major castes the Thakurs are still considered to be top in the social hierarchy, followed by the Muraos and then, with a substantial perceived gap, the Jatabs. The Muslim castes such as Dhobi and Teli are placed slightly higher than the Jatabs. While overt forms of untouchability are not practised any more, many subtle differences remain. For instance, a person of a lower caste is still not offered food in a Thakur household. Those belonging to higher castes attend weddings in Jatab households, but will eat food there only if it is cooked by a professional cook (*halwai*) of a different caste. They do not eat in the Muslim households either. During marriage ceremonies, an invitation is given for all members of the household of the same caste; but in the case of households of other castes, only one member from each family is invited. It was rare in the earlier survey periods for a Jatab to sit at the same level with a Thakur or Murao and discuss politics, but such political discussions and negotiations are now common in the village.

Women of one caste barely interact with women of other castes. While the interactions amongst men have definitely increased over the years due to the changing economy in the village, restrictions on women's mobility and the fact that very few women in the village are engaged in jobs outside their household or farm greatly limits opportunities for such interactions. At the same time, with almost all children in the village now going to primary school and many even to high school, in the younger generation the chance of meeting and socializing is greater.

However, there are strict rules and customs as far as inter-caste relations are concerned. Marriages are still strictly within the castes. Caste endogamy and clan exogamy is practised among Hindus.[10] Most of the marriages are arranged, with relatives playing the role of intermediator or matchmaker.[11] Dowry is still prevalent, and the rate depends mainly on the asset position of

[10] Standard marriage practices such as caste endogamy, village and clan exogamy, hypergamy (the groom's economic status to be higher than of the bride), and patrilocality (the wife moves to the husband's house after marriage) still remain in Palanpur as in most parts of rural north India. Among Hindus, marriages are arranged amongst the same caste (caste endogamy) and many times even sub-castes are important. However, at the same time, amongst most upper-caste Hindus in north India the bride and the groom must not be related to each other in any manner or belong to the same *gotra* (clan). This refusal to allow clan endogamy is in contrast to south India, where cross-cousin marriages are allowed. In north India, amongst Muslims, clan endogamy is usually allowed.

[11] Most marriages are still decided without asking for the consent of the girl. While the parents still made the decision on who their daughter should marry, in some cases women did mention that their parents would ask them for their consent before finalizing the match. However, this does not yet mean that the girl and boy get to meet and talk before the marriage, as is now happening in the case of 'arranged' marriages in urban India. One change that people did mention was that now there was a 'greater' demand for 'educated' girls, especially among Thakurs, and this was one of reasons why parents felt it was important to send their daughters to school.

411

the groom. The richer the groom's family is, the higher the dowry demanded. The dowry is also higher if the groom has a regular job, irrespective of asset position. The norm is also to marry a girl into a family which is economically better off or comparable. Most of the brides and grooms are from a catchment area of 40–50 kilometres from the village. However, there are some cases where men have had to go a long distance to find a bride. There are now five married women in the village from the Midnapore district of Bengal. These are women from poor backgrounds, and the marriage often involves payment of money by the groom, in other words a bride price. There is a middleman in the village who arranges these marriages. These marriages are generally arranged for men who are unable to get married, usually because they are very poor, physically handicapped, or elderly. These women are kept under veil during the initial years and are allowed to move within the village only after their children are grown up. During the initial years, these women are not allowed to participate in customary caste events, with most of them generally confined within the household.

11.5 Changing Social Relations: Religion

Muslims comprise 16 per cent of the population in the village, and their population share in the village has increased over the years. There are two main types of Muslim families in the village, Dhobis and Telis.[12] As mentioned in the previous studies on Palanpur, there are no overt tensions between Hindus and Muslims. The village has never seen a communal 'riot', and the two religious groups are linked to each other economically in several ways. At the same time, there are some undercurrents which do exist.

One of the issues of silent friction between the two communities is to do with the discomfort that many Hindu households feel with the Muslims exerting their religious identity. The nearest mosque is in the neighbouring village Pipli, which has a large Muslim population. This mosque also has a *madrasa* (religious school) where a number of Muslim families send their children for some initial learning of religious texts. The Palanpur Muslims have been demanding that they be allowed to construct a mosque in the village but so far the Hindu families have resisted any such proposal. They have no formal right to forbid construction of a mosque, but the social pressures can be overwhelming. Therefore, while there are four temples in the village, there is not a single mosque. This has led to some acrimony in the recent past, but there has not been any violence between the communities.

---

[12] Traditional occupational associations for Dhobis and Telis are washing and oil pressing. There are substantially more Telis than Dhobis in Palanpur.

An incident where these differences came to the fore was during the *panchayat* elections of 2012. The *pradhan* post was for women (only women could contest). One of the contestants was the wife of an influential Muslim man who was quite active in the village. Many appreciated his work, particularly in taking up village-related issues at higher levels, as he had some contacts with the local MLA.[13] However, when his wife decided to contest the elections, there was a consolidation of a Hindu position, especially amongst the upper castes, where one of the issues they campaigned on was that there would likely be a mosque in the village if she became the Pradhan. There is also some discomfort brewing because a number of Teli families, including this aspiring politician, have been amongst the most successful and entrepreneurial households that have diversified into non-farm occupations and seen an improvement in living standards. On the whole though, in spite of the changing environment between religious communities in the state of Uttar Pradesh and this western region in particular, Palanpur has, fortunately, not yet witnessed any major communal clashes.

11.6 Democratization and Participation

As seen in Sections 11.2, 11.3, 11.4, and 11.5, there has been some democratization of power relations and activities in the village with occupational diversification, greater monetization, and decline of agriculture. One of the institutional factors that has contributed to giving greater voice to the weaker sections in the village is the introduction of regular *panchayat* elections after the passing of the 73rd amendment to the Constitution.[14] Since 1995 the village has seen regular elections. Due to the system of reservations for SCs and women, by rotation, during the last two survey rounds Palanpur had first a Dalit Pradhan and then a female Pradhan. Further, recent years have also seen a huge expansion in the quantum of funds coming into the village *panchayat* as a result of central government policies favouring greater decentralization. Both these processes have led to more people being involved in public affairs. The caste *panchayats* which were earlier more influential than the village *panchayat* are now almost non-existent. At the same time, caste hierarchies, coordination, and politics still continue to influence both the outcomes of *panchayat* elections and decisions around allocations of funds. This was reflected in the way the upper castes in the village first supported a

---

[13] Member of Legislative Assembly (MLA). The Legislative Assembly is the legislature at the state level. The local MLA belonged to the Muslim community.

[14] The 73rd amendment to the Constitution was passed in 1992. It provided for a three-tier *panchayat* system in rural areas.

particular Dalit candidate in the village for the post of Pradhan and later themselves led a revolt against him.

The introduction of *panchayat* elections in the village has also led to a realignment of caste groups, in particular because a certain proportion of seats are reserved for OBCs and SCs. The post of the village Pradhan was reserved, for the first time, for SCs during 2005–10. During 2010–15 it was reserved for a female candidate. The village elections are generally fought along caste lines with large caste groups dominating the election process. During the 2005 election, the Thakurs aligned with Mahesh, who is a Balmiki,[15] in order to defeat the Jatab candidate, Ramjit. Balmikis are a small minority among the SC households in Palanpur that are otherwise dominated by Jatabs. The support to Mahesh was basically given to prevent the Jatabs from having a dominant role in village politics. Ramjit was supported by other caste groups including Muslims but lost by 13 votes to Mahesh.

After a couple of years Mahesh became so unpopular with his supporters that they eventually lead a mobilization to get him removed. The charges against him were that he did not do anything for the village and that he was very corrupt and usurped a large share of the funds earmarked for the village. The antagonism, however, was not purely because Mahesh did not undertake any development work; the previous headmen had not done much either. Nor was it that he showed favouritism in allocating government benefits. This was also the practice earlier. For example, many villagers reported that under the previous Pradhan one of the richest persons in the village, owning a tractor, thresher, mentha plant, and so on, got a grant under the Indira Awas Yojana (IAY) because of his close relationship with the Pradhan.[16]

Previous Pradhans had been both ineffective and corrupt without being thrown out. Two additional factors worked against Mahesh. First, he did not include any of the powerful people in the village in what he was doing, not even those who got him elected as Pradhan. It was during his tenure that the school midday meal was completely stopped, while most people knew that grain continued to be supplied for this purpose. It was rumoured that this was one of the main reasons for the fallout between the Pradhan and the local schoolteacher, another influential member of the village.

Second, he also indulged in petty corruption and offensive behaviour, with almost no patronage to anyone in the village. He asked for money or liquor even for the smallest things, like signing a document or certificate. He was also drunk most of the time and would pass lewd comments on women passing by.

---

[15] The Balmikis (also known as 'Bhangis') are traditionally 'sweepers' and are ranked very close to the bottom of the hierarchy.

[16] IAY is a scheme that provides a subsidy to help those who are poor and do not have a house construct one.

As a result, the level of anger among the entire village community was very high, and when a campaign began that he should be impeached there was widespread support for this. This became the principal topic of discussion in the village for a few weeks, with almost everyone except four or five households being against the Pradhan. Many women were vocal about how he needed to be removed, and many of them campaigned against him.

While a large number of people in the village wanted him removed, the process of impeachment was drawn out and required much effort by some of the villagers over more than four months. The villagers collected details of funds that came to the village using the Right to Information Act and filed complaints against the Pradhan at the Block Development Office (BDO) with detailed charges of irregularities.[17] An enquiry was ordered, and the team found that even on the date of enquiry, no midday meal was served at the school. Following this, an application for a no-confidence motion against Mahesh was submitted to the district magistrate in Moradabad, signed by 530 people from the village including all the *gram panchayat* members. Simultaneously a similar process was undertaken towards the removal of the Public Distribution System (PDS) dealer in the village. A vote was then held on this motion, and the Pradhan was finally 'impeached' by an overwhelming majority of 416 to 27.

Elections, which the impeached Pradhan contested, were held for a new Pradhan after three weeks. The post continued to be reserved for SCs for the remaining two years of the original five-year term. While there were a few other candidates in the fray, once again the 'elders' decided who would have their support. Ramjit, the Jatab candidate, who came a close second in the previous election, was chosen. There was intense campaigning by the earlier Pradhan, where he not only apologized for his previous misdeeds and promised to reform but also distributed a lot of liquor and allegedly cash as well. Nevertheless, out of 491 votes cast, Ramjit got 401 and was elected as Pradhan.

While the Jatabs felt increasingly empowered due to rising relative income and a favourable political environment in state politics, which was then ruled by the BSP, they could never establish a dominant role in village politics. Even Ramjit, who was elected after the impeachment of the previous Pradhan, was dependent on Thakurs and Muraos for the day-to-day running of village affairs. This was evident also in how the money for MGNREGS was spent; much of it was used to improve village roads around the Thakur and Murao households.

Ramjit completed Mahesh's term. At the end of this term the Pradhan's post was once again reserved, this time for a female candidate. Other than formally filing the papers in a woman's name, the entire contest and campaign was for

---

[17] Every state is divided into districts and districts are further divided into blocks. A BDO is the highest administrative officer at the block level.

and by the husbands. While one of the active persons in the village (Naseem, a Muslim), with a reputation of being honest and hard-working, filed a nomination in his wife's name, the post was ultimately won by a Thakur woman who lives outside the village. Naseem claimed that although he was promised support by many of the powerful people in the village, who also worked with him closely for the removal of the earlier *pradhan*, they ultimately ended up putting their weight behind an ex-army employee from the village who lives in Moradabad. In our discussions with some of the key people in the village, they said that they favoured the army officer because he lived outside, had worked in the army, and was already rich and therefore did not need to make money from the *panchayat*.

Therefore, while reservations seem to have given some voice to the Dalits, with first Mahesh, then Ramjit being a Pradhan in the village for several years, it is too early to suggest that this has led to a mainstreaming of the Dalits in the decision-making process.[18] While the village came together to overthrow the Dalit Pradhan, no such public outrage has been seen against the female Pradhan who was running the *panchayat* through proxy through her nephew. The female Pradhan lived outside the village. The nephew seemed to be as corrupt as the earlier Dalit Pradhan, but there were barely any protests against his inefficiencies and corruption in running the *panchayat*. Nor has the election of a female Pradhan changed anything materially as far as participation of women in the political process in the village is concerned.[19] They continue to remain marginalized in village politics.[20]

What both examples of *panchayat* elections in the village in the last decade show is that the regular conduct of such elections (with reservations), together with the large amount of funds (grants and centrally sponsored schemes) that are now directly handled by the *panchayats*, have contributed to changing caste dynamics in the village. While the Thakurs and Muraos still continue to

---

[18] On the role of caste in *panchayat* elections in Uttar Pradesh, see Kumar (2016). Kumar argues that the reservation in the *panchayat* system has given Dalits representation in the local politics, but has failed to change the caste relations in the village, with upper castes dominating the political process or colluding to capture it.

[19] Sathe et al. (2013) find a positive impact of reservation on availability of public services in Maharashtra in female-headed *panchayats* compared to male-headed *panchayats*. Chattopadhyay and Duflo (2004) also report greater investment in infrastructure in female-headed *panchayats*. While most studies (Bardhan, Mookherjee, and Torrado, 2005; Duflo and Topalova, 2004; Lindberg et al., 2011) report that reserved female political roles have a positive impact on village public services, Palanpur has not seen improvements in performance of the village *panchayat* during the term of the female Pradhan.

[20] Although they remain largely invisible in village politics, they were seen to be vocal during the impeachment of the earlier *pradhan*. Some even joined the protest demonstration to the district magistrate's office, travelling on tractors.

pull the strings, they now have to negotiate hard with the Jatabs and Muslims.[21] These two groups have become more confident; some of them have seen economic successes, and they have benefited from the wider UP political environment which, around 2009, the time of the most recent detailed surveys, was much in favour of these groups.

One of the reasons why the caste arithmetic within the village has such a great impact on village politics is that no political party has any significant presence there. There was some political consciousness among the Jatabs that they belonged to the same caste as the then-Chief Minister of Uttar Pradesh, Mayawati. Many in the village (including Jatabs themselves) observed that the Jatabs had become more vocal and were generally more confident in voicing their opinions after the BSP won the state elections with a large majority in 2007. However, there is no organized group or branch of the BSP in the village. Some Dalit households did paint their houses blue, a colour symbolizing their affiliation to BSP. Also, some villagers have access to political leaders and can call on them for help. For example, some of the Muslims have access to a minister from the same caste and they approach him sometimes, taking along villagers from other castes, when they need help. The general feeling in the village is that because it is a small place with not many votes, political parties are not interested in investing any time there.

We should note that the role of Pradhan was largely ceremonial when Bliss and Stern first came to the village in 1974. Politics around the role were not intense as it carried little power and dispensed very few resources.

11.7 Collective Action and Public Services

The increased flow of funds has certainly increased the interest of the villagers in the *panchayat*. Some impact of the increased financial status and strength of the *panchayat* is visible in the form of better roads and improvement in school meals. Most villagers admit to the increased public spending being useful but also complain about corruption and favouritism in the implementation of government schemes. Despite continuing failures of the public services, there has been no serious attempt to collectively set things right and demand accountability.

Palanpur was selected as part of the Agro-Economic Research Centre (AERC) surveys because of the presence of cooperatives in the village. The only

---

[21] Anderson et al. (2015) documents the role of elite minorities in the village in subverting pro-poor redistributive policies, in their analysis of *panchayats* in Maharashtra. Also see Bardhan and Mukherjee (2012).

element left now is the primary cooperative society, which does some lending. The cooperative seed store, which was the residence of the research investigators during the surveys in the 1970s, 1980s, and 1990s, and was then quite active, is now in a dilapidated condition. But even other cooperative institutions such as the sugar cooperative are now absent from the village. The decline of these formal cooperative institutions has partly been due to the government but also because of an absence of any institutional ownership among the villagers.

Although successive Finance Commissions have increased the money available to the village as untied grants,[22] these have rarely been used in the case of Palanpur; it would require calling a formal *gram sabha* (village assembly). The functioning of other programmes such as the MGNREGS, PDS, and social pensions, has been weak, with corruption still a major problem. Issues of exclusion of those who are genuine beneficiaries are often discussed informally by the villagers, but hardly ever become an agenda for public action. The same is true in the case of the functioning, or malfunctioning, of the village school and *anganwadi* centre.[23] The village school has seen large investments in infrastructure, being upgraded to offer education up to middle school (class 8), but there is little in the way of public discussion or pressure on the quality of teaching. Similarly, there is no discussion on the functioning of the *anganwadi* centre, which has no real presence, existing largely 'on paper'.[24] Other than the impeachment of a Pradhan, which, as explained, had as much to do with political power plays and corruption as with other considerations, there has not been any collective action taken by the villagers towards improving the state of their public services.

One of the complaints that women have expressed in recent years is the increase in instances of 'eve-teasing' or harassment of women around the liquor shop in the village. The liquor shop is located opposite the railway station, and, as a result, a number of outsiders also hang around the shop in the evening. Women have complained that the presence of the liquor shop in the village has led to men from the village spending more money on alcohol and gambling. However, their demand that the shop be removed has never become a strong or effective village issue.

Drèze and Sharma (1998), based on their work on the surveys of 1983/4 and 1993, had pointed to a few obvious, in their view, opportunities for collective

---

[22] These are established under the Indian Constitution to allocate financial resources between the states of India.

[23] The *anganwadi* centre is the early childcare centre at the village level. This is run under a centrally sponsored programme called the Integrated Child Development Scheme (ICDS) and provides health, nutrition, and education services aimed at pregnant and lactating women, adolescent girls, and children under six.

[24] See Chapter 9 for further details on the *anganwadi* centre in Palanpur.

action that could have helped to improve the quality of life for all. These included improving the village drainage system and coordinating in relation to sowing times. During this round of survey we observed failures of public services such as the stopping of the midday meal in the school, the irregularity of the nurse coming to the village, and other weaknesses of public services. These would seem to be situations evidently waiting for active engagement by the people of the village. Strong collective action could bring important improvements in the public service provisions for the village. Drèze and Sharma (1998), as well as Drèze and Gazdar (1997), postulate that one of the reasons for such lack of collective action is that the social stratification in the village limits the ability of people to come together around key issues. That also raises the question, however, of whether the stratification in Palanpur is any stronger than in other villages where collective action is more effective.

There exists in the village a small group of about 10–12 men who sometimes visit government offices at the block or higher levels if there is something that the village needs.[25] The group also exert some influence on how people vote at the *panchayat* elections and so on. It is also generally seen that anyone who has the support of these people can get away with a lot as well (for example, the schoolteacher). This is, of course, a simplistic presentation, and even within this group of persons there are differences and power struggles, often determined by caste affiliations. The balance of activity or strength differs from time to time depending on the issue and the personal interests of these individuals. When action on the issue in question could be beneficial to all the castes, collective action by villagers is more likely.

Other than the impeachment of the Pradhan, one instance where we saw the village come together collectively was their effort to get rid of the monkeys in the village. Monkeys were a major nuisance when we arrived for our survey in 2008. Villagers estimated that the number of monkeys in the village was almost double the human population. This was not a problem at the time of the previous survey held in 1993, and only developed later. The monkeys seem to have been attracted to Palanpur because of the presence of the station, as train passengers often fed them. It was also surmised that people from nearby villages got rid of monkeys from their own locales by bringing them to Palanpur. While this might appear to be a trivial issue, it in fact was causing severe disruption to daily lives. The monkey menace even changed the cropping pattern in Palanpur. People could no longer grow vegetables or groundnuts. Farms had to be constantly protected by humans before harvest. Someone

---

[25] The researchers involved in the 2008/10 fieldwork made a list of people they would put under this category. It was a list of 11 persons that everyone agreed upon. The group included one Muslim, one Gadariya, and one Jatab. The rest were Thakurs and Muraos. They were all male and heads of the households which were economically amongst the strongest in their respective caste groups.

had to stand guard all the time when women were cooking; this was usually the duty of children (with sticks). Eighty-four cases of monkey bites were reported in the one-year period before the survey. The monkeys were a constant menace even for those visiting the village for the survey; we always had to be careful if we were carrying any food with us.

Given this great inconvenience, it was surprising that there was no attempt to arrive at a collective solution to the problem. Villagers did not even try to stop those from other villages leaving monkeys in Palanpur. Some temporary solutions were worked out by those who could afford it. For example, in some better-off upper-caste homes, they built barricades around the cooking area, and for some farms people bought big guard dogs.

Through newspapers and the researchers, the villagers came to know that some neighbouring villages had managed to get rid of their monkeys. If the forest department was effectively petitioned, officials would come to the village, round up the monkeys, take them away, and release them in a natural habitat conducive to their survival. This motivated the village community to get together to tackle this issue. Under the leadership of a few influential people, the village collected funds from every household. A detailed formula was worked out where each family contributed according to their means. Many villagers volunteered time and joined the professional monkey-trapping team when it arrived. Trapping was done under the supervision of forest department officials and a doctor. The whole operation went on for a few days and according to the forest department's count, over 900 monkeys were caught by them and moved to a forest.

Both these examples, the Pradhan impeachment and the monkey story, show that collective action is possible when the issue affects most of the village population and also gets support from influential people.[26]

Currently, the one event that the entire village gets excited about and contributes to collectively is the Ram Katha that they organize once a year. The Ram Katha is an annual religious event organized jointly by the village, in which even Muslims contribute and participate. During the seven- to ten-day event, sermons are delivered by a priest who is invited from outside the village. He speaks on religious matters, good moral deeds, equality among men and women, and other related matters, and tells stories about the lives of Rama and Sita and how they are relevant in today's changing society. There is a segregated seating arrangement for men and women, and women have to keep their veils on. The villagers have to make individual contributions for the grand feast (*bhandaara*) organized on the last day, and the names, along with the amount of the contributions, are announced over a microphone.

---

[26] Also see Sinha et al. (2016).

The rise of caste and religious identities, particularly since 2013 in national and state politics, in the ways described has led to some polarization within the village community, although this has not yet manifested itself in any form of violence.[27] One consequence of the strengthening of such identities has been the absence of popular mobilization by political parties on issues of health, education, and other social issues. Similarly, Kumar (2016) also noticed increases in religiosity and the emergence of new sects in his study of Khanpur village in western Uttar Pradesh.[28]

11.8 Conclusion

The village has seen significant changes in both economic and social structures, which are closely related. The changes in agriculture, including *zamindari* abolition and the 'green revolution', were powerful forces of change affecting not just institutional structures, but also social and political dynamics. A remarkable feature of the village society has been the changing nature of institutions, which have quickly adjusted to the new realities. The emergence of new non-farm opportunities and increased mechanization of agriculture has been associated with the monetization of agricultural markets. For example, we see some switching away from 50/50 sharecropping towards cash rent and wage labour. This is consistent, too, with outside activity leaving less time for the supervision that share tenancy requires. And potential tenants previously excluded by social convention from hiring-in ploughing services with draught animals can now hire tractor services.

Social institutions such as caste, gender, and group alliances are changing too, not only via labour and land markets, but also in politics. Making a general assumption that because caste relations were centred on agricultural production these changes will unambiguously weaken the village hierarchy, would, however, be to oversimplify. Rather, there has been a re-emergence of caste as a proxy for trust in an increasingly informal and anonymized outside labour market. This is manifested, too, in credit and land markets, where a counter party from the same caste is often preferred.

Exogenous, or externally created, changes such as the introduction of *panchayat* elections mandated by the 73rd amendment to the Constitution,

---

[27] Religious and caste identities were also in play in the general elections of 2014 and in 2017 when the Bharatiya Janata Party (BJP) swept the elections. Despite Uttar Pradesh being a state with a 20% Muslim population, the BJP won the general election in 2014 and the assembly election in 2017 without giving any representation to Muslims. The caste-based polarization has also led to emergence of various caste outfits such as the 'Bhim Army', representing the Dalits.

[28] Kumar (2016) also attributes it to the increasing penetration of television and other forms of communication.

together with reservations for elected positions, have seen new alliances being built both to attempt to preserve power and also to challenge the hegemony of the existing village elites. The devolution of financial powers has also seen demands for accountability and transparency in the functioning of village institutions and greater involvement in village political processes, particularly the *panchayat*.

This 'democratization' of village society has been centred on particular public issues such as resources for school meals and on the monkey menace. But while it has grown, it is still sporadic and weak. There is potential for this to develop further and to emerge as an important point of contestation as well as cooperation in a fragmented society. Overall, Palanpur has not been able to get out of the ditch of extreme social divisions, collective inertia, dismal public services, and very poor social indicators. On the other hand, demand for services such as education and health are increasing amongst all groups. If the state continues to respond poorly, and the private sector is inaccessible or very costly for many, it is possible that mobilization will get stronger. We speculate further about the future in Chapter 12.

In this chapter, we have tried to put in context the changing dynamics between social groups in the village. As with the case of the economy, these are also changing continuously. First, it has been seen that the village has become more concentrated into the three largest castes, with the share of other groups declining and some smaller caste groups, such as the Passis, moving away altogether. This demographic change will likely have an effect on inter-caste relations in the future.

Second, linked to economic diversification, the rise of non-farm activities, and the relative decline in agriculture, is also a change in the relationships between different caste groups. Traditional ways in which hierarchies operated are breaking down, and new forces are at work, including several important ones that are external to the village. While there is some decline in certain kinds of social inequality, the gaps are still very wide. It is the upper castes, especially Thakurs, who are most rapidly moving away from agriculture and the village. Increasingly, those with the biggest personal stake in the village are the lower castes. Currently, upper castes retain their roots in the village in order to provide the security which can help enable their mobility. But over time as they move on, it may well be that the Jatabs and Muslims become most strongly rooted in Palanpur, plus possibly the Muraos, amongst the upper castes, depending on how persistent their commitment to agriculture turns out to be. What this might mean for relations between castes as well as village institutions is an interesting subject for speculation.

The changes in the village economy, society, and politics are happening at various levels. While it is premature to argue that village society is disintegrating (Gupta, 2005), there are certainly rapid changes in the way it has been organized. However, as Jodhka (2016), Harriss and Jeyaranjan (2016), and others have argued, village society is developing a changed identity for a new world in which the village is more closely integrated into the surrounding economy. It is difficult to characterize it solely on the basis of caste and class relations, but as they change they also remain strong. What is clear is that the structure of the village is changing and will change. As Kumar (2016) argues, the penetration of urban markets, communication and information flows, and the emergence of new networks have reconstituted the village into a multi-level and more open settlement. But more than the settlement, these profound external influences have changed the institutional structure which was the basis of economic, social, and political relations, with internal change being shaped also by culture and history. Old hierarchies are breaking down, class boundaries are becoming blurred, relations are changing, and new alliances and groupings are being forged.

Acknowledgement

This chapter was written by Himanshu and Dipa Sinha. We acknowledge the contribution by Dinesh Tiwari and Gajanand Ahirwal.

References

Anderson, S., Francois, P., and Kotwal, A. 2015. 'Clientelism in Indian villages', *American Economic Review* 105, no. 6: 1780–816.

Ansari, N. 1964. 'Palanpur: A Study of its Economic Resources and Economic Activities (No. 41)', Continuous Village Surveys 1958–9. Agricultural Economics Research Centre, University of Delhi.

Bardhan, P., and Mookherjee, D. 2012. 'Political clientelism and capture'. International Growth Centre Working Paper.

Bardhan, P., Mookherjee, D., and Torrado, M.P. 2005. 'Impact of reservations of panchayat presidents on targeting in west Bengal'. Bureau for Research and Economic Analysis of Development Working Paper No. 104.

Chattopadhyay, R., and Duflo, E. 2004. 'Women as policy makers: evidence from a randomized policy experiment in India', *Econometrica* 72, no. 5: 1409–43.

Drèze, J., and Gazdar, H. 1997. 'Uttar Pradesh: the burden of inertia', in J. Dreze and A. Sen (eds), *Indian Development: Selected Regional Perspectives*. New Delhi: Oxford University Press.

Drèze, J., and Sharma, N. 1998. 'Palanpur: population, society, economy', in P. Lanjouw and N.H. Stern (eds), *Economic Development in Palanpur over Five Decades*. New Delhi and Oxford: Oxford University Press.

Duflo, E., and Topalova, P. 2004. 'Unappreciated service: performance, perceptions, and women: leaders in India'. MIT Department of Economics. Available at https://econpapers.repec.org/paper/febframed/00233.htm (accessed 10 April 2018).

Gupta, D. 2005. 'Whither the Indian village: culture and agriculture in rural India', *Economic & Political Weekly* 40: 751–8.

Harriss, J., and Jeyaranjan, J. 2016. 'Rural Tamil Nadu in the liberalisation era: what do we learn from village studies?', in Himanshu, P. Jha, and G. Rodgers (eds), *The Changing Village in India: Insights from Longitudinal Research*. New Delhi: Oxford University Press.

Jodhka, S. 2016. 'A forgotten "revolution": revisiting rural life and agrarian change in Haryana', in Himanshu, P. Jha, and G. Rodgers (eds), *The Changing Village in India: Insights from Longitudinal Research*. New Delhi: Oxford University Press.

Jodhka, S. 2017. 'Non-farm economy in Madhubani, Bihar: social dynamics and exclusionary rural transformations', *Economic & Political Weekly* 52, nos 25–6: 14–24.

Kumar, S. 2016. 'Agrarian transformation and the new rurality in western Uttar Pradesh', *Economic & Political Weekly* 51, nos 26–7: 61–71.

Lindberg, S., Athreya, V.B., Vidyasagar, R., Djurfeldt, G., and Rajagopal, A. 2011. 'A silent "revolution"? Women's empowerment in rural Tamil Nadu', *Economic & Political Weekly* 46: 111–20.

Sathe, D., Priebe, J., Biniwale, M., and Klasen, S. 2013. 'Can the female sarpanch deliver', *Economic & Political Weekly* 48, no. 11: 50–7.

Sinha, D., Tiwari, D.K., Bhattacharya, R., and Kattumuri, R. 2016. 'Public services, social relations, politics, and gender: tales from a north Indian village', in Himanshu, P. Jha, and G. Rodgers (eds), *The Changing Village in India: Insights from Longitudinal Research*. New Delhi: Oxford University Press.

Part 4
Reflections

12

Future Prospects*

12.1 Looking Back and Looking Forward

'The farther backward you look, the farther forward you are likely to see' is an aphorism usually attributed to Winston Churchill.[1] Given that we have been examining evidence on Palanpur since Independence, if the aphorism has substance it invites us to look some decades ahead. In this chapter, on a few subjects and in a broad-brush way, we accept that invitation.

We start our speculations about the future, therefore, by reminding ourselves, in this section, of the key forces, trends, and outcomes that we have seen in Palanpur over the last seven decades. That will lead later in the chapter to questions concerning which forces at work in the past are likely to be of particular prominence in the future, and what other forces or trends, including from the economy and society as a whole, may develop. But before looking forward, we will briefly review our past speculations on the future, offered in our earlier books, Bliss and Stern (1982) and Lanjouw and Stern (1998). It is interesting to reflect on where we were on the right track and where we got things wrong, and why. That is the subject of Section 12.2.

In Section 12.3, we consider broad future forces and trends in the India and Uttar Pradesh economies concerning the pace and nature of growth and how these might affect Palanpur. We speculate on possible broad future outcomes for the Palanpur economy, which might arise from these forces and trends, including growth, integration with the outside economy, the future of agriculture, and general living standards. We suggest that the expansion of non-farm and informal employment (both casual and self-employment) based on the growth of smaller towns and cities will be a central feature of India's growth.

---

* This chapter has been written by Nicholas Stern, Himanshu, and Peter Lanjouw.
[1] Churchill himself had, in our view, a feeble understanding of India and its potential. And his forecasts for the future of India were dismissive, deeply gloomy, and, in key respects, badly wrong. But his observation here, as a historian, has substance. In looking to the future, it is important to reflect on the long story.

The first of our five key themes in this book has been that such growth has been vital to rising living standards and social change in Palanpur. We suggest that it will continue to be critical for Palanpur's future.

For Sections 12.4, 12.5, 12.6, and 12.7, our focus is within the village and structured on four other key themes from our analysis in this book. In Section 12.4, we discuss the future of poverty, inequality, and mobility; in Section 12.5, possible developments in institutions; in Section 12.6, human development; and in Section 12.7, entrepreneurship. Finally, in Section 12.8, we offer, in conclusion, a mix of optimism and anxiety.

From our earlier work on Palanpur, recall that in both of the previous books we emphasized three factors—population growth, technological change, and outside economic possibilities—as drivers of change. In this book, we have emphasized these same forces, but with different relative emphases since the 1990s/early 2000s.

We have argued that *non-farm opportunities* have been of ever-growing influence. They have increased strongly in scale, and their nature has, broadly speaking, become more informal and casual. They have been driven, in large measure, by the growth of nearby towns and often connected with construction. Their take-up has spread strongly across the social and economic structure of the village, with Jatabs, for example, involved in unskilled and informal labour markets in Moradabad, Chandausi, and elsewhere. Previously, outside activity was more formal and access skewed towards the better-off groups in Palanpur. Self-employment income from varied activities and places, from marble polishing to motorcycle repair shop to retail, has been a major driving force for growth. Some of these jobs have been within the village but they are all dependent on local, including urban, growth.

For these more recent decades in relation to agriculture, we have come to emphasize investment, changing cropping patterns, intensification of irrigation, mechanization, and monetization of input markets. In the first few rounds of surveys, our stress was on *technological change* associated with new varieties, irrigation, and fertilizers (occasionally under the heading green revolution), which in many ways took the form of land augmentation in a land-scarce economy. Now, whilst recognizing that technology and capital are intertwined and that land remains scarce, our focus has been more strongly on increasing capital intensity: tractors and other machinery replacing draught animals and labour power, electricity in place of diesel, and so on. Thus, farms and farmers have seen investment that releases labour for other activities.

Population growth, on which we laid strong emphasis, particularly in Bliss and Stern (1982), covering 1957 to 1975, has slowed, and outward movement, particularly in employment and to a lesser extent migration, is becoming more prominent. So, too, is education, although very much in its early stages. Our population story over the last two or three decades has moved towards the changing nature of the workforce, the society, and individual skills and attributes.

Overall, however, we must stress that the most powerful influence on development and change in the village is now the economy outside. The story of a village as a well-contained community, with its particular institutions shaped and driven largely by internal forces, is long gone, at least for Palanpur. In telling the story of change and understanding that change, in more recent decades we have drawn out five interrelated themes. Most of our speculation about the future can be structured around how the factors at work within these themes might develop.

In summary, our five themes have been the following: (i) the driving role of non-farm activities, including their informality; (ii) change in mobility, inequality, and poverty, strongly linked to non-farm opportunities, with the mobility they offer associated with rising inequality; (iii) development of Palanpur's institutions under the forces of economic change, including market structures and political and social institutions, together with the implications of the institutions and their change for economic change; (iv) human development, including in relation to education, health, and gender and to relatively slow progress; and (v) entrepreneurship in taking action to change lives and livelihoods, including its distribution and relevant obstacles. Sections 12.3 to 12.7 reflect these five themes.

12.2 Past Attempts at Forward Predictions

For the 1982 book we had three surveys and three decades as a basis for forward speculation; for the 1998 book we had five surveys and five decades (counting the 'thinner survey' of 1993). We did indeed indulge in some forward speculation in both cases. We are now in the position of having seven surveys covering seven decades and are tempted, and shall succumb, to speculate at somewhat greater length. But before we do this, let us look back on our previous speculations.

In the final chapter of Bliss and Stern (1982), we offered some forward speculation, also taking into account a revisit, after 1975, in August 1977. Our main thoughts, guesses, and anticipations were the following. We began, as noted, from the perspective of seeing the driving forces as population growth, technology, and outside jobs. Interestingly, in looking forward, we focused on response to rapid population growth and saw change and agricultural intensification within the village as primary amongst the responses. Indeed, we stated 'we doubt that there will be great scope for Palanpur to solve its population problems by migration. The difficulty is for migrants to obtain jobs.' We were right about agricultural intensification, both via inputs and switching to higher-value crops. We suggested a move to greater irrigation and mechanization, better varieties, and more cash crops. All that, broadly speaking, has come to pass.

We were, however, on the wrong track on relations with the outside economy. Such relations have indeed become very important for Palanpur, as we foresaw and subsequently have seen. What we did not foresee, at least not well enough, was the rise of informal employment, the rise of commuting as opposed to migration, and the rise of communication, in particular the mobile phone, as enabling travel and commuting to work with improved confidence of finding employment.

The growth of the informal sector and activities was not at the centre of economic analysis or understanding in the 1970s. Probably the economics profession as a whole underplayed that set of issues.[2] The growth analysis and models focused on employment outside agriculture as being more formal than it has turned out to be. Indeed, there are still many who see the formal sector and manufacturing as offering 'proper jobs' and as being overwhelmingly important as the key to the future. Palanpur's experience and that of India as a whole raises a question mark. Will Africa, for example, see structural change more like China, and perhaps Latin America, with stronger formal sectors, or will it be more informal, like India? And will the future of India see strong continuation of informal sector growth, much of it in services, including those related to construction, as the big driver of changing opportunities? If so, this would likely have profound implications for mobility, inequality, security, and for policy.

We argued also in Chapter 10 of Bliss and Stern (1982) that differential responses to opportunities could lead to rising inequality. Thus we suggested that some farmers would intensify activities before others. In retrospect, whilst that was not wrong, the bigger force for growth in inequality since the later 1970s has been associated with some taking up non-farm employment opportunities before others, and some being more successful in the new ventures than others. And in fact, we are now arguing more prominently than in the previous books that the expansion of irrigation that occurred during the 1960s was probably an important force of equalization. At least some of the substantial decline in inequality observed between 1962/3 and 1974/5 could be linked to that. The move from around 50 per cent of land irrigated to nearly all land irrigated in that period can be seen as a 'catch-up' at the lower end of the income distribution and of real importance. In contrast, the involvement

---

[2] It was not, of course, entirely absent. In the 1950s Peter Bauer's book on *West African Trade* (1954, 1963) and Albert Hirschman's book *The Strategy of Economic Development* (1958) did emphasize informality, but this perspective lost its prominence and played a minor role in the modelling of growth.

in outside activities is at an early stage, and its increase has led to rising inequality. These two phenomena taken together highlight what we might call the Kuznets insight: new opportunities at first increase inequality but, at a later stage, the diffusion of these activities is an equalizing force. We discuss this further in Chapter 13, in relation to theory.

We speculated that the birth rate would fall and that education would improve. These seemed 'fairly safe bets' in the late 1970s and, broadly speaking, have transpired. As we saw in Chapter 10, a 'modified' gross fertility rate (GFR) has dropped sharply since 1983/4 from 135 to 106 in 2009.[3] In the same period, literacy rates have increased from 26 per cent to almost 54 per cent. However, the rise of education is only now accelerating, after three or four decades, and has appeared much later than we anticipated in the 1970s.

The speculations on the future in Lanjouw and Stern (1998), especially Chapter 2, were largely written following a visit by Drèze and Sharma in 1997 and thus were formulated around 20 years later than those of Bliss and Stern. They were fairly gloomy and contrasted slow change and growth in Palanpur with the faster change in India as a whole. On p. 231, Drèze, Lanjouw, and Sharma spoke of 'this pattern of sluggish change...' (Lanjouw and Stern, 1998: 231). They wrote of the 'general pattern of the failure of public services...' (Lanjouw and Stern, 1998: 232).

The emphasis was also on the strong and '*persistent* inequalities relating to ownership, caste, gender, and education', and it was argued that these were dominant relative to opportunities around the 'green revolution and all that' (Lanjouw and Stern, 1998: 227). The 'persistent' factors have indeed been both persistent and important but, overall, that perspective around new opportunities in relation to inequality and mobility now appears to be too gloomy. Opportunities from changing circumstances outside the village, together with the entrepreneurship of villagers in response to them, have been of real importance in understanding economic change and income distribution. And such effects within farming have also been of significance.

At the same time, the notion of 'persistence' of inequality has acquired new meaning. Our assessment of intergenerational mobility cautions us against extrapolating too confidently from short-term dynamics to long-term (absolute and relative) welfare improvements. Essentially, when new opportunities appear, in this case outside the village or with regard to non-farm activities, some who take them will have had advantages in so doing, from family, from their social group, or from being better off. Others who take them are those with stronger initiative or entrepreneurial spirit. Both forces are at work and they interact. At earlier stages, whichever forces are at work, the fact that some take

---

[3] We used a modified version of the GFR, defined as the ratio of children aged less than one to women in the reproductive age group, in the absence of data on number of births.

new opportunities before others, and some are more successful in these, increases inequality. In this context, the language of 'persistence' may be overly static. Some of the forces creating inequality remain strongly at work, but the inequality itself changes, and new opportunities provide mobility.

It is interesting to compare those two sets of predictions, written with a difference of almost two decades. The first, Bliss and Stern, was written in the 1970s when many years of gloom over India (witness the picture painted by Myrdal (1968) in *Asian Drama* of long-term stagnation and villages and villagers as passive and without initiative) had given way to some optimism around the clear changes and entrepreneurship shown in the green revolution. Twenty years later, some of that optimism had dissipated. The reforms of the early 1990s in India as a whole were only beginning to bear fruit in industry and elsewhere and had had only small effects on the countryside. In understanding past predictions, context matters. So, too, perhaps, do the personalities of those making the predictions. All this should be borne in mind as we offer speculation some two decades on from the mid-1990s.

Again, for the second book, prospects for non-farm or outside jobs were seen as largely more formal than informal and tilted towards richer groups (Lanjouw and Stern, 1998: 300–11). So even in 1997, we were still underemphasizing the possibilities, which emerged in the subsequent two decades, outside the village, in informal jobs, accessed by commuting and with perceptions of possibilities of finding work informed by better communication. In particular, in discussing rising mobility and inequality (Lanjouw and Stern, 1998: 358–70), we emphasized the lack of mobility out of agricultural labour. It is this mobility out of such labour that has been such a striking feature since the late 1990s. We should not understate the importance of rising agricultural wages in helping to reduce poverty: the indirect effect of non-farm expansion on wages through labour market tightening implies that even the disadvantaged households who did not move into the non-farm sector may have benefited from the expanding non-farm sector. The translation of non-farm wages into agricultural wages does depend on the linking of the labour markets.

There was a little burst of optimism in predictions made in the 1990s around 'a possible take-off in the field of primary education' (Lanjouw and Stern, 1998: 232–3). That, however, may have been a false dawn, as there have been stutters and backward steps, as we saw in Part 3 of this book. Recent evidence suggests that perhaps, at last, it has started to move forward on a firmer basis.

Thus, our past attempts at speculating about the future have had mixed success. Our anticipation of agricultural change has been more or less on the mark. So too have our speculations about the continued weakness of social and political institutions, as we have seen in Part 3 of this book. And, as we suggested, population growth has slowed, and interaction with and openness to the world outside the village has increased. But what we missed or underestimated was the pace and nature of integration with the economy outside the village since the late 1990s. And we probably underestimated the entrepreneurship in reaction to opportunities as these develop, both from the population as a whole and from some within the lower social groups.

12.3 External Forces and Internal Forces

Let us now look ahead and offer, from 2018, some speculation a further 20 years on. We begin with the broad drivers of change. The three forces we have put centre stage across all our work over the years—population, technological change, and the outside economy—will surely continue to be of real importance. However, we would now put the strongest emphasis on non-farm activities and the outside economy. How will these develop? How easy will it be to take advantage of the opportunities? And what are the internal forces within the village which will drive agricultural change and facilitate the greater involvement in non-farm activities and the outside economy that now seems inevitable? How do the internal and external interact? And, importantly, what are the prospects for overall growth in incomes? This discussion is orientated around the first of our five main themes in this book, the importance of non-farm, informal activities. Distribution of incomes is the subject of the speculation in Section 12.4.

The outside forces in the Indian economy as a whole will likely include a decade or two of strong growth. Most or many economists would forecast economic growth rates of 6 or 7 per cent per annum for India during this period. Investment and savings are likely to stay high, there are many inefficiencies to be tackled, and labour force growth is strong. There is real 'catch-up' potential in technology. Some are still more optimistic and suggest that India is at a stage of development which will allow very rapid growth and might take India's income per capita in 20 years close to where China is now, in other words, a growth factor of around 4 over 20 years. That would imply growth rates in the region of 7 per cent or more. We should recall, however, that Indian policy-making and planning has a history of over-optimism on future growth.

Only around one third of India's population live in urban areas.[4] Urbanization is likely to be a powerful force, particularly as regards urban centres in rural

---

[4] Such numbers are subject to major measurement issues, as the distinction between urban and rural is far from clearly defined. This is further complicated by the rise of commuting, as we have seen in Palanpur (Chapter 7). Villagers make use of economic opportunities offered by neighbouring towns, without moving out from the village. Such numbers, thus, should be used only as a broad indicator of urbanization, with the knowledge that the linkages between urban and surrounding rural areas are deep and complex.

areas such as Moradabad and Chandausi (Tewari et al., 2015; World Bank, 2013). A number of writers have emphasized the potential of smaller towns and cities in driving India's growth and have warned against an overconcentration of attention on mega cities.[5] In the case of Palanpur, it is the towns of Chandausi and Moradabad that matter, rather than Delhi. The very dense population of the Indo-Gangetic plain, for example, and its many towns means that a corresponding statement is likely to be true for hundreds of thousands of villages across India.

The sectoral growth opportunities are likely to be strongest in services and construction as the urbanization process intensifies. Manufacturing is likely to pick up, too, but South Asia has not shown such a strong performance in these areas as East and South-East Asia. It is interesting that China's new and important strategy around 'the belt and road initiative' (BRI) has focused on infrastructure linking China and East, South-East, and Central Asia. This is in large measure a strategy to decentralize lower-cost manufacturing in some of its neighbours as wages rise in China, and it looks to export capital and skills. It is also seeking to link China to markets more broadly in Europe, Africa, and the Pacific. Much of the BRI investment is likely to be in competition with India. We do not yet know how India will react to that competition via the increasing spread of low-cost manufacturing to, particularly, other Asian countries. Or indeed the political aspects of these new and enhanced BRI linkages.

We can, however, be reasonably confident for India with respect to overall growth rates in services and in the continuing strength of construction and rapid urbanization, including of smaller towns and cities. All these point to increasing growth in demand for non-farm activities for villages like Palanpur and the likelihood that many of the opportunities will remain informal. Some of the new opportunities will likely demand some education, language skills, computer literacy, and understanding of finance. Others will be of a more menial kind, including parts of construction and transport.

Uttar Pradesh may or may not grow faster than India as a whole. After long periods of talking about BIMARU or sick states destined to grow more slowly than India as a whole,[6] perceptions have been changing. Some are arguing that a catch-up process is already under way, with signs that 'backward states' may grow more rapidly than India as a whole; states like Bihar and Madhya Pradesh have been amongst the fastest-growing states since the late 2000s (see Acharya, 2013; Aiyar, 2012; Planning Commission, 2014). On balance we see no strong presumption that Uttar Pradesh will grow faster or slower than India

---

[5] See, for example, Gibson et al. (2017), Lanjouw and Murgai (2014), Li and Rama (2015).
[6] BIMARU stands for the states Bihar, Madhya Pradesh, Rajasthan, and Uttar Pradesh. The Hindi word *bimar* means 'sick'.

as a whole. And a 1 or 2 per cent differential in India–Uttar Pradesh growth rates would not, in any case, change our broad-brush speculations on the future of Palanpur very much.

Overall, we would suggest that the growth of opportunities outside the village will accelerate and cover a spectrum of activities from service to manufacturing and from informal to formal. Whether formal or informal, it is likely that education will become an increasingly important requirement for accessing non-farm opportunities, as digital methods for operating activities get stronger and India's openness to the world continues to grow. The use of a smartphone, for example, requires some literacy and numeracy.

Changes inside the village may be, in large measure, reactions to those outside. However, population growth, although it is slowing, will continue to exert pressure, in part to seek outside jobs and in part to invest to increase productivity in agriculture. The release of labour to other activities is likely to involve a continuing intensification of agriculture. Palanpur's land and labour productivity continues to be low (as we saw in Chapters 5 and 6) relative to other parts of India, so there is substantial scope here. Part of this will be via investment but there is great scope for boosting agricultural productivity to narrow the gap with, for example, Punjab and other parts of western Uttar Pradesh. Much of this concerns agricultural skills and knowledge. As with most professions, some farmers are better at their work than others.

We would also emphasize strongly the great scope for more of the entrepreneurship and initiative we have seen in relation to self-employment in Palanpur. This has been largely around service and construction, whether it be motorcycle repair shops, retail, or construction. It is highly likely that such demand for services will grow. Palanpur's entrepreneurs have shown they can respond.

At the same time, one cannot ignore the environmental consequences of intensive farming, which have led to depletion of water tables and declining soil fertility in parts of Punjab. Similar concerns exist for the Palanpur economy, although they have yet to appear as obstacles to future agricultural growth.

How will these drivers, primarily external but also internal, change overall growth, productivity, and incomes in Palanpur? We have argued that the external opportunities will grow strongly, that the people of Palanpur have demonstrated their ability to respond, and that the processes of educational improvement is beginning. We would suggest, therefore, that the processes of growth and integration that we have seen drive economic change in Palanpur since the late 1990s/early 2000s will continue.

In our earlier attempts at speculating on the future, we laid excessive emphasis on the growth of more formal full-time jobs, for which relatively higher income and more educated groups in Palanpur would be at an advantage. This time, while we would not want to dismiss such jobs, indeed we suggest they will grow, we would emphasize as strongly, or more strongly, the growth of more informal and unskilled jobs. That is what we have seen as of particular importance in the recent past. And it seems that the manual and agricultural workers of the village, particularly the Jatabs, have been more likely to take on these jobs than those belonging to the higher social groups. We have argued that the strong growth of these jobs and of nearby towns and cities is likely to continue. If it fails or stutters, the prospects for income growth and poverty reduction in Palanpur would be damaged.

At the same time as the sophistication and urbanization of the economy grows and as education is now picking up rapidly in India as a whole, and to some extent in Palanpur, the likely required skills and qualifications for jobs across the spectrum will rise. And these more educated groups will have an advantage. The slowness of post-primary-educational advance in Palanpur could limit prospects of those from the village. Nevertheless, the demand for unskilled, manual, informal jobs, for example in construction, is likely to continue to grow strongly for some time. In other words, we believe the processes which have brought Jatab and others new opportunities will continue to be important, or indeed intensify.

Overall, a growth of income and wages outside the village at 6 or 7 per cent may start to boost the growth rates of income per capita in Palanpur substantially above the 2 per cent or so experienced since the 1980s. Indeed, as we move on from the early stages of involvement in new opportunities that we have described, one would expect aggregate growth rates in Palanpur to pick up.

12.4 Mobility and Inequality

Many studies of mobility and inequality of income in rural India have begun by emphasizing caste difference and inequality of land ownership; similarly with education. Ours is no exception, as indicated by some of the quotes, in Section 12.2, on past attempts at prediction. But as the internal structure of the village economy and society become less dominant in people's lives and employment outside the village grows, we would expect these forces to weaken. We should not be misunderstood here, and we would expect them to stay strong for a long time; we are talking about the weakening of these still strong forces, not their elimination or marginalization.

But there are now other forces at work, in particular non-farm and outside opportunities. We suggested in the Bliss and Stern 1982 study that differential paces of intensifying agriculture, by different households, in response to population growth would be a force for increasing inequality. Now we would argue that a strong force for inequality is different access, and speeds of response to, outside opportunities. Sometimes we can attribute these to differences in entrepreneurship, but in other cases there will be barriers, such as disability, family circumstances, or powerful social pressures. And we have seen that caste and other networks carry advantages for many of these jobs.

The process of some taking advantage of new opportunities before others will in its earlier stages work to increase inequality, much as in the Kuznets story of inverted 'U' curves for inequality over time. In later stages the same processes will work to reduce inequality. We should note that some people are more entrepreneurial and successful than others in new ventures. Recall that Kuznets also noted that urban income distributions were more unequal than rural.

For Palanpur and the forces of change from non-farm opportunities, we are surely still in the early stages. A critical question is whether, as a result of rising inequality, certain population groups become better placed, and more inclined, to lock-in the forces that perpetuate inequality. The example described in Chapter 11, of a shift to private education that could attenuate pressure to improve the quality of education offered in the village public school, could be similarly manifested in other domains. There is a concern that rising inequality could translate into declining mobility and increased inequality of opportunity.

A further interesting question is whether poor villages within Uttar Pradesh are catching up with the richer ones. Is there a process of convergence? Poorer villages might have a larger pool of casual wage workers and thus greater propensity to increase engagement in the non-farm sector. If this conjecture were to be valid, it could imply that rising village-level inequality combined with declining between-village inequality might result in overall inequality in Uttar Pradesh that could be stable or even declining. We hesitate to speculate on such a development.

12.5 The Future of Palanpur's Institutions

The weakness of Palanpur's public institutions has been a strong theme from 1972 onwards, even though in the 1950s and 1960s some institutional processes such as *zamindari* abolition and the early days of the seed store and credit union may have worked reasonably well. Once institutions deteriorate and cultures of graft or non-performance or non-presence develop, they are difficult to change.

Nevertheless, in Palanpur, there are occasional signs of improvement or willingness to act, such as the case of the 'impeachment' of the *pradhan*. Perhaps rising education will go hand in hand with a greater readiness to insist on rights, including a demand for better performance of Palanpur's schools. Greater integration with the outside economy may lead to greater awareness of what is possible or to be expected elsewhere. Greater exposure to media via television, smartphones, and internet penetration are likely to contribute to this process. We have already seen in India the Right to Information (RTI) increasingly being used to demand transparency and accountability of government offices. Increasing access to information is likely to contribute to rising aspirations and demand for accountability from the existing institutional structures. But how strong all these might be in Palanpur is open to question; we simply raise the possibility.

Forces the other way might include rising income inequality. We have indicated that we might expect inequality to rise, and some have argued (see also Chapter 11) that greater inequality can lead to less pressure for improved services that benefit poorer people. These arguments are more persuasive when structures are static and long established, but in Palanpur we have seen the beginnings of social change. If Jatabs as a group become stronger, they may push for better services reaching them. On the other hand, the rising inequality may also follow the path traced out by the Gatsby curve, resulting in declining intergenerational mobility as the elites within the village take active measures, including controlling or manipulating institutions, to prevent the remaining segments of the population from catching up or joining them. The growing tendency for the better-off segments to educate their children in private schools outside Palanpur, and to thereby 'defect' from lending their support to the strengthening of the public school in the village, might constitute an example of such active measures. Thus, whilst we have seen increased mobility causing increased inequality via differential movements in the taking of non-farm opportunities, we might in the future see increased inequality causing restricted mobility.

The strengthening and democratization of institutions such as the *gram panchayat* could, however, contribute to neutralizing such efforts at perpetuating inequalities, as reservations for backward castes, Dalits, and women continue. Change here is slow but possible and is likely to see a push from similar democratization of politics at state level. As the politics of Uttar Pradesh changes, it could lead to changes in the functioning of institutions at the village level. This is hard to predict but the 1990s and 2000s did see the emergence of the backward caste and scheduled caste (SC) parties such as Samajwadi Party (SP) and the Bahujan Samaj Party (BSP), which led to the Jatabs in Palanpur feeling somewhat more empowered. This particular force has seen a reversal in 2017 with the Bharatiya Janata Party (BJP) coming to power.[7] Whether the social change and political alignment will benefit the Jatabs, Muslims, and other castes is difficult to predict.

---

[7] Although the village has not seen direct conflict on the basis of religion during the long survey period, the western Uttar Pradesh area experienced communal riots in Muzaffarnagar in 2013. There are signs of an increased sense of anxiety among Muslims in Uttar Pradesh and elsewhere after the BJP came to power nationally in 2014 and won the state elections in 2017.

Economic forces, particularly around changing occupations, will continue to chip away at the rigidity of the old caste structure in the village. As economic opportunities in the outside economy grow, income might increase in importance relative to caste, although both factors are and will remain relevant. However, we suspect that caste will maintain its strong role as the moderator of social networks in the village for the decades to come. While its economic role might decline, its political and social importance will continue to keep it at the centre of the village's social and institutional life. Recent assertions of Dalit identity in Uttar Pradesh are probably an indicator of the social change that might occur in Palanpur in the near future. Such associations and economic progress from the Dalit community, together with increasing overall inequality, might bring tensions.

12.6 Human Development

The demand side for education is finally starting to build, as we saw in Chapter 9. Whilst it is still strongest for the Thakurs, it is growing across all caste groups, including Jatabs. And at last the gap between boys and girls in education, whilst still wide, is beginning to close. The forces that are driving this increase in demand, in terms of a recognition of the role of education in the ability to participate and compete in future labour markets, are likely to continue. And there is some mutual reinforcement in the demand for boys' and girls' education in that it seems that an educated boy might prefer an educated girl as a spouse and vice versa.

The problems are mostly on the supply side, and that is where the difficulties of prediction lie. There is a private sector supply which is responding to demand and is assisted in capturing that demand by the weakness of the public side. And it is the poorer parts of the community which are more dependent on the public side. Further, they are less willing to 'go private' for girls, particularly as the expense rises as they progress further through the educational system.

A critical question, therefore, concerns what will happen to public supply. That is a matter in part for public policy in the district, state, and country. It is also a matter of public priority in terms of insistence on raising the quality of delivery. As demand gets stronger, pressure at the local level for teachers to become reliable may rise. It is currently muted, however, by the willingness of the better off to go private; they thus have a smaller stake in the public.

We speculate that pressure in Palanpur for better performance in the public provision of schools will grow as demand continues to grow. That demand growth is still in its early stages. So, too, are the linkages with other areas and the world outside Palanpur. These forces point towards greater political and social pressure. It is very difficult to forecast, however, when that pressure will really become effective. We had anticipated some growing demand and pressure for education in our predictions of the 1970s and 1990s, only to be proved premature. Perhaps that is now starting to change, and we can expect much stronger expansion in both demand and supply in the coming two decades. As the great economist, Rudiger Dornbusch, was widely quoted by his friends and students as saying, 'Sometimes things take much longer than you think they would, but then happen much more quickly than you thought they could.'[8]

Demand for health services is more complex. Presumably we all want to be healthy in some sense, but it is not always straightforward to understand what it is that you should seek. This is true of all societies and certainly of Palanpur. Generally, however, the wish to seek professional help is increasing, whether it be for midwifery or vaccination; in some cases only slowly, but it is increasing.

Again the problems are on the supply side. And again, there is a growing private supply alongside a weak public sector, as we saw in Chapter 9. Here, along with the response from the supply side, there has been, particularly after 2008, an expansion in public services. A community health worker (Accredited Social Health Activist (ASHA)) has now been appointed in the village, people can call for an ambulance during emergencies, and there is a Primary Health Centre (PHC) with reasonable physical infrastructure in Akrauli just four kilometres away. However, the problems of irregular staff, vacant positions, undersupply of medicines, and so on continue. It is likely that the demand for curative health services will rise, but it is difficult to say how rapidly, in what form, and how it could be met.

At the national and state level there is debate on whether the public sector should expand the delivery of services or should invest in insurance schemes for poor people and leave the delivery to the private sector. While what is ultimately chosen will have implications, particularly in relation to equity in access to care, one can surely predict that expenditure (public and private) on health will increase in future.

With women's education increasing, general health conditions improving, and a reduction in infant mortality rates (IMRs), one can also predict that

---

[8] There are many versions of Dornbusch's iconic quote along these lines in circulation. There is something of an 'oral tradition'. Here is one he gave in an interview on the Mexican economy: 'The crisis takes a much longer time coming than you think, and then it happens much faster than you would have thought' (PBS, 1995).

there will be a continued decline in fertility rates. This is a pattern that has been observed in other parts of the country. With fewer children, families will be able to invest in their children more, and women's care burdens will be reduced. This could reduce the pressure on women's time and allow more time for the labour market. Here again, the trend is for fertility rates to reduce first amongst the upper castes; this is another possible factor contributing to perpetuating inequalities.

Two things are clear with regard to human development in Palanpur. First, both health and education services are weak, and that weakness shows strongly in health and education outcomes. Second, it is particularly weak for women and Jatabs. How all this changes, in what ways, and at what speed, is in large measure an issue for public policy and political priority in India. It is on developments at this level that outcomes in Palanpur will depend. It should, in our view, be centre stage in public action in India (see Chapter 13). At the same time, the people of Palanpur could do much more to exert pressure for better local delivery. We anticipate that they will move in this direction.

12.7 Entrepreneurship

Entrepreneurship and initiative have constituted key themes in our discussion.[9] We have seen villagers in Palanpur recognize opportunities, act on those opportunities, invest, and take risks right through the seven decades of study. This has been evidenced from investment in irrigation in the 1950s and 1960s, the green revolution technologies and methods in the 1970s and 1980s, increasing non-farm activities in the last 30 years, and continuing mechanization and investment in agriculture. They have invested in their homes and in equipment. Since the late 1990s/early 2000s, self-employment income in Palanpur has grown very rapidly and in large measure as a result of entrepreneurship and initiative from villagers responding to opportunities in service and construction created by the growth of the regional economy and nearby towns.

At the same time, some have moved faster than others. That is part of initiative: it is unequally distributed. At the same time, there are some whose education and social networks lend them advantages in recognizing and acting on opportunities. And some have been more successful than others.

---

[9] For a brief discussion of the definition of entrepreneurship, see Section 4.6 of Chapter 4. We focus on a definition of entrepreneurship encompassing decision, change, risk, and originality. The originality, or newness, in our understanding is 'new to the individual' and not necessarily some pioneering innovation in the sense of Silicon Valley.

Luck plays a role, but some are better entrepreneurs than others, and these differences come through at times of changing opportunity.

How will all this develop? With irrigation in the 1950s and 1960s, and in the green revolution period, we saw some of the earlier slower movers catching up, generating rising incomes and an equalizing force. There will be some catching up, too, in the new world of non-farm activities. But there is a long way to go in this process, and we shall continue to see the more entrepreneurial in Palanpur 'move out in front'. There are likely to be an increasing number who will recognize the attractiveness of the path set by Nanhe, who, after learning a trade (repairing machines and motorcycles), became self-employed and invested in his businesses. There will be others who seek out formal sector jobs after investing in education.

At the same time, we must recognize that there will be others who are able and willing to use contacts and networks to garner advantage. Any closing down of opportunities in this way would dampen the process of growth and opportunity.

The ability to become involved in new enterprises and initiatives will also depend on capital and education. While these have not yet played a strong role in Palanpur, jobs will become more skill-intensive as the economy is digitized and integrated with the urban areas. On financial inclusion, the penetration of banking access through the Jan Dhan Scheme and other measures has not yet led to a strong response in terms of using more formal outlets to save money. Nor has it been accompanied by increasing access to capital in the financial system. On education, notwithstanding improvements in primary education enrolment, the drop-out rates at higher levels are very high, with relatively fewer accessing technical education. For the next few years, it seems that entrepreneurship will be self-driven in response to overall opportunity. Formal attempts to facilitate either directly or through complementary inputs may be of only modest importance. However, some aspects of the modern economy, such as digitization of banking and public transfers, may arrive fairly quickly in Palanpur.

12.8 Conclusion: Optimism and Anxieties

Our picture of the future has strands of optimism: growing opportunities in non-farm activities outside the village, rising education, falling population growth, longer life expectancy. Upward movement has been from very low levels and has often been haphazard, but it is nevertheless a picture of growth and poverty reduction. As we have seen, such processes may well involve a period of rising inequality.

There are, however, a number of grounds for anxiety. The areas include: gender; public services and the development of institutions; inequality;

communal tensions; and the environment and climate change. While women's education is improving and can be expected to change things substantially, women currently have very little voice within and outside the household. Very few women in the village are working outside the household, and the absence of opportunities for them to participate in labour markets may dampen the desire to educate girls. This could hold up 'development' in a number of spheres for Palanpur.

We have emphasized key aspects of change in village institutions. They have indeed responded to not just economic changes but also to social and political stresses and changes, for example in the village *panchayat* and the behaviour and election of the *pradhan*. But these have not yet had any significant impact on the functioning of key public services, including the school and health services. The alternatives that are emerging are not equitable in the sense that the need for payment can exclude the poorer groups. The private options are not of high quality, but the public are worse. These weaknesses in public services are likely to limit access to skills and capital, two important ingredients enabling entrepreneurs to take advantage of the emergence of opportunities. Institutional weaknesses can create perverse incentives for corruption and rent seeking by the well-off. Whilst we are seeing some entrepreneurship, better governance, skills, financial services, and infrastructure could provide a real acceleration in response to the growing opportunities in the India economy as a whole. We comment on policy in Chapter 13.

Communal tensions have so far not been a serious issue in Palanpur, either between castes or religions. Can we be confident this will continue? We are not sure. The rising incomes and economic status of some Jatabs and Muslims may create tensions. Jatabs have begun to exert more influence in labour markets—and to some extent, also in land markets—as their bargaining position improves. Some Telis, who are Muslims, have been successful entrepreneurs. They have tried to exert political influence along with their increasing economic status. Population in the village is concentrating in the major groups, as some from smaller caste groups leave. National politics may feed tensions. Our guess is that some of these tensions will increase. Palanpur has shown itself as a fairly peaceable place, as regards communal affairs. But there have been several non-communal murders and acts of violence over the years, as we have remarked in our personal stories of households in various chapters. We hope that communal tensions will not start to become violent and speculate that past peacefulness amongst communities will continue, notwithstanding.

Environment and climate change have not yet been prominent and explicit issues in Palanpur. But it has suffered in ways common to many parts of India. Most cooking is done by burning dung cakes, wood, coal, or biomass. In-hut air pollution kills many millions around the world, particularly women. There can be little doubt that this is an issue in Palanpur. Looking ahead, Palanpur and this part of Uttar Pradesh may start large-scale stubble burning at the end of a cropping season, which is prevalent in Punjab, Haryana, and some of west Uttar Pradesh, and which has greatly contributed to the severe air pollution in Delhi. This practice arises with combine harvesting, which cuts higher than the hand harvesting we see in Palanpur. It is also influenced by the desire to plant crops quickly in order to take advantage of the next season. There are technical and organizational solutions (involving various seeding and cutting machinery which can be shared or leased), but they would have to be supported by public policy.

The water table has not yet reached levels which are dramatically low, but it has fallen sharply as a result of the intensification of irrigation in the region. Nearby factories (paper and sugar mills) have, from time to time, polluted water courses. Most trees have been cut down. Fertilizers have focused on nitrogen with little attention to other nutrients, and soil fertility will be under threat. Whilst the pressures from these developments have not appeared strongly, they could well increase.

Climate change is a major threat to India as a whole, and the Indo-Gangetic plain is very vulnerable. It depends, for its water flows and their patterns, on the snows and glaciers of the Himalayas. Most of these would vanish at global temperature increases of 3 to 4 degrees centigrade, as is a real possibility in the next 100 years or so, if we mismanage climate change and follow anything like business-as-usual. The result could be severe and extensive flooding as the holding ability of snow and glaciers vanishes. The monsoon could be disrupted suddenly and dramatically, undermining a central element in agricultural livelihoods. Later this century, temperature and humidity could rise in parts of north India to levels that humans could not tolerate (Eltahir et al., 2017). The future of the climate will depend on the world as a whole. India is a big part of that world, and its environment and people are very vulnerable. Some policy issues addressing these will be discussed briefly in Chapter 13.

We will conclude, however, on a note of optimism. Palanpur is changing, with difficulties, weaknesses, blemishes, and stutters, but it is changing. Living standards are far higher than 60 years ago, and progress is accelerating. Whilst the anxieties are real, good sense and good policies can deal with them. Policy matters. Policy depends on understanding. This study has tried to offer some understanding on the basis of the study of Palanpur. It is to the understanding of development economics and policy that we now turn.

Acknowledgement

Dipa Sinha contributed in various ways in developing some of the ideas discussed.

References

Acharya, S. 2013. 'Progress and poverty in Bihar', in N.K. Singh and N. Stern (eds), *The New Bihar*. Noida: HarperCollins.

Aiyar, S. 2012. Backward states growing fast, proving good economics can be good politics. *Economic Times* (online), 6 June. Available at: https://economictimes.indi atimes.com/swaminathan-s-a-aiyar/backward-states-growing-fast-proving-good-economics-can-be-good-politics/articleshow/13858556.cms (accessed 15 November 2017).

Bauer, P. 1954. *West African Trade: A Study of Competition, Oligopoly and Monopoly in a Changing Economy*. Cambridge: Cambridge University Press.

Bauer, P. 1963. *West African Trade: A Study of Competition, Oligopoly and Monopoly in a Changing Economy*, new edn. London: Routledge & K. Paul.

Bliss, C.J., and Stern, N.H. 1982. *Palanpur: The Economy of an Indian Village*, 1st edn. Oxford and New York: Oxford University Press.

Eltahir, E.A.B., Im, E.-S., and Pal, J.S. 2017. 'Deadly heat waves projected in the densely populated agricultural regions of South Asia', *Science Advances* 3, no. 8: p.e.1603322.

Gibson, J., Datt, G., Ravallion, M., and Murgai, R. 2017. 'For India's rural poor, growing towns matter more than growing cities'. World Bank Group Policy Research Working Paper No. 7994.

Hirschman, A. 1958. *The Strategy of Economic Development*, Yale Studies in Economics 10). New Haven, CT: Yale University Press.

Lanjouw, P., and Murgai, R. 2014. 'Urban growth and rural poverty in India 1983–2005', in N. Hope, A. Kochar, R. Noll, and T.N. Srinivasin (eds), *Economic Reform in India: Challenges, Prospects, and Lessons*. New York: Cambridge University Press.

Lanjouw, P., and Stern, N.H. 1998. *Economic Development in Palanpur over Five Decades*, 1st edn. New York and Oxford: Clarendon Press.

Li, Y., and Rama, M. 2015. 'Households or locations? Cities, catchment areas and prosperity in India'. World Bank Policy Research Working Paper No. 7473.

Myrdal, G. 1968. *Asian Drama*, 3 vols. New York: Pantheon.

PBS. 1995. 'Interviews: Dr. Rudi Dornbusch'. Frontline. https://www.pbs.org/wgbh/pages/frontline/shows/mexico/interviews/dornbusch.html (accessed 31 March 2018).

Planning Commission. 2014. Data Table on *Gross State Domestic Product (GSDP) at Current Prices (as on 31-05-2014)*. Government of India. Available at http://plan ningcommission.nic.in/data/datatable/index.php?data=datatab (accessed 10 April 2018).

Tewari, M., Aziz, Z., Cook, M., Goldar, A., Ray, I., Ray, S., Roychowdhury, S., and Unnikrishnan, V. 2015. 'Reimagining India's urban future: a framework for securing high growth, low carbon, climate resilient urban development in India'. ICRIER Working Paper No. 306.

World Bank. 2013. 'Urbanization beyond municipal boundaries: nurturing metropol-itan economies and connecting peri-urban areas in India'. World Bank Report No. 75734.

13

Lessons for India, Policy, and the Economics of Development*

13.1 Introduction

What can the study of Palanpur tell us about the future of India? What lessons or pointers might there be for economic and social policy? What insights can it bring to theories of, and stories about, the processes of economic and social development? Of course, our first objective in this study has been to characterize and explain growth and development in Palanpur itself over the seven surveys and sixty years of data, whilst placing it firmly in the context of change in India. But we think examining one place in great detail over such a long period can indeed provide us with, or at least suggest, ideas which are much more general.

What has happened in Palanpur both illustrates and reflects what has happened in India. Understanding the veins, arteries, and basic functioning in detail in one village or microcosm can add richly to our understanding of the bigger and broader picture. That is not to say the village is 'representative', but the processes at work in Palanpur are also at work in much of rural India. The workings of policies in relation to circumstances and institutions in Palanpur can raise questions about the way policies elsewhere might be modified, improved, created, or abandoned. And theories of economic and social development should be able, if they have real explanatory power, to help us understand the growth and development of a 'not particularly unusual' village in one of the most important developing countries in the world. Which ideas, singly or together, carry the strongest insights for Palanpur? Similarly, understanding growth and change in Palanpur should help us in understanding

---

* This chapter has been written by Nicholas Stern, Himanshu, and Peter Lanjouw.

how theories, singly or together, might be advanced or modified, and how and which priorities for new ideas might be set.

Accordingly, Sections 13.2, 13.3, and 13.4 of this chapter examine some implications of Palanpur for, respectively: India, past and future; policy; and the economics of development. There is much more research that existing Palanpur data could allow, and we hope to take the analysis of our data further in coming years. And there will be more Palanpur surveys. Possibilities for future research are discussed in Section 13.5. Concluding remarks are provided in Section 13.6.

The basics of Palanpur's experience were set out and summarized in Chapters 2 and 3 and emphasized the context of India's growth and change. The central ideas in economics and related disciplines that, *ex ante*, might carry some relevance and insights for change in Palanpur were presented and discussed in Chapter 4. And some speculations on the future of Palanpur were provided in Chapter 12. This chapter picks up themes and ideas from those earlier chapters. At the same time it draws on the details and specifics of Parts 2 and 3 of the book (Chapters 5 to 11), where, in Part 2, we examine agriculture and non-farm activities as drivers of income, mobility, and distribution, and, in Part 3, issues around human development, gender, society, and politics.

13.2 India

We do not attempt to describe the future of India over the coming years on the basis of the experience of one village. That would not be wise. What we do try to do is to highlight strands in the Palanpur story which might carry lessons and guidance for key features of the future of the Indian economy and society, particularly those of relevance for policy.

Central to the Palanpur story of the last 30 years has been the rise of off-farm employment, the informal nature of most of that activity,[1] strong links to the service and construction sectors, and commuting from Palanpur to reach the place of employment. This is very different from a picture where villagers move their residence to towns, that is, migration, a story that is often embodied in theories of development. Many of these theories point, implicitly or explicitly, to more formal sector employment, often, it is suggested, focused on manufacturing. This is a story of development sometimes told through a Lewis model, although we argued in Chapter 4 that Lewis' own story was

---

[1] Recall that we focus on the informal nature of the employment itself, largely remunerated by piece rates, such as number of bricks made and containers unloaded. Mostly the employer is an informal small firm, but in some cases, such as unloading containers, the employer will be a subcontractor of a large enterprise in the formal sector.

somewhat richer than that, particularly in his 1955 book, *The Theory of Economic Growth*. This formal/manufacturing route is often offered in public policy discussions as the most promising for growth in developing countries in general and India more specifically.

We should note also that non-farm employment for Palanpur has been focused on towns fairly near the village, and not the very big cities. Urbanization through small-town development with their generation of employment opportunities has been a major feature of India's growth (see, for example, Gibson et al., 2017; Lanjouw and Murgai, 2014; Li and Rama, 2015; Mishra, 1995).

The increasing mechanization of agriculture in Palanpur has helped release labour for work outside agriculture. The increasing marketization of agricultural activities has in part been a consequence of, and has facilitated, these processes.

What would be the implications of these processes of change in Palanpur if they were to be reflected in India as a whole? Will these forces continue? How might they change? We argued in Chapter 3 that important aspects of this picture of change in Palanpur have indeed been reflected in India as a whole, and vice versa. Further, the formal sector is still only a relatively small fraction of the economy. Indeed, most estimates point to the informal sector comprising as much as 40 per cent of the total economic output in India (and employing 90 per cent of the workforce).[2] And India is still only one-third urbanized. The non-formal, non-agricultural sector, much of it in rural areas, has been central to growth in India. There seems great scope for this to continue.

Is that form of growth something which should be regarded as a 'bad thing' and to be discouraged? We would suggest that such a perspective could be damaging. It is perhaps a form of growth, for all its inequalities, that may be less unequal than one which favours an elite, formal 'vanguard' of workers.[3] Perhaps this informal route to growth is not one to be encouraged indefinitely because, for example, workers' rights are important; so, too, are the tax revenues a formal sector can bring. But, for a while at least, one could argue that the growth of opportunities for groups like the Jatabs and Telis (Muslims) in Palanpur is of great significance and its potential should not be overlooked, discarded, or discouraged. And it would seem to be a form of growth that is flexible to changing circumstances and capable of moving at pace, as well as being potentially inclusive. This point of view, if accepted, could have implications for policy.

---

[2] See NSSO (2012).
[3] That form of inequality has indeed been a feature of a number of countries, particularly in Latin America.

Over time, we should see the beginnings of a move away from the form of labour demand we have seen associated with the growth of non-farm activities in Palanpur. As India's population, including its growing middle class, increases its demand for both services and education we might expect both the supply of, and demand for, higher-quality labour to increase. Much of this might occur in smaller, less formal enterprises such as those involving car mechanics, para-legal services, retail, taxis, construction, and so on. But over time, we might expect some increase in the formality of these activities. Probably, we suggest, the increase in quality will precede the increase in formality. Indeed, currently the former would appear to be moving faster than the latter. This whole process might be accentuated as India becomes a bigger player in the world economy. But all this remains unclear; what is clear is that the form of change we have described is also strong for India as a whole and likely to continue as a dynamic force.

Overall, then, the Palanpur experience and forecasts for the future of the village point to a strongly growing informal service sector, which will eventually improve in quality and become more formal. But it does not point to a model of growth being dominated in the short or medium term by a formal urban manufacturing sector. However rapidly the formalization emerges, the entrepreneurial spirits and embrace of change we have seen in Palanpur will be a key driver of Indian growth. We have emphasized that Palanpur is a backward village where growth could have been, and should have been, faster. So, too, should advances in human development, which have been particularly disappointing. But if the forces of change we have seen in Palanpur are strong, their potential is likely to be still stronger for India as a whole.

It is interesting and important to note that this is a story of development very different from China and its powerful emphasis on manufacturing growth and exports, initially through township and village enterprises (TVEs) and later in substantial formal firms. The world has changed, with new strong growth in the demand for services, very rapid progress in high-end technology, and, of course, the rapid growth in China and other emerging market countries. Further, China chose and was able, to exert much greater control on population and population movement than India. India is likely to follow a different path to prosperity. Harnessing domestic demand will be of great importance.

The village is no longer a self-enclosed society and economy, overwhelmingly focused on agriculture. It will become still more open to and involved with the outside world. And it is still less the inward-looking and closely structured society which was the preoccupation of anthropological studies a few decades ago. This increasing openness and external involvement will mean that institutions, attitudes, and demands will change. This process is already clearly underway in India as a whole,[4] and that it is happening in a backward village like Palanpur, albeit rather later than in many other places, indicates the power of these processes. Jatabs, with opportunities outside the village, are experiencing rising economic and political status. Telis are showing their entrepreneurship. Caste interactions are less based on traditional occupations, but are now relatively more about networks and trust. Networks, for example, are relevant in finding outside jobs. Trust matters for land, labour, and credit contracts, and often, for these reasons, intra-caste arrangements may be preferred. These institutional changes are the outcomes of the economic forces driving structural change away from agriculture and likely apply across India. They, in turn, influence economic outcomes.

The village, with its commuting inhabitants, will increasingly become, for many, a place of residence rather than a place of work. The commuting comes with the proximity of non-farm opportunities. The changing economic structure combined with the density of population, and thus the proximity of nearby urban centres, is likely to apply across India. Commuting can lead to migration with the greater knowledge it brings. But migration will generally carry greater costs and risks, including in relation to housing and alternative opportunities (the commuting household has its own home, within-village opportunities, and a sense of belonging within a community).

However, the quality of the public institutions in the village has stayed so poor for so long that we hesitate to be overly optimistic about Palanpur. The same would be true of our speculation on India. We would suggest that there is real scope for political, public, and community action, and that economic and social returns to stronger institutions could be very large.

All these processes of change are likely to mean that some political and social institutions in Palanpur and India have the opportunity to improve. This could include the quality of local governance and the supply of public services and entitlements. Some of these growing demands and forces of change are reflected in the enactment of various legislation around food security (National Food Security Act), employment (Mahatma Gandhi National Rural Employment Guarantee Act, MGNREGA), Right to Education (RTE), and the Right to Information (RTI) in the last decade. Most of these have emerged as a result of strong demand from the ground and political recognition of these demands. Most of them have not only provided greater access to resources from the government to the residents in villages, but have also generated new movements for accountability and transparency, now that they are legislative acts and therefore justiciable. This has also changed the balance of class forces and the caste alignments in the villages, with poorer households and

[4] Jodhka (2016), Gupta (2005), Harriss and Jeyaranjan (2016).

disadvantaged communities more likely to be at the forefront of demanding better services and greater accountability in the existing services than they have been hitherto.

Demand for education is already rising strongly, including for girls, and again this is a process that if it is happening, or is beginning to happen, in a backward village like Palanpur, must already be powerful, and will be still more powerful in the future, for India as a whole. Response to growing demands is already visible in the expansion in physical educational infrastructure in Palanpur. Crucially, however, the quality of education at all levels remains a concern.[5] The likely effect of pressure and political demand on the quality of India's educational workers could be large. And if the quality of education improved, there would be potentially substantial effect not only on the quality of labour, but also on the size of the workforce, as more women eventually enter the labour market. In the shorter run, some women who might have worked will be in education, and women's labour force participation could fall for this reason. And for some families, rising incomes may exert less pressure to work. But, over time, there is real potential to expand the quality and size of India's labour force, especially as rising incomes and demand for a skilled workforce will also lead to more women participating. Taken together with the fact that India's population is more youthful than some other parts of Asia, particularly China, this could give India a strong comparative advantage if other economic policies allow this labour to be used productively (see Section 13.3).

What would the forces and processes we have identified and stressed in shaping change in Palanpur imply for inequality and mobility in India as a whole? The taking of new opportunities off-farm, with some people moving faster than others, is likely to be a general phenomenon across India, although more advanced in much of the country than in Palanpur. In its early stages it can be a factor increasing rural inequality, but it could be equalizing in places where it is in later stages. Of course, in those less backward places other new opportunities with differential take-up may arise. Indeed, the emergence of new opportunities should be a powerful feature of strong development.

The processes at work clearly have implications for how we think about jobs and the growth of output and incomes. These observations suggest a

---

[5] In the last two decades, there has been large expansion in school infrastructure in India at the primary and secondary level as part of the Sarv Shiksha Abhiyan (SSA). There has also been an expansion in coverage of the Mid-Day-Meal (MDM) programme after it was made universal and expanded following Supreme Court orders. There is now a programme for expansion of middle and secondary schools along with emphasis on expansion of higher educational institutions. The number of universities in India has increased from less than 500 at the end of last century to more than 750 as of 2017. These have had impacts on the enrolment of children at lower levels, and slowly at higher levels, with primary school enrolment for boys and girls at nearly 100% in the 2010s.

two-pronged approach, fostering both informal and formal activities. The importance of such an approach is emphasized if we think of India as being in a very different position from where China was when it began its rapid industrialization, which was based on low-cost manufacturing. We return to this in Section 13.3.

In some respects, the experience in Palanpur with respect to the natural environment carries indications of the stresses of India as a whole. As the village expands, orchards and groves have been replaced by housing. There are also pressures for more available arable land. Thus, trees on Palanpur land have fallen dramatically in number. The mango grove close to where we lived in the village in 1974/5 disappeared long ago. Common land which was used for grazing has largely disappeared. Water has at times been reduced or polluted by lifting for irrigation in the region as a whole and by extraction from nearby paper mills followed by discharge of dirty waste.[6]

Nevertheless, it is probably the case that the environmental lessons from Palanpur are less strong than those occurring elsewhere in India. The Palanpur water table has probably dropped to about 40 or 50 feet now relative to the 15–20 feet or so in 1974/5. But in other parts of India we see far greater falls than this.[7] Crops such as mentha and sugar cane are heavily dependent on the availability of large quantities of water, and the lower or zero market prices for water can hide the true long-term costs of their cultivation. Other parts of India which gained from the green revolution technologies and methods, notably Punjab, are witnessing rapidly deteriorating soil quality due to misuse or to overuse of NPK (nitrogen, phosphorus, and potassium) fertilizers. Soil fertility in Palanpur is not yet a severe issue, although with increasingly similar usage patterns (to the rest of west UP) of chemical fertilizers we cannot rule out problems in the future. Air pollution inside the home is bad in Palanpur (as we mentioned in Chapters 3 and 12), but the village does not experience the terrible air pollution of India's cities. India's air pollution is the worst in the world, with, for the most part, Delhi being the worst of all.[8] Some of this air pollution arises from stubble-burning in Haryana, Punjab, and west UP, as noted in Chapter 12. India can learn from that difficult experience and work to prevent it spreading (see Section 13.3.). As we described in Chapter 12, India as a big and growing country is vital to the future of the world's climate and is very vulnerable to climate change.

[6] The small rivulet which encircled the village during the first survey in 1957/8 (Ansari, 1964) was already a small drain by the time Bliss and Stern were doing their fieldwork in 1974. By the time of the 2008/9 survey, there was no trace of the rivulet in the village.

[7] Kaur, Aggarwal, and Soni (2011), Kaur and Vatta (2015), Rodell, Velicogna, and Famiglietti (2009).

[8] See, for example, World Health Organization (WHO) data on pollution linked to PM2.5 pollutants.

We conclude our speculation on implications for India by looking a little beyond the direct experience of Palanpur, although Palanpur is relevant here, and asking about India's global role in the next 20 years. This is a period where India is looking to take a leading role in the world and lay the foundations for making this India's century.

India embarks on this course in a very different position from China in the late 1980s. At that time, emerging markets and developing countries constituted perhaps a quarter of world output. Now they are well over a half. Manufacturing exports are now dominated by emerging market countries— they have indeed emerged into the world trading system in a very powerful way. Thus, India's expansion into world trade must compete not just against the existing dominance of developed countries, but also against very strong competition from both established emerging market countries and those on the rise, such as Vietnam.

In our view, this observation underscores the argument that India will need a two-pronged strategy, with formal and informal feeding off each other. And it will need strong domestic demand and a central role for services, which already make up well over half the economy. Thus, a sound growth strategy for India cannot be one which is dominated by manufacturing and export demand. To avoid misunderstanding, we should stress that such demand will be an important element, but it will not be the dominant story to the extent it was with China.

All this emphasizes the importance of the informal sector, services, and internal demand in India. If this is to be India's century, the two processes of formal and informal must be intertwined and complementary. And internal demand will depend in part on demand coming from middle- and lower-income groups. India will chart an Indian route. It has its special characteristics, and the world is not the same as when China, the other giant, began its big push over 30 years ago.

13.3 Policy

Traditionally, production-side policy towards rural areas in India has, over the years, focused at various times on land reform, agricultural extension, agricultural procurement and prices (support prices, volatility, and so on), loans for agricultural investment, and rural public works. On the human development and social protection side, the focus has been on education and health, the Public Distribution System (PDS), and employment guarantees. A third broad area of focus has been public services and the functioning of public institutions, governance, participation, and social relations. A fourth area, which has seen less emphasis, is the environment. We consider these in turn. Our concern here is on lessons from Palanpur for policy. All four areas have, respectively, important distributional elements. In Chapter 12 and in Section 13.2., we have looked ahead for Palanpur and for India on the basis of our study. We now consider lessons for policy that would follow from or be suggested by the lessons from Palanpur.

Most of the lessons arise from recognizing the potential importance of the forces shaping lives and livelihoods in Palanpur, together with possible impacts of policy on those forces. Others arise from applying the notion of 'economist as plumber' suggested by Duflo (2017), where a key task of policy analysis is to try to understand the detail and contexts which enable policies to function well.

In this Indian route to growth and success which we have begun to sketch, it will be crucial that the country makes the most of its demographic dividend, that is, a period of expansion in the share of its workforce in the overall population in the context of a world, including China, with a strongly rising share of older people. If the demographic dividend is not to be a demographic burden, that means that employment must expand rapidly. Again this points to a strong role for domestic demand, services, and the informal sector.

13.3.1 *Production and Employment*

Land reform was a key factor in the 1950s with *zamindari* abolition. This set the stage for heavy investment in irrigation and the move to double-cropping. Agricultural extension played a key role for India as a whole in the green revolution period of the late 1960s and 1970s. However, in Palanpur, agricultural extension did not function well. Palanpur farmers learned from others and from seed merchants, although their information and use of it were often patchy. Nevertheless, seed varieties changed, the seed store did provide some new varieties, more fertilizer and irrigation were used, and yields rose, albeit by much less than their potential. Information which reached Palanpur had been influenced in some shape or form by agricultural research and extension in India.

Looking to the future, the further scope of land reform in India, as in Palanpur, is probably very limited. *Land redistribution* is now, 70 years after Independence, probably too difficult politically to achieve on any major scale. From Palanpur, we have seen that tenancy regulation is more likely to have more negative than positive effects. When we undertook the 1974/5 survey, we eventually took competent legal advice on the position of tenants in UP, post-*zamindari* abolition and the acquisition of land it enabled. The upshot was that the legal position on the ability of tenants to gain some security in their ownership rights, and thus landlords (many of whom acquired their land as a result of *zamindari* abolition) lose rights, was genuinely unclear. That can discourage investment in land and agriculture. After long spells during which nothing has happened to strengthen tenants' claims to ownership rights, anxieties of landlords and potential landlords have disappeared. Landowners are confident in their ownership, whether or not they lease-out, and investment in land improvement continues. There would be little point in reintroducing uncertainties. Nevertheless, those cultivators who lease-in can have difficulty in gaining access to credit for agricultural and other investment because credit schemes are organized for landowners, sometimes using the land as collateral. Credit for tenant farmers could be enhanced.

Land reclamation and rehabilitation could have real potential, as we have seen around the world, from China to Israel to Ethiopia. And it is likely to have a high priority as the world seeks to manage climate change; it will be imperative to capture carbon, and both soil and forests have real potential. It can also make an important contribution to food supply (see GCEC, 2014). The relevant nature and scale for India of these possibilities is an important issue for policy research.

The lesson that *land rights and tenure* matter greatly for investment and entrepreneurship is a very important one. For India more generally, there are important issues around forests and the rights of people, particularly 'indigenous people', in relation to forest usufruct and activities. India has long planned to increase its forest cover by around 50 per cent, and land rights would surely be fundamental to success.

There is evidence from around the world (see, for example, Gray et al., 2015; Stevens et al., 2014) that the management of *forest rights*, and the surrounding areas, can make a big difference to the health of forests and ecosystems, as well as to the livelihoods of those who live there. The potential for India in this area could be very large.[9] It can play a vital role, too, in the expansion of tourism, a labour-intensive industry in which India is underexploiting its potential.

Agricultural extension can, as India saw in the decade or so of the green revolution years, from the late 1960s, be important to technological change. India's land productivity is, in many areas, low by international standards. Many parts of UP are much worse in productivity terms than in neighbouring Punjab, for example. Hence there may well be scope for considerable strengthening. The experience of agricultural extension in Palanpur is weak; a lesson is that it is possible to do agricultural extension badly. Overall, for India, agriculture policy lessons reveal the importance of: (i) clarity and stability in land rights; (ii) land rehabilitation; and (iii) agricultural extension. Agricultural

---

[9] India enacted the Scheduled Tribes and Other Traditional Forest Dwellers (Recognition of Forest Rights) Act 2006 to give greater say to forest dwellers in the management of forests. However, the implementation of the Act remains a challenge.

extension could also be helpful in managing environmental impacts (see Section 13.3.4).

Procurement and price support may still have important roles to play in some circumstances. Increasing vulnerability due to price fluctuations remains a key reason for distress in farming in India. As recently as 2017, there were mass protests by farmers against the lack of price support for agricultural commodities.[10] Rising input costs and monetization of input markets have not been matched by increases in output prices, and integration with global markets has increased the speed of price transmission in crops with large external exposure.[11] While there is a political agreement among all national and regional parties on the need to provide remunerative prices to farmers for agricultural produce,[12] the nature of the operation of the minimum support price (MSP) operations has varied a great deal across crops and across regions.[13]

The challenges of providing reasonable returns and managing production and price risk cannot be anchored only to the MSP policies. Given the inefficiencies of the MSP system and the limitations of such an exercise for a large variety of crops, a superior solution could be better provision of access to markets that can help manage risk and provision of storage, both of which have received less attention than the MSP policies. The emergence of *futures markets* and forward trading have brought their own complexities, with demand for the regulation of such markets. While procurement operations have played a limited role in wheat and paddy production in Palanpur, farmers have benefited from a fixed MSP for sugarcane in Uttar Pradesh. On the other hand, farmers' experience in dealing with the mentha futures market in Chandausi has not been very encouraging. The policy lesson would be not to rely only on the MSP system, which in any case is applied only to a narrow range of crops, but to support measures for risk management along the lines described; these measures could include crop insurance. Good agricultural extension can promote practices which reduce risk. Further, government-induced policy risk from chopping and changing policies can

---

[10] The farmers' agitation in the summer of 2017 was a big political flashpoint with lakhs of farmers mobilized in Madhya Pradesh, Maharashtra, Uttar Pradesh, and Haryana. The street protests resulted in seven farmers being killed by police fire in Madhya Pradesh.

[11] The large fluctuation in mentha area in Palanpur has largely mirrored the price trend in international markets. While farmers in Palanpur did benefit from the rising prices of mentha until 2009, they have also suffered losses after that.

[12] Most political parties, including the incumbent Bharatiya Janata Party (BJP), have promised as part of their election manifesto to implement the recommendations of a National Commission of Farmers, 2005 regarding the fixing of MSP in relation to cost. Known popularly as the Swaminathan Committee formula (after the noted agricultural scientist M.S. Swaminathan who headed the commission), the formula promised to fix the MSP at 50% over and above the cost of production.

[13] As of 2017, the MSP operations have been effectively implemented only in the case of rice and wheat, and only in selected states such as Punjab, Haryana, Uttar Pradesh, Madhya Pradesh, Chhattisgarh, and Andhra Pradesh.

be an important source of destabilization, which should be avoided. Clarity and predictability in policies is of great importance.

Loans for agricultural investment, from official sources, have been important in the process of capital intensification in agriculture in Palanpur, although mainly for the purchase of equipment such as diesel pumps and tractors. This intensification played an important role in the release of labour to non-farm activities. Apart from the 1950s to 1970s seed- or fertilizer-related loans, other sorts of loans from official sources have had limited effect in Palanpur. However, there has been a push in India in recent years to increase the flow of credit in agriculture, particularly after 2004/5. Agricultural credit in India increased by more than four times in the eight years after 2004/5.[14] Various forms of incentives, including interest subsidies and the Kisan Credit Card (KCC) scheme, have helped increase the penetration of institutional finance to farmers,[15] although, as noted, tenant farmers can have difficulty accessing credit.

The increase in credit in agriculture has not been able to deal with the problem of default on loans, however, mostly during times of price collapse or droughts. In the last decade alone, several state governments have introduced loan waivers to ease the burden on farmers. That is a form of state insurance. The recurring nature of these loan waivers is now, however, turning out to be a serious problem. In 2017, the total loan waiver was expected to rise to 150,000 crores, which is a heavy financial burden on state governments. The Economic Survey 2017 has estimated the total cost of loan waivers at 0.7 per cent of gross domestic product (GDP).[16]

The problems go beyond the cost to the exchequer. First, there is the problem of moral hazard. By penalizing relatively rule-abiding farmers who pay on their loans, come what may, it promotes a rise in the tendency to default by farmers going forward, particularly when the loan waivers are not a one-time solution but are used repeatedly by policy-makers. The expectation that loans do not have to be repaid leads to a deterioration in the performance of banks and credit institutions more generally. Second, it is also highly unequal as it penalizes the relatively small and marginal farmers who are more dependent on non-institutional sources of loan such as the local moneylenders. The interest rates on these loans are higher, but these are excluded from any loan waiver scheme. Given the nature of collusion and capture of

---

[14] According to the Reserve Bank of India (RBI), institutional agricultural credit increased from around Rs 100,000 crores in 2004/5 to Rs 400,000 crores by 2012/13.

[15] There has been an almost equal increase in non-institutional loans. Based on the Situation Assessment Survey of the National Sample Survey Office (NSSO), 2013, the share of institutional loans in the total loan portfolio for agricultural credit has remained around 60% at the all-India level.

[16] See Indian Ministry of Finance's Economic Survey, 2017, Volume 2.

institutional sources of finance by well-off farmers, loan waivers create a perverse incentive structure for the financial system and also among farmers. The policy lesson is to manage uncertainty and risk better, as described, and use loan waivers much less often. Again, we should remind ourselves that some of the risk arises from instability in government policies and lack of reliability in their implementation.

Rural public works and infrastructure do make a difference. Inside Palanpur the improvements in lane surfacing and drainage have generated real improvements to sanitation and ease of movement and have been in part supported by MGNREGA. Transport links by road have improved and have helped with marketing and commuting. Although the programme has been plagued by the usual problems of delayed payments, leakages, and exclusion of some of the poorest households, it did help in creating infrastructure. The second-round 'multiplier impacts' in the village are becoming visible. Road improvement and increasing demand imply that now (since 2015) some auto-rickshaws have come to the village. Most commuting, however, is by rail, and here Palanpur has inherited the rail connections from the 1930s. Maintaining or improving the quality of the rail and other road transport links is very important to livelihoods via their enabling of job opportunities through commuting. There is considerable research across the world showing the productivity potential in improving rural roads for marketing, commuting, access to health care (including for births), and so on.[17] The policy lesson is that rural public works can make a big difference to lives and livelihoods. And in India, or at least Palanpur, MGNREGA has played at least a partial role in this.

The infrastructure of telecommunications has been, and will continue to be, very important, too. This has mostly been via private investment but, further, such investment, including in broadband, can make a big difference to lives in Palanpur. Rapid information on work opportunities and on market prices for outputs matters greatly. And broadband is likely to be increasingly important for education, too. Most phones in Palanpur are currently used for telephoning and text messaging, but the use of smartphones is expanding. Evidence from across India shows the importance of smartphones in people's lives. The policy lesson is that further expansion of broadband and telecommunications should have high priority.

We have seen that entrepreneurship and involvement in informal off-farm activities has been a source of rising incomes, therefore it is natural to ask how such entrepreneurship can be fostered in relation to these activities. Important elements will be better governance (including avoiding problematic regulation), skills, financial services, and infrastructure. We have touched on all

---

[17] See, for example, Asher and Novosad (2016), Lei, Desai, and Vanneman (2017), and Chatterjee, Murgai, and Rama (2015).

these but would suggest that the fostering of such entrepreneurship should be an important element in further policy research.

13.3.2 *Human Development and Social Protection*

The promotion and protection of capabilities and living standards on the side of individuals and households operating via the health and education systems have played an important role. These systems have seen strengthening of existing programmes through legislative routes or through judicial action in recent decades. The increase in provisioning of these services has led to expansion of expenditure and of physical infrastructure. This is visible in Palanpur as well. However, there has been a genuine concern regarding the quality of services provided, particularly with regard to the fact that the vulnerable and disadvantaged are often excluded from accessing them, while corruption appears to be rife. Attempts at removing corruption through technical means such as 'Aadhar' are underway, and whilst there is potential, there are also problems.[18] In Part 3 we saw that reforms in the provision of public health and education had been weak. The poor functioning of public institutions has also seen an exit of the relatively affluent towards private services. Private provision will no doubt continue to play a strong role, and transparent assessment of the quality of such provision could provide strong incentives to improve. But weak institutions are likely to exacerbate inequality along several dimensions, including on education and health, which are likely to play an important role in the future. The lessons from countries which have managed a successful transition towards better and inclusive human development outcomes point to strong and inclusive public provisioning. This will require better design of these services, with community participation and accountability.

In Chapter 8 we document the rise in income and of inequality in the village in recent years. While overall poverty has declined significantly, the nature of vulnerabilities among poor people remain, particularly for those households without any earning member. Single-member households, widows, and the elderly are particularly vulnerable in the absence of adequate *social protection* policies. While there are several programmes and schemes, most of these remain inefficient, with inadequate coverage and meagre assistance. PDS has functioned in a haphazard way, with extensive corruption and exclusion of households from the programme. Only 8 out of 233 households in the village

---

[18] 'Aadhar' is a biometric authentication system providing a unique identity number for every individual based on biometric uniqueness of fingerprints and iris scans. The question of Aadhar and whether it should be used for public service delivery is currently being adjudicated by the Supreme Court constitution bench.

were eligible for the subsidy, but even among these most were not receiving it regularly. The MGNREGA did increase access to employment opportunities, particularly for those unable to commute from the village, but it has been at the mercy of district officials. The same is true of the National Social Assistance Programme (NSAP), a programme for pensions for the elderly, widows, and the disabled. Very few in the village receive the NSAP pensions; corruption and exclusion beset the programme. The policy lesson is that it may be better to concentrate attention and resources on those policies which both support the worst off and are least prone to corruption and mismanagement. Amongst those, support for widows would be of high priority, as they are particularly vulnerable and can be relatively easily identified. Broadly, it is likely that digital and biometric identifiers will have a strong role to play; but care with design and implementation will be essential to take account of potential misallocation of benefits, fraud, and corruption, together with privacy and human rights.

13.3.3 *Public Services and Public Institutions*

As we have seen, public services around health and education in Palanpur have not performed well. *Public action and pressure* which might have yielded improvements in these services have been weak. This is an area where Palanpur carries strong lessons about the importance of change but, perhaps, fewer lessons about how to change. We have seen that public policy can influence *panchayats* and *pradhans* in terms of participation of social groups and women, but it takes local public pressure to make such participation function effectively.

The future opportunities in labour markets, as we have argued in Section 13.2, whilst currently mainly focused on unskilled jobs, are likely over time to become more demanding in terms of necessary education and skills. The expansion of quality education is both a high priority and problematic. This is probably going to be of particular importance in expanding future opportunities for women. Perhaps one aspect of public policy could be a national campaign and movement to encourage women to demand better public provision of education and health, particularly for themselves and girls. Change is clearly vital, and more pressure to achieve change is clearly needed.

13.3.4 *Environment*

We have argued in Section 13.2 that so far environmental issues have not been as severe in Palanpur as in, say, urban areas such as Delhi. An important qualification to this, as noted in Section 13.2, would be internal air pollution, as we know from various studies of India and elsewhere that the damage to health, particularly for women, is severe.[19] Whilst this applies to Palanpur, the lesson is not primarily from Palanpur.

On this subject, let us look more to the future and India as a whole rather than confining ourselves to Palanpur. Stubble-burning in Punjab, Haryana, and parts of western UP has contributed greatly to the very damaging air pollution in Delhi, the most polluted major city in the world. This has been associated with the rise of combine harvesting, which leaves much more stubble than hand harvesting, as in Palanpur, where the stalks are cut close to the ground. It is also linked to more intensive land use as farmers try to shorten the gap between harvesting and planting the next crop. Combine harvesting is likely to accompany more intensive agriculture across UP. It is important to look for new techniques which can avoid stubble-burning. These are emerging, such as the 'happy seeder', which simultaneously sows new seed and transforms stalks into mulch. In this way, as in many others, environment and technology are linked. But the spread of technology such as the 'happy seeder' requires policy to promote it. That may involve a combination of regulation against burning and promotion of organizational structures for sharing and efficient use of 'happy seeders', as well as some subsidy.

Of special importance to India is the monsoon, the flows of water from the Himalayas, and the level and reliability of ground water. Global warming and climate change could be profoundly disruptive. Studies at research institutes in Pune and Bangalore (Deshpande and Kulkarni, 2015; Goswami et al., 2006; Madhura et al., 2015) have shown that disruption to the monsoon could be substantial and sudden. Its whole nature and pattern could change dramatically. The effects on agriculture could be devastating both from the absence of a monsoon and increases in intensity. Recent research has suggested a link between the rise in temperature and the tragic phenomenon of farmer suicides in India (Carleton, 2017). Care here is necessary in drawing overly strong conclusions from current circumstances, but it is clear that climate change increases risk, its effects are present now, and risk contributes to stress. Flooding can devastate urban areas, too, and destroy infrastructure. The 2010 floods in Pakistan, for example, damaged almost 4000 kilometres of roads and 5000 kilometres of railways, besides causing severe disruption to the economy. The fragile economy of Nepal, too, suffers heavily from regular flooding.

The effects that we see now are associated with just 1°C global warming (increase in average global surface temperature since late 19th century, the benchmark). This increase is already very large and is taking us to the edge of the temperature of the benign Holocene period, the 10,000 years or so since the warming at the end of the last ice age. The average global temperatures in

---

[19] See, for example, Kankaria, Nongkynrih, and Gupta (2014); Sukhsohale, Narlawar, and Phatak (2013), and Duflo, Greenstone, and Hanna (2008).

this period have been in the range of plus or minus $1°C$ or so. This was the period when our societies matured or sprang up, with the domestication of cereals and the consequent growth of stable communities and food and agricultural surpluses, which enabled other activities. We are on a path to an increase of 3 or $4°C$ or more over the next hundred years or so, unless we take significant action. We have not seen $3°C$ for around 3 million years. The effects could be devastating, with possibly hundreds of millions around the world having to move (see, for example, Stern, 2015). The experience in South Asia of 'Partition' in the 1940s has shown the conflicts that can arise around large migrations. And more recently we have seen in Iraq and Syria, and in Myanmar, how drought can contribute to migration and conflict.

The melting of snows and glaciers in the Himalayas, in conjunction with disruptions of the monsoon, could lead to radical changes in flooding and the water table, with devastating effects on lives and livelihoods. Recent research (Eltahir et al., 2017) suggests that if we look ahead towards the second half of the century, temperatures and humidity across much of India could reach levels that would lead to death within hours or days. The Indo-Gangetic plain would be likely affected early and severely. The scope for universal air conditioning for the many hundreds of millions potentially involved might be limited, to put it modestly. The answer is surely to work to radically reduce the risk of all this happening. If it were to happen, it could not be reversed quickly, and adaptation, although necessary, would likely offer only small moderation of very large effects.

If India grows at 7 per cent or so for the next two decades (and current articulated intentions are for such growth rates) using current energy technologies, then its output and greenhouse gas emissions 20 years from now could be similar to China's today. That is around 11–12 billion tonnes of CO_2 equivalent per annum. And it would go on rising from there. That level of emissions would constitute more than half the total world carbon budget in 2050 (just 20 billion tonnes CO_2e) for a path that holds world temperature increases to below $2°C$. This is the international target agreed in the United Nations Climate Change Conference Conference of the Parties 21 (UNFCCC COP21) in Paris in December 2015, on the basis of very strong scientific logic in relation to the dangers. Indeed, the Paris target is 'well below' $2°C$. India was a key mover and supporter in creating this agreement.

India's greenhouse gas emissions are rapidly heading for an amount which will have a fundamental influence on its own well-being. It is already suffering severely from terrible air pollution. Radical change in the way India uses energy is fundamental to its future well-being. The good news is that the alternative technologies are already available and increasingly used in India. There is great potential in energy efficiency (Ahluwalia, Gupta, and Stern, 2016) and in the design of smart cities. Here, too, India is on its way. The combination of 'better growth and better climate' has great potential. But the future of Palanpur, as for the rest of India, depends hugely on the success of far-reaching actions being taken quickly.

We now see that substantial growth, effective poverty reduction, social inclusion, and climate responsibility can and must all come together. There is no serious and lasting high-carbon growth story. The new routes are feasible, cost-effective, and sustainable. It is in India's interest, and that of the world, to follow low-carbon growth, and there are many outstanding Indian pioneers leading the way. India has been part of the story of rapidly falling costs of solar electricity, both on-grid and off-grid. And its IT companies, such as TCS, Infosys, and Wipro, have provided many examples of the use of digital technologies in promoting greater efficiency. The transition to the low-carbon economy is the only viable growth strategy for the world as a whole, and emerging markets and developing countries more specifically, where the main expansion will take place. It is very attractive, including cities where you can move and breathe and strong and productive ecosystems. And, as well as sustainable, it can be much more inclusive and equitable than current patterns. It is surely the growth story for India for the 21st century.

13.3.5 A Broad Policy Message

Past policies towards rural areas have had a strong concentration on production, whether it be agricultural technology, farming equipment, or price support. *Increasing agricultural productivity* should continue as a major policy objective. But we have seen that opportunities in, and integration with, the outside economy has become extremely important in raising living standards in rural areas. That is a key lesson from Palanpur.

It is time to make *the promotion and facilitation of these informal, off-farm opportunities* a direct and central policy issue. This involves, as we have discussed, improving physical and communications links. Also, and particularly over the coming decades, investment in human capital will be of increasing importance, including bringing education closer to *skills of direct value*, such as vocational training. So, too, the avoidance of unnecessary obstacles to the informal sector: for example, by having simple calculation methods for the goods and services tax (GST).[20] Important also would be avoiding unnecessary regulation that creates opportunities for bureaucratic harassment and coercion. Reliable power supplies, or autonomous supplies, such as decentralized solar energy, can also be important.

---

[20] India's version of value-added tax, introduced in a reform of indirect taxation in 2017.

Effective investment in *education and health* in rural areas should move strongly up the list of priorities, not simply because they are part of development and human rights, but also because they will be critical to the participation of those in rural areas in the strongly rising incomes India anticipates over the coming two decades. Such investment in education and health—a core aspect of human rights and development goals more generally—would also contribute to the rights of and opportunities for women. Also, such advances, along with access to reproductive health care, can contribute to falling fertility and falling infant mortality rates (IMRs).

Further, and this must be stressed strongly, policy should take care not only to avoid inhibiting the expansion of demand and supply in the informal sector, but should also increase the emphasis on the *development of smaller cities and towns via their connectedness and infrastructure*. These towns and cities are crucial to driving rural non-farming opportunities.

Duflo (2017) has argued that there is merit in thinking of 'economists as plumbers' (following Keynes' comparison of economists and dentists). The argument is that economists should offer practical solutions based on testing and experience. The evidence and analyses presented in this book offer, we hope, some input into 'plumbing insights' for economists, policy-makers, and development practitioners. But we also hope the analysis might contribute to an understanding of how major structural and institutional changes in India's economy and overall policies can affect the dynamics of the polity and economy of the Indian village that goes beyond simply asking about the functionality of particular policy interventions, valuable though that is.

13.4 The Economics of Development

We have tried to put the subject of the economics of development, and other social sciences, to work in understanding economic change in Palanpur over the decades from the 1950s until today. At the same time, we have seen change in Palanpur take forms which point strongly towards particular drivers and outcomes in ways which have led us to reflect on and ask questions of the subject of development economics. Relevant parts of this subject were summarized in Chapter 4 on 'Theory and India', and we organize our reflections in relation to the key strands identified in that chapter. Our identification of these key strands in development economics were, in turn, partly influenced by our work on Palanpur.

We begin with the drivers of growth, then turn to the relations between growth and distribution and then link to mobility. We examine the interplay between changing institutions and changing economic outcomes. We comment briefly on sustainability and growth. Our emphasis is on dynamics and change;

that has been at the heart of this study with its wealth of longitudinal data. At the same time, with our surveys covering all households, mobility and inequality have been fundamental to the issues of change under analysis. To emphasize again the key motivation for so much of our work: the understanding of change in lives and livelihoods is what development economics should be about.

13.4.1 *Drivers of Growth*

Theories of economic growth have traditionally emphasized capital, labour or population, and technical progress, in the tradition of Solow and others (for example, Arrow, 1962; Lucas, 1988; Mankiw, Romer, and Weil, 1992). In agricultural economics, land inevitably plays a role. In theories of development there has been much discussion of sectoral change and the movement of activity and people from one sector to another.

None of this is fundamentally wrong. Indeed, in our earlier Palanpur studies we have emphasized technology, population, and outside activities as drivers of growth. But our experience of Palanpur, particularly since the late 1980s, has led us to emphasize key features of the growth process which give a rather different perspective. First, the growth of participation in outside non-farm activities which has been so important to rising living standards in Palanpur, including of some disadvantaged groups, has not taken the form of a wholesale switch from one sector or set of activities to another. Second, for many or most, change has not involved migration in the sense of a complete shift in residence. Rather, it has involved commuting. Third, the activities have been largely informal, particularly in the service sector. All this is very different from standard dual economy models of growth and from many broad discussions of structural change.

Further, the willingness or possibility to participate in new activities depends not only on transport and communication, which do indeed matter and have changed, but also individual entrepreneurship. Put simply, some individuals recognize and take advantage of opportunities before others and some do this better than others. Some are more entrepreneurial than others. Also, social and economic structures imply that some have better access to opportunities than others.

This story, if accepted, would lead us to suggest that theory should include much more examination of the mixing of activities and the drivers of entrepreneurship in the sense of recognizing and taking opportunities. This will involve close attention to the nature of opportunities, to how they are perceived and understood, how people learn about them and how to take them, and the barriers surrounding them that have to be overcome. Social and institutional determinants and the context of a person's ability to take opportunities are of great importance. In other words, we see great scope and need for integration of behavioural economics, institutional economics, labour economics, and growth theory in the task of understanding the processes of change such as those we have seen in Palanpur and which apply in large measure across much of India and the developing world. Much of that will involve economists being open-minded to and embracing other social sciences.

13.4.2 Growth and Distribution

The picture of change we have identified has powerful implications for mobility and the evolution of income distribution. Kuznets, in his seminal work on growth structure and inequality (see Chapter 4), emphasized movement from rural to urban settings and a switch of activity out of agriculture towards industry. He argued that urban areas have higher incomes and more unequal distribution. For both reasons he theorized therefore that inequality would rise in the early stages of transition. This story depends on the movement of people. It is a fruitful and important perspective and rightly has been influential.

However, our story is different in two important respects in relation to distribution. People do not necessarily have to make dichotomous choices between rural and urban or between one sector and another. And they do not have to shift residence to take advantage of opportunities. This puts the focus on how the changing combination of incomes from different choices drives changes in individual outcomes and inequality, and on the distribution of willingness or ability to find and participate in outside activity.

In Palanpur this has led us, in thinking about distribution, to place weight not only on land ownership and social structure (including caste, the traditional preoccupation of many analysts of rural India), but also on within-group variation.

It has also led us to change our views about the prospects for, and nature of, outside activity. We had previously (see Chapter 12, for our history of prognostications), laid emphasis on formal employment, which in retrospect misjudged the growth of informal activity. Since the late 1980s, the rising number of outside and non-farm opportunities have been largely of a casual nature, in the sense that employment contracts are informal, short-term, and offer little assurance of employment security. The work is also, frequently, physically arduous, hazardous to health, and requires little formal education. Wages, while typically higher than in agriculture, are markedly lower than the earnings received by the fortunate few with regular jobs in the non-farm sector. These features of expanding non-farm activities have meant that access for previously disadvantaged segments of Palanpur society has improved, while competition for such jobs from village elites, better placed to offer bribes and to tap into their more extensive networks of contacts, has been limited by the fact that many of the non-farm jobs are relatively unappealing.

Nevertheless, we have seen that higher castes, particularly Thakurs, have put their networks to use in assuring that some of the more attractive opportunities in the spectrum of unskilled informal activities come their way.

At the same time, many who have done increasingly well in Palanpur have done so via self-employment and small enterprises. Indeed, these have been the main source of the sharpest moves upward we have seen. In some ways, those with more capital and better networks have more advantages here, but there have been some outside of the dominant groups who have shown impressive entrepreneurship.

Many poor people in Palanpur have become active participants in the non-farm sector. Poverty has fallen, the consequence both of increased numbers of households with earnings from non-farm sources and higher agricultural wages, which have risen as a result of a tighter labour market within the village.

While poverty has fallen, income inequality has risen in recent decades. The uneven nature of access to, and pursuit of, non-farm employment, coupled with the heterogeneity of non-farm occupations and earnings, has translated into a greater dispersion of incomes across villagers. The processes behind these changes—which we are able to document for the village due to our collection of income data from all households—can remain largely 'invisible' from standard distributional analyses of large-scale household survey data. It is possible, in fact, for inequality trends at the state or national level to mask important changes occurring at the more micro or village level. Inequality trends at the village level do matter. A continued rise in inequality in Palanpur could undermine social cohesion, service delivery, and the functioning of local politics.

Overall, we must recognize the importance of the 'Kuznets insight' (see Chapter 4 for discussion of the Kuznets curve). We use 'Kuznets insight' to capture a broader notion than the narrower Kuznets curve. This idea, at its core, involves the phenomenon of some taking advantage of new opportunities before others, which, in the early stages of such a process, increases inequality. As these new opportunities are taken more widely in the population, at some point 'catch up' will imply that inequality starts to decrease. We saw these processes at work in Palanpur with the role of diffusion of irrigation in the first half of our period and the arrival of new activities in the second half. It is interesting to ask how these Kuznets-like processes would interact with the inflow of a whole set of new opportunities, emerging in different ways at different times. Change in inequality over time would be driven by the interaction of the newer opportunities arising, with the diffusion of the older ones.

13.4.3 Mobility

The rise of informal non-farm opportunities, the mixing of activities, and entrepreneurship or initiative, have led to striking examples of upward mobility in the village. Importantly, the upward mobility has been observed even amongst the weakest segments of the village. In the period up to 1983/4, for example, evidence seemed to suggest that the Jatabs, as a group, were falling ever further behind the rest of the village in income terms. In the subsequent 25 years this process reversed. As a group, Jatabs have benefited from higher agricultural wages, certain non-farm sources of income, and greater ease of access to land under tenancy. There has been a process of 'catch up' with the rest of the village.

Some Telis have shown real entrepreneurship and moved up significantly. In contrast, the Muraos have seen some decline in their relative status over the last three decades. This is, in part, the consequence of their focus on cultivation and having been later than the rest of the village to embrace the new opportunities presented by non-farm activities. The patterns of intragenerational mobility observed in Palanpur point to a good deal of relative movement within the income distribution from one survey year to the next. Over time, this movement appears to be accelerating.

An important qualification to this assessment comes from our examination of mobility across generations, and in particular how intergenerational mobility has evolved. An influential theme in the literature on intergenerational mobility concerns the existence of a 'Gatsby curve' which tracks intergenerational mobility against inequality (Corak, 2013). The internationally observed pattern, where countries with high levels of inequality display lower intergenerational mobility, is consistent with our observations for Palanpur. The rise in inequality observed between 1983/4 and 2008/9 has been accompanied by a decline in intergenerational mobility, relative to the previous 25 years. This pattern, in particular in light of its apparent contrast to the picture emerging from the scrutiny of mobility within generations, is striking, and has received little attention in the development literature to date. However, it can be readily understood given that mobility patterns in Palanpur were driven initially by an equalizing process associated with the expansion of irrigation to all farming households, and then by a process driven by the expansion of non-farm opportunities. This latter process did offer a route to higher household incomes for the poorer villagers, but access to the better non-farm jobs, some of them regular, remained largely the preserve of the wealthy. Indeed, there are reasons to believe that access by the poor to such high-return opportunities may become more, rather than less, restricted, given uneven improvements in education levels and the advanced position, in terms of contacts and networks, of those currently employed in regular non-farm jobs. The better-off may also have stronger chances in self-employment and small business, with better networks and more capital. Whilst many poorer households have broken into these activities, it is possible that over time it could become relatively more difficult for other such households to do so.

13.4.4 *Institutions, Behaviour, and the Economy*

Institutional economics has a long and distinguished tradition and has recently made valuable contributions to our understanding of drivers of growth and change (see Chapter 4). In large measure, in order to achieve identification of causes, it has looked for institutions that were exogenous, or whose change was exogenous, and has seen causality flowing from institutions to economic outcomes.

In Palanpur, we have recognized, indeed strongly emphasized, the influence of institutions on outcomes. For example, *zamindari* abolition, with its stronger land tenure for farmers, increased investment in irrigation in the 1950s and 1960s. And, until tractors came to the village, basically from the late 1970s, social restrictions on ploughing with bullocks on a field which another farmer was cultivating meant that the ownership of bullocks was a necessary condition in leasing-in land under a sharecropping tenancy.

But we have also emphasized how economic change in turn changes institutions. The arrival of tractors meant that the owning of draught animals was no longer a precondition for agricultural tenancy, thus opening up new opportunities to some disadvantaged groups. There was major change in the way in which a significant Palanpur market, tenancy, functioned. Markets are key economic institutions. Also, the possibility of outside activities has changed the nature of economic and social relations between Jatabs and higher castes. Looking to the future, it may be that stronger education and exposure to outside jobs could enhance the functioning of political institutions in Palanpur and in turn improve the quality of public services.

We have seen profound changes in the role of caste in economic activity. The link between caste and occupation has become far weaker, even though caste, through networks and trust, has been playing a strong role in mechanisms for finding non-farm work and in land, labour, and credit relations within the village. Social institutions adapt to economic change and, in turn, influence that change. And the combination of changes in social institutions and economic change both drives and is driven by changes in behaviour.

Self-employment in non-farm activities is now an important route upwards. Opportunities will depend on ease of entry to these activities and sectors. The ease or otherwise of entry will differ across groups. Networks and contracts have played a role, but current non-farm institutional structures have allowed entry from different groups; caste has not been a rigid barrier. We need to pay greater attention, in theory, to how institutional structures evolve in relation to new opportunities and departures.

Piece-rated contracts, particularly for team jobs, allow women to gain employment in family-run activities or enterprises. Piece rates have allowed them to participate in manual jobs which were less likely to be available to them. Here again is another line of research: How do incentives and labour contracts in a dynamic economy influence opportunities in relation to gender and how do these changes play through?

This kind of interplay and endogeneity between economic outcomes and institutions may not be easy to capture econometrically in formal modelling, but close study of the details and timing of change and how it occurs can provide strong pointers to the influences at work. Examples of individual, household, and community histories alongside the qualitative and quantitative data can be very valuable.

We would suggest that both theoretically and empirically there is great potential in examining this interplay between institutions and outcomes. It would have seemed a natural set of questions for the classical economists, including Smith, Ricardo, and Marx, and would not seem out of place to economic and social historians. This is one of the strongest of our conclusions for theoretical and empirical enquiry in our subject.

13.4.5 *Human Development*

Most studies of development and discussions of objectives now put economic and human development together at the heart of development goals. This has been very clearly embodied in the Millennium Development Goals (2000–15) and the Sustainable Development Goals (2015–30) of the United Nations (UN). Further, many aspects of economic development and human development can be seen as both ends and means (see, for example, Sen, 1999; Stern, Dethier, and Rogers, 2005), in the sense that they are both valued as objectives and each is a means to the other. In particular, human development, in the form of education and health, promotes economic development and vice versa.

Nonetheless, there have been discussions where some protagonists appear to prioritize one over the other. That might be one reading of interactions between Jagdish Bhagwati and Amartya Sen, in which Bhagwati has stressed economic growth as a priority which, he suggests, can provide the resources for investment in human development, and Sen has emphasized the importance of human development, both as end and means. Perhaps the differences have been exaggerated as both writers point to both goals, but there has nevertheless been a difference in emphasis.

What we see in Palanpur is that growth occurred without much advance in human development for 40 or 50 years. At the same time, the villagers of Palanpur have been largely restricted to unskilled jobs, which are by far the most commonly available, but the unskilled will likely be disadvantaged in future access to non-farm jobs as skill demands increase. Their weaknesses in education have diminished empowerment, capabilities, and the ability to advance their lives and influence opportunities. Overall, if there is a lesson for such controversies from Palanpur, it is that there is little to be gained by seeing human development and economic development as in some kind of horse race—both matter.

Palanpur is consistent with the many studies in economic development that have pointed to the weakness of the supply side for education and health, in terms of the functioning of public institutions. Even when investment in physical facilities occurs, delivery through the behaviours of staff can be very weak. Many teachers either do not show up, or teach in a listless or perfunctory way when they do. What we are seeing is a growing demand side too often frustrated by a weak public supply side, with villagers moving to the private sector.

What we have found in Palanpur, via this route, is that economic development has proceeded faster than human development in the sense that Palanpur, UP, and India, have seen human development increase less rapidly in relation to economic development than has been the case elsewhere. That puts the spotlight for our analyses of economic and social development on public delivery and public policy and public action for that delivery. In that respect, our subject has been progressing in a constructive direction by identifying the key issues, and the emphasis in the literature on delivery and performance is well founded.

13.4.6 Entrepreneurship

Entrepreneurship and initiative have not really been to the fore in analyses of economic and social development.[21] There are important exceptions, as we saw in Chapter 4, for example work by Hirschman and Schumpeter. Other economists, such as Myrdal, have been deeply and erroneously pessimistic about entrepreneurship and initiative in developing countries, particularly South Asia. Some discussions seem to present an evil system, tightly controlled by the rich, powerful, and entrenched, which inexorably squeezes out entrepreneurship and initiatives by others. Much of the discussion of entrepreneurship has been in relation to firms and enterprises. The concept applies also, and in our view strongly, to the individuals and households that have been our focus.

Palanpur is a backward village that has seen income per capita grow at a fairly modest rate of around 2 per cent per annum over six decades. When that is compounded it represents a major change, but Palanpur is still a backward village in the context of India as a whole. Nevertheless, entrepreneurship

---

[21] See Chapter 4, Section 4.6, for a brief discussion of the definition of entrepreneurship.

and initiative, from irrigation investment in the early years, to the green revolution technologies and methods, and to the advance of non-farm employment, including self-employment, and the associated mechanization of agriculture, have all required the recognition of opportunity and the willingness to take risks and make investments, all of which is innovative for individuals, families, and households. They have had to take difficult and risky decisions. Some have moved more rapidly and effectively than others. The implications for mobility and inequality have been strong.

We would argue that our subject should focus much more explicitly on why some do, or are able to, react more quickly and successfully than others. What are the circumstances under which entrepreneurship and initiative are more likely to flourish? How does membership of different social or economic groups influence willingness or ability to take the initiative?

Throughout the periods involved in our study, we have seen lessons and insights into these questions. In our view they should be much more prominent in our subject than they have been.

13.4.7 Agriculture

Understanding agricultural change was the first priority in the earlier studies from Ansari (1964) to Bliss and Stern (1982) to Lanjouw and Stern (1998). This was understandable in terms of its dominance in the economy of the village. Now it ranks below non-farm activities as a source of income. It has been the latter that have driven change. Hence, whilst agriculture has remained centre stage, much of our focus has shifted in the direction of non-farm activities. Nevertheless, change in agriculture has been crucial to wider change in Palanpur, including in recent decades, and has been core to our study. And it has carried many lessons. It was at the heart of entrepreneurship and investment both in the 1960s, in the advance of irrigation, and in the green revolution years of the 1970s. Further, the mechanization of agriculture has been critical to the release of labour to non-farm jobs and the management of population pressures in more recent years.

The role of agriculture in economics used to be prominent in courses on economic development; it is much less so now. However, we have seen that agriculture remains very important, indeed crucial, to incomes and employment in rural areas. It carries major lessons on entrepreneurship and initiative. It teaches us much about the importance of institutions in shaping investment and growth, providing profound lessons on how institutions change and markets develop.

In our view, there are far too few economic researchers working on and in rural areas, and on agriculture in particular.

13.4.8 *Sustainability and Development*

Broadly speaking, sustainability means providing future generations with opportunities at least as good as those of the current generation; it would also be assumed within this definition that the next generation acts similarly. The opportunities do not have to be exactly the same. One way of putting it would be that the set of endowments which are passed on, including physical, human, natural, environmental, and social capital, are capable of offering to succeeding generations opportunities for levels of well-being at least as good as was possible from the endowments the current generation inherited.

We would not wish to argue that Palanpur itself has provided special insights into the links between sustainability and development. We would, however, be remiss if we did not mention the importance of building analysis of these links into our theories. India, including Palanpur, is very vulnerable to climate change, to air, water, and land pollution, and so on. Some of these factors are local and some more global. In the past, the economics of development has underplayed these issues. So too has economic policy. Thus we emphasize here, as we did in Chapter 12 and in Section 13.3 of this chapter, that they will be vital to understanding the future of India and thus Palanpur.

All too often economists look at modelling, forecasts, and extrapolation of growth, population, geography, and living standards as if sustainability, environment, and climate were not significant issues. That is a serious mistake. A population projection for 2050, 2080, or 2100 should make explicit assumptions about climate and environment. For many climate and environment outcomes that are possible on current trends, it would not be possible to sustain population projections as they appear. Heat stresses, drought, monsoon changes, floods, sea-level rise, could make large parts of India uninhabitable. Environment and sustainability should be everywhere in analyses of economic development.

13.5 Future Research on Palanpur and Elsewhere

13.5.1 *The Subject of Development*

Our lessons for the study of economic and social development in Section 13.4 embody clear priorities for areas of study. These include, as indicated: a different approach to modelling and understanding growth; an examination of mobility from the point of view of the availability of, access to, and the taking advantage of new opportunities; the evolution and endogeneity of institutions; the interactions between behaviour, economic institutions, and development; how economic development leads and/or is fostered by human development; the role of entrepreneurship and initiative in driving change and the forces determining these; and the importance of sustainability and the environment throughout all. These are all potentially very rich research areas. They are not necessarily those that leap out of the literature. These suggestions for a research agenda in development have been determined, influenced, and shaped by our work on Palanpur. They are far from absent in the existing literature, but the Palanpur experience does involve valuable perspective and guidance on priorities.

13.5.2 Using Palanpur Data

We have by no means exhausted the potential of research on the Palanpur data we already have. Indeed, we are keenly aware that with more resources we could do so much more. Longitudinal studies require continual replenishment with young researchers, and they are welcome. Anyone who gets involved in such work should recognize, however, that it might become a lifetime commitment.[22]

The following areas are examples where we think there is much more to be done with the data we have. There is a core data set which is, in some respects, like a panel study. The length of time and the births, deaths, marriages, outside movement of people, and so on, imply that it cannot be seen as a standard panel data set. Nevertheless, we think there is great potential for further work of this nature on how and why households change activities and outcomes. And we can enrich that with the direct qualitative information we have on households and individuals, and knowledge of the village context and institutions, together with the evolution of outside pressures and opportunities. We can undertake more research on why people move down as well as up.

There is also much interesting work that could be undertaken on a portfolio approach to activities, including how risk is managed and its influence on the taking of opportunities. Households have a much broader and deeper portfolio of activities and opportunities than before and it would be very interesting to go deeper into how their choices evolve. Also, how do the institutions that help handle risk develop in this process? Whilst we have explored some of these issues, there is much more to do.

Our data set on agriculture is very rich. This can be seen from our discussions in Chapters 5 and 6. However, we have not analysed this as deeply as is possible. There are many questions around the choice of cropping patterns and the intensity of input application which could offer real insights into behaviour, both maximizing and otherwise. There are likely more Palanpur straws in the wind to inform future theorizing, investigation, and speculation more broadly in our subject.

---

[22] Those who might be thinking about getting involved should contact one of the three authors.

These are just some of the opportunities.[23] We have invested a great deal of work in creating data which are as comparable as possible and effectively linked across the years. It has been time- and care-intensive, particularly as the studies up to 1983 were not really designed as the very long-term longitudinal study they have turned out to be. We plan to continue that research and welcome collaborators.

13.5.3 Further Studies of Palanpur

We hope, and are planning for, future studies of Palanpur. We hope that we will continue to be able to say that 'we have one for every decade since Independence' for many decades to come. From here, where would we now see likely areas of priority for the next study, or perhaps next two studies? We have made forecasts in the 1970s, 1990s, and 2010s. How might we be speculating 20 years from now, and on what evidence?

One set of priorities could arise from the issues that have emerged strongly in this round. Prominent amongst these would be non-farm activities, commuting, and migration. The likely centrality of these to future development might mean that the next Palanpur investigation focuses much more strongly on data collection outside Palanpur. That must surely be a feature of how village studies will change. It will be necessary to spend more time with Palanpur's 'original' households or individuals outside Palanpur. We will need to learn more about their decisions around non-farm activities. What information did they have about such opportunities? What were the motivations? How were choices influenced by decisions in relation to the household as a whole, and how much were they about the individual?

We have speculated about the future of mobility and inequality. How far and long will inequality move as the process of acquisition of outside jobs and the expansion of non-farm jobs continues? It is possible that the question itself becomes more complex as relationships between the individual and the household begin to loosen. We may have to look much more closely at individual incomes with some separation from household incomes.

We have been somewhat agnostic about how institutions will develop, and in particular whether local public pressure will demand and obtain better performance from schools and health centres. That is an area we might want to study much more explicitly.

---

[23] Two doctoral students at the London School of Economies (LSE) are currently working on some aspects of the Palanpur data. Tom O'Keeffe is examining the role of networks in the process of structural change, including in migration and education. Milad Khatib-Shahidi is working on the gender preferences of parents.

Another set of priorities would be around building on what we have. For the 2008/10 and 2015 studies we were determined to learn much more about women and girls, and to involve more female investigators. We were also keen to do better in terms of data on health and nutrition. We now have good data in these areas which could provide a sound basis for comparisons over time. We are likely to be able to learn more about how women and girls take decisions individually and within households.

The future of education, and its relationship with employment, has been a subject on which we have speculated. The next 10 or 20 years will likely see education play a much stronger role. We would also hope to ask how education, and possible employment, is likely to affect the opportunities and status of women and girls. One interesting set of issues could be around the future of boy–girl ratios. Another factor that could contribute to changing gender relations is greater exposure to social media and increase in access to forms of communication such as television and newspapers, and so on. To some extent, this is already visible in Palanpur but could lead to changes in relationships not only within the household but also outside the household boundary.

Entrepreneurship and institutions constitute a subject we have made much more explicit in our discussion than in our earlier studies, as a result of our findings. We could design future work to investigate this much more explicitly around questions of discovery of, access to, constraints on, and the taking of opportunity. How do new ventures come about, prosper, and fail? Who are the entrepreneurs? Why is it they prosper or fail? What pressures are they under and what advantages or disadvantages do they have?

It is possible that environmental and sustainability issues may start to loom larger in Palanpur and that too is a set of issues we would wish to investigate.

Agriculture is likely to continue to decline in importance. But the way that it intensifies, its role in portfolio decision-making, and the lessons it provides around changing markets and institutions are likely to continue as important research questions. And, notwithstanding its relative decline, it will remain important in terms of income, employment, and risk far into the future.

While the areas of priority for research will develop as the economy and society develop, it will be important to retain the key elements of our longitudinal data around household, family, human development, and income. These are core to the great strengths of and research opportunities from this whole set of surveys.

13.6 Concluding Comments

The Palanpur data set is extraordinarily rich. The survey of 2008/10 was broader and deeper than those that went before. It has allowed more detailed comparisons with 1983/4 than was possible with earlier studies. But all seven data sets are of high quality and have allowed us to examine issues of development and change in a uniquely detailed and informative way. For most of the data there is no sampling: we can examine developments of the whole population at the individual and household level. The study of how lives and livelihoods change over time and generations is, in large measure, what the study of development is all about. The Palanpur data offer a very unusual, perhaps unique, opportunity to examine these questions; they have been at the heart of this study.

In these last two chapters, Chapters 12 and 13, we have drawn out our conclusions and have used them to think about the future of the village, of India, of policy, and of research on development. We have, we hope, established that the study of one village and its people over a long period of time can make a crucial contribution to the study of development, and can tell us much not only about the village, but also India, policy, and the subject of economic and social development.

Our prognosis for Palanpur in Chapter 12 was one of rising incomes and falling poverty. Probably incomes per head will continue to rise more slowly in Palanpur than in India as a whole, but its growth rate may pick up as involvement in non-farm activities continues to rise. And education is at last starting to move. In that sense, there is some optimism.

There are, however, a number of anxieties around inequality, gender, political and social institutions, social tensions, and the environment, which we have articulated. We trust that these will be subjects of our further research and data gathering. And we noted that there was much more to be done with the data we have.

There is one prediction that we make with some confidence. There will be more surveys of Palanpur.

Acknowledgement

Dipa Sinha contributed in various ways in developing some of the ideas discussed in this chapter.

References

Ansari, N. 1964. 'Palanpur: A study of its economic resources and economic activities (no. 41)', Continuous Village Surveys 1958–9. Agricultural Economics Research Centre, University of Delhi.

Asher, S., and Novosad, P. 2016. 'Market access and structural transformation: Evidence from rural roads in India.' Manuscript: Department of Economics, University of Oxford.

Ahluwalia, M., Gupta, H. and Stern, N. 2016. 'A more sustainable energy strategy for India'. eSocialSciences Working Paper 328. Indian Council for Research on International Economic Relations (ICRIER).

Arrow, K.J. 1962. 'The economic implications of learning by doing', *Review of Economic Studies* 29, no. 3: 155–73.

Bliss, C.J., and Stern, N.H. 1982. *Palanpur: The Economy of an Indian Village*. Oxford and New York: Oxford University Press.

Carleton, T.A. 2017. 'Crop-damaging temperatures increase suicide rates in India', *Proceedings of the National Academy of Sciences* 114, no. 33: 201701354.

Chatterjee, U., Murgai, R., Rama, M.G. 2015. 'Job opportunities along the rural–urban gradation and female labor force participation in India'. Policy Research working paper; no. WPS 7412. Washington, D.C.: World Bank Group.

Corak, M. 2013. 'Income inequality, equality of opportunity, and intergenerational mobility', *Journal of Economic Perspectives* 27, no. 3: 79–102.

Deshpande, N.R., and Kulkarni, B.D. 2015. 'Changing pattern of heavy rainstorms in the Indus basin of India under global warming scenarios', *Journal of Earth System Science* 124: 829–41, https://doi.org/10.1007/s12040-015-0570-0 (accessed 22 March 2018).

Duflo, E. 2017. 'Richard T. Ely Lecture: the economist as plumber', *American Economic Review* 107, no. 5: 1–26. DOI: 10.1257/aer.p20171153.

Duflo, E., Greenstone, M., and Hanna, R. 2008. 'Indoor air pollution, health and economic well-being', *Surveys and Perspectives Integrating Environment and Society* 1: 1–9.

Eltahir, E.A.B., Im, E.-S., and Pal, J.S. 2017. 'Deadly heat waves projected in the densely populated agricultural regions of South Asia', *Science Advances* 3, no. 8: p.e.1603322.

GCEC (Global Commission on the Economy and Climate). 2014. 'Better growth better climate: the new climate economy report', World Resources Institute, Washington, DC.

Gibson, J., Datt, G., Ravallion, M., and Murgai, R. 2017. 'For India's rural poor, growing towns matter more than growing cities'. World Bank Group Policy Research Working Paper No. 7994.

Goswami, B.N., Venugopal, V., Sengupta, D., Madhusoodanan, M.S., and Xavier, Prince K. 2006. 'Increasing trend of extreme rain events over India in a warming environment', *Science* 314: 1442–5.

Gray, E., Veit, P.G., Altamirano, J.C., Ding, H., Rozwalka, P., Zuniga, I., Witkin, M., Borger, F.G., Pereda, P., Lucchesi, A., and Ussami, K. 2015. 'The economic costs and benefits of securing community forest tenure: evidence from Brazil and Guatemala', World Resources Institute, Washington, DC, http://www.wri.org/forestcostsandbenefits (accessed 22 March 2018).

Gupta, D., 2005. 'Whither the Indian village: culture and agriculture in rural India', *Economic and & Political Weekly* 40: 751–8.

Harriss, J., and Jeyaranjan, J. 2016. 'Rural Tamil Nadu in the liberalization era: what do we learn from village studies?', in Himanshu, P. Jha, and G. Rodgers (eds), *The Changing Village in India: Insights from Longitudinal Research*. Delhi: Oxford University Press.

Jodhka, S.S. 2016. 'a forgotten "revolution": revisiting rural life and agrarian change in Haryana', in Himanshu, P. Jha, and G. Rodgers (eds), *The Changing Village in India: Insights from Longitudinal Research*. Delhi: Oxford University Press.

Kankaria, A., Nongkynrih, B., and Gupta, S.K. 2014. 'Indoor air pollution in India: implications on health and its control', *Indian Journal of Community Medicine* 39, no. 4: 203.

Kaur, S., and Vatta, K. 2015. 'Groundwater depletion in central Punjab: pattern, access and adaptations', *Current Science* 108, no. 4: 485–90.

Kaur, S., Aggarwal, R., and Soni, A. 2011. 'Study of water-table behaviour for the Indian Punjab using GIS', *Water Science and Technology* 63, no. 8: 1574–81.

Lanjouw, P., and Murgai, R. 2014. 'Urban growth and rural poverty in India 1983–2005', in N. Hope, A. Kochar, R. Noll, and T.N. Srinivasin (eds), *Economic Reform in India: Challenges, Prospects, and Lessons*. New York: Cambridge University Press.

Lanjouw, P., and Stern, N.H. (eds). 1998. *Economic Development in Palanpur over Five Decades*. New York and Oxford: Clarendon Press.

Lei, L., Desai, S., and Vanneman, R. 2017. 'Village transportation infrastructure and women's non-agricultural employment in India: The conditioning role of community gender context.' IHDS Working Paper 2017-2.

Li, Y., and Rama, M. 2015. 'Households or locations? Cities, catchment areas and prosperity in India'. World Bank Policy Research Working Paper No. 7473, https://openknowledge.worldbank.org/handle/10986/23445 (accessed 22 March 2018).

Lucas, R. 1988. 'On the mechanics of economic development', *Journal of Monetary Economics* 22, no. 1: 3–42.

Madhura, R.K., Krishnan, R., and Revadekar, J.V. 2015. 'Changes in western disturbances over the western Himalayas in a warming environment', *Climate Dynamics* 44, no. 3–4: 1157.

Mankiw, N.G., Romer, D., Weil, D.N. 1992 'A contribution to the empirics of economic growth', *Quarterly Journal of Economics* 107, no. 2: 407–37.

Mishra, P. 1995. *Butter Chicken in Ludhiana: Travels in Small Town India*. London: Penguin Books.

NSSO (National Sample Survey Office). 2012. 'Informal sector and conditions of employment in India: NSS 66th round, July 2009–June 2010'. Ministry of Statistics & Programme Implementation, Government of India, http://www.mospi.gov.in/sites/default/files/publication_reports/nss_rep_539.pdf (accessed 22 March 2018).

NSSO (National Sample Survey Office). 2013. 'Situation Assessment Survey of Agricultural Households, January–December 2013'. Ministry of Statistics & Programme Implementation, Government of India. http://mail.mospi.gov.in/index.php/catalog/157 (accessed 05 June 2018).

Rodell, M., Velicogna, I., and Famiglietti, J.S. 2009. 'Satellite-based estimates of groundwater depletion in India', *Nature* 460, no. 7258: 999.

Sen, A. 1999. *Development as Freedom*. Oxford: Oxford University Press.

Stern, N. 2015. *Why Are We Waiting? The Logic, Urgency, and Promise of Tackling Climate Change*. Cambridge, MA: MIT Press.

Stern, N., Dethier, J., and Rogers, F. 2005. *Growth and Empowerment: Making Development Happen*. Cambridge, MA: MIT Press.

Stevens, C., Winterbottom, R., Springer, J., and Reytar, K. 2014. 'Securing rights, combating climate change: how strengthening community forest rights mitigates climate change', World Resources Institute, Washington, DC, www.wri.org/securing-rights (accessed 22 March 2018).

Sukhsohale, N.D., Narlawar, U.W., and Phatak, M.S. 2013. 'Indoor air pollution from biomass combustion and its adverse health effects in central India: an exposure-response study', *Indian Journal of Community Medicine* 38, no. 3: 162.

Glossary

adda	A local, informal meeting place.
aloo	Potato.
anganwadi	Crèche.
bajra	Pearl millet (a coarse grain, grown in the *kharif* season).
batai	Sharecropping arrangement, involving equal output shares for tenant and landlord.
bhandaara	A large scale communal feast.
Bhangi	Caste of sweepers, also known as *Balmiki*.
bigha	Unit of land area; in Palanpur, there are 6.4 *bighas* in one acre.
chakki	Grinding stone; a small flour mill.
Chamar	A scheduled caste, with leather work as its traditional occupation. In Palanpur, the term has been discarded and replaced by the term Jatab.
chapatis	Bread made from a round lump of unleavened flour rolled out into the shape of a pancake.
chauthai	A variant of sharecropping, involving one-fourth share of gross output to the tenant.
chowkidar	Watchman.
crore	A unit in the Indian measuring system. One crore is 10,000,000.
dacoit	Robber; bandit.
dai	The village midwife.
desi	Country, hence local or traditional.
dhan	Paddy.
dharamshala	A public place meant normally as a resting place for pilgrims or other travellers.
DishTV	One of India's direct-to-home television operators. Colloquially used to refer to any direct to home dish antennae.
dharma	Law in the broadest sense, including the natural order as well as norms pertaining to human propriety and personal ethics; for an individual, duty or moral norm, specific to social status and stage of life; also religion in the conventional sense.

Dhimar	Caste of water carriers, formerly also called Bhisti.
Dhobi	Caste of washermen; washermen.
Gadaria	Caste of shepherds.
gehun	Wheat.
ghunghat	A cloth covering head and face, in part or fully.
ghutti	A local form of gripe water made with herbs.
godown	Warehouse.
gram	Village.
gram sabha	Village assembly, consisting of all adult village members. Officially, the *gram sabha* has supreme authority among village institutions and owns village public properties.
gram vikas	Village development officer.
halwai	Professional cook.
jajmani	Customary system of hereditary labour services (sometimes interpreted as patron–client relations).
Jatab	See Chamar.
jowar	Sorghum (a coarse *kharif* grain).
kaccha	Rough or unmade, the opposite of *pucca/pukka*.
Kayasth	A north Indian caste, with clerical and accounting work as its traditional occupation.
kharif	Monsoon or summer season in the agricultural calendar, lasting from June to November–December. This season accounts for most of the natural precipitation.
kirana	Grocery.
Kshatriyas	The second ranking in the Hindu four-tier arrangement of people. The Kshatriyas are the warrior caste.
lakh	A unit in the Indian measuring system. One lakh is 100,000.
Madarsa/madrasa	A Muslim religious school.
mandi	Marketplace.
Mahila Mandal	A women's association.
Murao	A caste, with agriculture (particularly vegetable-growing) as its traditional occupation.
Nayi	Barber.
nilgai	A species of antelope; literally 'blue cow'.
paisa(e)	A unit of monetary value. One hundred paise equal one rupee.
panchayat	Elected village council.
Passi	A caste of mat weavers, some of whom migrated to Palanpur from eastern Uttar Pradesh.

Peshgi	A sharecropping arrangement with a fixed cash rent.
pucca	A house or building, constructed of brick not mud. Hence, by extension, 'cooked' not 'raw', well made, proper, or correct.
purdah	Custom of a woman keeping her face covered with one end of her saree, or veil. By extension, the practice of female seclusion. Adherence to this custom varies between different castes and with age.
rabi	The winter season in the agricultural calendar, lasting from November–December to May. Rains are meagre in this season and cultivation is dependent on irrigation.
Raj	Literally, rule, hence sometimes the government of India by the British.
roti	See chapati.
rupee	The basic unit of currency in India.
sarpanch	Head of the *panchayat*.
Scheduled Castes	The caste groups mentioned in the constitution of India as meriting particular favour in view of their oppressed position. The untouchable groups are included here, as are tribal groups.
Scheduled Tribes	Tribal groups mentioned in the constitution of India as meriting particular favour in view of their historically disadvantaged position in society.
Shiksha Mitra	Literally, "education friend"; refers to a contract teacher hired by the government.
sirdar	Tenant of the state.
Sudra	A member of the fourth tier in the Hindu ranking of people. The Sudras are labourers and service groups of various kinds.
tehsil	Administrative and revenue unit below a district (Uttar Pradesh districts are divided into three to six *tehsils*).
tehsildar	Administrative head of the *tehsil*.
Teli	A caste of oil pressers or oil sellers.
Thakur	A martial caste, within the Kshatriya *varna*.
toli	A group or team usually consists of three or more members.
zamindar	Landlords or intermediaries, in north India, prior to land reforms initiated in the 1950s (bringing most cultivators in direct relation with the state).
zamindari	System of landlordism in which the *zamindar* is the crucial intermediary between the state and the cultivators (particularly in matters of revenue collection).

Name Index

Name Index

Lucchesi, A. 455
Luke, N. 230n

Madhura, R.K. 461
Madhusoodanan, M.S. 461
Maggu, A. 180
Mahajan, V. 238
Mahalanobis, P.C. 80, 107
Mahendra Dev, S. 245n
Malhotra, A. 399
Malhotra, N. 398
Malhotra, S. 397n
Malthus, Thomas 120
Mangahas, M. 226n
Mankiw, N.G. 465
Mann, Harold 22n
Mansuri, G. 225
March, J.G. 137
Marshall, Alfred 225
Marx, Karl 116, 118, 121, 123, 125, 128, 132, 150
Mason, K.O. 394, 395
Maurice, S. 131
Mayawati, K. 55n, 72
Maynard, A.K. 334
Mazzocco, M. 222n, 230
Meade, J.E. 132n
Meena, Gaurav 15
Mehrotra, S. 86n
Mellor, John 129, 130, 148, 244
Milanović, Branko 91, 118, 125–6
Miller, J.E. 371n
Milner, David 16
Miniere, Soline 15
Minnitti, M. 145
Mir, Banke 322
Mirrlees, J. 133
Mises, Ludwig von 147
Mishra, S. 59n
Mishra, V. 371n
Mistiaen, J. 323
Moestue, H. 371n
Mookherjee, D. 416n, 417n
Moore, M. 399
Morrisson, C. 124
Motiram, S. 91, 92, 333n, 337n
Mukherjee, A. 30n, 42n, 250
Mukherjee, R. 22n
Mukhopadhyay, Abhiroop 16, 283, 284, 296
Mullainathan, S. 118, 133
Munshi, K. 138, 230n
Muralidharan, K. 145
Murgai, Rinku 16, 86n, 88n, 89, 90, 91, 126, 127, 277, 434n, 448, 458n
Myrdal, Gunnar 146, 147, 150, 432

Nabi, I. 226n
Nagaraj, K. 23n, 26n, 288

Nanetti, R.Y. 136
Narayan, A. 86n
Narayanan, S. 189
Narlawar, U.W. 461n
Nehru, Jawaharlal 80, 107
Newbury, D.M.G. 226
Newman, A.F. 126, 133
Nilekani, N. 107
Nongkynrih, B. 461n
North, Douglas C. 95, 119, 136
Novosad, P. 92, 96, 458n
Nurkse, Ragnar 118, 122, 129, 133
Nussbaum, M. 143

O'Donnell, G. 117, 142
Ok, E.A. 131n
O'Keeffe, Tom 16, 475n
Olson, Mancur 141
Ostrom, Elinor 119, 136, 138n, 234
Otsuka, K. 230n
Özler, B. 39n, 323

Pal, S. 257
Palriwala, R. 361
Panagariya, A. 104
Pande, Priyanka 15, 299n, 344
Pandey, P. 137–8
Pankaj, M. 448
Pant, Chandrashekar 226
Parida, J. 86n
Parikh, Jyoti 16
Parikh, Kirit 16
Patnaik, U. 129n, 161n
Paul, S. 102, 337n
Pavoncello, F. 136
Pereda, P. 455
Perotti, R. 126
Persson, Torsten 119, 126, 137
Phatak, M.S. 461n
Pierre, Violaine 15, 361, 364, 365n
Piketty, Thomas 91, 91n, 92, 93n, 118, 125, 132, 132n, 305
Platteau, Jean-Philippe 16
Pollak, R.A. 229
Priebe, J. 416n
Pritchett, L. 304n
Putnam, Robert 119, 136

Quirk, Kerrie 16

Rafkin, C. 92
Rajagopal, A. 252, 416n
Raju, S. 361
Rama, M. 86n, 88n, 90, 434n, 448
Rama, M.G. 458n
Ramachandran, R. 102
Ramachandran, V.K. 16, 399

Subject Index

Please note that page references to Figures will be followed by the letter 'f ', to Tables by the letter 't';
References to Notes will contain the letter 'n' following the Page number